THE CAMERA IN THE CROWD

Filming New Zealand in Peace and War, 1895–1920

Flip Book: *Auckland's Expeditionary Force: The Minister for Defence Reviews the Troops, NTSV F38469.*

THE CAMERA IN THE CROWD

Filming New Zealand in Peace and War, 1895–1920

Christopher Pugsley
Foreword by Sir Peter Jackson

In association with Ngā Taonga Sound & Vision

Alla famiglia!
"T-T-To the family!"

— Johnny Cammareri, *Moonstruck* (1987)

Published by Oratia Books, Oratia Media Ltd, 783 West Coast Road,
Oratia, Auckland 0604, New Zealand (www.oratia.co.nz).
Copyright © 2017 Christopher Pugsley
Copyright © 2017 Oratia Books — published work
The copyright holders assert their moral rights in the work.

ISBN 978-0-947506-34-6

The publisher acknowledges the generous support of
Creative New Zealand for this publication.

The author acknowledges the support of the Literary
Trust of the National Army Museum over many years.

Jacket imagery

Main image: HRH Prince Edward being driven up Queen Street,
Auckland, 24 April 1920 (PA Coll-9055, ATL, Wellington).
Back cover (clockwise from top left): Still, *Scenes at the East End Annual
Picnic* (NTSV F2655); T.J. West filming at Whakarewarewa (F-54139-1/2,
ATL, Wellington); *The Kid from Timaru* poster (Eph-A-CINEMA-1918-01,
ATL, Wellington); Still, *With the New Zealand Expeditionary Force in the
United Kingdom Part I* (NTSV F1001).
Back flap: Author portrait by Harriet Bright (National Portrait Gallery).

First published 2017
Printed in China

Previous page: Returning home after reception for the American
officers of the Great White Fleet at the formal opening of the Rotorua
Bath House on 13 August 1908. Still from James McDonald's film
American Officers' Visit to Rotorua, on behalf of the Department of
Tourist and Health Resorts, NTSV F3033.

OTHER WORKS BY CHRISTOPHER PUGSLEY

Gallipoli: The New Zealand Story (1984; fifth edition 2014)
*On the Fringe of Hell: New Zealanders and Military Discipline in the
    First World War* (1991)
Te Hokowhitu A Tu: The Maori Pioneer Battalion in the First World War
    (1995; third edition 2015)
Ordinary People: New Zealanders Remember the Second World War
    (co-edited with Lindsay Missen and James Rolfe; 1995)
Scars on the Heart: Two centuries of New Zealand at war
    (with Laurie Barber, Buddy Mikaere, Nigel Prickett and Rose Young;
    1996. Revised as *Kiwis in Conflict: 200 Years of New Zealanders at
    War*, 2008)
The Anzacs at Gallipoli: A Story for Anzac Day (1999)
The New Zealanders at Gallipoli (1995; second edition 2000)
The German Empire and Britain's Pacific Dominions
    (co-edited with John Moses, 2000)
*The Anzac Experience: New Zealand, Australia and Empire in the First
    World War* (2001; second edition 2016)
*From Emergency to Confrontation: The New Zealand Armed Forces in
    Malaya and Borneo 1949–1966* (2003)
Operation Cobra: Battle Zone Normandy (2004)
Sandhurst: A Tradition of Leadership
    (co-edited with Angela Holdsworth; 2005)
Somewhere on the Western Front: Arras 1914–1918
    (with Jean-Marie Giradet, Alain Jacques, Jean-Luc Letho Duclos,
    Jean-Luc Gibot, Jean-Philippe Morange and Eric Sauvage; 2007)
*The Great Adventure Ends: New Zealand and France on the Western
    Front* (co-edited with Nathalie Philippe, John Crawford and
    Matthias Strohn; 2013)
Fighting for Empire: New Zealand and the Great War of 1914–1918
    (2014)
*A Bloody Road Home: World War Two and New Zealand's Heroic
    Second Division* (2014)
*Remembering Gallipoli: Interviews with New Zealand Gallipoli
    Veterans* (with Charles Ferrall; 2015)

Contents

Foreword

This is the book that I've hoped someone would write.

But I haven't been holding my breath. The amount of research and painstaking attention to detail required, in numerous film archives across the world, made it very unlikely — or so I thought.

I love old film — the silent black and white images that many people think of as jerky and 'sped-up'. New digital technology is arriving that can clean off the residue of time. Scratches can be removed, missing frames restored, the dancing film grain reduced, and the speed corrected.

Viewing these sharpened images is a startling experience, and it allows a new way to connect to our history — and to the New Zealanders who preceded us. I truly believe this technology will transform the way we regard these early films. But that is for the future; today we need to protect and preserve these valuable, often fragile, strips of film. These are so much more than old images — they are captured moments in the lives of early New Zealanders. Real moments that were lived then, and can live on for ever, but only if we protect and value them.

Did we even produce moving images in New Zealand 100 years ago? And if we did, what were they, and do they still survive somewhere?

Those are the questions Christopher Pugsley sets out to answer in this book, based on years of determined research.

New Zealand likes to think of itself as a young country, and I don't just mean that from a European perspective. Current historical thinking has us populated by birds, insects, lizards, and not much else, when William the Conqueror was making a name for himself.

But from the historical perspective of the moving image, we're no younger than any other country. In fact, we were right up there with the early motion-picture technology — as it was being invented, in some cases.

New Zealanders were looking into the peephole of the Kinetoscope a mere two years after Edison invented his 'amusement arcade' system. Based on a series of still images printed on a strip of moving film, and viewed through a revolving shutter, Edison's Kinetoscope is the stumbling birth of cinema.

Only a year after the Lumière brothers designed their Cinématographe projection system in Paris, Aucklanders were the first Kiwis to share in the wonder of a moving image projected onto a big screen.

Opposite page: Sydney Taylor in an Avro 504, with his camera mounted for aerial motion pictures. Taylor filmed the arrival of the Prince of Wales in 1920 on HMS *Renown* from a similar aircraft. Auckland War Memorial Museum M686.

Left: Capturing the moment of the big decision. Still from Brandon Haughton's *Taranaki Jockey Club's Annual Meeting*, 1912, NTSV F1465.

Less than two years after that, a motion picture cameraman in London filmed the first moving pictures of New Zealanders — or 'Maorilanders', as we were known back then. As the 19th century came to an end, Alfred Whitehouse had started touring New Zealand with a Kinematograph camera, filming moving pictures around the country.

There's a quote in this book describing these early movies as 'living pictures'. Today we should think of them as living history. We can see New Zealanders, born in the mid-1800s, moving, chatting, laughing. When these early movies are projected at the correct speed, our ancestors suddenly come alive as real people — just like us.

The Camera in the Crowd is the vital key to the mystery of unlocking this living history, unseen by most New Zealanders.

With this book, Christopher Pugsley has done New Zealand a great service. He has travelled the world, searching through numerous film archives for forgotten glimpses of our forebears. He has unearthed amazing surprises — for a century, the only 'known' moving images from the Gallipoli Campaign have been surviving fragments shot by an English journalist. But Chris has discovered not just one, but several more reels of Gallipoli footage, lying undisturbed and forgotten in English and French archives.

Not only does Dr Pugsley tell the many rich and entertaining stories of how motion picture cameras captured New Zealanders in the first turbulent decades of the 20th century, he provides us with all the links and archive information we need to peer into the past through this magical window of film.

You are holding a treasure trove in your hands. It's time to peer through that peephole, and see our country of 100 years ago come alive again.

Thank you, Chris.

Sir Peter Jackson
Wellington 2017

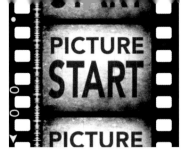

Introduction

This is the story of film in New Zealand for its first 25 years, 1895–1920, told largely through the film that has survived — mere fragments of the hundreds of films shot. It is the story of New Zealand and New Zealanders on film for the last years of the Victorian era and the first two decades of the 20th century: a period that encompasses great political, technological and cultural changes, including the cataclysm of the First World War. It tells of the cameramen or cinematographers (as they were known), of the film they took and how the public reacted to it, and of New Zealand in those eventful years.

Film is made to be seen on screen and this book reflects this by providing stills from the films discussed. Titles of surviving films are also identified by a small projector in the margin that allows you to access the film online and pause and have a look at what you are reading about (see the Using this book note that follows). Each page also includes a still from the 1914 film *Auckland's Expeditionary Force: The Minister of Defence Reviews the Troops* (NTSV F38469). You can see the complete film online, or you can enjoy this segment by watching the volunteers to the Main Body of the New Zealand Expeditionary Force (NZEF) march past by flipping the pages in the manner of the once very popular flip books. The film was possibly made by Frank Stewart, one of the stalwarts of early New Zealand filming, whose story is among the many told in this book.

Ngā Taonga Sound & Vision is New Zealand's audio-visual archive and is, as the name suggests, a treasure trove of New Zealand film. Many of these, including those of the First World War, disappeared from New Zealand collections through the disintegration of the highly sensitive and flammable nitrate stock, but many survived in overseas archives. Ngā Taonga has been actively seeking out and repatriating these treasures, but as you will see, many still are waiting to be returned. We are fortunate that many of these films are viewable online, but on the web nothing is permanent and so our films still need to come home.

As a boy growing up in Greymouth in the 1950s, going to the pictures was an integral part of my life. Saturday 'flicks' were at the Opera House or the Regent Theatre, and the matinee at the Opera House was my favourite, with visits to Frank Bell's and the Tip Top milk bars across the road. The Regent screened the feature film first, and if you had no money but hung round the foyer after the interval, the manager would often let you in for free to see the 'shorts'.

Opposite page: Brigadier-General F.E. Johnston intoduces King George V to Brigadier-General Herbert Hart, commanding the newly raised 4th New Zealand Brigade on Bulford Field. Lieutenant-General Godley commanding the New Zealand Expeditionary Force is on the left. A photographer captures the scene. Still from Sergeant Tommy Scale's first film as official cameraman, *His Majesty King George V Reviewing New Zealand Troops on Salisbury Plain*. NTSV F5540.

I started researching film and its history in 1983 as a by-product of my Gallipoli research, after being seconded to Television New Zealand from the New Zealand Army for 12 months as military advisor to the TV2 documentary *Gallipoli: The New Zealand Story*. Produced by Allan Martin, the director general of Television New Zealand, it was narrated by Lieutenant General Sir Leonard Thornton, directed by D.O.C. 'Doc' Williams, and had a script written by Maurice Shadbolt. We filmed on Gallipoli Peninsula and I spent a week in London viewing Gallipoli-related material at the Imperial War Museum, spending some hot days crammed into a viewing booth with Stephen Badsey, watching film on a Steenbeck film-editing table. Little could I anticipate that 11 years later I would be contributing my notes on New Zealand's official war film to the *Imperial War Museum Film Catalogue. Volume I: the First World War Archive* that Badsey was compiling; or that six years after that, we would be colleagues at the Royal Military Academy Sandhurst.

On Gallipoli I acted as military adviser and guide as well as clapperboard operator in the camera crew, marking the script, noting the timings and checking the camera for 'hairs in the gate' for Matt Bowkett, the principal cameraman. It was my one taste of what goes on in filming behind the camera. It was the year I completed my first book, *Gallipoli: The New Zealand Story*, and though I continued to serve in the New Zealand Army for another five years, this experience changed the course of my life. I found that I enjoyed both research and writing, and received great encouragement from Maurice Shadbolt, who read my draft chapters and set out the 'rules of the road' on how to finish the book.

I left the army in 1988 to become a professional historian. In 1989, to support my writing, I worked part-time as a consultant to National Archives on the National Collection of War Art. Under Ray Grover's direction as national archivist, Georgina Christensen and I put together *A Loss of Innocence*, a travelling exhibition on selected archives, paintings and drawings of the First World War to mark the sesquicentenary of the signing of the Treaty of Waitangi. It toured New Zealand for three years, with Sapper Horace Moore-Jones' *Sketches Made at Anzac* on loan from the Australian War Memorial. We thought there might be enough money for an exhibition video; we were dreaming, but at the New Zealand Film Archive (NZFA), as it was then, Bronwyn Taylor showed me the New Zealand official war films of the Western Front. They had not survived in New Zealand but had been repatriated from negatives held in the Imperial War Museum. (This has been ongoing; the most recent were returned through a funding grant from the Lottery World War One Commemorations, Environment and Heritage Committee.)

I had seen exactly the same images in the H-Series photographs that were the New Zealand official photographs taken on the Western Front and deposited in the Alexander Turnbull Library. The H-Series master photograph albums in the Alexander Turnbull number and date each image, with locations and principals also identified. Knowing this I was able to point out errors in the shot lists to the films. This led to a project funded by the Stout Research Trust to catalogue the NZFA's First World War films. They were paying me to watch movies. It was a consultancy that grew into a hobby and a delight that continues today, 27 years on. I worked with my researcher, Jean-Marie O'Donnell, guided by Elizabeth Street of the NZFA, researching and cataloguing both the war films and the pre-1914 military-related films. The weekly visit to the Archives, broken by 16 years overseas from 1997–2012, has led to many milestones along the way.

I was part of the team that, acting on a hunch by conservation manager Cushla Vula, identified Alfred Henry Whitehouse's *Departure of the Second Contingent,* which is now the oldest known film shot in New Zealand. Conservator Kurt Otzen's technical ingenuity devised a homemade steamer to soften the film enough for me to view it on the light table. Identification was aided by a team of New Zealand historians that provided confirmation while puzzling over the poor quality of the images that Kurt provided; one said that it could almost be film, but added that of course that was impossible. In this case the impossible was the reality.

Film was one of the projects I worked on in 1994 when appointed as writing fellow at Victoria University of Wellington, and I am grateful to the late Tim Beaglehole, Vincent O'Sullivan and the staff of the Department of History for their support in that most enjoyable year. In 1996 I worked with George and Anne Andrews on the television documentary *Journey to Arras* on the efforts of the New Zealand Tunnelling Company under the city of Arras during the First World War. We spent some days in Paris, including viewing engineering- and mining-related film of the First World War in the Service d'Information et de Relations Publiques des Armées (SIRPA) at Fort d'Ivry, Val du Marne.

During my time in the UK my colleagues in the Department of War Studies, Royal Military Academy Sandhurst assisted me when I road-tested some of my conclusions about Ellis Ashmead-Bartlett and his filming on Gallipoli. Director of Academic Studies Sean McKnight headed the committee that granted me sabbatical leave, and in 2008–2009 I returned to Taranaki Street for a delightful sabbatical during which I chronologically worked through and viewed all of the surviving New Zealand film of the period.

I am grateful to Roger Smither, Peter Simkins, Chris McCarthy, Toby Haggith and Philip Dutton, present and former members of the staff of the Imperial War Museum, who shared their knowledge and enthusiasm with me. The bibliographical note in the IWM War Museum Film Catalogue that mentions *The Camera in the Crowd* as an 'unpublished work in progress' can finally be updated.

Over the years I have viewed and catalogued film at various locations in Hunter and Tory streets and now Taranaki Street in Wellington. I have had the pleasure of working with the staff of the NZFA/Ngā Taonga Sound & Vision, enthusiasts all, over many years: Alex Burton, Virginia Callahan, Sarah Davy, Chris du Fall, Gareth Evans, Richard Faulkner, Kiri Griffin, David Klein, Jamie Lean, Leslie Lewis, Julian Millar, Johnny Morris, Mishelle Muagututi'a, Bryna O'Brien-Kiddey, Jane Paul, Diane Pivac, Zoe Robinson, Steve Russell, Peter Sarkey, Elizabeth Street, Mark Sweeney, Bronwyn Taylor, James Taylor, Sharon Trotter, Lawrence Wharerau, Amanda White, Tracy White, Cushla Vula and all. This was possible only with the support of the directors of the day: Kate Fortune, Cheryl Linge, Frank Stark and Rebecca Elvy.

The same applies to many other research institutions, libraries and archives. National Archives (now Archives New Zealand) and Ray Grover, national archivist, gave me a home after I left the army and set me on this journey. The manuscript and photography departments of the Alexander Turnbull Library, National Library of New Zealand freely shared advice and information over many years and I thank Joan McCracken and John O'Sullivan in particular. The National Library's Paper's Past website and digitised access to the photography and images collection have been vital research tools, both in my time overseas and from the wilds of Waikanae Beach. I extend my sincere thanks to Carolyn Carr and her team at the Defence Library in Wellington, Dolores Ho and the staff of the Kippenberger Library and Archives at the National Army Museum, Waiouru, and the librarian and staff at the Auckland War Memorial Museum. The BFI Library and Archives; Andrew Orgill and staff at the Library of the Royal Military Academy Sandhurst; Stephanie Boyle, George Imashev and Daniel Eisenberg at the Australian War Memorial; and Michael Kosmider and Simon Drake at the National Film & Sound Archive of Australia have all given

Gaumont Graphic shows the British public the first New Zealand soldiers to feature on newsreels in the First World War. Still from *Gaumont Graphic 380*, 12 November 1914, NTSV F914541.

generously of their time over the years. Michael has conducted important research into the filming of the Gallipoli Campaign, which continues. He and Paul Byrnes of the *Sydney Morning Herald* have both shared their own research with me and also reviewed my Gallipoli chapters.

During my time at Te Papa working on the *Gallipoli: The Scale of our War* exhibition, I enjoyed my engagement with Prue Donald and her team on the Ashmead-Bartlett film of Gallipoli. My thanks to Bill and Serpil Sellars for their friendship during our visits to Gallipoli over many years. Bill read some of the draft, allowed me access to his photo collection and shared his knowledge of the filming by Ottoman cameramen of prisoners during the August 1915 offensive.

In getting this book to publication, my mentor and good friend Ray Grover critically reviewed my draft as did Philip Dutton for the Gallipoli chapters. I am grateful to Sarah Davy, Jane Paul, Diane Pivac, Steve Russell, James Taylor and Lawrence Wharerau for reading and commenting on the draft. Natalie Marshall, curator of photography at the Alexander Turnbull Library, also read draft chapters and provided invaluable comment and advice. My good friend Mike Wicksteed in the UK also reviewed part of my draft and did important legwork for me in viewing film at the BFI Library.

I have worked closely with James Taylor, research coordinator at Ngā Taonga Sound & Vision, on researching and cataloguing repatriated First World War films from overseas film archives. It has been a partnership in exploration and discovery. Dr Lesley Lewis and Kurt Otzen continue to provide priceless gems from the nitrate collection and, together with Mishelle Muagututi'a and Tracey White, performed magic in producing all of the stills and photographs from the collection. I am very grateful to the present director, Rebecca Elvy, and the board for the provision of still images for the book from the Ngā Taonga library and film collection. I am also grateful for the support and friendship of the board chair, Jane Kominik, over many years.

I acknowledge and thank the institutions and archives that have allowed me access and permitted me to use images from their collections in this work. Alamy Images, Abingdon, UK; Alexander Turnbull Library, National Library of New Zealand, Wellington; Archives New Zealand,

Wellington; Australian War Memorial, Canberra, Australia; Auckland War Memorial Museum, Auckland; Bibliothèque Nationale de France, Paris, France; British Pathé Archives, London, UK; Canterbury Museum Collections, Christchurch; Gaumont Pathé Archives, Saint-Ouen, France; Hocken Library and Archives, University of Otago, Dunedin; Imperial War Museum, London, UK; Kippenberger Library and Archives, Lyttelton Museum, Lyttelton; Library of Congress, Washington, USA; National Army Museum, Waiouru; National Museum of Victoria, Melbourne, Australia; Ngā Taonga Sound & Vision, Wellington; National Film and Sound Archives, Sydney, Australia; Salvation Army, Fiji and Tonga Heritage Centre and Archives, New Zealand; Sir George Grey Special Collections, Auckland Libraries; State Library of New South Wales, Sydney, Australia; Tairāwhiti Museum, Gisborne; Tasmanian Archives and Heritage Office, Hobart, Australia; Te Papa Tongarewa, Museum of New Zealand, Wellington; Toitū, Otago Settlers Museum, Dunedin; Waddell Family; Whakatane Museum, Whakatane; Whanganui Regional Museum, Whanganui.

One name stands out in my endnotes and that is of the film historian Clive Sowry, who has been intimately involved with New Zealand film for almost half a century. With regards to New Zealand film he is the expert and I am the dilettante. During my research every time I thought I was breaking new ground, I would find his footprints ahead of me. I commissioned Clive to review my draft and gratefully received his copious notes and advice, all provided with his characteristic care and attention to detail. I am in his debt.

I acknowledge the ongoing support of the Literary Trust of the National Army Museum under its chair, David Moloney. The fund underpins research and publication across the spectrum of New Zealand's military endeavours and I appreciate the support it has given me over many years.

Peter Dowling at Oratia Books continues to bring out new editions of my existing works and accepted the challenge offered by *The Camera in the Crowd*, for which I am very grateful. Carolyn Lagahetau has been a superb editor, qualities matched by my copy editor Mitch Marks and proofreader Frances Chan, who also created the index. My daughter Susan Harris designed the book and, as you can see, when you flip the pages, it is like no other film book in bridging the gap between words and images so essential in a film history.

I am grateful to Sir Peter Jackson for his kind words in the foreword. We share a passion for the Gallipoli Campaign and it was a privilege assisting him on *The Great War Exhibition*, which also allowed me to glimpse a master film-maker at work. This led to my involvement with Sir Richard Taylor and his magicians at Weta Workshop, who combined with the equally talented Te Papa staff to create *Gallipoli: The Scale of Our War*, for which I was historical director. I always thought that the high point of my work on museum exhibitions about New Zealand at war would be the two years I spent with Rodney Wilson on *The Scars on the Heart* exhibition at the Auckland War Memorial Museum. I was wrong: working with the combined Weta/Te Papa team was like scaling Everest in terms of exhibition involvement. I have been so very lucky. In all of this endeavour I have been assisted by so many people, all of whom have my thanks. I have enjoyed this project and the mistakes are mine, but once again so is the delight.

Finally my love to Deanna, Joanna, Susan and David, our grandson Dylan, plus Ian, Camilla and all of the family. They have lived with my preoccupation with researching and writing books, my hobby and profession — something I have yet to get in balance, though perhaps there is still time.

Christopher Pugsley
Waikanae Beach 2017

Using this book

Ngā Taonga Sound & Vision, New Zealand's moving image and sound archive, has a treasure trove of material that can be accessed online (www.ngataonga.org.nz). Other film archives listed in these pages also contain New Zealand-related material. In each case where you see the projector image 🎥 enter the website and type in the catalogue number provided; this should enable you to view the film. For the full version of the Auckland's Expeditionary Force film shown in stills on each page, click on the Ngā Taonga website and enter the number F38469 into the Search box. Obviously websites continue to evolve and sometimes films can no longer be viewed. It is the long-term ambition to have all New Zealand-related material accessible through Ngā Taonga Sound & Vision, although in some cases items may be accessible only by visiting the access points listed on the Ngā Taonga website.

ACRONYMS

AAA	Amateur Athletics Association
ADS	Advanced Dressing Station
AIF	Australian Imperial Force
ANZAC	Australian and New Zealand Army Corps
ANZ	Archives New Zealand
ASC	Army Service Corps
AWM	Australian War Memorial
AWRS	Australian War Records Section
BEF	British Expeditionary Force
BFI	British Film Institute
BnF	Bibliothèque Nationale de France
CEF	Canadian Expeditionary Force
CEO	Corps Expéditionnaire d'Orient
CMG	Companion of the Order of St Michael and St George
DAQMG	Deputy Assistant Quartermaster General
DCM	Distinguished Conduct Medal
DCO	Draft conducting officers
DSO	Distinguished Service Order
FoL	Federation of Labour
GHQ	General Headquarters
IWM	Imperial War Museum
MDS	Main Dressing Station
MM	Military Medal
NAM	National Army Museum, Waiouru
NCO	Non-commissioned officer
NFSA	National Film & Sound Archives
NTSV	Ngā Taonga Sound & Vision
NZEF	New Zealand Expeditionary Force
NZFA	New Zealand Field Artillery
RAF	Royal Air Force
RFC	Royal Flying Corps
RMLE	Regiment de Marche de la Legion Étrangère
RNAS	Royal Naval Air Service
RNVAS	Royal Navy Volunteer Air Service
RSA	Returned Services Association
WOCC	War Office Cinema Committee

'A Marvellous Counterfeit'

There is of course no such thing as the 'motion picture', that is, a picture that actually moves. The illusion of continuous movement depends on a characteristic of the eye known as persistence of vision, which causes the eye to retain an image for a fraction of a second longer than it actually appears. Thus a number of pictures shown in very rapid succession are seen not as separate images but fused into a changing pattern ... In terms of cinematography this means that each frame on a roll of film is momentarily halted and projected onto the screen, then moved on and another picture substituted, all at the rate of sixteen frames per second for silent films and twenty-four frames per second for sound films. Thus the projection of each frame is fast enough for the eye to make the connection between one picture and the next, and so to create the illusion of continuous motion.[1]

THE MAGIC OF THE LANTERN

A shadow on a wall formed by the moonlight or by a torch in bed at night, and the stories that your imagination unfolds from this are part of most people's childhood. Shadows and shadow plays with shadow puppets have been with us for thousands of years. Projected images using 'magic lanterns' which projected glass slides onto a screen have been available since the 17th century. The lanterns were given that name even though they were nothing but a light source in the form of a candle and a lens; what the lantern did seemed 'magical'. It spurred the imagination and drew its audience into a world that was much richer than the simple image projected onto the wall. Magic lantern shows using painted images on glass were an integral part of the variety and vaudeville shows of the 19th century, being used to display the words to popular songs.[2] Various methods of levers and pulleys were also devised to make the projected images to move on the screen. Such machines have fascinated inventors over the centuries.[3]

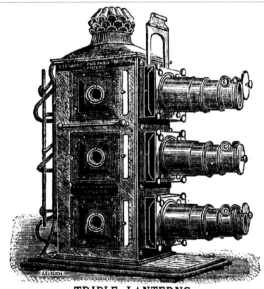

The advent of photography in 1827, using metal and then glass plates coated with chemicals, saw glass photographic slides of places and tableaux illustrating scenes of stories, plays and religious events incorporated into the magic lantern shows. In the 1890s these photographic and illustrated slide shows were a staple in a pastor's armoury for religious instruction, and for the travelling lecturer and raconteur speaking to rapt audiences of the wonders of the world or sharing details of the latest military campaign.

MAKING IT MOVE

Inventors endeavoured to discover how to create a machine that would record moving pictures of the world at large. The English photographer and experimenter Eadweard Muybridge (whose self-adapted name itself speaks of imagination and invention) was working in California when he perfected high-speed photography. He did this so that Leland Stanford, a railway baron and a United States senator, could determine whether his champion racehorse Occident ever had all four feet off the ground when racing.

In 1879 Muybridge invented the Zoopraxiscope. This machine projected a series of photographic images from a revolving disc containing successive phases of movement.[4] These images were obtained through the use of multiple cameras triggered by an electric current. After confirming that a galloping horse did have all four feet off the ground, Muybridge continued to photograph humans and animals in motion. In 1882 the Frenchman Étienne-Jules Marey, spurred on by Muybridge's work, used a round plate with 12 images per plate in a rifle-like camera with a clockwork motor. The instrument could take 12 pictures per second and capture the movement of a bird in flight.[5]

The next step forward was by George Eastman in the United States. He devised a system of coating rolls of paper with the light-sensitive chemicals needed to take photographic images. In

1888 he gave the Kodak camera to the world. From this followed the invention of the celluloid film roll, which Eastman developed in 1889.

It was now that Thomas Alva Edison, the 'Wizard of Menlo Park', where the Edison Laboratories were established, stepped into frame. Edison had become the 'businessmen's inventor' in the 1870s when he and his assistants developed a series of inventions in the telegraph, communications, power transmission and transportation that made him world famous. His invention of the phonograph to record and replay sound saw him take this concept and apply it to the development of a motion-picture system that shaped the work of other pioneers in the field.[6]

Thomas Edison testing his phonograph c.1900. ©Chronicle/Alamy Stock Photo.

Muybridge visited Edison in 1888 and discussed the possibilities for collaborating on combining the Zoopraxiscope with the phonograph. This was not pursued by Edison but it spurred him to examine how to achieve moving images on film. Using the phonograph as a model Edison saw the development of a device which would 'do for the eye what the phonograph does for the ear' — record and reproduce objects in motion. Edison called the invention a 'Kinetoscope', using the Greek words 'kineto' meaning 'movement' and 'scopos' meaning 'to watch'. Edison's team of inventors and designers led by Edison's assistant William Kennedy-Laurie Dickson, an "Englishman born in France but with family ties in the USA", developed a camera capable of recording successive images, using the celluloid negative film invented by Eastman. Edison's camera was the practical, cost-effective breakthrough that influenced all subsequent motion picture devices.[7] From 1891–92 Dickson's team designed not only the camera — using film stock that Dickson spilt and perforated to 35 mm, which, until the advent of digital, became the industry standard — but also the system needed to make it function as a commercial entity: camera, studio, laboratory to develop and print the films and then the means of projection — the Kinetoscope.[8]

The Kinetoscope was a peepshow machine that enabled the viewer to see moving pictures on a continuous looped strip of film lit by electric light, powered by battery. Each film allowed the viewer to see moving pictures for a brief and tantalising 20 seconds before the same scene was repeated. Film historian David Robinson writes:

> It consisted of an upright wooden cabinet, 18 in. x 27 in. x 4 ft. high, with a peephole with magnifying lenses in the top … Inside the box the film, in a continuous band of approximately 50 feet, was arranged around a series of spools. A large, electrically driven sprocket wheel at the top of the box engaged corresponding sprocket holes punched in the edges of the film, which was thus drawn under the lens at a continuous rate. Beneath the film was an electric lamp, and between the lamp and the film a revolving shutter with a narrow slit. As each frame passed under the lens, the shutter permitted a flash of light so brief that the frame appeared to be frozen. This rapid series of apparently still frames appeared, thanks to the persistence of vision phenomenon, as a moving image.[9]

Developed and refined in 1892–93, the Kinetoscope's commercial release was advertised for the Chicago World's Fair, or World's Columbian Exposition, which ran from 1 May to 30 October 1893 to commemorate the four-hundredth anniversary of Christopher Columbus's discovery of the New World. Chicago was a display — to the world — of American inventive commercial genius. Illuminated by electric light, the fair saw the introduction of Quaker Oats, Cracker Jacks, Aunt Jemima pancake mix, Juicy Fruit chewing gum, shredded wheat and, some say, the hamburger. Over it all towered the world's first giant Ferris wheel.[10] That Edison's Kinetoscope was not introduced as planned was due to the need for Edison's team to make what was outwardly a simple machine, robust enough to continuously show the loop of film without tearing or wearing out the film too quickly.[11] It was promised but did not arrive, but as it turned out there was a New Zealand salesman at the World Fair who did capitalise on Edison's inventions, a man who would become the pioneer of moving film exhibition in New Zealand — Alfred Henry Whitehouse.

ALFRED HENRY WHITEHOUSE: NEW ZEALAND FILM PIONEER

Whitehouse was born in Birmingham, England, in 1856 and came out to New Zealand with his parents around 1864 to settle in North Auckland.[12] At the time of his marriage to Eliza Davis in Auckland in 1878 he was working as a bootmaker. He set up business in Duke Street, Cambridge, "and is prepared to make all kinds of Boots and Shoes on the shortest notice — combining comfort with elegance and durability, at moderate prices."[13] By 1882 he had moved his business to Te Aroha and by 1890 no longer worked in his trade but acted as a travelling salesman, measuring clients for tailoring throughout the Waikato area for the firm of G. McBride Merchant Tailors, of Customs Street East, Auckland, who advertised that they were "The Largest Tailoring Concern in New Zealand".[14] Despite his wife's death and being left a widower with five children, it seems Whitehouse had a flair for salesmanship and his work for the company eventually extended to cover all of the North Island.

In 1895 Whitehouse gave an interview to the press on how he became involved with moving film.

I am not a native of this country, but have lived here since I was a child. My first trip away was taken two years ago, when I went to the World's Fair at Chicago, and was the only commercial traveller from New Zealand taking part, when 10,000 'C.T.'s' turned out in procession on commercial traveller's day at the Exhibition. I was given a leading position and treated right royally, and given a banner for my country. On my return I took to exhibiting the Phonograph which I had purchased while there.[15]

It may have been the Kinetoscope that drew Whitehouse to Chicago in the first place, but the delays in production meant that he had to be satisfied with the Edison phonograph which had been successfully toured in theatres, with the coin-operated version listened to on earphones in nickel phonograph parlours throughout the United States.[16] Selling was his business and Whitehouse took the phonograph on tour in 1894, concentrating on the areas of New Zealand where he was already well known as a commercial traveller. This proved rewarding enough for Whitehouse to take a further gamble, and in 1895 he set off back to the United States with the sole intent of purchasing Edison's latest invention — the Kinetoscope.

Viewing through a Kinetophone allowed the viewer to watch and listen to music at the same time. Whitehouse toured at least one of these machines. Edison, Library of Congress.

PHONOGRAPH AND VOCAL COM-
BINATION COMPANY.

FORESTERS' HALL, NEWTON.

TUESDAY NEXT, Oct. 23.
Introducing, for the first time in New Zealand,
Young's
AUTOMATIC REPRODUCER,
Or SOUND MAGNIFIER.
Just arrived by the last 'Frisco mail.

This invention increases the volume of sound
fully fourfold. Each item distinctly heard in
every part of the hall.

Monster Programme. Splendid selections of
Military, Orchestral, and String Bands; Cornet,
Piano, Banjo, Mandolin, and Piccolo Solos;
Songs by the leading professional artistes;
Gladstone's magnificent Speech.

The Phonograph Items will be interspersed
with Songs by Mr JOHN FULLER, Auckland's
favourite Tenor; Mr EDMOND MONTGOMERY,
and Mr A. H. WHITEHOUSE.

Admission, One Shilling Children, half-
price; Babies, One Guinea.

Pianist   ..   MISS McCLATCHEY.
Doors open 7.30, Overture 8 p.m.
A. H. WHITEHOUSE,
Exhibitor.

Above: Alfred Henry Whitehouse
in the *NZ Observer and Free
Lance*, 21 December 1895, p. 9.

Left: Three veterans of
entertainment in New Zealand
— John Fuller, Edmond
Montgomery and
A.H. Whitehouse.
Auckland Star,
20 October 1894.

> I left Auckland on the 15th June this year: stayed four days in ' Frisco, ten days in Chicago, and
> ten in New York, and only seven in the World's Metropolis, London. I came back via Suez, and
> landed back just seventeen weeks from the time I started, having travelled 28,000 miles, crossing
> four oceans, seeing many lands, many people, but feeling fairly satisfied that there is no place like
> New Zealand.[17]

One can see that Whitehouse had the 'gift of the gab', but more importantly his trip to the
Edison works and, no doubt, visits to working Kinetoscope parlours and exhibitions in the
United States, enabled him to come back with four machines with all of the associated batteries
and equipment and film to put them on the road as a touring exhibition.

Whitehouse became the first person to exhibit motion pictures in New Zealand when he
opened his Kinetoscope exhibition in the vestibule of W.H. Bartlett's studio at 322 Queen Street,
Auckland, on 29 November 1895.[18] His was a small-time shop-front operation that rented space
in the ornate and impressive foyer of Bartlett's photographic studios but its unique and unusual
nature soon gained a great deal of public interest. After paying one shilling (children sixpence),
adults could look into each machine in turn as the brief loop of film lit by electric light showed
films from the Edison studios. Whitehouse advertised this as his First Series, which included
The Barber Shop, *The Fire Rescue Scene*, *The Chinese Laundry* and *Annabelle's Butterfly Dance*. He

Barbershop, T.A. Edison.
YouTube.

Souvenir Strip The Edison Kinetoscope. *Eugene Sandow The modern Hercules.* Taken and copyrighted by W.K.L Dickson, 1894. Science History Images/Alamy Stock Photo.

Serpentine Dance. NTSV F2909.

Annabelle's Butterfly Dance had a touch of ankle to please the viewers. Edison, Library of Congress.

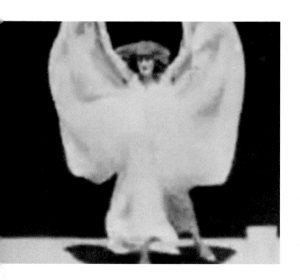

replaced these with a second series three weeks into the exhibition and also introduced his audience to the Kinetophone, "a combination of the Kinetoscope and the phonograph, which enabled viewers to see, for example, Annabelle perform her butterfly dance to music by the Paragon Trio."[19] You paid your money and then filed through looking at each peepshow in turn and for a brief 20–30 seconds you were in the world of moving pictures. It was something that you could only share with a companion once you were outside, the queues preventing any lingering or discussion, but it was a first and Whitehouse found himself with a novelty that everyone wanted to see and — equally important — was a commercial success.

His films were produced for the Kinetoscope under the direction of Edison's motion-picture expert, William Kennedy-Laurie Dickson. Most of the Edison productions were filmed in a specially constructed film studio at the Edison facility at West Orange. This was built on a revolving base so that it could be turned to follow the sun and was nicknamed 'Black Maria' as it was covered in black tar paper. In this studio films were made that now entranced New Zealand audiences and by 1895, the year Dickson left Edison, some 125 films were available.[20]

The Barber Shop shows a customer getting a lightning-fast shave for five cents and completed within the film's 20 seconds. *The Chinese Laundry* or *The Pursuit of Hop Lee* was some agile slapstick by the actors Robetta and Doretto. The scene and storyline is compressed into 20 seconds and so through the peephole we have a furious confrontation, a chase involving a revolving door, and Hop Lee's revenge. It still brings a chuckle from the viewer today. Of a different order were Miss Annabelle Whitford's dances for the camera.[21] She made many appearances in the Edison studio and both *Annabelle's Butterfly Dance* and *Annabelle's Serpentine Dance* show enough leg and ankle to excite the male audience of the day, while the hand-coloured images still have a beauty and magic to entrance the viewer.[22]

Whitehouse's set of four peepshow Kinetoscopes in Bartlett's Queen Street studio foyer was not considered mainstream theatre entertainment enough to be reviewed along with other theatre shows in the entertainment columns but its novelty value and commercial success could not be ignored. There was a clever little inclusion on the theatre review page of the *NZ Observer and Free Lance* on 14 December 1895 in the lead-up to Christmas. It read like a review but may have been a paid advertisement.

Most people, no doubt, have heard or read of Edison's latest, and, perhaps, most wonderful invention, the Kinetoscope; but until one has seen for himself, it is impossible to properly realise how perfectly living action is reproduced and presented to the eye of the wondering beholder. Talk about magic, why, magic isn't in it with this marvellous invention.[23]

It finished with the exhortation: "Everyone should see the Kinetoscope, which is exhibited by Mr Whitehouse, at Bartlett's Studio, Queen-street." Don't the words have a Whitehouse ring to them? It clearly brought in the crowds and this also led to Whitehouse's photograph appearing in the *NZ Observer and Free Lance* the following week on 21 December 1895, above the title: "Mr A. H. Whitehouse The introducer and exhibitor of Edison's Kinetescope [sic]", no small accolade, as at that time, photos were limited to usually a single inclusion per issue and then usually of local politicians and dignitaries.[24]

In February 1896 Whitehouse took his Kinetoscopes on tour through the North Island. It gave New Zealand a first glimpse of the magic of moving pictures. For Whitehouse it was a commercial triumph. His programme showed an extended range of Edison material including the original favourites showing a "Miss Annabelle of New York" skirt dance — "an exact reproduction of a graceful whirl" — and a cockfight giving the viewer "almost as much excitement as a genuine set-to".[25]

Whitehouse toured from town to town, judging the length of stay in each by the crowds that came. He was a one-man band, looking for empty shop space to set up business, no doubt using contacts gained from his previous tours with the phonograph, bringing in the heavy jukebox-sized Kinetoscopes — with all the batteries and equipment to keep them running — by horse-drawn wagon, employing local labour to help unload and set up shop, having primed the town with advertising in the local papers in advance. By American standards his four machines were 'small beer', but he had no competition in New Zealand and it proved to be a goldmine. There was a successful extended run in Wanganui in late May to early June 1896 where, according to his advertisements, over 2000 people viewed the show.[26] The exhibition promised "Several Highland Ladies Dancing, Boxing Cats, Napoleon's March, Scenes from Rob Roy, 34 characters on the stage in full Costume while the Band is seen and heard" and "Princess Ali, Native Dance or Haka".[27] This last title with its Maori ring has been adapted by Whitehouse to appeal to his New Zealand audience; the film itself shows an Egyptian belly dancer and musicians. However, by the end of the Wanganui season it seems that the crowd favourites were the cockfight and Annabelle's butterfly dance, where in her twirl, in addition to her ankles, a clear glimpse of a delightfully naked knee is also seen.[28]

Whitehouse arrived in Napier on 27 June 1896 and immediately attracted the crowds. His four machines were set up in a building in Hastings Street opposite the Bank of New Zealand, where for one shilling members of the audience could view each machine in turn: "Photographed from Natural Life and being reproduced in the Kinetoscope the characters

T**HE CROWNING TRIUMPH OF PHOTOGRAPHIC ART,** EDISON'S LATEST AND GREATEST ACHIEVEMENT, T**HE** K**INETOSCOPE.**

NOW ON VIEW AT BARTLETT'S STUDIO (By the kind permission of Mr W. H. Bartlett), Having just returned from a trip round the world (circling the globe in four months), taken solely for the purpose of bringing to New Zealand this emanation of genius.

THE KINETOSCOPE, Which reproduces motions of any kind with startling reality. The First Series of Scenes includes: The Barber's Shop — The Fire Rescue Scene — The Chinese Laundry — Annabelle's Graceful Butterfly Dance.

London *Daily News*, October 18, 1894 : —It is a living picture of a new order. A skirt dancer is seen among her flowing drapery, and she bends her knees, travels on her toes, and indulges in a giddy spin. It is just as one sees her on the stage.

Evening News and Post, October 24, 1894 : —Go and see the kinetoscope before you are a day older.

London *Morning Post*, October 18, 1894 : —The pictures are all perfect in themselves, are magnified in the machine, and illuminated by electric light.

All of which may be seen for ONE SHILLING.

A. H WHITEHOUSE, EXHIBITOR. Bartlett's Studio, Queen-street (formerly known as Tuttle's Studio).

NZ Observer and Free Lance, 4 January 1896. p. 6.

Sandow the Strong Man. NTSV F2628.

are perfect in every movement and detail; even a passing smile is plainly discernible."[29] To complement his machines Whitehouse also had his 'Splendid Phonograph' with a selection of 60 items from which one could choose and, for three pence an item, hear it through a set of earphones.

Whitehouse had to stop his programme for running repairs because after two days of continuous and profitable viewing the Kinetoscope batteries ran down and had to be recharged. The film, too, felt the demand and the very popular rooster film broke down. He also found that his Maori patrons monopolised the viewings and, mindful of the demand, Whitehouse extended his stay to almost a fortnight to "give Europeans an opportunity to view the only Kinetoscope in New Zealand".[30]

While Whitehouse had little competition in Napier and Hastings where he opened on 13 July 1896, his exhibition ran comfortably alongside the vaudeville and concert programmes in the larger towns with established theatres and halls, and brought something new to the smaller centres where it could be set up in rented space within a large local store.

Auguste and Louis Lumière were the first to perfect a system for taking and projecting moving pictures with their Cinématographe, which was given its first display in Paris on 22 March 1895. ©Photo 12 / Alamy Stock Photo.

THE LUMIÈRE BROTHERS PROJECT FILM

The Kinetoscope had encouraged inventors and mechanics around the world to achieve the projection of film onto a screen in the same manner as with a magic lantern. Auguste and Louis Lumière were the first to perfect a system for taking and projecting motion pictures with their Cinématographe, which was given its first display in Paris on 22 March 1895 and its first commercial public presentation to a paying audience of 33 people in the basement of the Grand Café, 14 Boulevard des Capucines in Paris, on Saturday 28 December 1895. There had been previous screenings to select private audiences. That of 11 July 1895 in the reception rooms of the Revue Générale des Sciences to an audience of some 150 people was described by André Gay:

The Cinematograph was illuminated electrically by means of a Molteni bulb. The images were projected onto a screen five metres distance from the lens, made of fine transparent cloth and stretched in the doorway between two of the rooms. On one side spectators saw the image reflected and, on the other, equally sharp but through the cloth. The first film showed trick riding by cavalrymen with all the skill of their kind; then a military joke; then a house on fire, flames engulfing the building, smoke in the sky, firemen arriving, drenching the house with water and putting the fire out. The next film showed life-like blacksmiths exercising their trade: the iron reddened in the fire, was beaten into shape, dipped into water to let off a jet of steam … A little girl, life-size [sic] was particularly popular. She was eating out of doors, in between her parents who were feeding her. Nothing prettier than the delightful expressions of a happy child enjoying the morsels her father was giving her and holding down her bib against the wind with her tiny hands. The same child delighted the audience in another film by trying unsuccessfully to catch goldfish in a bowl with the help of a spoon.[31]

Lumière's simple scenes on screen entranced every audience and led crowds to the basement of the Grand Café to see this wonderful magic. C. Francis Jenkins and Thomas Armat achieved the first projection of films in the United States. Armat, working separately, improved the original design and his electrically driven Vitascope projector was marketed under the Edison name, with its first public showing at Koster and Bial's Music Hall in New York on 23 April 1896, after which it rapidly became a craze throughout the United States. Rival firms raced each other to put projectors on the market in the United States and Europe. Edison, having reaped the benefit of Armat's original design, replaced the Vitascope with his own projecting Kinetoscope in February 1897.[32]

FILMS ON SCREEN COME TO NEW ZEALAND

It was inevitable that Whitehouse's initiative with the Kinetoscope was soon overshadowed by the first public screening of motion pictures in New Zealand, which was presented at the Opera House in Auckland on 13 October 1896 by 'Professors' Hausmann and Gow as part of the performance of Charles Godfrey's Vaudeville Company.[33] The conjurer and illusionist George Percy Hausmann was born in Christchurch in 1869. He made conjuring, his schoolboy hobby, his profession, going on the road as a magician's assistant at the age of 12. After stints behind a public bar and in acting, he headed his own show as a conjuror, touring New Zealand in 1888. He was always looking for something new and in 1896 he and John Gow of Dunedin imported the "first exhibition Rontgen X-rays apparatus, which he exhibited before the Governor and his Lady, Lord and Lady Glasgow at Government House".[34] Edison's projector was Hausmann's next imported novelty after he wrote to Edison, using the notepaper of the Metropolitan Hotel in Wellington, enquiring about this new invention. "Your name is as well known here as that of God Almighty himself and that is why I am sending for reliable information to yourself."[35] It worked. Hausmann and Gow bought an Edison Vitascope projector and a series of films and were signed up by Australasia's leading theatrical entrepreneur, Mr L.J. 'Daddy' Lohr, to tour with Charles Godfrey's Vaudeville Company projecting their films onto a screen between the live performances.

> Subjects including — Train in Full Motion — Sea Bathing — Electric Trams — Merry-go-Rounds — Dancing Girls — London Streets — and others too numerous to mention … Everything moved as though in life; in fact it was life reproduced. So natural was it that the moving pictures on the screen were cheered.[36]

'Professor' George Percy Hausmann, a magician and escape artist who later toured as Percy Verto 'The Handcuff King'. He and 'Professor' John Gow projected film onto a screen on 13 October 1896 in the first public performance in New Zealand at the Opera House, Auckland, as part of Charles Godfrey and his Vaudeville Company's performance. Australian Postal History & Social Philately. AusPostalHistory.com.

```
        Amusements.
O P E R A   H O U S E.
Lessee and Manager   ..  L. J. Lohr.
Business Manager     ..  Edwin Geach.

     TO-NIGHT.        TO-NIGHT.

CHARLES  GODFREY
CHARLES  GODFREY
        AND HIS
   VAUDEVILLE COMPANY.
Now terminating a phenomenally successful season
            in Auckland.

     LAST NIGHT BUT THREE.

CHARLES GODFREY TO-NIGHT,
In his intensely realistic Dramatic Scena, entitled,
          "DREAMS."
In conjunction with, by arrangement with
   Professors Hausman and Gow.
   EDISON'S LATEST MARVEL,
THE WONDER OF THE 19TH CENTURY.

THE  KINEMATOGRAPH.
THE  KINEMATOGRAPH.

At present the rage of London, Paris, and New
                 York.
MOVING FIGURES IN LIFE-LIKE ACTION.
A Truly Wonderful Development of Instantaneous
            Photography
Producing every action of Real Life with astounding
              fidelity.
   LIFE SIZE VIEWS AND SCENES
Everybody Astonished      Everybody Amazed
The Two Entertainments forming the Greatest
   Attraction ever offered to the New
          Zealand Public.

     Prices : 4s, 2s 6d, and 1s.
Box-plan at Wildman's.  Day Sale at Wildman's
          and Williams's.
Doors open 7.15 ; Commence at 8 ; Terminating at
              10.30.

SPECIAL NOTICE !
        SPECIAL NOTICE !

THE  KINEMATOGRAPH
THE  KINEMATOGRAPH

Owing to the Enormous Expense entailed in con-
nection with the engagement of Edison's Wonderful
Machine, it will be on view only until
          SATURDAY NEXT
Arrangements have been made, however, to have it
             exhibited
   DURING THE AFTERNOON
         at the hours of
   2    3    4    5
            O'CLOCK.
ADMISSION ...................ONE SHILLING
THIS AFTERNOON !  THIS AFTERNOON !
```

This New Zealand audience found themselves transported to a different world, a world away from where they lived — it was New Zealand's first taste of the wonders of film on screen. This experience involved the audience, who lived and shared the moment on screen and whose shared response heightened the experience, something that the peephole of the Kinetoscope could never do.

Veritable living pictures were thrown upon the screen, the effect being wonderful. In a bathing scene, the waves could be seen dashing in one after another on the beach, while the bathers dived and disported themselves. One of the most successful pictures was that of a skirt dance in which even the original limelight effects were reproduced in the picture. In another picture a train comes rattling up to the station, the doors open and people pour out, every detail of the busy scene being shown with marvellous fidelity.[37]

Godfrey's season at the Opera House lasted five days of packed houses with four matinees and an evening session daily at the cost of one shilling's admission. Later that month on 28 October the Australian showman Joseph F. MacMahon, the youngest of the three MacMahon Brothers, all well-known theatre entrepreneurs, exhibited 12 films at the Exchange Hall on Lambton Quay in Wellington, giving the capital its first taste of films on screen.[38] MacMahon, no stranger to New Zealand theatre and using another veteran showman John Tait as his advance agent, successfully toured his 'Cinematographe', which it seems was not a Lumière Cinématographe as the name suggests but simply MacMahon's renaming of his Edison Vitascope projector to distinguish it from the Hausmann and Gow machine. Having something different and reaching the audience first was everything. "Mr Macmahon [sic] has got ahead of the rival cinemat, now journeying from the north, and so he says he won't stay long with us, but will keep moving on."[39]

MacMahon acted as Master of Ceremonies and announced each film while a Mr Margery operated the projector, running the programme hourly six times a day.

First the living presentment of Sandow the strong man stood before us, and as he bent and turned like a living statue we saw the magnificent development of the muscles of his body. A burlesque highland fling by six 'stage Scotsmen' caused roars of laughter. An ambitious subject was the presentment of the execution of Mary Queen of Scots in all its gruesome details. The interior of a barber's shop crowded with moving figures … a wrestling match between a man and a dog, a champion lady shot firing at and breaking glass balls thrown into the air, a rescue by a fireman of children from a presumably burning building, a military operatic march, a broad-sword combat and a skirt dance by three 'Gaiety Girls' were each successive proofs of the capabilities of the invention. But the palm among the pictures must

New Zealand Herald, 14 October 1896.

be accorded the skirt dance by Miss St Cyr, the limelight effects of which were beautifully rendered, while the grace of revolutions far exceeded any dancing we have seen in New Zealand.[40]

Motion pictures had the same impact in Wellington as the films shown in Auckland. "Although Mac and his cine were here but a few days, the shivery-shakery photo affair managed to do as many turns as a bobby on his beat, and nearly as good business as Newhaven on the turf."[41] After a successful week MacMahon's show moved on to Christchurch and continued to successfully tour New Zealand into March 1897. Godfrey's Vaudeville Company with Hausmann and Gow's film programme followed him to Wellington showing many of the same films. Critics were quick to compare the quality of the two shows.

> The Cine-what is a real wonder, and hasn't the wobbles quite as bad in spots as the one that's spelt with a final "e". So real are the pictures, and so natural and alive the people in 'em, that you imagine for the moment you are the fellow on the other side of the road watching the busy street scenes, that you're by the seaside watching the bathers, and if you only whistle you'll be prepared to swear it was you made that chap turn round as he hurries up the street. It's realism, and the people are all alive O![42]

Carl Hertz, magician and cinema pioneer. *A Modern Mystery Merchant,* Hutchinson & Co. 1924.

Given that both MacMahon and Hausmann and Gow were using Edison machines, it seems the criticism of MacMahon's 'shivery-shakery' projection can be laid at its operation and maintenance by Mr Margery, the projectionist. However, its novelty more than compensated for faults in projection. Motion pictures were something new and showmen were always looking for the next technical fad to keep attracting the crowds. Leaving the Godfrey Company, Hausmann and Gow toured their Kinematograph and X-ray machine throughout New Zealand, before finally selling the machine and film stock: Gow continuing to tour X-rays, while Hausmann continued his mix of conjuring and film, touring as Professor Hausmann's Lumigraph Company.[43]

Film programmes were generally a choice of Edison, R.W. Paul or films taken for the Edison projector. The different perforations of the Lumière films meant that they could not be screened on Edison projectors. No Lumière films were shown in New Zealand until Wybert Reeve's tour in 1897–98. Films produced by the Lumière brothers were much more ambitious than those of Edison's more static productions, with Edison not producing a portable camera that could shoot outdoors until May 1896. The Lumière catalogue reflected the versatility of the Lumière camera, which could both take and project film. By 1896 Lumière agents were travelling the world, filming local scenes or 'actualities', showing them to local audiences to rapturous amazement, as well as sending prints back to the Lumière factory for worldwide distribution. Whether as a filler in a vaudeville show or as a dedicated film screening, film, first seen as a scientific novelty and to theatre managers as a passing fad, very quickly became a medium of information, showing images of faraway places with strange sounding names.[44]

Carl Hertz, the world famous American magician, 'prestidigitateur' and illusionist, had successfully toured New Zealand in 1892. He too used film as part of his act when he opened

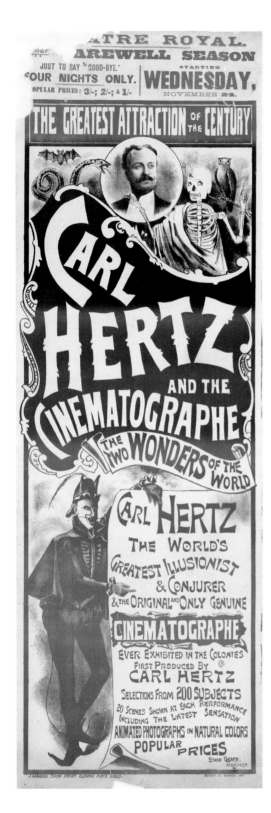

Carl Hertz and the cinematographe — the
two wonders of the world. Theatre Royal Hobart,
November 1897. This followed a similar pattern
to his programme in New Zealand. Tasmanian
Archive and Heritage Office. (See colour section.)

in Auckland on 20 February 1897 after a successful tour of Australia, where
he had been the first exhibitor in Australia to project film onto a screen in a
preview at the Melbourne Opera House on 17 August 1896.[45] Hertz used a
Theatrograph projector manufactured by the Englishman R.W. Paul, with film
shot by Birt Acres and Paul himself, as well as Edison material. However, after
a successful season in Wellington and Christchurch, where it did not hurt his
reputation that his manager, Edwin Geach, was fined five shillings for having
an overcrowded theatre, his show at the Princess Theatre in Dunedin was more
eventful when a reel of film was destroyed by fire during the Saturday evening
performance on 17 April 1897.

> [The] first indication that anyone in the crowded auditorium had of
> anything being wrong was a sudden blaze of light between the dress circle
> entrance and the barrier at the back of the seats. This was followed by the
> blazing of a baize screen which, enclosing the lantern, had been placed in the
> middle doorway immediately opposite the stage … There was a good deal of
> screaming by women, a large number of people rose to their feet and several
> persons made a rush for the stage; but Mr Hertz himself, running to the
> front of the circle, assured those downstairs that there was no danger, and
> members of the audience repeated his assurance and advised that all should
> keep their seats.[46]

It seems inflammable liquid had spilt on a couch near the lantern and had
caught fire, destroying eight films to the value of £200. It highlighted the
dangers inherent in showing film in an open theatre and the incident was
widely reported, but it did not stop the crowds wanting to see this new
marvel. Hertz was mindful of the risk and according to Clive Sowry he
then operated the projector from the rear of the stage onto a translucent
screen, minimising the danger of fire to the audience and also reducing
machine noise.[47]

   After the performance in Oamaru later in the month the theatre critic of
the *North Otago Times* wrote:

> When one can, by attending an entertainment by Carl Hertz, see the children
> playing on the beach at Brighton, the Boulevards of Paris, Charing Cross,
> and the dashing of a storm on the coast of Galicia, one must soon doubt the
> necessity for travel at all. And when Trilby, and the death of Svengali, and
> Loie Fuller in her inimitable skirt dance are so realistically produced the
> entertainment of Carl Hertz becomes at once a panorama, a theatre, and a
> music hall.[48]

Hertz made full use of this latest scientific marvel, playing to packed houses
throughout New Zealand in 1897 with repeated visits to every town with a
theatre large enough to warrant a profitable return, and enjoyed a successful
tour through India, Burma, Singapore, Hong Kong and the Dutch East Indies
into 1898.[49]

Whitehouse's Kinetoscope successfully toured the North Island throughout 1896, ending with a season at the Wellington Industrial Exhibition in the city and then at the Wellington A & P Show at the Petone showground. Christmas saw him at the Clifton Photo Studio, Willis Street, Wellington. Inevitably his Kinetoscope was compared to the projected film images already seen by Wellington audiences. The *Evening Post* reporter described it as a "Kinematograph in minature, and with much greater smoothness in its action as the Kinematographic views we have yet seen here".[50]

Whitehouse did good business but realised that any future in motion pictures was in projecting film.[51] He knew he had to keep abreast of the times, and projecting images would also move him from shop front to theatre hall and a much larger audience who would each pay the same price as individuals viewing the Kinetoscope. With the advent of projected images onto the screen in the United States, the Kinetoscope had gone through a similar cycle of boom then bust, and now it was time to move on.[52]

Whitehouse sold his machines and in 1897 once again travelled to the Edison studios where he met the great man and purchased the latest Edison projector with a stock of film and the latest phonograph.[53] He then travelled on to London for the Queen's Diamond Jubilee celebrations, the film of which he purchased, before returning to New Zealand, arriving in Wellington on 8 September 1897. The *Evening Post* announced his arrival on the *Ruahine*, reporting Whitehouse's purchase of "one of Edison's projecting Kinetoscopes which he has bought out to Wellington. The views are to be lighted by a special dynamo and engine bought by Mr Whitehouse in London." It also reported Whitehouse's personal interview with Edison "who gave him an autograph letter certifying that the machine was the first he has sent to the colony".[54] It may have been the first authorised Edison machine, but Whitehouse returned to a country avid to see this new invention — one that was quickly being acquired by every travelling showman keen to draw an audience.

The brothers Auguste and Louis Lumière's Cinématographe which combined a camera for recording the movement, a printer and, when connected to a magic lantern, a projector. It was lightweight and mobile. *Le Magazine du Siecle*, 1897.

THE PREMIERS VISIT TO HUNTLY (KING MAHUTA NEXT THE PREMIER) ESCORT KING MAHUTA BACK TO WAHI (PROTECTED BY 98) BEATTIE & SANDERSON, RUCKL

2

Whitehouse films
New Zealand

*I well remember the excitement with which the Low family sat — myself
spellbound — in the dress circle of the Christchurch Opera House to see this
marvellous new magic lantern which showed pictures that moved.*[1]

KING DICK'S GOD'S OWN

New Zealand in the late 1890s was the New Zealand of Premier 'King Dick' Seddon, who had
succeeded John Ballance as premier and leader of the Liberal Party in April 1893. Seddon was
Lancashire-born, and worked on the Victorian goldfields in Australia, following the gold to
Westland where he established himself as a storekeeper and publican, first in Hokitika and then
in Kumara. Local politics followed. Seddon was elected to Parliament as member for Hokitika
in 1879, later representing Kumara and then Westland. He was a gut politician who relied on his
instincts to know what people wanted.

> He seldom read anything not immediately relevant, his public speeches were rambling and
> verbose, he dropped his aitches, he was a jingoist, he was domineering and brash, a bit of a racist,
> even for that time, and the people loved him.[2]

This is how he appeared to the public and this is the image that has been passed down to us,
but it is evident that this apparent bluff ignorance was just that, a front, from a trained certified
engineer — whose book borrowings from the General Assembly Library and whose detailed
knowledge of parliamentary rules and procedures shows a clever mind — who understood
what the public wanted, and in a sense played down to their expectations. He was a man made
for the film age and instinctively recognised the advantages its advertising could give him.[3]

Seddon led the 'Party of the People' in a country emerging from the depression of the 1880s.
New Zealand under the Liberals was becoming a nation of small farmers, prices were improving
and there was rapid expansion in meat exports and dairying. The growth in education and
communications was matched by a growing national awareness that saw a staunch loyalty to
Britain accompany a growing consciousness of cultural identity imposed on New Zealanders

by the demands of the land in which they lived. Farming and breaking in the bush was hard, physical toil that demanded initiative and toughness to survive, let alone prosper. Seddon was a man for these times.

In 1886 New Zealand's population was just over half a million and by 1900 reached three-quarters of a million. In 1881 96% of the non-Maori population were British subjects and by 1886 the number of New Zealand-born equalled migrants born in Britain. Pride in Empire was matched by pride in what New Zealanders were carving out of the land. The rawness of a frontier society was being softened by the increasing move away from extractive industries such as gold towards smallholder farms, with an increasing percentage of women in the population, and accompanied improvements in education and welfare.[4]

Improved communications made New Zealand less isolated from the world and was a binding force within New Zealand itself. Seddon's Liberal ministry used the growth of post and telegraph, together with the expansion of the railways, as a means of giving this isolated colony — one where people living on the West Coast of the South Island found it easier to get by steamer to Sydney or Melbourne than to Auckland — a sense of themselves by linking communities. Film also brought the outside world closer and its impact was greatest in the small towns and rural settlements too small for touring theatre until the arrival of the travelling film show. Its arrival would provide the opportunity for New Zealanders to see themselves for the first time on the world's stage.

QUEEN VICTORIA'S DIAMOND JUBILEE

To mark the sixtieth year of Queen Victoria's reign on the occasion of her Diamond Jubilee, New Zealand sent its first military contingent overseas, not to war, but as the colony's contribution to the London ceremonies. Fifty-four New Zealanders were specially selected from hundreds of applicants from the mounted volunteer forces. Thirty were to be European and 20 Maori. Each was to receive a free uniform, return passage to England, accommodation and rations in England and a bonus of £40 for officers and £20 for men. 'Smart and good men' were nominated from every volunteer corps in New Zealand. The Maori Contingent was raised by the Native Affairs Department and enrolled in the Heretaunga Mounted Rifles, with Hoani Paraone Tunuiarangi, a chief of Ngati Kahungunu, in charge of the party, gazetted in the rank of captain.[5]

Lieutenant-Colonel Albert Pitt, a lawyer of Nelson, being the most senior district commander in New Zealand, became contingent commander. Captain Alfred William Robin of the Otago Hussars was made commander of the European Contingent.[6] Robin, a working partner in the family coach and carriage building business in Dunedin, had commanded the Otago Hussars since 1891. It was regarded as the most efficient of the volunteer corps, with Robin "the smartest Commanding Officer in the Colony".[7]

The Jubilee Contingent sailed for England on the SS *Tutanekai* as mounted infantry dressed as if on active service, in khaki jacket and trousers. The jacket had a scarlet collar, the pants a matching scarlet stripe, with brown gaiters and black-laced leather boots. Soldiers wore a brown leather waist-belt with a snake clasp, while the officers were distinguished with gold braid edgings to the collar and cuffs and brown leather Sam Browne belts. The Contingent wore what we would term a slouch or 'smasher' wide-brimmed hat with a plaited pagri, its brim turned up at the right and secured with a red cord to a button.[8] The men were each armed with a Martini-Henry rifle and bayonet and each officer with infantry-pattern sword and revolver.[9]

In London it was fete and celebration, the climax being the Queen's Jubilee Procession on 22 June 1897 where the 78-year-old monarch was escorted through the streets of London in a carriage, drawn by eight cream horses, to a celebratory service held on the steps of St Paul's Cathedral. The infirm Queen watched from her carriage and then was driven back through the streets to Buckingham Palace. Four members of the New Zealand Contingent formed part of the Queen's personal bodyguard, while the rest of the Contingent followed the carriage carrying Seddon, New Zealand premier, who was seated with the Queensland premier and his wife.

The day was also celebrated throughout the Empire and in New Zealand from 20–27 June 1897. It was a week of military reviews and civic processions in every town and district, displaying local achievements and loyalty to Queen and Empire. The return of the Jubilee Contingent on 8 September 1897 was an excuse to celebrate it again. They were feted as if heroes from wars returning, both in Wellington and in their home towns, with a grateful government gifting them their uniforms and weapons as a reward for services rendered.

THE DIAMOND JUBILEE FILMS

The Contingent did not return alone, bringing with them film of the London Jubilee Procession and celebrations. Not only did the country have their returned heroes but they could also see moving images of their 'boys' on parade in London, both protecting the Queen and escorting their premier through the heart of the Empire. It brought the world to New Zealand — "we at the end of the earth have been enabled within a few weeks of the happening of the greatest event in British History in the capital of the Empire, to participate to some degree at least with the inhabitants of London in a partial though most representative view of the procession on the Jubilee day is a triumph of science".[10]

OPERA HOUSE.

Under the Patronage of His Excellency Lord Ranfurly.

FOR A SHORT SEASON ONLY,

COMMENCING

MONDAY, 13TH SEPTEMBER,

THE GREAT

KINEMATOGRAPH

REPRODUCTION OF THE

DIAMOND JUBILEE PROCESSION.

Every movement in this, the most Gorgeous Pageant of modern times, reproduced with astounding fidelity. At the first reproduction in the Alhambra, London, on 26th June, a Scene of Wild Enthusiasm was provoked, and the identical exhibition, given for the first time in Christchurch on 19th August, met with an Ovation such as never before has been accorded to any performance in that city. The Theatre Royal was crowded and hundreds turned away at every subsequent performance.

For full particulars see bills.

Prices of Admission—3s, 2s, and 1s. Box plan now open at R. Holliday & Co.'s. Day sales at Abel's and Aldous's, tobacconists.

N.B.—In order to avoid confusion patrons are particularly requested to book their seats as early as possible.

E. E. TOWNSHEND,

Manager,

Kinematograph Company, Limited.

Evening Post, 8 September 1897, p. 6.

Every film promoter showed the Jubilee films, and fortunes were made because of their popularity with local audiences. In Wellington, Seddon and the governor, Lord Ranfurly, and Lady Ranfurly were in the audience at the Opera House on the opening night when the Kinematograph Company of Christchurch presented "the wonderful Kinematograph Reproduction of the Diamond Jubilee Procession". At the announcement by the master of ceremonies that the "Maorilanders would be shown with the New Zealand Premier. This was the signal for a louder burst of enthusiasm than ever, and when someone called for three cheers the call was heartily responded to." The reporter noted that the "cheering continued while the picture lasted. The view was shown again in reply to prolonged calls of the audience."[11]

These scenes were repeated everywhere the films were screened. In Christchurch when Seddon "was seen to gracefully wave his hand to the audience as the carriage trotted by a voice from the rear shouted 'Good man, Richard', and further applause followed. When the carriage bearing Her Majesty appeared on the scene the audience became most enthusiastic, those present rising and singing God Save the Queen and also giving three cheers."[12] There was the same public response at the Princess Theatre, Dunedin, and naturally enough there was keen interest in identifying Dunedin's sons — "When the Queen's escort was shown someone present called out to know where Captain Robin was, but of course none of the pictures were large

Still from R.W. Paul's Queen Victoria Diamond Jubilee film of 22 June 1897 showing Queen's colonial escort which included New Zealanders. NTSV F11225.

enough to allow the identification of individuals from the body of the theatre, though good pictures of Lord Wolseley and Lord Roberts as they rode past were shown."[13]

Perceptive showmen read the mood of their audiences and gave them what they wanted. On his return to New Zealand Whitehouse toured and featured his three short clips of the Diamond Jubilee Procession showing the 'Queen's carriage', 'Colonial Premiers' and 'Colonial Troops' and accompanied the scenes by singing Our Sons Across the Sea.[14] His selection of Diamond Jubilee film is both clever and obvious — he knew his market. It is likely that his audience joined in to rapturous applause and to keep the mood going, the 30–40 second-long film would promptly be run through again to more songs and more applause. These films were magical to New Zealand and those who had sent contingent members packed the halls to catch a glimpse of their boys, everyone craning to catch a glimpse or demand an encore as no doubt proud but red-faced contingent veterans in each town pointed out their place in the column as it quickly flickered past.

A fragment of the Jubilee film that was screened to New Zealand audiences has survived in the Ngā Taonga Sound & Vision archive. This is a fragment of that taken by the English film producer R.W. Paul who had three cameras covering the procession's route. His was one of 18 film companies, some with up to six cameramen, known to have been filming the event. It was a sophisticated film for its day, showing the sequence of the parade. Paul's film was originally some 480 feet in length but it was sold to film exhibitors in 12 x 40 feet (12.19 metres) sections to accommodate the wishes of the purchaser in selecting the scenes

Still from 'Sandow the Strong Man' who featured in the Kinetoscope film strips and in the first film screenings. NTSV F2628.

best suited to his audience.[15] The surviving film in the New Zealand archive is taken at the entrance to St Paul's Churchyard and corresponds to that taken by Paul, who positioned his Cinematograph camera, specially mounted on a tripod that enabled the camera to pan, in a window overlooking the parade route on the south side of the churchyard. Seddon's wave has gone and we get the briefest glimpse of 'King Dick' sitting opposite the Queensland premier and his wife, and then, in fours on horseback, our 50-strong contingent rides into New Zealand cinematographic history. At least it may be them ... the bandoliers strapped across the left shoulder also suggest it may be members of the Victoria Mounted Rifles Contingent who preceded the New Zealanders in the procession and who wore their hat brims turned up on the right the same as the New Zealanders.[16]

This was the first New Zealand Contingent to be sent overseas as representatives of New Zealand; it was also the first New Zealand body to be captured on film. To the audiences of the day the film was living proof that New Zealand was establishing itself as a presence in the world, albeit as part of the British Empire.

Whitehouse capitalised on this interest in the Diamond Jubilee. He advertised his new acquisitions, making particular emphasis that this was the only equipment sent to New Zealand that had been specially prepared by the Edison Company. Whitehouse was keen to advertise that he had a letter from Thomas A. Edison stating that: "I am very glad to confirm my verbal statement to you, that to the best of my knowledge you have the first Projecting Kinetoscope of my design and manufacture that has been sent to New Zealand. I hope the machine will meet with the same success it has achieved in this country and in Europe. Yours very truly, [signed] Thomas A. Edison."[17]

Whitehouse's projector was illuminated by electric light and his advertising reassured patrons "that the Electric Light used is perfectly under control, though the effects are startling and marvellous".[18] Whitehouse's programme followed the pattern established by the touring vaudeville shows with songs by various local artists alternating with phonograph and film.

Still from Edison's *The Widow's Kiss*, 1896. "They get ready to kiss, begin to kiss, and kiss and kiss and kiss in a way that brings down the house every time." Everett Collection Historical / Alamy Stock Photo.

 *The Widow's Kiss.* Library of Congress.

Advertisement in a souvenir catalogue of the Wellington Provincial Industrial Association (1896–97). The Pamphlet Collection of Sir Robert Stout, Vol. 75, Victoria University of Wellington Library, Wellington.

Nineteen short films were shown, few of which ran for more than a minute. Other than his three short films of the Jubilee procession, almost all were American in origin. The Edison films included the "Western Express which at one showing coming full end on from a distance at a rate of sixty-five miles an hour, and in such sort as to cause the downstairs audience to unanimously scream, jump out of the way, make room for it to pass through, when — bang! It vanishes into thin air, or rather the wondrous basket which receives these wondrous films."[19]

The May Irwin–John C. Rice screen kiss advertised as *The Widow's Kiss* was projected to "great amusement".[20] The programme concluded with Annabelle's *Sun Dance*. These crude flickering pictures accompanied by phonograph or piano were an enchanting novelty, so lifelike as to make the audience believe that they were "gazing at the actual incident, instead of a marvellous counterfeit of it".[21]

To New Zealand audiences the introduction of film fitted into a pattern of entertainment already established by the limelight magic lantern slide shows, and they responded in the same way with cheers and enthusiasm; singing along with the chorus when popular songs were sung by the master of ceremonies or when the phonograph scratched out Daddy Wouldn't Buy Me a Bow-Wow.[22] The films were so short that if the audience response demanded it, Whitehouse's Edison Projecting Kinetoscope was equipped with a 'spool bank', which looped the film and allowed it to be played again, with the audience again responding with song and applause.

Permanent picture shows were unknown. Charles E. Mackie of 286B Queen Street, Auckland, was probably the first New Zealand promoter to exhibit his British-manufactured Wrench Cinematograph in his own premises in February 1897, but this was unusual in an age of travelling shows. Mackie was an established figure in New Zealand theatre having previously toured with a magic lantern image projector as well as operating the limelight spotlights for stage productions at the Auckland Opera House. He also imported an X-ray machine that he demonstrated at the Auckland Industrial Exhibition. He, like his rival exhibitors, fitted this new wonder of moving pictures into their existing programme, with some of them, like Whitehouse, taking the plunge and venturing out into the provinces with the dual inventions of phonograph and film — acting as projectionist, master of ceremonies and songster as necessary; supplementing this with local musical talent if available. Films were shown wherever space could be booked in local town halls, theatres and schoolrooms, sometimes grandly naming them 'Salon Cinematographe' for the duration of the stay.[23]

Bob Fitzsimmons (left) versus 'Gentleman Jim' Corbett. Carson City, Nevada, 17 March 1897.
Glasshouse Images / Alamy Stock Photo.

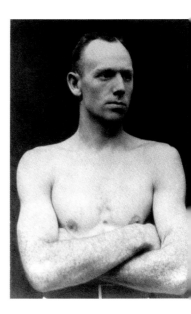

One of the outstanding boxers of his generation, Bob Fitzsimmons won three world titles at three different weights: middleweight, heavyweight and lightheavy weight. He became a figure of world renown with his filmed victory over 'Gentleman Jim' Corbett, knocking him out in the fourteenth round at Carson City Nevada on 17 March 1897. *Te Ara — Encyclopedia of New Zealand.*

With the ability of each promoter to purchase the same films, competition pushed each to present something new. In 1897, in Auckland alone, ten exhibitors ran film seasons with two returning again for another run during the year.[24] The films were too short in themselves to create more than an impression, one could view the sequence of the Queen's Diamond Jubilee Procession in the series of films available, but the story had to be sustained with narrative, music and song while each length of film was changed in the projector. As the number of exhibitors grew so did the public demand — more than the chance to see moving images as scientific curiosities, the subject of the film itself became an important drawcard.

BOB FITZSIMMONS: NEW ZEALAND'S FIRST SPORTING FILM HERO

Boxing films were popular, drawing a largely male audience. Edison included staged fights among his Kinetoscope output and to overcome the limits of the 40-second film length, developed a special Kinetoscope enabling the viewing of a 60-second film that allowed viewers to see a specially filmed, staged fight of six individual one-minute rounds viewed in sequence through each Kinetoscope in turn. The popularity of the first film fight between Michael Leonard and Jack Cushing, filmed in the Black Maria studio in 1894, led to the capturing of the six-round fight between the heavyweight champion James Corbett and New Jersey fighter Peter Courtney where, on cue, Corbett knocks out Courtney in the sixth round. Carl Hertz showed the Corbett fight film during his New Zealand tour.[25]

Film strip from Enoch Rector's Veriscope film of the Fitzsimmons–Corbett fight. The Veriscope name was emblazoned on the side of the ring to prevent counterfeiters.
http://collectauctions.com/1897-james-corbett-vs-bob-fitzsimmons-original-fi-lot6861.aspx.

Prize fighting was barred throughout much of the United States, but the skills of boxers such as John L. Sullivan and 'Gentleman Jim' Corbett gave a respectability to boxing, now fought with gloves under the Marquess of Queensberry rules, that it previously lacked. With the introduction of film projection combined with the draw of the featured fighter giving exhibition bouts, boxers and their managers realised that the potential gate from touring a fight film offered more money than the winner's purse from the fight itself.

In 1897 New Zealanders witnessed their boys parading for Her Majesty at the Diamond Jubilee celebrations in London, and, for those willing to watch a boxing film, they saw an adopted son of New Zealand win the heavyweight world championship. The freckled and balding 35-year-old Bob Fitzsimmons from Timaru triumphed in the first world heavyweight championship fight ever to be filmed. One of the outstanding boxers of his generation, Fitzsimmons won three world titles at three different weights: middleweight, heavyweight and light heavyweight. He became a figure of world renown with his filmed victory over 'Gentleman Jim' Corbett, knocking him out in the fourteenth round at Carson City Nevada on 17 March 1897. Cornish-born, New Zealand-raised and an American citizen when he won the world heavyweight title, Robert Fitzsimmons was claimed simultaneously by Britain, New Zealand, Australia and the United States, being usually referred to in the American press as an Australian — but the townsfolk of Timaru knew he was one of their own.[26]

At 11 stone 13 pounds Fitzsimmons conceded 16 pounds to Corbett, and he remains the lightest boxer to hold the world heavyweight title. However, despite spindly legs, his years as a blacksmith gave him tremendous upper body strength and a devastating punch.[27] The fight promoters had to find a state that would allow the fight to take place, and Carson City, with Wyatt Earp, Bat Masterton and other legends of the West in attendance, became that venue. The fight was filmed with a Veriscope camera specially made by Enoch Rector who ensured exclusivity by having the Veriscope name clearly shown on the side of the ring.[28]

News of Fitzsimmons' victory flashed by cable around the world and the film of the fight made fortunes for promoters and exhibitors. Reviewing the film in the *San Francisco Wave*, Mr Boswell Jnr highlighted the differences between the earlier Corbett–Courtney fight specially staged against a black background for viewing in the Edison Kinetograph and this 14-round epic taken from the viewpoint of a single camera — albeit three set up side by side to ensure no round was missed, all set back to enable the entire ring to be seen, with the crowd as backdrop and no possibility of retakes as this one was truly live.

There are plenty of imperfections in the films that stream across the field of vision like gigantic motes, and the oscillation is trying on the eyes. But taken as a faithful representation of the greatest 'pugilistic event of the century' the veriscope is a success, and the films of the last and most important round are fortunately the best of all. The lay spectator takes away with him the impression that honours were easy until the beginning of the fourteenth round. Both men had been taken turns in doing all the fighting, while at one time in the sixth and seventh rounds it even looked as though Corbett had Fitz going fast. In the middle of the last round Corbett sinks to his knee — the plexus punch is not visible to the naked eye — listens calmly and attentively till the timekeeper has counted seven seconds, starts to rise, and, to everyone's stupefaction, has trouble in doing so; he shifts his hand nearer his body to gain a better brace and in doing so raises it from the floor an inch or so, leaving his body unsupported for a fraction of a second. Instantly he goes over, gasping for breath, one hand over his stomach, and the crowd rush into the ring. [29]

> NEXT EMPIRE HOTEL.
> At 8 p.m. 2 Shows Nightly. 9 p.m.
> The Great International Glove Fight.
> BOB FITZSIMMONS v. JIM JEFFRIES.
> 11 COMPLETE ROUNDS. 11
> By Biograph.
> New Zealand v. America, as shown by the
> N.S. Club, London.
> Admission, 1s; Children, 6d.
> FRANK ST. HILL, Proprietor.

Evening Post, 15 February 1902.

Fitzsimmons had done the seemingly impossible. Arguments over whether Fitzsimmons fouled Corbett with a late punch to the jaw as he was falling, thereby deserving to forfeit the contest, guaranteed the film a worldwide audience. Some of the film survives, including the final round, and so as an American film reviewer foretold in 1897: "The ghosts of Mr. James Corbett and Mr. Robert Fitzsimmons [are] condemned for an indefinite period to go over again the scene of their deeds."[30] We can see these images today — Corbett the larger man, seemingly dominating, and then the knock-down with Fitzsimmons the new champion.[31]

Two showmen, Messrs Frank St Hill and Moodie, did good business touring the Corbett–Fitzsimmons fight around New Zealand in 1897–98. They recognised the money to be made in fight films and sports events, and annually showed the winning of the Melbourne Cup doing "enormous business", both in the larger centres but also in the mining districts of the West Coast and Central Otago. The partnership kept the Corbett–Fitzsimmons fight on the programme for 12 months, with Miss St Hill playing piano and Mr Frank St Hill entertaining the audience with his conjuring tricks while other acts came and went.[32]

The 35-year-old Fitzsimmons retired to the vaudeville stage but was lured back for a purse of £4000, only to lose the championship to a "young California Hercules" in the shape of 23-year-old James J. Jefferies, at night under arc lights at Coney Island on 9 June 1899 in the eleventh round of "hard and fast battling".[33] The American Vitagraph Company filmed the fight that was the first world championship to be filmed under lights. However, the intense heat generated burnt out the arc lights and filming abruptly stopped before the critical finale. The missing rounds were later re-enacted for film by the two fighters to ensure its screening before a worldwide audience.[34]

Fitzsimmons again fought Jefferies for the heavyweight world championship at San Francisco on 26 July 1902 and was knocked out in the eighth round. The film of the 1899 fight with its re-enacted scenes was still touring New Zealand to good houses. In February 1902 Frank St Hill, less Moodie, advertising his show as the St Hill Sporting Life Company, did ten weeks' business showing it twice nightly at the Empire Hotel in Wellington before taking it on the road, along with "Singers, Dancers, Musicians, Whistlers and Living Pictures" through the provinces.[35] One New Zealand reviewer noted that while in earlier rounds the referee tended to get in the way of the film audience, the later rounds were much clearer, not aware of course that these had been deliberately restaged for the camera.

Rounds 10 and 11 are the most exciting, and show Fitz going at the knees and returning Jefferies sledge-hammer blows in only a half hearted "I'm done" sort of style. With an under-

Fitzsimmons vs Corbett World Heavyweight Title Fight. YouTube.

O P E R A   H O U S E.

FOR TWO NIGHTS ONLY.
TWO NIGHTS ONLY.

TO-NIGHT (FRIDAY) AND SATURDAY,
10th and 11th inst.

THE THEATROPHONE.
THE THEATROPHONE.

Edison's latest marvel. The most perfect
Phonograph ever heard.

BANDS, QUARTETS, SONGS.

E. W. Favour's Comic Song—"The Forgotten Song, or What d'ye Call It?" with all
the power and clearness of the original.

Also,
WHITEHOUSE'S KINEMATOGRAPH,
WHITEHOUSE'S KINEMATOGRAPH,

Which will exhibit the first and only animated scenes taken in New Zealand.

The Opening of the Auckland Exhibition—
Uhlan Winning the Auckland Cup at
Ellerslie on Boxing Day—Maori Canoe
Hurdle Race.

An unbroken series of Thrilling War Scenes,
lasting twelve minutes; Grand Naval
Review; New York Harbour.

TWO HOURS' GENUINE ENJOYMENT.

A popular vocalist (Mr. George Girling
Butcher) will introduce Patriotic Song—
"Our Sons Across the Sea."

SPECIAL NOTE! SPECIAL NOTE!

Just landed by the San Francisco mail,
25th October, 1899, the THEATRO-
PHONE, Edison's perfected Phonograph of
1899—a model machine. This splendid instrument makes its first appearance in this
city.

REMEMBER—TWO NIGHTS ONLY.

Popular Prices—3s, 2s, and 1s.
A. H. WHITEHOUSE,
Proprietor.

Evening Post, 10 November
1899, p. 6.

cut and an upper-cut, Jefferies knocks the Timaru blacksmith out: the crowd who paid their dollars for a front view of the real fight depart into the biograph darkness, and the sixpenny audience at Sussex Hall grab their hats and make for the door.[36]

The same critic also noted that the film was going to be shown at Timaru later in the month.

How Timaruvians will take the smashing up of their fighting idol, or how the Biograph Company will take their smash-up should any friends of Bob Fitzsimmons get loose on the machine is hard to say. It is a biograph risk and the present company are prepared to take it. If the residents of Timaru are wise, they will pay their 6d, see the show, and go quietly home through the South Canterbury night, vowing nothing more than vengeance on the referee. [37]

At 41 years of age, Fitzsimmons won the world light-heavyweight championship on points over 20 rounds from George Gardner on 25 November 1903 in San Francisco, becoming the first boxer in history to hold three world championships at three weights. He lost the light heavyweight title to 'Philadelphia Jack O'Brien' in 1905, but continued to fight until 1914 while also appearing on the vaudeville circuit. Fitzsimmons visited New Zealand in 1908 to an ecstatic welcome, especially in Timaru. He remained a New Zealand icon despite settling permanently in the United States, touring as showman and evangelist, dying from influenza in 1917.[38]

Bob Fitzsimmons was the first New Zealand sporting hero whose exploits on the world stage were seen in New Zealand through the magic of film in a year where the first New Zealand military contingent sent overseas for the Diamond Jubilee celebrations of 1897 also starred on film. It set a pattern for measuring New Zealand achievement, discernible to this day.

WHITEHOUSE BUYS A CAMERA

To keep up with such competition Whitehouse imported a camera into New Zealand in 1898 and advertised that he had "the first and only camera in New Zealand for taking animated pictures for the Kinematograph".[39] Naturally enough he then filmed "the first and only animated pictures to be taken in the colony".[40] However, even though Whitehouse no doubt decided on the subjects to be filmed and was on hand at their taking, he was not the cameraman, instead he enlisted the support of W.H. Bartlett, the photographer who had leased him his premises in Queen Street for his first Kinetoscope exhibition. Bartlett, it seems, filmed all ten films that Whitehouse is believed to have taken with his camera.

Whitehouse's first advertised New Zealand films were of the opening of the Auckland Industrial and Mining Exhibition by the governor on 1 December 1898: a minute of film showing Lord and Lady Ranfurly entering the Exhibition buildings. The film was screened in the vestibule of W.H. Bartlett's in Queen Street on Christmas Eve 1898 and so the venue of the first Kinetoscope screening became the venue for the first public screening of a New Zealand film.[41] He followed this with a film of Uhlan winning the Auckland Cup at the Boxing Day

Meeting at Ellerslie on 26 December 1898, which in turn was screened at Bartlett's studio, together with the Auckland Exhibition films, for two nights on 30–31 December 1898. There was seating for 60 people at a time.[42]

In January Whitehouse explored the advertising opportunities of his Kinematograph camera by announcing that an "ANIMATED PICTURE" would be taken in Queen Street at an early date. "Tenders for the privilege will be received from Merchants who will appreciate the advertising advantage of scene being taken to include their premises as same will be exhibited at all our entertainments for ensuing year."[43] Nothing seems to have come from this initiative. Whitehouse then filmed the "dancing of the Maypole by Mrs Osborne's pupils at the Auckland Exhibition … The scene was successfully secured by Mr W.H. Bartlett supervised by Mr A.H. Whitehouse, who intends to accord the youthful performers an opportunity of seeing themselves as others see them."[44] The film was shown with other Auckland scenes, including the opening of the Exhibition, a regatta scene and a selection of Edison films, for two nights at St George's Hall, Newton. It shows that Whitehouse was filming around Auckland and also filmed canoe races on the Waikato River.

He toured the North Island with his 'Animated Pictures', bringing New Zealand to New Zealanders, and looked for subjects that captured audience attention. In the course of just over 12 months, Bartlett, his cameraman, filmed ten one-minute films.[45] In Tauranga he showed his films of the governor's visit to the Auckland Exhibition, but the film that caught audience attention was the "Maori Canoe Hurdle Race on the Waikato River, wherein were shown all the laughable and exciting features which invariably accompany this unusual form of sport".[46] During this visit Whitehouse was invited by Hori Ngatai and Arama Karaka to film the opening of the recently completed meeting house at Maungatapu, and although the opening was delayed, the week-long hui (gathering) allowed enough time for him to return and film "two animated photographs of 1250 pictures each of the haka and poi performances [This suggests film in 78 foot lengths; 75 feet (22.86 metres) useable. A maximum running-time at 16 frames per second of 1 minute 18 seconds].[47] Many of the leading locals and visiting chiefs took part, standing in the front rank of the haka party. Afterwards Mr Whitehouse entertained the Maoris with selections on his phonograph, which greatly delighted the listeners."[48]

However, Whitehouse found that filming New Zealand subjects was not enough in itself, because — then as now — New Zealanders were especially critical of the local product and measured them carefully against the standard of imported films. When Whitehouse exhibited at the Opera House in Wellington in November 1899 the *Evening Post* reported:

> Compared with the others, the operator, an Auckland photographer has yet something to learn, as his films are patchy and lack sequence, owning as much as anything to an endeavour to get in as much incident as possible. A Maori canoe hurdle race on the Waikato River was as good as any in the series, and Uhlan's win in the Auckland Cup last Boxing Day was realistic. The light was not particularly good and it required an effort of eyesight to see some of the pictures clearly.[49]

There were almost too many film shows doing the circuit. Many saw film as a fad that would soon fade away as audiences tired of the succession of brief novelties and of "third-rate kinematograph shows, which during the last few winters have time and again disappointed the public and so disgusted them that a good show could do no business".[50]

WAR IN SOUTH AFRICA

The British war in South Africa against the Boer Republics changed that, because the Empire, including New Zealand's boys, was involved, and film became the medium that brought images back to local communities. Seddon, after some initial reluctance, became the first colonial premier to offer a contingent to support the British forces in South Africa in October 1899, before the outbreak of war. He cleverly judged the public mood and the last months of the 19th century in New Zealand were dominated by talk of war and the upcoming election. Seddon's commitment to the first won him the second, by a handsome margin.

The first contingent to volunteer for the war in South Africa went into camp at Potter's Paddock in Karori and sailed from Wellington, 214 strong, on 21 October 1899. An estimated 60,000 well-wishers crammed the wharfs and every vantage point around the harbour to see off their boys. To the enormous delight of all New Zealanders it was the first colonial contingent to arrive in Cape Town, and was in action at Jasfontein Farm on 18 December 1899. It was also the first New Zealand contingent on active service in a military campaign to be filmed overseas. The First Contingent's arrival in Cape Town was captured on film by the South African impresario Edgar M. Hyman, who before the war had supplied films to Charles Urban's Warwick Trading Company in London. He was on hand to capture with his camera the arrival of the British forces in Cape Town and their move to the front. On 24 November 1899 Hyman filmed the *Departure of the New Zealand Mounted Rifles From the Docks*, which showed the newly arrived troopers leading their horses and walking from the docks towards the railway station. A second film titled *New Zealand Mounted Rifles Leading Their Charges After Disembarking* was a continuation of the first, and the 100-foot-long film (30.48 metres) appeared with the catalogue notes that pointed out "the splendid portraits of these Australians" who by the time the film reached England "had already rendered such valuable services in the field of battle".[51]

The misidentification by the British film company of New Zealanders as Australians would continue, to the chagrin of a country keen to promote its national effort. It echoed the feelings of Lieutenant-Colonel Albert Pitt, who commanded the New Zealand Diamond Jubilee Contingent in 1897. Pitt was "much struck with the want of knowledge concerning the Colony of New Zealand among the bulk of those of the English people with whom I came in contact". Pitt believed that the "presence of the Contingent at the Jubilee celebration has conducted very much to the creation of an interest in New Zealand, and has been a very excellent advertisement for the colony".[52] This world recognition was something that both Seddon and his ministers were working towards. But New Zealand audiences did not read the catalogue notes, all they saw when the films reached New Zealand was that it was their boys on screen.

The films themselves have not survived but had a similar impact on New Zealand audiences as did the film of the New Zealand Contingent at the Diamond Jubilee Celebrations in 1897. They cheered and applauded their boys on screen and eagerly awaited the next batch of films from the front. The travelling film shows suddenly had a subject that the public wanted to see and the Boer War killed any notion that film was a passing fad.

Northcote's Kinematograph and Unique Speciality Company, which billed itself as the 'Premier Picture Show of the Southern Hemisphere' did good business with its films of the war in the Transvaal, promising "War! War! War!", each film being "absolute and actual".[53] Messrs St Hill and Moodie's Kinematograph and Wargraph Company's focus reflected its name with the promise of 30 South African scenes including *The Armoured Train Fight: Pluck and Devotion of British Officers and Men* for the price of sixpence in all parts of the theatre.[54]

Second Contingent for the Boer War in camp at Newtown Park, January 1900, watched by spectators. Mrs A.J. Hutchison Album, PA1o-242-15, ATL, Wellington.

The news of the British army's defeats of 'Black Week' in December 1899 spurred recruiting in New Zealand. Four contingents sailed in 1900. This was visible proof that New Zealand was doing its bit for Empire. Huge crowds waved farewell at each contingent departure and their training attracted families to open days where displays and parades were performed before an admiring audience. The war was news with the latest from South Africa dominating the headlines, and British victories such as the relief of Ladysmith and Mafeking being celebrated with public holidays. Films and magic lantern slides of the war were eagerly sought as this was New Zealand's first contribution to an overseas war as part of the Empire.

WHITEHOUSE FILMS THE SECOND CONTINGENT

Whitehouse filmed the training of the Second Contingent in camp at one of the open days at Newtown Park. Trooper Twisleton captures the mood of the camp at Newtown Park:

> The few days before embarkation were spent in reviews of different kinds and festivities, the whole of the population vying with each other as to who could make the most of us. Every day coming in from parade or drill we were sure to find cases of fruit, sweets, cakes, pies, etc. in the tents left there by unknown enthusiasts. The camp was some three miles from the city itself, in a park belonging to one of the suburbs. It was a splendid situation too, from a spectators' point of view, being perfectly level for some eight or ten acres, surrounded by sloping land, covered with evergreen trees that formed a welcome shade. Thousands used to come daily, some from the remotest parts of the colony to see us learn the mounted drill.[55]

These are the scenes that Whitehouse's film captures. We see a troop of horsemen from the contingent circling in front of the camera on the last major open day 13–14 January 1900, with 13 January the most likely day of filming as this was the day of the advertised sham fight. In the

Still from A.H. Whitehouse's *Departure of the Second Contingent for the Boer War*, shot at Newtown Park by W.H. Bartlett, 13 January 1900. NTSV F22555 (see colour section).

background crowds of people ring the hills around Newtown Park. It is a simple film with the horsemen dressed in training jumpers and slouched or 'smasher' hats, so named because of the single fore and aft dent in the centre of the crown, walking their horses round in a circle so that each rider in turn passes close to the camera. The camera is placed in a single position outside the ring of circling horsemen. Bartlett's focus is on the approaching rider whose head vanishes out of frame as he rides immediately opposite the camera. The sequence continues for 45 seconds.[56]

As a film it lacks excitement other than the audience of the day's ability to identify each of the riders as they passed. If this is typical of Whitehouse's films and Bartlett's camera work, then one can appreciate the criticism of the Wellington reporter who in writing of his earlier screenings said that he "had yet something to learn". Bartlett took the film with a hand-cranked camera on its heavy tripod that provided a stable platform for the operation. One turn of the handle was geared to give eight exposures and so the normal speed of 16 frames per second required the cameraman to crank the handle twice a second, roughly judging the distance and the image by sighting alongside the lens as there was no sighting mechanism, and at the same time have a sense of the picture he was taking.[57]

The result shows that even though Bartlett may have run a successful photography studio and was regarded as an accomplished photographer, what survives of his film handiwork shows that these skills do not necessarily transfer to the demands of moving pictures. However, for all its simplicity and faults, it is the earliest known surviving film taken in New Zealand and its existence is a tribute to Whitehouse, New Zealand's film pioneer and Bartlett, New Zealand's first film cameraman.

Whitehouse advertised this film as the *Departure of the Second Contingent for the Boer War*, but they were not to finally leave until 20 January 1900, having loaded their horses the day before. However, in discussing the film with New Zealand film historian Clive Sowry it seems that Whitehouse was not prepared to pay the photographer's fee demanded by the Wellington

Departure of the Second Contingent for the Boer War. NTSV F22555.

Wharf authorities. Perhaps it was also the crush of the crowd crammed round the men as they lined the wharf to receive the blessing of the Bishop of Wellington with speeches from the Earl of Ranfurly, governor of the colony and 'King Dick' Seddon, the premier. Twisleton records: "None save private friends of the troops were allowed on the wharf from which we embarked, yet the crowd was enormous and the noise deafening."[58] All this Whitehouse avoided by choosing the last open day to capture the departure. Whitehouse himself must have had doubts on the quality of the film. In August 1901, 19 months later, the *Taranaki Herald* reported the arrival of Whitehouse's Biochronoscope and Theatrephone entertainment at the Theatre Royal, New Plymouth, including "a film of the Second Contingent in Wellington".[59]

Whitehouse's forte was being a showman front of house in selling his picture show, but even though he was now a step up from the shop-front Kinetoscope show he was still not in the major league. Whitehouse must have realised that film-making was not his particular talent and that this alone did not give him the drawing power to stay ahead of his competitors. He was now one of a number of travelling picture shows appearing in turn in the same towns, touting for business by tempting the same crowds with, often, the same films. The wide-ranging commercial potential of film display was not lost on enterprising salesmen and in July 1901 New Plymouth witnessed the "American Tobacco Coy's representative … giving tonight and ten following nights free exhibitions on Smart's Wall, Brougham-street of living pictures by the aid of their Vanity Fair kinematograph machine" while no doubt dispensing his products for the gathered clientele to sample.[60]

New Zealand's involvement in the South African War reinvigorated the film entertainment industry, transforming a technical novelty into a means of seeing images to complement the written news reports in the press. In early 1900 Whitehouse was touring the West Coast of the South Island closely behind Northcote's Kinematograph Company whose manager, Harry Abbot reporting from Greymouth of his 'money spinner' picture show and in particular the popularity of the war films with "the 'war spirit' very strong here — our pictures of 'Uncle Paul' Kruger being nightly greeted with hisses, while anything appertaining to the British is cheered to the echo".[61]

The intensity of the competition in travelling shows can be gained from a report in the *Otago Witness* from Harry Baxter who was touring the North Island with the Christchurch Kinematograph Syndicate. From Hawera, Baxter wrote of doing good business with their stock of South African War films and being "billed for race nights at Hastings and Napier" where they were sure to draw a crowd. The Thornton Stewart Kinematograph Company was also touring the same venues, and he writes of Edmund Montgomery who ran a similar travelling picture show "on his way to England looking for novelties" and noted that this was the "third kinematographist on the same errand — Montgomery, Whitehouse and Northcote. What price 'old iron'?"[62] What price indeed, and as he had done in the past, Whitehouse went overseas to see what was new over there to entice the New Zealand public.

Whitehouse went to the Exposition Universelle Internationale in Paris with the films he had taken of New Zealand scenes. The Paris World Fair featured the achievements of the 19th century and looked ahead to the new millennium with advancement in film as its special focus. Whitehouse requested government assistance to underwrite the journey and show his New Zealand films in Paris, but this was refused.[63] Compared to European production, Whitehouse's films taken by Bartlett were not of a quality that would interest the European market. What he had to show may have been of some curiosity value as exotic, from a faraway land, but little else, and indeed many of the subjects he had chosen were now being filmed by more competent cameramen.

Horopito with Mt Ruapehu in the distance. Small settlements such as this were part of the circuit for A.H. Whitehouse's Living Pictures. Photograph taken c.1912 by Frederick George Radcliffe. 1/2-006991-G, ATL, Wellington.

THE LIFE OF A TRAVELLING FILM SHOWMAN

Whitehouse's plea for financial assistance was a bold request and may have planted the seed for further government involvement in local film production, but this did not involve Whitehouse. He wrote from Paris that he "had picked up some novelties there for the entertainment of the colonial public". In particular he told the theatre columnist of the *Free Lance* that he had "secured the animated picture machine which won the Grand Prix for showing a moving picture with the least perceptible flicker, a set of life motion scenes of the Exposition, an extensive set of various pictures, and the concert grand phonograph which won the gold medal".[64]

He returned to New Zealand advertising a new Biochronoscope projector and a stock of films and continued to earn a living as a touring film promoter through the North Island, bringing the world on the flickering screen to small-town New Zealand. Dave McWilliams' articles on Auckland film history note that Whitehouse was showing the coronation of King Edward VII's pictures with lighting supplied by a portable electric outfit overseen by an electrician, Chas Manners, with one of his sons, Clarence Craddock Whithouse, acting as film operator.[65] Even though he made a good living, Whitehouse was essentially a small-scale outfit.[66] As competition grew he adapted accordingly and his itinerary increasingly concentrated on the Auckland suburbs and a North Island circuit. In December 1902 his show at the Opera House in Hawera reflected the changes that were occurring in film shows worldwide and how he adapted to the times.

> There was a good attendance at the Opera House last evening, when the Whitehouse Company gave their entertainment, and applause was frequent. Since his last visit, Mr Whitehouse has improved a good show; he has, in the first place, added a powerful engine which is responsible for giving finely illuminated pictures. Further, he is, by means of lengthy films, able to give patrons a continuous run of pictures, it taking on an average twenty minutes for the showing of each set. The pictures shown last evening were very good — some amusing, all interesting. The new series of war pictures pleased the audience, the procession of Lord George Sanger's huge circus was fine, while the comic and illusive scenes were excellent. Mr Whitehouse gave short lucid explanations, and told several humorous anecdotes. The phonographic items were clear and good. As a comic singer, Mr F. Pierce, secured encores for his ditties, which were well given. The entertainment was decidedly worthy of the patronage it received.[67]

Over the years the name would change to Whitehouse's Bioscope and Star Variety Combination in 1904 to Whitehouse Living Pictures in 1907. The common theme was that Whitehouse "always gave a good show".[68] In January 1908 we know Whitehouse was still touring as he advertised his travelling show in Ohakune and Horopito in the central North Island. These were both growing settlements benefiting from the work on the Main Trunk line that opened that year with an influx of workers and businesses.[69]

At Horopito there "used to be great excitement in the village when the travelling motion pictures came around, and not only among the children, the adults too enjoyed them. That afternoon the picture man would walk all around the village ringing a school bell and calling on the people to come and see the wonderful show. Previous to this there would be posters sent throughout the mail and they would be displayed in the shops or any prominent place."[70] Heating on the cold nights was always a problem in the crowded community halls when the pictures came to town. Initially it was provided by big kerosene heaters, "needing only a touch of a small boy's foot to begin flaring dangerously. Many small boys sat on the aisle seats, so those heaters were replaced by cylindrical stoves that worked well until drunks started using the red hot tops as frying pans for tinned herrings."![71]

The life of an itinerant showman was a difficult one. George Cain in his memoirs recalls Whitehouse's Living Pictures visiting the railway settlement of Manunui in the King Country sometime in 1909–10 and showing films in the public hall. Hiring a pony and cart to get his projector to the hall, Whitehouse got Cain to "run through the town ringing a bell and shouting the information that pictures were showing in the hall and had to name the main attraction over and over again". The chore was worth a free seat, and Cain remembers

Still from Brandon Haughton's film of premier 'King Dick' Seddon leading the returning All Blacks down the gangway onto the ferry at Auckland to a rapturous reception. *New Zealand Footballers*, NTSV, F4361.

Whitehouse using a hand-cranked projector with gaslight illumination which "worked well enough to attract vast clouds of moths, so many in fact that the show had to be stopped from time to time to clean the incinerated creatures out of the machinery … The hard-working showman did everything single-handed, cranking his projector with one hand while the other took money from arriving patrons who were left to find their own way to a vacant seat on a form."[72] This imaginative recollection contrasts to Whitehouse's son Clifton's account of hauling several tons of generator and plant by horse and dray from settlement to settlement in this period.[73]

In 1908 Whitehouse was still advertising his Edison connections. There is a flyer inviting "One Hundred Members of the American Fleet to Attend Nightly" at the "Picture Display and Social" in the Ponsonby Hall during the visit of the United States Navy's 'Great White Fleet' in August 1908.[74]

Whitehouse, like other travelling showmen, relied on buying new films to replenish his stock and maintain variety. "When these films lost popularity in a showman's territory, he would swap them with other showmen or import new titles and discard old ones."[75] A possible sample of an itinerant showman's film stock came to the Ngā Taonga Sound & Vision archive via the National Film Unit from the Museum of Transport and Technology, Auckland. The 12 films are an interesting mix of scenic, topical and story films all made in the period up to 1906 and would represent the sort of material that Whitehouse and his competitors carried.

The films include one important New Zealand production showing the return of the victorious 1905 All Blacks and their reception in Auckland on 6 March 1906. The film camerawork is credited to New Zealand photographer Brandon Haughton.[76] In a letter from Auckland, dated 16 April 1906, 'Our Special Correspondent' for *The Theatre* journal in Sydney, wrote, "As an animated picture it was one of the finest ever shown in Auckland, too much credit cannot be given to Bandon [sic.] Haughton, operator of the Chubb's Biograph Company, for the production of such a splendid film picture."[77]

The All Blacks had completed what was described at the time as "the most wonderful football tour in history". And that was certainly how New Zealand saw it, as the *Auckland Weekly* reported, "[b]etween September 16 and December 30 [1905] the New Zealanders played the strongest and best combinations in the Motherland and worsted all save one".[78]

The film was first shown throughout New Zealand on the final two nights of the Wellington performances of the very successful *Living London* tour. Shown at the Wellington Town Hall from 26 March 1906, the tour was managed by the Australian promoters J. & N. Tait.[79] It shows the scenes at the reception at the Devonport Ferry Company Wharf in Lower Queen Street as the 'Original All Blacks', captained by Dave Gallaher, are led off the Royal Mail Steamer *Sonoma* by Premier Richard Seddon onto the deck of the ferry boat *Eagle*. The team in 'white hats' are led down the gangway, each shaking the captain's and ship's officers hands as they descend with clouds of cigarette and pipe smoke rising from the reception committee on the ferry boat where they are taken to the wharf. "It was getting on for four o'clock when the team was landed … to the strains of 'See the Conquering Hero Comes' and the accompaniment of roars of cheering."[80]

It was one of those moments that Seddon relished. He had insisted that cables be sent back immediately to New Zealand giving the result of each game. The achievements of the All Blacks as they became known on tour were as important to New Zealand's sense of identity as that of the 1897 Diamond Jubilee Contingent and the New Zealand contingents to the Boer War. Seddon leads the 'white hats' through the thousands gathered to welcome them.

New Zealand Footballers: The All Blacks' arrival and reception at Auckland. NTSV F4361.

Acknowledging the cheers, the team and officials drive off in a pair of two-horse-drawn brakes behind a brass band for the reception in Philson's Square as mounted police control the crowd. At the reception where they were welcomed by the mayor of Auckland and the premier, Gallaher spoke after Mr Dixon, the team manager, saying that he had only one piece of advice "and that was to play the Welshmen first".[81] This of course referred to the controversial loss to Wales (0–3), the only defeat incurred on the tour. They won 32 out of 33 games, scored 830 points to 39, 103 goals to 6, 109 tries to 5, and became the measuring stick for New Zealand's international rugby performance ever since.

The other films in the collection include the *Entry of Scots' Guards into Bloemfontein* produced in 1900 and *Farrier Shoeing Horses in Camp,* 1899, both produced by R.W. Paul.[82] The first is particularly important as it is one of the few films showing genuine footage of the Boer War, taken for Paul by Walter Beevor, the Scots Guards' medical officer.[83] There is also an Edison film of *Mr Edison at Work in His Chemical Laboratory,* 1897, two scenic films taken from a train, one of which, taken in 1898, shows scenic views and the other, views of Windsor, a film of King Edward VII opening Parliament and a London street scene taken before the coronation of Edward VII in 1902.[84] The story films have been identified as R.W. Paul's *Cupid at the Washtub* of 1897 and G.A. Smith's production of *Hanging Out the Clothes* of the same year.[85] At some point this collection of films was stored away and forgotten, but it gives us a fascinating glimpse of a likely programme of the period.[86]

After his return from France it seems that there were no further efforts on Whitehouse's part at local film production, and in that sense, his moment in history had passed. He remained a travelling one-man film promoter with perhaps an assistant travelling with him, or equally likely, relying on hiring local help in each town. The arrival of permanent picture theatres in small-town New Zealand from 1910 saw his opportunities gradually disappear. Rudall Hayward recalls Whitehouse being the name of the projectionist at Hayward's Royal Albert Hall in Auckland and this may be how he ended his career.[87]

Alfred H. Whitehouse is of a type recalled in a series of articles for the *Auckland Star* in 1941 written by veteran film man, Dave McWilliams:

> Memories of those early days when we travelled by wagon to a township — 'swung the sheet,' pumped gas into a tank, 'dodgered' the town, or posted a day-bill on a corrugated iron fence, or on a cream stand at a cross-roads. We recollect also, how we spent hours in the pelting rain next day, digging the conveyance out of the muddy roads, to allow us to get to the next town in time to show that night — to find, perhaps, that it was too wet for the people to come out. Those were the days.[88]

ENOS SYLVANUS PEGLER FILMS THE FIRST LADY MAYOR OF THE BRITISH EMPIRE

Before going to France in 1900, Whitehouse sold his projector and camera with his film stock to Enos Sylvanus Pegler, a professional photographer "well known with family groups, taken at home" who had a studio in Onehunga, Auckland.[89] Pegler made a foray into the world of moving pictures by establishing the Zealandia Living Picture Company. On 5 July 1900 the *Auckland Star* reported the picture show at the St James's Hall, Wellington Street, Auckland, for two nights with further one-night screenings in Onehunga, Otahuhu, Pukekohe, Waiuku, Otaua and Papakura.[90] Pegler's show of 50 films concentrated on the Boer War in South Africa but also included a number of New Zealand films.

Entry of Scots Guards into Bloemfontein. BFI screenonline.

Mr Edison at Work in his Chemical Laboratory. youtube.com.

Enos Sylvanus Pegler with his camera and magic lantern. Auckland Libraries, Sir George Grey Collection, ID1053-5601.

The New Zealand pictures were all original and were exhibited for the first time. Those representing the departure of New Zealand's troops for South Africa were especially valuable records. The Auckland troopers were seen boarding the S.S. *Rotoiti* at Onehunga, and some splendid animated views were given showing the farewell at the Onehunga wharf as the vessel steamed away. Another picture showed the departure of one of the contingents in Wellington, over 200 troopers passing on the screen. These pictures evoked the warmest applause. The Rough Riders were shown in the Domain, and a good living picture was given representing the unfurling of the flag at Napier-street School.[91]

The Wellington material may have included Whitehouse's film of the departure of the Second Contingent, as the only known existing copy was donated by Pegler's descendants to Ngā Taonga Sound & Vision archive. However, the most important film that Pegler screened and which got star billing in the screenings in the Auckland District under the title *The World's First Lady Mayor* is one that has also survived and is now in the archive.[92]

One of the best living pictures shown, and one which created the greatest interest and amusement, was that of Mrs Yates, the ex-lady Mayor of Onehunga, and her husband, Captain Michael Yates. Mrs Yates (in a specially rehearsed scene) was shown standing and delivering an impassioned speech to the Onehunga Borough Council, with much waving of papers and gesticulations. Her husband was seen entering the room and taking his seat, while Mrs Yates went on haranguing the Onehunga Borough Fathers on their manifold iniquities. This film was highly original and very well produced, and it should excite the greatest interest throughout the Colony.[93]

The film features Mrs Elizabeth Yates who was elected mayor of Onehunga on 29 November 1893, just one day after New Zealand women became the first in the world to vote in a general election. She was not the first lady mayor in the world — that honour is accorded to Susanna Salter, elected mayor of Argonia, Kansas, USA, in 1887. However, she was the first lady mayor in the British Empire and at the time she became the centre of media interest and a public celebrity. She received congratulations from the premier, Richard Seddon, and also from Queen Victoria, but four of her councillors and the town clerk immediately resigned in protest. No other woman was elected mayor in New Zealand until 1957, when Annie Huggan became mayor of Petone.[94]

Pegler filmed Mrs Yates outdoors against a painted canvas backdrop that one can see flapping in the breeze. The film is exactly as described by the *Auckland Star* reporter. We see a woman in her fifties in Victorian dress talking animatedly to the camera while her seated husband looks on approvingly. It seems this was one of a number of films that Pegler shot in Auckland. It is a clever piece of camerawork and Mrs Yates is clearly enjoying the moment. The quality of the filming is in strong contrast to Whitehouse's film of the departure of the Second Contingent taken with the same equipment in February that year, which revealed Bartlett's limitations as a film cameraman. Pegler took his Zealandia Living Pictures on the road and in September 1900 it was showing in Midhirst in Taranaki, but now the emphasis was on the Boer War films. Pegler continued a pattern that he started in Onehunga of giving talks to schools about photography and film.

Still of Elizabeth Yates with husband from *The World's First Lady Mayor*, 1900, filmed by Enos Sylvanus Pegler. NTSV F90103.

In 1901 Pegler moved to Palmerston North where his father and a number of relatives were living. He ran the Photographic Supplies Store, which imported photographic materials and acted as agents for Edison phonograph records. Always active in local affairs, in July 1901 he managed the "First Popular Concert of the Season" at the Theatre Royal, which showed a series of Limelight slides of the visit of the Duke and Duchess of Cornwall and York, later His Majesty George V and Queen Mary. The various slides were accompanied by leading vocalists and the local member of the House of Representatives talked to the various scenes, with Mr H.J. Cornwall acting as piano accompanist.[95]

In 1907 he returned to Auckland and established a second branch of the Photographic Supplies Store. Pegler settled his family in Papatoetoe and was active in local affairs, including agitating successfully to have the local railway line extended to Papatoetoe. He shifted his business focus to land development and engaged in farm and real estate sales in Manurewa until a few years before his death in October 1938.[96]

His family was aware of his interest in photography and film and the story of him filming the first lady mayor in the world became part of the family folklore. What was kept were the two film canisters containing two small rolls of film. These were deposited by the family with the NZ Film Archive (now Ngā Taonga Sound & Vision) in 1993. The first of these to be identified was that of A.H. Whitehouse's film of the departure of the Second Contingent to the Boer War, now the oldest known surviving film shot in New Zealand. The second, which had to wait until 2016, was Pegler's own film of Mrs Elizabeth Yates that, as Clive Sowry notes, is "the oldest staged surviving film" in which she is seen "delivering an impassioned speech to the Onehunga Borough Council". This film is now the second oldest known surviving film shot in New Zealand, it is also the oldest complete film and the oldest New Zealand film to recreate an historic moment in New Zealand local politics. Pegler's brief foray into professional motion picture film has left us with a tangible record of New Zealand's first film-makers.

The World's First Lady Mayor. NTSV F90103.

Joseph Perry and the Limelight Brigade

"What's on at the Army tonight?" someone asks.

"Oh, the Biorama — Perry's Biorama — the citadel at eight," is the answer, and one individual at least makes up his mind to be present. The minutes are passing — people still pouring in ... At 7.35 the spacious building was more than three parts full, and by the time the hands slowly crept to eight, we gazed upon one of the finest crowds ever seen inside the Citadel at a limelight gathering.

Punctual to the minute, Major Perry ascended to the platform, said a few words of introduction, and then called upon the Company to give one of their male chorus anthems, "Hail to the Brightness," which was rendered excellently, and bespoke months of hard practice. After God's blessing had been invoked, the lights were lowered, and the great and imposing array of machinery was brought into action, and for two hours there was not a dull moment. Living pictures taken on the Continent and at the International Congress, German soldiery drilling, scenes in the City of Berlin, changing the Guard at the Kaiser's palace, Laplanders at the Congress, Commissioner McKie receiving messages from old Australians and New Zealanders prominently amongst whom could be seen the well loved forms of Commissioners Pollard and Estill, who were received with cheers.

A pleasant break came in the shape of a beautifully illustrated solo by Bandsman Stevens, entitled "Little Black Me." Another change — some of the finest slides ever shown in Christchurch — of scenes of the River Thames.

Opposite page: Salvation Army officer, possibly Joseph Perry, with film projector including electrical supply outside a local hall somewhere in New Zealand during one of the Biorama tours. 1/2-125505-F, ATL, Wellington.

Yet another spool of film — this time illustrative of the way the waifs and strays of the greatest city on earth manage to struggle through life — sleeping on the benches in the parks; despair; a mother leaving her baby in a doorstep; selling matches; finishing up with a real Whitechapel brawl, in which the constable suffered most, and called in the slum officers to do what he could not do.

Another break of a few minutes — lights up! — announcements, and an anthem by the Company, "Sun of my soul," which must be heard to be appreciated. Lights down once more, and we are transported by means of the bio-chrono, to Australia — a scene in the bush; camp surprised by treacherous blacks; settlers shot; black-tracker and troopers on the trail; capture of the murderer, and burning of their mia-mia.

Another song … The clock hands had been travelling very fast and now we come to the last film — some 800 feet long [so the Major said — and he ought to know] — "The great American train robbery," which was realistic in the extreme, and held the crowd spell-bound from start to finish. The moral was very apparent — that no matter how successful villainy may be for a time — the strong hand of Justice eventually must prevail and the wicked be punished.

The first Monday night programme of the Biorama Company met with unqualified approval, and as the great throng left the building, expressions of wonder and delight could be heard on every hand.[1]

Perry's Biorama Limelight performance at the Salvation Army Citadel in Christchurch at the opening of its tour through New Zealand on 6 March 1905 was an extravaganza on an impressive scale. However, in its mix of film, music and song it still reflected the general format of how picture shows were held in New Zealand until the arrival of the multi-reel feature 'star' film heralded with the Australian multi-reel film *The Story of the Kelly Gang* in 1906.[2]

Early picture shows were a mixture of film interspersed with music, song and comic, acrobatic or dramatic skits. The Salvation Army film shows were no different. Perry's Limelight of the Salvation Army were similar to other travelling companies of the day, bringing music and moving pictures[3] with a religious intent to small-town New Zealand, and did so in a format that their audiences expected and with which they were comfortable. Not only did it show a wide cross-section of overseas film showing scenic views and travelogues as well as the work of the Salvation Army, it also showed the first narrative films such as Edwin S. Porter's *The Great Train Robbery*, which thrilled audiences as far afield as Mangaweka and Greymouth — and not just for its moral message of the triumph of good over evil.

The Salvation Army Limelight Company was also the first picture show to consistently use films with local content as part of its programme. This became more sophisticated as the

The Great Train Robbery.
Library of Congress.

pattern of the tours developed. Initially, Perry's Biorama filmed local events on tour and then returned to Australia to develop them in the Melbourne studios of the Salvation Army. These were screened on the next tour to New Zealand, usually in the following year.[4] On the 1905 tour local films were taken, developed and screened during the Biorama Company's two- or three-day season in each town. Many of the small New Zealand towns that featured in Perry's films never received such attention again, but it conditioned New Zealand audiences to expect to see local faces on their picture screens and it was this that drew in the crowds. It was this

determination to reach the widest possible audience that saw the Limelight Department of the Salvation Army become the first large-scale commercial film producer in Australasia.

The Salvation Army was founded in 1865 by William Booth in his Whitechapel mission in the slums of London's East End.[5] An eloquent preacher and a skilled organiser, Booth believed that the key to reclaiming souls was to cure the social evils that trapped them in poverty and want. His Salvation Army was organised on military lines with Booth as its commanding 'General'. His corps took it upon themselves to raise the money to run schemes for "prisoner repatriation, low-cost accommodation, job placement assistance, cheap food supply, legal aid for the poor, a missing-persons bureau and a drug and alcohol rehabilitation programme."[6]

Booth promoted emigration to Britain's colonies as a way of escaping the evils of slum life and articulated this in *In Darkest England and the Way Out*. His Army migrated overseas with its followers and established itself in the Australian colonies in the 1880s and in New Zealand in 1883. All were in the grip of a severe economic recession with increasing unemployment, low pay and women and children working long hours in 'sweat shops'. The Army's arrival was not welcomed by the established churches or by the establishment at large. A writer in the *Otago Daily Times* reflected this when he wrote:

> Bringing the Salvationists to New Zealand will be another of the many mistakes of acclimatisation. It is the thistles, the sparrows, the rabbits over again. The Army will prove a nuisance as troublesome as these pests and as ineradicable.[7]

The open air street corner meetings of the Army led by members in their strange quasi-military uniforms became the target of gangs of youths determined to break them up with eggs, stones and fists. However, the Salvation Army's target was the unemployed, disadvantaged and dispossessed elements of society and they were prepared to battle for audience, gradually winning the grudging admiration of both society and the press for their willingness and determination. It was an army that was prepared to battle for souls using the methods that would best appeal to its working-class audience. Converts were immediately put to work and give public testimony in their own words about why they joined.

It was simple language from simple people that the listeners could identify with. Bands, tambourines, drums and flags and large billboards were used to advertise and proclaim the time and place for the next meeting, hymns were set to the tunes of popular songs. The conspicuous, often individually designed uniforms, the prominent 'Blood and Fire Badges' of the converted, and the names of the various corps, 'Wellington Warriors', 'Christchurch Conquerors' and 'Invercargill Invincibles' proclaimed that this was an army on the march; ready and willing to do battle. Salvation Army meetings reflected the variety and format of the music halls with stories and song interwoven for variety before building up to a fervent climax where everyone sung along to the accompaniment of a brass band, attracting audiences ostracised by the formality of established churches.[8]

JOE PERRY JOINS THE ARMY

The positioning of the Salvation Army at the forefront of magic lantern and film exhibition and production in both Australia and New Zealand was largely due to the vision and showmanship of Salvation Army officer Joseph Perry. Joe Perry was born in Birmingham, England, in 1864, and at the age of nine or ten came to New Zealand with his parents. He followed his father's trade as a bootmaker in Dunedin, before joining the Dunedin Fire Brigade. He witnessed the

A fire in 1896 on the same site in this picture destroyed Joseph Perry's magic lantern projectors and forced him to re-equip. *Auckland Weekly News*, Supplement, 5 September 1909, Auckland Libraries, Sir George Grey Collection.

first Salvation Army gathering in New Zealand on a cold wet Dunedin day on 1 April 1883 and was not impressed. As he watched the small group of uniformed preachers, Perry remembered it was April Fools' Day and thought with some wry amusement that "the meeting and those taking part in it suited the day very nicely".[9]

Despite this he was won over by their dedication and swapped his fireman's uniform for that of the Salvation Army. After some brief on-the-job training Private Perry was commissioned with the rank of lieutenant and trail-blazed for the Salvation Army through a succession of New Zealand towns. It was not easy, but these were people he identified with from his own working-class background. "He confronted hooligans trying to break up his services, closed down brothels after converting the prostitutes and had a number of released prisoners bunking down in his quarters as he tried to find them work."[10]

Joe Perry married Annie Laurenson in 1885 and together they ran the Salvation Army Corps in Lyttelton and then in Nelson before being transferred to Australia. After a succession of appointments the Perrys were sent to run a 'Prison Gate Home' for released convicts in Ballarat in 1890. Annie died in 1891 leaving Perry with three children under five.[11] A keen photographer, Perry set up a commercial studio to ensure an income for the work of his corps. He also bought a simple single lens magic lantern and used it to advertise the work of the Salvation Army. The use of magic lantern slides to project slides upon a screen was nothing new, but, as well as entertainment, it was already a popular means for churches to illustrate a talk or a sermon, of providing the words of songs and hymns, and through the increasing sophistication of the machines showing rudimentary movement, to bring a bible story to life to the delight of both children and adults.

It was this that caught the attention of Major Frank Barritt, the 'Special Efforts Officer' at the Army's headquarters in Melbourne. Barritt knew Perry from his time in New Zealand, and had Perry placed under him to assist with publicity for General William Booth's visit to Melbourne in 1891.

With a tall hat and long beard, General William Booth, the British founder of the Salvation Army, greets followers at the wharf in Wellington in March 1899. This was one of Booth's four visits to New Zealand between 1891 and 1905. Salvation Army, New Zealand, Fiji and Tonga, Heritage and Archives Centre, Lower Hutt, New Zealand.

Such was the success of the magic lantern advertising that Commissioner Thomas Coombs, head of the Australian Salvation Army, authorised a trial tour through New South Wales and Queensland using Perry's lantern to advertise General Booth's scheme to resettle British unemployed in the Australian colonies. Perry's slides illustrated the squalor of the slums and the work of the Army to relieve this. Barritt and Perry were an effective team working together, in Barritt's words as "a kind of spiritual Barnums, to the astonishment of all and sundry."[12]

The Limelight performances paralleled the vaudeville and touring theatre shows in intermixing song and story illustrated by slides. It included singers and band instrumentalists. Tours were for three or four months and were planned to follow the railway lines where possible, but cart, coach and steamships were also used, with local Salvation Army officers booking the largest available halls in each town on the itinerary and arranging advance publicity with posters pasted up immediately before the tour came to town. Barritt and Perry took the Limelight shows to an audience in outback Australia. Its aim was threefold: to evangelise and seek new members; to publicise the social work of the Salvation Army; and to solicit funds to make this social work possible.[13]

At Bairnsdale with a full house people started clambering through the windows in order to see the slide show. At Townsville the iron gate of the town hall was twisted out of shape by the crowd, and when Perry gave an open air performance in the Botanical Gardens with half the proceeds going to the local hospital — it became a gala occasion. Three brass bands and the fire brigade swept down the main street in a torchlight procession.[14]

This success led to the establishment of the Limelight Department in 1892 under Barritt, with Perry as his assistant and lantern operator. In the same year Barritt was promoted to head the Salvation Army in Tasmania and Perry succeeded him in charge of the Limelight Department. In 1893 Perry married Julia Lear who became an active member of Perry's Limelight, touring with him, looking after his two boys, Orrie and Reg, Eva his daughter and adding four children of their own in what became very much a family concern. The three boys, Orrie, Reg and Stan, followed in their father's footsteps in being able to play as musicians, acting as assistants to the lantern and camera operators, played bit parts in their father's narrative films or acted as models for his narrative slides, before graduating as skilled cameramen in their own right — first for the Salvation Army and then in commercial film in Australia.[15]

The magic lantern machines were professionally made and highly sophisticated pieces of equipment. Perry graduated from his simple single lens lantern to a double or a 'bi-unial' machine, illuminated by 'limelight'. This light source had been invented by Thomas Drummond in 1816 and was created by directing an oxygen and hydrogen flame on to a small cylinder of lime. It was used by lantern and film operators until replaced by electric arc sources that became available from 1897. Perry enjoyed the challenge that the technology presented. He had to produce his own supply of gas, and through experimentation developed equipment that produced the combustible gas, which was then stored in a tank and released to provide the illumination during the show. Some of the equipment he developed was patented with the rights assigned to the Salvation Army and became standard in the film industry throughout Australia and New Zealand.

From the beginning Perry was the Limelight Department. As well as producing his own slides to supplement those purchased from overseas, Perry experimented with the range of effects he could achieve with the lantern. In addition to 'fades, wipes and dissolves' that later became part of motion picture practice, it was possible to have ships "bobbing in a choppy sea or the rotating arm of a windmill".[16]

Touring was in Perry's blood, he enjoyed putting the shows together and then gained equal satisfaction from the audience reaction. He was to sustain this pace for 17 years, spending much of his life on the road or in preparing for the next tour. In September 1894 an interview in the Salvation Army journal *Full Salvation* reported that:

> Captain Perry has travelled pretty well all over the colonies, visiting nearly every corps in the territory, and to date of our interview had journeyed something like 29,057 miles. Of these 21,839 had been negotiated by rail, 6,074 by water and 1,144 by coach, cart or horseback. Including junior meetings, 522 exhibitions have been held, at which some 469 souls have been saved, and the nett proceeds to the war have been something like £748.12.10.[17]

This is the description of Perry's equipment that he took on a tour of New Zealand in January 1896:

> The apparatus in use is a bi-unial oxy ether lantern with tanks and fittings to the oxygen supplying the light. The fittings are, as the Adjutant [Perry] is fond of asserting, of the latest and most

---

THE SALVATION ARMY.
—
GENERAL BOOTH
Will visit Wellington as follows:—
WEDNESDAY, 29TH MARCH.

Public Reception at Jervois-quay between 10 and 11 a.m. His Worship the Mayor, supported by Sir Robert Stout, Mr. Duthie, M.H.R., and Mr. Hutcheson, M.H.R., will receive the General.
All Salvationists muster at Jessie-street 9 a.m. for March Wednesday Morning.
—
OPERA HOUSE, AT 7.45 P.M.
Address—"LESSONS OF MY LIFE."
The Right Hon. R. J. Seddon, P.C., will preside.
Tickets, 1s and 6d; other parts, Silver Coin.
—
THURSDAY, 30TH MARCH,
OPERA HOUSE,
The General will Address a Special Meeting at 7.45 p.m.
—
General Booth will be accompanied by his son, Commandant Herbert Booth, Commissioner Pollard, Colonel Lawley, 150 staff and field officers, and the famous Federal Band.
Silver Coin collection at the door; selected seat, 1s.
N.B.—Young children, with or without their parents, cannot be admitted to above meetings.
Box plan at Flockton's.

Evening Post, 28 March 1899, p. 4.

approved character. The various pictures shown are thrown upon a canvas screen some twenty-two feet square, and between 3,000 and 4,000 slides are now included in the collection. These include illustrative sketches of the General's "Darkest England" scheme, and the condition of the submerged classes …; scenes from the Life of Christ, these embracing some beautiful views of the Crucifixion and Resurrection, portraits of leading Salvation Army officers, and illustrations of such simple stories as "The Road to Heaven," "Neddy's care," Billy's Rose," and so forth. Adjutant Perry's practical acquaintance with the photographic art enables him to add to these slides from time to time, and occasionally in the towns visited, local views are taken and reproduced as circumstances permit, on the canvas at night. In this way he has accumulated quite a collection of views, which are as unique in their way as they are perfect, every colony in Australia being represented in the collection. The interest in the exhibitions is thus still further increased, and abundant use is made of the opportunities gained to enlist sympathy for our work, and above all wins souls for God.[18]

This programme with its clever mix of content cemented a pattern that continued with the introduction of moving pictures. Its mix of slide, song and sermon involved the audience and provided a variety that attracted families and kept the young involved. In a sense it provided accessible family entertainment that paralleled the familiar pattern one could find in the variety theatrical shows and vaudeville theatre of the day, but which were usually beyond the purse of a working family — Perry's Limelight made it accessible to all.

Perry's 1896 'Limelight Crusade' to New Zealand ended in disaster. After successfully touring the South Island it all came to an end in Marton on 1 May 1896 when a fire broke out in a cabinet-maker's shop, spreading to the surrounding buildings, including the Salvation Army Barracks — burning them to the ground. Perry's telegram to his headquarters in Melbourne detailed the loss:

> The whole of the Limelight plant reduced to ashes. We have sustained a severe loss; nothing now remains bit a few twisted and charred pieces of brass. Great sympathy shown by public, money being subscribed to replace loss, which means at least £500, with meetings ahead which must be cancelled. Leaving for Melbourne at once with great sorrow; five years hard toil gone. God will help! — Joe Perry, Wanganui.[19]

FILM AND SALVATION

The Marton disaster meant that Perry had to rebuild from scratch and he did so — purchasing a tri-unial magic lantern with a triple lens to replace the di-unial model lost in the fire, but soon another element was involved. In August 1896 Carl Hertz held the first screening of motion pictures in Melbourne. This was also the year that Herbert Booth, the charismatic 36-year-old third son of the Salvation Army's founder William Booth, was appointed commander of the Salvation Army in Australia and New Zealand. 'The Commandant', as he was known, was a keen photographer who recognised the crowd-pulling potential of motion pictures and encouraged Perry to include film in his limelight programme. It paralleled his father's ambitions, with the press reporting General William Booth's scheme of having an exhibition of living pictures in London to show converts from every nation.[20] Under Herbert Booth the Salvation Army in Australia and New Zealand would use the tools of theatre and vaudeville to gain souls and Perry's Limelight Department would be the agent to achieve this. Joe Perry made this plain in an interview in *The Victory* in August 1898 appropriately published under the title 'The Triple Alliance: The Graphophone, Cinematographe and Limelight on Salvation Service'.

Herbert Booth, the charismatic head of the Salvation Army in Australasia, encouraged Joseph Perry in the development of the use of motion pictures and lantern slides in support of Booth's lectures. Salvation Army, New Zealand, Fiji and Tonga, Heritage and Archives Centre, Lower Hutt, New Zealand.

The Commandant has a big idea of the future of this department, and since he took it specially in hand — practically creating it a department — things have moved quickly with us, I can assure you.[21]

Perry did not see the Hertz film programme as he was not in Melbourne at the time, but no one as involved as he was with photography and magic lantern exhibition would not have been aware of the development of motion pictures. A Kinetoscope parlour was operating near the Salvation Army headquarters in Bourke Street and Perry would have kept pace with this and developments overseas. In February 1897 the Limelight Department bought its first motion picture projector. This was a Watson's 'Motorgraph'; a small machine intended for amateur use which served as both camera and projector.[22] This was added to by the purchase of a Wrench Cinematograph, a British-made projecting machine that was efficient yet relatively inexpensive at £36. Perry purchased a dozen French films from a local distributor, each of no more than a minute in length, which were first shown in April 1897 during a limelight lantern tour of Western Australia.

The format followed that already tried and tested by the existing limelight shows. Film complemented slides that accompanied stories and song or were interspersed with hymn and sermon. Perry had already identified the drawing power of local places and personalities in his magic lantern shows, and Booth encouraged him to branch out into film production of local Salvation Army activities. Filming Army activities and local events naturally followed on from this and in 1897 Perry began making his own films showing the work of the Salvation Army. These were the first story films to be made in Australia and fulfilled Herbert Booth's vision of film's role in salvation.[23]

These means are employed by the worldling; they form a source of attraction in the theatres and music halls. Why should they be usurped by the enemy of souls? The magic power of light that can transpose by these instantaneous flashes of light pictures upon the film, and by the brilliancy of artificial light reproduce them magnified upon a screen, is the creation of God, and it can only honour Him and glorify his handwork, to utilise this invention for the salvation and blessing of mankind.[24]

By 1898 Perry's Limelight Department was producing slides and film with the ultimate goal of making the Salvation Army "independent of outside film altogether", developing and printing what was then the standard film roll of 75 feet [22.86 metres] in a darkroom, using a printing machine of his own design in the Salvation Army's Melbourne headquarters in Bourke Street.[25] In February 1898 Herbert Booth purchased the latest Lumière Cinématographe, which was Perry's first fully professional camera and projector. Its improved performance reduced the flickering motion of the images on the screen that gave moving pictures the nickname 'flicks'. A report in the *Australasian Photographic Review* in 1899 from an unnamed Salvation Army correspondent who was most likely to have been Perry, read:

> All our kinematographe films are taken with the Lumière outfit purchased from Baker and Rouse [the major Australian firm for the sale of film equipment and films] some 12 months ago, and I can safely say, no other camera, so far as I have seen or heard, can come within a "coo-ee" of the Lumière. It is a beauty, and as sure as the sun.[26]

The Limelight Department also had four lanterns, "including three bi-unials by leading French makers". Edison's graphophone, or cylindrical disc phonograph, had also been introduced into

Joseph Perry surrounded by his still and motion picture cameras, film projector and tri-unial magic lantern slide projector. Salvation Army, New Zealand, Fiji and Tonga, Heritage and Archives Centre, Lower Hutt, New Zealand.

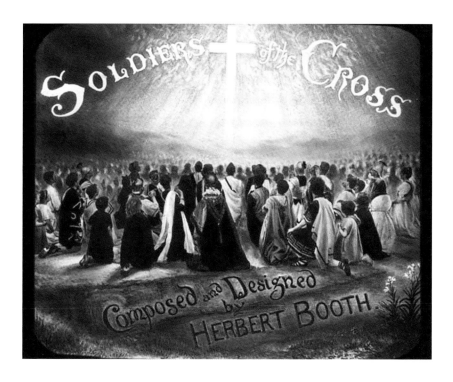

Soldiers of the Cross was specially scripted by Booth with musical arrangements for choir and orchestra. Illustrated with film and lantern slides, it caused a sensation when narrated by Booth on his Commandant's tour to New Zealand in May and June 1901. Salvation Army, New Zealand, Fiji and Tonga, Heritage and Archives Centre, Lower Hutt, New Zealand. (See colour section.)

Lectures.

THE SALVATION ARMY.

GARRISON HALL, DUNEDIN,
THURSDAY, JUNE 6.

SOLDIERS OF THE CROSS.
A Strikingly Original, Fascinating, and
Instructive Lecture
By
COMMANDANT BOOTH.

Soul-thrilling stories of the early Christian Martyrs. A Graphic Narration, Illustrated by over 200 Beautiful Pictures derived from Life Models, by Kinematograph and Bioscope.

TWO HOURS OF INTENSE AND SOUL-STIRRING INTEREST.

Doors Open at 6.30.   Tickets, 2s and 1s.

AGRICULTURAL HALL,
SUNDAY, JUNE 9.
COMMANDANT BOOTH,
Supported by many Leading Officers,
Will Conduct
A GREAT SALVATION BATTLE.

Otago Daily Times, 5 June 1901, p. 1.

the programme, in Perry's words, bringing some relief to the operator "who, under the old arrangement, had to talk half the night in explanation of the limelight views, and who, on top of that, had to pull his meetings in and often run the prayer-meetings as well". Now a programme could include "addresses by the Commandant, musical selections by the Headquarters Band and a quartette [sic] party, a Bible-reading by Colonel Peart, the record of an open-air meeting and others".[27]

In 1898 Perry filmed the procession of the Salvation Army Congress in Melbourne. Perry and Booth worked together on a series of films on the social work of the Salvation Army, which were shot in an attic studio established in the Salvation Army headquarters in Bourke Street in Melbourne. Film, lantern slide and graphophone record were combined to illustrate Booth's lecture on the work of the Army, which opened in Melbourne to packed houses in May 1898 under the title *Our Social Triumphs*.[28]

Perry came with Booth to New Zealand in 1898 in a tour that started on 21 November in Invercargill and moved north through both islands with the finale in Auckland. The Commandant's lecture was advertised in New Zealand as *Social Salvation*, being illustrated by "200 limelight views and 20 'kino films' all taken from life models under the Commandant's personal supervision".[29] The Theatre Royal in Invercargill was packed on opening night despite admission charges of one shilling, which was increased to two shillings if one reserved seats. Booth held his audience spellbound with "his lecture on the work of the Army amongst the wrecks of humanity. Marvellous was the interest aroused as the magnificent pictures

Perry's Salvation Army camera crews' most ambitious project was the filming of the Commonwealth of Australia's inauguration ceremonies. State Library NSW, Call Number: PXD 760. Published date: 1 January 1901, Digital ID: a186002.

were thrown upon the screen, beautifully the whole was illustrated by the Limelight and the Kinematographe" all of this being "excellently manipulated by Staff-Captain Perry".[30]

During this 1898 tour Perry is presumed to have filmed scenes at Otaki, although given the schedule and the brief stop made there by train this may have been of the Maori welcome to Booth at the Otaki railway station on 2 December 1898. "The blood-and-fire natives greeted the Commandant in characteristic fashion, nose-rubbing being indulged in *ad lib.*, to the delight of all concerned."[31] By coincidence Perry's film was shot the day after Whitehouse and Bartlett filmed the governor, the Earl of Ranfurly, arriving to open the Auckland Industrial Exhibition, which is accepted as the first film shot in New Zealand. Neither film has survived but from 1898 on, Perry shot film of local scenes on each of his visits to New Zealand.

In 1900 Booth and Perry collaborated on *Soldiers of the Cross*, which has sometimes been called the world's first feature film. It was not. It was a combination of some 200 lantern slides interspersed with film, illustrating the story and courage of early Christian martyrs during their persecution by the Roman Emperor Nero. Some of the slides were purchased from overseas, but many were specially taken with Salvation Army members acting out the various parts for slide and film. Two of Perry's sons appeared in the production, starting what would become lifetime careers in moving pictures. It was specially scripted by Booth with musical arrangements for choir and orchestra. It caused a sensation when narrated by Booth on his Commandant's tour to New Zealand in May and June 1901. *Soldiers of the Cross* came across to the audience as "almost painful, so realistic was the portrayal of the agonies endured by those who had warred [sic] a good warfare. It only wanted the cries of the infuriated and bloodthirsty mobs to resound through the building to complete the whole". All of this was played out to the "rattle and peculiar whirr of the Kinematographe, the movement of the conductor's baton; and out of the silence there would at regular intervals burst forth the strains of richest harmony from the choir".[32]

In the best of causes the Salvation Army was providing the most exciting and up-to-date entertainment in town. *Soldiers of the Cross* ran for two and a half hours and in Christchurch takings amounted to the record sum of £90. This was to be Perry's last collaboration with his Commandant. Herbert Booth and his Dutch wife, Cornelie, were virtual cult figures in Australasia, but the pace they set was exhausting and Herbert was frustrated by the ongoing need to seek approval from London for his plans in Australasia, and from what he saw as the unnecessary strictures imposed upon him by his elder brother Bramwell, in his role as Chief of Staff of the International Army.[33]

In 1902 Herbert Booth and his wife resigned from the Salvation Army. He and his wife left for the United States to become touring freelance evangelists. Booth negotiated the purchase of the slides and the film portions of *Soldiers of the Cross* together with the magic lanterns, which he took with him and incorporated into his preaching tours to American audiences. The *Soldiers of the Cross* illustrated lecture remained central to his preaching programme and was usually the 'grand finale' in each venue for the rest of his life. By the time he returned to New Zealand and Australia in 1919–20, on what was to be his final tour, it was solely a slide show, the film portions having long since been discarded or, more likely, simply worn out.[34] Selections from *Soldiers of the Cross* continued to be shown by the Salvation Army in Australia but, lacking Herbert Booth's charisma, it was a shadow of what it had been.[35]

PERRY'S BIORAMA

In 1900 the Limelight Department established the Biorama Company, which was derived from the 'Bioscope' name. This became the common name for the principal touring groups for the Salvation Army, the first of which under Perry initially numbered five members, including his wife, Julia. As the online history of the Limelight Department records: "Each person had the skill to be part of a string ensemble, a singing group or a small brass band, as well as operate parts of the projection equipment. Following the introduction of electricity generating plants, a steam tractor was often required to tow a Company's gear into town."[36] However, the success of the Biorama concept saw them grow both in size of party and number so that various Biorama companies toured throughout Australia under Perry's overall direction. The introduction of electricity-generating plants saw the name of the companies reflect this technology by becoming the Electric Biorama Company in 1905–06.

In the same way, Perry developed around him a number of expert cameramen such as Sidney Cook and James Dutton, who accompanied the companies taking film of local events or who could be gathered together and coordinated for the filming of major events such as the Australian Federation ceremonies and the visit of the Duke and Duchess of York to Australia and New Zealand in 1901, and later the arrival of the American 'Great White Fleet' in 1908.[37]

Joe Perry films the duke

My dear Mr Seddon

I have the honour to bring to your notice that we have at our Headquarters an up-to-date and well-equipped Kinematographic Studio, necessitated by our own requirements, but which also places us in a position to undertake such work for others.

We have wondered whether in connection with the approaching visit of the Duke and Duchess of Cornwall your Government would be desirous of securing some permanent memorial of the festivities, such as the processions, reviews, ceremonies, etc. which will doubtless take place in connection with same, in the way of Kinematographic film.[1]

Perry's film-making led to a number of commissions from Australian state governments for films to be taken of state events and public occasions. Perry filmed the departure of the Australian mounted contingents for the war against the Boers in South Africa, but his major undertaking was *The Inauguration of the Commonwealth* on 1 January 1901. Commissioned by the New South Wales Government, the finished film ran for 30 minutes and its production employed a number of specially deployed cameras to ensure that the sequence of events was captured on film. Perry had cameras sited on specially built platforms for unobstructed views. The tripods on the Lumière cameras had no pan or tilt facility and could only achieve static wide shots so Perry reconnoitred positions for five cameras to guarantee all events were recorded. Perry produced the plan and personally directed his camera teams, racing from position to position on a horse-drawn fire engine. *The Inauguration of the Commonwealth* was a skilled and carefully crafted exercise in coordinated film-making and has survived to be appreciated today.[2] The films were developed in the Bourke Street studios in Melbourne and first screened in Sydney at Her Majesty's Theatre on 19 January 1901. It was a great

Opposite page: The Duke and Duchess of Cornwall and York take their place on the dais at the Mayor of Auckland's reception on 11 June 1901. Perry's camera crew can be seen above the mounted trooper on the left of the photo. PAColl-9056_mm, ATL, Wellington.

commercial success and the Salvation Army sold prints across Australia, Britain and Canada. It led to the Salvation Army registering Australia's first film production company, The Australian Kinematographic Company, in 1901, and actively seeking more film commissions.

It seems that the revenue from the Federation Film Commission allowed Perry to upgrade his equipment with the purchase of the latest Warwick Bioscope cameras, which were available in two models. Model 'A' could handle reels of up to 1500 feet of film, or as it was advertised by the Warwick Trading Company, "thirty consecutive minutes without re-loading", which was a great advance over the 75-foot capacity of the Lumière model. Model 'B' was more compact and half of the weight of the 'A' machine and could accommodate 150 feet of film. Both machines came with a wide range of lenses and a new panoramic tripod head that gave the cameras a pan facility that allowed the camera operator to follow a parade or do a panoramic sweep of the scene from a single location. Bioscope cameras and projectors became the industry standard for reliability and the Bioscope name soon was used by the public to refer to any camera or film show.[3]

The first major commission with the new equipment was the visit of the Duke and Duchess of Cornwall and York to Victoria for the first opening of the Australian Federal Parliament in Melbourne. Having secured this, it seemed logical to suggest that the New Zealand Government be approached to commission a similar film for the New Zealand leg of the royal tour. The New Zealand premier, Richard 'King Dick' Seddon, was a guest at the Australian Federation ceremonies and would have been conscious of the prominence given to Perry's camera teams and no doubt made equally aware of the official purpose of the filming. His experience of the Diamond Jubilee films also made him very alert to the beneficial publicity.

In March 1901 Colonel William Peart, the chief secretary and essentially second-in-command to the Salvation Army in Australia, wrote to Seddon, describing the Salvation Army's modern and well-equipped Kinematograph studio that had been built in Melbourne and asked if the New Zealand Government wanted some permanent record in the form of moving pictures of the forthcoming visit to New Zealand of the Duke and Duchess of Cornwall and York. "The negatives of which could be placed among the archives of the history of the State so that at any future period the scenes which took place could be reproduced with the actuality of life and movement."[4]

Seddon gained great publicity with his attendance at the Diamond Jubilee celebrations in London in 1897 and requested a visit to New Zealand from the Duke and Duchess of Cornwall and York, Queen Victoria's eldest grandson and wife. The request was renewed in 1900 and this time approved by the Queen "to signify her sense of the loyalty and devotion which have prompted the spontaneous aid so liberally offered by all the colonies in the South African war, and of the splendid gallantry of her colonial troops" with the announcement that the couple would visit in 1901.[5] Queen Victoria died on 22 January 1901 and with the Duke of York now heir to the throne there were doubts that the tour would continue, but once these were overcome Seddon's ministry were determined to gain the maximum political mileage out of the visit.[6]

The Salvation Army approach to the New Zealand Government to commission a film of the royal visit could not have arrived at a more opportune time. Herbert Booth met Seddon during his 1898 tour and again in 1899 when his father General William Booth made his third tour of New Zealand and now Herbert Booth's third visit coincided with the visit by the Duke and Duchess of Cornwall and York. Perry and his crews came with Booth, and then split off from the evangelical tour, reconnoitred and prepared for the filming of the royal visit.[7]

JOSEPH WARD IN CHARGE

Planning for the tour became the responsibility of Colonial Secretary Joseph Ward, who was also minister of railways and postmaster general. Ward had a chequered political career, having lost office, humiliated, after the Colonial Bank bankruptcy in the 1890s, and he was also 'suspect' because of his Roman Catholicism. Yet with Seddon's support he overcame this and was now a central figure in the Liberal legislative programme. At the turn of the century Ward was an effective administrator at the height of his powers, capable of a prodigious workload matched only by his hunger for publicity. Michael Bassett writes in his biography of Ward that Seddon's "Liberal Government had always been ready to turn official occasions into semi-political rallies … By today's standards excessive speech-making was not only second nature to politicians but it was part of the entertainment available before radio, cinema or TV."[8]

'Progress' was Ward's clarion cry and, like his leader, keeping himself in the public eye was his forte. Under Ward's direction the post office and the railways became the principal instruments in the Liberal Government's programme of "drawing disparate towns and districts into one interconnected nation. New state operations such as advances to settlers' payments and old age pensions joined the multitude of tasks already handled by the Post Office staff." Telephone and telegraph services were very much part of Ward's "passion for gadgetry".[9] Ward was always keen to open new telegraph offices where he would "tap out the first telegram before a battery of cameras".[10] In the same way railways were taken under government control; fares reduced to increase passenger numbers and government attention focused on completing the Main Trunk line between Wellington and Auckland.

Seddon and Ward were, by their nature, men who centralised power to themselves. They saw this as the best way of achieving their political programme and in turn enjoying the patronage of power that flowed from it. What would be left to private enterprise in any other country became the business of the state in New Zealand by necessity due to a lack of private

capital to the benefit of the population who enjoyed ownership of the Public Trust Office, the Government Life Office, the telegraph services, the telephones and the railways.[11] Ward proclaimed, "If the ownership of such institutions was socialism then socialism was a great thing for this country."[12]

DEPARTMENT OF TOURIST AND HEALTH RESORTS

Ward was well-travelled enough to see the tourist potential of New Zealand's unique scenery and recognised that New Zealand also had the potential to share in the current European fad for thermal pools and spas. In 1901 he announced that a section of the Railways Department would be given the task of working up "a better and more widely organised tourist department". The official in charge would be sent to the various health and tourist resorts to see what improvements were needed in facilities and accommodation for them to attract overseas visitors.

> I share with my colleagues the opinion that every pound judiciously spent in making for the comfort of the visitors to the colony, and also for the comfort and pleasure of the people, who reside amongst us, will be recouped over and over again.[13]

A month later, against a background of fierce parliamentary debate, Ward persuaded Seddon to agree to the formation of a separate Department of Tourist and Health Resorts under the direction of its first general manager, Thomas E. Donne. When it opened on 1 February 1901 it was, as historian Margaret McClure points out, "the first government tourist department in the world".[14] It marked another intervention by Seddon's Liberal administration into a field that other countries left to private initiative. As they had acted on old age pensions, land settlement and factory reform, now the government intervened in the pursuit of "trade, tourism and overseas funds".[15] It was another example of New Zealand leading the world.

Ward's selection of his friend Thomas Donne as general manager of the new Department of Tourist and Health Resorts was an inspired choice. Born in Melbourne in 1859, he came with his parents to Dunedin in the 1860s. Now 41 years old, Donne was an interesting man. A keen hunter and fisherman, he was also a superb administrator with the knack of getting people to see his vision and share his goals — not the usual attributes associated with late 19th-century bureaucrats.[16] He progressed in the railways to the post of stationmaster at Wellington and then Auckland. Donne held the appointment of general manager of the Department of Tourist and Health Resorts and also acted as secretary of the Department of Industries and Commerce.[17] He had both the vision and the energy to put New Zealand in front of the world, and he also saw the importance of publicity in realising this goal. It was Donne who understood the value of the new technology of 'moving pictures' and who would be a powerful influence in New Zealand official film-making.

Thomas Edward Donne, the first general manager of the Department of Tourist and Health Resorts, was a visionary bureaucrat who saw film and photograph as the means of broadcasting New Zealand to the world. Photographer: James McDonald, Te Papa Tongarewa, C 025053.

Among the duties of the general manager of the new department were official visits, including arrangements for the royal tour for which Donne was appointed sole commissioner. Ward was acting prime minister when Seddon visited the Australian Federation ceremonies and found himself besieged with requests from every district for them to be added to the visit itinerary. It was Donne who put the programme together at Ward's direction and made sure that it went according to plan. Publicity was integral to this.

The government discussed with the Salvation Army the cost of taking pictures of the Maori gathering at Rotorua and "of say a quarter of a mile of a procession of each of the four principal cities".[18] This led the New Zealand Cabinet to approve the sum of £250, exclusive of the travelling and incidental expenses of the camera operators, for Major Perry to film the royal visit. Perry assured the New Zealand authorities that he would excel anything he had achieved previously on film, providing "we have favourable weather" as "I have two of the very latest cameras with me".[19]

PERRY FILMS THE ROYAL TOUR

Perry's camera team consisted of himself, Captain John Brodie, Adjutant Ebenezer Jackson and a Mr R. Gladding of Auckland who was attached as a temporary assistant camera operator, in effect a pair of strong hands. They were given "a free hand from the Government in the matter of taking kinematograph pictures … Platforms for the machine will be put up by the Public Works Department at various points along the route."[20] Perry met with the reception committees and arranged travel for his party from venue to venue by a mixture of government train and steamer, so that his crews could be on hand to film the royal couple when they arrived. Special passes and badges were printed for Perry and his assistants so that they had unrestricted access. He liaised with officials at every venue and in being seen to get this right he also stressed that he was available for any other 'kinematographic work' that the New Zealand Government may require.[21]

Perry and his party were at the arrival of the royal party in Auckland on 10 June 1901 and followed the party on its tour through New Zealand, travelling in turn to Rotorua, Wellington, Christchurch and Dunedin until 21 June 1901, shooting some 3360 feet of film (1024 metres) in the process. It included all of the principal events from the reception of the royal couple in Auckland by Premier Richard Seddon and Colonial Secretary Joseph Ward in front of 250 official guests in a specially erected stand at the bottom of Queen Street on 11 June 1901, to the welcome festivities by the Maori tribes in Rotorua, the royal party's arrival in Wellington, the march of the militia and South African War veterans through the streets and under the 'Westport' Welcome Archway, pictures of the escorting warships of the Royal Navy in Wellington Harbour and the stone-laying ceremonies at the Wellington Town Hall and the railway offices. Christchurch featured the civic reception in Victoria Square, the military review and medal presentations to the South African War veterans in Hagley Park and a stone-laying ceremony. Dunedin also had its medal presentation ceremony in the Octagon, the parade of the duke's police bodyguard and the departure of the royal couple's train from the Dunedin Railway Station.

All of this was detailed by Perry in his report to Seddon. Perry was very well aware of people's interest in seeing themselves on film and knew that politicians were no different. He had the measure of the man when he wrote to Seddon reporting that "amongst these pictures yourself and the Ministry figure very prominently, and on the whole the above will provide a very comprehensive and complete record of the Royal Visitors to New Zealand".[22] The government purchased two copies of Perry's film but unfortunately only fragments of this 'complete record' survive.[23]

Nothing remains of the tumultuous reception in Auckland. However, Clive Sowry's photographic research identified Perry's camera crew setting up one of the Warwick Model 'A' cameras in the crowd at the Mayor of Auckland's platform on 11 June 1901. On the extreme left of the picture we see Perry cheering the royal party as one of the crew mounts the camera on its tripod, and behind them both a cloth-capped Mr Gladding looks on, having done the donkey work in carrying the equipment up there.

Scenes survive of the royal couple's visit to Rotorua. On the morning of 14 June 1901 the royal couple were shown the scenic delights of Ohinemutu and Whakarewarewa. "Both the Duke and the Duchess were subjected to a veritable battery of cameras and the King's kinematographist secured a splendid film."[24] Perry's team was not the only camera crew filming. Film was also taken by the 'King's kinematographist', as he was titled. This was Chief Petty Officer McGregor, a photographer attached to HMS *Vernon*, the torpedo shore depot in Portsmouth, who was trained to use the kinema camera on behalf of Alfred West of G. West and Sons, whose *Our Navy* film series drew the crowds and was regarded by the Royal Navy as one of its major recruiting tools. West was hired to take a film record of the tour and McGregor acted as official photographer and cinematographer, hence his title.[25] McGregor's film was screened by West to the royal family at Sandringham in a 'Royal Command Performance' and it remained one of West's showpieces for the life of *Our Navy*.

A Mr George Hescott from Wanganui also filmed the Rotorua scenes. Hescott owned a Prestwich camera, and through the offices of Mr Willis, the Wanganui member of the house of representatives, secured agreement with the premier for the filming of scenes at Rotorua for a fee of £40. Three films were taken showing the Maori haka (124 feet), Pohutu Geyser (120 feet) and the poi dance (150 feet) and were judged by the Government Printer to be "quite as good as those of Major Perry".[26] Hescott had hopes of using the film to secure a position with Donne's department, but the general manager clearly had not been told of this particular commission, and was in no particular hurry to settle the account. Hescott, after lengthy and increasingly heated correspondence, finally had to be satisfied in gaining his fee alone, with little prospect of further employment, indeed, he also offered to sell the government his camera![27]

In the surviving film of the Whakarewarewa visit, guide Sophia, a survivor of the Tarawera eruption, escorts the duchess while her niece, Maggie Papakura, escorts the duke.[28] Seddon, as always, is the dominant figure in each scene. The group is led by a standard-bearer of the Tuhourangi carrying the 'Takitimu' flag. A smart Maori officer of the Wairarapa Mounted Rifles, most likely Captain Rimene (Te Rimene Witinitara Te Kaewa) the officer commanding, is prominent in the group seen in the surviving film. Formally dressed dignitaries in the group watch the geysers, but inevitably the presence of Perry's camera crew, cranking away behind them, draws their attention as they pause to turn and peer at this curious contraption. This distraction may have been heightened by Pohutu Geyser's refusal to perform despite being liberally soaped to encourage it into action. However, Wairoa Geyser performed to the satisfaction of the premier and the royal party.

The film shows scenes from the royal couple's impromptu visit to a dress rehearsal of the 'Grand Carnival of the Tribes' on the afternoon of 14 June after visiting Whakarewarewa. Perry's Warwick camera's tripod demonstrates its panning capabilities by sweeping across "Two parties of poi dancers and four matuas armed and costumed … The poi dancers were — Ngatirangi from Tauranga, and Ngatiraukawa from Otaki; and the tauas of warriors were Ngatirangi from Tauranga, Ngatiporou, from the East Coast; Ngatikahungunu from the

Hawkes Bay and Wairarapa districts; and the Ngatimaniapoto from the Waikato … some seven hundred strong."[29]

In film they face the grandstand and the royal party with the warriors in column: Ngatirangi on the right; Ngatiporou in the centre in white singlets, purple sashes with black loincloths and with spears; Ngatikahungunu next to them, bare-chested with flax piupiu, white albatross feathers and taiaha. On their left are the Ngatimaniapoto in scarlet loincloths and with spears. In front of the warriors are the lines of poi dancers. The Ngatirangi are in "long white mats enriched with tufts of feathers with variegated *piupius* at the waist and the white feathers of the albatross (toroa) in their hair".[30] The Ngatiraukawa dancers are in scarlet and white with piupiu and feathers. Above them fly the tribal flags, uniformed soldiers and police pass among the crowd, and the tribal elders and chiefs stand proudly to the fore in each group.

Onlookers are kept back by piquet ropes and marshals. Behind the gathering is the tented camp of the tribes, to the right the mounted khaki-clad horsemen of the Wairarapa Mounted Rifles, the self-appointed escort to the royal party. Perry's film captures the moment, albeit in black and white. All that is missing is the hubbub of excitement in the crowd as the royal party approaches, the shouts of warning from the lookouts, the call of "haere mai", the slap of flesh against flesh, the swish of the piupiu, the clash of spears, the chant of the poi and the music of the Tuhoe fife and drum band as they launch into the national anthem, God Save the King.

Dressed in splendid feather cloaks, the Duke and Duchess of Cornwall approach the camera, escorted by the premier with Mrs Seddon alongside, Joseph Ward and James Carroll, minister of native affairs. The welcome begins: "The Ngatiporou taua *'peruperu'* began with the ancient war-cry of the Ngatiporou: *'A ki waikurekure ha!'* … At the first word the *matua* leaped up as one man and a thicket of spears darted up above them." This is followed by the haka of the Ngatikahungunu with taiaha and tewhatewha [battleaxe].[31]

The visit to Whakarewarewa on 14 June 1901 with Premier Richard Seddon, the Duke and the Duchess of York, flanked by guide Sophia, a survivor of the Tarawera eruption, on the left, and her niece, Maggie Papakura, on the right. R.A. Loughnan, *Royalty in New Zealand*.

This was all a preview for the next day when a gathering of thousands would welcome the royal couple and, while this was caught on film:

> The camera and the kinetograph may reproduce what met the eye, but no theatre audience can ever rise to thrill of novelty or tenseness of expectation which held Royalty and gentle folk and commoner wide-eyed and open-eared when face to face with the last remnant on earth of primeval man in the ecstasy and frenzy of passion simulated till it was all but real — near naked and unashamed.[32]

There are interesting questions to be answered about the date that the Rotorua film was taken, the source of the surviving film and of the identity of the cameramen who filmed it.

Scenes from the 'Grand Carnival of Tribes' at the Rotorua Race Course, poi dances with Tuhoe Fife and Drum Band, 14 June 1901, R.A. Loughnan, *Royalty in New Zealand*.

As we know, in addition to Perry's camera teams Mr George Hescott and Chief Petty Officer McGregor filmed the Rotorua scenes. Certainly some of the sequences of the 'Grand Carnival of Tribes' judged by their background seem to have been taken on 14 June 1901, and while the opening pan of the tribes is undoubtedly Perry's, the tripods of his Warwick cameras alone having that capability, there is uncertainty as to whether Perry or Hescott took the remaining Rotorua material, although during the visit to the geysers we see a Salvation Army camera assistant identified by his distinctive hat, briefly move in front of the camera, suggesting that this too is Perry's film.[33]

Only glimpses exist of the Wellington visit but we know this is Perry's camerawork. Perry was confident at the time that he had "secured some excellent pictures … A commanding stand on the wharf was obtained by the operators and they got an excellent shot of the Royal party as it stepped ashore. Next they got the sunny side of the Westport arch, where about 270 feet of excellent film were secured."[34] Perry was not so happy with the Town Hall stand, but we can judge the quality of the film taken at the Westport arch.

The royal carriage passes along Lambton Quay beneath the Westport Arch "like some old Roman arch of triumph, with commemorative tablets; but instead of bronze … coal filled the openings; massive blocks of coal — the same that saved the *Calliope* from the Apia hurricane".[35] Lambton Quay is lined with infantry of the Volunteer Corps who present arms in salute as the royal carriage passes. The Wellington crowds cheer and wave as the duke salutes in acknowledgement. His aide de camp, Captain the Viscount Crichton, in breastplate and helmet of the Horse Guards, rides by his side. They are followed by Colonel Sommerville of the New Zealand Permanent Militia leading an escort made up of 1000 Mounted Rifle Volunteers. The film captures a test of horsemanship by one of the Volunteer officers when his mount is unsettled by the cheers of the crowd. Finally we glimpse the march past of the artillery brigade

The duke salutes as his carriage passes through the Westport Arch on Lambton Quay, Wellington, with his aide de camp, Captain the Viscount Crichton, in breastplate and helmet of the Horse Guards riding by his side. Still from *Royal Visit of the Duke and Duchess of Cornwall and York to New Zealand.* NTSV F2468.

and the six guns, 60 horses and 80 men of Wellington's 'D' Battery, with the gunners splendid in dress blue uniforms and Busby headdress.

No film was provided by Perry of the medal presentations at Parliament House in Wellington, but a photo in Loughnan's *Royalty in New Zealand* shows one of Perry's camera teams, smartly coated against the threatening rain, filming with a Warwick Bioscope Model 'B' camera from the foot of the steps as each man marches up to receive his medal from the duke on 19 June 1901. The crowd reserved the biggest cheer for the two Wellington nurses who served in South Africa, nurses Monson and Warmington, who were last in the reception queue to receive their medals.[36]

Nothing survives of the grand review of Volunteers at Hagley Park in Christchurch on a cold frosty morning on 24 June 1901, but we have photos showing the 10,700 Volunteers and school cadets marching past the waiting crowd assembled in the temporary stands. We also see the specially erected photographer and cameraman's platform built adjacent to the reviewing dais, so that Perry's camera crews could look directly down the line of the approaching troops as they marched past and then again as the Boer War veterans among them came forward in single file to receive their campaign medals from the duke.

It was a setting and an audience to delight 'King Dick'. A British journalist wrote:

> Socialist, Mr Seddon, the Premier of New Zealand, who represents the Radical sentiments and aspirations of the island, gave a fervent speech, uttered in his usual stentorian tones …
>
> "I would much rather," he shouted, "see all you mounted men finishing the Boer War than being reviewed in Hagley Park" (a sentiment that was loudly cheered), "for this war has to be finished at whatever cost of blood and treasure.[37]

Grand Review of Cadets and Volunteers at Hagley Park, Christchurch, on 24 June 1901. Perry's camera teams can be seen in their temporary stand on the right.
Photographer unknown, 8015, Canterbury Museum.

Medal ceremony at Hagley Park, Christchurch, 24 June 1901. Perry's camera team are in their stand at top left.
Photographer unknown, PA1-f-064-47-1, ATL, Wellington.

Seddon's message of loyalty to the Empire was a puzzle to the accompanying English journalists as they found it difficult to reconcile his unalloyed imperial support with the otherwise 'socialist' programme of his Liberal Party. Moreover, here was a junior member of the Empire that was prepared to back up its rhetoric with the considerable contributions of its contingents to the war.

Perry's film of the medal presentation in the Octagon at Dunedin on 26 June 1901 survives. We see the duke and duchess under a canopied dais presenting medals to the South African War veterans, with Sir Joseph Ward resplendent in formal dress in the foreground. In this case Nurse Ross was first to receive her medal. This is not on film, but we see the line of veterans, dressed in khaki, salute and receive their medal and salute again before returning to their place in the crowd.

One-armed Boer War veteran at the medal presentation in the Octagon, Dunedin on 26 June 1901. Still from *Royal Visit of the Duke and Duchess of Cornwall and York to New Zealand.* NTSV F2468. (See colour section.)

Perry's final filming of the departure of the royal couple by train from Dunedin for Lyttelton on 27 June 1901 to embark on the SS *Ophir* for Tasmania has not survived, but by then he had filmed some 5000 feet of film, totalling 83 minutes.[38] The fervent public support for the visit overwhelmed the royal party and is evident on the surviving film. Perry was pleased with what his camera crews had taken. On 27 June he told reporters that he had taken some 25 kinematograph pictures and thought "that the best view he took was that of the Christchurch military review, on which function he exposed about 400 feet of film".[39]

Sadly, fragments of the royal tour films are all we have of the hundreds of films that Perry's cameramen took in New Zealand between 1898 and 1910. The Duke and Duchess of Cornwall and York's visit to New Zealand was made as a gesture of thanks for the support the colony had given to Britain in the war in South Africa. It was convenient as it coincided with the inauguration ceremonies of the Federal Parliament for the Commonwealth of Australia. At the time of the visit, despite the fall of the Boer capital of Pretoria, the war was still being fought as the Boer commandos reverted to guerrilla tactics. New Zealand Mounted Rifle Volunteers were still riding the veldt in search of the Boer. There were parents in the crowds whose sons were still in South Africa, but they and the crowds around them were honoured in the presence of royalty in New Zealand. This was New Zealand's first overseas war and the country took pride in being the first colony to offer troops to Britain.

By the war's end in 1902 New Zealand sent ten contingents of Mounted Rifles to serve in South Africa with the Imperial Forces; a total of 6500 personnel and 8000 horses. Casualties were few with more dying of disease and from accident than from combat, but to the families concerned this cost was real and immediate. Perry's film of the Dunedin medal ceremony shows a bare-headed man in khaki receiving his medal and the observant viewer will note that he has lost an arm — part of the cost of war: a cost that would be greater still from 1914 to 1918. After

One of Perry's camera teams, smartly coated against the threatening rain, films with a Warwick Bioscope Model 'B' camera from the foot of the steps of parliament as each man marches up to receive his medal from the duke on 19 June 1901.
R.A. Loughnan, *Royalty in New Zealand.*

the First World War these film scenes would be paralleled by similar scenes when the Duke and Duchess of York's eldest son and heir to the throne, Edward, Prince of Wales, visited New Zealand to thank the Dominion for its part in a far more expensive war. But in 1901 all this was an unknown and to the public that cheered the royal couple; their presence was proof indeed that New Zealand was playing its part as a loyal member of the British Empire and for now that was enough.

THE BROWN BROTHERS TOUR THE ROYAL VISIT FILMS

At the end of the tour, Perry had his film and returned to the studios in Melbourne to be developed. Perry's cameramen had been busy with often two cameras being used to duplicate some scenes. As well as putting together the compilation for the New Zealand Government, some of the Perry material was offered for sale by the Melbourne firm of Baker & Rouse Ltd, who acted as agents in selling Salvation Army film in Australia.[40] A set of the complete royal tour film is known to have been purchased by the then New Zealand-based Brown brothers, John Henry and Walter Franklyn Brown, who toured it successfully throughout New Zealand. The elder brother, John, was an established Wellington photographer. His younger brother would change his name to W. Franklyn Barrett, becoming well known under this name for his scenic and news-event films of New Zealand and Australia, before becoming one of the leading silent film directors in Australia and involved in directing and filming fictional films in Australia from 1911 on.[41]

Frank, or 'Wallie' as he was originally called, was born in 1873 and brought up by an aunt in England after his father and elder brother migrated to New Zealand. A skilled musician, he played the violin for the Theatre of Varieties in Bath, trying out photography in his spare time. In 1895 he joined his father and elder brother in New Zealand, working as a clerk for his father's

OPERA HOUSE.
___

TUESDAY and WEDNESDAY, 14th and
15th July.

Harry Hall's Enter-
tainers !

A Show of Unexampled Brilliance (vide
Press).
A Startling collection of Biograph Novel-
ties, including—
The Famous Fire Walking in Fiji !
A Waikato Maori Regatta !
A Trip up the Wanganui River !
Maori Canoe Hurdle Racing !
New Zealand's Wonderlands, Rotorua !
Ally Sloper's Half Holiday (Scream-
ingly Funny) !
And a host of Other Subjects.
OUR CONCERT COMPANY.
The Latest Illustrated Story Ballads, by
Mr ALEX. FORBES.
The Newest Specialities by MISS OLIVE
FITZSIMMONS and Mr W. FRANK
BARRETT,
The Popular Comedian and Everybody's
Favourite, Mr HARRY HALL, late of
Montgomery's Entertainers.
Popular Prices—2/-, 1/6, and 1/-. Doors
open 7.30 ; Overture 8.
WALTER P. MONK, Representative.

W. Frank Barrett operated the projector and showed a series of films taken by himself and his brother. He also sang the latest popular songs.
Wanganui Chronicle,
10 July 1903; p. 7.

hatters business before once again working as a musician for touring theatre orchestras, all the while continuing to experiment with photography and film.[42]

The Browns claimed that they filmed the royal tour, but it seems that this was just good showmanship in drumming up publicity to bring in the crowds.[43] They used Perry's film, most likely purchased from Baker & Rouse, which included additional scenes to those Perry delivered to the New Zealand Government. This was given its first public screening by J.H. and W.F. Brown's Royal Bioscope Company for a short but profitable five-night season at the Opera House, Wellington, in late July 1901.[44] There was musical accompaniment, with a lecturer embellishing each scene as it appeared on screen and Master Tom Trowell, a young New Zealand cellist, playing Goltermann's The Dream.

The review in the *Evening Post* was critical of the small screen and the blurring of some of the film, but emphasised its historical importance showing as it did, "the last and greatest display of a real Maori ceremony of welcome" at Rotorua, but for Wellington audiences the particular drawcard was "the distribution of medals by the duke to members of the returned contingents. The men, full life-size, pass one by one before the audience, who can not only recognise those they know, but can mark the gratified smiles on their faces."[45] We have the image of the camera team filming from the bottom of the parliament house steps and the description of the film they took, but as we know these films were not included in the film Perry supplied to the New Zealand Government, which seems a curious omission.[46] The tour obviously did well financially and the elder brother John Henry Brown brought the royal tour film back to Wellington again in April 1902.[47]

J.H. BROWN AND HIS BROTHER FILM NEW ZEALAND AND FIJI

There were a number of other New Zealand films appearing in the programme including *The Fire Brigade 14 Seconds After Receiving a Call* and the *WRC [Wellington Racing Club] Meeting Featuring the 'Hutt Flying Handicap'*. These may have been Perry's films but we know the Browns were filming in 1901 and, while fire brigades were a subject familiar to Perry, it is less likely he was interested in horse racing and its gambling connections.

John H. Brown, who seems to have been known as Harry or Henry, was very active filming local events in this period, assisted by his brother Frank. In late October to December 1901 a series of films were taken for Linley and Donovan's Empire Specialty Company at the Federal Hall, Wellington.[48]

On 2 November 1901 a film of Tortulla winning the New Zealand Cup, "taken by our special photographer in Christchurch", was shown only two days after the running of the race — clearly a slick operation to get it before the public in that time. On the same day in Wellington, "A cinematographic picture of the march past was taken by Mr Brown for exhibition at the Federal Hall" of the parade of the Wellington School Cadet Battalion at Athletic Park for the Empire's hero, 'Fighting Mac' — Major-General Sir Hector Macdonald, who was visiting New Zealand fresh from his achievements in commanding the Highland Brigade in South Africa. The film of the New Zealand Cup was shown on the Monday, followed by the Macdonald film on the Wednesday. It seems one of the brothers shot the Christchurch film with the other shooting the parade for 'Fighting Mac'. It was a well-organised piece of travel, filming, developing and printing of the films on both men's parts.[49]

Smiling ladies board the 4:55 p.m. Wellington-bound train after a day at the Palmerston North A & P Show, 15 November 1901. Still from John Henry Brown's *Departure of the Wellington Train from Palmerston North Station after the Show.* NTSV F2142.

BIOGRAPH PICTURES OF THE PALMERSTON SHOW

Linley and Donovan transferred their show to the Lyceum Theatre in Palmerston North over the four days of the Manawatu Show, and biograph operator Mr John Brown "had some splendid opportunities to take pictures at the A. and P. show, and took many hundreds of feet, including a picture of Hutton, the champion chopper finishing a log".[50] The series of films titled *Biograph Pictures of the Palmerston Show* featured at the Federal Hall in Wellington on 20 November 1901. The films included "The Wood-chopping competition. The Grand Parade of Horses, Cattle, and Prize Winners of Events. The Leaping Competition (Steeplechase Style)" and *Departure of the Wellington Train from Palmerston North Station after the Show.*[51]

This last film survives. We see a crowded railway platform on a summer's day; men in straw hats and Stetsons, women in travelling clothes, and curious children peering towards the camera. The stationmaster and his bustling assistants help passengers aboard the distinctive American-style clerestory roofs of the Wellington and Manawatu Rail Company's carriages on the Wellington-bound train on Friday afternoon, 15 November at 4:55 (providing it was on time), at what was then New Zealand's busiest railway junction.[52] The crowded platform is made up of families returning from the show. Brown set up his camera alongside the train intent on capturing the people's faces as they went about their business. What stays in the memory is the animation and smile on the face of one of a pair of women as she walks to her carriage, oblivious to the camera.[53]

It is a marvellous piece of film-making, and you are aware that this is the first time in their lives that these people have seen a motion picture camera. This is New Zealand's oldest surviving film showing a railway station scene and, at present, the fourth oldest known surviving film taken in New Zealand. W. Franklyn Barrett today receives accolades as a pioneer cameraman, but in 1901–02 it was his elder brother who was the principal operator and cameraman, with his younger brother in the supporting role.

Other films followed. There was the "*Opening of the Swimming Season at Thorndon Baths* and several other films that our operator (J.H. Brown) is now engaged upon".[54] In December

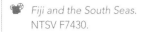

Fiji and the South Seas.
NTSV F7430.

1901 Linley and Donovan capitalised on the popularity of boxing films by commissioning the Browns to film a three-round fight, specially staged for the screen between 'Dummy Mace Carney' and T. McGregor, the champion featherweight boxer of New Zealand, for the Empire Specialty Company at Federal Hall, with Mace winning by a knockout.[55] 'Dummy Mace Carney' made his living in boxing sideshows and on the vaudeville circuit, and this was the first fight specially staged for film in New Zealand.

FIJI AND THE SOUTH SEA ISLANDS

The following year, 1902, was also busy. "Mr J.H. Brown of Wellington is to go to Fiji to take biograph pictures of the Coronation celebrations in the Islands for the American Biograph Company."[56] Some scenes of the film survives and is linked in with Rotorua Maori scenes also taken by the Browns. The Browns sold the film to Charles Urban who originally issued it in the United Kingdom in 1902. It was reissued in 1907 under the French Eclipse company that took over Urban's French franchise in November 1906.[57]

The film was taken during the special excursion of the SS *Waikare* to the Fiji Islands for the Coronation of the King of Fiji in 1902.[58] What we see today in *Fiji and the South Sea Islands* is a compilation of the Brown brothers' films originally screened in New Zealand by Harry Hall's Entertainers in a tour of the lower North Island in 1903. W. Franklyn Barrett featured in the touring party. He operated the film projector and also sang and gave comic turns. The advertising acknowledged his film-making skills. "Mr Harry Hall is the only manager of a theatrical company

Fijians prepare the bed of hot stones for the firewalkers. Still from John Henry Brown's *Fiji and the South Seas*. NTSV F7430. (See colour section.)

A canoe obstacle race on the Waikato River. Still from John Henry Brown's *Fiji and the South Seas*. NTSV F7430.

on tour in the colonies that carries his own biograph photographer, thus enabling the public a chance of seeing many remarkable sights that cannot be exhibited by any other company."[59] (This is the first time he used the name Barrett. To add to the confusion he still also used the name Brown.)

The advertised films included: "The Famous Fire Walking in Fiji! A Waikato Maori Regatta! A Trip up the Wanganui River! Maori Canoe Hurdle Racing! New Zealand's Wonderlands, Rotorua! Ali Sloper's Half Holiday (Screamingly Funny)! And a host of Other Subjects."[60]

The Fijian sequence originally ran for over 30 minutes and was originally titled *A Winter Trip in Summer Seas*.[61] In the surviving Urban version we see the pit full of heated stones being constantly turned and then, when hot enough, spread out to create a surface on which to walk. The firewalkers from the island of Beqa, Fiji, in their ceremonial dress, walk across and around the stones. They then throw their salu salus (flower necklaces) and ceremonial costumes of green leaves on to the stones as they step out of the pit. Foliage is thrown on to the hot stones and the firewalkers return and squat in the steam produced. As the firewalkers leave the pit, attendants place food baskets on to the hot stones to cook. All of this is filmed against a backdrop of watching European tourists.

This is followed by spectacular scenes of steam rising from Waimangu Geyser in Rotorua and the Wairoa Geyser, which was the largest at Whakarewarewa. (Waimangu was the biggest geyser in the world, playing to heights of 460 metres between 1900–04.) The film finishes with waka racing and canoe hurdling. This follows the sequence set out in the review of the screening at the Opera House in Wanganui:

> *A Waikato Maori Regatta.* These embrace the regatta procession, composed of all the competitors in canoes, ranging from the largest, containing 50 warriors to those holding only one. The war canoe race is a splendid spectacle of the skill the Maoris have acquired in the handling of their boats. A canoe hurdle race by wahines is a novel picture and shows the humorous situations and events that occur in this exciting pastime. The Maori men's canoe race is decidedly funny and also shows the champion team of the Auckland province, who negotiate the hurdle without hardly taking a drop of water in their canoe, while nearly every other competitor capsizes and gets into all sorts of ludicrous positions.[62]

The surviving film is how Fiji and New Zealand were seen by the wider world. All of this was fascinating fare for European audiences, which explains the film's re-editing and repeated

release. The film itself shows images of the first surviving overseas film shot by a New Zealand cameraman and collectively this and the Maori scenes represent the fifth oldest surviving New Zealand film. It is also the last film that we can attribute to John Henry Brown, because from now on it is his younger brother who takes centre stage.

CASHING IN ON ROYALTY

The veteran showmen Cooper and Macdermott's Kinematograph and Colossophone Entertainment also capitalised on the enormous interest in the royal visit. At the end of May 1901, before the royal arrival in New Zealand, they were already screening films with royalty as the theme at the Exchange Hall, "representing the Duke and Duchess of York's landing at St Kilda" from the Australian leg of the tour, moving the critic to write that "[t]his is wonderfully quick work" in putting it before a New Zealand audience, which it was.[63] At the Opera House in Wanganui on 31 July 1901 they added the 'Maori gathering at Rotorua' scenes to their 'Royal Visit' films; the day after the Brown brothers screened the 'Royal Visit' films in Wellington.[64] They also showed lantern slides but not film of the Auckland royal reception.

New Zealand was awash with films of the royal family. In July 1901, the month after the tour, the *Wanganui Herald* commented that there were 25 kinematograph companies touring New Zealand presenting pictures of the late Queen's funeral. These, together with Boer War film, are what the public wanted to see and the travelling showmen were keen to cash in on their interest.[65] It led to some interesting titles for the touring companies, such as Thornton Stewart's 'Royal War Kinematograph Company', where the name summed up the subjects on film, although in this case there was more, as "Mr Foley will give one of his clever ventriloquial [sic] turns"![66]

The government was also approached by a Mr John Stanley, who as the Lubin Biograph Company, c/- Chas Begg and Co., Dunedin, wanted to purchase a copy of the Perry government film for exhibition. It seems that he was unsuccessful but the New Zealand Government was in a quandary. At the end of a highly successful royal tour they had a commitment to purchase Perry's film but had no means of screening it, nor it seems, a clear philosophy as to what to do with the film afterwards.

PERRY DELIVERS THE FILM

On his return to Melbourne Perry advised the New Zealand Government that he had shot 3360 feet (56 minutes) of film and detailed the included scenes. The government was keen to purchase everything available and this increased the cost from £250 to £336 with an additional £107/10/- for the travelling expenses of the camera teams. The government negotiated the purchase from the Salvation Army Limelight company of two film projectors of the "very latest type enabling a large picture to be shown without flickering". The projectors were shipped with two copies of the film on the SS *Monowai* on 27 November 1901, together with a bill for the expenses of Perry and his camera crew, the cost of the film and projectors amounting to £729/15/.[67] Perry cautioned Seddon:

> I would strongly advise that none but a thoroughly competent and careful operator is entrusted with the handling of these films, as an inexperienced man might, in one exhibition, do them irreparable damage. Electric light is also to be preferred to Limelight, as with it a larger and much more brilliant picture may be obtained.[68]

On 2 April 1902 Perry's film was shown to a select audience in the Sydney Street schoolroom behind Parliament buildings. Mr Loughnan, who wrote the official published record of the tour, gave the commentary to an audience that included the governor, Lord Ranfurly, and his wife; premier Richard Seddon and his wife and daughter; Sir Joseph and Lady Ward, (Ward having been knighted by the duke for his endeavours during the Wellington section of the royal tour); Sir Robert Stout; W. Hall-Jones, C.H. Mills and others, including T.E. Donne who managed the tour arrangements so smoothly. "Repeated glimpses of the Royal visitors and numerous public personages evoked applause." One senses an element of anticlimax and this was mirrored in the *Evening Post* report: "Those who expect of them — minus as they are of so much of the colour and sound accompaniment — the completeness of the original pictures, will be disappointed."[69]

The Wellington screenings by the Brown brothers in July 1901 robbed Perry's film of its uniqueness. Now the premier and his colleagues, together with their families, saw it stripped of its ideal setting: a packed theatre. It lacked the music and cheering of the enthusiastic audience of the Wellington Opera House and the select group of viewers knew something was missing but could not quite identify what it was.

What was missing of course were the accompanying performances and the audience involvement that were an essential part of every touring theatre show that was now part and parcel of the wonders of kinematography. Perry followed the same structure in his tours. No showman would ever give 56 minutes of silent film accompanied by only a lecturer's address. Had there been, in addition to Loughnan telling the story in the manner of a good raconteur, some musical accompaniment — a piano at least, but more properly an orchestra, a good solo baritone singing patriotic songs, maybe a choir — there would certainly have been lots of audience involvement, spontaneous applause at the many appearances of the premier with the royal couple, with the house rising to its feet with demands for encores as the best bits were shown again. At the obligatory God Save the King everyone would have gone home happy that they had relived the tour of a lifetime.

The setting and the nature of the audience at the Sydney Street schoolroom lacked this, hence the government's muted response. They and the country were in a period of post-royal visit shock — the inevitable depression when the adrenaline stops pumping. Watching the film that survives one cannot fault Perry's film-making, yet James Mackay, the Government Printer, who was in the audience, no doubt voiced the feelings of the others present when he wrote to Pollen, the colonial secretary, expressing a certain disappointment that while the films were shown to advantage they "did not appear to be so perfect as they should be. The expert, however, was satisfied with them."[70]

As it turns out the expert was the photographer and senior half of the Royal Bioscope Company, John Henry Brown, who — at the request of the colonial secretary — inspected the films, projectors and accessories to ensure that the government received what it paid for. After the select screening the films and projectors were placed in storage under the care of James Mackay — "one copy being retained for the Government while the other has been sent to the Agent General in London, who will probably arrange their exhibition during the Coronation festivities".[71] Seddon was going to London for the coronation of King Edward VII and the visit included a Premier's Conference and a host of engagements where 'King Dick' continued to remind the Empire of his and New Zealand's willing role in the South African War. Politically he was at his peak — basking in New Zealand's status as a trailblazer in social democracy, and the government's royal visit film demonstrating New Zealand's loyalty to Empire was part of that message.[72]

5

Limelight and salvation

Every Bioscope machine requires the attention of an operator — a man who is competent to obtain the best results from the machine placed under his care. He must know every detail of his mechanism; what to do in an emergency and the quickest way of doing it, so as not to keep his audience waiting a moment longer than is absolutely necessary; he must be acquainted with all the latest and best methods of projection; the care of films, optical principles and fire appliances. He must be able to obtain the best results under difficult circumstances, and be competent to fit up his apparatus at a moment's notice.[1]

Regardless of any lingering government doubts New Zealand had its first official film, and it was the first of a number of films that Perry and his Salvation Army camera teams took of public events and then offered for sale to Donne's Department of Tourist and Health Resorts. On Saturday 9 August 1902, a public holiday, Perry filmed the massed schools and parade of veterans watched by a packed crowd of thousands at King Edward VII's coronation celebrations at the Basin Reserve in Wellington, having secured a "good position for kinoing the speech-makers as they delivered their orations. A number of pictures were successfully taken … on behalf of the New Zealand Government."[2] In September 1902 these were given their first showing in Wellington at the Salvation Army Barracks in Vivian Street. The screening also included "views incidental to the Duke's visit to the colonies" enabling New Zealand audiences to see films taken the previous year during the royal tour.[3]

PROMOTING NEW ZEALAND

Donne wanted to advertise New Zealand to the world and film was but one of the mediums. Pamphlets, postcards and lantern slides were distributed overseas through the tourist offices that were set up in Australia, the United States and in London. Donne represented New Zealand at the Louisiana Purchase Exhibition (1904–1905) at St Louis. The New Zealand Exhibit

The Triple Alliance of Graphophone, Cinematographe and Limelight were the key elements in Perry's Limelight Department.
Victory, August 1898, p. 300.

STAFF-CAPTAIN PERRY was surrounded by kinematographe films on the morning that the VICTORY representative invaded the sanctum of the Limelight Department, the studios being literally festooned with the newly-developed pictures which the chief departmental operator had been preparing for the future delectation of Salvation Army audiences.

"Busy?" queried he of the VICTORY.

"Never anything else on this flat," was the terse rejoinder of the Kinematographist, whose efforts had been so recently directed towards turning "negatives" into "positives"—an always congenial task to him. "Not that we are too busy to see gentlemen of the press," he continued cheerily.

"Then you are open to be interviewed?"

"Certainly; fire away!"

"Well, I want to know something about your department."

"In what way?"

"Mainly on the line of recent developments. You *have* developed, I presume?"

"Rather! The Commandant has a big idea of the future of this department, and since he took it specially in hand—practically creating it a department—

was mounted largely as the result of the joint efforts of his two departments — Industries and Commerce and Tourist and Health Resorts, together with contributions from private companies and individuals.[4] It earned several awards including a special award for the hunting and fishing exhibit — a particular interest of Donne. Film too played an important part. "Special films of New Zealand subjects also were screened … these films afterwards served a useful purpose in North American cities and afterward, too, in those of other English-speaking countries."[5]

Donne's approach was not governed by any thought of financial return, but to achieve the widest possible distribution. It is best illustrated by his reply to requests from his manager at Rotorua to restrict touting by commercial photographers at the entrance to Whakarewarewa village and thermal pools. He directed that "provided that the visitors are not subjected to undue solicitation I see no good reason for interfering with the sales. It must be remembered that from an advertising point of view the sale of photographs in any form to visitors from over-sea is good business, as every photograph sold becomes a standing advertisement for New Zealand's resorts."[6]

Donne was always looking for the opportunity. In 1905 the outstanding success of the 'Original All Blacks' tour of Great Britain created enormous public interest in Britain as well as in New Zealand. The trip had been underwritten by the New Zealand Government with the prime minister, 'King Dick' Seddon promising the New Zealand Rugby Football Union (NZRFU) that the government would pay the return fares if there was any shortfall in funds from the tour. George Dixon, the tour manager and a close friend of the prime minister, personally cabled him the results of each game, and it was Seddon who released the news through the post offices to the New Zealand public, with crowds gathering outside every post office after each match, anxious for the cabled results. Post offices were specially opened on Sunday mornings as the tour progressed to display the latest results.[7]

Donne, working closely with William Pember Reeves, the New Zealand high commissioner in London, capitalised on the tour's success with advertising in the British national press promoting "The Home of New Zealand Footballers". It pushed tourism: "The Land for Tourists: Deer stalking, trout fishing, beautiful lake and alpine scenery, excellent transit is provided by means of railways, coaching routes, and coastal steamers." New Zealand was also the perfect place to live and migrants were keenly sought: "A country with a fertile soil, well watered and a temperate climate. A great sheep, cattle, dairying, grain and fruit growing country … Passages at reduced rates granted to persons possessing small capital and approved by the High Commissioner."[8]

Seddon was also quick to promote New Zealand and its willingness to play its part within the Empire, capitalising on queries from the British press by replying to the *Daily Mail* that "[i]nterest respecting the contests taking place in Great Britain is awaited almost as eagerly as news of the late war in South Africa and the results are received with great enthusiasm".[9]

Films of the games were popular in Great Britain and even more so in New Zealand. John Fuller & Sons and T.J. West were two of the touring shows who arranged that films taken of the matches were purchased and sent to New Zealand, and in West's case he arranged for a camera team to film many of the games. The film of the match against Northumberland played on 14 October 1905 in which the All Blacks won 31–0 was screened in Auckland on 26 December 1905. Film of each test match was despatched on the first mail boat to leave for New Zealand after each match. Each touring film show endeavoured to have All Black films as a feature and it was not unusual for the film to be repeated at the same showing in response to the roars of the audience.[10] Even the film of the single loss on the tour continued to draw an audience, and in September 1906 The Stonham-Morrison Co. playing at His Majesty's Theatre, Dunedin, advertised "N.Z. Footballers in the match against Wales" as part of their programme.[11]

Dave Gallaher, captain of the Original All Blacks on their 1905 tour of the United Kingdom. The publicity from the tour was used by Seddon's government to promote New Zealand by advertising in the British national press "The Home of New Zealand Footballers". Films of the games were distributed throughout New Zealand. *The Complete Rugby Footballer* by D.Gallaher & W.J.Stead, published by Methuen, London, 1906 first edition.

New Zealand vs England 1905. NTSV F27366.

Dave Gallaher leads the All Blacks on to the field in the game against England at Crystal Palace on a "cold dull Saturday" on 2 December 1905. New Zealand won 15–0. Still from *New Zealand vs England.* NTSV no. 6 NZ1905.

Little has survived. There are scenes of the match against Cardiff and Glamorgan and perhaps two-thirds of the original film of the All Blacks versus England played at Crystal Palace on a "cold dull Saturday" on 2 December 1905. Such was the public interest that the ticket sellers were swept aside and thousands flooded into the grounds. In addition to the 45,000 who paid, it was assessed that there may have been another 50–55,000 people who crowded in, making it perhaps the largest rugby crowd in the history of the game. Among the crowd in the main stand was the Prince of Wales, later King George V, who had visited New Zealand as the Duke of Cornwall and York in 1901. Worried by the speed, skill and combination that the New Zealanders had displayed in their victories, the English game plan was to match the New Zealand system of 2-3-2 in the forwards, playing seven forwards with five three-quarters supporting the wings against a — by now — tired and past their peak New Zealand XV. It did not work. For New Zealand, McGregor on the wing would score four tries and Newton one, with no conversions in their 15–0 victory.

The surviving film captures Gallaher leading his men on to the field, the haka, and a run of scrappy play in which Gallaher seems ever-present. It ends midway through the second half, but the images at half-time, with the dejected body language of the English players in contrast to the smiles on the New Zealanders' faces with the score at 9–0, speaks of a game well under control.[12] It is interesting to compare the film to that of their return on the *Sonoma*; that quiet half-time confidence is still evident in a team that, despite the loss to Wales, knows that it has met the best the world has to offer and has triumphed.[13]

Both Perry and West's Pictures filmed the Christchurch International Exhibition. This still from West's *Sights and Scenes at the New Zealand Exhibition* shows one of his camera teams filming the Vice Regal party of Lord and Lady Plunket leaving the Exhibition entrance. NTSV F2656.

We also see Seddon basking in the glory of his returned heroes. In fact, he appears in three of the nine surviving films showing New Zealand-related subjects in the period 1897–1906. The tenth is of his funeral procession, filmed by W. Franklyn Barrett, leaving Parliament grounds in Wellington.[14] Even in death, his was the dominant part with his flag-draped coffin on the gun-carriage surrounded by cabinet ministers and followed by closed carriages carrying the governor and his successor Sir Joseph Ward, while members of the House of Representatives, judges of the Supreme Court and every public figure follow, watched by sorrowful crowds that press in from both sides. His is the presence in New Zealand's surviving film of the period in the same way he commanded New Zealand public life.

FILMING THE CHRISTCHURCH INTERNATIONAL EXHIBITION

In 1906 Donne approved Perry and West's request to film at the Christchurch International Exhibition in Hagley Park. Each sought exclusive filming rights but were unsuccessful. Both filmed, with T.J. West also setting up a picture theatre at the venue. The Exhibition had been a Seddon initiative that now became the stage for his successor, Sir Joseph Ward. A photo shows Perry's cameramen resplendent in uniforms: Major Perry with cane sits in front of five of his operators with an array of motion pictures and stills cameras, all in "Imperial Khaki Serge" uniforms covered with dress braid and wearing what today is instantly recognisable as a version of the Australian slouch hat.[15] It is a display that shows the resources of what was by now the largest film production company in Australia and New Zealand.

THE CAMERA OBSCURA
(Located near Maori Pa),
WHERE the whole of Exhibition Grounds
may be seen in
BEAUTIFUL COLOURED LIFE
PICTURES.
The Most Popular Entertainment in Exhi-
bition Grounds.
ADMISSION 6d.
Visited by over 10.000 Persons.   9534

The camera obscura presented coloured views of the Exhibition; its principles had been employed for
centuries and now incorporated the magic lantern projector. At the Christchurch International Exhibition the
old stood alongside the new with West's Pictures showing continuous pictures at the Castle Picture Theatre.
Photographer: Steffano Francis Webb, G- 5036-1/1, ATL, Wellington.

Perry reported that his crews "were successful in getting a fine series of the opening
ceremonies; the model geysers for which the Tourists and Health Department have received
great praise: the Fijians in their war-dance: the Maoris, with their hakas and 'poi' games. In
fact everything of interest, we set our machine on."[16] They were also part of the Exhibition
programme, and the Salvation Biorama Band had the "honour of playing at the opening of the
Christchurch (NZ) Exhibition, and of discoursing sweet music for several successive days to the
thousands who thronged the place each morning and afternoon. We were under the dome, and
were the only band in the Exhibition for several days."[17]

Perry's film has not survived but that taken by the film entrepreneur and showman T.J. West
has. In one of the scenes of the opening on 1 November 1906 when the vice regal party of Lord
and Lady Plunket are leaving the Exhibition entrance, one of West's camera crews filming close-
ups of the departing dignitaries is captured in the shot. They too are dressed for the occasion
in suits and top hats. It was a media event described in the *West Coast Times*: "Outside [the]
entrance there was a tremendous army of photographers and cinematographists, but they in no
way disconcerted his Excellency."[18]

It seems that West and Perry met at the Exhibition and found themselves of similar
temperament and equally driven by their love of film. They renewed that contact when West
shifted his base of operations to Australia and for a period some of West's news-event films were
developed in the Salvation Army studios in Melbourne.[19] West also offered to sell his film to
Donne's department and was quick to feature this in his advertising.

West's film also gives us a glimpse of what Perry's film would have shown with the pomp
of the opening ceremonies and the arrival and then departure of Governor Lord Plunket with
Prime Minister Sir Joseph and Lady Ward featuring prominently.[20] This is followed by the
'trooping of the colours' and the march-past of the scarlet-coated volunteer infantry of the

Canterbury Province parading behind their colours, several companies of blue-jackets from His Majesty's Ships *Challenger, Pioneer* and *Pyramus* that were docked in Lyttelton, and the school cadets. The scenes then change to the Wonderland with its toboggan slide, helter-skelter, water-chute, dragon-train and camel rides. A bewhiskered gentleman in a Stetson hat is prominent in the final scenes with the baby camels, and a comparison to surviving photos show that we may have T.J. West himself on film, allowing the world to see someone who was becoming the leading film entrepreneur in Australasia. The film was screened at West's theatre established in the Exhibition grounds and also featured in West's Pictures' tour through New Zealand with the Brescians, under the title *Sights and Scenes at the New Zealand Exhibition.*[21]

What we do not hear is the grand music of the Exhibition Ode specially composed by Mr Alfred Hill and performed by his Exhibition orchestra, the choir members of the Christchurch Musical Union and the Woolston Brass Band, mixed in with the "crash of the mimic cannon in the huge Cyclorama as the tremendous three-days battle of Gettysburg was fought again between blue coat and grey; … the voices of the merry-makers who shot the water-chute with shouts of laughter; or heard, perhaps, in an infrequent lull, from the distant dimness of the Maori pa, a high quavering waiata".[22]

This was the fourth in a series of industrial exhibitions to showcase New Zealand. Dunedin in 1865, Christchurch in 1882 and Dunedin again in 1889–90 had been privately sponsored but in 1906 the Christchurch International Exhibition was a government exercise and Seddon's brainchild. T.E. Donne was the workhorse in the organising committee. Two million people paid to see the show — over a million more than the population of New Zealand — and though it lost money, Ward saw it as evidence of New Zealand's growing prosperity and used his opening speech to announce the introduction of New Zealand's penny post and the ability to send "telegrams from end to end of the colony without any restriction for one halfpenny a word".[23]

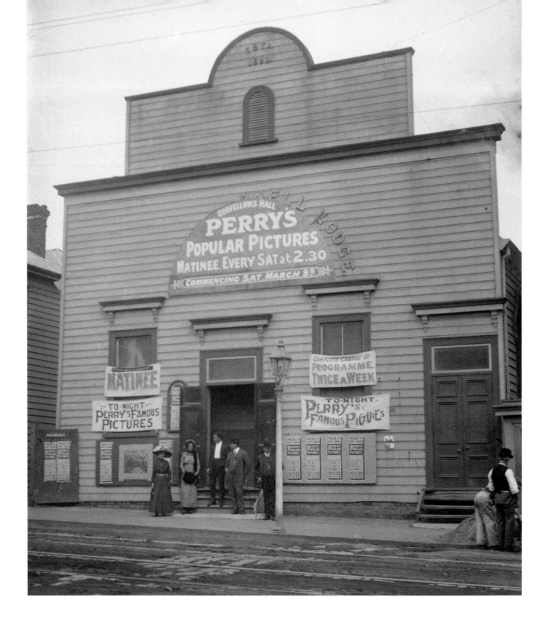

The staff of Will Perry's Popular Pictures standing in front of the Oddfellows' Hall in Parnell, taken in 1912. Auckland Libraries, Sir George Grey Collection, ID 902-9698.

In March 1902 Perry wrote to Seddon and told him that his cameramen were going to tour New Zealand over the next few months and "secure films of all the beauty spots of the colony for the use of the Salvation Army operations throughout the Commonwealth."[24] Perry is presumed to have taken his first film in New Zealand during Commandant Booth's first tour in 1898 when he filmed the Maori welcome at the Otaki Railway station. By 1900 the Salvation Army had become the biggest film producer in Australia and New Zealand. Following on from the disastrous fire in Marton in 1896, Perry returned with both lantern and kinematograph in the same year and then every year from 1901 up to 1910.

Perry, no doubt influenced by his Dunedin years, usually ran the New Zealand tours, though Sidney Cook toured the New Biorama in 1904. This was the year that Perry and Dutton visited Britain and Europe for the Salvation Army's International Congress. They impressed the audience with the sophistication and scope of the film and lantern shows. Perry and his team also filmed the Congress, before touring Europe to take films and photographs.

In England the Salvation Army first exhibited film in London from 1–13 February 1897 using a Lumiére Cinèmatograph, however, the bold plans of General Booth in 1896 were not realised until 1903 when Bramwell Booth, the general's eldest son and chief of staff directed that a Cinematograph Department be established and the first films produced. This never matched the sophistication and scale of Perry's Limelight productions but the mix of commercial and Salvation Army films had a similar impact on the audience, drawing in hundreds where before the meetings had numbered in their tens.[25]

In Australasia Perry toured to save souls and earn money to fund the Army's social projects, but it was also great entertainment and its success spurred imitators. In 1907 his brother, Will Perry, already an experienced tour manager, took advantage of the family connection and formed Perry's Biorama and Royal Speciality Company to tour New Zealand and capitalise on the Perry name.[26] Will Perry offered more than simply a name — which changed to Perry's Electric Biorama — and seemed to have the same skills as his brother. His tours received good reviews. "The programme submitted by this popular Company in the Town Hall last night surpassed all the excellent performances yet given by them. The pictures were realistically shown and demonstrated that the Perry Company are the premier picture company of the Dominion."[27]

The Salvation Army recognised the threat and during its stay in Wellington published a disclaimer in the local press stating that the company was "in no way whatever connected with the Salvation Army. Neither has it anything to do with MAJOR PERRY or his well-known and famous Biorama."[28]

The Salvation Army Biorama Company mounted ambitious tours on a scale that matched any of the travelling vaudeville and kinematograph shows. The first serious competition that the Salvation Army faced in terms of local filming was the arrival in New Zealand of the Hayward family and T.J. West, the entrepreneur touring as 'West's Pictures and the Brescians' in 1905. Despite a very lucrative tour the Haywards originally saw film as a novelty that would pass, but as we shall see they had second thoughts and became one of the powerhouses in the screening of films in New Zealand.

PERRY'S BIORAMA TOURS NEW ZEALAND

Perry's Biorama toured New Zealand for many months at a time, with usually no more than two or three days in any one town and often only staying for an overnight stop. For example, during the 1906 tour that travelled back and forth through both the North and South islands, Perry's report in *War Cry* gives us an idea of the scale of the enterprise: "We were twenty-four when we started, varying somewhat during the tour, but never went under fifteen in the orchestra, which was indeed a talented combination."[29]

The *War Cry* spoke of the Limelight Brigade's octopus-like tendencies, with Perry having Limelight and Biorama teams operating throughout Australia. In New Zealand his 'Territorial Biorama Company' became more and more identified with Perry himself and was advertised as "Perry's Pictures, Perry's Brass Band, Perry's Orchestra, Perry's Glee Party, Perry's Soloists, Perry's Illustrated Songs!"[30] Members included his wife and three of his sons, all of whom had active roles to play. He also took with him film shot in Australia as well as New Zealand film taken on earlier tours. "We took over a number of films that had never been seen in New Zealand before, one especially beautiful one 'Christ Among Men'. It comprehends the whole life of Christ in the form of one moving picture."[31]

All this was an enormous exercise in logistics with "tons of luggage". A steam traction engine, which drove the electric plant and powered the projectors, was hired locally with a trailer to carry the baggage. This was also used to publicise the tour by towing the Biorama Band, as they played under a publicity banner, down the main street of each town, advertising the night's performance. "The engine for driving our electric plant … has been the biggest hit

we have made to date, and has kept the Army head and shoulders above everything else in this line."[32]

Taking and screening moving pictures was Perry's life and this is evident from his report on the tour. Film opportunities included a biograph picture of 'Pelorus Jack', a famous dolphin some 15 feet long who escorted the Picton to Nelson ferry steamer as it sailed through French Pass. "By courtesy of the captain of the *Arahura*, a special platform was fixed over the bows of the steamer, down near the water, for our operators to 'snap' Jack. As we sailed through the French Pass our joy was complete when the monster made his appearance. You can guess the machine was soon set going."[33]

W. Franklyn Barrett also filmed 'Pelorus Jack' from a similarly erected platform when working as a Pathé cameraman in 1910. His Pathé colour-tinted scenic film the *Coasts of New Zealand* survives, showing the dolphin leading the ship through French Pass.[34]

It was the same on the return voyage to Australia, with Perry taking images of the Milford Sound that Barrett and others would also later capture to show New Zealand's wonders.

> Captain Neville, of the turbine steamer *Maheno* made it possible for us to do some good 'kinny' work. The Captain gave us the use of the ship's launch, and we cruised up the Milford Sound with the biograph apparatus going merrily. The *Maheno* waited for us for some hours. On our return to the ship we received the sad news that one of the stalwart sailors who had helped to lower our launch had dropped dead from heart failure. The same afternoon at 4 o'clock he was buried at sea. Sad and solemn as was the occasion, we could not refrain from making a record of such an unusual ceremony in these waters, and so a 'Burial at Sea' has been added to our splendid assortment of pictures.[35]

A storm en route provided another filming opportunity:

> Huge waves were breaking over the bows, the water flying clear over the hurricane decks in great showers; occasionally reaching the top of the navigation deck. Here was the material, I thought, for some fine pictures. Despite the danger of severe wettings, and other inconvenient experiences, one or two of the operating staff got to work with the cameras, whilst officers of the ship very kindly held the leg of the tripod. Orrie (my boy) secured a fine picture of the storm — and a good ducking into the bargain.[36]

Between 1902 and 1909 Perry repeatedly visited at some time or other every town and district in New Zealand where the Salvation Army had a corps with sufficient members to billet the touring party. Perry's orchestra and band also utilised the resident Salvation Army bands and musicians in each town. It set the standard for the many touring shows and, more than anything else, the Salvation Army Biorama Company brought moving pictures to small town New Zealand. Perry's filming of local scenes and personalities recognised the draw that such film would have. It established a pattern of film-making that characterised New Zealand film production during the silent film era.

A diary of Perry's 1902 and 1905 tour was published in weekly parts in the New Zealand *War Cry*, written by one of the members of Perry's company under the pseudonym 'Rambler', believed to be Captain John Brodie.[37] It constitutes the earliest detailed account of film exhibition and film-production in New Zealand, and it is worth sampling the 1905 tour to gain an impression of life on the road with Perry's Biorama that in 1905 numbered 17 songsters and musicians, some of who also assisted with limelight and projection.

Perry's programme may have been more spiritually uplifting than the travelling vaudeville and variety shows, but it followed the same structure of providing plenty of variety to keep the audiences interested. It was a mix of film, lantern slide and song, with the songs and music providing time for changing the reels of film, all cleverly building to a climax that allowed the paying audience to go home well content that they had got their money's worth — with a satisfying dose of salvation to boot. The film itself was drawn from overseas producers, as well as that produced by Perry's own Limelight Department. Films of the International Congress in London and of his travels through Europe featured in the show. Even the morally uplifting films of the work of the Salvation Army in London had all the classic elements of a good story that kept audience attention, with the pathos of life on the streets matched by a brawl where the constable is bested and the Salvation Army officers come to the rescue. This is repeated in the film set in the Australian outback that was filmed by Perry's cameraman in 1904; in this tale the 'Blacks' fall outside the hope of salvation and here it is simply a tale of crime and retribution.

Perry, like all good showmen, ended on a high note with the screening of Edwin S. Porter's production for Edison of *The Great Train Robbery*, which was advertised in Australia and New Zealand as *The Great American Train Robbery*. While the moral of the story was very apparent to 'Rambler', one can imagine New Zealand audiences leaving the Citadel buzzing with excitement after seeing the first of the Westerns with all the elements that would be repeated in its thousands of successors. It was a shilling well spent. Perry's Biorama preached salvation and at the same time provided entertainment of a standard rival tours could only envy.

Always the consummate showman, Perry varied the programme if the Company was staying more than one night in a town. On the second night in Christchurch in March 1905 the packed house saw a hand-tinted film of a coach-ride on the West Coast road. This had been shot on Perry's previous tour in 1902 when the Biorama Company visited some of the mining communities by coach.[38] This film of New Zealand from the road continued to grow as scenes were added with each visit, Perry calling it the longest coach tour film in existence. Once again we have to look to W. Franklyn Barrett's surviving films to gain some idea of what Perry's colour-tinted film may have looked like. Barrett's scenic travelogues *Coasts of New Zealand* and *Across the Mountain Passes of New Zealand* capture the images of New Zealand at the beginning of the 20th century. In the latter film we see a Newman's four-horse coach climb slowly up a narrow mountain road from the gold-mining community of the Lyell; perched above an arm of the Buller River at Lyell Creek, surrounded by mountains with its magnificent bush scenery all highlighted by Pathé's colour tinting.[39]

Perry assured his audiences that all of his films were "thoroughly up to date. Within a little over thirty days of their leaving London, they were being shown to a Melbourne audience, and that was not very long before the Biorama Company started for New Zealand."[40] Perry had the resources to purchase film from overseas producers as well as shoot and develop his own scenic, topical events and story films.

From March to October 1905 Perry's Biorama toured from town to town — first through the South Island, Mosgiel and Milton, all with packed houses, and "from start to finish the attention of the audience never flagged. Ripples of laughter one minute, a tear in the eye and a choke in the throat shortly after told only too well how picture and song can move a vast audience."[41] In Lawrence the Company took an "unparalleled balance of £20 for two nights" and also shot a "biograph picture of the local fire brigade who turned out and went through a number of drills for us."[42] Kaitangata, Balclutha and Gore followed. In Gore a packed house and

crowds of people waiting outside led to cries of "Go on boss run the programme, and then let us in, and start again."[43] There were 'bumper' houses in Kingston and Queenstown, and Perry shot "a most interesting panoramic view of Queenstown, which, no doubt will ere long be traversing the globe, as a great many more of our films are doing at present".[44]

In most towns it was good takings for the Salvation Army and the programme went down with local audiences "like ice-cream on an Australian summer's day".[45] Everyone turned out to see the show, whether they were seeking salvation or not, from the mayor to the local Roman Catholic priest. In May and June 1905 the Biorama toured Southland, the West Coast and Nelson and then through to Wellington with the previously described filming of 'Pelorus Jack' as they passed through the Sounds.

Wellington was the start of the North Island tour. Packed houses of 3000 were jammed into the newly opened Wellington Town Hall and hundreds were turned away.

Perry filmed wherever the opportunity offered; the fire brigade in Wellington and Maori in Otaki. Sometimes the negative was posted back to Melbourne and a print posted back to the touring company for screening before the tour's end — the *Turn-out of the Wellington Fire Brigade*, for instance; filmed in May and screened in September is an example. Otherwise the negative was held over for developing in the Salvation Army studios when the Company returned to its base in Melbourne.[46]

In Gisborne the week-long season starting on 9 August 1905 was the Company's longest single stay in one place. This allowed Perry to shoot, develop and screen his local films in the same week before they left town. On Saturday afternoon the Biorama Band "paraded in the main street, and the scientific end of the show perched themselves on a motor-car kindly lent to us by Mr Barker, and with a Kinematographe machine, we did a rapid run down Gladstone

Films of fire brigades at speed, such as the Wellington Fire Brigade, were popular subjects. 1/2-104840-F, ATL, Wellington.

Joseph Perry filming the re-enactment of Captain Cook's landing at Boat Creek on 16 August 1905. Photographer: William C. Crawford, Tairawhiti Museum, ID 061–4_WFC_1–4_4707–5.

Road taking in all the sights and scenes as we passed … We came back and got a good picture of the March-Past of a company of Maoris who also did some fine hakas."[47] Perry's crew spent the rest of Saturday developing the film as well as giving shows on Saturday night and Sunday.

> Monday was a day of hard and persistent work, getting the films printed and developed under exceedingly great difficulties to show the same evening. However pluck and perseverance gained the day, and at night we were well rewarded for all our exertions by the uproarious applause which greeted the local films. The hall was packed in every part, hundreds being turned away long before starting time.[48]

The Gisborne visit was a success and it was a formula that Perry repeated if time allowed at any of a tour's stops. Nothing drew an audience better than the chance to see themselves or people they knew on film. It was a drawcard that would be repeated by other touring film companies and also by local projectionists and photographers once permanent picture theatres became established.

It was not just motion pictures of crowds in the main street or the speed of response of the local fire brigade that interested Perry. He also knew the value of a good story. On 16 August 1905 at Boat Creek on the outskirts of Gisborne Perry filmed a re-enactment of Captain Cook's landing in Poverty Bay, showing:

> The boat coming into the creek, the Maoris resenting the landing, the fatal shot which killed the Maori and the first rifle shot heard in New Zealand, were all acted to the very life, and for the benefit of the insidious Kinematographe machine.[49]

Perry's filming of Cook's landing drew a number of interested spectators, including a local photographer, William Crawford, who took a series of photos of the filming. These include the Maori waiting with spear and taiaha on the shoreline, the approach of the ship's boat and the camera crew smartly dressed in their Salvation Army uniforms, all watched by an interested crowd of spectators and some puzzled dogs. This was shot on Perry's last day in Gisborne. It screened in Wellington about a month later, but Gisborne audiences had to wait a further 11 months.[49] Although the film itself has not survived, Crawford's photos have and they capture the filming of one of the first story films shot in New Zealand.[50]

Touring with Perry's Biorama was not without its trials and the first rule of any travelling show was that the show must go on. During the season in Dannevirke the company "did a run up the main street with the Kino camera, which was lashed to the front of a motor car kindly lent and ably manipulated by Dr. McKay, and were by its use, able to capture a picture of Dannevirke's High Street, which was shown the same evening — at least the negative of the same, there not being time to get the positive printed and dried. Perhaps at some future time we shall be able to return and show the people themselves as they appear kinematographically."[51]

This did not seem to disappoint a packed house in the Dannevirke Drill Hall and Perry cleared £32, which brought the total profit of the 1905 tour to that date close to £2000. The success was repeated in Wanganui and even though they found themselves "hard on the heels of West's great picture show, yet our reputation was such that once again the houses were full".[52] West's Pictures and the Brescians, combining the talents of the film entrepreneur T.J. West and the Hayward family, was one of the few travelling companies in New Zealand at the time to rival Perry's Biorama in variety and professionalism. The ability to sustain audience interest in the larger centres such as Wanganui signalled the beginning of a move to permanent moving picture shows and the inevitable decline of itinerant showmen with their travelling shows, except in the smaller country areas.

After touring the North Island the Biorama Company sailed for the West Coast and gave shows at Westport, Reefton and Greymouth. In Greymouth the band marched down the main street to drum up support for the evening's performance, while the camera crew took "a picture of Mawhera Quay. My word when our motor car came down the street, things fairly hummed, and the crowd came round all eager to be in the picture. What with the Band and crowd and one or two restive horses, we had a lively time."[53]

Perry's films, music, song and prayer packed the hall with a "record Saturday-night crowd. Folks from all round the place were there — Hokitika State Colliery, etc., the trains all being delayed until the close." Greymouth also marked a milestone for Perry's Biorama and a "new era as regards Kinematographic projection, for, in that town, we had our sheet illuminated for the first time by our own electric light, made by our own dynamo on the premises".[54]

The pattern and success of the 1905 Biorama tour was repeated again and again in the years that followed. On the tours Perry's party were billeted with Salvation Army folk or in hotels and boarding houses. The band, sometimes supplemented by local Salvation Army members, would march through the streets. Musicians, camera and lantern operators would perform to Perry's direction in local halls and theatres. They brought a quality of performance tinged with the promise of salvation that was seen only in the most professional of travelling shows.

At the end of the last show in each town, the sheet-screen would be lowered and packed with the camera equipment, film, lanterns and slides onto the drays or coaches and it was off to the next town and the next performance. Before they arrived the local Salvation Army Corps pasted posters and it would all start again with a Saturday afternoon matinee for the kids, and the evening shows that went on regardless of what fate threw at them. Like the time in Mangaweka during the 1902 tour when "the rain descended and the floods came and beat upon the hall and it stood … and not only stood, but was packed in every sense of the word. The front row had their noses practically against the sheet and those at the back were standing on the slide boxes and one man nearly sat on the tank."[55]

It did not matter that the rain drowned out both the singing and the voice of the lecturer; to the watching audience the magic was on the flickering screen because Perry's Biorama had brought the picture show to a town or rather country district 148 miles north of Wellington by rail, whose population was boosted by the workers and their families building the viaducts for the Main Trunk line between Wellington and Auckland.[56]

Thomas McKie, Herbert Booth's successor as Australasian commissioner, gave every support to Perry's film-making and touring. It was McKie who approved the construction of the Army's new film production studios in Malvern, a suburb of Melbourne. These studios opened in February 1909 and were glass-walled and glass-roofed for natural lighting, had adjoining dressing rooms, a carpenter's shop and a props storage area. In 1909 Perry completed two new 5000-foot-long films, *The Scottish Covenanters* and *Heroes of the Cross*. A reporter from the Australian *War Cry* visited the studios during the filming.

> THE SILVER BIORAMA!
>
> Under the Direct Management of
> BRIGADIER J. PERRY,
> Will give a Series of Entertainments in the
> SALVATION ARMY CITADEL,
> Vivian-street, on
> SATURDAY, SUNDAY, MONDAY, TUESDAY,
> 6th, 7th, 8th, and 9th November.
> SATURDAY, Opening Night, 8 o'clock.
> —Miscellaneous Programme.
> SUNDAY, at 3 p.m.—"The Scottish Covenanters."
> SUNDAY, at 7 p.m.—3000ft. Film, Depicting Scenes from "The Life of Christ."
> MONDAY, 8 p.m.—"HEROES OF THE CROSS."
> TUESDAY, 8 p.m.—Miscellaneous Programme.
> Magnificent Orchestra! Splendid Band!
> Beautiful Glee Party!
> Admission—Sunday, Silver Offering.
> Other Nights, Tickets 1s and 6d.

Evening Post, 6 November 1909, p. 6.

> One picture introduced the Procurator, seated on a dais, with the bodyguard of soldiers at right and left, in complete armour, and armed with their respective weapons. A petitioner was introduced. He was of the nobility and was praying the pardon of some condemned Christian. The entire action of the scene was rehearsed, improved and corrected over and over again, until the Officer instructing was satisfied, and then everything had to be repeated with the two cameras, (one moving and one still) so that every movement and expression was caught.[57]

Both *The Scottish Covenanters* and the *Heroes of the Cross* featured in Perry's Silver Biorama tour of New Zealand that started in August 1909. On their arrival in Wellington in November the show at Salvation Army Citadel, Vivian Street, featured in turn *The Scottish Covenanters*, alternating with *Scenes from the Life of Christ* and *Heroes of the Cross*. It was a superbly professional tour in every sense. Self-contained with its own electric plant, a stock of film from its own studios including the three featured pictures, and an "orchestra, band and glee party [that] is said to be one of the finest that has ever left the Army headquarters" in Melbourne. It was the pinnacle of Perry's work in taking entertainment in the name of salvation to the masses. It would never be as good again and, as fate dictated, *The Scottish Covenanters* was only screened in New Zealand during this tour and never shown in Australia.[58]

Brigadier Perry's film empire was now the Biograph Supply Department and had grown to six depots throughout Australia and New Zealand consisting of five staff officers and ten commissioned officers, 15 operators and 35 employees. They had seven Biograph film cameras and 35 Biograph film projectors powered by electric light.

> Two first-class triple-cylinder engines are now possessed by the Department, making it possible for our biographists to run electric biograph exhibitions in the smallest township or most out-of-the-way spot in Australasia wherever an ordinary vehicle can safely make its way.[59]

The Salvation Army was already adapting its Biorama performances to accommodate the arrival of permanent picture theatres and in the major centres there were regular picture shows in the garrison halls. "In some of our largest halls, especially on Saturday nights, many hundreds of the poorest boys and girls of our great cities take advantage of these meetings, present themselves with their penny, and, judging from the enthusiasm they show, greatly enjoy the two hours' programme provided for them."[60]

COMMISSIONER HAY TURNS OFF THE LIMELIGHT

In 1909 McKie was succeeded by Commissioner James Hay who embodied the winds of conservatism that had already gripped the Salvation Army movement in Britain and who now exerted a similar influence in Australia and New Zealand. Hay represented the growing belief that it was impossible to completely remove the 'harmful tendencies' that existed in films, even though they were being used for spiritual good. As principal of the Army's International Training College, Hay had been instrumental in closing the Cinematograph Department in Britain in 1908 and in early 1910 he directed the closure of the studio in Melbourne, the branches throughout Australia and New Zealand and the touring companies. Hay believed that "cinema as conducted by the Salvation Army, had led to weakness and a lightness incompatible with true Salvationism and was completely ended by me".[61]

Perry was touring New Zealand with the Silver Biorama when the directive came to disband the Department to which he had given his life. Perry resigned from the Salvation Army and for a time toured New Zealand towns as Perry's Biorama and Cinephone.[62] An advertisement appeared in the Hawera papers in June 1910 informing readers that "Major Perry, who for so long was connected with the Salvation Army has launched out into the animated picture business".[63] There is more than a hint of sadness in Perry's announcement to his Hawera audience that with his next screening he had hoped to show the parade of Hawera schoolchildren taken on his previous Biorama visit, but now he was just a travelling picture showman showing stock films and playing songs on a cinephone, without the resources and the band that had been his to command in his Biorama days.

Buckingham Concert Co. were typical of the travelling picture shows running a mix of films interspersed with songs and recitations. Eph-E-CINEMA-1907-01, ATL, Wellington.

Perry's attempt to continue touring was short-lived because the business was changing and permanent picture shows were coming to the larger towns. Two of his sons were already established film cameramen in Australia. Perry gave up touring, joining the management of Johnson & Gibson film exhibitors and distributors in Australia.

By 1910 the era of the touring picture show was passing. Permanent picture theatres had arrived and the primacy of the Salvation Army Silver Biorama Companies would have to change with the times and decline was inevitable. Between 1898 and 1910 the Salvation Army Limelight teams and Territorial Biorama companies under the guidance of Joseph Perry played a pioneering role in the filming and screening of films in Australia and New Zealand. In these years the Salvation Army took moving pictures to every part of New Zealand, and in turn filmed in many New Zealand small towns. In these years the Salvation Army was the largest film-maker in Australia and New Zealand — it had the resources and the professional staff that served to advertise New Zealand to the world. Its success saw the appointment of a dedicated official New Zealand kinematographer. The tragedy is that of all of the hundreds of films that were made by Perry's camera teams of New Zealand in those years, all that is known to have survived are fragments of Perry's film of the royal visit of the Duke and Duchess of Cornwall in 1901 — New Zealand's first official film.

> ## MAJOR PERRY'S BIORAMA AND CINEPHONE COMPANY.
>
> ### SCHOOL OF MUSIC.
>
> ### SATURDAY, SUNDAY, & MONDAY NEXT.
>
> ### AN OLD TIME ENTERTAINMET,
>
> ### WITH NEW SUBJECTS.
>
> ### WATCH THE PAPERS!! 3411

Colonist, 27 October 1910, p. 2.

High Street, Hawera, c.1907–1912. Hawera was a prosperous Taranaki town. This image was taken about the time of Joseph Perry's last visit with his now private 'Biorama and Cinephone Company'. Photographer: W.A. Price, 1/2-000967-G, ATL, Wellington.

6

The government appoints a kinematographist

The value of "living pictures," too, is well recognised, and the Department's photographer is also an expert cinematographer operator, who secures bioscope records of geysers in action, Maoris in their dances and the many picturesque incidents of life in these islands that lend themselves particularly to reproduction by kinematograph.[1]

PASSING THE BATON

On 9 August 1908 16 battleships of the United States' 'Great White Fleet' steamed up the Rangitoto Channel and anchored in the Waitemata Habour off the City of Auckland. Their arrival was watched by thousands who crammed every vantage point. This was the start of 'Fleet Week' in Auckland, the only New Zealand port of call. It was a week of receptions and pageants as Auckland hosted the fleet on behalf of New Zealand, and every city and town had its banner of welcome on display in Queen Street as the officers and sailors of the fleet came to town.

James McDonald, the official photographer and kinematographer for the New Zealand Government, was not the only motion picture cameraman filming the events of Fleet Week. His film of the official landing of Rear Admiral Sperry and his officers of the United States fleet is the only one to have survived, yet as McDonald panned his camera across the gathering of the dignitaries and the assembled United States marine and naval officers around the specially erected dais at the bottom of Queen Street, he caught on film another camera crew filming the same events. Two men, the camera operator wearing a Salvation Army hat and his assistant in a cloth cap, are seen changing film boxes on top of their camera.[2] This was a camera team of the Salvation Army under the command of Major Joseph Perry. In one sense the McDonald film of the Salvation Army film crew captures the passing of the baton, as it was his appointment as official government photographer and kinematographer that saw the New Zealand Government begin the filming and production of films for the Department of Tourist and Health Resorts.

American Fleet at Auckland. NTSV F10262.

Still from James McDonald's film of the reception to Rear-Admiral Sperry and his officers of the 'Great White Fleet' at the bottom of Queen Street, Auckland, on 10 August 1908. As he pans across the gathering of American officers he catches the Salvation Army camera team in the foreground. *American Fleet at Auckland*, NTSV F10262.

All of New Zealand had contributed to the ornate palm-frond archways and the banners of welcome that festooned Queen Street and all of New Zealand wanted to see and share in the excitement. Film offered that opportunity and by 1908 New Zealanders were beginning to see major local events on film. Leaf through the illustrated papers of the day; in almost every panorama photo of the race meetings, Dominion Day parades, Defence Volunteer parades, union meetings and every public gathering imaginable, you can see photographers hovering on the fringe of events, and when you look closely you can sometimes see kinematograph or Biograph cameras, as they were known.

Moving pictures were becoming an integral part of New Zealand life, and on every big occasion there was always a camera in the crowd. Films had grown in length from the barely one-minute-long glimpses and once the novelty of seeing moving images on screen began to pall, fictional narrative films became part of the staple fare and would quickly come to dominate the American market. However, narrative films did not totally dictate the New Zealand moving picture scene, what films 'featured' in the newspaper advertisements were those that drew in the crowds and increasingly it was just as likely to be a film of a local event as much as the latest American, French or British-sourced narrative film.

Following on from the European experience, what were later termed 'actualities' found their niche as visual newspapers showing places and people of current interest. These news-event films were staple fare for New Zealand picture shows and by 1910 evolved into the Pathé-devised newsreels, which had a much greater share of the market in Australia and New Zealand than they did in the United States. With few exceptions all of New Zealand's film production was of actualities where the civic parade, sports gathering, coach ride or steamer trip through natural wonders became the story. Local audiences were as entranced by views of inaccessible New Zealand and glimpses of their daily lives on screen as they were by scenes and events in Europe and the wider world.

JAMES INGRAM MCDONALD

James Ingram McDonald (1865–1935) is best known today for the ethnological films on Maori life that he made between 1919 and 1923 in company with Elsdon Best and Johannes Anderson.[3] Little attention is paid to his activities as the government official kinematographist between 1907 and 1912, nor is it appreciated how active he was as a film-maker in his six years in the appointment.

'Mac', as his friends knew him, was a man of many talents. He was a portrait painter in oils, sculptor, cartoonist, illustrator, model-maker, draftsman, photographer, film-maker and sponsor of Maori arts and crafts. He was hard-working with a reputation for getting things done and one who matched a practical hands-on ability with that of being a capable administrator. It may have been this that made him the ideal assistant or second-in-command, a role that he fulfilled in many appointments including that of deputy director of the Dominion Museum and secretary of the New Zealand Society of Arts. Because he was called upon to use all of his talents he was never to reach pre-eminence in any one, and even today his reputation in film and photo is based on one aspect of his surviving work.

McDonald was born on 11 June 1865 at Milton, or Tokomairiro as it was then called. His father, Donald, had been a crofter on the Isle of Ulva in Scotland before arriving in New Zealand in 1863 and working as a ploughman. James evidently demonstrated a talent for art and, after two years at Otago Boys' High School, attended art classes in Dunedin before leaving for Australia to study at the National Gallery of Victoria's school of design in the 1880s under the painter Frederick McCubbin and the sculptor C. Douglas Richardson, director of the life class. His contemporaries at the school included Sir John Longstaff and Max Meldrum.[4]

McDonald married Mary Brabin of Hawksburn on 29 April 1891 and listed his occupation on the marriage licence as 'accountant', which indicates the realities of life for a young artist in Australia and New Zealand in those years. He worked as a sculptor for a number of studios in Melbourne, principally that of his teacher, C. Douglas Richardson. He also worked as an illustrator contributing cartoons and sketches to the Melbourne *Punch* and *The Beacon*. The 1890s were the depression years in Victoria and could not have been easy for McDonald with a growing family — a son and three daughters. McDonald returned to New Zealand with his family in 1901.

It is not clear how McDonald was employed in his first years back in New Zealand. It seems that he first worked as an illustrator and artist for the Wellington illustrated weekly *The New Zealand Mail* and it may have been this that drew him back. In March 1904 he may have been employed in some capacity at the Colonial Museum, which was then sited in Museum Street behind the Parliament buildings, and he may have worked as a photographer on contract to the Department of Tourist and Health Resorts. His position as draughtsman and artist was confirmed from 1 July 1905. The *Government Gazette* entry for 1907 lists him as 'Draughtsman and Artist' in Wellington with three years of service being paid a salary of £275 that is "Paid out of Item for Advertising".[5] The director, Augustus Hamilton, was responsible for his employment. During this time McDonald worked on the scale model of a Maori pa that is still part of the collection of Te Papa Tongarewa, the Museum of New Zealand.

McDonald demonstrated skill as a photographer, and also contributed paintings and drawings to illustrate museum bulletins written by Elsdon Best. It was an appointment that

James McDonald on secondment as art assistant at the Colonial Museum working on a major sculptural group for the Christchurch International Exhibition 1906–1907. PAColl-6348-27, ATL, Wellington.

Thomas Edward Donne, general manager Department of Tourist and Health Resorts, in his element on the Franz Josef Glacier. Photograph by James McDonald, Te Papa Tongarewa Museum of New Zealand Collection, C025051.

suited his range of talents. It seems that in the small world that was Wellington he came to T.E. Donne's attention, perhaps due to his friendship with the writer and journalist James Cowan who worked closely with Donne, writing and editing the many brochures and pamphlets that were the stock-in-trade of Donne's department.[6]

Perhaps then it is not surprising that on 27 February 1906 McDonald transferred to the 'artistic staff' of the Department of Tourist and Health Resorts.[7] McDonald, in the company of Cowan and Donne, set out on a "prolonged tour of the West Coast and the Sounds district of the South Island" taking photographs. We have Cowan's recollections of these trips made by the three men.

"Mac" was not only a good artist but a good sport, a capital travelling mate, always cheerful, resourceful in camp. I write with knowledge and affection for "Mac" for we travelled some thousands of miles together and camped in all sorts of queer corners in those days. There was the faithful trio of us, with T.E.D. to boss the party in his genial capacity as official head. I see them now, "Mac" jogging along on his horse with a brace of cameras slung over his shoulders; far down the bush tracks of Westland — we had a wild week of it there once, a hundred and fifty miles from the Franz Joseph Glacier over the Haast Pass and out to civilisation again at Lake Wanaka.[8]

Cowan did not have to add, but he did, that this was: "Rough country! There was only one bridge in all that journey, and there was a swift alpine river to ford every few miles. All the better for picture making, was 'Mac's' point of view."[9]

It is a fascinating picture, Donne as departmental head with two of his employees, but in reality, soulmates and close friends, leaving the day-to-day grind and the minutiae of government bureaucracy behind to trek off into the unknown and difficult country of South Westland, a land where there were no roads and, once south of Okarito, few trails. The Haast's remoteness is still evident from the roadside today, and it would have been even more so then. One can almost sense the regret of the three when they reach 'civilisation' on the shores of Wanaka and the small settlement of Pembroke with its one hotel "but no private boarding".[10]

Donne, Cowan and McDonald shared kindred interests. All three loved the New Zealand outdoors, with Donne being a "fine sportsman, a keen angler and successful deer-hunter". Like his compatriots he was fascinated by this country and the Maori, collecting artefacts and rare books on Maori culture. In Cowan, whose family farm had included the site of the Orakau battle, he had a friend whose father fought in the New Zealand Wars and who was raised on the frontier of New Zealand as it was then. Cowan was fluent in Maori, a working journalist and author steeped in the history of the Maori and of the wars of the 1860s, and who later wrote the still definitive history of those events in his two volume *The New Zealand Wars*, first published in 1922.[11]

The origin of McDonald's love for things Maori is less evident. It may have been his art tutors in Dunedin or it may have been the influence of McCubbin in Melbourne who drew on national and colonial themes in his paintings. But he too was fascinated by things Maori, and set out to capture a people's art and traditions in his photography and film as well as drawing on Cowan's stories of the wars to furnish subjects for his paintings and sculpture. After the grind of making a living as an artist and raising a family in difficult years, McDonald suddenly found himself working with people who saw the world as he did. He must have been in heaven.

Donne was one of the vice-presidents and executive commissioner of the organising committee for the Christchurch International Exhibition in Hagley Park. When one looks at the list of other vice-presidents — which includes ministers of the Crown and the mayors of the principal cities of Dunedin, Wellington, Auckland and Christchurch — it is obvious that he was the 'working' member of the group who made it happen. Ensuring its success was a focus for his department and his two companions were equally involved as employees, with Cowan producing the official record.[12] McDonald was seconded back to the Colonial Museum as 'art assistant', working on a series of pieces for the Exhibition, including a major sculpture of a Maori group for display in the main exhibition hall.[13] The two photos of him working on this in the casting room of the Canterbury Museum show a thick-set man immersed in his work. Attention to detail was his hallmark. Perspective and balance were very important. He framed everything with a photographer's eye, and this detail can be seen in his oil paintings of Maori life and of the skirmishes and battles of the New Zealand wars, which fascinated him. His sculpture of the Maori group was intended to be the centrepiece for the Grand Hall and McDonald no doubt shared Cowan's view that it "somewhat suffered by the change [of position] to the Main Corridor".[14] However, Cowan ensured that the work of his friend was given deserved justice in the official report.

> The two principal figures were a Maori man and woman, standing, the *wahine* finely draped in a long *korowai* mat and carrying a baby *pikau*-fashion on her shoulders. Seated were a youth, playing a *putorino* or flute, a carver at work, a beautiful girl (modelled from a young Canterbury half-caste girl) making a *poi*-ball, and on the western side an old warrior, *mere* in hand, gazing with introspective eyes to the past. On each face of the pedestal was a panel, two of which represented the ancient art of cutting green-stone, the other two the olden-practice of *hika-ahi* or producing fire from wood by friction. A heroic emblematic Maori group of this kind, based on Mr McDonald's ideas, would be a remarkably appropriate sculpture set, at any future New Zealand Exhibition.[15]

One can see that McDonald shared Cowan's romantic vision of the Maori, and the warrior's introspective eyes gazing to the past effectively represented the views of McDonald the artist and of Cowan the writer.

OFFICIAL KINEMATOGRAPHER

After the Exhibition closed in 1907 McDonald must have convinced Donne that it was more cost-effective to employ him to do both still photography and motion pictures, and in 1907 McDonald became the government's official kinematographer, the first to hold this appointment in New Zealand and one of the first official government film-makers in the world.[16]

In the New Zealand fashion it was very much a one-man operation. The history of filming in this country was never a thriving large-scale industry, as we lacked the population to

James McDonald filming, official government kinematographer, 1907–1912. A. Salmond collection, NTSV S5928, no. 2.

support it. It shows it was always a one-man band and, in McDonald's case, film-maker and photographer were one and the same person: he would be hung with cameras and film boxes, perhaps hiring a boy to help carry some of the gear, then taking the photos and film back to the office and darkroom to carry out the developing and editing. McDonald toured New Zealand from 1907 to 1912 visiting towns, scenic attractions, all the major industries, being the camera in the crowd at principal events so that the images could be distributed to the world to make it more aware of distant New Zealand.

In December 1907 there was a private screening of McDonald's films from a recent visit to Rotorua. A reporter from the *Dominion* was in the audience and reported that the "Government owns a kinematograph and employs a kinematographist, in Mr J. McDonald, the artist-photographer of the Tourist Department".[17]

At the invitation of Mr T.E. Donne a DOMINION representative was present at a private show of the results that have been so far achieved in depicting those features of our picturesque country that lend themselves to animated photography. Some of these are exceptionally interesting, and if exhibited abroad, should provide a valuable advertisement. One depicts a healthy corps of Maori girls executing the poi dance with the never-resting Waikite geyser playing continuously in the background; another deals with an amusing Maori canoe race with plenty of Native colour, and still another is a particularly graphic picture of the steaming cliffs of Lake Rotomahana, and the government launch manoeuvering in the boiling waters of that historic lake. The Tourist Department intends sending several series of these views to England and America.[18]

McDonald's first films were of New Zealand scenic locations; a constant theme in local film-making. There was a ready overseas market in Europe and America for scenic films of exotic faraway places, and the Tourist Department was keen to exploit it. From the start McDonald's film was for export; to show New Zealand to a world market, its people, its industries, its attractions and its suitability as a prospective home for new migrants. The Department's annual report in 1909 stated that "greater attention has been paid to the securing of Kinematograph pictures. A number of these have been sent to the High Commissioner in London, also to the Melbourne office where arrangements have been made for their exhibition."[19]

McDonald's principal output was of still photographs that were reproduced as postcards and illustrations for the Department's publications and tourist pamphlets and brochures. The illustrated pamphlets published in 1908 contain the results of McDonald's first year as official photographer. The titles carry the clue as to contents: *Making a Home in New Zealand, New Zealand, New Zealand in the Nutshell, Wakatipu* and various viewbooks and postcards, including a special publication on the Rotomahana round trip. In 1909 the Department reported that 3331 lantern slides and 10,037 photographs "have been issued … for the purpose of illustrating newspaper articles published abroad and for exhibiting in shipping offices, steamer saloons, and other places where they will be brought under the notice of travellers".[20]

A number of McDonald's films from this first year of filming have survived. These include some of the scenes from McDonald's *New Zealand's Thermal Wonderland*, which shows a group of tourists being escorted to the Waimangu thermal area. They are shown crossing the Frying Pan and as they emerge from the steam, we see a photographer plying his trade as they view the thermal areas. It closes with a brief glimpse of two Maori women at Whakarewarewa. The film shows how safe it is to visit these sights, showing well-dressed European men and women in what might otherwise appear as dangerous surrounds, but the ever-present thermal activity and the glimpse of Maori life speaks of the exotic and the strange — enticing the audience to visit something different: indeed the purpose of the film.[21] The film *Maori Women Performing Action Song at Pohutu Geyser* may also be from this period as it may show the Waikite Geyser that is mentioned in the *Dominion* report.[22]

There is also film of poi dances at Whakarewarewa, taken about 1910 (and possibly a McDonald film). It shows a group of women in piupiu, white blouses and greenstone pendants. They perform various poi dances against a background of steaming geysers, directed by the kaumatua Mita Taupopoki of the Arawa tribe who was a ubiquitous presence in New Zealand film for over 20 years, first appearing in Perry's film of the Rotorua welcome for the Duke and Duchess of Cornwall and York. The chief, distinctive in his headdress, is seen leading a line of young women onto the performance area, against the background of Whakarewarewa village with its store and watching tourists.[23]

It parallels similar film taken by Whitehouse, Perry, Franklyn Brown (later Barrett), T.J. West's cameramen and by McDonald and others. These were scenes that the public never tired of, but, as with the films of the large Maori canoes (waka) on the Waikato during the Ngaruawahia regatta, these films broke through the cliché of being simply a photo opportunity to give an insight into Maori achievement for those who cared to notice.[24]

New Zealand's Thermal Wonderland. NTSV F31561.

Poi Dances at Whakarewarewa. NTSV F3990.

Maori Women Performing Action Song at Pohutu Geyser. NTSV F30560.

Maori War Canoe Race. NTSV F5035.

SHACKLETON'S *NIMROD* SAILS FOR ANTARCTICA

There is also the marvellous film of the departure of Ernest Shackleton's ship *Nimrod* for the Antarctic, which though taken in 1908, falls into McDonald's first 12 months of filming. On New Year's Day 1908 McDonald was in Lyttelton filming the departure of Shackleton's British Antarctic Expedition. This was a Donne initiative. He saw the opportunity that the publicity of the departure would generate in Great Britain and determined to take advantage. After getting approval of his minister he directed that the manager of the Tourist Office in Christchurch give every assistance to McDonald, who he despatched to Lyttelton at short notice.

Lieutenant Shackleton
"Nimrod" Lyttelton

Sir
The bearer, Mr. James McDonald, is the photographer for this Department, and he has been sent to Lyttelton to endeavour to obtain Biograph films of the departure of the "Nimrod" for your great Antarctic Exploration. These films if satisfactory will be exhibited throughout Great Britain and in all probability brought directly under notice of His Majesty the King.
I shall esteem it a favour if you will afford Mr. McDonald facilities for obtaining pictures of the officers and crew of the "Nimrod" also some deck scenes. Mr McDonald will accompany the "Nimrod" to Lyttelton Heads in a special steamer or launch.

Yours faithfully
T.E. Donne
General Manager[25]

Still showing intertitle from James McDonald's *Departure of the British Antarctic Expedition*, NTSV F8202. (See colour section.)

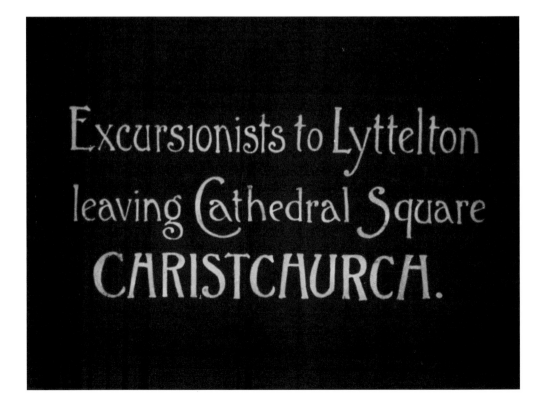

On 2 January 1908 the district agent reported back to Donne on his efforts.

> As instructed in your telegram which was not delivered until 7.35 pm on 30th December, I made the necessary arrangements for Mr McDonald to take the biographic pictures of matters in connection with the departure of the Nimrod. We first went to Quail Island on Tuesday and got films of the Manchurian ponies and Equimaux dogs being transported. I made arrangements with Admiral Fawkes to take the final departure of the Nimrod from H.M.S. *Powerful* which was lying at the Heads. It was a most difficult matter to engage a launch at such a late hour, and to get one at all I had to incur an expenditure of £4. For this I am sending a voucher per Mr McDonald. I also enclose voucher for my out of pocket expenses for two days at Lyttelton for 13/6.[26]

One can read in these lines the frustrations of the district agent but the surviving film more than repays his troubles. We see the exercising of the dogs and the difficulties in loading the Shetland ponies from their quarantine on Quail Island in Lyttelton Harbour.[27] There is the bustle and excitement of Shackleton's departure. It was Regatta Day and the port was packed with people to see the *Nimrod* off. Three ships of the Royal Navy's Australasian Squadron were also in port. Admiral Sir Wilmot Fawkes flew his flag in the HMS *Powerful*, a 14,200 ton armoured cruiser, together with the light cruisers *Pegasus* and *Prometheus*.

One of Shackleton's officers, A.L.A. Mackintosh, writes of "[c]rowds of people gazing at us from the Quay: and the deck or what is left of the deck is crowded with visitors". McDonald was one of the crowd, first on the deck and then on the quay filming the scenes. He had the knack of capturing the detail of faces of people going about their business amidst the bustle of a march-past, or in this case a departure. We see it in his shots of a relaxed Shackleton escorting Admiral Sir Wilmot Fawkes over his ship. It is an intimacy, heightened by the positioning of the camera above the principals, that is rare in film of the period. It exemplifies McDonald's skill as a cameraman.

Departure of the British Antarctic Expedition, 1 January 1908. NTSV F8202.

Shackleton's *Nimrod* is towed out of Lyttelton Harbour to the cheers from crowded ships in the harbour. Still from James McDonald's *Departure of the British Antarctic Expedition*, NTSV F8202.

At 4 p.m. the *Nimrod* sailed. Her "crew are up in the rigging on top of boats, singing We Parted on the Shore and similar appropriate airs. The crowd on shore are cheering us continually: remarks are passed such as 'Goodbye Kate' from the crew; and 'Bring us a chip of the Pole', or 'Don't forget to come off the Pole when you are up there', from the crowd." The harbour is crowded with ships, each packed with holidaymakers who cheer the *Nimrod* as she passes. "We were followed by two of the Union Steamship Company's steamers, the *Waikari* and *Monaki* and also smaller steamers, the *John Anderson* and the *Cygnet*. The steamers were simply packed, and the crowds on them continually cheered us."[28] The *Nimrod* received gun salutes from the batteries at Fort Jervois on Ripa Island and from Battery Point near Godley Head as she passed. The crew of HMS *Powerful* lined the decks and gave "Three cheers for the Nimrod". The band also struck up and played Hearts of Oak and Auld Lang Syne.[29]

McDonald shot all of this from Fawkes' flagship HMS *Powerful*. It is a superb piece of film-making carefully edited to tell the story of the departure. The packed steamer decks are alive with arms waving farewell, as the steamers seem to tilt alarmingly with the weight of passengers at the ship's side. The film ends with the view of the *Nimrod* now under tow to the SS *Koonya* disappearing out into the South Pacific.

New Zealand played a major role in re-equipping *Nimrod* for the retrieval of Shackleton's party in 1909 and he returned to New Zealand to a hero's welcome having gone further south than any man. At Lyttelton, "[s]teamers came out to us crowded with people, guns firing and flags waving".[30] He was immediately cast in the role of Imperial hero, at a time when England and the Empire needed such a man.

> Lieutenant Shackleton is in that rank of heros whose names go down to posterity … when we are all feeling a little downhearted at seeing our supremacy in sport and in more serious matters slipping away from us, it is a moral tonic to find that in exploration we are still the kings of the world.[31]

It is an interesting contrast to the film showing the return of Captain Robert Falcon Scott's *Terra Nova* to Lyttelton on 12 February 1913 after being beaten by Amundsen to be first to the South Pole, and the death of Scott and his party on return. This is more sombre in tone, showing the flag flying at half-mast from the ship's rigging and then the people of Canterbury entering the Christchurch Cathedral for his memorial service.[32]

Shackleton got permission from Donne to use the government darkrooms to develop cinematographic film taken in Antarctica, and being told of McDonald's film asked to purchase it and add it to film taken in Antarctica.[33] Donne recommended to Ward that the negative be gifted to Shackleton.

> There is no special advantage to the Government holding this film. It could no doubt be sold elsewhere as it has more or less an historical interest, but if in the hands of Lieutenant Shackleton copies would probably be distributed throughout Great Britain, and from it New Zealand would certainly get a very excellent advertisement. I would therefore suggest for your consideration that the Government should present Lieutenant Shackleton with the negative film and all rights of reproduction thereof. The Government would still hold the positive film available for exhibition on the limelight projector.[34]

This indicates Donne's view of McDonald's role as a film-maker, taking films of opportunity in addition to the standard scenics that together may be used to make the world more aware of this distant place. Ward saw it the same way and on 15 April 1909, Lieutenant E.H. Shackleton at the Wellington Club was notified of the gift of "600 feet of cinematograph film shewing [sic] the departure of the Nimrod from Lyttelton, with the compliments of the New Zealand Government".[35]

Back in Britain Shackleton embarked on a gruelling but highly successful lecture series and his film of the expedition was released by Gaumont to enormous business, which was equalled when it was released by Cosens Spencer in Australia and New Zealand.[36] How much of McDonald's film was included is not known. We are fortunate that the positive copy survives so that we can assess McDonald's film-making.

It is a film of heroes departing, continuing the theme first filmed by Whitehouse with his scenes of the Second Contingent at Newtown Park, Wellington. In McDonald's film we also see New Zealanders who enlisted for the expedition. It is a theme that would be repeated again with the troopship sailings during the First World War and mirrored by the films of returning heroes, already seen in Perry's film showing medal presentations by the Duke and Duchess of Cornwall and York, and in the film of the return of the 'Original All Blacks' to New Zealand.

The Terra Nova.
NTSV F1547.

VISIT OF THE AMERICAN 'GREAT WHITE FLEET'

In August 1908 McDonald was in Auckland filming 'Fleet Week': the arrival of the United States' 'Great White Fleet' commanded by Admiral C.S. Sperry. This grand world tour of 16 major warships of the United States Navy was the initiative of President Theodore Roosevelt to demonstrate America's blue-water naval strength as a counter to Japan in the Pacific. It included a visit to Sydney in response to a request from Australian Prime Minister Alfred Deakin. Auckland became the New Zealand port visited by this fleet of white-painted battleships with their attendant escorts and transports.

Deakin's actions reflected Australia's growing concerns about Japanese naval strength in the Pacific and the comparative absence of the Royal Navy. Australia's invitation to Roosevelt caused intense anger in British government circles as it was customary that the invitation be extended through the British Government and not directly to the United States.[36] It reflected both Australia and New Zealand's public disquiet over the nature of the 1902 Anglo–Japanese Naval Agreement. Deakin's act was a step leading to Australia's decision to form a Royal Australian Navy, while Ward sought to bind Britain closer to New Zealand with the offer of a Dreadnought-class battleship for the Royal Navy — an offer that would take Britain, Australia, Canada and the Empire, as well as the New Zealand public, by surprise.

However, there was no escaping the enthusiasm with which both Australia and New Zealand greeted this show of American naval strength. On 10 August 1908 McDonald filmed the official reception of Admiral Sperry and his officers at the bottom of Queen Street. We see the arrival of the dignitaries — Sir Joseph Ward, Lady Ward and their two daughters passing between the Guard of Honour and the cheering throng, with McDonald's camera positioned to capture the faces of the crowd as the admiral and his officers in full dress uniform move towards the dais.[37]

McDonald's camera also films a group of New Zealand War veterans, including one displaying a chestful of medals — George Rowley Hill, who won the New Zealand Cross defending Jerusalem Pa against Te Kooti's followers in 1869.

We cannot hear the words of the speeches but then, one suspects, neither could most of the crowd at the time. McDonald filmed each dignitary in turn and then would have paused in cranking the camera handle in order to get each one briefly on film during their extended orations to the select group on the dais, while the reporter seen sitting on the stairs at their feet captured every word in his shorthand notebook. King Mahuta, who had been barred from a similar welcoming role with the Duke and Duchess of Cornwall and York in 1901, is introduced to the admiral and with three hearty cheers the film ends with the dignitaries being driven up Queen Street through excited crowds, while messages of welcome from every town in New Zealand flutter on banners overhead.[38] The waving New Zealand Wars' veterans, driven by horse-drawn charabanc, depart as the massed bands plays "bars from the American, British, and National Anthems, and other airs as the official party left the wharf".[39]

Once again Donne was responsible for the reception arrangements and the official party travelled by train from Wellington on the Main Trunk line on the 'Parliament Special' on a hastily finished temporary track in advance of its official opening. It seems that McDonald did not accompany them and there is no mention of the journey being filmed. It was obviously more important that the government cameraman got to Auckland in advance to arrange his camera locations for the official reception, rather than risk being stranded and not getting the film.

On the same day McDonald filmed the "Boys of King's College, Auckland marching during the visit of the American Fleet".[40] This has not survived, but later that week he travelled to

Rotorua with the official party and the visiting American officers for the formal opening of Government Bath House on Thursday 13 August 1908.

Rotorua, 'the metropolis of Geyserland', was the jewel in the crown of the Department of Tourist and Health Resorts and a focus for McDonald's filming and photography. As Donne recorded, "[i]t is the only state-owned and State controlled town in Australasia", occupying as it did Crown lands with all the "hotel proprietors, boarding housekeepers, and other business people and residents" tenants of the Crown. Special legislation was passed in 1907 making Donne's department responsible for the municipal administration of the town. This gave the department control over the "Baths and Sanitorium and surrounding gardens and parks, the whole of the streets and roads and their maintenance, the water supply, lighting and drainage of the town".[41]

Sitting in carefully landscaped gardens, advertised as the "most beautiful landscape in New Zealand", the new bath buildings were the centrepiece of the mineral baths that the government were promoting worldwide for their "curative propensities". These were under the control of Dr Wohlmann, government balneologist, who had a staff of massage experts and bath attendants, as well as nursing staff, at the government sanitorium in the spa grounds.

Bath House was a jewel among jewels with the department controlling the celebrated geysers of Wairoa, Pohutu and Waikite as well as Tarawera, Rotomahana, and Waimangu thermal areas and the beautiful Lake Okataina.[42]

Despite its impressive facade Bath House was still not finished, but the opportunity to advertise Rotorua's delights to the world was too good an opportunity for Ward's government to miss. The only regret was that instead of the full uniform finery of the official reception, the American officers travelled south in civilian clothes. A fragment of McDonald's 400-foot film survives showing scenes on the grass embankment in front of Bath House as the Arawa chiefs Mita Taupopoki, Kokori Anaha Waharoa and Tarakara welcome their visitors.[43]

The speeches are translated by a youthful Te Rangi Hiroa (Peter Buck), the Native Health Officer, formally dressed in frock coat and top hat. The elders "bade Admiral Sperry and his officers a hearty welcome to their midst … they welcomed as men who go down to the sea in ships and they did not forget to remind them that Maori at one time owned the Pacific … all of it was Polynesian territory once … they were one with the Arawa people, one with the Maori race and with the people of New Zealand". All of this was to a backdrop of "warriors in piupiu mate and loin cloths or knee britches, and the wahines in white blouses".[44] Once again McDonald achieves a sense of intimacy by positioning his camera within the Maori welcoming party on the lawn looking up to the dignitaries on the bank above. He gets the same effect in the final surviving scenes showing the official party leaving the grounds, his camera focusing on an animated Te Rangi Hiroa, oblivious to the camera, totally engaged in briefing Sir Joseph and Lady Ward.

What is missing from this film may be guessed at — the visit to Ohinemutu village and the hot springs, which "beat everything" one of the visiting US officers had ever seen. The formal welcome at the sanitorium grounds, the challenge, the poi and haka leading up to the surviving portion was not seen. The film would also have included the opening of Bath House, the visit to Whakarewarewa and the soaping of the geyser by the guide Maggie Papakura. It was a great day for Rotorua, echoing the visit by the Duke and Duchess of Cornwall and York in 1901.

Films of the Great White Fleet were shown in picture shows throughout the country. Already during Fleet Week, Fuller's Advanced Vaudeville Company appearing at the Theatre Royal in Wellington were advertising:

American Officers' Visit to Rotorua. NTSV F3033.

The US FLEET. The Mighty Armada As now in Auckland will be shown TO-NIGHT as it appeared in 'Frisco on and during its visit there.[45]

McDonald's film was also seen by New Zealand audiences. Fuller's World Wide Pictures screened it at the Theatre Royal in Wellington under the title of *American Officers' Visit to Rotorua* with the acknowledgement that this was "by arrangement with Tourist Department".[46] Donne no doubt sent copies of the films to his agents in the United States knowing that the American content would add to the interest.

DOMINION DAY CELEBRATIONS

A month later on 26 September 1908 McDonald was in Wellington filming the Dominion Day celebrations. This was the first anniversary of New Zealand becoming a dominion and it is almost certain that McDonald filmed similar scenes the previous year, as we have the image of a camera in the crowd in front of Parliament buildings as Prime Minister Sir Joseph Ward reads the proclamation of New Zealand's dominion status.

Three of his films survive from this very busy day. In the morning he filmed the children's gymnastic demonstration at the Basin Reserve where a "living representation of the *New Zealand Ensign*"[46] was performed by 3000 schoolchildren.[47]

The power of the government kinematographer is evident in the film when a row of women in magnificent hats can be seen in the front between McDonald's camera and the official dais for the arrival of Sir Joseph and Lady Ward, but when Governor Lord Plunket arrives, the women have been moved so that McDonald has an unobstructed shot for his filming. That

Dominion Day Celebrations (Wellington): Children's Demonstration. NTSV F8276.

Dominion Day Celebrations (Wellington): March of Volunteers Past Government Buildings. NTSV F5064.

Dominion Day Celebrations (Wellington): Newtown Park. NTSV F8277.

New Zealand War veterans parade along Lambton Quay on the first anniversary of Dominion Day. Still from James McDonald's *March of Volunteers past Government Buildings*, NTSV F5064.

afternoon McDonald filmed the march along Lambton Quay of the volunteers and veterans of the New Zealand Wars from the Whitmore Street corner.[48] Six-horse teams pull the guns of Wellington's 'D' Battery, New Zealand Artillery leads the parade with its members in a mix of khaki and formal blues uniform. The young Bernard Freyberg was a member of 'D' Battery in 1908, and he may be one of the young men self-consciously avoiding looking at the camera. Veterans of the New Zealand Wars and of the many Wellington Volunteer Corps follow, with the Wellington Navals, Petone Navals, the Electric Light Company and Cycle Corps, the latter each providing their own bicycle in the same way that each of the Mounted Rifle Volunteers provided a horse. Each corps marches in its own distinctive dress, followed by cadet units from the Boys' Institute and the various Wellington schools, all conscious of the camera, smiling and hoping to see themselves on film. Once again McDonald positions the camera just above head height, capturing both the marching men but also the crowd, all intent on seeing their boys and all largely unaware of the camera.

McDonald then hurried to Newtown Park for the 'Grand Review of Troops' at 3 p.m. where the Wellington Volunteers marched past the governor before an enthusiastic crowd of some 12,000 people. It was:

> Fanfare and rumbling guns, white cockades, prancing horses, scarlet tunics, big busbies, Highland bonnets, boys in blue and the hundred concomitants of a grand parade of all arms.[49]

As the papers reported, it was spoilt only by "any fool with a camera [who] was allowed to wander all over the place, to spoil the ensemble and generally make himself a curse".[50] Wandering photographers are evident in the film but McDonald would have seen himself in a

Photographers among the Dominion Day Commemoration crowds at Newtown Park, 1908. S.C. Smith Collection, G19902-1/1, ATL, Wellington.

 *Proclamation of King George V, Wellington.* NTSV F4102.

very different category to those complained of in the press. He was there on official business.[51] We have McDonald's film of the proclamation of King George V on the steps of Parliament.[52] While he clearly enjoyed being the official photographer at important public events, McDonald's photography and film work was mainly concerned with scenic films for both New Zealand and the overseas' tourist market. In this he obviously met Donne's expectations reflected in a report written by Donne for Ward on the progress of the Department.

> In the Department's active work of securing publicity for New Zealand and all that is therein, pen and pencil and camera are actively employed. The Department has its own photograph section, and a stock of thousands of photographic negatives covering all features of life and industry and scenery in these Islands. These pictures are sent all over the world in the form of photographic prints and postcards, and in the descriptive books issued by the Department. The value of "living pictures," too, is well recognised, and the Department's photographer is also an expert cinematographer operator, who secures bioscope records of geysers in action, Maoris in their dances and the many picturesque incidents of life in these islands that lend themselves particularly to reproduction by kinematograph. Lately a set of films of this character, illustrating life in geyserland, travel and scenery on the Wanganui River, amongst other things was despatched to London, for use at the Franco-British Exhibition.[53]

WORLD SCULLING CHAMPIONSHIP ON THE WANGANUI

Film survives from 1909 of Sir Joseph and Lady Ward at home in Wellington that was taken by McDonald — it follows the style of the series of Pathé formal pieces on prominent New Zealand politicians produced in 1912.[54] McDonald also filmed the world professional sculling championship between Dick Arnst and William Webb on the Wanganui River on 22 June 1909. Both were Canterbury-born, but Webb lived and trained in Wanganui and there was a move to rename the town 'Webbanui' when he defeated the reigning world champion, Charles Towns, on the Parramatta River near Sydney in 1907. This was filmed and shown as part of Fuller's vaudeville show at the Theatre Royal, Wellington, to crowded houses. The *Free Lance* reported:

> The biograph varieties have been enhanced by the capital reproductions of the world's championship sculling race on the Paramatta river, Sydney. The film is an admirable one, and the dense crowds on the banks of the river, the congested mid-stream traffic, and the race between Webb and Towns are very clearly shown throughout.[55]

Webb successfully defended the title against Towns on the Wanganui in 1908. This race was watched by a crowd of some 25,000 including Prime Minister Sir Joseph Ward.[56]

Dick Arnst, the pride of Tai Tapu near Christchurch, took the title from Webb on the Wanganui in December 1908, and now for a purse of £1000 Webb set out to win it back, in

William Webb of Wanganui, former world, who set out to regain his title against Dick Arnst of Tai Tapu on the Wanganui River, 22 June 1909. *Auckland Weekly News*, 30 September 1915.

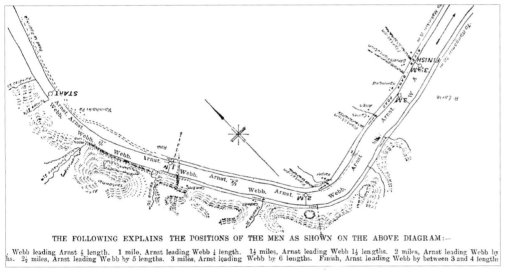

THE FOLLOWING EXPLAINS THE POSITIONS OF THE MEN AS SHOWN ON THE ABOVE DIAGRAM:—

Webb leading Arnst ¼ length. 1 mile, Arnst leading Webb ¼ length. 1½ miles, Arnst leading Webb 1½ lengths. 2 miles, Arnst leading Webb by hs. 2½ miles, Arnst leading Webb by 5 lengths. 3 miles, Arnst leading Webb by 6 lengths. Finish, Arnst leading Webb by between 3 and 4 lengths

The race explained. *Wanganui
Chronicle*, 23 June 1909, p. 5.

*World's Sculling
Championship Wanganui
River*. NTSV F41774.

a sport that at the time attracted worldwide interest. His opponent Dick Arnst, an all-round athlete, initially made his name as a successful cyclist, but wealthy backers, and no doubt betting men, sponsored him to train in Sydney under George Towns, where he showed his class in winning handicap races on the Parramatta River.[57]

The race was also important because it featured the Wanganui River, which the Department of Tourist and Health Resorts advertised as the 'Rhine of Maoriland'. The purse itself may have been partly donated by Australian-born Alexander Hatrick, whose firm A. Hatrick & Co. ran the steamer service on the Wanganui. Starting in coastal shipping, Hatrick introduced a regular service on the Wanganui in 1892 that at its peak employed 12 steam and motor vessels as well as three motorised canoes on the river, taking passengers and cargo as far upriver as Taumarunui.

Hatrick was the mayor of Wanganui from 1897–1904 and the town benefited from his energy; the Opera House was built and the Gas and Water Works were developed.[58]

Tourism was very much Hatrick's business. In 1904 he had the houseboat *Makere* built to his own specifications, with 18 cabins and a dining room, smoking room and lounge on its verandahed upper deck, and positioned it midway between Pipiriki and Taumarunui. He was also instrumental in enlarging 'Pipiriki House' into a tourist stopover at the Pipiriki landing, where a rough road link existed to Ohakune and Raetahi. Hatrick did good business out of the sculling championships as it was his steamers that carried the spectators upriver to line the banks. For those willing to pay a little more they could keep the scullers in view from the steamers' decks as they followed them to the finish line.

Hatrick ensured that McDonald had everything he needed to take the best pictures possible. On the day of the race hundreds lined the banks above Upokongaro along the three-and-one-third mile course (5363 metres), while five Hatrick steamers packed with onlookers followed the race. Fares were £2 return on the umpires' boat, £1 return on the press boat and 10/- return on each of the other three steamers.[59]

McDonald's film opens with close-up shots of local dignitaries gathered on the open foredeck of the SS *Waimarie* with the bowler-hatted Hatrick prominent in the foreground, McDonald positioning his camera on the bridge to achieve a balance between his subjects and the background activity of the other Hatrick steamers. The steamers *Waione* and the paddle-steamer *Wairere* are shown packed with spectators, before the focus shifts to the two scullers, Arnst in black and Webb in white, waiting for the race to begin. The scullers are then shown sculling upstream with the film ending before Arnst on the right, or eastern bank-side, pulled ahead to win — but not before Webb made one final effort.

> Arnst's friends shouted encouragement to their man, as Webb drew closer and the champion responded grandly although it was plain he was tiring rapidly and his rowing was not so neat as that of his opponent's. Webb maintained his plucky effort … However it was not to be as the same powerful stroke which has made Arnst champion of the world enabled him to last long enough to retain his title, and he flashed past the post.[60]

McDonald was evidently pleased with his efforts and the *Wanganui Herald* reported that "Cinematograph pictures of the race were taken and are expected to prove really excellent, as the conditions were favourable."[61] They were not to be disappointed. McDonald returned to Wellington to develop and print the film that was first shown by John Fuller and Sons in the Theatre Royal in Wellington on Saturday 3 July 1909. "The picture is a triumph in cinematography and a credit to the operator."[62]

Dick Arnst capitalised on his celebrity status and appeared in person narrating to McDonald's film at local theatres throughout the country. He toured himself as the 'Dick Arnst Picture Company' and advertised that he had purchased the "Sole rights for New Zealand of the Webb-Arnst Boat Race Pictures".[63] He combined his talk to film with a lecture on physical fitness and demonstrated this with "an exhibition of chest expansion which showed that he could expand about 12 inches [30.48 cm]".[64]

Arnst appeared before Wanganui audiences at the Opera House on 23–24 August 1909 to a "good audience" on the first night and a "fairly good" audience on the second before moving on to Hawera. These were not the packed houses that may have been expected had the local man, Webb, won. However, there were no complaints about the quality of the filmed scenes "which are very fine and many local celebrities can be easily picked out of the groups". Certainly as far as the local audience were concerned McDonald had achieved his principal aim as the film "cannot help serving as a splendid advertisement for Wanganui and its famous river".[65]

Arnst would remain world champion until 1912, defeating the champion English sculler Ernest Barry on the Zambesi River, with one of Arnst's brothers armed with a rifle, preceding him by boat, ready to shoot any crocodiles that threatened to disrupt the race. This was filmed and released by the Warwick Trading Company with one of the final scenes showing Arnst and his brother hoisting the New Zealand flag bearing the dates of Arnst's previous championship victories.[66]

Arnst would lose to Barry on the Thames in 1912, but reclaimed the title nine years later. He would successfully defend it against Pat Hannan on the Wairau River, Blenheim, on 11 June 1921 in a race filmed by Sydney Taylor, McDonald's successor, before losing it to the New Zealand Expeditionary Force (NZEF) sculling champion, Darcy Hadfield, on the Wanganui River in 1922.[67] A consummate sportsman, Arnst then devoted himself to competitive shooting and did so successfully in New Zealand, England and the Continent.[68]

A REFORMED DONNE.

Taking advantage of a large gathering of women, Mr T. Donne, of the High Commissioner's Office, London, paraded a number of sandwich boards calling the attention of passers-by that New Zealand wanted servant girls.

Duke Donne: Got to show this new Reform Party that's come into power that I've got brains and am working for my screw.

DONNE HEADS FOR LONDON

Ward drastically trimmed and reorganised the Civil Service in 1909 and the Department of Tourist and Health Resorts, which had been a constant target of opposition criticism, was absorbed into the Department of Agriculture, Industries and Commerce in April 1909 with Sir Thomas Mackenzie as its minister.[69] It was becoming more and more difficult to defend a department that was not making a profit on the basis of the indirect benefit to "hotel keepers, shop-keepers, shipping companies, coach drivers and the railways", who in the words of James Cowan, the department's publicist and journalist, "all shared the traveller's gold".[70]

Donne may have recognised that his days as a free agent were over and that the future would be far more circumscribed. He stood down as general manager and transferred to the New Zealand High Commission in London. He would never live permanently in New Zealand again but his presence at the High Commission sees him remain as an important player in this story of New Zealand film.

Donne departs for London. Cartoon from unknown New Zealand illustrated weekly. Author's Collection.

However, there were many who appreciated what Donne had achieved.[71] The fruits of his determination to put New Zealand on the map were seen both in tourist numbers but also in the screening of New Zealand-related films overseas. In late 1909 Cosens Spencer's Theatres in Sydney ran a "fine series of New Zealand views shown by special arrangement with the New Zealand Government, in praise of which the press are very eulogistic … These films are now drawing big business."[72]

FIELD MARSHAL LORD KITCHENER'S VISIT

The planned expansion of the kinematographic and photography section of the department was put on hold in a period where many public servants lost their jobs. McDonald remained as busy as ever. Field Marshal Lord Kitchener visited New Zealand in February–March 1910 at the invitation of the government to report on the defence organisation, following a similar tour of Australia. Kitchener inspected the Volunteer Corps throughout the country where he was feted everywhere as the hero of Khartoum and of the Boer War. Having a married sister in New Zealand made him in a sense one of us, although his expressionless visage discouraged such familiarity. Every aspect of his visit was photographed and filmed and McDonald accompanied the official party filming the various presentations and parades on behalf of the government.

Ward was determined to gain the greatest possible benefit from the publicity associated with the Empire's greatest soldier. Kitchener arrived in Bluff from Australia on 17 February 1910 where he was met by the prime minister. Not everything went according to plan; there

School cadets march past Field Marshal Lord Kitchener of Khartoum at Hagley Park. Still from James McDonald's *A Day with the Boy Scouts*, NTSV F6076.

was a hitch in arrangements in Dunedin where the prime minister's carriage was not provided and Ward quarrelled with the mayor of Dunedin in trying to usurp the mayor's place in Kitchener's carriage.[73]

Fragments of two of McDonald's films survive. On 20 February Kitchener inspected a parade of school cadets, Boy Scouts and Boer War veterans at Forbury Park, Dunedin, at 3 p.m. The cadets, gathered from the Otago Province, numbered 2648 from 63 companies. They were joined by 203 boy scouts from Otago and Southland. The film begins appropriately enough with the pipers of the Dunedin Garrison Band and the march-past. After this an impassive Kitchener presents colours to the battalion of high school cadets against a background of photographers.

What McDonald does not record is the mobbing of the Empire's hero by the Dunedin crowd, "the few police on the ground being entirely unable to control the movement … the parade ground was invaded and Lord Kitchener surrounded by a pressing mob of people. The crowd became worse and worse and more and more insistent and curious … The dust of the ground rose in suffocating clouds." All of this Kitchener endured until he was rescued and escorted with cheers from the grounds.[74]

Fragments also exist of McDonald's film of the Christchurch parade of cadets and boy scouts before Lord Kitchener, which he filmed on 22 February 1910.[75] The cadets are seen marching down Rolleston Avenue to the park, wreathed in clouds of dust on what was clearly a very dry, hot day. McDonald placed himself in the stands at the Addington Showgrounds and looks down on the "remarkably picturesque crowd at one of the most cosmopolitan of public gatherings". He captures the moment that Kitchener and his entourage enter the grounds "and instantly there was a craning of necks and straining of eyes to capture the earliest possible sight of the Field Marshal".[76] Members of the elite Canterbury Yeomanry Cavalry (CYC) in white helmets and scarlet tunics ride through the crowds of men and women in summer finery. It is a sea of white dresses and summer hats, women wheeling perambulators and couples strolling together on a glorious summer's day, while in the background one can glimpse the march-past of school cadets and boy scouts.

'TAM' MACKENZIE'S PERSONAL CAMERAMAN

Thomas Mackenzie, both as Minister of Tourist and Health Resorts and of Agriculture, Industries and Commerce, recognised the power of film in attracting an audience and was quick to use it a political tool. McDonald was his agent in this, taking film of Mackenzie's projects and acting as projectionist in screening them at Mackenzie's talks at local meetings.

Mackenzie and McDonald had much in common, both shared a love of the New Zealand bush and fiordlands "and no one did better work than he [Mackenzie] in the opening up of the tourist tracks between the Cold Lakes and Milford Sound". He also headed the unsuccessful search when Professor Mainwaring Brown of Otago University was lost in the mountains at the head of Lake Manapouri.[77] Equally importantly, Mackenzie was as adept as Ward at self-promotion through photo and moving picture. A photo album, presumably taken by McDonald, exists of a Mackenzie trip to the fiords as minister for agriculture and there is a segment of a Pathé newsreel from about 1912 showing the *Honorable T. Mackenzie, A Minister of Many Portfolios* in what appears to be his backyard in Wellington, that screened throughout New Zealand and Australia.[78]

McDonald's surviving work diary of 1912 shows how busy he was kept meeting the needs of his new master. In June he was in Dunedin filming a gathering of the Gabriel's Gully

A Day with the Boy Scouts: Kitchener Inspecting Boy Scouts in Dunedin. NTSV F6078.

A Day with the Boy Scouts: Inspection by Lord Kitchener, Hagley Park. NTSV F6076.

Living New Zealand screened a selection of McDonald's films taken for the Department of Tourist and Health Resorts. *Evening Post*, 23 May 1910, p. 8.

LIVING NEW ZEALAND!
LIVING NEW ZEALAND!
LIVING NEW ZEALAND!
LIVING NEW ZEALAND!
LIVING NEW ZEALAND!
LIVING NEW ZEALAND!

At the

TOWN HALL
TOWN HALL

TO-MORROW, 24th MAY,
TO-MORROW, 24th MAY,
TO-MORROW, 24th MAY,

(EMPIRE DAY)

At 8 p.m.   At 8 p.m

AND FOLLOWING NIGHTS,

THE UNIQUE
THE UNIQUE

ANIMATED-PICTURE-PAGEANT
ANIMATED-PICTURE-PAGEANT

OF EMPIRE
OF EMPIRE

UNDER THE SOUTHERN CROSS.
UNDER THE SOUTHERN CROSS.

By Direction of New Zealand Picture Company.

IF THERE
IS ANYTHING
IN THE WIDE WORLD

That will stir the soul of man or woman and set the pulses throbbing, it is the sight of men fully equipped and ready to do battle for their country

TO-MORROW NIGHT every company of our Wellington defenders will make a Pictorial March along Lambton-quay, and will Parade before His Excellency the Governor at Newtown Park. We want every member of each company to come along and see how well he marches.

And then
MRS. M. SUTCLIFFE

Will recite the patriotic and soul-stirring piece, "THE MIDNIGHT CHARGE," by Clement Scott. You certainly 'must come and hear that.

TO-MORROW NIGHT

We will also show you a picture which we secured on Saturday afternoon of a Boy Scout holding the New Zealand Flag, and what a magnificent type of Young New Zealand he is—a boy who will surely be a leader of men. We are certain that every mother's heart will swell with pride as she gazes on the picture of this sturdy young New Zealander.

We intend also to conduct you through Rotorua, Waimangu, and the Wairakei Valley, and show you quite a number of interesting sights. Life on a Sheep and Cattle Station will give you some idea of the sure foundations on which the prosperity of the Dominion is based, and show you the possibilities for expansion that exist. The Huka Falls and Aratiatia Rapids will be particularly interesting to those whose thoughts turn to the utilisation of Nature's energy; but it is the sight of the mighty seething, twisting Waikato that will charm you. We doubt if any such scene has ever been more perfectly pictured. And there are many other pictures which you must see.

'Dunstan Miners' Jubilee Celebrations. NTSV F6536.

goldfield veterans, and then developing the film to screen at Mackenzie's lecture in the Wellington Town Hall.[79] The *Evening Post* reported: "Led by a piper, with the streamers of his pipes drooping in the rain, over 100 of the Gabriel's Gully diggers marched in procession this afternoon from the Early Settlers' Hall to the Winter Show, where they were guests of the A. and P. Society. As they marched along, hooching to the skirl of the bagpipes, a Government cinematographer, brought from Wellington for the purpose 'took' them as they trudged by the Queen's statue."[80]

In August he was south again in Milton and Balclutha filming the Bruce Woollen Mill, developing and again showing the film at one of Mackenzie's lectures. In November he was in Clyde filming the Dunstan miners' Jubilee celebration on behalf of the Department of Mines.

In 1912 McDonald was 47 years old. It was the year he lost the second of the patrons who supported his film-making. Mackenzie was chosen to succeed Ward as prime minister following the Liberals' election setback in 1911, but as Tom Brooking notes, Mackenzie "lacked either the charisma or the vision to lift the Liberals out of their lethargy and seemed almost relieved to hand over power to William Massey and the Reform Party in 1912".[81] Almost immediately after this he was appointed high commissioner in London to the United Kingdom.

The nature of McDonald's work had also changed. Until Donne's departure in 1909 McDonald's film was sought after by local moving picture shows. However, 1909 saw the beginnings of permanent picture theatres. Henry Hayward opened Pathé Pictures at the Theatre Royal in Christchurch on 13 March 1909 and with his brother Rudall, in partnership with T.J. West, he purchased the Royal Albert Hall in Auckland and began a permanent picture show there on 26 April 1909.

In 1910 Henry Hayward's and John Fuller and Sons' competing circuits of picture theatres throughout New Zealand were hungry for film. On 23 July West–Hayward Pictures announced the first of the Tourist and Health Resorts Department's 'Living New Zealand' series in Auckland, at the Royal Albert Hall, and this was followed by a further series later in the year.[82] It included film taken by Perry's Biorama and by McDonald of 'God's Own Country' showing: "Visit of King George V. and Queen Mary to N.Z. 1901. The late Right Hon. Richard Seddon. Life on a Sheep and Cattle Station. Mail train ascending the Rimutaka. A Day with New Zealand Boy Scouts including inspection by Lord Kitchener. Our Rockbound Coast. The Waikato River: its falls and rapids", and concluded with "Carnival at Rotorua" featuring Maori at the boiling pools, the canoe races, the Wairoa geyser, the haka and dances.[83]

'Living New Zealand' films was screened throughout New Zealand through the Hayward picture theatre chain in 1910–11. It was a review of a decade of government-sponsored film-making and its success showed the country's appetite for seeing itself and its recent past on screen. Hayward also announced that the films were being sent to T.J. West's head office in London "to be shown throughout the United Kingdom".[84]

Permanent picture theatres were constantly demanding local actualities to go with the supply of overseas film and while, as the 'Living New Zealand' series shows, McDonald's film was eagerly sought, local photographers and theatre projectionists-cum-cameramen increasingly stepped in and filled this role. By 1912 McDonald found himself more and more on the margins, filming gold mining reunions or industries for possible overseas distribution and then having to screen it to accompany ministerial talks in the constituencies. He was more and more a factotum to politicians and less and less at the cutting edge of New Zealand film-making.

SYDNEY TAYLOR REPLACES MCDONALD

It is perhaps an indication of McDonald's frustrations that he successfully applied for the post of art assistant with the Dominion Museum, a position he previously held in 1904. McDonald's replacement as government photographer and cameraman was Sydney Benjamin Taylor, employed by the Department of Agriculture, Industries and Commerce. Taylor's achievements have been overshadowed by McDonald's, but, as we shall see, he too made a major contribution to filming in New Zealand in the period he was official photographer and kinematographer.

Born in Port Chalmers in 1887, Taylor's first employment was as an apprentice blacksmith before being apprenticed to a Wellington engraving firm in 1902. He then moved to the *New Zealand Times*, which was one of the first daily papers in the country to successfully print photographs. Taylor branched out from doing the etching and hand-engraving to taking photos. Featuring regularly in the Wellington press, his talent led the secretary of the Department of Agriculture, Industries and Commerce to offer him the position of photographer with the department. He, according to Taylor "sent for me and enquired would I put in for the position … and arranged then and there that I was to get the position. Most of my work was movie pictures of N.Z. industries and farming and showing pictures in different places in the country districts."[85] Government photography and film for the purpose of attracting tourists and migrants would fully engage him for the next 13 years before he joined the *Otago Daily Times* as principal photographer in 1925.[86]

In London, Donne, with Mackenzie's backing, negotiated with Pathé Frères for the release of New Zealand Government-produced film through the Pathé circuits, and asked for copies of all available film to be sent to London. McDonald also tried to hold on to some official film work in his new museum appointment. An inter-departmental meeting was held in September/October

A woman peers through a camera at Rotorua. This image is an example of James McDonald's skill as a photographer. James McDonald, Department of Tourist and Health Resorts, 1903. F111562 –1/2 ATL, Wellington.

1912 between the secretary of the Department of Agriculture, Industries and Commerce, the general manager of the Department of Tourist and Health Resorts, the assistant under-secretary for Immigration, the secretary for Internal Affairs and the director of the Dominion Museum to establish a policy of supplying film to the High Commissioner in London.

It was agreed that Taylor, the new cameraman, would do the ordinary photographic work, and that McDonald would attend "the most important functions or ceremonies held during the year, in order to take cinematograph views which may be of use to the High Commissioner". It was anticipated that this would involve McDonald for two months of each year. In the first year the Department of Agriculture, Industries and Commerce would pay one-fifth of McDonald's salary of £300, but after this it would be a charge against the Department of Internal Affairs, that would also be responsible for communicating with the high commissioner on the provision of photographs and films.[87]

In addition McDonald was tasked to develop a positive and a negative copy of films that he had shot but not yet developed, hold the positive in New Zealand and send the negatives to London "so that the High Commissioner may be able to develop as many films as desired".[88] Twenty-one films were sent, covering topics on all aspects of the New Zealand agricultural industry to sports and scenic films. Ten were films of New Zealand agriculture covering ploughing techniques and the work of the department's instructional farm at Ruakura, including films on the pastoral and woollen industry of New Zealand, life on a sheep and cattle station, and the Mosgiel Woollen Mills. The sports topics consisted of the Metropolitan Trotting Club's New Zealand Cup in Christchurch, won by Lady Clare, and curling and skating in Central Otago. The remaining nine films covered New Zealand scenic attractions, including *A Launch Trip on Boiling Water*, Lake Rotomahana, the mail train on the Rimutaka Incline, a number of films on the Milford Sound, a trip to Akaroa by motor car and coach, a coach trip over the Arthur's Pass to Westland and river steamers on the Wanganui River. In addition, McDonald noted that there were not yet fully completed films on the timber and mining industries, forestry, scenic views of Hamner Spa and Sanitorium; the alpine regions, falls and rapids of the Waikato River; thermal action in the Wairakei Valley as well as the Ngaruawahia regatta and Maori poi dances.[89]

It is some indication of his output in six years of prolific film-making. The *Free Lance* reported:

> Mr James McDonald who used to photograph and kinematograph all things bright and beautiful for the Tourist Department has had about as many changes lately as any fellow wants. He was transferred from the Tourist people to the Agricultural Department and under Minister Tom Mackenzie he scoured New Zealand for pictures of colossal turnips and elephantine moo-cows and other staple products of our backblocks, and between whiles did kinematograph accompaniments to Minister Tom's lectures on our Magnificent Country. Now he has been shifted on some more, this time to the Dominion Museum, which will keep him pretty busy photo'ing the Maori in his savage lair.[90]

McDonald, being the man he was, made a wishlist of film subjects for overseas distribution that included the chief city centres with up-to-date views of the main street scenes, principal country towns, a typical agricultural show in each of the North and South islands, the kauri gum and flax industry, tourist resorts throughout New Zealand, a general film of New Zealand tourist attractions and a film on the frozen meat industry — but it was his successor Taylor who increasingly ended up doing both official functions and the 'ordinary' work.

The newspaper reporter was right in that McDonald found that museum demands prevented him from continuing part-time official film-making to the degree he wished. He filmed the visit of HMS *New Zealand* to New Zealand in 1913, which was one the principal events of that year, but no known copy of the film has survived.[91] He also filmed the Otago Boys' High School Jubilee celebrations in Dunedin over 1–5 August 1913 showing the "High school boys (past and present)" marching from the school's original site in Dowling Street to the present school, followed by rugby at the Caledonian ground. Being an old boy of the school, this must have been a particular delight.[92]

We also have one film from 1912 attributed to him relating to his work with the museum. This is of the veteran Maori warrior Tutange Waionui of Patea demonstrating the fighting methods used when he fought with Titokowaru at Te Ngutu-o-te-manu in 1868 when Gustavus von Tempsky was killed.[93] It is an invaluable glimpse of a veteran fighter demonstrating the tactical skills that made the Maori such a dangerous opponent, and despite his age, the brief seconds of film allows us to imagine Tutange as a much younger man in his prime doing battle with the Pakeha. It is the first of McDonald's known surviving Dominion Museum films capturing the traditions of Maori life.[94]

McDonald became indispensible to the museum as well as acquiring other responsibilities such as becoming Assistant Film Censor in August 1918. Only occasionally could he escape on filming[95] expeditions upcountry with Elsdon Best and Johannes Anderson. Today it is for his films taken on these trips, showing the detail of Maori traditional life and craft, that he is best remembered and we will meet him again in this role in the final chapters. But, as his surviving films from 1907–1912 demonstrate, he deserves recognition as New Zealand's first official photographer and kinematographer.

1863–1913 Otago Boy's High School Jubilee Celebrations. NTSV F28248.

T.J. West conquers Australasia

If a mud-hole breaks out in the North, a West operator snaps it. The defence cadets of the colony have come under his camera. He has a man dodging round after the New Zealand footballers at Home. Shortly a man who uses every effort to give the people something new merits the success he achieves.[1]

WEST'S PICTURES AND THE BRESCIANS

When Perry's Biorama arrived in Wanganui on their 1905 tour they found themselves "hard on the heel of West's great picture show".[2] At that time T.J. West's touring party was the only touring film and variety show equal to Perry's Biorama in variety and professionalism. West's first tour of New Zealand in 1905 signalled the arrival of two of the names that had a major impact on the film industry in Australia and New Zealand. 'West's Pictures and the Brescians' was a combination of two companies, T.J. West's and the Hayward and Martinengo families, the latter families having successfully combined film and concert in Great Britain before coming to the colonies to make their fortune.

The musical and concert element was provided by the 'Brescians' led by Henry Hayward and his brothers and their wives, who were a "group of solo singers and orchestra" drawn from the two family groups, taking their name from Brescia in Italy, the hometown of the Martinengo family.[3] As a group of talented singers and musicians they offered, as Henry Hayward later wrote, "beauty to the eye, artistry in song and solo, with plenty of laughter, and for years they were a household word in entertainment in hundreds of cities and towns throughout Britain".[4]

Hayward's partner, Thomas James West, an Englishman, was an itinerant entertainer who had been in the business since 1873, first touring with a panorama, and then lecturing and touring with a triple lantern and slides, before adding film to his entertainment programme.[5] West had been entranced by a magic lantern show as a schoolboy in Bedford and on leaving school as a 12-year-old "went to London to carve out [his] fortune". He began in the ticket office of St James Hall, which was showing a panorama illustrating the opening of the transcontinental railway from New York to San Francisco. West toured with the show, working up from ticket office to tour manager and after two years he purchased his own panorama. The

magic lantern followed "and then came the kinematograph. I used it almost immediately … and at once recognised that every other form of picture entertainment as known at that date must give way to the kinematograph."[6]

T.J. West's Modern Marvel Company advertised itself as "pre-eminent in the Animated Picture World. Everything that money can buy, or science achieve, has been lavished to produce that perfection in Pictorial Projections, which has placed WEST at the head of the Cinematographic Entrepreneurs. The absolute absence of flicker, the marvellous optical clearness, and the artistic stereoscopic effects, creates a beauty that enchants the eye and charms the intellect."[7] As Henry Hayward recalled West would "pick up and exhibit scientific novelties showing them as entertainment". This included X-rays, colour photography and then, with a R.W. Paul projector and films, moving pictures screened on a bare wall in a side room after the regular show, for 6d extra. Despite the machine breaking down at every show, "the wonder of the pictures held them spellbound".[8]

The success of 'Living Pictures' saw West do "roaring business" in Glasgow and Edinburgh and Scottish provincial towns "sending out concert and vaudeville turns as time fillers, with the Living Picture as the draw".[9] In March 1902 his Méliès' films of Edward VII's coronation and of *A Trip to the Moon* shown on his Imperial Coronascope (obviously named for the subjects shown) drew the crowds at Exeter and did so again with his "New Coloured Animated Pictures" in September 1903.[10] He toured the provincial towns of England and Scotland, returning each year for the Christmas season to the Queen's Hall in Edinburgh and, after his first appearance in 1891, for similar extended seasons at the Shaftesbury Hall in Bournemouth.[11]

T.J. West, *The New Zealand Graphic*, 26 October 26 1906, p. 17.

West happily benefited from the public associating him with Alfred West of G. West & Son, marine photographers in Portsmouth, who specialised in photographing and then filming images of the Royal Navy at work and play. Alfred West's film and magic lantern programme titled *Our Navy* was enormously successful and toured through Britain before finding a permanent home at the Polytechnic Theatre in Regent Street, London, opening on 14 October 1899 and running for 14 years. Its value as a recruiting agent was quickly recognised and supported by both the Admiralty and the Royal Navy League with Alfred West able to film all aspects of 'Jack Tar's' life afloat and ashore.[12] It capitalised on public interest in the sailors' lives and pride in the evolving technology of the Royal Navy with the introduction of submarines and the launching of the HMS *Dreadnought* in 1905. West also established strong links with the royal family as demonstrated with his training and despatch of the king's kinematographer to accompany the royal tour of 1901.

Our Navy did great business throughout the Empire and T.J. West was often mistaken for the originator of this programme. He did nothing to correct the impression; indeed he encouraged it.[13] The real Alfred West considered 'T.J.' an "absolute impostor", but West removed himself to the colonies with the Brescians where he found fame and fortune in his own right and it was

His Majesty's Theatre, Dunedin. ❦ Commencing Monday, April 1'n, 1905

THE BRESCIANS.
ORCHESTRA AND SINGERS

West's Pictures and The Brescians.

Programme for West's Pictures and the Brescians, His Majesty's Theatre, Dunedin. Deposited by Ramai Hayward, NTSV MA0099.

this success that allowed him to build up a similar reputation in England from 1909.[14] What is evident is that T.J. West was a natural showman and raconteur who could hold an audience, with a head for business as well as being an accomplished film-maker and producer.

As with Hayward's memories of the Brescians it sounds grander than it was, but, while there is no doubt about the Brescians' musical talents and West's entrepreneurship, in Britain they were just another company competing for business with many other equally talented touring parties. With the Hayward family having a married sister in New Zealand, the temptation to seek their fortunes saw them sail to Dunedin, the Edinburgh of the South.[15]

The West and Brescians Company sailed on the RMS *Corinthic* in what was then termed the Second Saloon, which listed West's Picture Company as Mr T.J. West, Mr E.J. Hardy, Mr T.N. Lax and Mr A.M. Miller and also named the ten strong Brescian's Orchestra and Singers.[16] During the voyage West presented his "series of Coloured Cinematograms" to passengers and crew, with West acting as lecturer, his cameraman, E.J. Hardy, as projectionist and T.N. 'Tommy' Lax playing the piano. The programme's proceeds were donated to seamen's charities.[17] Naturally enough West proclaimed that this was the first time films had been screened at sea.

The company had a successful tour starting in Dunedin, for an unheard of length of four weeks taking "one hundred pound nightly" from packed houses. Henry Hayward's advance publicity whetted Dunedin's appetite and the combined show fulfilled expectations being in the words of the *Otago Witness* critic, "the most attractive [show] of its kind ever seen in Dunedin".[18] West's mix of scenic and narrative films interspersed with musical and comic items climaxed with Georges Méliès' hand-coloured fantasy *A Trip to the Sun*, which even today captures one's imagination.[19] It tells the story of how "the numerous friends of an eminent scientist pay a visit to this uncommon tourist resort. They journey by train as far as the Swiss

Alps when the train is suddenly forced off the line by means of balloons, landing the party in space, and finally after a 'cloudy' passage, they arrive at their destination. The Sun is represented as being a humourist who treats the whole affair as a huge joke, for, becoming dissatisfied with the influx of earthly travellers to his territory, he resorts to fire and brimstone to get rid of them, the result of which being a hurried descent to the bottom of the sea."[20]

It drew critical praise as "a marvellous picture ... If this Cinematograph included nothing else it would merit public patronage."[21] It did and crowds flocked to see the show. One of the lads sitting entranced during a matinee performance was the future politician and writer, John A. Lee:

> I didn't know I was witnessing the birth of a new sort of … entertainment and the death of vaudeville … the start of an age in which we became lookers rather than performers.[22]

West's equipment included the latest Bioscope projectors developed by Charles Urban and he also had an agreement with Urban's company for a supply of films.[23] The projectors were driven by a portable generating plant and, uniquely for New Zealand at that time, were housed in a portable, fully-enclosed fireproof projectionist booth that lessened the fire risk inherent in operating projectors in an open hall. When the projection booth was erected in His Majesty's Theatre, Auckland, West was very concerned that it involved taking out two rows of seats in what promised to be a season of full houses, and was very much against losing that income. However, Rudall Hayward recounts a fierce argument between West and Edwin Hardy, his chief projectionist and cameraman. Hardy told his boss "that unless the portable operating box went in he would catch the next boat back to England and so in due course the operating box was built".[24]

Rudall Hayward's first job in film was in the projectionist booth:

> They [the projectionists] were, of course, still hand cranking them in those days, but all our projectors had take-up spools on them and when the take-up spool didn't work they always employed somebody to turn the bottom spool and that's how I started as a boy, sitting at the feet of the projectionist, turning the bottom spool. If the take-up was a little faulty that was my job. If I got too interested in a film and forgot to turn I would be gently kicked in the pants for failing in my duties.[25]

The enthusiastic audience response to West's Pictures and the Brescians was repeated throughout New Zealand, the Wellington *Evening Post* reporting the films being "one of the best exhibitions in the cinematographic line yet seen here, giving equal accolades to the Brescian singers and musicians … On the whole, one would not like to award the palm to either the Pictures or the Brescians. They are not rivals but complimentary."[26]

West's Pictures and the Brescians made a profit of £13,000 from their first tour of New Zealand having responded to audience demand by revisiting some venues.[27] They left for Australia early in 1906, returning to Christchurch for the New Zealand International Exhibition in 1906–07 where West ran pictures daily at half-hour intervals in a small hall known as the Castle Theatre.

On 15 February 1907 the *Bush Advocate* reported that the evening's performance would be the 1107th consecutive display since opening in November 1906. "Mr West has now put through one and a half million feet of film, or over 285 miles, and some 25 million photographs have, he states, been projected on the screen. He claims that this is a world's record likely to stand for some time."[28]

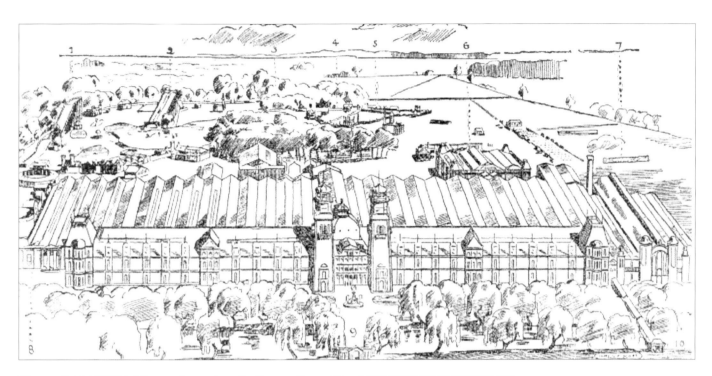

Bird's-eye view of the buildings and grounds of the New Zealand International Exhibition in Christchurch.
1. Toboggan-Helter Skelter.
2 Water Chute-Pike-Aquarium.
3. West's Pictures. 4. Fernery.
5. Maori Pa. 6. Art Gallery.
7. Machinery Hall.
8. Canadian Court.
9. Main Entrance.
10. Covered Entrance.
Evening Post, 1 November 1906. 19873261, records, ATL, Wellington.

Dragon train at the New Zealand International Exhibition, Christchurch, 1906–07. Still from West's Pictures. *Sights and Scenes at the New Zealand Exhibition*, NTSV S2793, no. 2.

It featured West's own film of the exhibition. "The opening ceremony, reception by Maoris to Sir John Gorst, axemen's carnival, and other events were all cinematographed, and West's are now showing to crowded attendances, excellent moving pictures of these functions."[29] This highly successful picture season in Christchurch was separate again to the main touring party, with West's Pictures and the Brescians on the road throughout the North Island over Christmas 1906–07, including appearances in the Concert Hall at the International Exhibition.[30]

WEST'S PICTURES CONQUERS THE DOMINIONS

After the second profitable New Zealand season the partnership was dissolved. Henry Hayward saw film as a passing fad and sailed for London to arrange a tour for the magic show Maskelyne and Devant's Mysteries, which he brought out first to Australia and then to New Zealand beginning in Auckland in November 1908. West continued to tour his pictures throughout

Wash day at Whakarewarewa. Still from West's Pictures. *Sights in New Zealand*, NTSV F3005.

West's Pictures filming Wairoa Geyser at Whakarewarewa. Two motion picture cameras are in action with West operating the camera on the left. Wairoa Geyser was the largest in the field, but it did not erupt regularly and sometimes was induced with soap. This film was released as *Sights in New Zealand* and sold to Charles Urban in the United Kingdom. *Evening Post* Collection, C9582, ATL, Wellington.

Sir Joseph Ward 'addresses the scholars' at the Terrace School, Wellington on the Dominion Day Anniversary on Monday 25 September 1911. The cameraman may be Brandon Haughton who was filming for Fuller's at this time. The film *School Children addressed by Sir Joseph Ward at the Terrace School*, screened at Fuller's His Majesty's Theatre, the following day. John Dickie Collection, G34742-1/2, ATL, Wellington.

Australia and New Zealand winning both public approval and financial success. If the town had a hall big enough to attract an audience then West's Pictures, assisted by De Groen's Vice-Regal Orchestra, would screen there.

The *Hawera and Normanby Star* advertised West's two-night season at the Opera House in Hawera in October 1908 by reporting the Wellington papers' reception of the latest programme of West's films.

> Many centuries have rolled by since Mahomet went to the mountain because the mountain
> refused to come to Mahomet, and with the advance of years there seems to have come about a
> great change. Not many Wellingtonians have ever had the fortune to visit the Tyrolean Alps, and
> there are few who ever will. The Tyrol therefore came to Wellington last night, and — per medium
> of West's Biograph — was shown in all its grandeur and its quaintness in the Town Hall. There can
> be nothing more interesting, such fine views of a little-known land as were exhibited last night.[31]

The Tyrolians would have said the same about New Zealand and indeed the view of strange lands that one would never otherwise see was a fascination for film audiences throughout the world.

West's Pictures also recognised the powerful audience appeal of local films and filmed local events and scenic attractions that were shown throughout New Zealand. In 1905 *The Parliamentary Picture*, featuring scenes of Parliament buildings in Wellington with a number of members of parliament including Premier Richard Seddon, guaranteed the premier's attendance and that of Wellington society at the first showing. *Living Auckland* made a similar impact in that city. As Rudall Hayward later noted, "I know that the regular thing was to include some local scenes amongst the programmes that they were showing the public."[32]

The young Rudall Hayward remembers Mr Edward Hardy, West's cameraman/projectionist, filming the school cadets of Auckland Grammar School parading up Wellesley Street. West was keen on 'firsts'. Hayward recalled West filming the "first electric tram in Christchurch, a

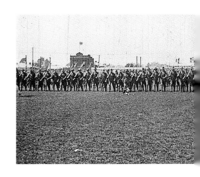

harvest scene in Canterbury, and the most famous scene was the driving of a horse and trap up the Cathedral steps in Nelson … which was considered quite a feat of horsemanship in those days".[33] The films have not survived but we have a 1905 photograph of West's camera team filming the horse and gig driven by the intrepid and obviously skilled Mr F.N. Jones as it nears the top of the steps. This feat was included in West's film *Sights in New Zealand* that was released worldwide by Charles Urban.[34]

There is the full-page photo spread in the *Otago Witness* of 4 October 1905 headed "'West's Pictures' cinematographing Maori scenes at Rotorua".[35] We see his two camera teams filming a poi dance with West in his Stetson hat, Hardy, his principal cameraman, surrounded by Maori elders and curious onlookers, staring back quizzically at the photographer. There are also shots of canoe races and a larger shot of West's cinematographic teams filming the dancers performing on the marae. The Rotorua scenes — of the hot springs, Maori dances, canoe races and wood chopping — were also some of the 16 different scenes included in *Sights in New Zealand* screened to audiences throughout New Zealand and Australia, and then to the world, through Urban's distribution network.[36]

Some of West's scenic films were purchased by Donne's Department of Tourist and Health Resorts. West also sold some of his film negatives to Charles Urban who was always seeking scenic films and actualities from around the world, which he sold from his own trading company, Urbanora, and from his French production company, Eclipse.[37]

West's success led the Haywards to change their views on the future of film.[38] Henry Hayward records how he and West came to an arrangement that "he should stay and devote himself to the cinema in Australia and I should apply myself to New Zealand".[39] The two agreed to mutually benefit from joint purchase of film for each enterprise and West agreed that Hayward could continue to use the title 'West's Pictures' in New Zealand and West–Hayward's Pictures gradually evolved into Hayward's Pictures. The division may not have been quite as clear-cut as Hayward remembers. West maintained a strong interest in New Zealand, eventually building permanent picture theatres in each of the main centres, usually in connection with local business interests and using the Hayward's film distribution circuit. Henry and his brother Rudall opened the Royal Albert Hall in Auckland in August 1909 and advertised itself as West's Pictures.

West went to Australia at a time when moving picture exhibition was moving from the margins to the centre of social life around the world.[40] In France, there was Charles Pathé, a butcher's son who began his career as a travelling entertainer with the new-fangled gramophone before expanding his business into gramophone production and the Pathé record label. Film exhibition followed and in 1896 he and his brothers established the Pathé Frères Company encompassing films, gramophone production and sound recordings. It became a public company the following year and in 1902 acquired the Lumière patents, expanding film production with a large processing facility at Vincennes, experimenting with coloured film — Pathécolor — and the synchronisation of film and gramophone recordings. Two years later it claimed a 12,000-title film catalogue and began opening distribution offices worldwide.[41]

In November 1906 Charles Pathé and Edmond Benoit-Levy went into partnership with the foundation of the Omnia cinema chain of permanent picture theatres, moving away from the itinerant fairground circuits that until then had been the major focus for their film sales. By 1909 Pathé had 200 permanent cinemas throughout France.[42] Pathé expanded throughout the world, opening their 41st branch in Melbourne on 1 July 1909 — the opening event attended by Australian prime minister Alfred Deakin — and later opening an office in Wellington for the New Zealand market.[43]

The growth of film production gave the picture showmen the ability to change programmes every week or more and this drew audiences back again in the same week. Permanent picture theatres became a feature of the larger centres and then spread out into the suburbs and small towns. West became Australia's first notable exhibitor and the first to open large permanent picture theatres specially constructed for that purpose.

In 1909 Henry Gee, West's general manager in Australia, detailed the growth of West's Pictures in an interview for *The Bioscope*:

> As you know, it is about four years since we landed in New Zealand with West's Pictures. We opened in Dunedin, and had a successful provincial tour. Operations were then extended to Sydney and Brisbane, and the provinces in the Eastern States. Then we took a lease of the Sydney Glaciarium, which holds 4,000, and is crowded each Saturday night of the season. For seven months of the year that building is utilised for the show, the remainder being spent at the Palace Theatre. Business has expanded so that special halls are to be built in the different States … West's Pictures are now established in Brisbane, Sydney, Melbourne, Adelaide, Perth, Fremantle and Kalgoolie. There are also touring shows in Western Australia, New South Wales, Queensland and New Zealand. Business in the Dominion has been so satisfactory that on my visit there I entered into contracts for the expenditure of about £50,000 for the erection of picture halls in Wellington, Christchurch and Auckland. The expansion of West's Pictures is shown by the fact that there are over 300 employees, of whom 140 are musicians.[44]

T.J. West, the film colossus straddling the United Kingdom, Australia and New Zealand. Supplement to *The Bioscope*, 22 September 1910.

By 1910 West controlled 14 permanent cinemas throughout Australia with an estimated nightly audience of 20,000.[45] Each cinema had its own orchestra to give life to the silent films, with West having a predilection towards military-style brass bands, with his advertising boasting that his programmes consisted of "pictures and instrumental music only, no extraneous aid, such as songs, etc, being allowed".[46] Both West and his initial major competitor Cosens Spencer built picture theatres in Australia that were "as like the ordinary theatre as possible, a place where a man could take his wife and family on State occasions."[47] West boasted that his New Olympia Theatre in Melbourne that opened in 1909 with 4000 seats was the largest theatre in the world exclusively designed for film exhibition, and priced accordingly, charging between one and three shillings a seat, offering one evening session each day and two matinees a week.[48]

The exhibition battle in Australia became a fight between West and Spencer, which, in the words of one of Spencer's film buyers, "was almost war to the knife". The fray was later turned into a three-way tussle for the public purse by J.D. Williams whose 'continuous pictures' unashamedly drew in a working-class audience, forcing seat prices down.[49] All three sought exclusive films to draw the crowds in a period when a series of Australian narrative films 'featured' in Australian picture theatres. West concentrated on news-events, travelogues, scenic

and actualities in his film production, relying on imported film for the narrative content of his shows, having purchased exclusive distribution rights to Pathé's *Film d' Art* series offering "adaptions of famous classic and contemporary plays with renowned stage actors".[50] He never shifted from his belief that local content attracted the crowds and drew upon Pathé's Australian production and his own cameramen to provide his cinemas with a steady diet of Australian-sourced actualities as well as featuring films shot in New Zealand. Spencer matched this with similar scenic films shot throughout Australia by his camera crews under the direction of his head cameraman, Ernest Higgins.[51]

Films of Melbourne and Sydney, agricultural shows, Australian Rules Football, "Quaint Australasian Dances, interesting customs and glorious travel scenes", *Yachting on Sydney Harbour*, *Surf Sports at Manly*, *Australia's Boy Scouts* and *Catching Crocodiles* were all part of West's bill of fare.[52] His beauty contest on film travelled from suburb to suburb, town to town, titled *Beauty by Biograph,* promising "Living, breathing, true to life pictures of Sydney's fairest daughters". West ran a similar contest in Auckland in 1911.[53]

HAYWARD'S PICTURES

In New Zealand Henry Hayward followed his partner's example and capitalised on the West name. His first picture show, Pathé Pictures, opened in the Theatre Royal, Christchurch, on 13 March 1909 and rapidly grew from there. He wrote of the difficulties in finding venues for his picture shows:

> Our first picture theatres were empty shops, old warehouses, schoolrooms, and deserted churches … at Wanganui, Louis Cohen, Will Jameson and I ran the first regular cinema at the auction mart; at Napier, in partnership with Messrs. Thompson and Payne, I opened the initial 'pictures' in an old garage. Fullers' first permanent movie house was a horse bazaar in Christchurch; whilst Wellington's venue was a deserted church.[54]

Henry Hayward's first permanent theatre was in partnership with his brother Rudall. Henry settled in Auckland and his brother Rudall settled in Waihi. Their theatre in Waihi was the first permanent theatre in what would become the Hayward chain.[55] This was followed by Royal Albert Hall in Albert Street, Auckland, opening on 26 April 1909, running nightly performances first as Pathé and then as West's Pictures. "'Everything new,' is Mr Hayward's motto, and a special installation of up-to-date plant is now erected whilst weekly batches of the freshest gems of the film manufacturer are on the way from Europe and America."[56] Hayward also screened films at the Tivoli Theatre in Karangahape Road in what was previously a vaudeville theatre, with Fuller screening pictures on a regular basis at the Opera House and then opening the King's Theatre in Upper Pitt Street, being the first purpose-built picture theatre in Auckland.

Competition was intense and waged as fiercely between Fuller and Hayward in the provincial centres as it was in the main cities. It was a battle for venues and the cost of hiring existing theatres was usually with the proviso that film screening was suspended for pre-booked touring shows, but going to the pictures was becoming the most popular and affordable entertainment for families. It was public demand that led to the establishment of permanent picture theatres.[57]

On 10 November 1910 Benwell's American Pictures started 'continuous pictures' at the old Federal Hall on Wellesley Street West, Auckland, renaming it the Gaiety Theatre, but it was off the beaten track for pedestrian traffic and soon closed. Hayward opened the Lyric Theatre on

6 November 1911 as Auckland's premier picture palace, complete with the Lyric Symphony Ladies Orchestra conducted by Chas Parnell and with its grand entrance, marble stairways and armchair seats; it was the last word in luxury, intent on drawing a middle-class audience into film.[58]

On 25 November J.F. MacMahon in partnership with Arthur Lodder opened the new Queen's Theatre in Queen Street running from 11a.m. to 11p.m. as a continuous theatre.[59] James MacMahon was one of the MacMahon brothers who were veteran theatrical entrepreneurs well known throughout Australia and New Zealand. They had introduced the viewing of film with the kinetoscope to the Australian colonies and had then moved into film projection, being among the first touring film shows in both Australia and New Zealand. They then got into film production. *Robbery under Arms* in 1907 and *For the Term of his Natural Life* in 1909 broke records at theatres throughout Australasia.[60] In 1912 they set up the Dominion Picture Theatres Co. in New Zealand, opening cinemas in Auckland and Wellington, and began a film-renting agency buying or "hiring a wide variety of exhibitors' unwanted stock, allowing travelling showmen to rent films at a fraction of the cost of buying films outright".[61]

New Zealand also attracted the West Virginian, James Dixon Williams, trading as J.D. Williams Theatres, who expanded his successful continuous pictures from his Sydney base, where with Spencer and West he was one of the big three cinema promoters, to having four theatres in New Zealand and a film rental agency.[62]

Picture theatre followed picture theatre in the cities and the suburbs, expanding in the suburbs with the growth of suburban train and tram services. They seemed to change their names as often as they changed managers, to the confusion of future film historians. Gordon Ingham wrote of "small halls which screened only occasionally [but which] adopted grandiloquent titles and then departed the scene forever".[63] It seems that Oddfellows' Halls were popular for occasional screenings in the Wellington area while elsewhere, including Auckland, Foresters' Lodges were favourites.[64] These were one- or two-man affairs, usually with a local pianist hired to provide musical accompaniment.

West's Pictures hoarding on the site of the post office at the bottom of Queen Street, Auckland, featuring L. De Groen's Vice Regal Band. Extract *Auckland Weekly News*, Auckland Libraries, Sir George Grey Collection, 7-A1752.

One of the first 'all-picture enterprises' on Queen Street, Auckland, was adapted from a sideshow at agricultural shows. A shop near Wellesley Street East was fitted with an oscillating floor for an audience numbering about 50, who paid their shilling to see films of scenic views as if they were travelling in a train or tram through the city or the countryside. The programme ran for about 20 minutes, continuously, and you "stayed until you had obtained value for your money".[65] This was similar to and no doubt adapted from the Hales Tours and phantom ride films that were popular in the United States and Europe.[66] It capitalised on the moment and then, like the skating rink craze that raced through the United States, Britain, Europe, Australia and New Zealand over the same period, ran out of steam as people's interest turned to the greater variety offered in moving picture theatres.

Henry and Rudall Hayward's first picture theatre was in Waihi, which at that time, with the gold mines in full production, was the second-largest town in the Auckland province. The miners were getting regular wages that they were keen to spend. Once established in Waihi, as his son and film-maker Rudall Hayward remembered, "he began to spread himself to other places. He had a circuit of small towns of which the town of Hamilton was a one-night stand. The other one-night stands were Te Aroha, Thames and Tauranga. He spread himself with portable shows all around the goldfield in the Waikato."[67] Film exhibition in New Zealand became a mix of permanent picture theatres in centres with the population large enough to support nightly viewings and touring shows in the smaller centres.

In July 1910 Henry Hayward formed Hayward's Picture Enterprises and by 1912 controlled 33 picture theatres throughout New Zealand with an established film renting agency. This still honoured Hayward's original agreement with T.J. West on the joint purchase of film to the benefit of each and through West's Pictures in Australia enabling Hayward's to have exclusive rights to first screen films for many of the leading film-makers in Europe and America.[68]

JOHN FULLER AND SONS

The major competition that Hayward's Pictures faced was from John Fuller and Sons. A professional singer in England, John Fuller arrived in Auckland from Australia as a tenor soloist with the Albu Sisters in 1893. Recognising an opportunity for promoting and singing ballad concerts, which was his field, he stayed on and prospered by running a series of 'People's Popular Concerts' in the City Hall Theatre. His family was soon included in the programme.

This developed into a touring show that grew from its Auckland provincial base into a New Zealand-wide tour under the title of the Myriorama Company, consisting of a magic lantern programme accompanied by commentary and songs. Fuller added a hugely popular waxworks show that occupied the foyer area of the theatre and operated simultaneously in the four main centres. Success saw Fuller became more and more centred on engaging performing artists and managing the family's vaudeville circuit. The logical next step was the purchase of the theatres in which the company performed in each of the main centres, Auckland, Wellington, Christchurch and Dunedin. Fuller's sons Benjamin and John junior increasingly took over the day-to-day management and had a firm finger on the public's tastes in entertainment, with John junior becoming the firm's spokesman on film business.

By 1900 the John Fuller and Sons Vaudeville Circuit phased out the waxworks and were importing the best in variety and music-hall entertainment from around the world, with new shows opening weekly and touring their four

John Fuller's Myriorama Company developed into John Fuller and Sons, which dominated live theatre in New Zealand. *West Coast Times*, 27 April 1899, p. 3.

PRINCESS THEATRE.
Two Nights and Sunday Concert.
FRIDAY, APRIL 28TH
Mr John Fuller's
MYRIORAMA COMPANY
First Production
ROSE, SHAMROCK, & THISTLE.
First appearance here of Mr Will Watkins and Mr Arthur Hahn, together with the old favorites, including Mr John Fuller.
Price, 1s ; Children, 6d ; Resrvd Seats, 2s
MATINEE—Saturday 2.30., " Aladdin " Prices—Children 6d & 3d · adults

Fuller's Star Theatre, Newtown, Wellington. John Fuller and Sons rivalled Hayward's Pictures in New Zealand. 1-2-139943-F, ATL., Wellington.

theatres. Short films were shown between acts and proved so popular that in 1908 the Fullers transformed some of their vaudeville houses into picture theatres and for a period closed down their vaudeville shows.[69] As it turned out the ongoing popularity of vaudeville saw Fuller develop two separate circuits with dedicated theatres for film and theatre throughout New Zealand and Australia.

Fuller's circuit dominated New Zealand live theatre and became equally prominent in Australia in competition with J.C. Williamson. Dowling Street, Dunedin, where the company had two theatres operating including its first freehold theatre, the Alhambra, became known as 'Fuller's earth'.[70] Unlike Hayward who leased his sites, Fuller owned the freehold of their theatres. They wanted to be as dominant in film as they were in live theatre and set up Fuller's Wide-World Pictures at the same time establishing The Biograph and Amusement Supplies Co., which was New Zealand's first film distribution company for the hiring of film and the selling of projectors and other related materials.[71] There was intense rivalry between the two firms, with the MacMahon brothers and J.D. Williams being the lesser players in New Zealand.

Both Fuller and Hayward raced each other to show something different and new. In 1911 it was Kinemacolor — the world's first successful natural colour film system, invented in England by G.A. Smith, patented in 1906 and successfully marketed by Charles Urban. The process relied on either multiple coloured lenses converging on to a single image, which was the basis of Gaumont's Chronochrome system, or coloured filters rotating in front of the image at higher projection speed, which was the Kinemacolor system developed by Urban. Both competed with each other but both suffered and eventually failed commercially because each required special film projectors and specially trained operators.[72]

Fuller and Sons were first to show Kinemacolor at the Theatre Royal in Wellington. The *Evening Post* reported:

> Kinemacolour presented through the enterprise of Messrs. John Fuller and Sons, for the first
> time in New Zealand, by means of Messrs. Urban and Smith's kinemacolour patents, is, simply,
> natural colour kinematography, a result achieved by a delicate and intricate process of light filters
> with very beautiful results. The pictures screened last night were an unqualified success. From a
> spectacular point of view nothing could have been finer than the pictures of the investiture of the
> Prince of Wales and the recent coronation processions.[73]

Fuller had the licence for the Urban system when the two companies opened colour film in their Auckland theatres on Boxing Day evening 1911. Hayward advertised their system as 'colourmatography' but this was simply the Gaumont equivalent of the colour stencil process already used in Pathécolor using standard film projectors. The coloured scenes of George V's coronation drew in the crowds to Fuller's picture theatres but the need for special projectors and the limited supply of films meant that it remained a curiosity and became an occasional event for a special feature usually with its own lecturer and projecting team rather than standard fare.

Initially there were no exclusive film rights. As Rudall Hayward recalled:

> Everybody could buy the films and did so … You knew that Fullers had the same films as
> the Hayward's had and so the great thing was to try and get your films through the country

as quickly as possible to get ahead of the opposition. A programme of films would be made up in Auckland and immediately it finished its [weekly] season … it would be split up and half of it would be sent to Wanganui and half to New Plymouth or Napier and in that manner they hoped to get ahead of the Fullers.[74]

Vaudeville and live theatre suffered from the impact of 'pictures' and some of its stalwarts had no option but to move into the new business. One was Tom Pollard, whose professional Opera Company was a New Zealand institution from the 1890s. Pollard closed it down with a final performance on 13 April 1910 and then earned a living, until his death in 1922, running Pollard's Pictures at the Princess Theatre in Hokitika and at the Public Hall and then the Opera House in Greymouth: all venues showing live shows, with films becoming more and more the staple fare. It seems that he ran them with his two brothers, Jack and Pat O'Sullivan; Pollard having changed his surname when he married the daughter of J.J. Pollard, owner-manager of the original Pollard's Opera Company, after playing second fiddle in the company's orchestra![75]

Others were absorbed into the Fuller's or Hayward's chains. One of these was the actor and playwright Barrie Marschel who successfully toured New Zealand with his own touring company throughout the 1890s and early 1900s. A prolific playwright with some 31 plays to his credit, those toured by his company included *Murder in the Octagon* in 1895 with a Dunedin setting and *Humarire Taniwha*, or *The Greenstone God*, in 1898.[76] The advent of moving pictures saw Marschel as master of ceremonies and raconteur front of house to dramatic films such as *The Battle of Waterloo* in November 1913 and *Sixty Years a Queen*, on the life of Queen Victoria, that drew in the crowds in 1914.[77]

---

92   *THE BIOSCOPE.*   OCTOBER 27, 1910.

WEST'S PICTURES

Universally admitted as the Finest (as it is certainly the Largest) Organisation of ANIMATED PICTURES in the World, employing over 800 persons.

Under the Direction of Mr. T. J. WEST.

Central Home Offices — PICCADILLY MANSIONS, LONDON, W.

ENGLAND

BOURNEMOUTH : Shaftesbury Hall	Manager, Mr. T. W. KINGSTON
BLYTH : West's Pictures Palace	Manager, Mr. JAMES HAYWOOD
READING : New Forester's Hall	Manager, Mr. H. BATTERSBY

SCOTLAND.

EDINBURGH : Queen's Hall (intermittently)   Manager, Mr. T. HADDOW

CHANNEL ISLANDS.

JERSEY : West's Pictures Palace   Manager, Mr. GEORGE FRANCIS

Regarding WEST'S AUSTRALIAN and NEW ZEALAND ENTERPRISES.

The following is a List of the Extensive Enterprises and Tours controlled by Mr. T. J. WEST in the Antipodes.

NEW SOUTH WALES.
1.—SYDNEY : Glaciarium, in the Summer.
2.—   ,,   Palace Theatre, in the Winter.
3.—   ,,   Bijou Theatre.
4.— No. 1 Touring Show, Western District.
5.— No. 2 Touring Show, Southern District.
6.— No. 1 Suburban Weekly Circuit, Sydney.
7.— No. 2 Suburban Weekly Circuit, Sydney.
8.—MANLY : Open Air Theatre.
9.— A new Theatre in course of erection at Paddington, Sydney.

QUEENSLAND.
1.—BRISBANE : West's Olympia.
2.—GYMPIE : Olympia.
3.—IPSWICH : Touring Circuit.
4.—NORTH QUEENSLAND : Touring Circuit.

VICTORIA.
1.—MELBOURNE : West's Palace.
2.—No. 1 Touring Show, Western District.
3.—BENDIGO : His Majesty's Theatre.

SOUTH AUSTRALIA.
1.—ADELAIDE : West's Olympia.
2.—No. 1 Touring Show.

WESTERN AUSTRALIA.
1.—PERTH : Queen's Hall.
2.—FREMANTLE : His Majesty's Theatre.
3.—KALGOORLIE : Cremorne Gardens Theatre.
4.—BUNBURY CIRCUIT.

NEW ZEALAND.
1.—WELLINGTON : King's Theatre.
2.—CHRISTCHURCH : King's Theatre.
3.—AUCKLAND : Albert Hall.
4.—DUNEDIN : Building in course of erection.

HEAD OFFICE:

Piccadilly Mansions, London, W.

'Phone : GERRARD 579.   Grams : "WESTOGRAPH, LONDON."

The Bioscope, 27 October 1910, p. 92.

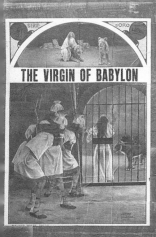

Advertising for 'Fullers' Pictures', Nelson, March 1911.
Photographer, Frederick Nelson Jones, (1881–1962),
G-11836-1/1, ATL, Wellington.

A GLIMPSE OF FILM IN 1911

Fred Jones' photograph of a pasted wall of bill posters advertising 'Fullers' [sic] Pictures' in a Nelson street in the first week of March 1911 gives us an indication of a typical film programme at the time. The posters feature the star films, two from Italy, a news-event of the Sydney Street siege in London and a scenic of *Picturesque Sydney* together with two American films from the Vitagraph Company. The two Italian films reflect the strength of the European film industry at the time, although both were distributed through Vitagraph. *The Virgin of Babylon* (1910), with its English title pasted over the French-language version (*La Vierge de Babylone*), is a one-reel (14-minute) historical drama made by the Ambrosio film company in Turin as one of its 'serie d'oro' or golden series. This started in 1908 with *The Last Days of Pompei*, which found a ready market around the world, making Ambrosio one of the largest film producers in Italy with over 200 titles a year by 1912.[78] *La Première Bicyclette de Robinet* (titled in English *Tweedledom's First Bicycle*) is also an Ambrosio film of 1910 featuring Marcel Fabre, the Spanish comedian and clown, who, as Robinet, acted the part of a shameless Casanova who inevitably gets involved in a chase on some mode of transport, whether aeroplane, car or, in this case, his first bicycle, dealing mayhem and destruction to all in his path.[79]

The two Vitagraph Company films are also typical one-reel (14-minute) productions of the time. *Jean the Matchmaker* from 1910 is one of the first of the series featuring Jean the 'Vitagraph dog' who, directed by his owner Larry Trimble, featured in some 18 one-reel films for Vitagraph from 1910–13.[80] The love interest in the film is the actress Florence Turner, known to the viewing public as the 'Vitagraph Girl', who was singled out as "A Motion Picture Star" by the *New York Dramatic Mirror* in June the previous year; bringing the phrase into public consciousness for the first time.[81] *A Life for a Life* was a one-reel melodrama. Both films were advertised by their accompanying international posters that featured the Vitagraph logo with the titles emblazoned in German, French and English; indicating the global reach of the company, which was the largest film-producing company in the United States at the time and second-largest in the world after Pathé Frères.[82]

Picturesque Sydney is a Cosens Spencer production of 1910 when West's Pictures and Spencer were locked into a battle for audiences with their Sydney theatres; West producing a series of scenics on Sydney made by Pathé under the title of *Living Sydney — the London of the South,* while Spencer countered with a series on *Picturesque Sydney* — 'Australia by the Australians' in a not-too-subtle dig at West's head office being in London and of course the Pathé French connection, ignoring the fact that Spencer was English-born.[83] Hayward had first call on West's films and so Fuller purchased Spencer's productions. In this case *Picturesque Sydney* was a 40-minute long multi-reel film that took top billing when it featured at His Majesty's Theatre, Wellington, for three nights in December 1910.[84]

The news-event film *Battle with Anarchists* is of the dramatic scenes captured on film when two Latvians, earlier involved in the shooting of three London policemen, are besieged in a house at 100 Sidney Street on 3 January 1911. A Pathé newsreel survives showing policemen and soldiers firing from windows and alleyways at the house, while the home secretary, Winston Churchill, directs operations (although in this case, while he appears on the inter-title he cannot be positively identified on film). Bullets are seen hitting walls and the house is seen ablaze, killing the two besieged men, while police hold back the crowds. It is dramatic footage and enthralled New Zealand audiences.[85]

Sydney Street Siege, British Pathé, 2961.31.

8

The permanent picture show

The picture should appear on the curtain white and brilliant except for the natural shades of photography and it should be uniform in color — that is to say, no shadows, top, bottom or sides … It is of prime importance that the operator bend his every endeavor to getting clear, white light on every portion of the picture, and, having succeeded in this, if his machine be in proper adjustment, there is little more he can do save grind out the right speed. But don't forget this: the really good operator the one who really understands his business and wants to produce the best possible results, never takes his eye from the curtain from the time he starts until the tail piece comes into view.[1]

GARNET SAUNDERS: FILM KING OF TARANAKI

The shift in interest from live theatre to film and the opportunities this presented drew many into trying to cash in on the film business. As P.A. Harrison describes, outside of the Fuller and Hayward chains, it was a business attracting "innumerable, often part-time, small town and city suburbs exhibitors, operating either in single locations or local circuits".[2] One such independent entrepreneur was Garnet Hornby Saunders, who established a thriving film circuit in Taranaki.

Adelaide-born Saunders was a shoemaker by trade, a musician who played cornet in a brass band, and a showman by inclination. Working for Fitzgerald's circus as a musician he came to New Zealand in 1902, lured by the Waihi gold mines. With the opportunity to start a shoe repair business Saunders moved to New Plymouth in 1904 and, as Brian Scanlan wrote in the *Taranaki Herald*, "the town was never quite the same after he arrived".[3] He threw himself into the life of the town, joining Garry's Band as solo cornet player, before later becoming conductor, while also playing in the Taranaki Garrison Band. In 1910 he bought out the plant of the Hewitt Picture Company and set himself up as Saunders' Biograph Pictures, leasing the Theatre Royal for six months to project moving pictures when it wasn't needed for other shows. His wife Kitty

worked the ticket booth and Saunders played in the three-strong orchestra as well as managing the theatre.

> A new Warwick Biograph which is considered the best English-made machine has been
> purchased and arrangements have been made to obtain the very latest supply of films …
> There will be a strong orchestra each evening composed of Mr Golding (pianist), Mr Salt
> (violinist) and Mr Saunders (cornet).[4]

It was an immediate success. Included in the first programme was a Biograph production by then-unknown director D.W. Griffith, *A Corner in Wheat*, which is now regarded as one of his early classics. There is a dramatic final scene of a businessman suffocating and drowning in the wheat he had cornered at the expense of the poor.[5] Hundreds came to see film of Edward VII's funeral and the footage of the Jack Johnson–Stanley Ketchel heavyweight fight drew similar crowds, despite letters in the local papers from a concerned citizen who thought women had no place in an audience that watched "brutal punching".[6] At the times when the Theatre Royal was booked for other productions, Saunders showed films at Waitara and Stratford.

Saunders prospered with the town and in 1911, after a period in the Whiteley Hall, leased the Empire Theatre and started regular film screenings on 23 December 1911. Renamed the Empire Picture Palace it was the town's first continuous picture theatre. The success of the venture was marked by increasing his 'symphony orchestra' to four players. Hundreds attended the opening day's shows, which screened from 11 a.m. to 11 p.m. One of the first films that drew the crowds was French film-maker Victorin Jasset's three-reel film of the master criminal Zigomar, which followed on from the director's success with the *Nick Carter, King of Detectives* series.[7] This was three times the length and time of the standard one-reel 14-minute films of the day; although the time taken to show a reel would vary. Film projectors were hand-cranked and a skilled projectionist would judge the speed to the subject, and if necessary speed things up if time was short and they wanted to finish the programme. Studio Éclair's four Zigomar films were great successes, and three years later Kitty and Garnet's first-born son was nicknamed 'Zig'. Their children all grew up in the picture theatre, helping out until they were tired and then sleeping out in the back during performances.[8]

BRANDON HAUGHTON FILMS TARANAKI

Saunders was always looking for something new to draw the crowds, whether staging an attempt at the world record in endurance piano playing, employing acrobats or escape artists, or — with more enduring success — frequent films of local events. Caleb Wyatt, who himself became a film projectionist, recalled going to town in 1915 on a Saturday, market day in New Plymouth, and seeing "this big open car driving down Devon Street, Garnet Saunders driving it, a 35 mm movie camera fixed up in the back seat, and a man called Brandon Haughton turning the handle, filming everything".[9]

In 1915 Brandon Haughton ran the photo studio next door to the Empire Theatre and was a skilled and experienced cameraman. Haughton is a model for the many photographer/cameramen/projectionists who underpinned the film industry in New Zealand throughout the silent era.

Haughton was New Zealand-born from Wellington, but spent many years in Australia during which time he improbably claimed to have "produced the first film to be shown in Australasia that was of Australian manufacture".[10] In January 1906 he toured New Zealand

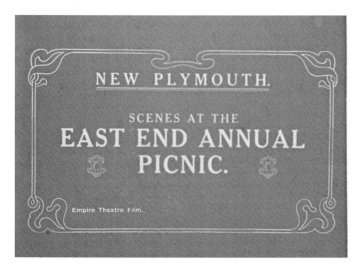

as the Biograph operator with Mr Roland Chubb's Biograph and Combination Company, where his singing skills were also appreciated. At the Phoenix Hall in Morrinsville, "Brandon Haughton fairly brought the house down with his new and splendid rendering of 'the Man behind,' 'St Louis,' and 'Girls, Girls, Girls,' and was encored many times".[11]

In 1907 Haughton was the 'Biograph Expert' with Will Perry's Biorama and toured with him for a number of seasons.[12] Here he met and married Ida Brady, one of the singing Brady sisters who were part of the show.[13] In 1909 he took over as manager of Pathé Pictures in Gisborne and imported the latest Pathé camera and film production equipment. In an interview with the *Poverty Bay Herald* he talked about his experience in film-making and also his approach to filming:

> Questioned as to what would form the subject of his first film here. Mr Haughton said in all probability it would be the Labor Day demonstration, which takes place next week. "That occasion," he added, "will supply me with any amount of scope for good work that will be of interest to our local audiences. I intend taking the procession in the morning, and to spend the afternoon in a visit to the Domain, where I expect to secure film of the sports, also a special panoramic picture of the spectators, as I know the public will be most anxious to see themselves on the screen, not as they appear as they consult the mirror, but as their friends see them walking about in daily life."[14]

In 1911 he worked as a cameraman for John Fuller and Sons but in January 1912 "Mr Brandon Haughton, biograph expert and camera artist" was engaged by Garnet Saunders for the Empire Theatre in New Plymouth. "It is the intention of the management of the Empire Theatre to secure a number of interesting films of local events each week."[15] Haughton worked as cameraman for Saunders, producing films attributed to the Empire Theatre Film Company and for the Egmont Film Company, neither of which were registered companies.

Saunders engaged Haughton to capture Taranaki life on film and in 1912 local events became a regular feature at the Empire. Most of these films have survived and each indicates Haughton's considerable skill and eye for a scene, with cleverly structured films edited to tell a story with the minimum of intertitles. *Scenes at the East End Annual Picnic, New Plymouth* was shot on 25 January 1912 and screened on 31 January.[16]

Left: *Scenes at the East End Annual Picnic,* filmed by Brandon Haughton for the Empire Theatre. NTSV F2655. (See colour section.)

Chewing gum race. Still from Brandon Haughton's *Scenes at the East End Annual Picnic,* 1912. NTSV F2655. (See colour section.)

Scenes at the East End Annual Picnic, New Plymouth. NTSV F2655.

🎦 *The Production of the Taranaki Herald and Budget.* NTSV F4106.

🎦 *Taranaki Jockey Club's Annual Meeting.* NTSV F1465.

Advertised as *New Plymouth at the Seaside*, it drew an "immense crowd".

> Long before 8 o'clock the pit and the unreserved part of the rest of the house was crowded … The building is meant to accommodate 630 people with seats. The number present last night when the 1ˢᵗ picture was thrown upon the screen must have been nearer 800 and the only disappointed ones in the huge crowd were those who could not gain admittance … As scene after scene was unfolded before the audience, parents joyfully recognised their own particular 'Jimmys' and 'Nellies' and some groups of merry makers gave vent to their feelings in little suppressed exclamations of satisfaction.[17]

Screened at the same time was *The Production of the Taranaki Herald and Budget* showing the complete process of putting out the newspaper.[18] "View of main building, office and staff; a peep at the editor; stereo room, linotype room, compositors' room; Foster single-reel printing press at work (printing capacity, 17,000 8-page papers an hour)." It is one of the rare surviving industrial films from the period and the advertising emphasised, "THE WHOLE FILM IS TONED THROUGHOUT".[19] The local reporter stressed the commitment that Saunders was making:

> The advantages that this class of film have as an advertising medium will clearly appeal to every resident that has any interest in the advancing of Taranaki. Enterprise is a much misused and libelled word, but it can certainly be credited to the manager of the Empire Theatre, as the erection of a plant to do this kind of work is extremely costly, and the expense of producing pictures is far heavier than the general public are aware.[20]

This was followed by the marvellous crowd scenes of the Taranaki Jockey Club's annual meeting filmed on 14 February 1912 and then developed overnight to be screened the following day.[21] As the *Taranaki Herald* reported, Saunders made sure that it capitalised on every local market before being sold to Fuller for national distribution. In this way New Zealand got to see the delights of New Plymouth, which proudly advertised itself as the "Garden of New Zealand".[22]

The linotype operator. Still from Brandon Haughton's *The Production of the Taranaki Herald and Budget*, 1912. NTSV F4106.

At the start. Still from Brandon Haughton's *Taranaki Circular Road Race*, 1912. NTSV F9312.

The whole picture is beautifully clear, and yet a further tribute to the Empire Theatre Enterprise. It is interesting to note that the famous Seaside Picture has already been shown in Waitara, Stratford, Inglewood, Eltham, Manaia and will next week be seen in Patea, Kaponga, Opunake and Hawera after which it goes to John Fuller and Sons, Wellington. That the Cup Picture will be an equally good advertisement for New Plymouth can be gauged from the fact that Mr Saunders has booked the picture in three towns before it was out of the developing bath.[23]

Saunders' filming was driven by his determination to fill his picture theatre. Any wider audience was a welcome by-product, particularly in terms of additional cash flow but always secondary to the need to keep his theatre seats full. His success spurred rivals, with films being shown by competitors at the Theatre Royal. In New Plymouth and throughout New Zealand, it was the financially astute cinema manager who kept his business going when many others chasing easy money on the latest craze went out of business.

TARANAKI CIRCULAR ROAD RACE

One film that was guaranteed to have New Zealand-wide interest was the second running of the annual Taranaki Circular Road Race around what was then Mt Egmont, now Mt Taranaki, a distance of over 104 miles (167 kilometres), which the organisers claimed made it the longest circular road race in the world.[24] It was run on 5 September 1912 with 57 of Australia and New Zealand's most experienced riders taking part, spurred by the prize of the Britannia Tyre Challenge Cup valued at 50 guineas, prize money of £50 and a gold medal valued at £5.

"An excellent series of kinematographic views were obtained by Mr Haughton, the expert for the Egmont Film Company, and these are being shown at the Empire Picture Palace."[25] Haughton ensured that the advertisers who sponsered the race all had their hoardings prominently featured, as are the place-getters with their prizes.

Last shown is A. Danielson of Palmerston North, nervously wiping his nose on his sleeve for the camera. As third-placed rider he won £10 cash and a 1912-model road racer.[26]

Taranaki Circular Road Race. NTSV F9312.

Boys and girls create intricate designs around the flagpole. Still from Brandon Haughton's *Grand School Carnival.* NTSV F4154.

GRAND SCHOOL CARNIVAL

Both the Theatre Royal and the Empire Theatre screened Haughton's film *Grand School Carnival* showing the Central School's "Grand Gymnastic, Equestrian, Military, Carnival" held at the Recreation Sports Ground, Pukekura Park, New Plymouth, on Thursday 21 November 1912. Saunders' Empire Theatre advertised it as a film taken by the Mt Egmont Film Company, while the Theatre Royal is a little more coy, saying that it was "Reproduced by local cinematographers". However, at a repeat screening in December the Theatre Royal management acknowledged that it was screened with Saunders' permission.[27]

The film captures the events of the day including the grand march.[28] The "Continuous Round of Gaiety from Noon till Sunset" ends with school children executing a series of involved and intricate movements around the maypole. It was all captured by Haughton and his camera positioned high in the terraces among the watching spectators.

The *Taranaki Daily News* reported:

> The picture taken by the local Egmont Film Company of the Central School Carnival last Thursday will be shown tonight at the Empire Theatre and the Theatre Royal. The picture is a very fine production, and outside of its local interest should prove a splendid advertisement for the progressive Egmont Film Company. It will interest our readers to know that his company also have in hand a film of Mt Egmont taken during the depth of winter, and another of the breakwater and wharf, including some magnificent rough-sea-scapes taken during the heavy gales some weeks ago. The first picture of Mt Egmont, also Pukekura Park and the Sea-Side Picnic has already been accepted by one of the leading British film agencies, and Mr Saunders has received advice that they will be pleased to receive and handle any and all of the company's future pictures. This means that the local pictures will receive worldwide screening.[29]

Grand School Carnival. NTSV F4154.

The Sports Recreation Ground at Pukekura Park, Mt Egmont and various scenes of Taranaki featured in Haughton's productions in 1912. The film *Scenes in Taranaki New Zealand,* which survives in the archive, with its panorama of the town, the local oil industry, Pukekura Park and "Waves breaking on the Coast" is not one of Haughton's films.[30] This was taken by the Wanganui-based cameraman Charles Newham.[31]

This spate of local production was not sustained. Locally made films were more expensive to make and became few and far between from 1913 on. Taranaki film-goers were fed the latest feature films from overseas and a steady diet of newsreels with the occasional New Zealand film. Brandon Haughton ran his photography studio next door to the Empire Theatre and this now became his main occupation. On the night of 31 October 1919 a fire destroyed his studio and equipment with his losses estimated at £600 in excess of his insurance cover.[32] In 1922 he moved his photography business to Hawera by purchasing an established studio in the town.[33] In 1928 he was in Wellington operating a studio in Riddiford Street offering "modern portraiture" at "moderate charges".[34]

The growing supply and variety of films allowed for regular changes in programme and this variety attracted regular patronage by families, for whom film-going became the regular weekly entertainment: having their night at the 'flicks' and booking the same seats each time. It prompted the growth of permanent picture theatres and was the start of a theatre-building boom.

THE KING'S THEATRE, WELLINGTON, NEW ZEALAND'S FIRST PURPOSE-BUILT 'PICTURE PALACE'

On Wednesday 16 March 1910 the King's Theatre opened in Wellington as New Zealand's first permanent purpose-built 'Picture Palace'.[35] This was one of the four picture theatres constructed by T.J. West's Picture Proprietary in association with local business interests in each main centre, in this case the veteran vaudeville and film show partnership of Linley and Donovan trading as the Royal Pictures Syndicate. The opening advertisements emphasised its comfort and safety. As the name suggests it was intended to be a theatre fit for a king.

The new theatre is fireproof and has a seating capacity for 1500 people, of which 800 seats have been apportioned to the dress circle and front stalls, in which divisions there are tip-up chairs of the latest patterns. In the back stalls there are comfortable seats with backs. The dress circle is noticeably spacious, with four passages each four feet wide; in fact, it is the first built in the Commonwealth or Dominion in accordance with the New London County Council by-law. The dress circle is also the first ferro-concrete one built in this part of the world. Every seat is screwed to the floor. There is no danger from a stampede as there are three exits to Little Taranaki street on the ground floor, four exits into the side passage on the ground floor, and three exits from the dress circle. The theatre could empty in two minutes … Electric lighting is installed everywhere … The biograph plant is enclosed in a ferro concrete box outside the auditorium at the rear of the dress circle, with walls 18 inches in thickness and with drop shutters, and a steel door for the operator. This will prevent risk from fire at the lantern.[36]

Souvenir programme from the opening of the King's Theatre, Wellington, 16 March 1910. Original held in NTSV collection.

 *Scenes in Taranaki New Zealand.* NTSV F55926.

Construction of Queen's Theatre, Hereford Street, Christchurch, 1911. Steffano Francis Webb, G-3988-1/1, ATL, Wellington.

On Wednesday 16 March 1910 the Royal Pictures Syndicate's King's Theatre opened in Dixon Street, Wellington, as New Zealand's first permanent purpose-built 'Picture Palace'. The syndicate was a partnership between T.J. West and Linley and Donovan. Bennie Album, F139928-1/2, ATL, Wellington.

Fire remained a real risk particularly with the smaller travelling film shows in local halls. The *Southland Times* reported on the first and perhaps the last film show of a would-be film entrepreneur at Waikaia in Southland.

> After a couple of films had been exhibited 'bang' went the machine, and acetylene gas threw fire in all directions. The audience, which was of fair dimensions, made a wild rush for the doors, and a crush ensured, in which some ladies fainted, and one was trampled on. Several members of the audience were singed by the flames, but the fire was speedily extinguished and no great damage done, except that the machine was wrecked and the operator received some nasty burns.[37]

Throughout New Zealand local authorities brought in fire restrictions. In Dunedin the city by-laws imposed strict conditions on the use of "any machine or the display of animated pictures in which a light is passed through a rapidly moving inflammable film".[38]

The King's Theatre opening was a grand affair with Prime Minister Sir Joseph Ward and Lady Ward in the audience. Silk souvenir programmes were given out and many were turned away from the full house. West's and Royal Pictures relinquished their lease on His Majesty's Theatre the previous night, and not to be outdone this was taken over by John Fuller and Sons, as the entertainment column of the *Evening Post* made very clear. "'Fuller than ever' was reported at His Majesty's Theatre before eight o'clock last night." Fuller, having provided the Royal Syndicate at His Majesty's with film for the previous two years, was determined to fight the threat posed by the King's Theatre that now came under Hayward's distribution chain.[39]

SOUNDS OF THE SILENTS

West provided an orchestra of six players for the opening of King's Theatre and reflected the reality that silent film was rarely silent. Sydney-based Louis de Groen, 'Australia's Souza', was West's chief musical director, responsible for the 'de Groen's Orchestra' for each of West's theatres and touring circuits throughout Australia and New Zealand.[40] De Groen, through regular visits, personally supervised the standard of each of his orchestras.

> Fitting the music to the picture is an art of some difficulty … I have had a lot of experience at it since joining Mr West … A great point is contrast in tone and time. By attending to this the music may be made to interpret the emotions of the actors in the little plays depicted on the screen.[41]

It was rare to have a film show with no musical accompaniment and it was likely that in these circumstances there would be a master of ceremonies talking to what the audience could see on film. Music was integral to every film screening, from the three- to four-person orchestra under Garnet Saunders at the Empire in New Plymouth, which was mirrored more or less at picture theatres throughout New Zealand, to the single pianist doing the day shift at the continuous picture houses.

A travelling showman may be restricted to a gramophone, or a locally-hired pianist contracted on a regular basis when the picture show came to town. Competition bred sophistication in the picture theatre trappings offered to the public, and the size and accomplishment of the theatre orchestra was one of the draws. Songs and music were often interspersed between films in the programme, as well as playing accompaniment to each film. In 1908 Fuller's Pictures engaged the Edgar Collins' Orchestral Band to accompany the films in Wellington, and in 1912 for Hayward's Pictures in Wellington "the Adelphi Ladies Orchestra discoursed sweet music".[42]

The larger theatres had sophisticated sound effects behind the screen that unerringly captured the patter of rain, thunder and wind, or the clatter of horses' hooves. Some films came with recommended musical accompaniment and, in the case of the D.W. Griffith epics, with their own score. George Tarr had the incidental music of New Zealand composer Alfred Hill performed when he toured *Hinemoa* in 1914–15, and as pictures grew in length and sophistication greater care was taken with musical arrangements played for them.[43]

The boom in picture theatres offered employment for musicians who previously feared redundancy with the downturn in live theatre. We can see this with L.D. Austin's contract with the People's Picture Palace in Manner's Street, Wellington, where he was to perform as the night pianist for a period of six months from 9 June 1915, and then on a monthly basis, for the sum of £5 a week.[44] One suspects that the pianist on the day shift at the People's Picture Palace did not get the same money, but the work was there and every theatre had its music and musicians.

Thirty-eight-year-old London-born Louis Daily Irving Austin was entranced by theatre from boyhood, his father being secretary and literary associate to the actor and theatre manager Sir Henry Irving, who became Louis' godfather. An accomplished pianist and theatre habitué, Austin taught piano in London before marrying Hilda, a barmaid (or as the entry in the *Dictionary of New Zealand Biography* primly puts it "a licensed victualler's assistant at the Railway Hotel in Bromley").[45] Together they migrated to Australia in 1908 where he played for picture houses in Newcastle and then at an open-air picture theatre at Manly.

Louis Daily Irving Austin, a professional musician who played the piano for picture theatres. Above is his contract with People's Palace Pictures for £5 a week for the position of night pianist. Contract, 41468_ac_1_1; Image, 41472_ac_1_1, ATL, Wellington.

View of the exterior of the Globe Continuous Pictures theatre, 260 High Street, Christchurch. The theatre opened on 20 May 1912 with seating for 329. Steffano Francis Webb, G-3991–1/1, ATL, Wellington.

An unknown projectionist with his hand-cranked projector, possibly at the New Empire Theatre in Nelson. Frederick Nelson Jones Collection, G-11360-1/1, ATL, Wellington.

One of his Manly stories relays a day when a southerly bluster blew away the music sheets, stopping the orchestra but he improvised and played on through the film. His reward was a contract at West's King's Theatre in Christchurch, New Zealand, which he took up in 1910.[46] After two-and-a-half years he and his wife moved to Wellington where Austin became "pianist-conductor of a Grand Symphony Orchestra — cornet, violin and piano — which played for one of Fuller's cinemas in the old skating rink in Vivian Street. On crowded nights the screen was placed in the middle of the rink and patrons sat on both sides, with those behind it holding mirrors to correct the image."[47]

After an interlude touring with J.C. Williamson, Austin found work playing the 'night piano' from 6.30 to 11 p.m. with the People's Picture Palace, which showed continuous pictures.[48] In 1915 Austin played at the King's Theatre in the afternoons and Everybody's Picture Theatre in the evenings doing whatever was needed, dependent on the film. Sometimes he was a solo pianist and occasionally musical director for big shows such as *Neptune's Daughter* in October 1915, which featured the Australian swimmer Annette Kellerman. The advertising announced that music would be provided by an "Augmented Orchestra" with "Magnificent Music specially arranged and conducted by L.D. Austin".[49]

By 1911 picture shows were "everywhere ... in the city and suburbs, and all of them doing big business".[50] Continuous pictures were being shown in specially built cinemas. At the start of the picture boom prints of films could be bought by any exhibitor and it was a race to get the films to the audience first, "but by 1911 leading exhibitors such as Fuller's Pictures and Hayward's Picture Enterprises had obtained exclusive rights to certain films and screened them in the chains of theatres under their control and rented them to independent exhibitors. The pattern of cinema organization was established."[51]

PICTURE THEATRE PEOPLE

The picture industry attracted a particular breed of people who were often
initially employed for a technical skill and then found that they had the
entrepreneurship to flourish in the business. Mr E. Trevor Hill was one such
who moved ashore, after working as a ship's electrician, to take the job of
electrician and operator for Henry Hayward's Enterprises. His first position was
at the Empire Theatre in Auckland, a suburban theatre seating 1000 patrons
with tickets a shilling in the circle, sixpence in the stalls and three pence for
children at the Saturday matinee. Hill saw advertising as the key to running a
successful cinema. 'YMCA' became his motto — 'You Must Constantly Advertise'.
At the Empire he started what he believed was the first house magazine in the
Dominion, *The Empire Call,* and then with Phil Hayward filmed some of the
news film for *The Auckland Animated News,* which was the first topical newsreel in New Zealand.

    His next move was to the Foresters' Hall at Birkenhead, which brought in the money 'like
hot cakes', before becoming operator-manager of Fuller's Wide World Pictures at the Royal
Pictures in Dargaville, which "was down and out and losing money fast". With his gift for
advertising he turned it round, giving himself the title 'The Film Man of the North' into the
bargain. In 1914 Hill was promoted to take over the newly opened King's Theatre in Thames,
a Fuller's theatre, which he ran with a staff of six: himself as manager, an operator, pianist, two
checkers and Mr G.R. Maltman who did the programme advertising, producing the weekly
theatre magazine.[52]

    The nature of the film shows were changing, with 'Star' or 'Feature' films — almost always
an overseas fictional narrative — fronting the programme, supported by a number of shorter
films including comedies, scenics and news-events, and it was here that local content remained
important. These local event films rarely if ever scooped a news item, that was the role of the

FEATURES

Every Week Beginning March 8th

WEDNESDAY, MARCH 12th, 1913   FRIDAY, MARCH 14th, 1913

"The Grim Toll of War"
Two Reel Kalem.

FREDERIC DOUGLAS returns from a diplomatic mission abroad and falls in love with his daughter's governess. Just before the Civil War breaks out they are married. The wife endeavors to hide the identity of her brother, Clel, who is a Secret Service agent. Clel secretly visits his sister. The meeting is witnessed by Douglas who, believing his wife unfaithful, enlists, receiving a commission of Colonel.

Ellis is captured by the Confederates, but escapes closely pursued by the enemy and makes his way towards Colonel Douglas' camp. Mistaken for a spy, he is mortally wounded. After discovering his error the Colonel personally rescues Ellis and brings him to camp. A battle ensues. The Confederates are driven back. Ellis has been carrying a letter written by his sister. Douglas finds it and learns the relationship between the two.

The Colonel returns home after the war and endeavors to make amends by a life of devotion to his faithful wife.

"Loved by a Maori Chieftess"
Two Reel Melies.

A NOVEL and spectacular film produced in New Zealand and enacted throughout by Maoris, under the personal direction of Gaston Melies.

Just after the Maori uprising of 1870, when the bitter feeling against the British was growing, a young English trapper was taken captive by a Maori tribe. The influence of the Chief's daughter who loved him to the point where she believed him the man she was predestined to marry, saved him from death by burning. Their escape through the treacherous land of hot geysers, recapture and final union are told in a series of exciting scenes that make the film a real thriller.

TO BE RELEASED SOON

"Notre Dame"
(Patheplay)

A notable production of Victor Hugo's famous work, in three parts—three full reels of *colored photography*.

"Exposure of the Land Swindlers"
(Kalem)

A sensational motion picture masterpiece with Detective Wm. J. Burns and Alice Joyce in the leading roles. 3 reels.

FILM CO.

Moving Picture World, 8 March 1913, p. 1037.

press, but they put an image to current events in the same way as the illustrated weeklies. They also placed local audiences at the heart of what was happening in the town, showing public involvement in the annual fetes and shows, at the races and at visits and openings by local dignitaries in a way that papers could not.

CONSOLIDATION — NEW ZEALAND PICTURE SUPPLIES LIMITED

On 28 April 1913 John Fuller and Sons, Hayward's Picture Enterprises and J.D. Williams — the major film distribution and theatre-owning companies — formed New Zealand Picture Supplies Limited, making it the dominant firm in the New Zealand film distribution industry, providing film to both the Hayward and Fuller chain of theatres, which continued to trade as before but with the exclusive rights to the major overseas film titles guaranteed.

This partnership mirrored a worldwide trend of consolidation in the film industry. In Australia Johnson and Gibson had merged with J. and N. Tait to form Amalgamated Pictures in March 1911, which merged with West's and Spencer's to form the General Film Co. of Australia in November 1912. In January 1913 General Films merged with The Greater J.D. Williams Amusement Company to form the exhibition company Union Theatres and the distribution company Australasian Films Ltd, controlling 29 theatres.[53] The 'Combine', as it was known, dominated Australian film distribution and exhibition, but retained its existing distribution agreement with New Zealand Picture Supplies in New Zealand.

West's Pictures acquired the sole rights in Australia and New Zealand to the distribution of Pathé films. The production of the *Pathé Animated Gazette (Australasian Edition)* continued under the 'Combine' and it absorbed the various weekly newsreels distributed by member companies.[54]

The formation of the 'Combine' had a major impact on the production of Australian multi-reel narrative film that had prospered since the Tait brothers' production of *The Story of the Kelly Gang* (1906), which was made in partnership with the firm of Millard Johnson and W.A. Gibson. Both firms previously successfully collaborated in touring Charles Urban's multi-reel *Living London* throughout Australasia in 1906, and now this sophisticated four- or five-reel film on the exploits of Ned Kelly and his gang exceeded that success, drawing huge audiences in both Australia and New Zealand in 1906–07.[55] The years 1906–12 saw a period of innovative Australian film-making in multi-reel narrative film equal to the best of Europe and usually in advance of American and British production at the time.

This suddenly ceased as the 'Combine' concentrated on distribution and limited production of actualities and news-events, refusing to distribute Australian films shot by independent film-makers.[56] The establishment of the 'Combine' and the merging of Spencer, West and Williams' film interests saw West's name gradually disappear from public awareness in Australia and New

Zealand. No longer the dominant force and no longer a theatre-front name in Australia, he retained his share in the 'Combine' and continued to run what was a comparatively small circuit of theatres in Britain from his London office until his death in December 1916.[57]

It was Henry Hayward who paid tribute to T.J West, his former partner "who may be described as the father of the picture show business in Australasia … Deceased was recognised as a very successful businessman whose word was his bond. He was also deeply religious and during his life gave very largely to charities. During the years Mr Hayward was in partnership with Mr West there was no legal agreement, the only document being a few lines written on a sheet of notepaper, which was never after referred to, as there was not a single dispute between the two."[58]

GASTON MÉLIÈS VISITS NEW ZEALAND

New Zealand-based fictional films were extremely rare events. But in 1912 the exotic nature of New Zealand as a location drew Gaston Méliès (older brother of Georges), who with the diminishing interest in Méliès fantasy films, had gone out on his own and set up Star Films in the United States. Initially its purpose was to ensure an end to the illegal copying and sale of his younger brother's films, but from 1909 he went into film production, which increased as his brother's film output declined.[59] His Star Film Company in 1910 produced a film a week, usually a one-reel western melodrama first from San Antonio, Texas and then from California. In 1912 in a bold attempt to reinvigorate the output of his company, Méliès sailed the Pacific visiting Tahiti, New Zealand, Rarotonga, Australia, Java, Cambodia and then Japan. Méliès set out with 17 members of his company, his cameras and equipment searching for novel ideas for films — "there is nothing for it to get something fresh, but to sail on the Pacific for the land of the sunny south".[60]

Arriving in Wellington on the *Aorangi* from Tahiti on 12 September 1912 Méliès willingly told the press of his plans to film stories in a New Zealand setting. "The scenarios are written by an expert journalist, Mr Ed. Mitchell, who travels with the company and composes appropriate stories and scenes for the occasion … It is understood that the chief scene of operations will be Rotorua, where the Maoris will, no doubt, participate gladly in the drama to be unfolded among lakes and geysers." Méliès stressed that his "pictures will be not only dramatic, but also educational, and there are two different sets of apparatus with the expedition. The films are developed in a portable darkroom and forwarded to New York where they will be printed and distributed."[61]

Méliès met with Mr B. Wilson, T.E. Donne's successor as the general manager of the Department of Tourist and Health Resorts. No doubt on Wilson's recommendation he hired the journalist James Cowan "the authority on Maori legend and custom" to act as "general advisor and interpreter to the Méliès Picture Expedition".[62] On arrival in Rotorua he met and worked with the Reverend F. Bennett's concert party who provided him with his Maori cast and whose members adapted easily to the demands of film-making.[63] Sadly he found that New Zealand as a setting did not live up to his hopes. He had troubles with his American actors, most of whom he sacked, and relied on Bennett to provide his principal characters.[64] He wrote to his son Paul: "We're in a foul country, cold, rainy, windy, and we can only work between the downpours, but it's so interesting because of the Maoris, their villages and the geysers."[65]

Moving Picture World reported that while "dramatic picture stories were being made at and around Lake Rotorua, numerous educational films were being taken by other members of the Méliès staff in various parts of New Zealand … Altogether New Zealand, as it was and is, will be shown with thoroughness never attempted before and only possible now with the advancement of cinematograph enterprise."[66]

Gaston Méliès with his Maori
cast drawn from Reverend F.
Bennett's concert party
at Whakarewarewa.
NTSV, Méliès, Gaston [2]
No. S5962.

Three narrative films — the two-reel *Loved by a Maori Chieftess* and *How Chief Te Ponga Won His Bride*, and a one-reel film version of the popular Maori legend *Hinemoa* — were filmed in Rotorua, with the star role played by Maata (Martha) Horomona.[67] Méliès wrote that "I had only to explain very slowly to Martha what I wanted from her and she would immediately do it with a natural grace."[68]

The films received favourable comment in *Moving Picture World*: "One will find in these folklore stories a quality something like the stories of Homer. A Maori girl loves a warrior and finds a way to make him win her in spite of her father. It is beautiful and delightful and we can find nothing but good to say of it."[69] *Loved by a Maori Chieftess* was particularly well reviewed and "will be admired by all … who are interested in the wonders of remote lands and in the customs and character of a people so wholly and strangely different from ourselves".[70] *How Chief Te Ponga Won His Bride* received less attention, being "Another of this companies folk-lore stories played by Maori people in New Zealand … The photography is clear in most of the scenes: in some it is poor." It was a split-reel film sharing a reel with *A Trip to the Waitomo Caves of New Zealand* "giving some views of New Zealand back-country and a glimpse or two of a cave".[71]

Méliès' New Zealand scenic films, mostly shot by Mr George Scott, all featured prominently in the trade press with full page advertisements. *The Maoris of New Zealand* was: "An interesting study of one of the most wonderful but least known, races in existence."[72]

Intersection of Riddiford and Rintoul streets, Newtown, Wellington, 1909–11, advertising Fuller's Star Pictures in Newtown. Photographer: S.C. Smith Collection, G19563-1/1, ATL, Wellington.

A Trip through the 'North Island' of New Zealand from Auckland to Wellington showed "in detail the beautiful city of Auckland and its environs; the Kauri log industry; a New Zealand ostrich farm; a present day Maori village; and the great seaport of Wellington — the outlet of New Zealand".[73]

None of the films from the Pacific venture were initially released in New Zealand, although Méliès received an offer from Hayward's Picture Enterprises to take three or four copies per week at £17 per 1000 feet, which was bettered by J.D. Williams in Sydney who negotiated the exclusive rights for Australasia. For some reason neither offer was finalised, and so New Zealand never saw the most concentrated burst of narrative and scenic film-making ever undertaken in this country.[74]

The films were released through Vitagraph in the United States, Méliès having sold 50% of his company in a deal that included all of Méliès' negatives, with Vitagraph taking over the distribution.[75] *Loved by a Maori Chieftess* was released on 14 March 1913 and was met with a reasonable response with 50 prints being sold.[76]

Hinemoa was released on 27 March 1913. *The River Wanganui* went out as a split-reel with the melodrama *Stolen Tribute to the King*, filmed in Tahiti and released on 3 April 1913. *The Maoris of New Zealand* was released on 10 April 1913 as a one-reel. *A Trip to the Waitomo Caves of New Zealand* was released as a split-reel with *How Chief Te Ponga Won His Bride* on 24 April 1913. *A Trip through the 'North Island' of New Zealand from Auckland to Wellington* was released as one reel on 8 May 1913.[77] The one-reel documentary *In the Land of Fire* was the last of Méliès' New Zealand films to be released on 21 August 1913.[78] By this time Star Films was in trouble and the number of prints sold plummeted; the releases from July onwards sold on average nine prints of each film.[79] It was financial disaster. The 60-year-old Méliès, after filming in Japan, returned to the United States. The strains of the tour "proved too much for his health" and he "was a wreck of his former self".[80] He closed the company and sold the studio and equipment before retiring to Corsica where he died in 1915.[81]

Gaston Méliès' visit was a flicker of overseas film interest that would be repeated fitfully in the years ahead, but his films were only belatedly seen by New Zealand audiences and, with increasingly meagre sales, by few people overseas.[82]

Charlie Newham films Wanganui

Something may here be said about topicals, or "newsy" films, including such things as processions, pageants, reviews, athletic displays, opening ceremonies, cricket or football matches, and so on. Quite the most important consideration with such subjects is the selection of a good standpoint. Sometimes this may be arranged beforehand by application in the right quarter, or by making friends with officials, but more often the operator has to put up with the best he can get and to take his chance with the public.[1]

PATHÉ FRÈRES COMES TO NEW ZEALAND

Pathé Frères in France was the first company to produce a regular film journal of topical events with its weekly 15-minute *Pathé-Journal* in 1908, which logically followed on from the establishment of its chain of picture theatres. Pathé established an office in Australia in July 1909 and its representative, Monsieur Leopold Sutto, visited New Zealand and discussed filming New Zealand scenes with the Department of Tourist and Heath Resorts.[2]

By 1910 Pathé Frères had the lion's share of topical and scenic film production in Australia and in the same year introduced its regular weekly film newsreel. There was a strong link between Pathé and T.J. West and his picture theatre chain in Australia. As we have seen, West continued to emphasise local films shot by his camera teams in his programmes in Australia. By late 1909 West "appeared to have signed the world's (then) largest producing concern, Pathé Frères, to what we would now call a 'city first run' agreement for Australia and this gave him exclusive access to the Film d' Art series of narrative films distributed by Pathé. West thus became the first Australian exhibitor to feature Pathé's films of Australian industries made for the Commonwealth government."[3] The Hayward chain in New Zealand also benefited from this link as Hayward and West "made mutual arrangement for the joint purchase of what film we could purchase, which lasted through the rapid growth of pictures until they practically swept both the legitimate drama and vaudeville out of the payable market of entertainment".[4]

Opposite page: A cameraman moves position after filming the parade of school cadets visiting HMS *New Zealand* alongside the wharf in Lyttelton. It was taken on Saturday 23 May 1913 and was published in *The Weekly Press* of 28 May 1913. *Christchurch Press* Collection, G2284-1/1, ATL, Wellington.

Pathé was voracious in its demands for local content to feed into its worldwide network. In establishing itself in Australia Pathé sent out its operators to local theatres in Australia and New Zealand to shoot local news events and scenic films.[5] Small towns were asked to underwrite the cost of the cameraman, with the lure of putting the town on the map with the possibility of the film being syndicated through Pathé to the Australasian market. There was also the prospect of excerpts being included in the *Pathé Animated Gazette*, the British edition of the Pathé newsreel that started in 1910. This was adapted by T.J. West in Australia to *West's Journal of Daily Events* and released on an occasional basis with local items included. This was absorbed into the *Pathé Animated Gazette (Australasian Edition)* and released weekly from 28 November 1910 as a collection of local items covering mainly Australia, with some New Zealand inclusions. The newsreel was of variable length but usually about a ten minute duration. In Australia it was colloquially known as *The Australian Gazette* and after May 1914 this became its official title. It became *The Australasian Gazette* in 1916.[6]

Mr T. Gerald Fitzgerald of Pathé Frères established a branch office in Wellington in June 1911 with the expressed intention of seeking government support in advertising New Zealand to the world through the medium of scenic films as well as working on a scheme to show educational films in state schools.[7]

FRANK BARRETT FILMS NEW ZEALAND

W. Franklyn Barrett, a pivotal figure in film-making in Australia and New Zealand, was one of the cameramen contracted by Pathé from 1909 to 1911. We last met him as W. Franklyn

Walter Franklyn Barrett, one of New Zealand's film pioneers. *Australian Dictionary of Biography.*

Brown who with his elder brother, John Henry Brown, toured the film of the visit of the Duke and Duchess of Cornwall and York through New Zealand in late 1901. His brother was initially the prominent cameraman in the pair, but filming and film exhibition became Frank's overwhelming passion, while his brother concentrated on his photography business.

In 1901 Frank's photographs won a Thornton-Pickard camera prize worth £15. This led to his returning to England where he worked for the Charles Urban Trading Company Ltd during which time he sold Urban a number of scenic films. He spent 1904–05 in Australia and then on his return he lived at 180 Willis Street, Wellington, with his brother. In 1905 he gave his occupation as 'musician', although he was very active in film production and projection with various touring companies, including his own.[8] It was in this period that 'Wally' Brown became 'Frank' Barrett.

From very early on Barrett experimented with fictional narratives. In 1902–03 he and his brother most likely shot the comedy *Ally Sloper at Days Bay*, also advertised as *Ally Sloper's Half-Holiday*, which was based on a popular English comic character that was toured with a number of the Brown brothers' films with Harry Hall's Entertainers. In the same period he made a fictional film of *A Message from Mars*, Robert Ganthony's very popular stage play that the Charles Hawtrey Theatre Company toured through New Zealand to packed houses in the same year.[9] The film was screened by the Chas Cooper and W.J. Macdermott Imperial Biograph Company, one of the stalwarts among the touring picture show companies in New Zealand at the time. But, while the film was listed in the advertising, it was never given top billing.

The funeral cortege of the late Right Hon. R.J. Seddon leaves St Paul's Cathedral in Wellington, 21 June 1906, as a cameraman captures the scene. Postcard Jones & Coleman publishers, Collection Te Papa Tongarewa.

'KING DICK'S' FUNERAL

Barrett travelled throughout New Zealand and Australia in 1906 with the Wide-world Pantoscope Company, which again included his own films, billing himself as "Australia's first operator".[10] One of the films featured during the New Zealand leg of the tour was his film of 'King Dick' Seddon's funeral in Wellington.[11] It was first shown the day after the funeral at the Opera House, Palmerston North, on 22 June 1906. "The films were taken by the Company's own operator and the rare achievement will be effected to-night of enabling the people of Palmerston to witness the pictorial reproduction of the great event within a few hours of its taking place."[12]

On Thursday 21 June 1906 the funeral cortege of Richard John Seddon made its way from Parliament grounds en route to St Paul's Cathedral through streets massed with mourning New Zealanders.

The company capitalised on public interest in Seddon's death by also showing "pictures of the returning footballers to Auckland, in which the late Premier is a prominent figure. This is the last living picture of Mr Seddon and was taken by the Company's own operator on their latest machine."[13] In fact, the All Blacks arriving in Auckland was taken by Brandon Haughton, but obviously purchased by Barrett and screened in Wellington where he also showed a selection of his New Zealand films, including that of Seddon's funeral, with his own touring show Globe Syndicate Pictures for a six-day season at His Majesty's Theatre.[14]

In 1908 Barrett travelled throughout Australia, filming life on the trawling boats in the Bass Strait, the wool industry courtesy of Dalgety and Company, surfing at Manly and Coogee beaches in Sydney and taking film of industrial meetings in Melbourne.[15]

OPERA   HOUSE.

NEXT

MONDAY, TUESDAY, WEDNESDAY.
June 25, 26, 27.

WIDE-WORLD

LIVING PICTURES.
LIVING PICTURES.
LIVING PICTURES.
LIVING PICTURES.
LIVING PICTURES.

The Pictures that have created such a sensation at the

TOWN HALL, WELLINGTON.

Thousands are talking of them, and their return visit is already eagerly looked for.
The Press says they are the best Pictures ever seen in New Zealand.

THE RETURN OF THE FOOTBALLERS to Auckland, with a striking Picture of

THE LATE PREMIER

in a prominent position. This is the last living picture taken of him.

FUNERAL SCENES

at the Interment of the late Right Hon. R. J. Seddon, P.C., specially taken by our own operator.

ILLUSTRATED SONGS

by Miss NOVELLO, the famous Australian Contralto, and many others.

ADMISSION—3s., 2s., 1s.
Box plan at H. I. Jones and Son's.

WORLD-WIDE PANTOSCOPE COMPANY.

Wanganui Chronicle,
22 June 1906, p. 7.

 Funeral Procession of The Late Rt Hon. R.J. Seddon. NTSV F31276.

View from above a train, with three steam engines, rounding a bend on the Rimutaka Incline, showing the special middle track required for the Fell system, c.1910. This was one of the scenes filmed by W.F. Barrett during his time in New Zealand. Photographer: Albert Percy Godber. APG-0151-1/2-G, ATL, Wellington.

BARRETT DOES THE COUNTRY

In December 1909 Barrett was back in New Zealand to make a series of scenics and travelogues for Pathé's Melbourne office. His arrival, particularly as a former Wellington resident, was reported in the *Evening Post*. It announced that he was in New Zealand on behalf of the French cinematograph firm, Pathé Frères, Paris.

He is going to "do the country" with a ninety-five pound camera. Beginning at the West Coast Sounds, which he will reach by steamer, he will go overland along "the finest walk in the world" to the lakes. After that he will visit the Franz Josef glacier, the Westport coal mines, Nelson and the French Pass in order to take "Pelorus Jack." Then he will go northward into the Kauri country of Farthest Auckland, and take timber subjects from the tree to the finished plank; also the gum-digging industry will be dealt with. Rotorua and its Maori life and volcanic incident will receive cinematographic treatment, and Mr. Barrett will work southward via the Wanganui River in a canoe. The Rimutaka Incline will find its place on the film and suitable agricultural subjects will receive due attention. After New Zealand Mr. Barrett will go to New Guinea in Sir Rupert Clarke's yacht in order to "do" that gentleman's rubber plantations. Fiji, Samoa, and Rarotonga will follow. The finished pictures as they appear on the screen will be seen in their natural colours — the outcome of a process upon which Pathé Freres have been working for some time.[16]

During this visit and until his return to Australia in July 1910, Barrett shot a series of films for Pathé Frères, two of which survive in the Ngā Taonga Sound & Vision archives and are characteristic of the material that Pathé sought for worldwide distribution. The two films, *Across the Mountain Passes of New Zealand* and *Coasts of New Zealand*, exemplify Barrett's skills

Coasts of New Zealand.
NTSV F41776.

as a cameraman and his eye for framing a scene. Released in Pathécolor, they show the "softly
coloured land filmed for others to see". A perfect advertisement for the mystery and adventure
offered to the intrepid tourist who would journey to this distant land of New Zealand.[17]

In his interview with the *Evening Post* reporter, Barrett stressed the importance of the
Pathé approach to film production and we gain a glimpse of the process by which Pathé Frères
dominated the pre-war film market throughout the world. "From Mr. Barrett, who has worked
in the Pathé studio in Paris, it was learned that every picture taken, no matter where or on what
subject, is 'edited' by M. Charles Pathé and passed or rejected. Afterwards it is examined and
directions given for its printing, the length of exposure and other details being attached. The
brains of three people only are concerned in any picture — namely, those of the photographer,
the 'editor', and the examiner, in that order. The rest is all automatic. There is one chemical
formula, one pattern lens, one type of camera for use all over the world. Everything, in fact, is
standardised in order to secure absolute uniformity in results. The gigantic business works like
clockwork, yet in Paris alone over 2000 hands are employed."[18]

Barrett's filming tour through New Zealand attracted great interest and was reported in
the local papers. It provides a running commentary on his progress and captures the intensity
of the filming and the bubbling enthusiasm of the cameraman who is besotted by what he
witnessed and filmed.

Asked for a brief outline of the views he had taken, Mr Barrett told the *Dominion* that he went
round the Sounds on the first trip of the Waikare and got some splendid bits of Milford Sound;
bottled up the scenery from Sandfly Point to Lake Ada; and took the Giant's Gate Fall and the
Bowen Falls. The full view of the Bowen Falls he took from the steamer's deck. Then he went

Still from W. Franklyn Barrett's *Across the Mountain Passes of New Zealand.* NTSV F10078 (see colour section).

ashore and clambered up a 1000 feet, and got a splendid section of the top section of the falls — the elbow. Several panoramas of the different sounds were taken — they should be magnificent pictures. Returning, Mr Barrett travelled to Christchurch — took several street scenes, Cathedral Square on New Year's Day, boating on the Avon, trotting at Plumpton Park, a cycle meeting at Lancaster Park, and an exposition of wire jumping by some 'chasers just outside Christchurch. This is a novelty as far as other countries are concerned.

Barrett then left for the West Coast. The torrential rain in the Otira Gorge prevented any filming and he went on to Hokitika.

There he was waited on by the Westland Scenic Society, who desired him to make a trip to the Franz Josef Glacier, and offered to pay all expenses for the expedition. Mr Barrett did not intend to go so far down, but he thought the offer so generous and patriotic (as against some quite opposite views he had encountered in some quarters of New Zealand) that he "took it on," and was not in the least sorry that he did.

Barrett took every opportunity to film.

An industrial picture was secured at Malfroy's sawmill at Hoko, near Hokitika, from the felling of a tree to the plank stage after it leaves the mill and is stacked for seasoning. Some good views were also taken in the Buller Gorge and the Valley of the Murchison. Throughout the coach trip, Mr Barrett was franked through by Mr Newman, the coach proprietor, who declined to allow Mr Barrett to pay his fare. Mr Newman also placed any variety of conveyance at Mr Barrett's disposal when in Nelson.

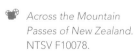

Across the Mountain Passes of New Zealand. NTSV F10078.

The highlight of his extended filming tour was in the ship voyage through French Pass.

> Perhaps the most interesting picture secured throughout the trip was that of "Pelorus Jack" taken from the trip of the *Pateena* from Nelson on Friday last. The ship's officers very kindly rigged a large platform over the side of the bow of the vessel, and as "Jack" kept faith with the ship a splendid view of this unique denizen of the deep was caught. Mr Barrett said that he got about 150 feet of the film, so that the incredulity with which the story of "Pelorus Jack" has been received elsewhere is likely to be permanently removed through Pathé Frères.[19]

The generosity of Barrett's patrons was well rewarded in the films that survive. *Across the Mountain Passes of New Zealand*, New Zealand's earliest known surviving colour print, is a wonderful example of Barrett's filming and of Pathé's production and colouring techniques. It shows Newman's coach and horses in the rugged beauty of the Buller Gorge. The coach passes through the gold-mining settlement of Lyell carrying passengers and collecting the mail with "diligence" along the banks of the "glittering river."[20]

Coasts of New Zealand includes the glacier and alpine scenes that Barrett described to the *Dominion* reporter. This includes the shots of the dolphin 'Pelorus Jack' as the animal accompanied the SS *Pateena* as it steamed through French Pass. The films screened throughout New Zealand in the Hayward and Fuller theatres in 1911.[21]

LIVING WANGANUI

On 30 June 1910 Frank Barrett wrote from Wanganui on Pathé Frères letterhead to Maurice Bertel at Pathé's Melbourne office.

> By this mail I am forwarding a parcel of film for development. I cannot get a darkroom here … the film will be slightly underexposed as there was bad light. I have tested each parcel and I find that by forcing the development a little there is quite enough to make a good print.
> I am leaving New Zealand for Australia on 8 July, and I can assure you I shall be glad to get back. In N.Z. the weather is something frightful — rain and floods everywhere.

> Please do your best with these films for me. It is needless to ask that, for I know you always
> do — but the people of this town have paid the expenses of the trip, and I should like to have
> something to show them.[22]

In August 1910 Henry Hayward continued the *Living New Zealand* series of films that had
drawn from the stock of New Zealand Government films with the *First Series of Pathé Frères
Living New Zealand*. Titled *Living Wanganui*, this is almost certainly Barrett's film. "See the
Glorious Beauties of the New Zealand Rhine. A Ride through the Avenue — The Racecourse —
Beautiful Studies of the Swans — Motoua Gardens — Loading Frozen Mutton — A Trip on the
upper Reaches of the River — Maori Studies — Climbing the Rapids."[23]

Here we see Hayward successfully replicating what worked for West in Australia. The
advertising at West's Pictures at the Royal Albert Hall, Auckland, under the direction of
"Hayward's Enterprises Ltd. By arrangement with Mr T.J. West", highlighted the ongoing
association between West and Hayward and also West's association with Pathé Frères.

A fragment of film, though badly decomposed, survives. It is not Barrett's film but it is
representative of the many films taken on the Wanganui River in this period. It shows the
Hatrick steamer SS *Wakapai* that plied between Pipiriki and Hatrick's Houseboat, an 18-cabin
floating hotel with electric light and flushing toilets, situated as an overnight stop at Ohura
Junction at Maraekowhai on the way to Taumarunui.[24]

Barrett is one of many — West, McDonald, Meliès and others — who filmed the Wanganui:
the 'New Zealand Rhine'. By the time Barrett completed his film the town already had a
photographer who, perhaps spurred on by Barrett's filming, would over the next four years
become identified as New Zealand's leading professional cameraman, and who later worked
with Barrett on multi-reel feature filming in New Zealand.

Frank Barrett's films were of the quality that fulfilled T.E. Donne's dream of putting New
Zealand's attractions in front of a worldwide audience. This was now happening through
Pathé Frères, which also absorbed the efforts of James McDonald and Sydney Taylor, his
successor, the government kinematographers, as well as those of local cameramen who
responded to both local interest and Pathé's increasing demands for film. Evidence of this
is the quantity of film from this period that survives in the vaults of the Ngā Taonga Sound
& Vision archive, some 70 films covering 1910 to the outbreak of war in 1914, compared to
the 20 films identified in the period from 1900–09 — a minute fraction in each case of those
actually filmed.

CHARLIE NEWHAM OF WANGANUI

Wanganui, with its sizable population, had been on the itinerary of the travelling pictures shows
from the beginning with films being shown at the Opera House in 1900, the year it opened.
By 1909 films were being screened on a regular basis and permanent picture shows came to
Wanganui in 1910. Thompson-Payne screened at the Opera House on 13 May and was followed
by Zealandia Pictures, managed by Mr J. Stirton who enlisted the services of a Wanganui
photographer, Charles Newham.

> Mr Newham the local photographer has secured a cinematograph camera and proposes to take
> various scenes in and around Wanganui. Weather permitting he will take a picture of the Avenue
> next Saturday. The whole process connected with the films, developing, printing, etc will be done
> in Wanganui and the finished product will be first shown in Wanganui in the Opera House.[25]

*Wanganui River
Steamboat Trip.*
NTSV F31567.

The film *Picturesque Wanganui* was screened at the Opera House on 9 September 1910 and was greeted according to the advertisement in the local papers with "thunders of applause and acknowledged by all to be without equal". The advertising also made great play of the fact that, perhaps in contrast to Frank Barrett's recent visit, this "is the first time that a film of this kind has ever been taken by a local man and projected by local people".[26] It met all the critical requirements to make it a success with the "people in the street and on the car" being "easily recognisable". The public responded accordingly. The general feeling was that it was "far ahead of previous pictures and should be shown elsewhere as an advertisement for the town".[27]

Charles Frederick Newham was born in Wellington in 1880. In 1902 he established a photography studio in Wanganui with John Brady and traded as Newham and Brady at 188 Victoria Avenue, opposite the Technical School. A number of their photographs featured in the Auckland and Wellington illustrated weeklies. Newham took over the business on his own in 1907.[28] At some point Newham purchased a kinematograph camera and increasingly found himself more and more committed to meeting the demands of the local picture shows. His first film was made for the Zealandia Picture Company, managed by Mr J. Stirton who had taken a short lease at the Opera House. Its success was not lost on Hayward's Pictures that ran the Lyceum Theatre, which at the time was the only permanent picture theatre in the town. The *Wanganui Chronicle* announced on 14 October 1910 that Hayward's Pictures "have arranged with Mr Newham to take an animated picture of the opening of the rowing season tomorrow afternoon. The picture will be screened at the Lyceum on Wednesday evening."[29] Part of the film survives and gives us a glimpse of Newham's early work. We see the fun and frivolity of the opening of the new season on the foreshore near the boating club as "'The Darktown' Crew led by their Chief declare proceedings open."[30]

The pages of the *Wanganui Chronicle* document Newham's activities in filming local events, including the Wanganui Show in November, and in December the review of the Boy Scouts at Feilding by Lord Islington, the governor, followed later in the month by Palmerston North Racing Club meeting. In 1911 film followed film: the Manawatu Cup followed by the Annual Grocer's Picnic, an "Animated Beauty Competition — for young ladies over 16", and in April the affair of the 'harem skirt'.[31]

> An adventurous young lady attired in a harem skirt and closely attended by a couple of escorts, attracted a very great deal of attention on the lawn at the Feilding races on Monday. She was followed up and down the enclosure by a crowd of several hundred people, who at times became rather demonstrative, but on the whole the "barrack" was humorous rather than hostile to the innovation. The visit of the lady was due to the enterprise of a Feilding picture proprietary for whom Mr Newham secured views of the commotion created.[32]

On the same night Hayward's Pictures at the Lyceum advertised that a model would display "THE HAREM SKIRT", which would be worn by "a real live lady" and advised patrons to "come early and avoid the crush!" It did what was intended and drew the crowds with the *Wanganui Chronicle* reporting the following day, "Hundreds turned away last night" and that such was the interest that "She occupied the stage for nearly ten minutes." Naturally enough those disappointed the night before would have their chance as the "sensational costume will be again exhibited" on that evening's programme.[33]

A harem skirt suggests bare midriffs but this was far more daring than a country audience of 1911 would ever accept. A Pathé newsreel film survives of the display of similar skirts or pants

Opening of the Wanganui Rowing Season, Wanganui River, 15 October 1910. NTSV F384827.

in Melbourne. It shows two women modelling harem skirts outside of George's Department Store in Collins Street, attracting the interest of the women shoppers as much as the men, before driving off in a chauffeured car. One of the women is then shown pirouetting around in a pair of loose harem-style trousers, which is the only departure from otherwise very proper attire, all of which is suggested from the titling as being of the latest Paris fashion. It seems that in 1911 this was enough to almost start a riot at a New Zealand country racecourse! It certainly drew in the picture theatre audience and so achieved its commercial aim.[34]

Many of Newham's films were distributed throughout Hayward's chain of theatres and in March 1911 the *Wanganui Chronicle* reported that Pathé Frères, which had opened a Wellington office, had written to Hayward's Pictures "stating that the films of the Wanganui Races, opening of the boating season, and the Wanganui Show, which were taken by Mr Newham, have been accepted by them for their animated Gazettes. Messrs Pathé Frères stating that providing the standard submitted is adhered to, Mr Newham's success is assured and he will receive their hearty cooperation. They have also decided to take all films turned out after they have been presented at the Lyceum." It was a coup for Mr Jameson, Hayward's local manager and "should prove a great advertisement for Wanganui, as these pictures will be presented in nearly every part of the world where pictures are shown".[35]

A DAY AT THE RACES

Newham's film of the 1911 Feilding Spring Hurdles captures the mood of the day; the horse-drawn open carriages and expensive motorcars stopping at the entrance, and the crowds moving through the turnstiles with both the men and women dressed for the occasion. The Spring Hurdles was won by Reumac who would also win the following year.[36]

A second film of the Feilding races also survives and what's interesting about it is as the horses return to the parade ring after the race, a cinematographer and his camera can be seen in the background; so even in Wanganui and the Manawatu there was enough local film business to attract rival cameramen. Clive Sowry's fascinating research into the physical characteristics of the film stock and the positioning of the intertitles identifies the film as that taken by Monsieur Dahmen from Pathé's Wellington office, who was engaged to film the event by Hayward's Pictures at the Lyceum Picture Palace, while Percy Price who ran Price's Permanent Pictures at the Feilding Drill Hall hired Newham to film the race meeting, and so we have Charles Newham in profile cranking away on film taken by a rival cameraman.[37]

Newham's film *Pictures of Feilding Races* was first screened at Price's Permanent Pictures on 1 December 1911. "The picture — one of the Newham series — was hailed with enthusiasm. A crowd of faces of well-known people appeared on the screen."[38] Hayward's Pictures at the Lyceum Theatre promised that the Pathé Frères film of the races would be worth the wait. *Feilding Races* was screened on 7 December 1911. "The scenes open with a capital picture of the fleet of motor cars and the arrival of the President of the Racing Conference (Sir Geo. Clifford), and then myriad faces of Feilding and other folks poured onto the screen — people on the lawns, along the fences, in front of the totalisator, thronging, jostling, chatting, greeting each other, picking winners and losers and friends, and generally (so far as the ladies were concerned) wearing pretty frocks or (these were the men) absorbed looks."[39]

There is also Newham's film, with its distinctive Maori-motif titling, of the 1911 *World's Championship Axeman's Carnival, Taumata Park Eltham New Zealand* that was commissioned by Charles Wilkinson whose hardware firm had a branch in Eltham and who, in 1910, opened

Wilkinson's Pictures in a specially built hall, which could also function as a skating rink.[40] This gem of a film is complete and starts with the arrival of the contestants by train at Eltham station (with one of the travellers throwing out his gunny sack as the train pulls in), the gathering at the park, the bicycle races and the axemen's competitions with George Thomas McCauley winning the World Championship with a 'Collie King' axe, and there is no doubt about the axe, its name on some of the contestants' singlets makes it quite clear — obvious advertising for the cinema age and makes one wonder if Mr Wilkinson, the theatre owner, was also the agent for 'Collie King'.[41]

The World Championship was first competed for at Eltham in 1906, having begun in Tasmania, and soon became the "most popular sports gathering in New Zealand".[42] It is a marvellous film, full of great faces, close action and a sense of a small New Zealand community proudly showing itself to the world. Wilkinson no doubt appears among the many shots of the 'busy officials' and the film was shown at Wilkinson's Pictures in Eltham two weeks later in January 1912 to a no doubt appreciative crowd.[43]

Newham found himself in constant demand as a cameraman. He continued to live in Wanganui, juggling his photo studio work with his growing film commitments as he ranged across the North Island of New Zealand producing scenics, travelogues and topical items for both local theatres and Hayward's Pictures, which were distributed New Zealand-wide.

In 1911 Newham went to Napier at the invitation of George Tarr who ran Hayward's Empire Theatre. Thompson-Payne Pictures, under Harry Thompson's management, were in partnership with Hayward in Napier. On 17 December 1911 the Empire opened as Napier's first purpose-built picture theatre, under Tarr's management. Like many others who went into the moving picture industry, Tarr's background was in show business. Sydney-born, he worked New Zealand and Australia as a scenic artist (having recorded his occupation on his marriage certificate as 'signwriter'), actor and vaudeville song and dance man with the touring companies and magic lantern shows first visiting New Zealand in 1902. "I was a vaudeville artist ever since

World Championship Axemen's Carnival, Taumata Park, Eltham New Zealand. NTSV F1152.

Local pictures taken by their 'own townsman'. *Wanganui Herald*, 26 March 1913, p. 1.

Fishing Industry in New Zealand. NTSV F97914.

I was a child. I was seven and a half when I went on the stage."[44] Tarr moved into moving pictures as an itinerant showman screening *The Great Train Robbery* around Australia and New Zealand, settling in New Zealand in 1907 when he joined the Taylor–Carrington Company with whom he toured with for the next few years.[45] He worked with Benwell's American Pictures with his wife Alice or 'Darcie' as she liked to be known, accompanying the films on piano at the Gaiety Theatre in Auckland during its brief life in 1910, before moving down to Napier.

I was managing for Haywards down in Napier. And I thought the business wanted kicking along a bit, so I thought we'd introduce some local stuff. So I sent for … Charlie Newham from Wanganui. And then we … made the trawling industry in Napier and we got two trawlers out one Sunday morning at the same time and we stayed out all Sunday in a big swell and we made the trawling industry. Well Charlie's contract with that was to retain the negative which he sent to America and for years afterwards that picture was running … I paid him for it out of the takings … After that we made a picture of the gannets at Cape Kidnappers, and it was a glorious picture too. Well he put that out the same way and sent it to America.[46]

What worked in Wanganui worked equally well in Napier. On 4 October 1911 Hayward's Empire Theatre announced the screening of *Napier Day by Day*. "Mr Newham Head Photographer for Hayward's Enterprises Ltd has filmed many of Napier's notable buildings, scenic spots, and its fishing industry."[47] This film was purchased by Heron in the United Kingdom who released it as *Trawling in Napier, New Zealand* in 1912. It was released again as *Fishing Industry of New Zealand* by the New Agency Film Company in the United Kingdom in 1916 and found its way back to New Zealand. Similarly, Newham's *With the Gannets at Cape Kidnappers*, which was made on a later trip to Napier in 1913, was released throughout New Zealand and sold overseas and found its way back home when it was screened in Napier in December 1918.[48]

NEWHAM GOES FULLTIME

On 14 May 1912 Newham took the gamble and went into fulltime film-making, selling his photography studio to H.S. Litchfield who then traded in Wanganui as Falk Studios. Newham became one of the few professional film-makers in New Zealand, setting himself up as the principal of the Dominion (NZ) Film Manufacturing Company and working on contract throughout the North Island. Wanganui and the Manawatu continued to feature in his films that he filmed for Hayward's, Fuller's and local picture theatres.

The pages of the *Wanganui Chronicle* faithfully recorded his film-making forays further afield. One of his first films after going fulltime survives. This is his film of the wreck of the 4623-ton refrigerated steamship *Star of Canada*, pride of the Tyser Line, which ran aground at Gisborne on the night of 23 June 1912 in a fierce southerly gale. Attempts to refloat the ship and salvage its cargo captured New Zealand's attention. The clue to Newham as the cameraman's identity is that it was made by the Dominion (NZ) Film Co. Wanganui, which is proudly emblazoned on each intertitle. It is a tight, cleverly shot and edited film that obviously kept audiences entranced.[49]

Diver descending to inspect damage to the *Star of Canada*, which ran aground off Gisborne on 22 June 1912. Still from Charles Newham's *The Wreck of the* Star of Canada. NTSV F38455.

Films of shipwrecks were always popular, particularly so as they had more than a local interest. This is evident from Wanganui audience reaction in May 1913 to Newham's film of the wreck of the steamer *Indrabarah* that ran aground on the Rangitikei shoreline near Bulls.

> Never has Mr Newham turned out a better picture. It gives one just as good an idea of how
> the steamer is placed as if one were on the spot. Photographically, the picture could not be
> surpassed. It gives views of the *Indrabarah* from all positions. It shows the sandy, tussocky hills
> which fringe the sea coast, and one can form a very good idea of how far the steamer is away.
> The waves are seen rebounding off the broad iron side, and yet through it all the big steamer
> seemed to be lying quite peacefully with smoke rising lazily from the funnel. Some interesting
> views are given of the improvised tent and the members of the crew who came ashore. The
> gallant Adcock, who saved two lives is also shown; though he only caste a disgusted look at the
> camera and then goes on with his business.[50]

In these films Newham captures the drama of the event and the personalities involved, nothing staged or contrived, simply the knack of capturing people as they go about resolving a crisis. He is the shadow in the foreground, sometimes earning a disgusted look but filming the moment for New Zealand audiences to see.

NEWHAM GOES TO AUCKLAND

On 30 May 1913 the paper announced that "Mr C.F. Newham and family left for Auckland yesterday. Mr. Newham as representative of the Dominion Film Co. has been commissioned to carry out work for the [Auckland] exhibition, and will reside in Auckland till that big event is over."[51] Auckland became Newham's home for the next seven years where he established himself as New Zealand's most experienced film-maker. His job was to film events, both big and small, as he had done in Wanganui, those moments that drew the crowds into the picture theatres. Consolidation in the film business ensured that his films would be seen countrywide in all of the major picture theatres.

The Wreck of the Star of Canada. NTSV F38455.

NEWHAM FILMS THE NEWS

On 2 September 1912 the first issue of Hayward's Theatres monthly newsreel *Auckland Animated News* launched. It ran until May 1913, then on 16 November 1913 the *New Zealand Animated News* — the weekly newsreel of New Zealand Picture Supplies — had its first release, and continued to screen until 1914. It was the start of local topical newsreels. These complimented the *Pathé Gazette* and other overseas newsreels from Gaumont and Topical.

The *Auckland Animated News* was produced by Phil Hayward, who ran the Lyric Theatre at the top of Symonds Street in Auckland. Filmed by Newham it came out monthly and screened throughout the Hayward circuit of cinemas. "Charles Newham did the whole thing. He did the photography and he processed them and at times I went out with him to photograph things. I remember going out with him on one occasion into the Auckland Domain to photograph a parade and I was just a boy helping him carry his gear and learning all I could from him."[52]

In this recollection, Rudall Hayward gives us a glimpse of the busy life of a professional cameraman and film-maker such as Charles Newham, who, in the nature of New Zealand film-making was a 'one-man band', having to do everything himself and, as we have seen with Brandon Haughton in New Plymouth, would shoot, develop and edit the film and then often as not screen it as projectionist for the local theatre.

> He [Charles Newham] was a tall angular sort of man who had really graduated from still photography. He'd been a fine still photographer and had taken up motion picture work. He was a fine technician. He used to develop his own film and he was always meticulously careful in the handling of his negatives and in the developing of them and in his printing. He achieved a very high standard in the days when it was extremely difficult, he worked in little back room offices and he developed his film in pin trays. A tray or trough made probably of wood which would be three or four inches deep and the film was wound on arms of wood which had sections of wood driven into them like pegs — a series of pegs. Thin dowling was used for this purpose. A number of holes were drilled in the arms of the pin tray and sections of dowling inserted and the film was wound in and out of these pegs starting from the centre of the pin tray and wound laboriously round the pegs until it reached the outer edges and then the whole thing would be dipped into the developer and developed for a time and lifted out and put into the fixer and then the wash and then wound on to a wooden drum and dried. From that the film would be edited and printed on the printing machine and then the process would be repeated with the positive film which would be put back on the pin tray and re-developed again to make the positive prints. He was most careful with his film and many years afterwards when you examined his negatives they were still in excellent condition. They had been thoroughly fixed and washed and they lasted a long period. I always remember the titles that he made so carefully. He used a Maori carving — the front of a meeting house — to make a border for the lettering that he inserted for the titles and because of cheapness he used rubber stamps, letters, to print the titles and the title was inserted in this outer border of the Maori carving of the front of a meeting house. Then the whole thing was tinted the same colour as the ochre of a Maori Meeting house. So you could always tell Charles Newham's films whenever one of these bordered titles came on screen.[53]

There are a number of films that can be definitely traced to Newham's Auckland years. There are also a number of films that seem to have his style but equally there were a number of very competent Auckland cameramen so identifying who did what is often wishful surmise.

Cricket and yachting in the summer, rugby and rugby league in winter, racing with the Auckland Cup covered by teams of cameramen from competing film distributors, and sports days often connected with events such as the St Patrick's Day parade, provided constant fare, keeping Newham busily employed along with a number of other cameramen.

We have Newham's film of the crash of the Auckland-bound Main Trunk express train that due to a signalling error ploughed into a 41-truck goods train at Whangamarino Station, south of Mercer, causing the death of three passengers and seriously injuring a further five. The film *Main Trunk Express Smash* is identified to The Dominion (NZ) Film Manufacturing Co. with Newham's distinctive Maori-patterned border, and in one of the scenes the shadow of the cameraman filming can be seen. Interesting touches such as selective hand-tinting of the train roof show the care that Newham took developing his film, despite the necessary haste to get it to the screen.[54] Viewing his film makes it clear that it was more than a job; he loved film and filming and attended to each film's development and printing with an artist's care.

The film *Trawling in the Hauraki Gulf* is attributed to Newham and is believed to have been shot on the trawler *Countess* owned by Sanford Ltd. There are intimate shots as the men haul in the nets choked full of fish, the fisherman who, aware of the camera or not, tweaks the watching cook's chin, the clever touch showing the captain viewing through his binoculars and then cutting to the binocular-masked shot of approaching the Auckland wharfs with the vehicle ferry loaded with its mix of motor and horse-drawn vehicles leaving for the North Shore.[55]

We have also the 1912 Auckland Cup scenes at Ellerslie Racecourse, ladies parading in their finery, the packed grandstands and the clever interplay between the two cameramen involved; cutting between views from the track and those taken from the top of the grandstand, finishing with a view of the winning horse Bobrikoff ridden by F. Jones.[56]

There is also the film of the professional sprint races at the Auckland Domain during the St Patrick's Day sports in 1912, between the two Australian runners; world champion Jack Donaldson, 'The Blue Streak', against the former champion, Arthur Postle, 'The Crimson Flash'.[57] Postle regained his champion's crown, defeating Donaldson at 75 yards, 150 yards

and 200 yards; equalling the world record in the first two and setting a new world record in the third. For once the film, taken for John Fuller and Sons, concentrates on the racing to the exclusion of the crowd. Donaldson and Postle were stars in a period when professional running was of worldwide interest and their achievements were confirmed in the picture theatres.[58]

Sports were popular subjects for local film and the faces of the crowds always featured. They are a strong element in the film of the Plunket Shield cricket match at Lancaster Park, Christchurch, in 1912.[59]

At least half of the surviving film of the Great Britain versus Auckland rugby league game at the Auckland Domain Cricket Ground on 25 July 1914 is devoted to various panning shots and close-ups of the 8000-strong crowd, giving them a reason to see the film, perhaps in compensation for a convincing British win by 34 points to 12. The test game played on the same ground on 1 August 1914 was a much closer affair with New Zealand losing to Great Britain by 13–16, however, Monday's report in the press was overshadowed by the news of European mobilisation for war.[60]

HMS *NEW ZEALAND*

There is a fragment of Newham's film of the big New Zealand event of 1913. This was the arrival of the battlecruiser HMS *New Zealand* in Auckland, which he filmed on 29 April 1913 for screening the next day in Hayward's Lyric Theatre and which also screened simultaneously at the Globe Continuous Pictures and Queen's Theatre. The warship's arrival was visible proof that New Zealand was playing its part as a junior partner in the British Empire.

New Zealand's gift to the Empire was the impulsive gesture of Prime Minister Sir Joseph Ward, and his offer to "buy one first-class battleship and if necessary two" surprised the British Government as much as it surprised the New Zealand public.[61] It reflected growing concern in New Zealand and Australia about the declining power of the Royal Navy in the Pacific. The public feared the growing power of Japan, an Asiatic or 'Yellow Peril' in the public mind that was not calmed by Japan's treaty with Great Britain. Public anxiety was also heightened by Germany's naval ambitions. Our worries in New Zealand reflected our perceptions of Pacific security, but it paralleled similar concerns of the British public regarding Kaiser Wilhelm II's determination to make Germany a major naval power by building a battleship fleet capable of challenging the Royal Navy.

The launching of the battleship HMS *Dreadnought* in 1905 revolutionised battleship design making all existing battleships obsolete. It provided an even playing field, giving Germany a chance to catch up with Britain in its number of Dreadnought-class battleships. It was this, prompted by a consciousness that his government was losing its appeal, that led to Ward's gesture on 22 March 1909. He did not have Seddon's magic and his ministry was losing its grip so he looked for diversions to take public attention away from his growing political weakness.[62] Ward's commitment of £1,700,000 to buy a battleship for the Royal Navy did not win universal approval, but certainly captured public imagination.

HMS *New Zealand* was not a battleship, but a battlecruiser of the Indefatigable-class. She was the second series of this type built for the Royal Navy and the last with 12-inch guns. She carried a crew of 806 that were drawn from personnel of the Royal Navy and never numbered more than a handful of New Zealanders.[63] Its construction and its launching on 1 July 1911 by Lady Ward, using a bottle of Whangarei wine to break on its bow, was avidly followed in New Zealand and featured in the picture theatres.[64]

Plunket Shield Cricket Match Auckland v Canterbury/Domain Fete Christchurch. NTSV F3985.

Football: England v Auckland, 25 July 1914. NTSV F27357.

New Zealand Leads the Way/Scenes on Board HMS New Zealand/Britannia Rules The Waves. NTSV F 4387.

HMS *NEW ZEALAND*'S GRAND TOUR

Films survive of the formal visits to the ship at Portsmouth prior to its departure for New Zealand. The first is a compilation of three films covering events around King George V's formal inspection of the ship on 5 February 1913, the day before her departure. The first sequence shows Mr Thomas Mackenzie, high commissioner for New Zealand, and his family, with Colonel James Allen, New Zealand minister of defence, and a party of 300 New Zealand visitors boarding the ship for the unveiling of a plaque of the New Zealand Coat of Arms on 5 February 1913. The Coat of Arms was designed by James McDonald and it is almost certain that T.E. Donne is among the visitors; so in a very New Zealand way all of the principals in the story of New Zealand filming keep intersecting with each other. Mackenzie, distinctive in beard and bowler hat, is followed by Mrs Mackenzie in fur stole being met by Captain Lionel Halsey, the ship's captain. The sequence ends with a queue of New Zealand visitors all in Sunday best, but one sees at least one wide-brimmed farm hat in the crowd, while in the background is the special train that brought them down from Waterloo to Portsmouth.[65]

The next sequence is the visit of King George V on 5 February 1913. Three versions survive, all taken by Jury's Imperial Pictures. The more detailed shows the King being received by the commander-in-chief in Portsmouth and then escorted by Captain Halsey, inspecting the Guard of Honour and touring the ship accompanied by First Lord of the Admiralty Winston Churchill, with Admiral Jellicoe, New Zealand Minister of Defence James Allen, Thomas Mackenzie and Sir Joseph Ward, now leader of the Opposition. A formal photo is taken under the New Zealand Coat of Arms and the King is introduced to the ship's mascot, a bulldog named 'Pelorus Jack'. The final scenes show the crew polishing the guns, with the brass barrel caps of the 12-inch guns prominent, displaying 'NZ' below the relief of the crown. This last scene was also issued as a Pathé newsreel clip.[66]

British papers reported the king's visit to the ship, noting the lack of formality and his good humour. On inspecting the bakery and the production of white bread the King "recalled that when he was first at sea, the bluejackets had to put up with weevily biscuits and maggoty flour". Later, "On seeing the mauve, white and green upholstery in the gun-room His Majesty remarked that it was more like a Lady's boudoir than a gun-room. This led to general laughter when someone pointed out that the upholstery was in the suffragette colours." The *Daily Telegraph* spoke of the ship being "an emblem of a new era, the first gift of the daughter-lands to the Navy on which every Imperial interest depends". Appropriately enough, the film was released throughout New Zealand with scenes of British battleships manoeuvring at sea.[67]

HMS *New Zealand*'s reception in New Zealand was unprecedented. It had echoes of the return of the 'Original All Blacks', the sending and return of the Boer War contingents, and the tour by the Duke and Duchess of Cornwall and York, all rolled into one. En route she called at Cape Town and Durban where some 113,000 visitors trod its decks, almost 10,000 came aboard in Melbourne, but in New Zealand everyone wanted to visit the ship. Wellington was its first port of call and from 12–23 April 1913 it received 98,170 visitors, ferried out to where it was anchored in the harbour. Numbers often reflected its ability to dock alongside the wharf; 16,750 went aboard in Napier with its population of some 11,000, 3210 in Gisborne with a population of 11,000, 94,616 over ten days in Auckland from a population of 110,000 and a staggering 132,365 in Lyttleton while Christchurch's population at the time numbered some 80,000, and so it went on — 2127 in Akaroa (which was added to the schedule at the insistence of the acting minister of defence, W. Heaton Rhodes),[68] 330 in Timaru, 3306 at Otago Heads, 7494 in Nelson, which had a borough population of some 8000, and 7578 in Picton.

HM The King Inspects "The New Zealand" at Portsmouth. NTSV F29375.

Auckland's Reception to the Battleship HMS New Zealand. NTSV F10484.

Schoolchildren were brought in special trains to see New Zealand's contribution to the Royal Navy. All of New Zealand wanted to see their battleship and a total 376,084 trod its decks in its visits to every port in New Zealand. Where no berthing alongside was possible and lack of ferries or conditions necessarily limited visitors, everyone crammed vantage points to see their ship.[69] Over a third of New Zealand's population had walked its decks and perhaps that many again had seen it from the shore.

EVERYONE FILMS HMS *NEW ZEALAND*

Newham was commissioned to film HMS *New Zealand*'s arrival in Wellington for John Fuller and Sons and His Majesty's Theatre advertised *The Arrival of HMS New Zealand in Wellington* with the description that "special arrangements have been made to take the Battleship and Fleet as they steam up the harbour. The film will be printed, developed and produced THIS EVENING".[70] With the ship anchored in the harbour for its 12-day stay in the capital, the Monday press reported that the "picture showing the battleship New Zealand entering Wellington Harbour, was responsible for His Majesty's Theatre being packed on Saturday evening". The Saturday night crowds may also have been influenced by the programme including exhibition of the latest dance craze, 'The Turkey Trot'. Similar films "by our own operator" were also screened at West's King's Theatre.[71]

After its season in Wellington, the film of the Wellington arrival was toured through the provinces. The *Nelson Evening Mail* of 29 April 1913 had the management of the Theatre Royal, Nelson, apologising for the picture missing the post but promising it would be shown the following evening. It was shown on 30 April and 1 May 1913 and the advertising proclaimed: "An event never to be forgotten by all New Zealanders. Your own Dreadnought brought to your very doors", all of which was "keenly appreciated and enthusiastically applauded by the vast audience".[72] The film continued to do good business in the country halls and theatres, including

Charles Newham's distinctive Maori motif title design. Still from *Auckland's Reception to the Battleship, HMS New Zealand.* NTSV F10484.

Takaka, in late May.[73] Certainly everyone who had not personally seen the ship had the opportunity to see it on film.

Newham was in Auckland on 29 April for the arrival of the battlecruiser and his film *The Arrival of HMS New Zealand in Auckland* was screened at Hayward's Lyric Theatre the following evening. "The launch of the battleship was first shown. The battleship's arrival at Auckland, and the procession of the launches up the harbour, was next shown, and this was followed by the landing of Captain Halsey at the wharf, the procession up Queen Street, and the illuminations. All the pictures were remarkably clear and were received with loud applause."[74]

A fragment of the film with Newham's distinctive titling survives in the national archive. On a day that the *New Zealand Herald* reported was a "gift from the Gods", we see the ship steaming into harbour "three massive funnels then all the huge grey bulk of the battlecruiser … sullenly majestic, awful in portent, relentless as death itself". We get a sense of the clamour of the city's reception by the swarm of small boats that surround it and the merchant ships decked with festive flags. "Launch followed in the wake of launch. Ferry-boats and steamers crowded on their sterns, intrepid men and boys tugged at oars of tiny dinghies and rowing boats, rowers in outriggers joined in the procession until so great was the traffic and the bewildering array of craft that the water was churned into white-crested waves and the smaller craft were tossed about like so many corks."[75]

The government kinematographer, this time James McDonald, also took a detailed film of the ship tour around New Zealand titled *HMS New Zealand*. It was later shown throughout New Zealand by patriotic societies in local halls for fundraising.[76] The Wellington sequence of this visit was shown on 21 July 1913 to members from both houses in the Parliament House tea rooms together with the series of films of farming taken by Taylor, "which have been prepared for the Agricultural Department".[77] The *New Zealand Times* reported that that the films of life on New Zealand experimental farms were "shown in England and Scotland in connection with the campaign for immigrants".[78]

There are two film segments of *HMS New Zealand*'s stay in Dunedin taken by Charles Newham's Dunedin equivalent, Henry Gore, a photographer turned cameraman/projectionist. We have a magnificent shot of the battlecruiser steaming into Otago Harbour and the only surviving film showing visitors on board the ship during its New Zealand tour.[79] This was screened throughout New Zealand along with other topical items filmed by Gore. His films *The Wreck of the* SS *Tyrone* and of the views of *HMS New Zealand* at Otago Heads at the Lyric Theatre in Nelson were reported as a "splendid tribute to the ability of the photographer, Mr H.C. Gore of Dunedin".[80]

HMS New Zealand continued to feature on film until scrapped in 1922.

HMS *New Zealand* in Waitemata Harbour surrounded by a fleet of launches and yachts. Still from Charles Newham's *Auckland's Reception to the Battleship HMS New Zealand*. NTSV F10484.

HMS New Zealand. NTSV F38483.

10

Local, topical and professional

HENRY GORE IN OTAGO

From 1900 to the end of the silent picture era, Henry C. Gore was at the heart of film-making and screening in Dunedin and Otago. His family had made its fortune in brick-making and building and were well-established Dunedin identities; his grandfather being mayor of Dunedin, and his father, mayor of St Kilda. Henry's obsession was photography and from the beginning he was fascinated by moving pictures and its technology. He imported a camera and projector, mastered their construction and workings and began filming local events. His grandfather sponsored his travel to Europe, but he cashed in his ticket and worked his passage as a ship's waiter getting as far as South Africa where he worked as a projectionist before returning to Dunedin in 1905.[1]

He married Ellen Willis in 1911 and his passion and his wife's forbearance are seen in the names of their first children, his first two daughters being named Zeita and Koda Edis — 'Koda' after Eastman's Kodak camera and 'Edis' after Thomas Edison.[2] He set up a family-run photography studio in Dunedin and was appointed manager of Hayward's Pictures at Burns Hall when it opened as a permanent picture theatre in October 1910. In 1913 he became 'chief operator' at the Plaza Picture Theatre, which was run by Cinema Enterprises Limited.[3] This private company numbered Gore as one of the shareholders.[4] During the First World War he journeyed to the United States where he worked as a projectionist and also in the factory manufacturing Simplex projectors. On his return to New Zealand in 1916 he was principal projectionist at the newly opened Queen's Theatre in Cuba Street, which boasted two Simplex projectors of the "very highest class … The operator at the Queen's Theatre is Mr H. Gore, lately of Dunedin, who has had experience in America, not only as an operator, but in the big factory where the 'Simplex' machines are made."[5] By 1919 he was back in Dunedin filming the peace procession and local events.

Gore, like Haughton in New Plymouth and Newham in Wanganui, filmed local events to draw in the crowds, which he fitted in with his running of the photography studio and his work as projectionist. We have his film of the Brass Band Contest for bands from the Otago and Southland provinces held at Carisbrook Park, Dunedin, on a rainy October Saturday in 1912. Each band is identified in turn and marches past in quick time. An army warrant officer judging

Opposite page: The motion picture camera in the crowd. Fete at Wellington Boys', Institute children's public playground looking across Riddiford Street, Newtown, Wellington, in 1914. There is a large Salvation Army presence. Photographer unknown, C16693, ATL, Wellington.

Henry Gore with the staff
of Hayward's Picture
Enterprises, Burn's Hall,
Dunedin, 1910. Henry Gore
is seated centre, middle row.
NTSV, Henry Gore Collection,
S5743, no. 6.

the standard of the drill as the Citizens Dunedin, St Kilda, Caversham, Kaikorai, Balclutha and Dominion Invercargill bands are each put through their paces. However, Gore ran out of film before the performance of the winning band, Blenheim, which does not appear on screen, much, one imagines, to the frustration of its band members. Despite this, after a private screening the members of the Band Contest Committee expressed pleasure on the quality of the filming.[6]

Gore gave the intertitles a nice orange tint and one can imagine the musicians at the New Queen's Theatre and the St Kilda Coronation Hall playing some popular marches to accompany the film that featured in both programmes.[7]

We also have Gore's film of sightseers disembarking from the Port Chalmers harbour ferry *Waireka* after being taken along to Rerewahine Point to see the wreck of the SS *Tyrone* of the Union Steamship Company, which ran aground on 28 September 1913 and later sank.[8] Films of the wreck were screened at New Queen's Theatre, the Octagon Theatre and Fuller's Princess Theatre, Dunedin, from 1 October 1913, all three being exclusively filmed by their 'Special Operator'.[9] As we have seen with Newham's films, shipwreck scenes were guaranteed a New Zealand-wide distribution.

CHARLIE BARTON IN WELLINGTON

In Wellington Newham's equivalent, also working freelance, was Charlie Barton, who would become New Zealand's only native-born official war cameraman, albeit only after the Armistice and sadly with question marks over what survives of his work with the New Zealand Expeditionary Force (NZEF). Charles Donald Barton was born in Dunedin on 25 January 1887. He worked as a professional photographer in Wellington and like Newham was fascinated by moving pictures and its possibilities. We have three surviving films attributed to Barton from this period, all identified with his closing signature, "Kinematographed by

Dunedin Brass Band Contest, Quickstep.
NTSV F9933.

Wreck of the SS Tyrone.
NTSV F1208.

Pilot Reggie White going solo on his introductory flight in the Fisher monoplane's first flight. Still from Charles Barton's *The Fisher Monoplane*. NTSV F7306.

Reggie White takes to the sky in the Fisher monoplane. Still from Charles Barton's *The Fisher Monoplane*. NTSV F7306.

Barton, 10 Willis Street, Wellington New Zealand" — a building he shared with a couple of dentists, another photographer, and Harry H. Tombs, who is listed as the proprietor of the *Progress* (newspaper). The surviving films were shot in June–July 1913 and, as with Newham and Gore, we can see that Barton was equally busy capturing local events to satisfy public demand. These films were fed into either the Hayward or Fuller circuit and the New Zealand Picture Supplies national distribution network and then in selected cases overseas through Pathé Frères.

THE FLIGHT OF THE FISHER MONOPLANE

Barton's first surviving film is of a New Zealand first: the flight of the Fisher monoplane on 21 June 1913. The *Dominion* reported, "A kinematograph display representing a series of flights made recently by a monoplane designed by Mr Percy Fisher, of Wellington, was given in the tea-room of Parliament Buildings last night. The film commenced with a picture of the machine, with planes [wings] folded back, being towed along the road by a motor car at a fairly smart pace — this is to show that the little machine is easy to transport. The machine, piloted by Mr Reginald White, of Wellington, rose to no very great heights, but it seemed to be quite under the pilot's control, and it certainly did fly."[10]

The flight of the Fisher monoplane was the third successful flight to take place in New Zealand and the first by a completely New Zealand-made airplane. The plane, modelled on the Bleriot-type, was designed and assembled by David Percival Fisher, better known as 'Percy', an engineer of Wellington who spent two years designing and building it. Once completed he and his team of helpers looked for a suitable airstrip to test it. They initially set up camp at Pigeon Bush near Featherston, but found the proposed airstrip too rough and moved to 'Middlerun' station at Gladstone in the Wairarapa.

The Fisher Monoplane.
NTSV F7306

The first flight took place on Saturday 21 June 1913. The pilot, Reggie White, was an engineer who worked with Fisher on the plane. This was also a first for him as he had no previous flying experience and had to learn on the job. We see him check the plane, pose for the camera, straighten his beret and then fly. The first attempts are, as one would expect, tentative affairs with the plane 'bunny-hopping' down the paddock. Each shot shows White getting bolder as he gains confidence and we see him soaring over us as the film ends.[11]

Any audience could not but take the pilot to their hearts and share the excitement of his endeavours. The news of the flight came out in a special edition of the Wellington papers and Barton's film, titled *Experimental Flights of the Fisher Monoplane*, featured in the week of 10–14 July to "standing room only" crowds at the People's Picture Palace in Manners Street, Wellington. The press were particularly complimentary, reporting that the "technique of the film is equal to that of any aviation picture seen here, and reflects great credit on the local kinematographer, Mr Barton".[12]

The film had a special screening at parliament as Fisher was keen to see if he could interest the government in purchasing the plane, and this is why the ease of towing the aircraft from likely airstrip to airstrip was emphasised, showing its military potential. It was a step the government was reluctant to take. It had already been gifted an airplane, the *Britannia,* and had sent one of its permanent staff corps officers, Lieutenant W.E. Burn, for training at the Farnborough Aircraft Factory in Britain. With so much being spent on raising and equipping the Territorial Force and with the need to meet its annual subsidy towards the Royal Navy as well as paying off the cost of the HMS *New Zealand*, Massey's government was wary of further commitments: Fisher's initiative was refused.

The film kindled Barton's interest in the economic potential of aircraft and he was one of ten investors who each purchased one share to the value of £50 to raise £500 to form the working capital of New Zealand Aviation Limited, with the purpose of "exhibiting aeroplanes in New Zealand".[13]

Politicians always sought publicity and perhaps filming in the Wairarapa of the Fisher monoplane alerted Barton to both a pageant and a welcome home of a local politician, Sir Walter Buchanan, member of parliament, at Carterton, that was newsworthy enough to merit filming. It would certainly draw a local audience and the film may have been commissioned by the local cinema manager who made it worth Barton's while to return to the Wairarapa. The film itself touches all bases; the many speeches of welcome in front of a large crowd, Sir Walter's equally lengthy reply, the cheers of the crowd at the end. The filming then shifts to the showgrounds with women and children watching from the grandstand, the presentation of a large bull — a Highland "Stirk" — to Sir Walter, the local Caledonian Pipe Band and teams of locals in shirt sleeves straining against each other in a tug-of-war contest. There is a pan across an impressive line-up of motor cars giving some clue to the wealth in the district, before finishing with two girls' hockey teams, Dalefield versus Greytown, playing each other. All enough to ensure strong audience interest in the local picture theatres.[14]

THE 'RED FEDS'

The years leading up to the First World War were marked by periods of intense industrial unrest in New Zealand, which saw a resurgence of trade unionism that had been dormant since their defeat in the 1890 maritime strike. The wave of strikes that marked union attempts to overturn what they saw as an employer-biased Industrial Conciliation and Arbitration Act was played out throughout New Zealand from 1908–14. The successful 11-week-long 1908 Blackball Mine strike on the West Coast galvanised unionism throughout New Zealand and led to the formation of the New Zealand Federation of Miners at the instigation of Bob Semple, Paddy Webb and Pat Hickey. This organisation changed its name to the New Zealand Federation of Labour (FoL) and was strongly influenced by events in Australia and the activism of the Industrial Workers of the World (IWW) or 'Wobblies' in the United States. The slump of 1909 and sharp rise in unemployment exacerbated conditions. The FoL was seen to be increasingly under the control of a radical element and in 1912 the Wellington tramway's dispute saw the FoL labelled the 'Red Feds' by the Wellington *Evening Post*.[15]

In 1912 the miner's strike at Waihi divided the community when the company brought in non-union labour and the newly elected Massey government used the strike as a test of its political strength in taking on the unions. Backed by the government and with a strong police presence, the mining company hired in non-union labour that was organised into a union whose members were known as 'Arbitrationists' as they would abide by the Arbitration Act.

Picture theatre fortunes reflected those of the community from which they drew their audience. Rudall Hayward was 12 years old in 1912 and his father's picture theatre in Waihi was badly hit by the strike. The miners' families, now on limited strike pay, could not afford to go to the weekly pictures and Hayward's Pictures was hurt, along with other local businesses, by a community divided and fighting within itself.

> [The strikers] came to my father and said, "We want you to keep these scabs out of the theatre … We will boycott you unless you stop the scabs coming into the theatre." My father's answer to that was that he was a showman and that he couldn't refuse anybody admission regardless of their political viewpoints. His theatre was open to anybody and he was very sorry indeed but he couldn't accede to their request and so our theatre was boycotted and although we had done everything we could to help the miners — we had given them free shows, we had contributed funds and done everything that a citizen of a town might do to try and help them, but still the feeling was so high that the strikers realised that if they attended the pictures and the arbitrationists or scabs were there in the theatre it might end up in a fight … As things got more grim my father lost money hand over fist. He kept his show going but his capital was being reduced all the time … and it was only with very great difficulty that we kept the show still going night after night.[16]

It was a period of sustained violence with Massey's government determined to break the power of the unions. Strikers were hunted down and beaten up in the streets, the miners' store was sacked. The climax came on 12 November 1913 when the Arbitrationists raided the miners' hall and a policeman was shot in the stomach. A pitched battle erupted in the streets that led to Frederick George Evans being beaten and truncheoned so badly that he later died from his injuries. The mine company, backed by the government, gained control and set out to drive the unionists and their families from the town. It is said some 1800 people left in a hurried exodus that saw miners' families seek shelter in neighbouring mining settlements.

Rudall Hayward remembers an incident involving Mr Teddy Dye, a prominent unionist, who "afterward became a member of the Legislative Council … but at that time he was a strong unionist and one of the leaders of the striking miners and he was a marked man and the arbitrationists were after him. They chased him to his house and he climbed up on the roof and then eventually got on a horse and escaped from his house. He rode through the streets with a number of arbitrationists after him on horses. I was at the theatre in Waihi … and I watched this real wild west show take place before my eyes and I climbed up to the roof of the theatre

to the searchlight tower, where we had a searchlight for advertising purposes — I suppose it might be 40 feet above the ground and from that eminence I watched this wild west scene in New Zealand with Teddy Dye riding for his life through the streets."[17] Hayward also recalled a later incident again involving Dye that saw Hayward's father lock the iron doors of the theatre to keep out the Arbitrationists, who were trying to get to him, before phoning the police in the police station around the corner who "took him into custody to save his life".[18]

The climax came in October 1913 with wharf strikes that paralysed New Zealand ports when a dispute over the payment of travelling time to shipwrights developed into a major confrontation between trade unions and the government. Some 13,731 workers were involved, including waterside workers, painters, labourers, carpenters, miners, bakers and brewery workers. Massey's government responded by first attempting to use military force but then by enrolling thousands of special constables, known as 'Massey's Cossacks', from the farming community to maintain order. This in effect was a de facto mobilisation of the newly created Territorial Force who rode into town on horseback under a command structure that would take them to war in 12 months' time. But for the present, the country had come to town to save the nation from the 'Red Feds', and were barracked and accommodated in mobilisation camps in racecourses and parks, which again became a feature of 1914. It was an unanticipated dress rehearsal for the coming mobilisation for war.

Little has survived on film but we do have photos of motion picture cameras in the crowd capturing events that then screened at local cinemas. The *Wanganui Herald* reported Newham filming the strikes in Auckland and, as the illustration of the tramway strike in Wellington shows, we have a lonely camera with a cameraman and his assistant at Newtown Park in Wellington. The speaker is haranguing a small crowd in the foreground; the relaxed cameraman is possibly waiting for the crowd to grow large enough to justify his filming.

The cameraman and his assistant wait for the crowd to grow big enough to merit filming at the tramway strike mass meeting, Newtown Park, 1 February 1912. S.C. Smith Collection, G-19771-1/1, ATL, Wellington.

Delegates from the trade unions gather for the Unity Congress held in St Peter's Hall, Ghuznee Street, Wellington, in July 1913. Some ignored the camera, others doffed their hats. Still from Charles Barton's *Federation of Labour*. NTSV F1956.

There is one trade union-related film from this time and this is Barton's film of the parade of participants of the Unity Congress held in Wellington in July 1913 to unify sections of the Labour movement in the face of strong government opposition. It was the most "representative Labour gathering ever held in New Zealand or even, as was claimed at the time, in the southern hemisphere".[19] The Unity Congress drew the attention of the New Zealand press and was the subject of intense media debate in July and August 1913. The film itself does not live up to its historic importance. We see the march-past of delegates with the men, either smiling and doffing their hats, looking bemused, or determinedly avoiding looking at the camera, with the ubiquitous schoolboy staring from the pavement as they pass into the hall of St Peter's School in Ghuznee Street. The film ends symbolically enough at a fence with the sign 'Unity Congress' in the background, while the assembled delegates watch the camera on what is a very wet Wellington day.[20] It screened in the picture theatres in late August. The Queen's Theatre in Queen Street, Auckland, advertised it under the title: "FEDERATION OF LABOUR. The largest Congress South of the Line. Delegates of the Labour Unity Congress held in Wellington, New Zealand, July 1 to 10, 1913". After this came the words "THINK OF IT, THINK OF IT"; it is not clear if this refers to the fact that the ticket prices for adults is sixpence and children threepence, or it relates to the significance of the events filmed in Wellington.[21]

Perhaps the one film that does give us a sense of these times is that taken in December 1911, aptly titled *Wellington. 'The Elections'. A Dash of Politics at Lunch*, which shows David McLaren, Labour candidate for Wellington East, electioneering in Post Office Square, opposite the entrance to Queen's Wharf, which later became one of the flashpoints during the 1913 wharf strike. McLaren, a Scottish-born bootmaker, was founder and long-time secretary of the Wellington Wharf Labourers' Union. In 1908 he was elected as the first true Labour MP for Wellington East but lost his seat in the 1911 election. In 1912 he became the first Labour mayor of Wellington city.[22] In the film McLaren is talking to a workingman's crowd, smartly dressed by today's standards, and is seen haranguing the crowd from the tray of a horse-drawn wagon.

Federation of Labour.
NTSV F1956.

This captures two of five electioneering speeches he gave this day, 5 December 1911, but the fascination is in watching the mood of the crowd and especially the antics of the boys around the camera. It is a tight, effectively shot and edited on camera scene in an atmospheric film.[23]

The 1911 election itself was inconclusive with an uneasy balance between Ward's Liberals and Massey's Reform Party with four Labour–Socialist MPs elected. Ward, recognising the inevitable, resigned as prime minister. Thomas Mackenzie briefly replaced him as prime minister in a Liberal administration that stumbled on for a further three months. The Liberals' 21 years in office ended when Mackenzie lost a no-confidence motion in the house on 6 July 1912. It was replaced by William Ferguson Massey's Reform Party ministry that would govern until his death 13 years later. Ward and Mackenzie were adept at using film to further their political ambitions; during his years in power Massey showed the same skill.[24]

There is a 1910 West's Pictures' film of the Labor Day parade through Auckland, though the lack of any motor vehicles makes it seem earlier. There is also a curious film segment from a Pathé newsreel entitled *Auckland Bakers' Strike: Procession of Chinese Bakers in New Zealand*.[25] The scene is of the 1912 Labor Day parade passing up Queen Street through a holiday crowd. There is a mix of races, showing a series of highly ornate horse-drawn floats and includes a large circular loaf topped by the Union Jack, a wonderfully decorated crown and then bakers working in front of a brick oven; banners proclaim 'Defence not Defiance', which was a Labour movement catch-cry. A sole figure in what may be traditional Mongolian dress gives a touch of the Orient. One wonders if the pattern of industrial turmoil and strife at the time convinced the Pathé editor to pick a somewhat exotic and different New Zealand parade scene to put the message across about New Zealand's industrial unrest.

The rise of militant labour in New Zealand paralleled events overseas, particularly Australia. Already in Australia in 1908 West's Pictures presented audiences in Sydney and Melbourne with footage of the 24 July Sydney tram strike, including "the violence of an angry mob; the derailing of a stationary tram car in George Street; inspectors returning the cars to the depots; and a car worked by 'blacklegs' with troopers patrolling the streets".[26]

An Auckland Labor Day parade passing down Queen Street in about 1912. Auckland Libraries, Sir George Grey Collection, 1-W1163.

TERRITORIALS ON FILM

We have seen the excitement generated by Field Marshal Earl Kitchener of Khartoum's visit in 1910 and military parades and camps were a magnet for local film-makers. The fruits of Kitchener's visit saw the establishment of a citizen Territorial Force under compulsory military training. The provincially based military units became a popular subject in local cinemas. Newham filmed the military tournament in Palmerston North in 1911. It was an impressive series of competitions involving the volunteer companies before the formal changeover to the new territorial organisation. Filmed exclusively for Hayward's Pictures, it featured throughout New Zealand. As the *Nelson Evening Mail* advertised, "Watch College Rifles fording Manawatu River, Maxim Gun and Field Artillery Competitions, Tent pitching and striking, Daring feats on horseback, etc, etc". All the sensational feats by local lads who were identified by their titles emphasised the local connections and so each town could promote their own territorial unit if it featured in the programme. It drew the crowds and the paper reported, "The film of the recent military tournament at Palmerston North was exceptionally interesting and the same can be said of the Manawatu racing fixtures."[27]

The Territorial annual camps became an attractive subject for local cameramen, particularly so in 1914 during the visit to New Zealand by General Sir Ian Hamilton, the British Army's inspector general for overseas forces. Hamilton was assessing the state of readiness of the New Zealand Territorial Force, having already done similar inspections in Australia and Canada. To allow Hamilton to see as much of the Territorial Force as possible, Major-General Alexander Godley, commanding the New Zealand Defence Forces, directed that each military region hold divisional camps for each of the four military districts, Otago, Canterbury, Wellington and Auckland. This included both the mounted rifles and infantry brigades for each district and the artillery, engineers and supporting units.

Given that the system had only been effective since 1912 and was not planned to be fully effective until 1916, it was an ambitious undertaking. Having the camps so late in the year, in late April–May, also meant that the weather was likely to play a part. It did. Wet conditions at Takapau led to disciplinary problems among the infantry that were reported widely in the press as a 'riot', but Godley was determined that Hamilton be able to see and assess the effectiveness of the Territorial Force. Between late April and May, Hamilton toured New Zealand and, as with Kitchener, was the subject of film-makers' interest, but none featuring him have survived.

The Wellington camp was held at Takapau in the Hawkes Bay. The Thompson–Payne Picture Company, who ran the Gaiety Theatre in Napier and held regular screenings in the Forester's Hall in Masterton, and whose letterhead declared the company to be 'The King of Cinematograph Entertainers', wrote to Godley requesting exclusive permission to film the annual training camp. This was being held for both the Wellington Mounted Rifle Brigade and the Wellington Infantry Brigade and the film company stated that, "such a picture would be a great and valuable advertising medium in England, and at the same time prove to the whole world the advanced state of the New Zealand Territorial Movement, placing at the same time on permanent record the largest encampment held in the Dominion".[28]

Godley was happy to give permission but would not grant exclusive rights, as everyone was interested in filming the camp and Godley wanted as much publicity as possible. The Auckland brigades camped at Hautapu near Cambridge. Charles Newham filmed the camp and the film then circulated through the Hayward and Fuller chains. Godley, Hamilton and James Allen, minister of defence, saw the film at the King's Theatre in Wellington. They were impressed by what they saw and negotiated with New Zealand Picture Supplies to purchase copies of the film,

 Auckland Bakers' Strike: Procession of Chinese Bakers in New Zealand. NTSV F46203.

A parade day involving soldiers at Newtown Park before a packed Wellington crowd, c.1912–13. A motion picture camera is in position to the right of the flagpole waiting for events to begin. S.C. Smith Collection, G20323-1/1, ATL, Wellington.

less some of the camp scenes where some of the boys had imbibed too much and were clearly drunk on camera.

Two copies of the 1000-foot-long film, showing the camp, the march-past, the field exercise showing the whole force on operations and a leg amputation scene demonstrating the medical corps in action, were purchased at sixpence a foot, a total bill of £50. One copy was sent to Colonel Sam Hughes, the Canadian minister of defence, for screening in Canada and the second was sent to the New Zealand high commissioner in London for exhibition throughout Great Britain. Godley had no doubts about the value of the film as they displayed "the citizen soldiers of the country in the mass, in working kit, carrying their packs like soldiers, and performing field operations in the same manner and on the same scale as the troops of any other country, and this is what we think would be of value to be shown at home and in the other Dominions".[29]

It seems that James McDonald asserted his right over Sydney Taylor to do the big events and filmed General Hamilton's inspection of the Territorial and Cadet Forces at Newtown Park in Wellington on the king's birthday.[30] It was decided that this and the Hautapu Camp film would be circulated throughout New Zealand under the auspices of the Navy League, "the intention being that the films will be loaned to each centre for a week, and that the proceeds of at least one evening's entertainment shall be devoted to the Patriotic Fund".[31]

None of these films are known to have survived, but we have a 1913 film titled *2500 Territorials Marching Home from Camp* showing the four battalions of the Canterbury, Nelson, Marlborough and West Coast Infantry Brigades marching in fours into Christchurch from the Easter Camp at Yaldhurst on 26 March. It was filmed at Hospital Corner as the soldiers turned into Montreal Street. The press reported, "A solid knot of people and the 'cinema' man greeted the soldiers … and raised a cheer."[32] It was screened by "West–Hayward Pictures"at His Majesty's Theatre and at the Sydenham Pictures, Christchurch, on 31 March 1913 as one of "Our Local Films".[33]

Led by a military band we see an impassive Godley riding at the head of the column of Territorial infantry in their 'smasher' hats and 'Long Tom' Mark 1* Lee Enfield rifles that had been purchased second-hand from Canada. The cameraman is keen to get as many faces in close-up as possible but in setting up his camera misjudges the height and we only get a glimpse of the hats of some of the smaller boys. What stands out to the viewer is the age of the boys fully uniformed and kitted out but not yet old enough for war. In 17 months' time, many would lie about their age to join up for the 'Great Adventure'.[34]

The films were popular fare throughout New Zealand and also served a wider purpose in showing the other dominions and the Mother Country New Zealand's defence preparedness and her willingness to serve as a junior partner in Empire. By the end of May 1914, Hamilton had inspected 18,807 Territorials and 17,868 cadets — a total of 36,675 or 70% of the New Zealand defence forces. He had seen the citizen soldiers engage in a series of field days and concluded that "the military machine in New Zealand had been subjected to a severer trial than that of any portion of the Empire" ever inspected by him. "It is well equipped; well armed; the human material is second to none in the world; and it suffers as a fighting machine only from want of field work and want of an ingrained habit of discipline."[35] This could only be made good by the prolonged mobilisation of the forces and operational service in the field — for many of New Zealand's young men this was only months away.

2500 Territorials Marching Home from Camp. NTSV F56660.

Major-General A.J. Godley leads the Territorials of the Canterbury Infantry Brigade into Christchurch for a parade in Hagley Park at the end of the Easter Camp at Yaldhurst on 26 March 1913. Still from *2500 Territorials Marching Home from Camp*. NTSV F56660.

11

New Zealand goes to war

That memorable 3rd of August, 1914, was a bank holiday in Nelson, and we went for a glorious tramp up the Dun Mountain track. We stopped to boil the billy at a waterfall away beyond the big clearing and, having exhausted the subject of our chances in the rugby final (first things first), we turned to the question of enlisting in the proposed expeditionary force if, as seemed inevitable, Britain declared war on Germany. It was agreed that it was the urgent duty of every able-bodied man to consider the question of enlisting, and that self-interest would be no excuse for staying at home. The prospect of seeing service gave us a thrill of pure joy, and indeed the feeling throughout New Zealand was mainly one of pleasurable excitement.[1]

As Cecil Malthus records, the talk of war in Europe dominated the headlines in August 1914. Images of European mobilisation were matched by similar pictures in the New Zealand illustrated papers including scenes on the steps of the old parliamentary buildings in Wellington at 3 p.m. on the afternoon of 5 August 1914 with 10,000–15,000 Wellingtonians crammed into the forecourt, waiting for the governor the Earl of Liverpool to announce Britain's declaration of war on Germany and the Austro–Hungarian Empire. Britain had spoken for us and that was enough.

JOSEPH 'VANIE' VINSEN, KING'S THEATRE CAMERAMAN

Ubiquitously, the photographers on their stands took their photographs and among them cinematographers cranked their handles as they filmed that assembly of New Zealanders hearing that they were now at war. The following day, 6 August, the King's Theatre announced that the evening programme would show *The Proclamation of War by the Governor*.[2] Joseph Sylvanus Vinsen, or 'Vanie' as he was known, was the 31-year-old 'expert' cinematographer at the King's Theatre. His family came from the West Coast of the South Island where his elder

Opposite page: Joseph 'Vanie' Vinsen, King's Theatre cameraman. Photo taken in Wanganui in 1923. Tesla Studio Collection, F-17471-1/1, ATL, Wellington.

On the steps of the old parliamentary buildings in Wellington, on 5 August 1914, up to 15,000 Wellingtonians crammed into the forecourt to await the announcement of Britain's declaration of war on Germany and the Austro–Hungarian Empire. S.C. Smith Collection, 1/2-045239-G, ATL, Wellington.

brother was a photographer in Westport. Vinsen obviously shared the same interest and in 1912 worked as a projectionist for Royal Pictures at the Theatre Royal in New Plymouth before moving to Wellington where his father, in retirement, chaired the 'West Coaster' Association and his sister ran a fruiterer's shop in Adelaide Road.[3] He established himself both as cameraman and projectionist at the King's Theatre.[4] By 1918 he was New Zealand Picture Supplies' chief cinematographer in charge of their film department and also responsible for taking the film censorship titles that was the compulsory government film censor certificate of approval on every film shown in New Zealand.[5]

That evening,

> Willis-street, Lambton-quay, Manners-street, and Cuba-street became so densely crowded in places that it was difficult for the ordinary traffic to get through. The crowd outside *The Evening Post* office was especially dense throughout the whole of the evening, the posters on the window being read with the greatest interest, and the special war edition being rushed with unprecedented eagerness … The majority … displayed general confidence in Great Britain's ability to hold her own and a determination that in whatever happened everyone was prepared to see it through.[6]

Meanwhile, with the excitement in the streets around him and with the projectors running the evening performance, Vinsen, in the developing room of the theatre, had more immediate concerns developing and editing his film of the afternoon events.[7]

Vinsen probably worked long into the night to ensure that the next day the King's Theatre could show *The Proclamation of War by the Governor* as advertised in the daily papers and that copies could be despatched to other theatres.[8] As he worked, cinema and theatre audiences were caught up in the emotions of the moment. Mr Alexander Watson appearing at the Wellington Town Hall asked the audience to stand at the end of his performance while he recited the last verse of Kipling's poem *The Recessional*, which he gave "with great sincerity and earnestness" before leading the audience in singing the national anthem. At the picture theatres patriotic films were shown and at the King's Theatre, the well-known New Zealand actor and playwright Mr Barrie Marschel "read the latest war news from The Post's special edition, and the audience rose and sang the National Anthem".[9]

Both Massey, the prime minister and Ward, the leader of the Opposition, with elections approaching, sought to benefit, although each stressed to the cheering crowds that this was no time for politics. Massey's "We are all staunch Imperialists, and party is dropped for the time being", was matched by Ward's similar declarations. "New Zealand," added Sir Joseph, "will do her part in assisting the Empire cheerfully and well as she has done in the past. (Loud cheers.) She will do it to the last man and the last shilling if called upon to do so."[10]

GEORGE TARR AND *HINEMOA*

War in Europe took many New Zealanders by surprise. One of these was George Tarr who we met managing Hayward's Empire picture theatre in Napier in 1911 and who then managed the Opera House in Gisborne in 1913. There had been some problems between Thompson–Payne Pictures and New Zealand Picture Supplies in 1913 that led to legal action to recover outstanding film hire costs. How Tarr featured in this is not certain. In 1914 he was no longer managing for Hayward but was looking to finance a film based on the Reverend Bennett's Rotorua Maori Mission Choir and Entertainers' highly successful touring show on Maori life, "The Maori. At home! At Play! At War!"[11]

TUTANEKAI AND TIKI.

George Tarr's *Hinemoa*, a multi-reel film that opened at the Lyric Theatre, Auckland, on Monday 17 August 1914 in the second week of the war. NTSV Collection.

In 1914 I conceived the idea of making a Maori picture with the Reverend Bennett lecturing it and taking it to England. It was going to be a fairly financial thing and of course it was going to cost some money … the president of the Chamber of Commerce, Mr Anderson of Auckland … was the man that was financing the venture … I met him in Queen Street one day and he said to me: "Well Mr Tarr, "he said, "I'm afraid that we'll have to postpone that little business venture of ours." I said, "Why? What's the matter?" "Well," he said, "The War." I said, "What War?" He said, "War with Germany."

"But," I said, "We're not going to war with Germany are we?" He said, "Yes. I've just come away from the heads … and war might be declared anytime." … "But," he said, "If you've got anything in a smaller way that we might do … just tell me and I'll finance it …" So I went straight up to the library; that was about ten o'clock in the morning … and I read "Hinemoa" backwards and forwards, and forwards and backwards and I wrote a scenario. And I took this scenario down at eight o'clock that night to his office … 'Well here's my 'smaller thing' as you call it." I said, "I'd like to do 'Hinemoa'. The Story of Hinemoa and Tutanekai."

"Well!" he said, "Let's hear it!" So I got out my book and read him the scenario. I told him about the sunsets, the going down of the sun and the coming up of the sun, and what the Maoris would

do, and what they wouldn't do. I think he was a bit dazed at the finish because he said, "Well that's perfectly all right. Just tell me when you're ready." So I said, "Well I'm ready now. I want a cheque. I want to go away in the morning to Rotorua." "Well," he said, "all right, how much do you want?" … "I want fifty pounds to go away." And he wrote me a cheque out for fifty pounds. An open cheque. So I went down in the morning and I changed it, and I got on the train for Rotorua. I arrived in Rotorua, and that night I went to see the Maori concert. And I saw several people there I thought would do me quite fine for the cast. And I saw the Reverend Bennett … and he was quite excited about it … But he got his Maoris together and he told them … "You do for Mr Tarr just the same as you would do for me." And the Maoris did that, and they did everything I asked them. So I started in, and within four days I was out at Whaka and they were having a big hangi, and I supplied food for them …[12]

Tarr selected Hera Tawhai and her husband Rua for the main roles of Hinemoa and Tutanekai. It was a logical choice as the concert included a tableau on the legend and this led to Hera's part in the film.

Mr Tarr took me and an auntie of mine to Kawaha. That's where I listened to Tutuanekai's flute. After that listening I got into the water, swam. A little way of course. But in the picture — miles! Then after swimming then, we landed over at Mokoia Island just beside Hinemoa's bath now. I got off again from the boat, the launch, and swam a little way. When I got ashore I was exhausted, tired, swimming all that way … I thought it was all good fun![13]

Tarr worked with Charles Newham as his cameraman and they agreed to go into partnership for the film and each take a share of the profits. Tarr put it together with the minimum of editing. "I've been on stage all my life, you see, and I've been in drama and musical comedy and everything and I made it per the script. And I did it as much as possible with the scenes following each other."[14] Tarr worked through the Reverend Bennett in selecting the cast. He paid the men eight shillings a day and the women six shillings.

I finished the picture in about eight days, as I thought, and took it back to Auckland. And I went to see Mr Hayward. I said, "I have a picture for you, Mr Hayward, I've made." He said, "You made a picture? … What is it?" I said, "It's Hinemoa and Tutanekai … I want you to give me a preview." That was [at] the Lyric Theatre which was the biggest theatre in Auckland at that time in 1914. So he made the day for a Wednesday … afternoon. And when I got there I was quite surprised to find the Mayor there, and all the heads of Auckland were there. There were about fifty people in all, so I went on the stage and ran the picture through. It wasn't completed of course. I ran it through and told them what I was going to do to finish it. And they gave me a big hand and when I went down to the front Mr Hayward met me and put his hand on my shoulder and he said, "Well look, Mr Tarr, I'll put that picture on right away. And," he said, "I'll give you the same terms as I'm paying now for Antony and Cleopatra, which is showing at the present time."[15] Well, of course that was good enough for me. If it was good enough for Antony and Cleopatra, it was good enough for me. So we made that arrangement, but I said, "I've got to go to Rotorua to finish it." So we went to Rotorua on the Sunday. And then, my little dear sweet Hinemoa, of course, she'd swum across the lake and she'd dived into the boiling bath and I found that she was laid out with two doctors … So I went round and found a cousin of hers. And this cousin was, very, very much like her, especially profile. So I made it in semi-darkness and profiled her.

Anyway I finished the picture and titled it and we finished up in Auckland, and we opened in
Auckland, in the first week of the First World War. [16]

In fact, Tarr's memory is at fault. *Hinemoa* opened at the Lyric Theatre, Auckland, on Monday
17 August 1914, in the second week of the war. Hayward did it justice advertising it as New
Zealand's "First Photo-play yet produced in N.Z. by entirely local enterprise" and acknowledging
both the producer George Tarr and the cinematographer Charles Newham. The *Auckland Star*
reported: "The story is so well known that it is unnecessary to recapitulate what may be termed the
Maori version of Hero and Leander. The details have been well arranged and the picturesque native
costumes and the natural scenery of Rotorua are well calculated to ensure a good result. Added
interest is given by the fact that the characters are all represented by members of the famous choir
party of the Rev. A. Bennett of Rotorua, direct descendents of the hero and heroine of the story."[17]

We were the only theatre in Auckland that was getting any business at all. And we did very big
business with it. And at the end of the season in Auckland, Mr Anderson came to us, and he said
he was very pleased with the picture. He said as far as he was concerned … if we could pay him
the money that he had just paid out on it, the production of it, we could have all of his shares …
So that of course gave just the three of us the interest in the film. So we put it on. I took it right
through New Zealand. I travelled for about five months with it in New Zealand.[18]

Tarr, Newham and two others shared the profits from the film, after paying out Mr Anderson's
advance of £50. While the Auckland film critic was guarded in his comments, the Wellington
reviewer was more positive during its run at the King's Theatre, praising the quality of
Newham's camera work, noting that "while the film is being screened appropriate selections of
Mr Alfred Hill's compositions are played by the orchestra".[19] Rudall Hayward remembers seeing
it at the cinema. "It was a very fine film, beautifully made. The photography was first class and
as far as I remember the acting was of a high order."[20]

It did a week at each of the main centres and then toured to packed houses around
the circuit. In terms of New Zealand narrative films, it was an auspicious beginning but a
beginning in a very New Zealand way; fictional films remained rare events, driven by individual
inspiration that worked once, but were rarely successfully repeated.

HER BROTHER'S REDEMPTION

The success of *Hinemoa* tempted Tarr to make *Her Brother's Redemption* in early 1915; "A New
Zealand Film play written, acted and photographed by New Zealanders".[21] Tarr acted in one of
the four named parts and this time the cameraman was Frank Stewart.[22] It was released in the
picture theatres in late April 1915. This melodrama of New Zealand settler life did not have the
same impact on audiences as did *Hinemoa* and it seems the film reviewers tried to be positive
about it when it was released "calling it a sensational drama … which is well up to standard",
but apart from this had nothing to say.[23]

The film did not have a well-known legend to sustain it and one suspects that its content led
it to be compared to the staple dramas from overseas that were the film theatres' stock in trade.
Other than being filmed and located in New Zealand, there was nothing that made it stand out.
It was Tarr's last fictional film venture and he returned to theatre management before enlisting in
the New Zealand Expeditionary Force (NZEF) serving overseas in the NZ Machine Gun Corps
on the Western Front where almost inevitably he was co-opted to run pictures and other shows

Her Brother's Redemption. George Tarr's second feature film released in late April 1915. NTSV Collection.

in the field.[24] Local and general news events and scenic films remained the staple fare of New Zealand cameramen and were always in demand, even though overseas multi-reel fictional feature films increasingly dominated the theatre programme.

However, in August 1914 war was the news and picture theatres throughout New Zealand adjusted their programmes to ensure that they had suitable pictures that captured contemporary events in Europe. In Auckland, Fuller's Pictures at the King's Theatre advertised *The British Army of 1914,* which was a compilation from existing stock that included the Trooping of the Colours on the Horse Guards parade "screened nightly to the accompaniment of deafening and patriotic cheering". Hayward's Pictures showed scenes of *Our Navy,* the following week it was Fuller's who screened *Our King's Navy,* which included replaying Newham's film of HMS *New Zealand* entering Auckland Harbour, then Hayward's screened *Soldiers of the King* at the Lyric.[25]

OFF TO THE FRONT

What captured public attention was the mobilisation of the NZEF. An advance party formed from the Territorial Force and drawn from the main centres of Auckland and Wellington was immediately mobilised to seize German Samoa. This task had been planned for by the staff of the New Zealand Defence Force and immediately put into effect on the receipt of a telegram to the New Zealand Government requesting the capture of the wireless station at Apia "as a great and urgent Imperial service". Friday night was the Territorial Parade night in Wellington and Auckland. By 11 August the Samoan Advance Party consisted of 1383 composite forces made up almost entirely of Territorial volunteers commanded by Colonel Robert Logan, a regular officer of the New Zealand Staff Corps who commanded the Auckland Military District. They were a three-infantry company-strength battalion, two companies drawn from 5th Wellington and one from the 3rd Auckland Regiment: all volunteer soldiers based in the two large urban centres. In addition, there were two obsolete 15-pounder field guns and two six-pounders as the artillery of the force, engineers that included signallers volunteered from the Post and Telegraph Department, a company of railway engineers and four trained ship's officers to command four motor patrol craft that were embarked with the force.[26] Supply services were provided by the Army Service Corps. The field ambulance of six officers and 67 other ranks included two dental surgeons, an addition that was unique to the New Zealand Medical Corps. Attached to this were six nursing sisters and chaplains.[27] This Samoan Advance Guard, as it became known, concentrated in Wellington and was a tribute to the effective planning that had taken place before war was declared.

Photographs showing the mobilisation and departure featured in the illustrated papers and film of these events featured in the picture theatres. "Patriotic feelings are intensely

Coaling HMNZT No. 1 *Moeraki* prior to its sailing for German Samoa. A Territorial soldier self-consciously guards an obsolete 15-pounder field gun on its deck. Still from *Off to the Front*. NTSV F38442.

stimulated by an excellent specimen of New Zealand made film titled 'Off to the Front'. The recent departure of the advance guard of this Dominion's Expeditionary Force from Wellington by the steamers 'Moeraki' and 'Monowai' has been splendidly recorded commencing with the preparations at the Buckle street barracks and terminating with good-byes as the transports cast off from the wharfs."[28]

Little of this detail survives on film. The two New Zealand transports, 'His Majesty's New Zealand Transport' (HMNZT) No. 1 *Moeraki* and HMNZT No. 2 *Monowai* are shown being coaled for the voyage at King's Wharf in Wellington Harbour. It is an atmospheric shot as steam wafts over the workers on deck as dockers use large buckets to pour coal into the ship's bunkers. A soldier in uniform self-consciously stands guard over an obsolete 15-pounder field gun from Wellington's D Battery and its limber on the ship's deck. There is a detailed pan along the length of both ships and the number '2' can be clearly seen on the side of the *Monowai*.

This film fragment ends with soldiers in shirt sleeves and braces loading straw-filled canvas mattresses onto one of the transports.[29] It is one of only two remaining film fragments showing the troop departures from New Zealand in the First World War. *Off to the Front* was first screened at the King's Theatre in Wellington on 11 August.[30] It was a commonly used phrase during the war and the title was given to a number of films. The ships sailed on 15 August 1914. The day before both were inspected by Prime Minister William Massey, together with James Allen, Minister of Defence, accompanied by other cabinet ministers and Major-General Sir Alexander Godley, commanding the New Zealand Defence Forces. "Accommodation for the men is necessarily limited, and bunks have been erected in every conceivable part of the ships." Nevertheless: "The men are very cheerful and look forward to an interesting experience."[31] The departure was delayed because of the threat posed by the German East Asiatic Squadron, which included the two powerful armoured cruisers the *Scharnhorst* and the *Gneisenau*. Initially the protection for the New Zealand transports were the two obsolete P-class cruisers HMS *Philomel*

🎞 *Off to The Front*. NTSV F38442.

and *Psyche* and the initial route was changed so that the convoy called into Noumea where it received the added naval protection of the Indefatigable-class battlecruiser HMAS *Australia* and the French armoured cruiser *Montcalm*. The New Zealand force rowed ashore at Apia, German Samoa, on 29 August 1914 and occupied it without any resistance. It was the second German territory after Togoland to fall to the Allies in the First World War.[32]

MOBILISATION OF THE MAIN BODY, NZEF

Film survives of the mobilisation of the Auckland, Wellington and Otago contributions to the Main Body of the NZEF in 1914. Each centre focused on what their local boys were doing, but also screened pictures from the other centres in this New Zealand-wide endeavour. In Auckland all the picture houses vied with each other to capture the patriotic fervour sweeping the country. At the Queen's Theatre *In the clutches of the Ku Klux Clan* took second billing to *Off to the War* showing the departure of the "Second Contingent of Auckland Territorials comprising 281 officers and men, left for Wellington, yesterday afternoon by Special Train. Taken especially for the QUEEN'S and PRINCESS THEATRES. Come and see the Great Send-Off of our Noble Territorials."[33] This was the departure of the final elements of the Auckland Contingent for Wellington where they would link up with the Advance Guard of the NZEF.

Frank Stewart, one of New Zealand's pioneer cameramen, in 1915. NTSV Collection S6169, no. 2.

The Main Body of the Auckland Contingent for the NZEF went into camp at Alexandra Park Racecourse where they were inspected by Minister of Defence James Allen on Saturday 19 September 1914. The papers reported: "The weather was glorious, and there was a large attendance of the public. The inspection took place in the Alexandra Park enclosure, but as the parade ground was some distance from the grandstand, most people preferred to stand by the rails, nearer to the scene of operations. At the saluting base a space had been roped in, and here a large number of officers' wives and civilians were seated. The march past made quite an imposing spectacle, and called forth the hearty applause of the onlookers."[34]

The film of this parade survives and was shown in Auckland theatres in the week starting Monday 21 September under the title *Auckland's Expeditionary Force: The Minister for Defence Reviews the Troops*.[35] The cameraman (possibly Frank Stewart) positioned himself to the right of the saluting dais with One Tree Hill in the background.[36] This is perhaps the best film we have that gives us a glimpse of what each of the military districts sent to war. Lieutenant-Colonel C.E.R. Mackesy, a Territorial officer from Whangarei, commanded the parade. In peace he commanded the 11th North Auckland Mounted Rifles Regiment, whose acronym 'NAMR' was known as 'Nearly All Mackesy's Relations'. He came to war with his son and nephews numbered among his horsemen. 'German Joe' Mackesy proved to be an outstanding commander in the field, first on Gallipoli and then in the campaign in Sinai and Palestine. We have the report from his troopers of their commander who, on reaching the border

March-past of the Auckland Infantry Battalion of the NZEF at Alexandra Park, Auckland, on 19 September 1914. Still from *Auckland's Expeditionary Force: The Minister for Defence Reviews the Troops.* NTSV F38469.

with Palestine, gave thanks to God that he was about to enter the Holy Land. Mackesy saw himself in the mould of the Crusaders and was larger than life to all who met him.

The march-past allows us to see the scale of New Zealand's military effort in 1914. "The first to pass the saluting base were the mounted squadrons, under Major Chapman: they marched past in column of troops. Then came the [Auckland] Infantry Battalion in column of platoons, under Lieutenant-Colonel A. Plugge. Following on came the Motor-cycle Corps, the Army Service Corps, in line, under Captain H.G. Reid, and the Field Ambulance Company, under Lieutenant-Colonel C.M. Begg, in column of sections."[37]

Lieutenant-Colonel Arthur Plugge is remembered in history by Plugge's Plateau that looms over Anzac Cove, so named because it is here that Plugge had his headquarters on 25 April 1915. A Territorial officer and headmaster of Dilworth School, he proved to be an earnest but mediocre officer in war. He objected to being passed over for command of a brigade in France and Russell, the New Zealand divisional commander, removed him from battalion command after the Somme in late 1916. In deference to his position as the last surviving original Main Body commanding officer he was made divisional sports officer before being returned to New Zealand. He was one who, although honoured, was destroyed by war. Separated from his family he became a sharemilker at Taupiri, living alone in a lean-to shack alongside the milking shed.[38]

Many of those marching past on film were to die on Gallipoli and in France. Mackesy's son Harry was killed in the August 1915 offensive on Gallipoli, as was the 56-year-old sheep farmer and South African War veteran Major Frank Chapman, killed on Chunuk Bair commanding the Auckland Mounted Rifles on 8 August 1915.[39] Begg would become director of Medical Services of the NZEF and die as much from exhaustion as influenza in Britain in 1919.[40]

What we do not see is what follows immediately after the march-past when Allen addressed the men, now formed into a hollow square, "making a very fine speech, in which he told them that they carried the honour of New Zealand in their hands, and that both the friends they met and the enemies they fought would form their opinions of New Zealanders from them.

Auckland's Expeditionary Force: The Minister for Defence Reviews the Troops. NTSV F38469.

'Therefore, see that you are as brave as you are honourable and modest, and courteous as you are brave.'[41]

The film featured at MacMahon's Queen's and Princess theatres in Auckland, together with two other topical films relating to the Auckland Contingent of the NZEF. The first was *Sammy, My Old Friend Sam*, the Manx collie presented by Mrs Joe MacMahon as a mascot to the New Zealand Army Service Corps. Mrs MacMahon was the wife of theatre proprietor, Mr J.F. MacMahon, who with his two brothers had been pioneers in both film-making and screening in Australasia. The second film was *The Mounted Rifle Regiment Passing Down Queen Street*.[42]

Neither of these films survive but we do have film of the Auckland Mounted Rifle Regiment marching down Queen Street on 22 September 1914. This was included in Ken G. Hall's 1928 Australian drama *The Exploits of the Emden*, which was a combination of documentary film and dramatised scenes recreating the battle between the cruiser HMAS *Sydney* and the German cruiser *Emden* off Cocos Island in November 1914.[43] The scene titled 'New Zealanders marching through the streets of Auckland' shows the troopers of the Auckland Mounted Rifles Regiment in their greatcoats marching down Queen Street with their rifles at the shoulder on a wet Auckland day. Crowds watch them pass from the cover of shopfront verandas while trams and vehicles pass by. Some boy scouts and in one case two women, no doubt accompanying a family member, walk with them. The fact that the regiment is dismounted, and the weather, indicates that this is the march down Queen Street after the farewell parade for the Auckland Contingent in the Domain on Saturday 22 September 1914. Their horses were already loaded on the transports in the harbour and they sailed the following day, only to be recalled because of the potential threat of the German Asiatic squadron that included the *Emden*.[44]

The surviving scenes in Hall's drama were originally screened in the Auckland theatres at the end of that week showing the final parade and embarkation of the Auckland Main Body of the NZEF under the title *The Farewell to the Auckland Expeditionary Force*. The Arcadia Theatre advertised: "THE FAREWELL TO THE AUCKLAND EXPEDITIONARY FORCE. 'Our Camera Man Was There'. Yesterday's Big Review and Parade — At the Domain — Marching Through the City — The Huge Crowds — Scenes at the Wharf — Embarking for the Front — A Complete Film of yesterday's big muster, specially taken and exclusive to the Arcadia."[45]

It was a pattern that continued for the rest of the war.

The despatch of the advance party of the NZEF for Samoa appeared alongside the advertisements for George Tarr's *Hinemoa*.[46] By early October 1914 the popular actress Mabel Norman in *Mabel at the Wheel* featured at the Lyric in Auckland alongside 'A Budget of War Items' that included the departure of the Auckland Contingent showing the march down Queen Street and the final review in the Auckland Domain. Other theatres showed scenes of the Wellington parades and a patriotic procession in Christchurch, all being highlighted in the entertainment columns of the daily papers.[47]

JUST AS THE SUN WENT DOWN

The Auckland papers also advertised that the Arcadia Theatre in Karangahape Road was screening the film *Just as the Sun Went Down* from Monday 5 October 1914. Like *Hinemoa* this was a New Zealand-made two-reel fictional film that was prompted by the outbreak of the war, and, like *Hinemoa*, was made on a shoestring budget and rushed into theatre. The *Auckland Star* reported:

> The opening is of a particularly charming nature, a touching farewell by a New Zealander,
> who is ordered to the front, being taken in ideal scenic conditions in Auckland, followed by

the training of the Expeditionary Forces, a march through Queen Street, and a farewell, reflecting the greatest credit on the photographer, Mr Frank Stewart. The second part takes us — in imagination — to Belgium with New Zealand troops, who take part in many thrilling incidents in the great campaign, the capture of German trenches being a most vivid and realistic portion of the film. The two principal characters, Jack and his pal, have many hair-raising adventures in their attempt to cut their way back to the main column, and the film depicts Jack, fighting all the way, carrying Sergt. Cross out of the firing line. The conclusion of the picture is of an emotional and touching nature, showing two heroes, mortally wounded, "bidding farewell to the dear old flag, just as the sun went down."[48]

The film was directed by Australian actor Frank Devonport (real name Frank Jones), who was a well-known face on the New Zealand theatre circuit as an actor-director-playwright.[49] The title originally featured as a popular song with an American version recorded and sung by Dudley and Macdonough for Edison in 1899.[50] It was adapted to British music halls during the Boer War and entrepreneurs in New Zealand such as Cooper and Macdermott toured country areas with a Myriorama or magic lantern slide programme that illustrated the story as a singer or raconteur delivered patriotic songs such as Dolly Grey and Tell Mother I Am Not Coming Home. The climax was Just as the Sun Went Down with the pictures "portraying an artillery battery dashing forward; a mortally wounded gunner falling onto the veldt and the following limber driver making a hasty decision; he galloped the limber over the casualty Just As the Sun Went Down".[51]

Devonport was working with the Cyclorama at the Auckland Exhibition in 1914 and, like Tarr, recognised the moment and seized it. He took the words of the song and made it the basis of his plot.

> Just at the din of the battles o'er
> Just at the close of day
> Wounded and bleeding upon the field
> Two dying soldiers lay
> One holds a ringlet of thin gray hair
> One old a lock of brown
> Bidding farewell to the stars an' stripes
> Just as the sun went down.

The advertising shows how cleverly Devonport achieved a cast of hundreds if not thousands at little or no cost for 'New Zealand's Own War Drama'. He injected his characters into the actual training at the mobilisation camp at Epsom, into the march-past down Queen Street and the departure at the wharf gates. It rightly proclaimed that the film was "Supported by the entire Auckland Contingent of the Expeditionary Force", and so naturally enough the public flocked to see their boys and themselves on film. "See the cheering Auckland throng! See yourselves as others see you!"[52] It did good business in Auckland and throughout New Zealand but, as with *Hinemoa*, no fragment of it appears to have survived.

ARCADIA ———— THEATRE,
ARCADIA ———— THEATRE,
KARANGAHAPE ROAD.
CONTINUOUS PICTURES.
TO-NIGHT!   TO-NIGHT!   TO-NIGHT!
Final Screening of
THE RANGE WAR,
And Present Programme.
ANOTHER TREMENDOUS SCOOP
MADE BY
———THE ARCADIA———
—THE ARCADIA——
The Arcadia, famous for exclusiveness, has again scored a Terrific Triumph by securing the most talked of War Picture of the year.
—— MONDAY NEXT ——
—— MONDAY NEXT ——
WE OFFER THE BEST YET.
A Drama of the Moment.
JUST AS THE SUN WENT DOWN.
JUST AS THE SUN WENT DOWN.
A Gigantic Local War Drama, founded on the Present Campaign.
A Magnificent Production. Produced by Frank Devonport.
Acted by a Specially Selected Cast. Supported by the Entire Auckland Contingent of the Expeditionary Force.
JUST AS THE SUN WENT DOWN.
A Story of Love and War.
OUR BOYS IN THE FIRING LINE.
—— MONDAY NEXT. ——
—— MONDAY NEXT. ——
FIRST SESSION COMMENCES AT 2 P.M.
In Addition,
THE LATEST LONDON TOPICAL, PICTORIAL NEWS FROM THE FRONT SPECIAL ORCHESTRAL EFFECTS.
NO ADVANCE IN PRICES—
6d and 3d Everywhere.

Auckland Star, 10 October 1914, p. 10.

Frank Stewart, the cameraman, was another pioneer in film-making in New Zealand and Australia. He worked on film in Australia for Cosens Spencer and claimed he was part of Ernest Higgins', camera crews that filmed the world title bout between Tommy Burns and Jack Johnson in Sydney in 1908, which ended when the police entered the ring and stopped the fight in the fourteenth round; the film then did great business throughout the world.

Like many of his contemporaries Frank Stewart managed picture theatres and filmed when the opportunities presented themselves. In 1910 he managed Thompson–Payne Pictures at the Opera House, Palmerston North.[53] In 1911 he went out on his own as Stewart's Pictures and Orchestra at the Tivoli Theatre, Newton, Auckland.[54] In August the papers reported that, "During the week an additional picture of local interest will be shown this being a cinematograph representation of the skaters at the Windsor Rink which was taken last week by Mr Frank Stewart."[55] Local skating rinks were doing excellent business. Stewart wanted to draw in some of this crowd to the mutual benefit of the rink, who would attract more skaters in the hope of being filmed and to Stewart's picture theatre where the skaters would go to see themselves on screen.

Stewart ran into financial difficulties in 1911 and into 1912 and there were constant reports of claims against him for unpaid debts. The climax came in September 1913 when 25-year-old Stewart was committed to the Supreme Court for trial on fraud charges in borrowing £15 by credit. Stewart was apprehended in Sydney and returned to New Zealand. He was "charged with attempting to leave New Zealand without providing his wife with adequate maintenance. As he had entered a bond for 50 pounds for his future payments and had paid all costs and expenses, this charge was withdrawn."[56]

On 10 September 1913 Stewart was again charged with fraud in that on 5 and 6 June he had cashed two cheques with Mai Candy for 25/- and £5 "by a false pretence".

Mai Candy, cashier at the Queen's Theatre, said she had known Stewart for about two years, and on 5 June she cashed a cheque for 25/- for him. The following morning she cashed his cheque for £5. The cheques were returned 'Account Closed', and she had to pay the money out of her own pocket. She "had never given Stewart cash without some acknowledgement. She had told him about the matter, and he had said he would fix it up. She was satisfied that he would, until he left New Zealand, though she would not have paid the money had she known the cheques were worthless. Since he came back, the accused had made arrangements to refund the money, and had, in fact, paid the money last Monday."[57]

His ability to make good his debts saw the case withdrawn and by 1914 Stewart was in demand as a cameraman.

NEW ZEALANDERS FOR THE FRONT

It seems James McDonald was the cameraman who took the surviving film of the farewell parade and departure of the Wellington Province's section of the Main Body NZEF on 24 September 1914. The illustrated papers show a stout man in a white suit behind the camera, filming from the position that equates to the camera's viewpoint.[58] It certainly does not seem to be a young Sydney Taylor, the official cinematographer for the Department of Agriculture, Industries and Commerce, and so it appears that this was one of the 'important events' that McDonald decided to film for himself. It may be that Taylor filmed the march along Adelaide Road and along Lambton Quay; we do not know. However, it is almost certain he was filming somewhere and that every cameraman throughout New Zealand was filming the mobilisation scenes. McDonald's film paralleled those filmed by Barton and Vinsen in Wellington, Gore

in Dunedin, Newham, Stewart and others in Auckland, and indeed everywhere that the local photographer or picture theatre projectionist had a motion picture camera. As the photographs in the illustrated papers demonstrate one can find the camera in the crowd in many of the parades scenes.

McDonald was certainly one of a number of cameramen capturing the farewell scenes in Newtown Park that day on Thursday 24 September with 2500 men on parade before Governor General Lord Liverpool, and watched by a packed crowd of 25,000–30,000 people. The 2500 citizen soldiers included the men of the Wellington Infantry Battalion who can be seen on the right of the parade, prominent in their 'lemon squeezer' headdress, designed and adopted by their commanding officer, Lieutenant-Colonel W.G. Malone, when he was commanding officer of the 11th Taranaki Rifles. The hat's shape was a perfect foil to a wet Taranaki summer in allowing the rain to run off rather than collect in the dent that was the standard pattern of the 'smasher' hats worn by New Zealand Territorial Force. In justifying his decision to Godley when he commented on the unofficial headdress, Malone also explained that it mirrored his regimental badge in representing the shape of the volcanic cone of Mt Egmont. On his selection to command of the Wellington Infantry Battalion of the NZEF, Malone decided that this would be the battalion headdress. Now he stood on parade among his officers and men all wearing lemon squeezers, making up 1000 of the 2500 on parade in hollow-square.

The Wellington Mounted Rifles faced them while the Field Artillery Brigade and Ammunition Column together with engineers and signallers filled in the centre facing the dais. The papers reported: "The ceremony was as dignified as it was impressive. At 2.30 pm when His Excellency the Governor (Lord Liverpool) arrived the whole of the assembled troops came to the Royal Salute and the bands played the National Anthem. His Excellency was accompanied by the Prime Minister (the Right Hon. W.F. Massey), the Minister of Defence (Hon. J.H.

Farewell to the Wellington Contingent of the NZEF at Newtown Park on 24 September 1914. Note the photographer in a white suit to the left of the flag. *Auckland Weekly News*, 1 October 1914.

Allen), the Leader of the Opposition (Sir Joseph Ward), and the Mayor (Mr J.P. Luke) …
His Excellency then inspected the Force after which he delivered a stirring speech in which
he bade the troops goodbye."[59]

As one would expect all the other dignitaries also made speeches, the hymn O God, Our
Help in Ages Past was sung and prayers were read — to the irritation of Lieutenant-Colonel
Malone who noted in his diary that evening that there was "too much speechifying and
praying". However, there was enormous public pride in Wellington's sons parading for war.
Most were drawn from the rural areas outside of Wellington City itself, which had despatched
its contribution with the Samoa Force, "from the Tararuas and Ruahines, and from Taranaki,
the King Country, and the Manawatu. They are squatters' sons, small farmers' sons, the sons
of artisans and business people in the smaller country towns; there are backwoodsmen and
stockmen among them; and they are largely the sons of soldiers (Maori War veterans and
others) and the fighting blood in them."[60]

We see the gathering of dignitaries at the bottom of the steps at the northern end of the
park. Prime Minister William Massey is prominent in his bowler hat, as is James Allen, minister
of defence, in his trilby hat and winged-collared shirt. The inspection follows with Lord
Liverpool in his formal blue uniform being escorted by Major-General Sir Alexander Godley,
commanding the New Zealand Defence Force, who is now about to take the NZEF to war. They
pass along the ranks of the troopers of the Wellington Mounted Rifles in their 'smasher' hats
escorted by their commanding officer, Lieutenant-Colonel W.J. Meldrum. Among the gaggle
of military officers following them, we see the men who would carve New Zealand military
reputation over the next four years of war, including Colonel E.W.C. Chaytor, the assistant
adjutant general of the NZEF and Lieutenant-Colonel W.G. Braithwaite, the GSO1 or principal
operations officer.[61]

The Governor, the Earl
of Liverpool inspects the
Wellington Mounted Rifle
Regiment. He is followed
by Commanding Officer
Lieutenant-Colonel William
Meldrum with Major-General
Sir Alexander Godley on the
right. Behind them are Prime
Minister William Massey (in
bowler hat), James Allen,
minister of defence, and other
staff. Still from *New Zealanders
for the Front: Official Farewell*.
NTSV F1820.

The 6th Reinforcements march down Lambton Quay before embarking on SS *Tofua* on 11 August 1915. This is a fragment of the only reinforcement troopship sailing film that survives. Still from *New Zealanders for the Front: Official Farewell.* NTSV F1820.

Godley would command the NZEF for the entire war, rising in rank to Lieutenant-General and a corps commander of the ANZAC Corps on Gallipoli, II ANZAC Corps in France and XXII Corps in 1918 after the concentration of the Australian divisions into the Australian Corps. A clever and efficient administrator, he established both the New Zealand Territorial Force and the NZEF on a sound administrative basis that was critical to its survival and functioning in the years to come.

Diplomatic in his dealings with government ministers and military superiors, his men never warmed to him, or, outwardly, he to them, although his writings show that he was proud of their achievements and had a high regard of his New Zealanders. They rightly suspected his tactical failings on Gallipoli in 1915 and this dislike hardened during the years on the Western Front. As corps commander he was always a distant figure to the men. It was his determination to please British Commander-in-Chief General Sir Douglas Haig that led to the botched and tragic attack before Passchendaele on 12 October 1917.[62] Godley recognised the power of publicity and had been at the forefront in advertising New Zealand's citizen army; he would continue that policy overseas and shared the government's determination to show New Zealand, the British Empire and the wider world what this small country was achieving.

The film scene shifts to Adelaide Road, Newtown, as the crowds leave the park and trams pass towards the city centre. This is where the film of the Main Body ends, what follows seems to flow on, but in fact is film taken of the departure of the 6th Reinforcements who sailed from Wellington on 11 August 1915 on His Majesty's New Zealand Transport No. 28, the SS *Tofua*, a 4345-ton Union Steamship Company passenger ship that normally plied the Pacific Islands run from New Zealand. One can see the distinctly different mood of the soldiers crowding her decks and rigging. The enthusiasm and expectation clear with the Main Body is absent. The first casualties had returned from Gallipoli and it was evident to all that this was no longer a short

New Zealanders for the Front: Official Farewell. NTSV F1820.

war that would be over by Christmas. Sadly, of the many departure films taken at Wellington's wharfside, this alone survives.

In this added-on fragment of film we are looking down on Lambton Quay as the Wellington Infantry Battalion march in column of fours, with bayonets fixed, marching "through dense crowds of enthusiastic well-wishers, the bands playing Tipperary and other tunes popular at that time". It is then to the wharfs as stores and horses are loaded on board the transports.

This was an army dependent on horse transport and 3817 horses went with the Main Body to war; the troopers of the Mounted Rifles regiments had to provide their own horse and saddle, which if found suitable were purchased by the Crown at market value. "Such value should not exceed £20. Horses for Mounted Rifles must be from four to seven years of age, practically sound, from 14.2 to 15.2 hands in height, but animals under 14.3 hands will only be accepted if otherwise especially suitable. No greys, duns, or light chestnuts will be taken. Geldings are preferable to mares."[63] In addition to the trooper's chargers, light and heavy draft horses were purchased for artillery and to pull the standard Army Service Corps general wagon (GS).

The departure of the Main Body was reported in great detail in all the papers and filmed. The King's Theatre, Wellington, showed: "A panorama of Wellington Harbour showing the troopship march of the Field Artillery Brigade through the city, shipping guns, horses and foodstuffs, coaling operations, fitting up the troopships, inspection of troops and Governor's farewell at Newtown Park, the long march to the ships, embarkation. The latter section taken by a special apparatus was the only picture of the event secured."[64] It seems that the King's Theatre cinematographer, 'Vanie' Vinsen, had some form of special lens. Whether this was true or not, what it does emphasise is that cameramen were filming these events throughout New Zealand and there was competition to get them into the theatres, the next day if possible. Any suggestion that one theatre had something more to offer than another was eagerly used as advertising to attract the crowds.

While every picture theatre had its film showing the parade and departure of the Main Body, for the departing soldiers on board ship it was all anticlimax for, after pulling into the stream, they found themselves still in harbour the next day. The threat of the German Asiatic squadron operating in the Pacific and the New Zealand Government's concern at the lack of escorting warships led to a postponement. On 28 September the transports pulled back into the wharf, this time joined by the four ships of the South Island Contingent. The Mounted Rifles and their horses were disembarked; the infantry remained on board, training ashore during the day and no doubt visiting the picture theatres during the evenings to see and enjoy the films of their own farewell parade and departure!

OTAGO–SOUTHLAND GOES TO WAR

Henry Gore's films of the Otago Contingent also survive. A film of the parade of the Otago Contingent of the Expeditionary Force through Dunedin screened at the Plaza Picture Theatre on Friday 4 September 1914 under the title *Otago Contingents Parade through Dunedin*, emphasising the "Clear Picture. Everyone Recognisable". This has not survived.[65] The Plaza Picture Theatre took the lead in showing scenes of the Otago–Southland section of the NZEF in camp at Tahuna Park including "splendid" pictures of the Otago Mounted Infantry Regiment. Fragments of this film have survived.[66]

The film shows the civic reception at Tahuna Park on 16 September.[67] Gore captures the faces and the mood of the crowd as his camera pans across the gathering. We see the Otago

New Zealand Permanent Staff (NZPS) warrant officers with Territorial soldiers of the 4th Otago Company of the Otago Infantry Battalion at Tahuna Park on 16 September 1914. Still from Henry Gore's *Civic Farewell at Tahuna Park Section 1*. NTSV F1147.

Apprehensive faces among the crowd at Tahuna Park for the civic farewell on 16 September 1914. Still from Henry Gore's *Civic Farewell at Tahuna Park Section 1*. NTSV F1147.

Civic Farewell at Tahuna Park Section 1. NTSV F1147.

Civic Farewell at Tahuna Park Section 2. NTSV F54107.

Infantry Battalion commanding officer, Lieutenant-Colonel T.W. McDonald of the New Zealand Staff Corps, pass through the crowd and being congratulated by local dignitaries. The Dunedin Liedertafel choir sings, the moderator of the Presbyterian Synod and then the mayor of Dunedin, Mr J.B. Shacklock, address the crowd; we can imagine the singing of God Save the

King and Oh God, Our Help in Ages Past. Gore captures the evident cheerfulness of the men in contrast to the apprehension on the faces of the women. The tension is broken by a shift to scenes in the camp and the staged actions of the sergeant cook in an off-white apron and bandaged arm directing the work of his cookhouse fatigues, all of whom seem to be puffing on pipes as they go about their duties.

There are scenes from the open day at the park with two soldiers pillow-fighting on a greasy log while being photographed by a civilian photographer.[68] We can imagine Otago theatre audiences craning to identify themselves in the crowd and going home well pleased in seeing themselves and so many people that they knew on film on such an historic occasion.

OUR BOYS EN ROUTE TO EGYPT

The Main Body of the NZEF sailed from Wellington at 6 a.m. 16 October 1914, "the fourteen great grey ships, their smoke trailing away over the port quarter before a fresh wind, passed down the wild rocky gap of the entrance. The grey seas rolled in a long swell, grey flying clouds hid the eastern mountain tops. The passengers of an in-bound steamer had hurried on deck, clad lightly against the chill wind, and sent a faint cheer to each passing ship."[69]

Sailing followed sailing as reinforcements were raised, trained and despatched overseas every month, all appearing in film at the picture theatres.

New Zealanders featured on film in Great Britain in 1914. The response to the declaration of war saw a wave of jingoistic fervour sweep through the British Isles and a public desire to help 'brave little Belgium'. Thousands flocked to the recruiting halls and the country cheered off the British Expeditionary Force (BEF) as it embarked for France. In London many New Zealand expatriates applied to the high commissioner's office and this raised a 200-strong New Zealand Contingent, many of whom like the New Zealand artist, Horace Moore-Jones, were over-age but who, adding dye to their hair and adjusting birthdays accordingly, signed up in London and joined the NZEF in Egypt before Gallipoli. The New Zealanders marched in the Lord Mayor of London's parade and featured in the newsreels.[70] This was seen in New Zealand in January 1915 in a *Gaumont Graphic* newsreel titled *New Zealand Infantry*.[71] It gives us a glimpse of these mainly over-age New Zealanders wearing their 'smasher' hats with the brims turned up like the Australian-pattern slouch hat as they proudly march into film history.[72]

"We were very conspicuous in our slouch hats in the streets and the little boys used to gape at us a lot. We had New Zealand in white on a crimson ribbon on both arms just below the shoulders and one little paper boy looked hard at it and slowly and laboriously spelt it out, looked into my face, then said to his mate 'New Zealand and Gor Blimey 'e's white!'"[73] Anzac participation in the Lord Mayor's show continued throughout the war.[74]

TE HOKOWHITU-A-TU: THE NATIVE CONTINGENT GOES TO WAR

One segment that has survived in the Pathé vaults shows a reinforcement draft marching to the wharves through the streets of Wellington.[75] What is important about this film is that it shows the departure of the original Maori, or Native, Contingent as it was titled. We can identify Major H. Peacock, NZSC, Maori Contingent commander leading his officers and men. It was taken on Saturday 13 February 1915 and shows the 3rd Reinforcements numbering 1712 personnel, consisting largely of mounted riflemen and infantry for the two brigades of the NZEF in Egypt and the 509-strong Maori Contingent or Te Hokowhitu-a-Tu marching down Adelaide Road and through the city to the wharfs where they would depart the following day for Egypt on the SS *Warrimoo*.

Te Hokowhitu-a-Tu: the Maori Contingent, led by Major H. Peacock, parade through Wellington on
13 February 1915. Still from *Pathé Gazette: New Zealand Reinforcements Leaving*. NTSV F245692.

The Maori people had attempted to send a contingent from the tribes to the Boer War but
had been refused by the British government and this happened again in 1914 on the grounds
"that the Maoris should not take part in the wars of the White Race against a White Race".[76]
However, this argument vanished with the deployment of Indian Army units to France and so
permission was given for a special Maori Contingent, half of which was to go to Samoa and the
other half to Egypt as garrison. The uncomfortable realities of Maori garrisoning Samoa was
soon realised and it was decided that the Maori Contingent should join the NZEF in Egypt. It
was raised and trained at Narrow Neck Camp, Devonport, Auckland, and organised into two
250-strong companies; 'A' Company, drawn from the West Coast of the North Island, north of
Auckland and the South Island; 'B' Company, drawn from the East Coast of the North Island,
and commanded by a Pakeha New Zealand Regular Officer Major Henry Peacock, NZSC.
The highest ranked Maori officer was the contingent's medical officer, Captain Peter Buck, 'Te
Rangihiroa', already seen in McDonald's film of the officers of the United States 'White Fleet'
visiting Rotorua in 1908.

On 10 February they paraded through the crowded streets of Auckland to the wharf and
sailed for Wellington. On Saturday 13 February 1915 they disembarked and marched with the
3rd Reinforcements of the NZEF to Newtown Park for the official farewells. Their families and
the Maori members of parliament who had engineered their existence had no doubts about
their potential.

The Europeans, who had seen that 500 march, have never forgotten: they still speak in high praise of them, of their splendid condition of the men, of their marching and of their general appearance which compared favourably with the best troops in the world. Some went as far to say that they were even better than the white soldiers seen at Newtown Park. It is only right that it should be so. The heritage of their ancestors had been inherited by them, such as the haka, the tutu-ngarahu, canoe-paddling singing the performance of which in those days meant the rhythmical motion of the legs and swinging of the arms and the singing of the 'waiata'. That quality was already in them while they were learning these 'hakas' of the white races.[77]

It was a time when the papers were full of the bombardment of the Turkish forts guarding the straits of the Dardanelles and of the Turkish attack on the Suez Canal that would see New Zealanders in action for the first time. It was against this background that the contingent received their farewell. George Knight of the Otago Regiment, who sailed on the *Aparima* with the 3rd Reinforcements, at the same time as the Maori Contingent, recorded his impressions of the final parade at Newtown Park and the sailing.

> We marched up the back streets & arrived about 2.30 there was a deuced of a crowd there & the streets toward the latter part were thronged. The Governor didn't keep us waiting long & he inspected us & gave a speech as also did Bill Massey, J. Allen & two Maori Members. Then we marched back to boats through the main streets which were thronged. Lots of people gave soft drinks, papers, cigarettes, fruit etc. We got down to the wharf and saw Dossie, Mrs Varnham, Mr V., Gladys and Barie got our tin & parcel. The people were not allowed on the wharf until we had embarked. The crowd at the gates was awful. Senior cadets had to keep the people back with their rifles. Several ladies fainted and had to be rescued. We got to the side of the ship & when the crowd broke in we talked to the girls & gave them all my brasses for broaches … The ship pulled out into the stream about 7 o'clock & we anchored in the stream all night. Sunday was very fine & the sea was very calm. We lifted anchor about 30 minutes to eleven & made for Egypt via Lord only knows.[78]

Some of this is captured in this newsreel. We see the families crowd round the Wellington members of the reinforcements as they march to the wharf, walking with them, clasping hands with loved ones, and smiling bravely at the camera. The crowd thins for the Maori Contingent and their escorts are school-aged lads happily marching alongside. The last view is from a cameraman on the rooftop looking down on Post Office Square at the junction of Jervois and Customhouse quays and we see the long line of horse-drawn wagons GS, manufactured by local industry to military specifications, being driven to the wharf for loading. These and the horses pulling them were part of the reinforcement with 317 horses, including 140 draught horses, sailing with the transport.[79]

It immediately featured at the local cinemas and was advertised as *Our Maori Contingent (Native Volunteers for the Front)* "which vividly depicts our native volunteers for the Front as they appeared last Saturday afternoon". It was screened repeatedly in the cinemas in the main centres until late March 1915.[80] This film of the Maori Contingent found its way into the *Pathé Gazette* as it no doubt caught the editor's eye because it was something different among the many films of troop departures from New Zealand.

REINFORCEMENT SAILINGS

Every reinforcement departure was reported in detail with photos in the illustrated papers and films of the official farewell at Newtown Park, the march through the streets, embarkation and shipside farewell. The cinema camera in the crowd is in its usual place near the flagpole in the illustrated news photo of the official farewell to the 2nd Reinforcements at Newtown Park on 12 December 1914. This and every farewell featured in picture theatres around New Zealand.

The advertising always emphasised 'intimate shots' that showed the soldiers' faces. In May 1915, with New Zealand abuzz with the news of Gallipoli, the King's Theatre, Wellington advertised *The Departure of the 4th Reinforcements*, no doubt taken by Vinsen, which "shows the troops leaving the city. Many of them were very close to the camera and are easily recognisable by relations and friends."[81] It was what the audience demanded, and the departure films continued to circulate around local theatres in the Hayward and Fuller circuits for the duration of the war until no doubt they were worn out with repeated screenings. This may explain why one wharfside departure film only survives.

In January 1917 the *Akaroa Mail* advertised that Hayward's Weekly Pictures in the Oddfellows' Hall was "showing the departure of the Maori Contingent and the Third Reinforcements for the Front", two years after the event, but, no doubt, for those in the audience throughout New Zealand whose sons and loved ones had left with the 3rds or the Maori Contingent, this film and those of the other departures never dated as long as their men remained overseas, and for the families of those who died the images remained etched in memory forever as: "They swing across the screen in brave array."[82]

The 2nd Reinforcements for the NZEF drawn up in review order at Newtown Park, Wellington, on 12 December, when they were inspected by his Excellency the Governor (the Earl of Liverpool). The motion picture camera is to the right of the flagstaff. *Auckland Weekly News*, 24 December 1914, p. 43.

12

Sailing off to see the world

LIFE ON NEW ZEALAND TROOPSHIPS

On 16 October 1914 New Zealand's sons sailed for war; 8547 men and 3818 horses on ten transports crammed with stores and equipment including ten million rounds of small arms ammunition and 6000 artillery shells. On board HMNZT No. 12 the Commonwealth and Dominion Line, SS *Waimana*, carrying part of the Auckland contingent, the ship's master, Captain Holmes, was also a keen amateur cameraman and cinematographer.[1] Lieutenant Colvin Algie, an officer in the 6th Hauraki Company of the Auckland Infantry Battalion wrote in his diary on 25 October 1914: "We had church parade on the after running deck this morning and after that the officers paraded for a photograph by the captain. The latter also took a cinema picture of the officers which may possibly be screened in New Zealand some day. It will be very interesting to go to the pictures say in London and find oneself figuring on screen."[2] This film more than met Algie's expectation. The scenes of shipboard life for the soldiers, the Auckland Infantry Battalion on the wharf at Albany, Western Australia, and the sailing of the ships of the Australian and New Zealand convoy from King George's Sound on 1 November 1914 provide a unique historical record of the New Zealand Main Body. The surviving film opens with the animated faces of a soldier crowd on deck watching a wrestling match between two older men in singlet, trousers and braces. These two veterans know what they are doing in contrast with the eager keenness and raw strength of the two young soldiers that follow. But the film's fascination lies in the faces of the crowd.

We witness the return of the Auckland Infantry Battalion from an eight-mile route march through Albany on 29 October 1914. Lieutenant-Colonel Arthur Plugge, a large man, towers over the rest of his officers, while alongside him the battalion band plays the troops home as each company in turn marches back, halts, orders arms, turns to face the ship and are 'stood easy'. This is the first glimpse New Zealanders at home would have of New Zealanders on a foreign shore, albeit Australia, in the First World War. Most of who we see here would feature in the Gallipoli casualty lists in 1915. The major part of the film concentrates on the sailing of the 36 transports carrying the soldiers of the Australian Imperial Force (AIF) and the New Zealand Expeditionary Force (NZEF) from King George's Sound on 1 November 1914. We see the cruisers HMS *Minotaur* and HMAS *Sydney* lead the way on a "Beautiful summer's

Opposite page: Sailing off to see the world. The ships of the New Zealand convoy en route to Egypt. Morison Album, NAM 1992.758.

Life on New Zealand Troopships. NTSV F1147.

A wrestling match on the SS *Waimana* carrying the Auckland Infantry Battalion, filmed by the ship's master, Captain Holmes. Still from *Life on New Zealand Troopships*. NTSV F1147.

Overseas in London. The British Contingent of the New Zealand Expeditionary Force march in the Lord Mayor's Procession before joining the Main Body in Egypt. Still from Gaumont Graphic, *380, New Zealand Infantry*. NTSV F194541.

🎞 *Joining the Flotilla*. http://anzacsightsound. org/videos/the-first-troopships-depart.

morning with a clear sea". They are followed by the Australian transports, distinctive with the letter 'A' before the identifying number and still painted in their civil colours, "all in their glory of greens, blues and yellows", unlike the New Zealand transports that are painted a uniform grey.[3] The Australian transports glide past in single file forming up in three lines led by the A3, SS *Orvieto*, carrying Major-General William Throsby Bridges, commanding the AIF, and his staff, until finally the New Zealand ships follow them in a long line out into the Indian Ocean where they form up in two lines behind the Australian ships. One of the last images is of the escort cruiser HMAS *Melbourne*, smoke belching from two of its four funnels, as it waits to herd the convoy along.

The film was taken from the bridge of the *Waimana* and in the final pan the cameraman's heavy officer-pattern coat and still camera can be seen on the railing.[4] What is missing from these silent reels are the cheers and 'coo-ees' as the ships pass each other, before being whipped away by the wind. There was also at least one cameraman on the *Orvieto* and possibly a second on one of the other Australian transports because two films survive at the Australian War Memorial showing shipboard life on the *Orvieto* as well as similar scenes of the sailing of the convoy from King George's Sound. One of these cameramen is likely to have been the professional cinematographer employed by the Commonwealth government, Bert Ive. He travelled with the convoy from Melbourne to Albany and is the most likely candidate to have filmed the departure of the convoy from King George's Sound from a small boat.[5]

The New Zealand public had to wait until the cameraman from the *Waimana* returned to New Zealand with his film before these images were seen.

The film of shipboard life and the convoy leaving King George's Sound featured in New Zealand picture theatres in early 1915. The Empress Theatre in Wellington advertised *Life on New Zealand Troopships* in January 1915 and it featured again at the People's Picture Palace in March when it was advertised as *Our Boys en route to Egypt*.[6] The *Evening Post* reporting that the scenes were "greeted with spontaneous applause by crowded houses at all sessions".[7] The films were released again and again to make up for a scarcity of films from the front itself and the voyage to Egypt, with some adapted intertitles, soon became the voyage to the Dardanelles to make up for a lack of film from Egypt.[8]

STANDING BY IN EGYPT

The first year of the war saw the NZEF embark for the war in Europe, only to find them offloaded in Egypt with Turkey's entry into the war as an ally of Germany. The voyage was heightened by the Australian cruiser HMAS *Sydney*'s sinking of the German cruiser *Emden* off Cocos Island, which showed how right Massey's concerns were for the protection of the convoy and resulted in the initial delayed sailing from New Zealand. The transports docked at Alexandria after passing through the Suez Canal on 3 December 1914, seven weeks to the day after sailing through the Wellington Heads.

Over the next week men, horses and equipment were taken by train on an eight-hour journey through the Nile Delta to Cairo where a camp was established at Zeitoun, a proposed housing development on the edge of Cairo where streets were laid out but nothing had been built. Only the empty sandy expanse of the desert greeted the new arrivals. Tents were erected and a camp grew and with them a row of souvenir shops and a tent cinema, all run by a local Egyptian entrepreneur who had won the service contract for the camp. The Australian infantry brigades were camped at Mena under the shadow of the pyramids and the Australian Light Horse were at Medi.

These citizen soldiers sorted themselves out and went straight into hard training over the desert sands, while at night they went on leave into Cairo, ogling and sampling delights and opportunities undreamt of in New Zealand or Australia. Fred Waite's history captures the mood of those days. There was a pub and café for every town and district in New Zealand and Australia with names that changed overnight to suit the clientele.

> Owing to the war, the tourist season had failed — the rich Americans had stayed at home — but in the well paid Australians and New Zealanders the astute merchants found suitable substitutes, whom they could proceed to bleed most unmercifully. Out into the streets they came with their wares … walking sticks and swagger canes by the thousands; antiques made out of the Nile mud; ancient Dervish weapons with the dust of Birmingham still upon them; foreign postage stamps on sheets; scenic postcards and questionable pictures; dainty little fly-whisks and "pieces of the true Cross." … Eating houses purveying the fried steak and eggs and tomatoes, together with imitation Scotch whisky and Greek beer, came forth in all their glory of calico signs inscribed "The Balclutha Bar," this with a fine disregard for the prohibition tendencies of the Southern town; "The Waipukurau Reading Rooms," and the "Wellington Hotel — very cheap and breezy".[9]

The two forces, consisting of the New Zealanders and of the AIF made up of the 1st Australian Division, commanded by Major-General William Throsby Bridges, were formed into the Australian and New Zealand Army Corps under the command of Lieutenant-General Sir William Birdwood who at 49 was an experienced and ambitious Indian Army officer with service in South Africa and on the Indian northwest frontier. He was already regarded as a likely future candidate for commander-in-chief, Indian Army. The acronym 'ANZAC', initially used as the stamp on incoming correspondence and then as the telegraphic address, became the abbreviated title of the Corps and was to gain worldwide recognition in the weeks to come.

Godley, the commander of the NZEF, found himself commanding a mixed division of New Zealanders and Australians; there were not enough New Zealanders by themselves, 8500 in total, to form a viable division that normally numbered between 15,000 and 20,000. Colonel Harry Chauvel's 1st Australian Light Horse Brigade and Colonel John Monash's 4th Australian Infantry Brigade were added to the two New Zealand brigades — the New Zealand Infantry Brigade commanded by Colonel F.E. Johnston and the New Zealand Mounted Rifles Brigade commanded by Colonel Andrew Russell — to form the New Zealand and Australian Division (NZ & A). It was a most curious combination being two brigades of infantry and two brigades of mounted rifles, lacking the normal amount of artillery and missing many of the specialist units normally found in a division.

The natural antagonism and competitive spirit characteristic of the relationship between New Zealanders and Australians was equally evident in Egypt over Christmas–New Year 1914–15 but now they found themselves among the forces of the Empire. The 42nd (East Lancashire) Division, the first Territorial division of the British Army to be sent overseas, was camped alongside the New Zealanders and equally evident were the soldiers of the Indian Army: "picturesque bearded Sikhs, the native cavalry and infantry from every frontier State, and the alert Ghurka with his familiar slouch hat and short trousers".[10]

OUR BOYS IN EGYPT

The New Zealand public was hungry for news. The papers were full of events from the Western Front and every picture theatre vied to get scenic film of Egypt to show where our boys were training. The first film shown of New Zealanders was of the voyage out and then on 28 April 1915 the *Evening Post* advertised at the King's Theatre:

> Our Boys in Egypt — A Grand Parade of New Zealand Forces in Cairo before Major General Godley. General Birdwood and Mr T. Mackenzie. Infantry, Mounted Ambulance, Transport, etc, all New Zealand's sons are in it, also the Australian Boys.[11]

New Zealand infantry of the Wellington Infantry Battalion line the streets of Cairo with the New Zealand ensign flying over them on 23 December 1914. This parade was filmed and was the first film of New Zealand troops in Egypt seen by the public at home. Morison Album, NAM 1992.758.

Eighteen-pounder field guns of the New Zealand Field Artillery parade through Cairo on 23 December 1914. Still from *A.H. Noad Film*. F00176, AWM.

The film screened in New Zealand cinemas in the same week that news arrived of the landings on the Gallipoli Peninsula. The papers had been full of expectation of the forcing of the Strait of the Dardanelles, with reports of the bombardment of the outer forts in January–February 1915 and the failure of the naval attempt to force the strait on 18 March. The positioning of forces on islands off the coast and the formation of the Mediterranean Expeditionary Force under General Sir Ian Hamilton led to vigorous media debate on the difficulty of an army landing on Turkish soil, with much conjecture on possible roles for the New Zealanders and Australians.

The film is of the parade of Australian and New Zealand soldiers through the streets of Cairo in December 1914 taken by a French cameraman. Only a fragment survives. This is the earliest known filmed images of New Zealanders in Egypt and it survives in a post-war compilation in the Australian War Memorial, which is best known for its Gallipoli scenes.[12]

The parade took place in Cairo on 23 December 1914. It was a show of force involving contingents from all of the Imperial forces based in Egypt and followed on from the proclamation of a British protectorate in Egypt on 18 December.[13] What is important about these images is that they are the first taken of New Zealand soldiers in Egypt and as such constitute the only known surviving film showing New Zealanders taking part in this parade. Here we see New Zealanders on active service overseas parading under the New Zealand flag for the first time in their history.

Shortt's Star Theatre in Newtown and King's Theatre in Wellington screened it in late April 1915 and it was shown throughout New Zealand. It was followed in July 1915 with the screening of the final parade of the New Zealand and Australian Division before sailing for the Dardanelles. These two films and the film taken on the New Zealand convoy became the most viewed films in

A.H. Noad Film/Gallipoli. AWM F00176.

The New Zealand Mounted Rifles parade in Egypt for General Sir Ian Hamilton as part of the New Zealand and Australian Division, 28 March 1915. This was the last major parade before embarking for the Dardanelles. Still from *Inspection of the New Zealand and Australian Division*. NTSV F6824.

March-past of the Signal Company of the New Zealand Engineers. The bicycles would go to Gallipoli and remain on the beach. Still from *Inspection of the New Zealand and Australian Division*. NTSV F6824.

Inspection of the New Zealand and Australian Division. NTSV F6824.

New Zealand in 1915, capturing as they did the last glimpse of a body of New Zealanders who, in four months from late April to late August 1915, suffered almost 100% casualties. It is sobering to think that three out of every ten New Zealanders seen on this parade would be dead by the end of the year and most of the rest wounded and maimed or convalescing from enteric fever and dysentery.

The Cairo parade film was screened in New Zealand in the same week that news arrived of the commitment of the NZEF to the landings on the Gallipoli Peninsula. This was the last view of the New Zealand boys before they landed on Anzac Cove on 25 April 1915 and because there was no film of the Anzac troops ashore on Gallipoli shown that year, these films of the parades in Egypt became its substitute.

PARADE OF THE NEW ZEALAND AND AUSTRALIAN DIVISION

A second and almost complete film taken by the same French cameraman survives in the archives. The film is one of soldiers marching over the desert sands. It shows the inspection of the New Zealand and Australian Division on 28 March 1915. It was a repeat of the previous divisional inspection of 22 March 1915 and was the last parade of the NZEF before embarkation for Gallipoli in April 1915.[14]

Major Herbert Hart, 2IC of the Wellington Infantry Battalion, wrote in his diary:

> 20,000 troops on parade again, and we had the biggest dusting there since reaching Egypt. The sand is worked into such fine dust near the camp, that it now fly's everywhere whenever the troops move over it. We had dust in our ears, eyes, mouth, nose and everywhere, it fell from our pug-garees, pouches, pockets and from all our clothes.[15]

It was the second parade of the Division in the week as Hamilton assessed the capability of the troops that would soon take part in the greatest amphibious landing in history to that time. Both were impressive showings and reported in detail in the New Zealand press.

The camera is set on the edge of the parade area and as the horsemen of the Otago Mounted Rifles trot past the horses raise clouds of sand, choking and masking the formed ranks of infantry standing in the background. Each unit follows in turn, the signal detachment of the New Zealand Engineers, the dispatch riders with their rifles strapped to the bars of their bicycles, followed by the engineers with their horse-drawn bridging pontoons. The Mounted Rifles Brigade trot past followed by the medical orderlies of the Field Ambulance, without weapons, and with white armbands with red crosses on their left sleeve. The cameraman, conscious of his potential market, attempts to get close-ups of the faces but is defeated by the dust clouds. It is an impressive showing; the Wellington Battalion in their lemon squeezers, the 18-pounder field guns of the New Zealand Field Artillery, the supply wagons of the divisional train and a glimpse of the slouch hats of the Australian engineers, the Signals with cable drums mounted on wagons and, standing out with their pith helmets, the Maori Contingent. One cannot make out the New Zealand high commissioner to London, Thomas Mackenzie, among

THE   KING'S   THEATRE.
———
HAYWARD'S PICTURES.

HIS SON'S ACCUSER !   A
HIS SON'S ACCUSER !   Story
HIS SON'S ACCUSER !   of
HIS SON'S ACCUSER !   Human
HIS SON'S ACCUSER !   Frailty and
HIS SON'S ACCUSER !   Redemption.

A tragic yet romantic theme, produced with the classic artistic characteristic of Pathe's best.

OUR BOYS IN EGYPT !
OUR BOYS IN EGYPT !

A grand parade of N.Z. Forces in Cairo before Major-General Godley, General Birdwood, and Mr. T. Mackenzie. Infantry, Mounted, Ambulance, Transport, etc., all N.Z. sons are in it, also the Australian troops.

HOGAN'S SPREE (Keystone).

HELEN'S INTERVENTION (Child Study).

News from the Battlefronts, etc., etc.
———
1s, 6d, and Reserves at Bristol Piano Co., 1s 6d.
———
ELECTION RESULTS WILL BE ANNOUNCED FROM THE SCREEN.

Evening Post, 28 April 1915.

The haka of the 1st Maori Contingent, Te Hokowhitu-a-Tu, Egypt, 3 April 1915. Still from *Inspection of the New Zealand and Australian Division.* NTSV F6824.

the VIPs but, as we will see with many of the films from England and the Western Front, he invariably appears for the camera.

A haka by the Maori Contingent ends the film and the cameraman takes full advantage of the drama of the war dance. They had just arrived and to their chagrin found that they were to go to Malta for further training, well away from the fleshpots of Egypt, while the remainder of the Division, less the Mounted Rifles, were earmarked for Hamilton's landing force. Hart wrote in his diary:

> On the 3 April the Maori contingent gave a haka. The Maori have been giving displays, haka, etc to Generals and other big guns since their arrival. Today one exhibition was witnessed by Sir H. McMahon, Chief Commissioner, General Maxwell, Birdwood, Godley and all the chief people of Cairo — and myself. On Monday the Maori go on to Malta for more haka displays presumably.[16]

Hart's cynicism is evident, but the Maori, too, wanted to be more than a sideshow. The *NZEF War Diary* reported:

> During the entertainment one of the officers, Capt. Buck made a speech on behalf of the Maori asking that their claims for seeing active service may be favourably considered. At the conclusion of his speech, Sir John Maxwell [Commander-in-Chief Egypt] replied that they might rest

assured that in due course they would be given an opportunity of proving their worth on the battle field, which statement met with universal approval.[17]

Buck's plea included the words:

> Though we are only a handful the remnant of a remnant of a people, yet we consider that we are the old New Zealanders. No division can truly be called a New Zealand Division unless it numbers Maoris amongst its ranks.[18]

As we know the spirit of the plea was admired, but the authorities had made their plans and the Maori were sent to Malta on what seemed like something of a travelling show, "a kind of Williamson company" as one of the soldiers said.[19] Naturally none of these undercurrents are evident on the film. We cannot distinguish Buck, who we have already seen on film at Rotorua in 1908 at the meeting of Maori politicians in the Pathé newsreel of 1912 and more recently in the film of the Maori Contingent in Wellington, but we will see him again in France.

In many ways, other than the setting, we see a repeat of the parade films we have already seen in New Zealand but this time there is an important difference. Previously in New Zealand the films were of the Otago, Wellington and Auckland contingents to the NZEF, now it is the NZEF on parade, no longer marked out by their provincial distinctions, but now a New Zealand force overseas alongside the Australian and other forces of the Empire. We went to war as Otagos, Aucklands, Canterburys and Wellingtons but found out that we were New Zealanders in the eyes of those we met and served alongside. Egypt was the first step in that process. We do not know who took the film but we know from Godley's correspondence that it was a French cameraman. Pathé Frères first opened a picture theatre in Cairo in 1906 and there were a number of local cameramen making news event films and scenics that easily found overseas markets.[20]

The film's purchase by the New Zealand Government was at Godley's initiative. He wrote to Allen on 10 April 1915 while his division was preparing to move to the Dardanelles: "As regards to the cinematograph films which I cabled to you about, we have had to pay for them, as the man who took them is off to fight in France. Pending a reply to my cable, we are keeping the offer open for you and the Australian Government, but [Brigadier-General Andrew] Russell and [Captain Tahu] Rhodes [Godley's Aide de Camp (ADC)] have paid for them. There will be a good deal of money to be made out of it and, therefore, though they were anxious to have it as a private venture, I said they must give the Governments the opportunity first."[21]

Thomas Mackenzie was one of the VIPs on parade inspecting the New Zealanders and no doubt agreed with Godley's decision. The 'world rights' of the 505-metre film were purchased for £160 and it was despatched to New Zealand on the SS *Willochra* addressed to the Tourist Department, arriving on 16 July 1915.

Along with film of the troopship departures, the voyage out and the parade scenes both of the New Zealanders and the Australians at Mena, this footage was edited and re-edited, titled and re-titled, and released over and over again throughout the year of the Gallipoli Campaign. The public wanted more but although advertisements promised "GENUINE PRESENT DAY WAR PICTURES — not Spectacular Parade and Review pictures taken years ago", all that was available was just that, the same pictures seen before. Despite this the promise of the chance to recognise "relatives and friends who are fighting for our liberty" usually worked, and the crowds came, because there was nothing else to see.[22]

TOWN HALL.

COSY CONCERT CHAMBER!   COSY CONCERT CHAMBER!
COSY CONCERT CHAMBER!   COSY CONCERT CHAMBER!

SATURDAY, MONDAY, TUESDAY,

2nd, 4th, and 5th OCTOBER.

THREE NIGHTS ONLY!   THREE NIGHTS ONLY!
THREE NIGHTS ONLY!   THREE NIGHTS ONLY!

Direction Armies of Europe War Films Co., Earl's Court-road, London.

EXTRAORDINARY ENTERTAINMENT!   COMPLETE PROGRAMME!

ARMIES OF EUROPE AT WAR!

8000 FEET GENUINE WAR PICTURES TAKEN ON THE ACTUAL BATTLE-
FIELDS OF FRANCE AND BELGIUM, AND WITH AN

N.Z. TROOPSHIP TO THE DARDANELLES!

SOMETHING SPECIAL THAT WILL INTEREST YOU!

COME AND RECOGNISE YOUR RELATIVES AND FRIENDS WHO ARE
FIGHTING FOR OUR LIBERTY!

SHOWN FOR THE FIRST TIME IN NEW ZEALAND!

JAPANESE, BRITISH, AND AUSTRALIAN NAVIES ESCORTING OUR
BOYS!

Everyone is interested in the doings of our own gallant heroes, and you know you
will want to see them. BOOK YOUR SEATS EARLY to save disappointment.
These Pictures are GENUINE PRESENT-DAY WAR PICTURES — not
Spectacular Parade and Review Pictures taken years ago, but

WAR OF TO-DAY!   WAR OF TO-DAY!

Although the Cinematograph is used to graphically portray the daily news of
the present Great War, this is NOT A MERE PICTURE SHOW. It is

AN ENTERTAINMENT WITHOUT RIVAL.

MAGNIFICENT MUSICAL PROGRAMME.   FULL AND AUGMENTED
ORCHESTRA.

Songs—One of New Zealand's Leading Tenors (Signor Abel Rowe) will Sing—

"The Firing Line."   "We Mean to Fight Like Gentlemen."
"To Guard Thy Liberty."   "England Calls for Men."

Lecture—One of the ACTUAL CINEMATOGRAPHERS will describe each scene
as it HAPPENED BEFORE THE CAMERA!

TOWN HALL!   COSY CONCERT CHAMBER.   TOWN HALL!

SATURDAY, 2nd OCTOBER.
MONDAY, 4th OCTOBER.
TUESDAY, 5th OCTOBER.

PRICES—Circle, 2s; Reserved, 2s 6d; Body of Hall, 1s. Box Plan at The
Bristol Piano Co.

Evening Post, 30 September 1915.

Within two months of war being declared New Zealand sent 1413 men and nurses to Samoa, and 8499 personnel with the Main Body NZEF to Egypt. This was only possible because of the Territorial Force scheme that Godley had put in place and the anticipatory planning carried out by him and his staff. This planning also included discussions on the number of reinforcements necessary to maintain the NZEF at full strength. The 1st Reinforcements sailed as part of the Main Body in October and New Zealand agreed to provide the 2nd Reinforcements numbering 20% of the total force six weeks later. This force of 61 officers and 1913 other ranks sailed on 14 December 1914. It was anticipated that a further 5% per month would follow after that, but the heavy casualties received by the BEF in France saw this percentage rise to 15% for infantry and 10% for mounted rifles, and the 3rd Reinforcements that sailed on 14 February 1915 was based on these figures.

It was possible to get film of New Zealanders training in Egypt and England, but pictures of New Zealanders from the battlefield were rare in 1915–16. What battlefield film that came concentrated more on the doings of the British and French armies on the Western Front. Film-making on the battlefield in 1914–18 was also limited by the technological restrictions imposed by the tripod-mounted camera, and the difficulty of filming war as it had become. Usually there was nothing to see. To stand up and peer over the parapet in the trenches on Gallipoli or in France was to risk a sniper's bullet, and if one filmed further back then there was an empty battlefield devoid of movement or they would see only specks that indicated men or brief puffs of smoke indicated bursting shell. A cameraman risked his life standing up to film and for his pains got little more than a blurred glimpse of landscape. However, the major impediment was the strict censorship imposed by military authorities.

KINEMACOLOR FILLS THE GAP

What filled the gap were pre-war compilation films of the European armies engaged in the war. The Kinemacolor film *With the Fighting Forces of Europe* toured New Zealand from July to October 1915 using its own equipment and a Charles Urban operator imported with the show from Britain. It was independent of the picture theatres and ran its programme in the town halls. It was a three-hour extravaganza shown in parts and was a compilation largely of

pre-war parade and peacetime manoeuvre films covering the armies of Europe, Japan and the British Empire, accompanied by a lecturer with a soloist and an orchestra playing to the film and providing interlude music during the breaks.

The *Armies of Europe at War* also showed in New Zealand, opening in July 1915 and touring until March 1916. It was not a Kinemacolor film but one that was extensively tinted and toned, and used the standard theatre projectors. It toured with a lecturer, a Mr Holmes, whose claim to fame was that he was one of the photographers who had taken some of the film. It was a show in itself, 8000 feet (2438.4 metres) of film together with the signing of military songs during the film changes and an orchestra.[23]

Both films received good reviews. The *Armies of Europe at War* drew the following comments from a reviewer in the *Evening Post* in Wellington. "These pictures were terrible in their truthfulness. Nevertheless they should prove powerful agents for recruiting, inasmuch as they show the enormity of the crime of those responsible for the war and the necessity even at such tremendous sacrifices as the allied nations are making to prevent the perpetuation of such horrors for the sake of the lust for ambition and power."[24] The reviewer's warnings on their "terrible truthfulness" was warranted. There was government concern that they may have a negative impact on recruiting and, as we have seen, steps were taken to censor war films. However, *Armies of Europe at War* ran for 42 days in Auckland and did equally good business everywhere else in its nine months on the circuit.

There was an enormous demand for press reports, photos and moving film of 'Our Boys' overseas. Apart from one or two films from Egypt this was largely unfulfilled and enterprising film exchanges, recognising the public mood, reissued what was available, editing in each reinforcement sailing, showing every travelogue available on Cairo and Egypt, doing everything possible to suggest something new and exciting in the way of film had arrived, when the reality was that certainly for all of 1915 all that was available with one exception were the films of men in training, the departures and then, from mid-1915 on, films of the wounded returning.

An historic occasion: prime minister W.F. Massey reading the message from His Majesty's Government advising the participation of New Zealand troops in the military operations at the Dardanelles, at Wellington, 29 April 1915. Note the photographer on the left. *Auckland Weekly News*, 6 May 1915, p. 35.

13

The French film
the Dardanelles

WITH THE ALLIED FLEETS IN THE DARDANELLES

It was the general belief that there was only one film taken of General Sir Ian Hamilton's Mediterranean Expeditionary Force in the Dardanelles in 1915, and that it was taken by the British journalist Ellis Ashmead-Bartlett. Recent research has led to the discovery of a number of films featuring the Dardanelles taken by French cameramen. The first and most influential of these at the time was filmed by a Gaumont cameraman attached to the French fleet in the period March to May 1915.

The outbreak of war badly affected the French film industry. Many film-makers, along with all eligible males, were immediately mobilised to join their regiments. Nitrate and cellulose were key ingredients of explosives and became difficult to obtain. The French government closed cinemas and places of entertainment and so film production almost completely stopped. It would end the dominant position that the French film industry had earned in the global market and this would never be recovered.

Rigid censorship regulations limited what could be shown on screen. However, in February 1915 a representative of Pathé Frères convinced the French military authorities that film was a potentially important element in boosting public morale and was also necessary to record French achievement in the war. It was agreed that the four principal film companies, Pathé, Gaumont, Eclipse and Éclair would each provide cameramen to form a Service Photographique et Cinématographique des armées (Cinematic Section of the Army). The companies would jointly decide which cameramen would be deployed to which locations. The film would be commercially processed and edited, after which the censors would view and clear the material for commercial release.[1] Gaumont sent cameraman Pierre Perrin to the front, where he joined three colleagues, each of them working for a different news company: Albert Machin for Pathé, Georges Maurice for Éclair and Pierre Emile for Eclipse. These men would later form the core of the photography and film division of France's armed forces.[2]

It seems that one of these cameramen was attached to the French fleet in the Mediterranean and filmed at least two major films of the Gallipoli Campaign in April–May 1915. A third film was shot in December 1915–January 1916 recording the French evacuation, but this seems not

Opposite page: The French gun crew strain to load a shell in the 24cm *modale* 1876 coastal gun which was one of four similar heavy guns used by the French at Cape Helles. They fired over the Strait at Ottoman artillery on the Asiatic side. The remains of these guns are still in their original positions on Gallipoli. One of these guns was nicknamed "L'Express d' Orient." Still from *Gaumont Actualities No. 5022. Gaumont Pathé*, 2000GS05022.

Admiral Émile Guépratte decorates one of his officers with the Croix de Guerre on the deck of his flagship, the French battleship *Juaréguiberry*. Still from *With the Allied Fleets in the Dardanelles*. NTSV F29386.

British signallers attached to the French battleship *Juaréguiberry*. Still from *With the Allied Fleets in the Dardanelles*. NTSV F29386.

With the Allied Fleets in the Dardanelles. NTSV F29386.

to have passed censorship and was not released until 1920, by which time there was no longer any French interest in the Gallipoli Campaign.

The film *With the Allied Fleets in the Dardanelles* is one of the most important films of the First World War held by Ngā Taonga Sound & Vision.[3] It is a very rare film, with the British Film Institute (BFI) having perhaps the only other copy known to exist.[4] It is the first known

The French battleship *Suffren*. Still from *With the Allied Fleets in the Dardanelles*.
NTSV F29386.

OPERA HOUSE
FULLERS' PICTURES.

TO-NIGHT. TO-NIGHT. TO-NIGHT

A Powerful and Extraordinary Drama.
A Vitagraph Production of Merit:
REGAN'S DAUGHTER.
REGAN'S DAUGHTER.
Politics v. Love.
SYMPATHY SAL.
SYMPATHY SAL.
Stirring Western Drama.
WITH THE ALLIED FLEETS
IN THE DARDANELLES.
Impressive and Inspiring
ABSOLUTELY AUTHENTIC.
AMBROSE'S NASTY TEMPER.
Just a little Keystone.
AUSTRALIAN GAZETTE.
CHAMPION BEAR SLAYER.
Prices: Circle, 1s; Stalls, 6d.
Half-price to Circle 9 o'clock. 317

HAYWARDS' PICTURES.

TO-NIGHT —— At 8 —— TO-NIGHT

Last Screening of the Nordisk Star:
CHILDREN OF THE CIRCUS.
CHILDREN OF THE CIRCUS.
Magnificent Mounted Filmic Treat.
THE MAHENO. Arrival in Auckland
THE MAHENO. with sick and
THE MAHENO. wounded from the
THE MAHENO. Dardanelles.
"A Life in the Balance," "Gazette,"
"Fatty's Married Life."
Prices: 6d and 1s. 318

film taken of the Dardanelles Campaign and the only one to receive public screenings during the campaign. It was filmed by a French cameraman attached to the French fleet with the focus on naval operations. He also filmed French troops ashore at Mudros Harbour on Lemnos Island: the staging point for the attack on the Gallipoli Peninsula. The film also showed scenes of French troops on Gallipoli — these have not survived in the New Zealand copy, but survive in the BFI copy.

The initial filming was around the period of the British and French naval attempts to break through the Strait of the Dardanelles that ended with its failure on 18 March 1915. This led to the decision to seize the Gallipoli Peninsula by a combined British and French ground forces assault with the support of the Allied fleet.

The primary landings were in the south at the tip of the peninsula by the British 29th Division. The French would land at Kum Kale on the Asiatic shore at the mouth of the strait, both as a feint and also to suppress Ottoman artillery firing on the British landings. The Australian and New Zealand Army Corps (ANZAC) would land north of Gaba Tepe further up the peninsula with the object of securing the high ground of the Sari Bair Ridge and then cutting land communications by advancing across the peninsula.

Birdwood's ANZAC landing on 25 April 1915 saw the 1st Australian Division carry out the landings with the New Zealand and Australian Division in reserve. The hoped-for success did not happen and the Anzacs were committed to an eight-month campaign. The high casualty lists, the publicity, the growing mythology of Anzac achievement and its commemoration each Anzac Day has become one of the central tenets in the image of ourselves as New Zealanders. Film played a significant part in this.

The film *With the Allied Fleets in the Dardenelles* appeared in picture theatres at the same time as New Zealand sick and wounded were being filmed on their return to New Zealand. *Dominion*, 24 August 1915, p. 7.

FILMING NAVAL OPERATIONS

With the Allied Fleets in the Dardanelles was shot in April–May 1915. Released through Gaumont, it was screened throughout New Zealand from August to December 1915. Given the time taken for the cameraman to return the film to France and then ship it around the world, it reached its audience in New Zealand remarkably quickly. It was the only significant film of the Dardanelles Campaign screened in 1915 and had a major impact on the New Zealand public.

The film reminds us that the Dardanelles Campaign was planned as an entirely naval operation. First Lord of the Admiralty Winston Churchill's initial plan was to use obsolete pre-Dreadnought battleships of the Royal Navy to bombard the outer forts protecting the Strait of the Dardanelles, then break through the strait into the Sea of Marmara and, unless the government surrendered, threaten the Ottoman capital of Constantinople with bombardment. Ground forces were an afterthought and were originally intended to secure the strait and the forts once the naval ships passed through.[5]

The film gives us an important glimpse of Britain's usually overlooked partner in the Gallipoli enterprise. France had the primary role on the Western Front, but at the Dardanelles Britain was the lead player. France was conscious of this and was determined to have a stake in the game.

The French, who had their major fleet in the Mediterranean, offered a squadron of four obsolete battleships under the command of Admiral Émile Guépratte to be part of this enterprise. Meanwhile, the main French fleet concentrated on bottling up the Austro–Hungarian Imperial Fleet in the Adriatic by blockading the Strait of Otranto.[6] Admiral Guépratte was highly regarded by his counterparts in the Royal Navy. He had the reputation of being a 'fire-eater' and there is a sense of this in the scene in the film where we see him present the Legion of Honour to one of the French naval pilots on board his flagship.

Evacuating French wounded on the wharf at V Beach. The village of Sedd el Bahr is in the background and the beached steamship *River Clyde* is on the right. Still from *The Allies in the East*. NFSA 323.

The film's screening in New Zealand in August 1915 coincided with the August offensive and the New Zealand Expeditionary Force's (NZEF) involvement in the battle for Chunuk Bair, which resulted in heavy casualties. The screenings were advertised in newspapers, full of the Gallipoli Campaign. Casualty details often appeared on the same page as 'Amusement' columns advertising the film. The Christchurch *Star* reported on 17 August 1915:

> 'With the Allied Fleets in the Dardanelles', a film which is intensely interesting to all New Zealanders screened at the Queen's Continuous Picture Theatre for the first time yesterday. The opening scene was on the deck of the French battleship, the "Jaureguebeerry," [sic] where the French Headquarters staff were shown conferring with the Admiral of the fleet for the further co-operation of land and sea forces. The Allied Camp at Mudros and the forts of [de] Totts, now held by the French, were shown in detail. A little steam launch was shown scouting for submarines, and views were given of the ill-fated Goliath at close quarters. Battleship scenes showed H.M.S. *Canopus* firing her heavy guns, the French cruiser *Suffren* and the H.M.S. *Agamemnon* bombarding a battery on the coast. Other incidents of this excellent film were views of a sinking transport and Turkish prisoners on Gallipoli.[7]

The *Dominion* in Wellington claimed it was "photographically excellent, and each of its many splendid sections made a strong appeal upon spectators".[8] A month later the *Wanganui Chronicle* was also effusive in its praise for the film. It claimed the film "shows some of the most interesting pictures ever taken of a fleet in action. Whilst looking on the screen one imagines he is actually on board one of the warships and in the midst of battle."[9]

The intertitles allow us to date when the various scenes were taken. The obsolete French battleship *Juaréguiberry* was based at Port Said in Egypt from February 1915 but was not deployed to the Dardanelles until after the failure of the naval attempt to break through the strait on 18 March 1915. In this attempt two British battleships, HMS *Ocean* and *Irresistible*, were sunk by mines and a third, HMS *Inflexible*, was badly damaged. The French battleship *Bouvet* was also sunk by a mine with the loss of some 600 of its crew. The two French battleships *Suffren* and *Gaulois* were damaged by artillery fire. These losses amounted to one third of the strength of the 17 battleships and one modern battlecruiser, HMS *Inflexible*, of the Allied fleet that took part in the attack and put out of action three of the four French battleships involved.[10] The *Juaréguiberry* sailed for Lemnos Island on 25 March 1915 and became Admiral Émile Guépratte's flagship after his previous flagship *Suffren* returned to Toulon for repairs accompanying the more seriously damaged *Gaulois*.[11]

THE CORPS EXPÉDITIONNAIRE D'ORIENT (CEO)

The failure of the naval attempt to break through on 18 March 1915 meant that General Sir Ian Hamilton's Mediterranean Expeditionary Force now had the task of securing the Gallipoli Peninsula to allow the navy to pass through. This major amphibious assault would be the largest in history to that date. It would involve the ANZAC forces in Egypt, the Royal Naval Division (raised by Churchill from surplus royal marines and seamen from the Royal Navy), and with much reluctance on the secretary of state for war, Field-Marshal Earl Kitchener's part, the involvement of the 29th Infantry Division, the only regular division of the British Army not yet committed to the Western Front.

France would also initially contribute the equivalent of an infantry division that was called the Corps Expéditionnaire d'Orient (CEO). General Joffre, the French commander-in-chief

refused to release any of the French divisions serving on the Western Front and so the CEO was made up of whatever forces were at hand. (In the same way, he appointed General Albert d'Amade to command as he wanted to get rid of him after removing him from corps command on the Western Front). An ad hoc division of some 23,000 personnel was raised.

The organisation of a French division was of two infantry brigades, each of two infantry regiments, each of three battalions: a total of 12 infantry battalions, the same number as a standard British infantry division. The 1st Division CEO consisted of a 'brigade métropolitaine' with 175 Regiment of Infantry (RI) drawn from the French training depots, and its second regiment (6 Mixed Colonial Regiment) a mix of Zouaves raised from the French colonies in North Africa and a Foreign Legion battalion. The second brigade was a 'brigade coloniale': a colonial brigade made up of two regiments (7 and 8 Mixed Colonial regiments) each containing one European and two Senegalese Tiraillieur battalions. The division was supported by eight artillery batteries plus combat and supply units.[12]

The 1st Division CEO arrived at Mudros from France on 18 March, moved to Alexandria in Egypt to await developments and then sailed again for Lemnos on 15 April. A French regiment landed at Kum Kale at the mouth of the Dardanelles on 25 April 1915. This was to act as a feint but also to suppress Ottoman artillery batteries from interfering with the British landings that could be seen across the strait. It redeployed to the peninsula on 27 April and the complete division took part in the initial attacks by Hamilton's forces to take the village of Krithia and the heights of Achi Baba. Both British and French forces suffered heavy losses.

The scene in the film of the meeting of the French commanders-in-chief, General d'Amade and General Henri Gouraud, with Guépratte, on the flagship is not just for the cooperation of the 'land and sea forces' as the intertitle suggests. It is in fact the handover of command of the CEO. General d'Amade, the original commander of the CEO was replaced by General Gouraud on 15 May 1915, three weeks into the land campaign.

A second division, the 156th Infantry Division, but known as the 2nd Division CEO, also of two infantry brigades, arrived with Gouraud and joined the 1st Division on 15 May 1915.[13] It was of similar composition to the 1st Division, consisting of a metropolitan brigade and a colonial brigade. Unlike d'Amade, Gouraud was highly regarded by General Hamilton. Gouraud insisted on more artillery being provided for his army corps of two divisions and established V Beach, next to the fort of Sedd el Bahr, as the principal base for the CEO while the British used W Beach for their logistic support. A major logistics depot was established at Mudros on Lemnos and 400 tonnes of supplies were landed at V Beach each day to sustain the French forces.[14]

The scenes in the film of the windmills and the villages on the heights above Mudros Harbour on the Greek island of Lemnos were taken at this time, but the film does not show the scenes, mentioned in the film review, of De Tott's battery on the promontory where the Turkish National Memorial to the Çanakkale or Gallipoli Campaign now stands. These scenes confirm that the cameraman was ashore with the French forces after 27 April 1915 when they re-embarked from their original landings at Kum Kale on the Asiatic shore and took over the eastern flank of the southern front alongside the British divisions of the Mediterranean Expeditionary Force.

HAMILTON'S PLAN

This southern front at Cape Helles was Hamilton's main axis of attack with his initial aim to secure the modest (though dominating) heights of Achi Baba (Alçitepe) near the village of Krithia before advancing to secure the Kilid Bahr plateau. The beaches on the southern tip of Gallipoli Peninsula were the landing points for the 29th Infantry Division in daylight on 25 April 1915. Stubborn resistance by vastly outnumbered Ottoman infantry caused heavy casualties at V and W beaches: the main landing beaches. Inaction and a failure to take advantage of little resistance at the other beaches meant that little progress was made. The Ottoman forces were able to reinforce and deny the high ground of Achi Baba, and so from 27 April 1915, any advance from the south became a combined British and French operation in a series of costly frontal attacks. Hamilton's British forces lacked both field artillery and ammunition and so were dependent of French artillery support that proved critically important throughout the campaign.

The French faced the most difficult ground with the deep and heavily defended gully of Kereves Dere blocking their access to the heights of Achi Baba. They were also under constant Turkish artillery fire from the eastern shore across the strait. The final scenes showing the transport being escorted by French and British warships presumably was taken in April, as are the shots of the Turkish prisoners under escort at Mudros.

THE ANZAC LANDING

Birdwood's ANZAC Corps landed before dawn on 25 April 1915. The Anzacs came ashore around the headland of Ari Burnu, north of their intended landing beach near the promontory of Gaba Tepe. The Australians of the 1st Australian Division made the initial landings and overwhelmed the some 200 widely dispersed Ottoman defenders and advanced inland. However, the leading Australian commander redirected the second brigade to land to reinforce him around the Lone Pine area on the southern flank of the bridgehead. This weakened the northern flank facing towards the high ground of Chunuk Bair and it was here that the Ottoman counterattack threw back the Anzac line. It was this fighting on the northern flank around the heights of Baby 700 that saw New Zealand infantry from the Auckland and Canterbury Infantry battalions come into action from about 2 o'clock on in support of the overstretched Australian line.

The rapid insertion of Turkish reinforcements saw the Anzac situation deteriorate so that by nightfall on 25 April they were holding on by their fingernails to a small bridgehead around what became known as Anzac Cove. General Birdwood recommended evacuation to Hamilton, but Hamilton directed the ANZAC to dig in and hold on. None of this is part of *With the Allied Fleets in the Dardanelles* but it gave the New Zealand public its first filmed images of the Gallipoli Campaign.

NEWSREELS OF THE DARDANELLES

Gaumont and Pathé also released a number of newsreels containing brief clips of the Dardanelles Campaign during 1915 and these may have been screened in New Zealand. There is a Gaumont newsreel clip of the battleships *Bouvet* and *Gaulois* at anchor at sea that was released in 1915 prior to the 18 March naval assault or otherwise it would have mentioned that the *Bouvet* had been sunk and the *Gaulois* badly damaged. This may be stock footage or scenes taken in the Dardanelles.[15]

There is also a Gaumont newsreel showing a French Naval Air Squadron embarking at Marseilles for the Dardanelles. The French navy's seaplane carrier *Foudra*, the first warship to be adapted to an aviation role, was already in the Mediterranean with its Nieuport seaplanes. This joined the Anglo–French fleet in the Dardanelles. It was joined by the Royal Navy seaplane carrier, HMS *Ark Royal,* and the tethered balloon carrier, HMS *Manica*. The Royal Navy also deployed a squadron of aircraft commanded by Wing Commander Charles Rumney Samson

The Wairarapa Age, 12 May 1916, p. 1.

of the Royal Naval Air Service, a character as colourful as his name, to command 3 Squadron Royal Naval Air Service (RNAS). Samson was one of the first British naval aviators and was the first person to fly an airplane from a moving ship. He also pioneered the use of armoured cars in British military service and his RNAS armoured car squadron was deployed to Gallipoli.[16] No. 3 Squadron RNAS consisted initially of 18 aircraft of five different types of British and French manufacture. It was based on the Island of Tenedos where it would fly reconnaissance and artillery-spotting flights for the naval ships providing naval gunfire support to the land forces. Both the British and the French authorities saw an important role for aircraft to locate Turkish batteries and then use wireless to communicate with the ships and subject them to effective naval gunfire.

Not to be outdone, the French raised 'L'escadrille MF 98 T (Ténédos)' in France under the command of Captain Antoine Césari, a veteran of the Battle of the Marne.[17] His unit consisted of eight pilots to man the eight Maurice Farman MF XI aircraft that were crated and sailed from Marseilles on 28 March 1915. The newsreel shows one of the crated aircraft being swung precariously by crane onto the transport. This is followed a close-up of Captain Césari surrounded by his pilots and key personnel. You can identify the winged propeller insignia for officers on their shoulders and the winged star collar insignia of French military aviation.[18] The clip finishes with shots of smiling squadron personnel boarding the transport with their kit.[19]

The most important of these news clips is a Pathé newsreel showing French soldiers doing their laundry in the field. There are three short scenes, one of which shows French Zouaves washing clothes in a stream in a steep-sided gully. If, as the visible terrain strongly suggests, this scene was taken on Gallipoli, it would make it the most important in the film. We see their individual equipment and weapons stacked at the side of the gully. This brief glimpse of French infantry ashore on Gallipoli dates from April, early May 1915. We can guess this from the appearance of the French soldiers in the film. They are obvious new arrivals and do not show the wear and tear of a prolonged campaign. This confirms that a French cameraman was ashore at the very beginning of the land campaign.[20]

It shows that film was an important aspect in French reporting from the beginning of the campaign, and in the case of *With the Allied Fleet in the Dardanelles* resonated strongly with New Zealand audiences. To the French public these films were glimpses of a sideshow to the major endeavours on the Western Front, but to New Zealand audiences the Dardanelles Campaign was our one significant contribution to the war and the focus of public attention.

THE ALLIES IN THE EAST

The Gaumont cameraman continued to film on the island of Lemnos and at Cape Helles in April–May 1915, but the English-language version of the film was not released until early 1916 with its intertitles adapted to an English audience. Titled *The Allies in the East*, it screened in New Zealand from April to September 1916 but had little impact. It seems to have been deliberately kept out of the cinemas in the major centres, touring the provincial areas and

getting very little interest.[21] This may be because at the same time the British journalist Ellis Ashmead-Bartlett was in New Zealand giving his lectures on the Gallipoli Campaign. His film of the campaign was also screening in picture theatres and both were heavily touted in press advertisements. This may explain why so little attention was given to *The Allies in the East* both then and since.

In April 1916 the *Southland Times* reported: "The Allies in the East' is an authentic film of great interest, showing unique panoramic views of Gallipoli Peninsula, the French, Colonial and Indian troops and conveying the wounded to Alexandria."[22] This is the most detailed of the reports on the film in New Zealand papers. A copy of the film exists in the British Film Institute. It is a superbly shot and a very revealing film, which as the title suggests concentrates

on the allied forces fighting with the French in the Dardanelles. This was adapted by Gaumont's editors for the English edition by providing intertitles giving it a more British Imperial flavour. However, the structure and the opening and closing sequence makes it clear that we are watching a French film.

It opens with French wounded being loaded onto a small coastal steamer with the hustle and bustle of the large tented encampment that has grown up at V Beach between the old village of Sedd el Bahr and the castle walls. The wounded are carried or hobble down the jetty that runs alongside the hull of the beached steamship *River Clyde*. French soldiers are shown landing from a barge near what seems to be S Beach, below the headland where the Turkish national monument now stands.

The scene then shifts to the airfield on the island of Tenedos and we see a hangar being erected and an overview of the airfield and the camp occupied by Samson's No. 3 Squadron of the Royal Naval Air Service. The film returns to the airfield a number of times and we can admire the airmen and groundcrew's myriad ways of protecting themselves from the heat of the day. We see an impromptu boxing match and then a game of soccer between the squadron personnel. The film shifts back to Cape Helles and we see a busy British Army signal centre with men, obviously happy to be on film, rapidly coming and going as they deliver messages especially for the camera. The lines of the Indian Mule Corps show the various ethnic groups making up the Indian forces contrasting the different regiments of Indians and Gurkhas.

There are scenes of a row of Australian soldiers, distinctive with their slouch hats, sitting on one of the dismounted Ottoman coastal guns in Fort No. 1 overlooking V Beach. They play up to the camera and the man on the extreme left turns his back and 'moons' for the camera. Their presence indicates that it was filmed in May 1915 when both the New Zealand Infantry Brigade and the 2nd Australian Brigade were sent south from Anzac and attached to the British forces at Cape Helles for the Second Battle of Krithia, where they took part in the attack on 8 May 1915 with both brigades suffering heavy losses. They then remained there working on the roads and at the beaches with the 2nd Australian Brigade returning to Anzac on 17 May with the New Zealand Infantry Brigade returning on 19 May 1915.[23]

An impressively large French field kitchen is shown in the village of Sedd el Bahr, reminding us that V Beach was the main French logistics base on the peninsula. The extent of the camp at V Beach is seen with a panorama from the grounded transport SS *River Clyde*.

We see wounded being carried down the gangway of a hospital ship at Alexandria. The film then returns to Mudros Harbour for scenes of 'An English Hospital' with wounded of all nationalities, including a New Zealander among a group of Australians at the front of the crowd, and the officers' mess tent with a mix of naval and army officers including a RNAS pilot. Turkish prisoners are seen with tools walking up a hill towards the camera at Mudros under casual escort. The harbour scenes and panoramic shots from *River Clyde* and that of the Turkish prisoners capture the scale and the intensity of the logistic support for the campaign; it is all movement. The camera captures the subject in the foreground but one is increasingly drawn to the activities going on all around.

The final scene shows shipping moored in Mudros Harbour at sunset with the title: 'The Sun never sets on the British Empire'. However, the nearest warship flying the Tricolour is a French battleship and it may be the French flagship *Jauréguiberry*.

The intertitles proclaim the achievements of the British Empire, but the strong French elements betray its origins.

Zouaves, with their equipment packed, playing around at V Beach, Sedd el Bahr. Still from *Gaumont Actualities No. 5022*. Gaumont Pathé, 2000GS05022.

Lowering the Tricolour immediately before the final evacuation. Still from *Gaumont Actualities No. 5022*. Gaumont Pathé, 2000GS05022.

THE FRENCH FILM THE WITHDRAWAL FROM GALLIPOLI

The Gaumont Pathé Archive in France has a number of films of the Dardanelles filmed in 1918–19 taken by French cameramen when France was one of the occupying powers in Turkey. These show fascinating scenes of the remains of the *River Clyde* and the blockships at Cape Helles and views of the fortifications and towns inside the strait and of Constantinople itself.

The most important and interesting of these, though dated as being released in 1920, is in fact a film showing the French forces on Gallipoli at the time of the withdrawal from the peninsula in December 1915–January 1916. This was at the same time that the British forces, including the ANZAC, were evacuating Suvla Bay and Anzac. The final British evacuation from Cape Helles occurred on 9 January 1915.

This marvellously detailed film of the French logistics base at V Beach near the village and old castle of Sedd el Bahr provides a comprehensive view of the evacuation of the CEO in the last weeks of the campaign.[24] The 2nd Division CEO had been withdrawn and redeployed to Salonika together with the British 10th Division, leaving the 1st Division CEO as the sole French division at Cape Helles. The two regiments of Senegalese infantry were withdrawn from 12–22 December. On 24 December 1915 the only French infantry remaining on the peninsula was a French Colonial Brigade consisting of four battalions of Zouaves and two Metropolitan battalions, together with the French artillery, all of which were successfully evacuated except for a battery of French heavy guns that were disabled and left behind on the last night.[25]

It opens with scenes of V Beach at Sedd El Bahr showing the SS *River Clyde* aground surrounded by the roads and wharf developed by the CEO. The hulk of the French battleship *Massena*, which was towed from Toulon and sunk to form a breakwater on 9 November 1915, together with the former French passenger liner SS *Saghalien*, that was sunk the following day, were positioned to protect the harbour from the winter storms. In the foreground there is the light railway, with wagons loaded with heavy artillery shells, that leads up towards the front lines. It is interesting to contrast how it appears with the similar scenes of V Beach and the French logistic base taken in May and shown in *The Allies in the East*.

Gaumont Actualities No. 5022. Gaumont Pathé, 2000GS05022.

This mass of artillery shells are in front of a series of temporary huts and tents. Every available metre of space has been utilised and the sheer scale of supplies and ammunition needed to sustain the French force is self-evident. The scenes include a mix of British and French soldiers posing on the Ottoman coastal guns at Fort No. 1 that overlooks V Beach. We see soldiers of the British 52nd (Lowland) Division stack their equipment in the tent lines as they move in to occupy the French area in anticipation of the French withdrawal. A group of Zouaves of either the 1st or 2nd Regiment 'de marche d'Afrique' in their distinctive headdress, pantaloons and belts, happily act up when they see the camera.[26] The regimental number can be seen on the coat collar of the soldier playing with his pet dog in the foreground. They have their webbing and equipment stacked near them as they wait for the order to march down to the boats. The village and the battered walls of the old castle of Sedd el Bahr are in the background.

Similarly, a Zouave working party file past their stone shelters with the beached SS *River Clyde* and the blockship *Massena* in the background. Their single file is disrupted when they see the camera and they promptly start dancing and play-acting for the camera. There is a sense that everyone is keen to get away.

A motor boat sails into the harbour at V Beach. The film is taken from the seaward side and we see the panorama of the harbour with the quays and large canvas storehouses holding forage and stores in the foreground and the storehouses and tented camp beyond climbing up the hill to the village of Sedd el Bahr on the skyline with the walls of the old castle on the right of shot. It is a mass of stores, dumps and supplies with men working on the wharf as horses and carts move among them. It is a fascinating contrast to the scene today where this area is now taken up by holiday homes overlooking a quiet beach occupied by bathers, still bordered by the old village and the walls of the castle.

French officers lead a file of heavily laden French soldiers, or 'poilus' (hairy ones) as they called themselves, of one of the metropolitan battalions, carrying their rifles and equipment. They file past a row of dugouts dug into the trench wall. The Krithia plain with its trees and fields stretch towards the front line. This is the landscape of battle at Cape Helles in contrast to the rugged hills and gullies at Anzac. Perhaps the most important scene is that where senior French officers salute as the Zouave guard of honour presents arms as the Tricolour is lowered in front of the French headquarters marking the final phase of the French withdrawal. It reminds us that this a failed campaign. It is unusual to have such graphically filmed images in this detail of a military evacuation from a hostile shore, and certainly not one taken as early as 1915.

One of the last scenes is the firing and the reloading of one of the four obsolete French 24 cm 1876 *modale* coastal guns, each weighing 16 tonnes. The gun is fired and then the breech opened and a shell is winched into position and loaded into the chamber. The intense labour involved in crewing these guns is evident. This battery was used to suppress Ottoman artillery across the strait on the Asiatic shore. French artillery continued to fire until the final British withdrawal from Cape Helles on 9 January 1916. Three of the four guns were disabled immediately before the evacuation but the demolition charge disabling the fourth gun failed. The guns are sited forward of where the British Memorial at Cape Helles now stands. All four guns are still in position today, hidden among the olive groves, and rarely visited.

The focus on the 'withdrawal' of French forces may be why this film was not released until 1920. Defeat at the Dardanelles was not something that the French or the British authorities wished to display in the cinemas and so this remarkable film remained in the vaults and was never publicly viewed until placed online.

JAMES WADDELL OF THE FOREIGN LEGION — NEW ZEALAND'S FRENCH CONNECTION

These French films with their emphasis on the French expeditionary force on Gallipoli are important not only for their images of Gallipoli but in reminding us that at this time France, with its film production houses of Gaumont and Pathé, dominated the world newsreel market. There is also a unique New Zealand connection with the French commitment to the Dardanelles. The battalion of the French Foreign Legion on Gallipoli was commanded by a short, nuggety New Zealander, the son of an old pioneering family from Cromwell in Central Otago, until his wounding in July 1915.[27]

James Waddell died in comparative obscurity in Palmerston North on 18 February 1954 at the age of 81 and is buried in the Levin Soldiers' Cemetery. Among those gathered at the graveside for his funeral was the French ambassador to New Zealand, who spoke of Waddell's achievements as an officer in the French Foreign Legion and French Army, but who also admitted to being baffled as to how a New Zealander could become one of France's most decorated soldiers of the First World War.

It is a tale that defies belief. James Waddell, the son of a saddler, was born in Dunedin in October 1872. A bright student, he won a scholarship to Otago Boys' High School and in 1895 was the first New Zealander to pass the open examination for an officer's commission into the British Army. The 24-year-old Waddell joined the 2nd Battalion, the Duke of Wellington's West Riding Regiment in South Africa in 1896. It was not a happy time for the young man. His social background, lack of height (being only 1.6 metres tall), university education and the fact that he was a colonial meant he was not accepted by his fellow officers. He endured a six-month regime of constant bullying and hazing. This became the subject of a military court of inquiry that led to his commanding officer resigning his command. However, Waddell stuck with it and went with his regiment to India in 1898. Here he met and fell in love with a French woman, who he married. Waddell resigned his commission and moved with his wife to England. It is obvious that the lady had powerful connections because in April 1900 Waddell was accepted into the French Foreign Legion and was commissioned as a sub-lieutenant in the 2nd Regiment of the French Foreign Legion, something unheard of for a foreigner.

Waddell had been a trailblazer at great personal cost with his commission in the Duke of Wellington's West Riding Regiment. He now had to prove himself again in the Legion. The Legion also did not want him and viewed him with equal suspicion. It was a hard road as indicated in this early report from his commanding officer. "Sub Lieutenant Waddell … is a young man of timid aspect, slow-witted character, mild demeanour, wanting to do good service and striving to learn French. Finding our regulations for manoeuver difficult to assimilate. His joining is not seen as of value to the Legion."[28]

Capitaine James Waddell, French Foreign Legion, 1913. Waddell Family.

In 1919 this French military cameraman returned to V Beach, Sedd el Bahr, and filmed the wrecks from the walls of the castle. W. Sellars Collection.

Waddell's performance changed this perception. In the years before the First World War he proved his worth as a soldier in one of the world's toughest and most demanding of military organisations, seeing active service in the Boxer Rebellion in 1900–01, and in Algeria, Morocco and Tonkin. On the outbreak of war in August 1914 he had risen to the rank of captain and become a French citizen. He had divorced his first wife and married again. His reports indicated that he was now regarded as an outstanding officer. "Demonstrates authority over the troops he commands with brilliance but with firmness."[29] He was awarded the rank of chevalier of the Legion of Honour for his work in Indo-China.

In mid-May 1915, three weeks after the initial landing, Waddell landed with 347 legionnaires at V Beach at Cape Helles to reinforce the legionnaire battalion that formed part of the 1st Regiment 'de marche d'Afrique' in the 1st Metropolitan Brigade of the 1st Division CEO. The reinforcements brought the battalion up to strength and with the wounding of his predecessor, Waddell found himself appointed commanding officer. Waddell's legionnaires held the Gouez sector facing the Ottoman front line along the western crest above the deep gully of Kereves Dere, which angled across the French front and presented a major obstacle to any advance on the high ground of Achi Baba.[30] Fort

Gouez had been one of the four heavily defended and entrenched redoubts protecting the Ottoman front line. Taking and holding each position involved constant attack and counterattack and heavy casualties to both sides.

On 30 May and in the failed attack on 3–4 June 1915 Waddell's battalion withstood a series of fierce counterattacks and held their ground, despite the fort being almost completely destroyed by Ottoman artillery fire. In the French offensive on 21 June 1915 the French attack was driven back after initially occupying the Ottoman front trenches. Waddell led his battalion forward and secured the enemy trenches, holding them against strong counterattacks. For this he was awarded his first Croix de Guerre on 4 July 1915 by General Gouraud.[31]

Waddell's legionnaires were part of the Allied attack on 12 July. The aim of the legionnaires was to seize the Le Rognon redoubt that was the key to the Ottoman front line trenches in this sector. In the first rush, Waddell's men seized the western half of the Rognon defences.[32] Waddell, as always, led from the front and was wounded twice in the attack. However, he stayed forward with his men until the counterattacks were defeated and the position consolidated. Gouraud was seriously wounded by artillery fire near his headquarters at V Beach and it was his successor General Bailloud who awarded Waddell the Croix de Guerre with bronze palm leaf.

Waddell was evacuated to a hospital in Algeria and then to France where he recuperated at his home in Nice with his second wife. Coincidentally, one of Waddell's two brothers also served on Gallipoli with the NZEF. David Waddell, a schoolteacher from Raes Junction, served as a trooper with the Otago Mounted Rifles. He fell sick at Anzac in June 1915 and was evacuated first to Alexandria and then to England. Declared unfit for active service, he returned to New Zealand on the SS *Athenic* in April 1916.[33]

It was not until April 1916 that James Waddell returned to duty and was appointed commanding officer of the 2nd Battalion of what was now the 'Regiment de Marche de la Legion Étrangère' (RMLE) that formed part of the Moroccan Division.

He later commanded a battalion at Verdun and on the Somme. Waddell continued to display outstanding leadership and a complete disregard for danger. By the war's end in 1918 he had been awarded the Croix de Guerre with seven palm leaves, and made a Commander of the Legion of Honour. In 1918 he was part of the French Mission serving with the United States Army, and in May 1918 transferred from the Legion and commanded a French regular battalion in the 169th Infantry Regiment, receiving three awards for his bravery in three months before being wounded in August 1918.

On Gallipoli Waddell sought out and met with his fellow New Zealanders, particularly when the New Zealand Infantry Brigade was stationed at Cape Helles in May 1915. His making contact is mentioned in various diaries. This continued throughout the war. He visited London a number of times and in December 1916 met with Sir Joseph Ward who he knew from his volunteer days in Invercargill. This and his achievements in the French Army were reported in the New Zealand press.[34]

After the war he commanded a district in the French zone of occupation in Germany, and served in Tunisia before retiring in 1926. In 1950, after the death of his third wife, Waddell returned to New Zealand with a married daughter. His achievements in the First World War were now forgotten. He died in 1954 and is buried in the Levin Soldiers' Cemetery. The films of the French at the Dardanelles serve to remind us of an amazing New Zealander's story, a story that has remained largely unknown in New Zealand.[35]

Ashmead-Bartlett films Gallipoli

I remember the first day ashore we collected souvenirs, you know bayonets and bullets that the Turks had. But we soon dropped those. All over the hillside were beautiful cameras, cameras galore, just thrown off because you had to travel light. You would travel with practically nothing, just a rifle, bayonet, ammunition and a trenching tool.[1]

WAR REPORTERS AT GALLIPOLI

In 1915, with the exception of the single film *With the Allied Fleets in the Dardanelles* that showed a glimpse of the French ashore on the Gallipoli Peninsula, it was the written word and photograph that the New Zealand public had to rely on for news from the battle front. Possessing a camera and taking photographs was forbidden by military regulation with the threat of court-martial.[2] Although in early 1914 on all fronts this was observed more in breach than in practice; it was soon clamped down on in France and Belgium, but never on Gallipoli and the press received enough photos from private sources on the peninsula to meet public demand for images. Many of 'Bill Massey's Tourists', as they termed themselves, had cameras and one of the most vivid images conjured up for me in the interviews I did with Gallipoli veterans in the 1980s, such as with Russell Weir who was a private on the headquarters of Godley's NZ & A Division, is that of the beach and slopes above Anzac Cove being littered with cameras on the evening of 25 April 1915; the first Anzac Day. When I queried this, I was told that suddenly cameras were less important than food and ammunition, they were hastily thrown aside as men rifled through the packs on the beach looking for essentials. Luxuries like cameras were discarded. Photography never became the disciplinary issue that it did in France. It was shortage of film and the impossibility of replacing it, or the death or wounding of the owner that abruptly stopped an individual's photographic chronology of the campaign.

Official reporters, including Ellis Ashmead-Bartlett from England and Charles Edwin Woodrow Bean from Australia with the Australian Imperial Force (AIF), were attached to the contingents and it was their reports of the secondary landing of 25 April 1915 that captured

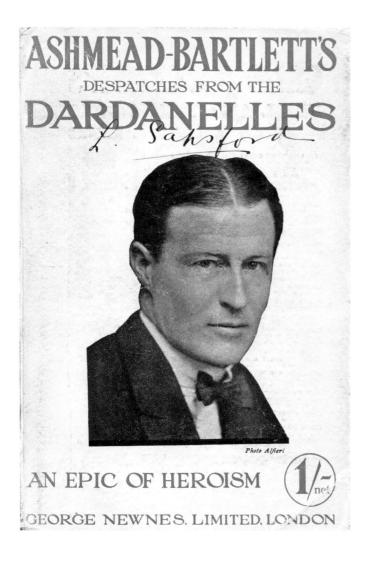

ASHMEAD-BARTLETT'S
DESPATCHES FROM THE
DARDANELLES

L. Sahsford

Photo Alfieri

AN EPIC OF HEROISM   1/-net

GEORGE NEWNES. LIMITED. LONDON

Ellis Ashmead-Bartlett's *Despatches from the Dardanelles* inspired the legend of Anzacs being natural soldiers. Author's Collection.

the imagination of the Empire and overshadowed the main landings of the British and French forces at Cape Helles. Ashmead-Bartlett's despatches, vividly 'eyewitnessed' from a battleship offshore, cemented an image of Anzacs as natural soldiers that the Australian and New Zealand public wanted to believe and his role as an official British correspondent gave it a validity that no Australian or New Zealand reporter would have earned. Ashmead-Bartlett wrote of Australians that day, but his report was given a universality to include the New Zealand contribution both in editing on board ship and by the press in New Zealand.[3] This was matched by C.E.W. Bean's reports, but a New Zealand voice was missing and this was belatedly supplied by Malcolm Ross.

MALCOLM ROSS: NEW ZEALAND'S OFFICIAL WAR CORRESPONDENT

Malcolm Ross, the official correspondent for the New Zealand Expeditionary Force (NZEF), was a late addition who did not get to Gallipoli until June 1915. His first despatches of the campaign were sent from Egypt using information drawn from the wounded arriving from the peninsula. Ross, although 52, was very fit for a man of his age; he had a love of the outdoors and a reputation of being a skilled and highly respected mountaineer. He was vastly experienced as a parliamentary reporter, being accredited to both the *Otago Daily Times* and *The Times* in London, but was a controversial choice as official correspondent in an age when New Zealand papers were identified by their party affiliation. A friend of Massey's, he was seen as Reform Party-biased. Despite having previous experience in Samoa during the fighting in 1899, his personal initiative in seeking out Godley to become the official reporter attached to the Samoan Expeditionary Force in August 1914 was somehow seen as government-engineered, and vigorously attacked by Ward and Opposition members in Parliament.

Massey's protestations simply heightened the Opposition's conviction that Ross was a government man. This suspicion stuck to him for the rest of the war. Despite his selection by a panel of press editors as the best man for the job, Opposition MPs took every opportunity to criticise what he wrote, using any delay in its arrival, and emphasising his cost to the taxpayer. As Palenski notes, Ross was subject to a "war-long campaign of derision and disdain" from the Auckland weekly newspaper the *New Zealand Observer*, which was solidly aligned to Ward's Liberal Party.[4] It is this criticism that has lingered on and clouds today's views of his writing and effectiveness. A skilled photographer, his dapper image already appeared alongside the cameras in the crowd in the illustrations of many of the New Zealand public ceremonies at Parliament before the war. He is the forgotten man of New Zealand journalism from this period, yet his is the ubiquitous presence with the NZEF, first on Gallipoli and then in France and Flanders, both with his writings and his presence in photograph and film accompanying dignitaries on visits to the troops.

His terms of employment from the New Zealand Government demanded that he "remain as near as possible to the New Zealand Forces at the seat of the war, and to write regularly detailed accounts of events in which the New Zealand Forces are engaged, and of matters of special interest to New Zealand". He was to be tasked by the government and also by the high commissioner for New Zealand, and "must comply with any specific directions received".[5] This was unlikely to trouble Ross. In 1888 he accompanied Thomas Mackenzie into the unexplored reaches of Lake Manapouri and the Fiordland sounds while with the *Otago Daily Times,* as part of the search party for Professor Mainwaring Brown of Otago University, and shared Mackenzie's love for the rugged bush and mountains of the South Island.

Of more concern was his work being subject to censorship imposed by 'Imperial Authorities' but once again Ross saw this as an expected wartime reality. Despite his age and his stylish looks, he was a man inured to 'roughing it' and with his background in the bush and mountains, accepted the reality of plans not always working, putting up with bureaucracy in all its forms, and of getting the story in to the press whatever the difficulties. Despite the criticism he was the ideal choice for the job he was sent to do.

The greatest restriction placed on Ross was Massey's government's unwillingness to pay for the cost of cabling the news. "He is to send his despatches as frequently as possible by course of post to the High Commissioner in London" where they would then be despatched to New Zealand. When in Egypt and on Gallipoli, Ross's despatches were posted directly back to the Department of Internal Affairs in Wellington. This guaranteed that anything Ross wrote would feature at least six weeks after the event, and certainly long after the cabled news reports of his fellow official correspondents. Ross would be damned for these delays in the New Zealand press but it was beyond his control, New Zealand Government penny-pinching ruled that "he will not use either cable or telegraph".[6]

Ross sailed for Egypt with his wife and fellow reporter Forrestina (or Forrest) Ross.[7] Their son Noel, also a journalist, had enlisted in the Canterbury Infantry Battalion, so they, like many other New Zealand families, had a vested interest in the efforts of the NZEF. They arrived in Egypt to news of the wounding of their son, just as the boatloads of wounded from the Dardanelles swamped the hospital facilities and of the New Zealand medical arrangements in particular. Rumour of casualties with contradictory reports reaching New Zealand of who had been killed, wounded or missing, with many reported wounded who could not later be found, caused enormous anguish in New Zealand, which grew into anger at perceived military bureaucratic ineptitude.[8] It reflected the chaotic reality ashore on the Gallipoli Peninsula within the Anzac perimeter as the landing by the ANZAC Corps came perilously close to failure on the 25 April 1915.

The two divisions of the ANZAC Corps were fighting for their lives, clinging on to a tiny foothold of Turkey. Most of the dead of the initial day's fighting lay on ground now held by the Turks and those wounded in the first 24 hours were despatched out to the transports offshore pell-mell and without record.

The battalions ashore, fighting for their lives, had no knowledge of who was dead or who was wounded and often got it wrong in their belated reports. It was weeks before any semblance of what happened, or who was likely to be where, was established. The brunt of this was borne by the government in New Zealand as private cables sent from wounded arriving in Egypt contradicted official reports.

Groups of mothers besieged politicians urging "immediate improvement in the system of notifying casualties and the progress of wounded soldiers in hospital. Cases were quoted

showing the inadequacy of the present arrangements, and complaints were made of the non-delivery of parcels sent to soldiers."[9] The political implications were obvious with the press cautioning the government to "Keep sweet with the mothers."[10] This was not lost on Massey who was in political difficulties, having just held on to power in the December 1914 elections. Massey's playing of the patriotic card, "calling on people to support the government in time of crisis", left him vulnerable to calls for a wartime 'national' government, which came into effect in August 1915. This was after months of bargaining with Ward's Liberals and Massey's Reform ministers equally dividing the expanded number of cabinet posts.[11] In August Massey sent his former cabinet minister W. Heaton Rhodes to Egypt and Gallipoli to report on a wide range of issues covering "any matters affecting the well-being and comfort of New Zealand soldiers' as a much needed response to growing public concern".[12]

SEARCHING FOR NOEL

Opposition members pilloried Ross for his and his wife's concern in running around Cairo to locate their wounded son, Noel, of the Canterbury Infantry Battalion. But their actions and the difficulties they faced, which Ross detailed in his press reports, were what New Zealanders wanted to read to better understand why they had not heard about their own sons. Ross, although his news on the landings was superseded by cabled reports from Ashmead-Bartlett and Bean and abbreviated by New Zealand editors, still struck a chord with his detailed stories from the front that he gained from interviews with the wounded in Egypt, giving names, chapter and verse on how New Zealanders fought and died. It was exactly what every New Zealand family wanted to read and while the Opposition MPs criticised Ross's preoccupation with finding his son, they missed the point as his words were eagerly read in homes with sons and fathers at the front who wanted reassurance on hospital conditions and casualty reporting. They desperately wanted to know that Chaplain Taylor of Nelson was giving "decent burial" to the dead and that there was a chance "that a mother or a father in Australia and New Zealand" will receive what was in the pockets of their son or husband, "from one perhaps a pipe, from another a few letters or the family photographs, or from still another a man's pay-book, often as not stained with his own blood".[13]

'TINY' FREYBERG OF THE ROYAL NAVAL DIVISION

Ross was first to break the news of the achievements with the Royal Naval Division of the New Zealand-raised 'Tiny' Freyberg, "who, as a schoolboy, was a champion swimmer" and well known in New Zealand. Now a lieutenant-commander (major-equivalent) in the Royal Naval Division, Freyberg objected to a planned feint that would see three boatloads of his men land on the Turkish-held beaches at the northern junction of the Gallipoli Peninsula with European Turkey. He believed that "this meant sacrificing the lives of his men, not one of whom would be likely to return alive, and he suggested that he, himself, should be allowed to swim ashore."[14] He did this on the evening of 25 April. Freyberg swam the half-mile to the beach, crept inland below the Turkish trenches, lit a flare before diving back into the sea and repeated this two more times along the stretch of beach, prompting the Turks to open fire. The destroyer that dropped him returned fire to simulate support to a landing party while Freyberg, now bitterly cold and suffering from cramp, swam back out to sea in the pitch black night and by some miracle reached the ship's cutter searching for him. He was awarded the DSO for this exploit. This was detail that never dated and Ross's letters, often printed in successive issues over the course of a week, each covering two or three columns, reported to a public hungry for news.[15]

ROSS AT GALLIPOLI

Ross got to Anzac Cove on 26 June but his first despatch was not published in New Zealand until 14 August 1915.[16] It is not to be wondered that his first impressions of a "rather quiet day at Anzac" sat uncomfortably alongside Ashmead-Bartlett's and C.E.W. Bean's cabled news of the August offensive and the long casualty lists featuring names such as Lieutenant-Colonels Malone and Bauchop that heralded the near destruction of the NZEF in the August fighting. Censorship soon prevented the publication of names but Ross painted enough detail for his New Zealand readers to identify the principal New Zealand personalities he wrote about. His letters were delayed in getting to Egypt and then had to wait for the mail boat home and he was criticised. But, other than published personal letters, his despatches were the only source of regular New Zealand detail and, if out-of-date, still gave information that was avidly sought by those wanting confirmation of what happened and of the conditions faced by New Zealand's sons.

Ross's despatches of the August offensive were not received until 13 October when they appeared in the *Evening Post*, but what he wrote was again printed in full. Despite the lack of names, readers already knew that the Otago colonel who died leading his men in the night attack was Arthur Bauchop, as that had been reported weeks before, but they still devoured every word that Ross could tell them.[17]

At the front Ross was part of the war correspondents contingent consisting of Ellis Ashmead-Bartlett, C.E.W. Bean, Henry Nevinson and others, working under the conditions imposed by Hamilton's headquarters and located alongside his headquarters at Cephalos on the island of Imbros. He, with the official Australian correspondent, C.E.W. Bean, determined to spend as much time at Anzac as possible where they stayed. This was despite constant attempts to concentrate all correspondents offshore with Hamilton's Mediterranean Expeditionary Force headquarters. Ross accepted the realities of the restrictions placed upon him as a correspondent. In September he wrote to Allen detailing what these were, but stressed everyone was treated similarly.

> All our despatches are severely censored, and it is very difficult to make them interesting in regard to the intimate details that New Zealanders would like to read about … I shd [sic] have liked to have written about Bauchop and Malone and many other gallant fellows who have gone, but mention of names is absolutely interdicted. You might let the Cabinet know all this in confidence. I don't think anything can be done unless the War Office can be got to make an exception in the case of N.Z. because of her distance away.[18]

Ross detailed to Allen his impressions of the campaign and in his private correspondence unhesitatingly gave both blame and praise. He was highly critical of New Zealand medical arrangements in Egypt and blamed the personalities in charge. He had nothing but praise for the New Zealand performance on Gallipoli, but was disparaging of the medical arrangements and of the British forces at Suvla.

> Our own men have fought splendidly and have well earned their spell. Godley, who has not spared himself in any way, is well and doing good work. We very narrowly missed a big thing on Chunuk Bair and later also with the Mounted Infantry under Russell, who is capital. The K. [Kitchener] Army on the left made a mess of things and were too slow and not tenacious enough. You will hear — or have heard — that the wounded were badly cared for after the Chunuk Bair fight; but <u>our people</u> were in no way responsible for that.[19]

A glimpse of Anzac Cove at its northern end looking towards the New Zealand Ordnance Depot above the beach, with stacks of stores on the beach itself, men bathing, and the hustle and bustle of a busy port. Filmed by Ashmead-Bartlett with his portable Aeroscope camera. Still from *With the Dardanelles Expedition/Heroes of Gallipoli*, Weta Digital Restoration, AWM F10581.

He also highlighted the debilitating effects of the endemic dysentery, shared by soldiers and journalists alike. "Pretty nearly everyone from the General downwards has suffered from the prevailing diarrhoea which after three or four days leaves one very weak and not caring a damn whether a shell gets you or not." Ross also pointed out that while the New Zealand casualties were very heavy in killed, wounded and sick, "we have not suffered any more than other divisions, and probably not so much as the 29th [Division]".[20] This was a counter to a growing feeling in New Zealand that both the Australians and New Zealanders were being asked to do too much; a mood increasingly reflected in the soldiers' letters home.

In New Zealand Ellis Ashmead-Bartlett was seen as the trusted official voice from Gallipoli complimented by the Australian, C.E.W. Bean, both of whose cabled despatches gave the first news from the peninsula with Ross's letters filling in the New Zealand details, six weeks later. Ross accompanied both in their visits to the trenches and was occasional witness to Ashmead-Bartlett's filming. Ross continued in this role as the sole New Zealand official correspondent on the Western Front and continued to attract vociferous criticism in the opposition press.

ELLIS ASHMEAD-BARTLETT FILMS GALLIPOLI

Ellis Ashmead-Bartlett is an interesting character. He was eldest son of the distinguished lawyer and politician Sir Ellis Ashmead-Bartlett, who championed the importance of Turkey and the Ottoman Empire to Britain's security in the Middle East. The 16-year-old Ellis junior travelled with his father as guests of the sultan during the Greco–Turkish War of 1897. A fine writer, he served as a volunteer in the Boer War, then as a war correspondent in the Russo–Japanese War in 1904–05. As Reuter's special correspondent he reported on the French Army in Morocco in 1907–08, the Spanish in Morocco in 1909 and the Italians in Tripoli in 1911. In between Ashmead-Bartlett attempted a political career by twice unsuccessfully standing for parliament. He covered the Balkan Wars of 1912–13 for the *Daily Telegraph*.

Medical grounds frustrated his attempts to enlist in the army in 1914. However, the 33-year-old Ashmead-Bartlett was selected by the National Press Association as the London Press Association correspondent for the Dardanelles Campaign.[21] He was the obvious choice and was by far the most experienced war correspondent in the Dardanelles. Ashmead-Bartlett lived life to the full. His inveterate gambling and womanising meant that he was always close to bankruptcy and his outspokenness tended to get people's backs up. Nevertheless in 1915 he became the trusted eyewitness of the Dardanelles Campaign for readers throughout the Empire and his despatches of the landing by the ANZAC Corps on 25 April 1915 became the foundation stone of the Anzac legend.[22]

Ashmead-Bartlett was accommodated on board the battleship HMS *Majestic* that was anchored as guard ship off W Beach on 27 May 1915 when it was torpedoed by the German submarine U-21, commanded by Commander Otto Hersing. Ashmead-Bartlett lost almost all of his belongings including his diaries. He returned to England to replace his kit and when offered the chance to supplement his income by taking motion pictures of the campaign, seized the opportunity. Bankrolled by the London theatrical entrepreneur Alfred Butt, Ashmead-Bartlett stood to profit from the release of a film of the campaign.

Although, as he admitted, he knew nothing about the Aeroscope camera he was given or indeed how to load and care for the 10,000 feet of film he was entrusted with.[23] He had some brief lessons on what was one of the world's first portable cameras, albeit a bulky box affair that operated by compressed air and was considerably larger than the Lumière Cinématographe of some 20 years earlier. Its portability came from its method of operation. "It is an automatic machine which winds up, and you just turn it on when you have something to take."[24] Air was pumped in by a simple hand pump that allowed the operator to hold it with both hands and concentrate on filming the scene. The compressed air allowed some ten minutes of filming and the camera had the capacity for 400 feet of film.[25]

Ashmead-Bartlett's Gallipoli filming was a chore undertaken where financial need, rather than any real interest, determined motivation. Assisted by Ernest 'Baby' Brooks, the Royal Navy official photographer, he filmed scenes on the peninsula but had no way of knowing how successful he was with his Aeroscope camera or 'cinema' as he called it. He learnt on the job and, despite his inexperience, was very fortunate because the freedom given to him with his filming would not have been allowed in France. Ability rather than opportunity limited what has survived. Despite this, the combined endeavours of Ashmead-Bartlett and Brooks resulted in some of the most vivid combat war footage that survives of the First World War, and what was thought for many years to be our only Gallipoli footage.[26]

FILMING HELLES

Arriving back on the Gallipoli Peninsula in late June 1915, he teamed up with Brooks, who agreed to assist with the filming.[27] Their first outing together was not promising. Viewing the Krithia battlefield at Cape Helles on 12 July, Ashmead-Bartlett sought a good vantage point to see the Allied attack.

> Finally I found what looked like a very favourable spot, and apparently as safe as any in the neighbourhood, in a deserted observation post of 42nd Division. But, strange to say, it became the focus for several Turkish guns. Brooks was enchanted by the panorama of the battle, the bursting of countless shells, and the infantry attacks. Then, by a strange irony, he was hit behind in a soft spot by a shrapnel bullet. It seems incredible that a bullet could have come in at such an angle, and I think he believes to this day that I arranged it on purpose. He dropped his precious camera with a yell, and "the subsequent proceedings interested him no more." However he was more bruised than wounded and soon recovered his equanimity when he discovered he was very much alive.[28]

FILMING ANZAC

The wounding resulted in Brooks returning to England and throughout July Ashmead-Bartlett attempted filming alone. On 22 July he visited Anzac with Henry Nevinson and was escorted by Aubrey Herbert, intelligence officer on Godley's staff. "We visited Quinn's and Courtney's Posts, where I took a number of cinema pictures. Colonel Malone, a hardy old New Zealand officer and ex-South African veteran, showed us round."[29]

Ashmead-Bartlett was wrong in thinking Malone had served in South Africa, but he was one of the outstanding fighting commanding officers ashore on Gallipoli. It was his personal drive and determination that transformed the situation at Quinn's Post; the critical and vulnerable apex of the Anzac position where at its closest point the Ottoman and Anzac trenches were five metres apart. It was also Malone's initiative that saw the best New Zealand and Australian

With the Dardanelles Expedition; Heroes of Gallipoli. AWM F00069.

With the Dardanelles Expedition; Heroes of Gallipoli. Weta Digital restoration, AWM F10581.

marksmen employed as sniping teams to seek out and kill the Turkish snipers who until now dominated no-man's land and who had caused deadly havoc among the lines of men carrying supplies up Shrapnel Valley and Monash Gully to the front line positions along Second Ridge.

Malone put on a show for Ashmead-Bartlett and we see this with the surviving shot of the two snipers. The New Zealand observer, wearing a battered lemon squeezer, is sighting a target through his periscope, while his Australian counterpart loads and aims his rifle mounted on a periscope frame — an Australian soldier's invention that allowed accurate fire over the parapet without exposing the firer. It is an important piece of film history, a sniping team at work on Anzac or indeed anywhere else during the First World War.

Given the nature of the Australian perceptions of the Anzac legend there is gentle irony in the smartness of the uniform of the Australian sniper; he is most probably the neatest of anyone appearing in the Anzac scenes filmed by Ashmead-Bartlett. From his colour patch on his shoulder he appears to belong to the 2nd Australian Division. The first elements of this arrived during the August offensive and this sniper may have been a member of an advance party in late July/early August 1915. He is clearly a crack shot and from his dress may be a regular officer or warrant officer or possibly the machine gun officer on a preliminary reconnaissance. This may be wishful thinking and if not then this sequence must have been filmed in August–September, which raises questions on its location, as the Wellington Battalion was withdrawn from Quinn's Post on 5 August 1915.

Malone noted in his diary:

> Ashmead-Bartlett the English W/Cpdent [sic] came with the others, and actually kinematographed part of the Post, at back, taking in the terrace and the men at work etc. Then I took him into the fire trench and he took some more pictures. He seemed a bit swollen-headed,

Toiling up Shrapnel Valley from Hell Spit, a New Zealander in 'lemon squeezer' is on the right. Still from *With the Dardanelles Expedition/Heroes of Gallipoli*, Weta Digital Restoration, AWM F10581.

Bicycles above the beach at Anzac Cove in anticipation of a war of movement that never happened. Still from *With the Dardanelles Expedition/Heroes of Gallipoli*, Weta Digital Restoration, AWM F10581.

A New Zealand soldier, wearing the 'lemon squeezer' hat, acting as observer for an Australian officer or warrant officer. The Australian is wearing 2nd Australian Division shoulder flashes. The scene is presumably at Quinn's Post. Still from *With the Dardanelles Expedition/ Heroes of Gallipoli*, Weta Digital Restoration, AWM F10581.

and full of his own importance. I gave him a couple of thrills, by taking him to place open to Turkish fire at about 300 yds range, and then pointing out to him the Turks trenches. I had asked him if he wanted to see them. But generally they are looked at thro' a periscope.[30]

The scenes of a headquarters dugout and the file of men passing through a covered walkway includes that of a New Zealand soldier in lemon squeezer hat that identifies him as a member of the Wellington Infantry Battalion who were at that time the only New Zealand infantry battalion to be wearing that distinctive headdress. This confirms that this was filmed at Quinn's Post most likely on 22 July 1915. Historians have also speculated that the presence of

a neatly dressed officer with pith helmet and tie also indicaties that this was filmed at Quinn's Post because Malone was a stickler for neatness and order for his officers and men alike. However, it is more likely that Ashmead-Bartlett enlisted the assistance of those visiting the post with him to feature on camera; a more likely candidate for the pith-helmeted officer is that of Lieutenant-General Birdwood's aide de camp, the Victorian grazier, Lieutenant Robert Gordon Chirnside, who features in a number of photos taken at Quinn's Post and locations on Second Ridge, and who looks remarkably similar to the well-dressed officer in the film.[31]

The following day, 23 July 1915, Ashmead-Bartlett visited the New Zealand manned outposts along the beach, including No. 1 Outpost, or the Maori Pa as it was known, held by the Maori Contingent.

> The latter are magnificent physical specimens of manhood, but they have not yet been tested in action. I stayed out at No. 3 Post all the morning examining the enemy's lines. I lunched with some of the officers of the staff and spent the afternoon taking cinema pictures, but whether they will come out only time will show.[32]

Ashmead-Bartlett's reservations were justified. The surviving film has a brief image of signallers erecting telephone lines along the Great Sap, the communication way dug by Maori Contingent labour between Walker's Ridge and the outposts, but no other images survive that can be attributed to this day's filming.

July 24th was spent filming at Anzac Cove. Ashmead-Bartlett positioned himself on the jetty in the centre of the beach exactly opposite Birdwood's headquarters, panning his camera across the lower slopes above the beach with Plugge's Plateau on the skyline. He captured the hustle and bustle of this gold rush town in appearance, hurriedly established on Turkish shores, home to 25,000 inhabitants and all manner of stores, essential to their survival, as well as those no longer required, like the line of bicycles visible above the beach, now very much surplus to their needs. Another view of Anzac Cove may have been filmed on the same day. It shows the view over Anzac Cove taken from the slopes of MacLagan's Ridge looking north along the beach. It emphasises how small the beach is and how crowded the conditions. We see soldiers swimming and at their ablutions while the bustle continues around them. It is the only scenes showing the beach at Anzac Cove from higher ground. Ashmead-Bartlett wrote at the time:

> July 24th. I spent the whole morning at Anzac on the beach trying to get cinema pictures of the shells bursting among the bathers. It was exciting work and finally the bathing had to stop when a shell killed twenty men and wounded fifteen others — so I am told. They started firing again just as Nevinson and I were leaving, but we managed to get aboard the lugger safely.[33]

There are no scenes of shelling, and no close-ups of the bathers, but the stacks of head high forage and boxes of corned beef and biscuits down the centre of the jetty as protection for working parties against artillery shrapnel fire, with men filing up and down on either side, shows that the danger was real.

From 30 July to 1 August, Ashmead-Bartlett with Ross and Nevinson visited the British positions at Helles, and over the three days Ashmead-Bartlett filmed the panoramic views from the *River Clyde* overlooking V Beach, the armoured car scenes in their earth bunds manned by personnel of the Royal Naval Air Service (RNAS), and the shots of British infantry on their way out of the line from the front trenches facing Krithia. Much more was filmed but like many of his filmed attempts at Anzac, these were unsuccessful or have since been lost.[34] It was on 4 August visiting the seaplane carrier *Ark Royal* that he met "a real cinema operator on board, who came over ... to explain several points about the machine of which I was ignorant. I am afraid the films up to date will be of small value as I have not been taking them correctly."[35] However, enough survived to provide his Cape Helles and Anzac Cove material.

FILMING THE SUVLA BAY LANDINGS

On 6 August Ashmead-Bartlett filmed the preparation and embarkation of the men of the British 11th Division on Imbros Island who were part of the Suvla landing by Lieutenant-General Sir F.W. Stopford's IX Corps on 7 August 1915. His film captures the scale of the operation; the line of First Sea Lord Jackie Fisher's armoured amphibious barges or 'Beetles', so named from the shape of the distinctive arms either side of the bow ramp that were designed for operations in the Baltic; the work of the Egyptian labourers and Turkish prisoners loading stores; and the mass of fully equipped men patiently waiting as they filed slowly forward onto the landing craft and ships.[36]

That evening Ashmead-Bartlett, with Henry Nevinson, embarked on the liner *Minneapolis* and filmed the invasion armada sailing from Imbros. The next morning he captured the scenes as the convoy approached the landing beaches at Suvla Bay, the first-ever filmed scenes of an amphibious military landing in the history of warfare. Mules are hoisted from the hold onto barges and we have film of the beaches: a Beetle run up onto the shore with its ramp down, men struggling ashore with stores, as heavily laden men mass on the beach itself.

Ashmead-Bartlett records this first day ashore in his diaries:

> Nevinson and I seized the first opportunity of going ashore and landed at Ghazi Baba. Here we found hundreds of bluejackets and soldiers hastily unloading stores and ammunition ... We then set off to explore the country, passing round the long northern arm of Suvla Bay until we came to the sand spit which separates it from the Salt Lake. The scenes en route resembled rather the retreat of a routed army than the advance of a victorious one. Everywhere we encountered stragglers returning from the firing line in a state of pitiful exhaustion from fatigue and thirst, hastening to the beaches to find water at any cost. Many had their tongues hanging from their mouths blackened with thirst. When they reached the bay they found the water lighters but no adequate means of filling their bottles. The water was pumped ashore through hose-pipes, but there were no receptacles, and the men were expected to fill bottles a quarter of an inch wide at the spout from a hose three or four inches in diameter. Naturally, more was wasted than drunk. The hoses were leaking in dozens of places. But I have since learnt that this was due to holes bored by the impatient infantry, who would no longer wait their turn at the spout. The men with whom I spoke seemed dazed and depressed. No one could tell a coherent story of what had happened, or what was happening at the front. Lack of sleep, thirst and physical fatigue had killed their interest in the operations.[37]

These scenes survive on film. The crowded beach. A dense mass of soldiery, washing, eating, waiting, all part of a British Corps struck by command inertia at brigade, division and corps-level; paid for in blood, heatstroke and confusion by the soldiers appearing on film.

Combat footage filmed by Ashmead-Bartlett from the front trench looking towards Scimitar Hill on 21 August. The scrub-covered foreground has been set on fire by artillery shells. The wounded who could not crawl fast enough were burned to death. Still from *With the Dardanelles Expedition: Heroes of Gallipoli*, Weta Digital Restoration, F10581, AWM.

There are contrasting scenes ashore, an infantry battalion officers' mess with its officers, Ashmead-Bartlett among them, sitting in the open dining al fresco, two trenches with a bench of earth providing the seating, with the unexcavated earth between the table, enamel mugs and plates, plain fare but still fresh bread, rare on Gallipoli, and a wave of acknowledgement to the camera manned by Brooks. Stretcher bearers struggle down the jetty with wounded to the barges waiting to ferry them to the hospital ships offshore.

The Suvla landings surprised the Turks, but the bravery, determination and resourcefulness of a small Ottoman force that included two battalions of gendarme, the Bursa and Gelibolu battalions, along with two battle-weakened battalions of army troops, 1/31st and 2/32nd, under the overall direction of a German major, held back until further Turkish reinforcements arrived. A priceless opportunity was lost.

FILMING COMBAT AT SUVLA

Ashmead-Bartlett was intent on capturing the realities of combat on film. On 9 and 21 August he filmed the desperate British attacks on Scimitar Hill. These are some of the most graphic battle scenes ever shot during the First World War. Ashmead-Bartlett's images caught the realities of modern warfare, no scenes of massed men charging, but pictures of fiercely burning bush and scrub intermixed with the smoke of exploding artillery shells on the fiercely contested Chocolate Hill and Scimitar Ridge at Suvla, and the knowledge that within that fiery maelstrom wounded men, unable to move, were burning to death.

His experiences on 21 August encapsulated the risks run by film cameramen.

About 5.30, the Turkish artillery fire on Chocolate Hill having diminished, I endeavoured to set up my cinema above the parapet of the partly destroyed trench to get some pictures of the wonderful panorama of the shellfire and the burning scrub. The gunners were on me like a flash. I could not believe that they could have picked up a target so quickly. One shell whizzed past my head and stuck in the back of the trench without exploding. Then came another. I saw a bright flash and found myself in total darkness.

I struggled to get clear but realised that I was buried. Shortly afterwards a spot of light appeared and I became conscious that I was being dug out. My benefactor turned out to be a soldier who had seen my mishap and who immediately ran to my assistance. I found the fuse of a high explosive shell lying on my legs but I had not received a scratch. My belongings did not fare so well. Owing to the heat, I had taken off my coat and placed it beside me with my small camera, walking-stick, field glasses and water-bottle. They were probably blown to smithereens, and, in any case, disappeared for ever. The infernal old cinema, of which I was now heartily tired, the cause of all my troubles, had of course survived and I was reluctantly compelled to drag it back to camp.[38]

On 2 September, Ashmead-Bartlett and Brooks again visited Suvla and as we see in his description of his visit to an Irish battalion on the front line, captured perhaps the most vivid trench fighting sequence ever filmed in the First World War, with Ashmead-Bartlett himself visible on camera as he tries to move past the line of riflemen.

I left for Suvla Bay, armed with my cinema, accompanied by Brooks, the official photographer, who has returned from England. I landed after a very stormy voyage, the precursor of what is to come. I found things much quieter than usual and very little shelling ... We went out beyond Chocolate Hill into the front trenches, where the Turkish lines were about fifty yards away. We were out after pictures and nearly caused a battle. Finding a trench occupied by an Irish Battalion, Brooks asked them to assume positions just as if they were resisting an attack. But the men would look round at the cinema. Brooks said "That is not realistic enough." "Oh!" exclaimed an Irishman, "I'll make it realistic." Whereupon he started to shoot at the Turks, followed by all his comrades. The day being perfectly quiet, the latter imagined we were about to attack, and replied furiously. A sustained duel then began and in the excitement the Irishmen forgot all about us. Soon the Turkish artillery joined in, and it looked as if we had started a battle all along the line. They telephoned down from brigade headquarters to find out what was happening, whereupon one of the N.C.O.s replied, "Oh nothing, sir, it is only the cinema." But I though the matter had gone far enough, so we crept away to avoid the wrath of the divisional headquarters.[39]

Brooks took a number of photographs that showed a quiet day in the trenches of the 5th Royal Irish Fusiliers. He then took over the filming while Ashmead-Bartlett can be seen on film moving along the trench to stir up the firing line and then hurrying back out of shot. Ashmead-Bartlett noted how successfully this scene turned out. The images were eagerly claimed by C.E.W. Bean, (who re-edited the film before Bartlett's diary extracts were published,) as scenes of Australians firing on the Turks. The Irishmen Fusiliers are scruffy enough, except for their officer, to fit our image of Anzacs, but how they appear is the reality of any soldiers after a prolonged stint in the trenches during a Gallipoli summer. But film by its nature triggers the imagination and what one wants to believe becomes as important as the reality. In fairness to Bean, it was an assumption that was made by audiences in Britain, Australia and New Zealand wherever the film was screened in 1916. Everyone watching the film willed them to be 'their boys'.

Soldiers of the 5th Royal Irish Fusiliers in action on 2 September 1915 in the front line near Green Hill after being encouraged by Ashmead-Bartlett with back to camera, while Ernest Brooks filmed. Still from *A.H. Noad: Gallipoli Film*, AWM F00176.

This scene of soldiers in action may have been inspired by the presence of the two cameraman but it is not a fake scene, which is what we have with the iconic images of British infantry attacking through the barbed wire entanglements in the film *The Battle of the Somme*. In it we see two men fall in the wire and as they move forward a further two go down. It confronted British audiences with the reality of death at the front. Only much later was it discovered that it was staged for camera on a firing range in France and that the dead would rise again and joke with one another over their ability to play dead.[40] Ashmead-Bartlett's filming of the Irish firing and the Turkish response gave us real images where any consciousness of camera by the participants vanished in the intensity of this small but real trench battle.

Bean's diary entries tell of Ashmead-Bartlett's determination to capture on film the explosion of artillery fire. He achieves this during the August fighting at Suvla with the images of naval gunfire bursting on Hill 112 during the British attempts to take Scimitar Ridge and W Hill.

By the end of the August fighting at Suvla, Bartlett had filmed scenes at Cape Helles in the south, at Anzac and at Suvla. He filmed sniper scenes at Quinn's Post at Anzac, but his successful battle filming all took place with the British forces at Suvla. The implications of this imbalance continues to resonate to this day.

This sequence is not the only one that we know was filmed by Brooks. Ashmead-Bartlett mentions that on 9 September Brooks went off to Anzac filming while he visited Hamilton's headquarters.[41] It was during this visit that Ashmead-Bartlett was told by Hamilton that the "War Office had cabled out forbidding anyone to take photographs except the official photographer. As I have been taking them for the last six months, this seems rather a belated move. I wonder who in the War Office has the time to think over the matter and to come to this great decision. Sir Ian frankly declared that he considered this regulation absurd, and told me I might go on, as far as he was concerned. His attitude was extremely kind, and he went out of his way to make himself agreeable." Bartlett noted that "[t]hese journeys to G.H.Q., since our failure, are like visits to the tombs of the dead ... The General and his Staff realise that their position is precarious, and sit round like condemned criminals, on tenterhooks of expectation, awaiting execution or a reprieve."[42]

For Hamilton the failure of the August offensive led to his removal from command, an act in which Ashmead-Bartlett played a role. By September 1915 Ashmead-Bartlett was as exhausted as the tired men of the Mediterranean Expeditionary Force whom he was writing on and filming. Disenchanted with the conduct of the campaign, he wrote a critical report in a personal letter for H.H. Asquith, the British prime minister. This he sent back safe hand with the Australian correspondent Keith Murdoch who had briefly joined the band of journalists on a five-day visit. Someone informed on Ashmead-Bartlett to the military authorities. Murdoch was intercepted at Marseilles and the letter confiscated. Murdoch substituted an equally critical letter, intended for the Australian prime minister, on the conduct of the campaign. This was shown to David Lloyd George and was given to Asquith. It led to Ashmead-Bartlett's recall and was one element in the series of events that saw Hamilton's removal on 15 October 1915.

Hamilton was replaced by General Sir Charles Monro who reviewed the situation and recommended that the campaign be abandoned. The ignominy and potential consequences of this step led to Kitchener visiting Gallipoli in mid-November. He too recommended evacuation and eventually led to an agonised decision by Asquith and his war cabinet where the reality of failure at Gallipoli was reluctantly accepted. This evacuation was conducted by 20 December 1915 at Suvla and Anzac and by 9 January 1916 at Cape Helles. The latter was captured on film in crisp detail by a French camera team. It was the one outstanding military success in an otherwise botched campaign.

ASHMEAD-BARTLETT TOURS AUSTRALASIA

Having got the film back in stages to the theatre impresario Alfred Butt and being paid his money, Ashmead-Bartlett dismissed the exercise. It seems apart from providing shot lists he took no part in the editing process. In early 1916, and now permanently out of favour with the British military authorities, he accepted a speaking tour of Australia and New Zealand organised by the Australian theatre entrepreneurs J. & N. Tait. This was on the understanding that his film would not be shown in any centre where he was lecturing lest it detract from audience numbers. Ashmead-Bartlett arrived in Sydney on 11 February and found himself the centre of media attention. "The papers are full of everything I say and do. I lecture this evening for the first time at the Town Hall that holds some 3,500 people. The booking has been enormous."[43]

He impressed his audiences in Australia but, while he enjoyed the travel, he soon grew tired of the lectures. Golf, cards, gambling, women and dancing became his escape. He was quick to praise Australian achievement in his lectures but was far more critical in his diaries.

The whole community seems drunk with the joy of living and the joy of sport. It permeates every section of society. No sooner is business over for the day than practically the entire population rush off to amuse themselves. They are tremendous motorists, others love golf, others cricket, football, prizefighting. The entire population spends hours in the sea. There are innumerable Theatres, Music Halls and Cinema Shows which always seem to be packed. The level of the

BURNS HALL

SATURDAY NEXT, at 8.

ONE LECTURE ONLY.

"There is no man better qualified to speak on the subject than the brilliant representative of the British press in the Dardanelles operations."—Sydney Morning Herald.

J. and N. TAIT Present

THE GREAT WAR CORRESPONDENT, Mr

ASHMEAD BARTLETT,
ASHMEAD BARTLETT,
ASHMEAD BARTLETT,
ASHMEAD BARTLETT,

In His

FAMOUS WAR LECTURES,
"WITH THE ANZACS AT THE DARDANELLES."

Illustrated by
150—WONDERFUL VIEWS.—150
A Vivid, Thrilling Story of
AUSTRALIANS AND NEW ZEALANDERS MAKING HISTORY.
SPECIAL NOTICE.
BOX PLANS OPEN THIS MORNING
BOX PLANS OPEN THIS MORNING
BOX PLANS OPEN THIS MORNING
AT THE BRISTOL.
On account of the limited accommodation at the Burns Hall, intending patrons would be well advised to secure seats early.

Otago Daily Times, 4 May 1916, p. 1.

PEOPLE'S PICTURE PALACE
PEOPLE'S PICTURE PALACE

MONDAY (And all Next MONDAY
MONDAY Week). MONDAY

By arrangement with
FRASER FILMS.
FRASER FILMS.

THE BIGGEST EXCLUSIVE SCOOP
THE BIGGEST EXCLUSIVE SCOOP

EVER MADE IN PICTURES—

WITH

THE DARDANELLES EXPEDITION!
THE DARDANELLES EXPEDITION!
THE DARDANELLES EXPEDITION!
THE DARDANELLES EXPEDITION!
THE DARDANELLES EXPEDITION!
THE DARDANELLES EXPEDITION!

The ONLY MOVING PICTURES taken
with the ANZACS AT GALLIPOLI.

Showing

THE LIFE, DEEDS, and DARING OF
OUR BOYS MAKING HISTORY.

Synopsis:

Disembarking Troops, Suvla Bay
General Staff Headquarters, Suvla Bay
General Birdwood Snatches a Meal in a
     Dug-out, Suvla Bay
In the Trenches
Collecting Discarded Kitbags after a
     Charge
8th Australian Light Horse
Imbros Island
Embarking the Wounded
Anzac Beach, near Suvla Bay
A Snap from the Beach
Shrapnel Gully, showing Main Communi-
     cation Trenches to all Positions
14th Australian Batt., Walker's Ridge
7th Brigade, Aust., New Zealanders, and
     Tommies Repelling an Attack
Turkish Guns Shelling Position, Lone
     Pine
Walker's Ridge
Effect of Bombardment at Cheeseboard
     Trenches
A False Alarm—Men Taking Cover
Anzacs Surfing—Imbros Island
3rd Brigade Anzacs—24th New Zealand
     Battalion—And many other import-
     ant events.

BIG SUPPORTING PROGRAMME!

Advertisement for *With the Dardanelles Expedition* with details of scenes added by Fraser Films to appeal to an Australian and New Zealand audience. *New Zealand Times*, Wellington, 8 April 1916, p. 3.

theatres is however very low and the good shows few and far between …
The people are mad about the Cinema and will take a pleasure in any rubbish shown them.[44]

Continuing on to New Zealand, he praised the New Zealand performance and singled out Lieutenant-Colonel Malone of the Wellington Battalion for particular mention.[45] Authorities in Australia and New Zealand were worried about the criticisms that Ashmead-Bartlett might voice, and each country placed a military minder and police note-takers in attendance at every lecture. They had no need for concern. His lecture 'With the Anzacs at the Dardanelles' sometimes given with magic lantern slides, sometimes without, held his audiences in rapt attention. It also won praise in the press who used the journalist's concluding words in telling New Zealand what it wanted to hear:

It is a wonderful tale of gallantry and endurance in which any country can be proud to have participated and I don't believe that in the end New Zealand will regret having sent her men to take part in that glorious effort.[46]

Ashmead-Bartlett was less complimentary in his diaries:

You speedily grow tired of New Zealand. The people are not nearly so lively as in Australia. There is little to do in Wellington and there is absolutely no social life outside of the clubs. I have visited one or two houses but the people are not at all interesting … The New Zealanders hate the Australians and look down on them because of the Convict settlements. There were never any in New Zealand. As a matter of fact I have found the Australians far more intelligent than the New Zealanders. They dislike the New Zealanders and declare the country to be dead. This is certainly partly true. There is a terrible wave of "Wowserism" sweeping over the country and parts of it have gone dry altogether. The sleepiness of the people is extraordinary. The streets are full of people mooching about. They walk with that sloppy gait which is so peculiar to Colonials. There is little or no intellectual life. Some-one described the people as farmers [bred] out of servant girls.[47]

Unaware, New Zealand applauded him in the press, broadcasting his opinions on the war, while Ashmead-Bartlett grumbled on in his diaries. He enjoyed Auckland because of the female company, thought the Christchurch audience "sleepy and stupid", spent three days in Wellington losing money playing poker in the Wellington Club before leaving on 16 May 1916 with the words: "Thank God I shall soon see America and England again."[48]

WITH THE DARDANELLES EXPEDITION

War Office censorship delayed the release of Ashmead-Bartlett's film titled *With the Dardanelles Expedition* until after the evacuation of Gallipoli Peninsula in January 1916. Butt's editor structured it so that it could be shown complete or

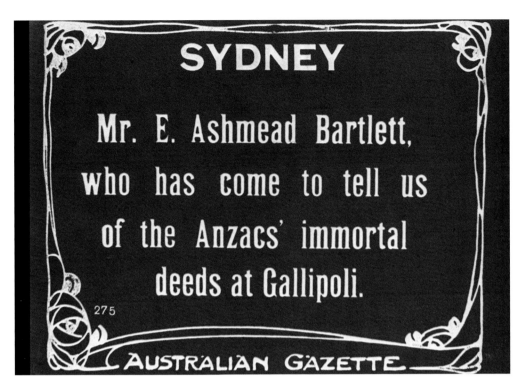

In February 1916 Ellis Ashmead-Bartlett arrived in Sydney to undertake a lecture tour with J. & N. Tait, the theatre enterpreneurs. Still from *Australian Gazette* -275, February 1916, NFSA, 102837.

Ellis Ashmead-Bartlett on his arrival in Sydney in February 1916 on the start of his lecture tour with a representative of J. & N. Tait. Still from *Australian Gazette* -275, February 1916, NFSA, 102837.

in three parts, dependent on the picture theatre manager. Once released it did good business in the United Kingdom. Butt, keen to get a return on his considerable investment, sold prints to Fraser Films in Australia who released it throughout Australia and New Zealand at the same time that Ashmead-Bartlett was on his lecture tour. The release of the film in Australia got Ashmead-Bartlett into trouble with the Tait brothers who were already concerned about declining numbers at his lectures. This led to some tense negotiations before the issue was resolved: "and they have now written me a letter saying they will take no further notice of the technical infringement of my agreement with them which has of course done them no harm. In fact advertising these films was in reality a very good advertisement in advance of my lecture."[49]

Historically the film is of priceless importance because it is our only glimpse of British Empire soldiers in the firing line at Gallipoli. The original title *With the Dardanelles Expedition* was used in New Zealand but Fraser Films advertised it in Australia as *Ashmead-Bartlett's Pictures of the Dardanelles*.[50] Its advertised title was changed by local theatre managers in Australia into variations of the following: *Australia's Field of Glory — with the Anzacs at the front* (Sydney, Theatre Royal); *The Battlefields of Gallipoli — being authentic pictures of Australia's Field of Glory* (Melbourne, Paramount Theatre); *Ashmead-Bartlett's Motion Pictures of Gallipoli and Anzac — Australia's Field of Glory* (Brisbane, Strand Theatre); and *Ashmead-Bartlett's Battlefields of Gallipoli — Australia's Field of Glory* (Adelaide, Wondergraph Theatre).[51]

It reached the New Zealand public in April 1916 when "By arrangement with Fraser Film's Historical Moving Pictures — 'With the Dardanelles Expedition'" was shown throughout New Zealand.

> A notable series of war pictures, taken with the Anzacs at Gallipoli is the feature attractions of this week's programme at the People's Picture Palace. The pictures are splendidly taken and give a vivid idea of the country that witnessed one of the most glorious feats of arms ever known in history. The film opens showing the SS *River Clyde* beached to land troops at Suvla Bay on 25 April 1915. A general view of Suvla Bay, the surroundings, the crowds of transports, and the general headquarters staff. From Suvla Bay the spectator is taken to the trenches and sees some of the places made famous. A fine picture is the shelling of Lone Pine by the Turks. Our boys are seen repelling an attack and firing through sandbags, whilst others refill the cartridge clips at the rear. Other views include Anzac Beach, Lemnos Harbour and transports, the ruined forts at Seddul Bahr, ANZACs surfing, the water transport service and various battalions and troops.[52]

Fraser Films' advertising emphasised the "enormous difficulties" experienced in taking the film. It said that this made it impossible for an ordinary tripod camera to be used, "so a new invention, the 'Aeroscope' Camera was employed. A camera that is worked by clockwork and steadied by a gyroscope."[53] The review of the film in the *Poverty Bay Herald* in Gisborne on 27 June 1916 provides important detail of the film's original structure. As the advertising indicates it was a random series of pictures of the campaign without chronology or storyline.

> The whole series of pictures take up 2000 feet of film and cover a screening period of 35 minutes, and among the places and incidents shown are: — S.S. *River Clyde*, beached to land troops of the 29th Division, on 25th April, 1915; Disembarking Troops and Mules at Suvla Bay; General Staff Headquarters at Shrapnel Gully and Landing Beach; General Birdwood and Staff snatching a meal in a dug-out at Suvla Bay; In the Trenches; Imbros Island and Harbor; the Sunk Road; Dead Man's Gully; Embarking the Wounded; the 29th Division; Anzac Beach, near Suvla Bay; Lovat's Scouts; a Sap from the Beach; Shrapnel Gully, showing main communication trench to all positions; the Destroyed Fortress, Seddul Bahr, Cape Helles; Turkish Guns Shelling Position at Lone Pine; Walker's Ridge; Mule Corps, Anzac to Lone Pine; Effect of Bombardment at Chessboard Trenches, Olive Grove: the Water Barge; Saps at Walker's Ridge: Drawing the Enemy's

Fire; Horses and Mules in Trenches; a False Alarm, men taking shelter; Turkish Prisoners; Steamer with Landing Party; Anzacs surfing at Imbros Island; and a number of others.[54]

The reviewer also reported that "Mr E. Ashmead-Bartlett in an autograph letter accompanying the pictures apologises for the photography, but the screening reveals a series of views well up to the best in topical pictures, the only fault being that the various sections pass too quickly".[55]

What is important about this review is that our diligent reviewer seems to have listed each intertitle heading in sequence. His Majesty's Theatre in Gisborne, advertised it as *Ashmead-Bartlett's Authentic Pictures of the Dardanelles Expedition*. This holds a clue to the nature of the film, because from the reviewer's list of scenes, that is what the audience saw on screen; a series of images with intertitles but not in chronological order.[56] The original *With the Dardanelles Expedition* was not a sequential documentary of the Gallipoli Campaign as we would expect today, but some unique moving snapshots in random order: a Gallipoli potpourri. That random order has been spelt out for us by the Gisborne reviewer and it jumps from Anzac to Helles to Suvla and back again, ignoring any sense of chronology or even any grouping by location. It was this random grouping of pictures of the campaign that allowed it to be shown in three parts.

This review is also important because it tells us that the film was 2000 feet in length and screened for 35 minutes. Even allowing for the Gisborne projectionist slowing down the speed so that viewers got the maximum impact from each scene, the 18 minutes of images and intertitles that survive today shows that a considerable amount of the film has been lost compared to what the public saw in 1916. The reviewer uses the term 'and a number of others' to cover intertitles that he missed, and a prominent scene that stands out here as part of that list is that of the RNAS armoured car sequence at Cape Helles.

There is no surviving copy of the original sequence of *With the Dardanelles Expedition*, but in structure it was simply a series of Gallipoli images with intertitles that may or may not have been accurate: the film editor in London simply matched images to Bartlett's shot list as best he could. It is evident from Fraser's advertising in New Zealand that some scenes were retitled in Australia to reflect Australian performance before they reached New Zealand and one imagines that this local flavour was added wherever the film was screened. To the audiences, particularly those whose loved ones had fought in the campaign, these images met a universal need to know about where 'Our Boys' had fought and died. None of this concerned Ashmead-Bartlett, who may have never viewed the film he shot.

The Gallipoli casualty lists and the delay in reporting details of the wounded, missing and dead impacted on all areas of New Zealand society in 1915. In early 1916 those 'missing in action' were formally reported as dead. These images of Gallipoli in *With the Dardanelles Expedition* put images of the Anzacs in the landscape where they fought and died. For New Zealand the Gallipoli experience was the equivalent to what the British public would experience on 1 July 1916 when the citizen divisions of Kitchener's New Armies attacked on the Somme. The impact of those 60,000 casualties and 18,000 dead reverberated through the length and breadth of the country: no community was unaffected. Here too, lengthy delays in casualty reporting led to public disquiet and complaint. The release of the film *The Battle of the Somme* had an enormous impact because its picture of brave young men preparing for battle and then the aftermath with the dying and wounded put a human face to the realities of modern war and its impact on society at large. The film *With the Dardanelles Expedition* had done that already for the public in New Zealand and Australia.

HEROES OF GALLIPOLI

A copy of *With the Dardanelles Expedition* was purchased by the Australian War Records Section (AWRS) in 1919. On 3 January 1919, Major J.L. Treloar, the head of the AWRS and later first director of the Australian War Memorial, wrote to Ashmead-Bartlett inquiring about any film taken on Gallipoli or during the campaign. Ashmead-Bartlett replied on 7 January confirming that he had taken some film and suggested that Treloar approach Sir Alfred Butt for a copy. A lengthy correspondence ensued between Treloar and Butt leading to the purchase of a 35 mm positive print of the film in June 1919. The film length was 1874 feet and cost £21.9s.6d. This purchase was on the understanding that it was for the historical record only and no commercial screening was allowed without further negotiation on fees. It is the edited version of this film that is now in the Australian War Memorial (AWM) collection.

The AWRS also contacted the official photographer Ernest Brooks, who had carried out some of the filming for Ashmead-Bartlett on Gallipoli, to see if he knew of any other films taken on Gallipoli. Brooks discussed this with Captain G.H. Wilkins, the official cinematographer for the AIF in France and stated that he did not know of any other Gallipoli film.[57] They were not aware of the French films of Gallipoli that had been screened in 1915–16. It consolidated the belief that continues to this day, that Ashmead-Bartlett's film was the only one taken on the peninsula during the campaign.

The AWRS copy of the film *With the Dardanelles Expedition* was edited by C.E.W. Bean, the former AIF official war correspondent and now official AIF historian. Bean had coordinated work of the official photographers and cameramen attached to the AIF on the Western Front. In 1916 this involved working with attached British Army photographers and cameramen. Bean was determined to capture and record the Australian efforts during the battle for Pozières on the Somme and worked closely with the camera team to ensure he got what he wanted on film. He then gave an edited shot list and sequence to the William Jury's Topical Film Company who handled the production of all official war film "in order [to make] a thoroughly true, interesting film of the Australians in France".[58] It was not until a year later that he saw the finished film and was shocked and dismayed by the result. His directions to achieve an accurate portrayal of the battle had been ignored. "The whole of our Pozières cinema work has gone for nothing. Thanks to these British and their private enterprise."[59]

It made Bean concentrate on having photographs rather than film for the historical record. By now he had dedicated Australian photographers and cameramen working to his direction. Here too he battled with the Australian photographer and cameraman Frank Hurley who, frustrated by the difficulty of capturing shell burst and combat images, believed in 'composite images' where he added in effects to create a battle scene in his photos. Bean regarded these as fakes leading Hurley to resign and go to the Sinai Peninsula and Palestine where he filmed the Australian Light Horse. Bean tasked the AIF official photographer Captain Hubert Wilkins to capture photographs and film for the historical record of the AIF, which he did brilliantly and bravely for the rest of the war.[60]

Bean's reputation as a historian was built on his rigorous insistence on accuracy and so his edited film *Heroes of Gallipoli* is regarded in the same manner. As a result film researchers and historians have been reluctant to question Bean's identifications in his film. There was no one more knowledgeable about Gallipoli and its landscape than Bean. In addition to the copious notes and interviews he did during his time on the peninsula during the campaign, he returned to the peninsula in 1919. He led a small Australian party that included George

Lambert, the artist, and Hubert Wilkins, the official photographer, to examine the ground in detail, retrace the landing and the fighting that followed for the duration of the campaign. With the assistance of a Turkish officer, Major Zeki Bey, he was able to assess Ottoman operations against the Anzacs. An account of this was published in *Gallipoli Mission* in 1948.[61]

Bean obviously decided that the title *With the Dardanelles Expedition* did not capture the flavour of Australia's achievement during the Gallipoli Campaign and renamed it *Heroes of Gallipoli*. Bean restructured the film into a story that unashamedly extolled Australian achievement. Sadly no original copy of *With the Dardanelles Expedition* was kept.

Two different versions of the Bean-edited film exist in the AWM film collection. Both are contained on the same film-print under a common catalogue number but show two versions: the first, a more formal version, consists of the title *Heroes of Gallipoli* and what appears to be a complete sequence of intertitles and a few scenes. At some stage most of the film images were transferred to a second version that follows the same sequence and intertitle wording, but which omits some of the images and intertitles relating to British forces at Cape Helles and Suvla. This gives the second version of the film an even more Australian focus. The omitted British scenes remain on the first version.

It suggests that at some time either Bean or someone working for the AWM determined a more Australian-oriented version than Bean's initial edit and made the second edit, which is in some respects in terms of the quality of the intertitles, a cruder version than that of the first. We know that Bean continued to work on the editing from sometime after the film was acquired and it was still not completed to his satisfaction when the record of his editing ends.

It was the first version with more complete intertitle sequence that was used as the basis for the digital restoration of the film for the AWM by Sir Peter Jackson's Weta Digital.

A.H. Noad Film.
AWM F00176.

Completed in time for Anzac Day, 25 April 2005, the film includes all of the available filmed scenes in the sequence in which they were first compiled by Bean.[62]

Bean took the series of moving picture scenes and organised them into a story of the Australians on Gallipoli within the context of the wider campaign. He gave the images a structure and a storyline that starts in May 1915 and with the use of intertitles takes it through to the evacuation in December 1915. The surviving footage at the AWM consists of 945 feet of images and 855 feet of captions, a total of 1800 feet, but this includes the duplicated captions, which indicates that perhaps some 500–600 feet of images were missing from *Heroes of Gallipoli* compared with the original *With the Dardanelles Expedition* film screened in 1916.[63]

The New Zealand review in the *Poverty Bay Herald* described the film as being 2000 feet or 35 minutes, which is slightly longer than the film purchased by the AWRS in 1919. It seems that Bean either discarded some of the scenes in the original film or that the copy of the film sold by Butt to the AWRS was missing some of its detail. Both reasons may have contributed to the missing length. Bean had not completed the edit to his satisfaction when he ceased work on the film. It was also not unusual for a film having finished its commercial tour to have lost scenes through cuts and repairs to wear and tear or through having been mined for action sequences that were cut out and transferred to other films.

Bean faced a dilemma when editing *Heroes of Gallipoli*. In examining the nature of the visual images that survives in the Bean version, one can break it down into 3 minutes 26 seconds of Anzac-related material, showing scenes of Anzac Cove, Shrapnel Valley and the trenches along Second Ridge including Quinn's Post. There are 2 minutes 50 seconds of Cape Helles material showing the British forces at Cape Helles and 5 minutes 50 seconds of Imbros and Suvla-related material.[64] Bean found that of the 3 minutes 26 seconds of Anzac material there was only one sequence that related to the August offensive and this was the 22-second scene of Australian soldiers on Walker's Ridge. He had a story to tell but when it came to the principal Anzac offensive including the battle for Lone Pine, he did not have the images to tell it.

Because of this he accepted the decisions made by the original editor of the 1916 version. As seen in the various newspaper descriptions, action scenes were given titles to accommodate the nationality of the audience. Bean accepted this in his editing but knew that these descriptions were wrong and this may explain the incomplete edit. Bean used the scenes of the logistics area on Suvla Beach to provide images of the 'Chessboard', the critical ground on the forward slope of Baby 700. This was attacked at such great cost by the 8th and 10th Regiments of the 3rd Australian Light Horse Brigade across the Nek on 7 August, and was the subject of the climatic scenes in Peter Weir's feature film *Gallipoli*. He then used the burning scrub scenes on Scimitar Ridge to show the fighting at the Chessboard.[65] Anyone as familiar as Bean with the landscape at Anzac and Suvla knew that these images were not correct. Similarly, he used the scenes of the 5th Royal Irish Fusiliers near Green Hill to represent "Australians firing from newly won Positions" and the Royal Navy bombarding Hill 112 to represent the bombardment of Lone Pine.[66] Pith helmets were sometimes worn by the Australian Light Horse but Bean was aware that Ashmead-Bartlett filmed at Suvla and the smartness of the officer in the shot would have raised question marks. It was the same for the bombardment of Hill 112, it is similar ground in appearance to Second Ridge but the lack of any trenches or development on the facing slopes should have also have raised serious question marks with Bean. He accepted the editor's judgement in *With the Dardanelles*

Comparison of Ellis Ashmead-Bartlett's Gallipoli footage in AWN Films F00069 With the Dardanelles Expedition: Heroes of Gallipoli and F00176. A.H. Noad Film. AWM F08484.

Expedition, and ignored any doubts that his own encyclopaedic knowledge of the ground should have raised.

Borrowing this one minute of film gave him the sequences he needed to tell his story of Australian endeavour. In effect he gutted the Suvla action scenes to tell the Australian story.[67] Ashmead-Bartlett and Brooks's filming of Imbros and Suvla in August 1915 presents us with the first moving camera footage of a major amphibious operation from its mounting with the embarkation of 11th Division at Imbros; the battle scenes for Scimitar Ridge on 21 August; to its consolidation with the trench scenes of the 5th Royal Irish Fusiliers in action near Green Hill in September 1915. This history is not told in the Bean editing of *Heroes of Gallipoli*.

If Bean's vision of Australian achievement in *Heroes of Gallipoli* left out critical parts of the British story at Suvla, it completely omitted the New Zealand story and there is no reference to them in his edited version. However, there are images of New Zealand soldiers among the carrying parties in Shrapnel Valley, and it is the New Zealanders who are identifiably in residence at Quinn's Post. Bean was aware of this and despite the obvious presence of a New Zealander as one of the sniper pair, he deliberately omitted the New Zealand contribution to the campaign.

Mindful of Bean's position in the pantheon of Australian 'Anzac' historiography and his careful attention to detail in every other aspect of his work, there has been a tendency by historians to bend over backwards to explain his use of images in *Heroes of Gallipoli*. We should not; Bean faced a conundrum and ignored the evidence before his eyes. He knew what he was doing and decided that the story he was telling was more important than historical accuracy in placing the images he was using and broke the rules he himself insisted on in his own supervision of filming on the Western Front.

What survives today is the Bean-edited film that was given the combined title *With the Dardanelles Expedition: Heroes of Gallipoli* by the AWM. It combines the two Australian versions of the film derived from a positive print bought by the AWR Section from Butt in 1919.

Research conducted by film curatorial staff at the AWM indicates that the Bean version of the film was never shown. There was no commercial release of *Heroes of Gallipoli* as that was not permitted under the terms agreed on its purchase from Sir Alfred Butt. It first came to public attention in the 1960s when extracts were copied and used for the BBC *Great War* series. In 1965 on the occasion of the 50th anniversary of the Gallipoli Campaign a copy was donated to the Imperial War Museum. It was about this time that AWM staff transferred the positive print to safety film and the original nitrate was destroyed.[68] The film "eventually had its first public screening in its entirety on the 85th Anniversary of the Gallipoli Campaign. It premiered on the 5th of August 2000, during the Gallipoli conference held at the Australian War Memorial."[69]

A.H. NOAD/TINSDALE'S *GALLIPOLI* FILM

In 2007 AWM staff identified further Gallipoli-related material in a compilation film acquired by the memorial from a Mr A.H. Noad in 1938 and identified by that name. The film is succinctly described by the AWM as "a patriotic montage from various sources" relating to the Gallipoli Campaign.[70] Much of it is drawn from Ashmead-Bartlett's filming but two scenes: one of Anzac Cove from McLagan's Ridge and the gathering of a mass of men on the beach at Suvla on 8 August — are not in the AWM *Heroes of Gallipoli* film. This discovery sparked further research into the A.H. Noad film. Careful comparisons between the Bean version and the Noad

Pathé Journal Actualité: Guillaume Ii En Turquie. 191529.

film showed that many of the scenes in the Noad film were different in both length and detail than those in the Bean version.[71]

Research by the Australian film historian and journalist Paul Byrnes established that the Noad film was a film produced by Arthur C. Tinsdale, an Australian film-maker working in the United Kingdom in the 1920s.[72] Noad somehow acquired a copy of the film and sold it to the AWM in 1938. Originally titled *Anzac Crusaders*, it was released under the title *Gallipoli* in 1928 by Tinsdale's Embassy Films. Tinsdale's production of the film was widely reported in the press in both Australia and New Zealand but while it was released in Australia it does not seem to have been screened in New Zealand.[73] Byrnes established that the Ashmead-Bartlett Gallipoli sequences in the film were acquired in the United Kingdom from an original copy of *With the Dardanelles Expedition.*

The identification of additional Gallipoli-related scenes in the A.H. Noad film held by the AWM added considerably to our knowledge of the AWM copy of Ellis Ashmead-Bartlett's film *With the Dardanelles Expedition: Heroes of Gallipoli*. It sparked further research by Michael Kosmider, then a member of the AWM staff. He identified further Ashmead-Bartlett material in other compilation films in the AWM film collection. It confirms that the copy of *With the Dardanelles Expedition* purchased by Treloar for the AWRS in June 1919 was missing some of the images originally circulated in 1916. It also confirmed that Bean also omitted some images from his *Heroes of Gallipoli* that were later used in other AWM compilations of the First World War and which were inadvertently destroyed with the destruction of the nitrate by the AWM. This research is ongoing and we are yet to see a final compilation incorporating all of this new material.[74]

FILMING GALLIPOLI

Aspects of the campaign were also filmed by Turkish cameramen. The Central Army Cinematography Office (Merkez Ordu Sinema Dairesi) of the Ottoman Army was established in 1915. Sigmund Weinberg was its director, Fuat Efendi the assistant director, and there were two co-workers, Mazhar Efendi and Cemil Efendi. Films were taken of the Gallipoli Campaign. There is surviving footage showing Turkish troops, including mounted troops, moving through the village of Büyük Anafarta, just to the east of the Suvla Plain.[75] The footage was taken in winter, as can be clearly seen from the terrain, bare trees and the troops in greatcoats. We know from the Australian journalist's William Sellars' research into Australian prisoners of war in Turkey that film was taken of Anzac and British prisoners of the August fighting when they were paraded in Constantinople. Private S.J. Drake, 14th Battalion, AIF, was captured on 8 August 1915. Writing of his time in Constantinople soon after capture he says: "About a week after our arrival we were paraded and drilled (platoon drills) by and English officer (Captain Dyson, West Riding Regiment). A cinematograph operator took pictures of us at drill. Afterwards we were put into groups and photographed. I bought one of these photos in Constantinople after the Armistice."[76]

In October 1917 the visit of Emperor Wilhelm II of Germany to Turkey was also filmed. The emperor visited the Gallipoli battlefield where he was escorted by General Esat Pasha who was the corps commander responsible for the Ari Burnu sector, which included the Anzac area. We see the emperor being briefed on the campaign. He then strides out to his car from a camouflaged tent in the area where the Commonwealth War Graves Depot is now situated near what was No.1 Outpost on Ocean Beach. We see views back along Ocean Beach towards the distinctive high ground of Plugge's Plateau and the headland of Ari Burnu that is

British, Indian, Australian and New Zealand prisoners of war
paraded in Istanbul after the August 1915 fighting, filmed by
cameramen of the Central Army Cinematography Office (Merkez
Ordu Sinema Dairesi) of the Ottoman Army. The office was
established in 1915; Sigmund Weinberg was its director, Fuat
Efendi the assistant director, and there were two co-workers,
Mazhar Efendi and Cemil Efendi. W. Sellars Collection.

at the northern tip of Anzac Cove. Esat Pasha briefs the Kaiser while General Otto Limon von
Sanders, who commanded the Ottoman 5th Army in the campaign, stands in the background
and looks towards the camera.[77]

Given the paucity of British film of the Western Front in 1915, one can argue that
Gallipoli was a comprehensively filmed campaign with three important French films that
span both the initial naval operations, the early days ashore at Cape Helles and the evacuation
in December 1915–January 1916. The overview of British operations and the August offensive
is provided by Ashmead-Bartlett's *With the Dardanelles Expedition*.

Ellis Ashmead-Bartlett's *With the Dardanelles Expedition: Heroes of Gallipoli* is a very
important film, but it is only one of four major films on the campaign. In its present form it
is central to the Australian 'Anzac' legend that was deliberately fostered by its editor C.E.W.
Bean. However, the filmed images also tells other stories that have yet to be fully appreciated:
that of the British landings at Suvla in August 1915 — the first amphibious landing to be
filmed in the history of warfare; and also the Gallipoli experience of those that provided the
'NZ' in ANZAC.

15

Filming the camps

Shift, Boys, shift we're on the shift again,
First, we shift from Trentham to Tauherenikau plain;
Then we start our shooting, and back we shift again;
First we live in Huts, and then again in tents —
They're not so bad in summer but in winter watch the rents,
It's shift, shift, shift, we're on the shift again.
The shifting might be good for us, but the good ain't very plain;
We're "Massey's Travelling Circus" — in wind and storm and rain
The Boys of C19, Massey's Travelling Circus[1]

Throughout 1914–15, the news from Egypt, the abortive Turkish attack on the Suez Canal and then the Allied landings on the Gallipoli Peninsula saw a constant stream of volunteers apply at Territorial Recruiting Depots throughout New Zealand. Once attested and medically examined these recruits were sent back to their homes to continue work and await call-up into camp, which until September 1915 involved 2000 men every two months and by 1916 would become 2000 men a month.[2] Every street in every town and district sent someone and volunteer numbers from each district were compared and debated in the press and were a subject of intense local pride.

ESTABLISHING THE CAMPS

Hasty mobilisation camps had been set up on local racecourses to cope with the raising of the Main Body. The number of camps was now rationalised and a training camp was established at Trentham in the Hutt Valley. In Auckland camps were established at Avondale and at Narrow Neck. A camp for training medical personnel was established at Awapuni racecourse at Palmerston North with a camp at Papawai in the Wairarapa. Initially all of these were tented camps with most of the all-arms training being conducted at Trentham, then a very thinly populated country district that offered some 400 acres of flat land in the Hutt Valley next to the

Opposite page: The daily scene outside the recently erected recruiting station in Auckland, fronting Queen Street and Victoria Street West. A scruffy non-commissioned officer with his jacket unbuttoned cajoles the crowd for volunteers. *Auckland Weekly News,* 16 March 1916, p. 37.

rifle ranges of the National Rifle Association. What also made it attractive is that it was near the Wellington Racing Club's Trentham racecourse with its convenient railway station built to cope with the large numbers coming out of Wellington by train for a day at the races.

The camp expanded rapidly throughout early 1915 with men under canvas, eight to a tent. Herbert Knight's letters to his family capture the mood of the times.

> It's just like being back at school again … The drill is very stale — it's only 'left turn' 'right turn' etc and it's great to see some stiff old fellow of about 35 or 40 jumping about like a cat on hot bricks … We get up about 5.30 and fall in for gym for 1 hour at 6 o'clock — breakfast at 8, fall in again at 10 to 9 — dinner 12 — 20 to 2 knock off again after 5, tea about 6pm, lights out at 10pm so we have plenty of slack time although we don't really seem to have much time on our hands.[3]

There was plenty of leave into Wellington with special trains each night and weekends for one shilling return fare. Recreational facilities sprang up to cater for the thousands of men. "There's quite a tin town here now. The different societies have put up halls, a tailor, a jeweller, 2 photographers, post office, store sheds, canteen, billiard saloon & shooting gallery, 2 barber shops and a fruit store — so you have plenty of opportunity of spending money."[4]

SYDNEY TAYLOR FILMS TRENTHAM

Filming the training camps became a substitute for the lack of film on the New Zealand Expeditionary Force (NZEF) from overseas. Already in January 1915 the official government cinematographer, Sydney Taylor, was tasked by his general manager to "visit the defence camps … for the purposes of completing cinematograph films of the Defence Forces of New Zealand."[5] This initiative came from both Thomas Mackenzie in London as "there is a very great demand for such

Auckland volunteers for overseas service are cheered off to camp at the Auckland Railway Station. Auckland Libraries, Sir George Grey Collection, *Auckland Weekly News*, 21 October 1915, p. 37.

Still from *Vast Training Camp* taken in early 1915 by government cameraman Sydney B. Taylor showing Trentham Camp, then largely a tented camp. NTSV F245691.

Still from *New Zealand Recruits* taken in 1915 by Sydney B. Taylor showing New Zealand volunteers drilling at Trentham Camp. NTSV F245691.

a film" and from Godley in Egypt who was keen that the effort that New Zealand was making was shown to the Empire.[6] Taylor visited the new camp at Trentham and a copy of the film "depicting the training of the Main Expeditionary Force at Trentham and its departure for the front" was sent in late 1915 to the high commissioner. Film clips showing Trentham Camp in early 1915 and reinforcements on parade are in the Pathé collection and are likely to be part of Taylor's film.

The high commissioner, Mackenzie, no doubt working through Donne, passed it to Pathé who selected the clips as *Gazette* items.[7] The film shows the tented camp in its very early days with its neat rows of bell tents with the gaggle of canteens, kitchens, stores and shops of 'tin town' in the centre of camp, with Trentham racecourse in the distance, while in the foreground, moving black dots of soldiers, carry out training. The film title suggests that it was taken from the air, but it is a panoramic shot taken from the Hutt hills above the camp. No doubt, Taylor and his assistant struggled and sweated up those slopes with his camera, tripod and film boxes to get the shot. His film of the drill parade captures the 'left turn' 'right turn' that Knight describes and shows the keenness of the reinforcements of all ages, shapes and sizes to get it right in their determination to get to war.

The pleasant summer conditions at Trentham seen on film soon gave way to the rain and damp in May 1915. A lack of duckboards, drying facilities for clothing and serious overcrowding led to a 'malignant' measles epidemic. This was followed by an outbreak of spinal meningitis that swamped the meagre facilities of the tented marquees of the small camp hospital and soon overwhelmed space available in the Wellington Public Hospital. The spate of deaths saw public concern turn to anger at men being hospitalised in tents in midwinter. Wool stores at Kaiwharawhara and the Trentham racecourse buildings were appropriated, with the circular tea kiosk accommodating 150 beds and even the horse boxes being used to accommodate a total of 603 cases out of 7498 in camp. To break the cycle of the disease the camp was evacuated on 10 July 1915 and its numbers reduced to 2000 with men railed to

Vast Training Camp. NTSV F245690.

New Zealand Recruits. NTSV F245691.

Rob Millington and his fiancé, reputedly filmed by a young Rudall Hayward. He would volunteer and lose his life in the English Channel when the ship he was radio operator on was torpedoed. Still from *Personal Record Hayward, R.*, Wellington, October 1916, NTSV F27365.

Another member of the Hayward staff in uniform, ready to do his bit. Still from *Personal Record Hayward, R.*, Wellington, October 1916, NTSV F27365.

satellite camps in the Wellington district until the camp was repositioned away from the marsh closer to the racecourse and better facilities were built.

Defence medical services were reorganised and a Commission of Enquiry publicly grilled Defence staff before confirming the inadequacy of the camp medical services, the overcrowding and lack of sanitation.[8] This reverberated throughout New Zealand, while at the same time the country absorbed the news and the implications of the Gallipoli Campaign.

Immediate reforms were initiated. By late 1915 Trentham had hutted accommodation for 4500 men with a further 1200 men under canvas. To cope with the numbers, Featherston Camp in the Wairarapa was established in January 1916 and grew to accommodate 4500 men in huts and 3000 under canvas. After that, Trentham received infantry and engineer reinforcements for their initial five-week training and Featherston received mounted rifles, artillery and specialists. After the first five weeks the Trentham reinforcements were railed to Featherston where they completed their eight weeks, doing specialist training before marching back the 48 kilometres over the Rimutaka mountain range to Trentham to complete their final musketry course and prepared to embark for overseas.[9] None of this survives on film, but we have a brief clip of soldiers marching down Molesworth Street in Wellington on a wet day during the war. It is not a farewell parade, bayonets are not fixed and the disinterest of the passers-by shows that this is simply a route march.[10]

The patriotic associations and the communities of Wellington and the towns in the Hutt Valley adopted Trentham Camp and the farming communities of the Wairarapa adopted Featherston. It became a point of honour that local communities provided refreshments to each sweating reinforcement draft as they reached the summit on the trek back over the Rimutakas. Under the aegis of the Red Cross and other societies every community raised money for comfort funds, knitted socks, caps, comforters, mittens and cholera belts, and sent Christmas parcels to the soldiers overseas.

Providing Christmas dinner at Trentham became an annual feature for the women of Wellington. Naturally enough it was filmed, most likely by 'Vanie' Vinsen, for New Zealand to see. "Tonight's performance at the King's Theatre promises to be a memorable one … there will also be shown a special set of pictures taken at Trentham yesterday, showing 4,300 soldiers, eating their Christmas dinner, and being waited upon by Wellington ladies. There are also many other interested glimpses of camp life. The Trentham Band will march from Lambton Station to the King's Theatre, and will play outside until 8 o'clock."[11]

FILMING MAORI REINFORCEMENTS

Maori reinforcements continued to be trained at Narrow Neck Camp at Devonport in Auckland. Two brief clips from *Gaumont Graphic* newsreels survive of the inspection by Major-General Henderson, Director-General of Medical Services, of the 2nd Maori Contingent in September 1915. In the first we see the contingent in tropical dress, shorts and pith helmet, fix bayonets and being inspected by Henderson accompanied by Colonel J.E. Hume, NZSC, Commanding Auckland Military District and Captain H. Peacock, NZSC. Peacock was originally appointed commanding officer of the 1st Maori Contingent but fell sick and invalided back to New Zealand. He established a close rapport with his soldiers, something his successor Lieutenant Colonel Herbert who commanded the contingent on Gallipoli failed to do.[12] Peacock was appointed camp commandant at Narrow Neck Camp, where he trained each Maori reinforcement draft. The contingent are then shown at rifle and bayonet practice.[13] The item was filmed on 15 September 1915, and released in *Gaumont Graphic No. 485*. Its London release date was 15 November 1915. The second, obviously taken at the same time, shows immaculately dressed and drilled Maori soldiers parading outside their barracks at Narrow Neck, but this item was not released in London until 20 December 1915 when it appeared in *Gaumont Graphic No. 495*.[14] The newsreels were distributed around the world in both English and French-language versions.[15]

TRAINING PILOTS FOR THE ROYAL FLYING CORPS

One other area of training that attracted the interest of film-makers was the training of pilots in New Zealand. Two flying schools were established during the war, both privately financed. The first was the New Zealand Flying School in Auckland in 1915 followed in 1917 by the

Looking North up Molesworth Street.
NTSV F38467.

Major General Henderson Inspects Maori Troops.
NTSV F48604.

Parade by Second Maori Contingent.
NTSV F246326.

The 2nd Maori Contingent in training at Narrow Neck Camp, Devonport, Auckland, on 15 September 1915. Note the photographer in shot. Still from *Major-General Henderson Inspects Maori Troops*. NTSV F48604.

Canterbury Aviation Company at Sockburn, Christchurch. The New Zealand Flying School, using seaplanes from its base at Mission Bay, Kohimarama, Auckland, was set up by Leo and Vivian Walsh with financial support from Mr R.A. Dexter, an engineer and aviation enthusiast who ran the Cadillac dealership in Auckland. The Walsh brothers negotiated with the Royal Aero Club for certification and gained approval from the British Government that its certified pilots would be accepted as candidates for the Royal Flying Corps. The cost of the £100 private tuition was offset by the War Office's grant of £75 towards the cost of qualifying and that all expenses connected with the training and subsequent passage to England would be met by the Imperial authorities. This approval, granted in October 1915, led to a flood of applicants whose acceptance was determined by the limited number of aircraft available.

The Walsh brothers, both engineers, were pioneers in New Zealand aviation having together built the first New Zealand assembled aircraft the *Manurewa* ('Soaring Bird'), a British-designed Howard-Wright biplane, from imported plans, engine and materials. Its brief flight of 400 yards at a height of 60 feet at Glenora Park, Papakura, with the 23-year-old Vivian at the controls on 5 February 1911 was the first officially recorded flight in New Zealand.[16] A crash and a falling out with their financial backers led the Walsh brothers to begin again but this time by building a seaplane. Backed by Dexter, in their spare time the Walsh brothers took 15 months to build New Zealand's first flying boat, which made its initial flight with Vivian at the controls, from the waters of Orakei Bay on New Year's Day 1915. It was this machine that underpinned their bid to train pilots for the Royal Flying Corps.[17]

The initial school was established at Orakei below Fort Bastion with the seaplane housed in a hangar made from used car cases provided by Dexter and the first three pupils living in tents with Leo and Vivian living in a bach near their machine. Training began on 2 October 1915 for Geoffrey Callender, an engineering graduate, Keith Caldwell, a bank clerk, and Bertram Dawson. The flying boat was dual controlled but its ten-cylinder Anzani radial engine was so underpowered it could barely get airborne with two people on board. On 28 November 1915 both Callender and Caldwell were judged ready for their first solos, and by winning the toss of a coin, Callender became the first New Zealand-trained pupil to fly solo. Keith Caldwell later reflected on this initial training.

> Our very limited air instruction ended in December 1915. The boat was underpowered with two on board, but Callender and I each made some useful 'hops' and at least got the feel of the controls by fast taxiing. After some serious thought on the part of the Walshes — who had to choose between letting us go off on our own or risk losing other pupils if we didn't — Callender and I went solo. I think they made a very brave decision.[18]

Both would go on to earn reputations as pilots in the Royal Flying Corps; Callender rising to the rank of captain with the award of the AFC and the Silver Star of Italy for bravery in action. 'Grid' Caldwell rose to major's rank in command of No. 74 Squadron on the Western Front during 1918, during which time its pilots accounted for 140 enemy aircraft destroyed and a further 85 sent down apparently out of control; Caldwell was awarded the DFC and Bar, MC and the Croix de Guerre, and twice mentioned in despatches.[19]

In late 1915 the flying school moved to the former Melanesian mission station at Kohimarama and set up camp around the stone mission buildings on the foreshore in what was still a country area. As the number of pupils grew, a formal training programme replaced the more relaxed system Vivian employed with his first three pupils. On passing their flying tests they were to be medically boarded and granted a commission in the New Zealand Force before sailing to England for further flying training. The flying tests consisted of passing three separate qualifications; two of which consisted of flying for five kilometres without touching the water in an uninterrupted series of five figure-of-eight turns over a set course. The third test consisted of an altitude test by climbing to at least 100 metres and descending with the motor cut off and landing within a set distance of a moored buoy. All of this was to be carried out under the observation of two military observers. In addition to the first seaplane, a Caudron airplane was adapted to a flying boat and in 1916 they imported a Curtiss flying boat with a powerful 90 HP engine. These three aircraft, 'A', 'B' and 'C' became the instructional craft for the 14 pupils who would fly daily. Twenty-four-year-old George Bolt, who had previously built and flown gliders from the Cashmere Hills in Christchurch, enrolled as a pupil at Kohimarama in 1916 and on graduation was engaged as an instructor. He was later joined by Bob Going and Marmaduc Matthews with Vivian Walsh taking on a coordinating role.

In December 1917 Vivian Walsh took Bus 'C', the Curtiss flying boat, to Napier for the summer carnival. On 'Aviation Day' or Boxing Day, would-be passengers queued up with their £5 on a 'first come first served basis', while hundreds more paid sixpence to board the coaster *Arahura* or one shilling on the *Tangaroa* to gain a good view of the flying. The day's festivities appeared on film at the local theatres.[20] But the trip was marred with bad weather on New Year's Day and an attempt to tow the seaplane to a safer anchorage led to it capsizing with the wings being smashed and the body holed in four places. Napier rallied to raise funds to repair the seaplane. The wrecked craft was shipped back to Auckland and was back in commission within four weeks.[21]

AUCKLAND FROM THE SKIES

Charles Newham filmed life at the school on 16-17 February 1917. Hugh Blackwell, a trainee pilot wrote in his diary, 'Cinematograph down taking films all day.' We are fortunate that the 35-minute film survives as a brilliant tribute to his skill as a cameraman.[22] It was released under the title *Auckland from the Skies* and according to the *New Zealand Herald*, showed "views of the aviation school at Kohimarama: flying school grounds; seaplane sheds, workshops and pupils' camp; principals, staff and pupils now on active service; construction shed and engine workshop; tuning up a 90hp Curtiss engine; launching a seaplane; recreation at the school; pupils receiving flight instruction; a pupil undertaking test flights for his pilot's certificate; and views of the suburbs taken from the air".[23]

The film captures the pioneering spirit of the school. Everything from training to repairs and maintenance of aircraft was done on site and improvisation and initiative were the keys to success. We see the pupils at work and play. It opens with pupils being taught and practising Morse code for their role as aerial observers to call down artillery fire on identified enemy positions that they spot from the air. There is the lighter side of life: young men and dogs gambolling in the sea and aquaplaning behind the school's rescue motorboat, diving off a moored seaplane with Rangitoto in the background. There are shots of Vivian Walsh the chief instructor and his staff including George Bolt and Leo Walsh the manager and chief engineer, as the three seaplanes are pushed on trolleys on rails from the aircraft hangars to the sea. Planes take off. A formal seated photo of all of the staff from cooks to mechanics leads into the detail of working on and maintaining the aircraft in the hangars with trainee pilots assisting mechanics as the struts are tensioned, wings fabricated and aircraft engines assembled.

For some reason the film was not released until April 1918. George Bolt was disappointed when he saw the film. He wrote in his diary on 14 April 1918. "All the high views of the city were

Trainee pilots at the Walsh brothers' flying school enjoying the water at the former Melanesian mission station at Kohimarama. Still from *Auckland from the Skies*. NTSV F7556.

The three seaplanes outside their hangars at Kohimarama, ready for the days flying. Still from *Auckland from the Skies*. NTSV F7556.

An aerial view of the Auckland coastline filmed by Charles Newham in a seaplane flown by George Bolt. This is the earliest surviving film taken of New Zealand from the air. Still from *Auckland from the Skies*. NTSV F7556.

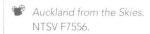

Auckland from the Skies. NTSV F7556.

cut out because they were blurred, but Walsh says the chap will be going up again and a decent piece will be tacked on before the film is shown in other places."[24] It seems that either Bolt was either being too critical or the extra aerial shots were later taken and added to the film, as the print gives the first superb views that we have of New Zealand from the air showing the coastal suburbs of the city. The film itself confirms Newham's skill as a cameraman and his ability to capture a story of young men at the cutting edge of technology venturing to fly.[25] The film *Auckland from the Skies* is Charles Newham's surviving masterpiece.

MENCE FILMS FEATHERSTON

As the war progressed there were moves to ensure that the record of New Zealand's achievement with its training camps was preserved on film for posterity. In January 1917 Charles Wheeler, a press correspondent with the parliamentary gallery wrote to James Allen, as acting prime minister, suggesting that a series of films be taken by the government cinematographer operator "as an historical record" showing all aspects of training in New Zealand. Wheeler listed what he believed should be in the film and also saw it as an opportunity to offer his own services. "If you think my journalistic and photographic experience will be of value in carrying out this scheme, I will be glad to assist."[26]

Both were declined but, perhaps prompted by the arrival of the first official New Zealand films from France and England, a similar initiative was taken up by the Dominion Museum who wrote to the Defence Department in December 1917 saying that: "The Department of Agriculture have offered to place their photographer at the disposal of the department for any photographic or cinema work in connection with war films for historical and other purposes. The Minister of Internal Affairs has accepted the offer and is desirous that the scheme should include films that could be shown throughout New Zealand for patriotic purposes. It is now desired to obtain films showing the camps and training as at present, the hospital ships, the return of the wounded and their treatment in Sanitoria and the internment of enemy aliens."[27]

An ambitious programme of filming was drawn up but there was a clash over dates as Taylor was engaged in filming in the South Island and was not available until April 1918. It was agreed that once Taylor became available "a conference between Col. Gibbon, Mr Robinson, Chief Clerk, Agricultural Department, who controls Mr Taylor's movements, Mr Taylor, Mr MacDonald, formerly Government Photographer and now on the Museum staff and myself (J. Allen Thomson, Dir Dominion Museum) be held and that a definite programme be thereafter

Bayonet training at Featherston Camp in the Wairarapa. Still from L.W. Mence's *Snow Man's Land*.
NTSV F1475.

A snowman on a cold winter's day with the battle about to start. Still from L.W. Mence's *Snow Man's Land.*
NTSV F1475.

drawn up".[28] Meanwhile, Mr L.W. Mence, one of the many commercial photographers working
at Featherston Camp heard of the project and offered film of camp life that he had taken over
the previous two years.

As it turned out, despite frequent correspondence, Taylor never found the time to take
the film and in 1919 the Mence film was shown to Minister of Defence Sir James Allen, in a
screening at the censor's office. Added to it was a filmed snow fight scene taken in August 1918,
when Featherston and the Wairarapa lay under a chilly blanket of white, released as a 300-foot
short, *Snow Man's Land.* Mence complained to a parliamentary committee that he was unable
to sell his films. He was told by the companies that the public did not want them and he could
not get the picture shows to accept them.[29] Mence's film was a comprehensive view of camp life
with scenes of the march over the Rimutakas, men going on leave, a church parade, artillery in
training and a live shell practice, physical drill, signalling, machine gun practice, officers leaving
the officer's mess, the hospital, stables, a mounted kit inspection and the training of Mounted
Rifles.[30] It was agreed that film to a total of 5000 feet should be purchased at a cost of £80.[31]

Only fragments of Mence's film that we now title *Snow Man's Land* survive, principally the
snow fight itself, where a snowman outside the huts at Featherston is demolished in a gleeful
melee of snow balls between soldiers and camp staff. The cold bleakness of Featherston in
winter dominates but there are also brief scenes of staff training on the Lewis light machine
gun on the camp 25-yard range and bayonet drill, all taken in the summer with the men in
shorts and singlets. The rest of the camp routine detailed in the correspondence has vanished
with time and what survives is our only record of training at Featherston. It is a glimpse only of
what was perhaps one of the most efficient reinforcement training systems that existed in the

Snow Man's Land.
NTSV F1475.

British Empire at the time and perhaps of any citizen army in the world during this war. This guaranteeing that New Zealand would send its quota of 2000 trained men a month to sustain its forces in Egypt and on the Western Front, come rain, snow or shine.[32]

Some of Mence's scenes appear to have survived in other films. We have shots of the Fell engines pushing loaded sheep wagons and passenger carriages over the Rimutaka Incline while very smart soldiers in lemon squeezers, no doubt going on leave, walk the rails and are seen having tea in the railway tearooms.[33] There is also a sequence in the film of New Zealanders training at Sling Camp in England, showing New Zealand engineer reinforcements dragging a GS wagon across an improvised bridge over what is clearly a braided gravel-bed New Zealand river, most likely the Tauherenikau, during training in New Zealand. This was one of the tests to see that the bridge worked, a further shot shows them marching over the bridge, followed at a safe distance by the senior instructor. Although not specifically listed in the Mence material, it is one of the scenes that Taylor was going to film had he had the time, and this would be an obvious sequence to be included in the Mence compilation.[34]

With 17,000 men overseas and 8000 in training in 1915 New Zealand geared itself for a long war with the passage of the National Registration Bill that imposed a census on all males between the ages of 20 and 40 years and determined their willingness to serve at the front. It was a national stocktake of manpower to properly assess New Zealand's capacity to send men to war while still maintaining essential national industries.[35] By the year's end the Trentham Regiment, later the New Zealand Rifle Brigade (Earl of Liverpool's Own), 5000-strong, had been raised in Trentham as the third infantry brigade needed to bring Godley's New Zealand and Australian Division up to strength by increasing the present two brigades, the New Zealand Infantry Brigade and the 4th Australian Infantry Brigade, to three brigades. This brought the division in line with the authorised strength of a British Infantry divisional-organisation.

There was a growing awareness throughout the country that this was not enough. The expansion of the ANZAC into two separate ANZAC Corps to accommodate the expansion of two Australian divisions to four and then five divisions and an entirely separate New Zealand division of three New Zealand infantry brigades demanded a manpower commitment beyond what Allen, the minister of defence, had ever thought possible. Providing enough trained reinforcements for the duration became his principal concern, while cautioning Prime Minister Massey against making any further manpower commitments. The experience in France in 1916 and the losses on the Somme in September–October 1916 confirmed this. New Zealand became one of the first countries in the Empire to follow Britain's lead and introduce conscription for overseas service.

FILMING THE BALLOT

The Military Service Act of 1916 was cleverly introduced into practice. Its implementation triggered at the end of 1916 by a shortfall in the number of volunteers necessary to maintain the supply of 2000 men a month for the front. The first ballot was conducted at Routh's Building, Brandon Street, Wellington. "The Government Statistician (Mr Malcolm Fraser) was in charge of the operation and the supervising magistrate was Mr S.E. McCarthy SM. The invited spectators were — The Mayor (Mr J.P. Luke), the President of the Trades Council (Mr M.J. Reardon) and six press representatives." This included Harry Holland representing *The Maoriland Worker*. "No one else was present who had not work to do in connection with the ballot, save for two photographers and a Cinematograph operator. Nowadays everything is recorded for the moving pictures, and the first ballot under the Military Service Act was no exception. The cinema came and was clicking away busily."[36]

Government statistician Mr Malcolm Fraser with the supervising magistrate (Mr S.E. McCarthy SM) conducts the first ballot to conscript for overseas service in New Zealand in November 1916. Still from Sydney Taylor's *Ballot at the Government Statistician's Office*. NTSV F3484.

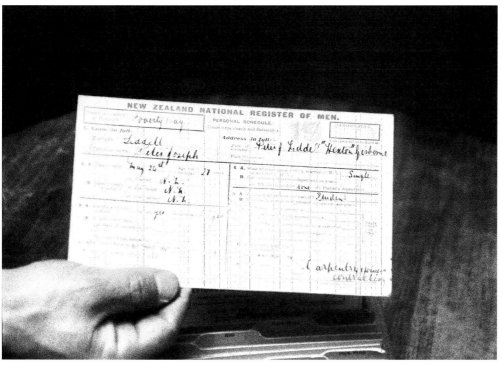

An example registration card for Peter Joseph Liddell whose name does not appear on the personal files of those enlisted into the NZEF. Still from Sydney Taylor's *Ballot at the Government Statistician's Office*. NTSV F3484.

Syd Taylor, from the Department of Agriculture, did the filming of New Zealand's "first gamble in human life" to make up 1300 shortages in the 23rd and 24th reinforcements that was carried out by Mr Fraser and his staff. The event was followed by a morning tea for the ladies "who it is quite possible will draw their sweetheart's cards" and a gathering on the building's roof on what was visibly a windy Wellington day, which Taylor also filmed.[37] *The Ballot at the*

Ballot at the Government Statistician's Office. NTSV F3484.

Government Statistician's Office was not publicly released at the time, although the illustrated papers recorded the photographic details of the occasion.[38] It seems that most of the original film has survived. It is a marvellous record of the event taking us in stages through the setting out of the 194 drawers containing the names in alphabetical order of the men of the 1st Division, who were single men without dependents, being positioned by clerks on two long tables. Each drawer was balloted so that none of the female clerks, each responsible for four drawers, except one with two only, could anticipate the names that she would administer. Fraser, the government statistician and McCarthy, the magistrate, are conscious of the historic nature of the event and stiffly perform to camera, as do the young male clerks whose work it seems was more to position the drawers, while their female colleagues type the call-up lists of balloted men.

There is a similar film from 1940 showing the first ballot of New Zealanders for that war, where in this case Minister of Public Works Robert 'Fighting Bob' Semple, once considered the most dangerous of the 'Red Feds', is seen drawing the first marble from what seems to be the same ballot box and the same procedures as were used in 1916; a certain irony given Semple's imprisonment for his opposition to conscription in the First World War.[39]

In 1915 New Zealand found itself mourning its casualties from Gallipoli but enjoying an economic boom brought on by the war and the British Government's purchase of our entire output of wool, frozen meat and dairy produce. Labour was scarce and wages soared along with the cost of living, but for those not limited to fixed pensions, these were prosperous times with money in most people's pockets. Race meetings and theatres were crowded, so much so that the picture theatre building boom continued despite the war.

The female clerks type up the call-up notices while the male clerks look on. Still from Sydney Taylor's *Ballot at the Government Statistician's Office*. NTSV F3484.

A breather while women volunteers provide refreshments at the top of the range in the march from Featherston to Trentham Camp in the final phase of training. *Auckland Weekly News*, 12 October 1916, p. 37.

This sat uncomfortably alongside the news from the front, where the casualty lists, incongruously positioned alongside the entertainment columns in many papers, constantly reminded the public that New Zealand was at war. The *Evening Post* on 23 September 1915 advertised the delights of Annette Kellerman in *Neptune's Daughter*, Mary Pickford in *Such a Little Queen* and Charlie Chaplin and Marie Dressler in *Tillie's Punctured Romance* placed alongside the 'Roll of Honour' which on this day listed another 28 deaths, mainly those killed in the battle for Hill 60 at Gallipoli on 27 August 1915.[40] This included the name of Sergeant John Walter Wilder of the Wellington Mounted Rifles, whose diary read: "We go for a flutter this afternoon. Just missed a trip to Alexandria, Colonel would not let me go, sent McIver instead."[41] It was his last entry.

16

Filming Diggers on the Western Front

They swing across the screen in brave array,
Long British columns grinding the dark grass.
Twelve months ago they marched into the grey
Of battle; yet again behold them pass!

One lifts his dusty cap; his hair is bright;
I meet his eyes, eager and young and bold.
The picture quivers into ghostly white;
Then I remember, and my heart grows cold!
Florence Ripley Mastin, At the Movies[1]

THE NEW ZEALAND DIVISION IN FRANCE

The first film showing New Zealanders in action was Ashmead-Bartlett's *With the Dardanelles Expedition* seen by New Zealand audiences from April to September 1916. Withdrawn to Egypt, the rapid expansion of the Australian Imperial Force (AIF) to five divisions saw the New Zealand Government reluctantly endorse the formation of a New Zealand Division of three infantry brigades commanded by New Zealander Major-General Sir Andrew Russell totalling 20,000 men.[2] This consisted of the original New Zealand Infantry Brigade now titled 1st New Zealand Infantry Brigade (1st Brigade), a newly raised 2nd New Zealand Infantry Brigade formed out of reinforcements and recovered convalescents and given some experienced officers and non-commissioned officers (NCOs) by cross-postings from 1st Brigade and a third brigade raised in New Zealand. Originally titled the Trentham Regiment, it was raised at Trentham Camp outside Wellington and now titled 3rd New Zealand (Earl of Liverpool's Own) Rifle Brigade (3rd Rifle Brigade), which acknowledged the governor's regimental service in the Rifle Brigade.

At the time *With the Dardanelles Expedition* was being shown in New Zealand picture theatres, the New Zealand Division was arriving in France, going into the line for the first time in the so-called 'Nursery' sector at Armentières, where new divisions were blooded in a quiet

Opposite page: The 1st Auckland Battalion led by Lieutenant-Colonel Arthur Plugge march through Marseille on their arrival in France. *Auckland Weekly News*, 6 July 1916, p. 38, author's collection.

New Zealanders in a model support trench on moving into the front line in the Armentières sector. IWM, Q666.

sector of the front. General Sir Douglas Haig now commanded the British Expeditionary Force (BEF), which numbered four armies, and prepared for a joint Anglo-French offensive on the Somme that was the boundary between both groups of armies, in 1916. During 1914–16 Britain was very much the junior partner on the Western Front but was growing in strength with the move of the divisions of Kitchener's New Army to France. The original divisions of the BEF were shadows of the regular divisions of 1914 and now filled with new reinforcements. The New Army divisions were also inexperienced as were the Australian and New Zealand divisions of the two ANZAC Corps. The Battle of the Somme was the first large-scale offensive mounted by the BEF and the first with Haig as commander-in-chief. The German offensive at Verdun in February 1916 reduced Marshal Joffre's ability to provide French forces for the Somme battle and when it started on 1 July 1916 it was the first Anglo-French battle on the Western Front where the British Army played the leading role.

As it turned out it was anything but quiet in the line at Armentières for the New Zealanders and Australians of what were now two Anzac Corps: I ANZAC commanded by Lieutenant-General Sir William Birdwood, the British commander of the AIF, and II ANZAC, commanded by Lieutenant-General Sir Alexander Godley, the British commander of the New Zealand Expeditionary Force (NZEF). With the build-up for the coming offensive all sectors were deliberately active to prevent German reinforcements being released to the Somme. This meant battalions held extended frontages of the front line for prolonged periods in a time of intensive patrolling and trench raids that tested inexperienced officers and men to their limits and beyond.[3]

CAMERAMEN AT THE FRONT

Until July 1916 cameramen were forbidden from filming British forces on the Western Front. The British Topical Committee for War Films comprising the seven most prominent newsreel and documentary film companies was finally granted official status to film on the Western Front by the War Office in return for a share of its profits being given to War Office charities. The first two official cameramen left for France in November 1915. The Canadian Expeditionary Force (CEF) sent out its first official cameraman in July 1916. Both Australia and New Zealand had to rely on the British official cameramen to film their activities in 1916 but this was as much by luck as good judgement, because there were two to three cameramen available to film what was now some 50 infantry divisions.[4]

We have glimpses only of New Zealanders in photograph and on film and at the front in 1916. The first image to appear in the New Zealand illustrated papers showed the 1st Battalion, Auckland Regiment marching through the streets of Marseilles with flags on their bayonets and carrying bouquets of flowers presented by the watching French crowds. They were led by their commanding officer, Lieutenant-Colonel Arthur Plugge. He was the last of the original New Zealand commanding officers of the Main Body NZEF still commanding his battalion. Lieutenant-Colonels D. McBean Stewart of the Canterbury Battalion and W.G. Malone of the Wellington Battalion were killed on Gallipoli and T.W. McDonald of the Otago Battalion was invalided back to New Zealand from Egypt. Plugge was not an effective commanding officer and the demands of the Western Front on top of the strain of his Gallipoli experience saw him perform poorly in France. Russell, the divisional commander, was mindful of his reputation as one of the last commanding officers of the original Main Body. On removing Plugge from command after the Somme, Russell appointed him director of sports and physical training for the division, a position that suited his talents and saw his frequent appearance in photo and film.

ARMENTIÈRES AND THE NURSERY SECTOR 1916

Even for Gallipoli veterans, trench warfare at Armentières was a learning experience. Lance Corporal Fred Cody in 1st Canterbury wrote on 22 May 1916:

> This is a very different sort of trench life to Gallipoli. The place is in a hell of a mess and Jerry's snipers make it unsafe to show an eyebrow over the top, though he must be a couple of hundred yards away. Some of the fire bays are smashed to blazes and you have to dodge around the back of the parados [the raised earth or sandbagged mound at the back of a trench — the parapet being at the front] to move about. The Wellingtons told us to look out for Parapet Joe and by cripes they were right. He has got a machine gun on a swivel or something and fairly belts the devil out of the sandbags on top of the firebays at night. You never know what hour of the night he is going to turn the hose on. Something will have to be done about him. Another pest is the shave and clean up for inspection each morning. Not an empty cartridge or piece of paper to be left about. They ought to ask Fritz not to throw his shrapnel around like he does and make the place untidy.[5]

A brief glimpse of Armentières on film while the New Zealanders were in residence in May 1916 was taken by a French cameraman.[6] We see the centre of the town with the clock tower and the time fixed at half-past eleven, the moment that a German shell stopped the clock. It became 'Half-past eleven square' for the rest of the war, and a phrase that featured in New Zealand letters and diaries. The distinctive lemon squeezer hat is evident on the few soldiers to be seen and the lack of damage to the buildings shows that it was taken early after the New Zealand arrival in May 1916. By the time the New Zealanders were withdrawn in late July, the town was badly battered by intensive German artillery fire. The intensity of the New Zealand Division's initial experience in the trenches is measured by the 2500 casualties including 375 dead from May to August 1916.[7]

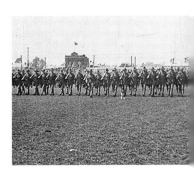

Ruines — Arras, Bailleul, Nieppe, Ypres, Albert, Béthune, Armentiéres. NTSV F253663.

With The Australian Forces In France. IWM Film IWM 138 (from 0:08:30 - 0:11:48).

The same film also shows the towns and villages that became familiar to New Zealanders as the war progressed including Bailleul, which was a major logistics and hospital centre and the location of Godley's headquarters II ANZAC in 1916–17. The Bailleul Communal Cemetery Extension Nord has 252 New Zealand graves including those of two New Zealand brigade commanders, Brigadier-General C.H.J. Brown, commanding 1st Brigade, killed by artillery fire at Messines on 8 June 1917 and Brigadier-General F.E. Johnston, commanding 3rd Rifle Brigade, shot by a sniper on 7 August 1917. The town was captured during the German offensive in April 1918 and was reduced to rubble by November 1918.

We also see the destroyed churches in the villages of Nieppe and Neuve-Église, which were the sites of New Zealand medical and logistic units in 1916–17. Nieppe was the home of the 'Kiwis', the New Zealand Divisional Entertainers, for nine months in 1917. Both churches feature in the paintings of the New Zealand official war artist, George Edmund Butler, with those of the ruined church and cemetery at Neuve-Église being particularly evocative.[8]

The first film we have featuring New Zealanders on the Western Front was taken on 21 May 1916 by a British official cameraman. This shows a wood-chopping competition between Maori axemen of the Pioneer Battalion against Australian and Canadian axemen, with the prizes being awarded by Lieutenant-General Sir William Birdwood, commanding I ANZAC.[9] "The New Zealand axemen were drawn from Lieut. Maclean's party of bush-fellers at La Motte: all were Maoris. The New Zealanders won two out of four contests and were second in the other two — a splendid performance considering some of their opponents were drawn from the ranks of the finest woodsmen in the world."[10]

TRAINING FOR THE SOMME

The British official cameraman Geoffrey H. Malins filmed riflemen of 1 Rifles ('Diamond Dinks') 3rd Brigade on 14 August 1916 in a rest area at Steenwerck waiting to entrain.[11] It was the end of their tour in the trenches at Armentières. The first two rifle battalions were withdrawn and went by train to the training areas around Abbeville to prepare for the commitment to the Somme battle. The term 'fair dinkum' was used initially in a derisive sense to describe the members of the Rifle Brigade, because those already at the front who had served at Gallipoli thought they had taken their time before enlisting. It was taken up by the Rifle Brigade themselves and they used the term proudly, shortening it to 'Dinks', which in their minds suggested they were a better class of soldier than those of the Main Body. The term 'Diamond Dinks' comes from the 1½ inch square of black cloth worn diamond fashion on both the shoulders and on the side of the hat. We see them entrain into the passenger carriages. Each man is carrying steel helmets, full packs and rifles and one senses that these soldiers have had a long and tiring stint in the trenches.[12]

It was while they were waiting to entrain that they were informally inspected by HM King George V with scenes of them cheering the King as he passed. We can date this because they are wearing smasher hats, with the fore and aft dent in the crown. This would all change on 7 September 1916 when the soldiers of the New Zealand Division would reshape their hats into lemon squeezers.[13]

This was seen by New Zealand audiences in the film *The King Visits His Army in the Great Advance*, which screened in December 1916 and was still appearing in local theatres in June 1917.[14] *The New Zealand Herald* entertainment column reported: "The sections devoted to the portrayal of New Zealand troops in the official war picture *The King Visits His Armies in France*, at the Strand Theatre show our soldiers on one of the roads at the rear of the trenches.

The excellent photography makes it a simple matter to recognise the units of the troops."[15] It ensured that families with soldiers in the Rifle Brigade would inevitably flock to the theatre and scan the faces.

Episode 5 of *Sons of Our Emprie* shows New Zealanders on the Somme. We now see our 'Diamond Dinks' in lemon squeezers. They are in a mixed group of British and New Zealand soldiers gathered around a captured German artillery piece.[16] This was shot in the week 7–15 September on the Somme as the New Zealand Division assembled before their attack on 15 September 1916. It was detached from Godley's II ANZAC and fought on the Somme as part of the British XV Corps. The 'Dinks' played a prominent role on 15 September 1916 and the

3rd Brigade suffered almost 50% casualties over the course of the battle. Many of the New Zealanders shown here would be among the killed and wounded. Captain Lindsey Inglis whose rifle company would seize the furthest New Zealand objective on the day of the attack spoke after the battle of the cost of "three and a half weeks of strain and exposure". Losses in his company were 42 dead and nearly 150 wounded out of its strength of 240. The 3rd Brigade had 1773 casualties, an average of 15 officers and 420 other ranks in each of its four battalions.[17]

This is the only glimpse we have of New Zealanders on film during the battle. However, there is a sequence of photographs taken by the now commissioned Lieutenant Ernest 'Baby' Brooks who had last filmed and photographed New Zealanders on Gallipoli, and now ran into them again on the Somme. Brooks shot an important series of photographs that show the arrival of the division on the Somme, including the infantry, field ambulance and artillery. He then went forward in the New Zealand sector on 15 September and captured the faces of New Zealanders in the newly won positions of the Crest and Switch trenches taken from the Germans.[18] This is now the site of the New Zealand Memorial. Brooks' photographs appeared in the New Zealand illustrated papers. The first image showing New Zealand motor ambulances made no mention of the New Zealand connection and only the most discerning viewer would have identified the white silver fern on the black circular background on the side of the co-driver's compartment that identified it as a New Zealand Division vehicle. In the following weeks, images of New Zealand soldiers in their lemon squeezers moving forward to the battlefield, or steel-helmeted in battle on 15 September, digging in forward of the Switch Trench or moving forward towards the village of Flers, provided the public with what are now iconic images of New Zealanders in their first major battle on the Western Front.

The New Zealand Division attacked with four tanks in support (the first time tanks were used in battle) on 15 September 1916 and gained more ground than any other division on that

New Zealanders of the 1st Battalion, 3 New Zealand Rifle Brigade mix with British soldiers round a captured German gun on their arrival at the Somme battlefield. Still from *Sons of Our Empire*, Episode 5, NTSV F246428.

day. It played a major part in suppressing German resistance in High Wood on its left flank and in regaining the village of Flers on its right after the 41st Division were driven back. It was a day of hard fighting and heavy losses. The New Zealanders would remain in the line from 15 September until 2 October 1916, the longest unbroken spell of any division in the battle of the Somme. It reflected its continued success in a series of small-scale operations that eventually exhausted the division. Its efforts earned the division a reputation for fighting. Godley proudly wrote to Allen on the New Zealand performance and the praise it had received from the higher command, "and a thing with which they were all particularly pleased, was that the Division, though it was kept in the line longer than any other Division has been yet, made no bones about it and did not ask for relief. They also told me that a thing they liked very much was, that after they got their orders, nothing more was heard of them, till a report was sent that they had gained their objective."[19] A workmanlike silence from a division that became known as 'The Silent Division' — a title used in its first unofficial post-war history.[20]

The New Zealanders also gained a nickname on the Somme. The British Armies in France awarded the title 'Digging Battalions' to those units who excelled at digging in when an objective was gained and who also then linked it up with the old front line by digging communication trenches. That accolade was awarded the New Zealand Engineer field companies and the (half-Maori, half-Pakeha) Pioneer Battalion who coordinated the digging of two of the longest communication trenches on the Somme battlefield. They called themselves 'Diggers' and this became common within the New Zealand Division. In 1917 it spread to the Australian divisions in I and II ANZAC. Australian official war correspondent and historian C.E.W. Bean acknowledged the term's New Zealand origins in his official history of the AIF in France.[21]

Soldiers of the New Zealand Division at the end of their trek to the Somme battlefield in early September 1916. Photographed by Lieutenant Ernest Brooks who last met the New Zealanders on Gallipoli. Q1243, IWM.

Riflemen of the 3rd New
Zealand Rifle Brigade pass
through the remains of Crest
Trench on the morning of 15
September 1916. British official
photographer, Lieutenant
Ernest Brooks, Q188, IWM.

THE BATTLE OF THE SOMME

It was the British Government official film *The Battle of the Somme* (five-reel, 5000 feet), that
again brought home the realities of war to the New Zealand public. This film was shot by the
two British official cameramen Geoffrey H. Malins and J.B. McDowell, showing principally the
men of the 7th and 29th British divisions in the days leading up to 1 July 1916, the first day of
the Somme offensive. Instead of the film footage being used in a series of short films as had
been the case to date, it was edited by Charles Urban into the first 'big battle' film. In the words
of Stephen Badsey, who catalogued it for the Imperial War Museum (IWM) collection, it was
the "only British official film to have a major impact on the perception of the war, both at the
time and in historical terms."[22] It shows the expectation and anticipation on the faces of the
soldiers of Kitchener's New Army divisions as they prepare and move forward to the line in
what they anticipated would be the climatic breakthrough battle on the Western Front on 1 July
1916. Sixty thousand casualties on this day would end that dream and the battles of the Somme
would continue until November 1916 before petering out in the winter mud. That failure would
see the Australian, Canadian and New Zealand forces committed to the Somme in turn along
with almost every British division in France.

The film of the battle reached New Zealand audiences in October 1916 just as the New
Zealand Division finished its part in the battle. Advertisements for *The Battle of the Somme*
were displayed on the same pages as the obituaries of the soldiers that died there. The New
Zealand Division numbered 7959 casualties, 2111 dead and some 5848 wounded. As Andrew
Macdonald details in his important study of New Zealanders on the Somme, "More than half
of the dead — 1272 or 60 per cent, to be precise, have no known grave … Roughly one in
every seven New Zealand soldiers who fought on the Somme was killed, while about four out
of every ten were wounded."[23]

Telegrams arrived at New Zealand doorsteps at the same time as families were seeing
graphic scenes of cheering men before going 'over the top' to be followed by lines of exhausted
men bringing back the wounded and the realities of the dead and dying. *The Battle of the*

 *Battle of the Somme.*
NTSV F231397.

Somme, competing for audience attention with D.W. Griffith's *The Birth of a Nation*, had an enormous impact on New Zealand with its "awe-inspiring reproduction of the terrific events in which our brothers, our sons, and fathers are gloriously playing their parts this day. If anything were needed to justify the existence of the cinematograph, it is to be found in the wonderful series of films of the opening of the British attack on the Somme on July 1."[24] The film shocked New Zealand audiences and continued to do so as it toured circuits throughout New Zealand for the duration of the war. A perceptive reviewer for the *Ashburton Guardian* mirrored the thoughts of many New Zealand families when he wrote that while there were many impressive aspects about the film in the scenes of preparation and the actual attack, it was what followed that was most important.

> Thereafter the picture is terrible in its story. The dead are shown as little as maybe; but a host of wounded — friends and foes — are seen, and the sacrifices of war thus pictured cannot readily be forgotten. Great numbers of German prisoners were secured by the British, and the state of many of these men, with their nerves shattered, and obviously in a state almost of dementia, due to the terrific bombardment to which they had been subjected, is shown with terrible plainness. It is in this part of the picture, when the price of victory — so much more easily paid than the price of defeat — is clearly seen, that the spectators grip something of the wholesome truth about the war.[25]

New Zealanders who fought on the Somme had similar reactions, Signaller Harold Constantine Ferrand was a projectionist for Tom Pollard in Greymouth. He wrote to his former boss after seeing the film in the United Kingdom.

> I went to see the most wonderful film I have ever seen "The Battle of the Somme." When released in New Zealand, don't miss it, as it is a Government official film; but [it] will not suit everyone as it is too real. In places it is ghastly, but true and shows real warfare which is hell with the lid off.[26]

Taranaki Herald, 27 October 1916, p. 1.

This and the release of *The King Visits His Armies in the Great Advance* in late 1916 increased public pressure on the government for films showing New Zealanders at the front. The success of both these films saw the creation in London of the War Office Cinema Committee (WOCC) consisting of Lord Beaverbrook, who became the minister of information in February 1918, Reginald Brade, the permanent secretary at the War Office, and Sir William Jury who took over the production of official film through his own company, Jury's Imperial Pictures. The WOCC became the dominant organisation with a monopoly on the production of official film on all fronts including the Home Front.[27]

In December 1916 the New Zealand Government cabled the New Zealand high commissioner in London, Sir Thomas Mackenzie, asking if they could get the sole New Zealand rights to British official pictures taken at the front. The War Office replied that the WOCC would grant the New Zealand Government sole rights to cinematographic films taken at the front providing that they took two copies of each film issued at five pence per foot. They also offered to take films and photos of New Zealanders at the front at no cost to New Zealand by using their own

cinematographers, "the photographs only with exclusive New Zealand rights would be supplied at cost price" and the film would be available under the first arrangement. The other option would be to share a photographer with the Australians. The New Zealand Government baulked at the cost of providing its own photographer and opted to take advantage of the War Office offer and also purchase sole rights to the film as suggested.[28]

The creation of the WOCC was aimed at providing a rational system for filming on the Western Front. This was the plan but it did not work. There was one formal visit of the British official cinematographer to the New Zealand Division and a detailed visit's programme was put together to ensure as full a picture of the division and its activities was filmed.[29] "A Cinematograph operator will be attached to the Division for about one week from Thursday next … for the purpose of taking typical scenes in the daily life of the New Zealand soldier. Brigade and other commanders will render him every assistance."[30] It was shot during 8–15 March 1917 with the division in the line opposite Fleurbaix in Northern France immediately south of Armentières as part of Godley's II ANZAC. The film gives us a rare overview of New Zealanders in the front line.[31]

REVIEW OF NEW ZEALAND TROOPS BY SIR WALTER LONG

The film *Review of New Zealand Troops by Sir Walter Long* opens with the arrival of Sir Walter Long, secretary of state for the colonies who is met by Godley, commanding II ANZAC and Major-General Sir Andrew Russell, the divisional commander, all the while accompanied by a retinue of staff officers and reporters. On 9 March 1917 they inspect battalions of 2nd Brigade on the Armentières–Bailleul Road. The brigade was commanded by Brigadier-General W.G. 'Bill' Braithwaite, a crusty demanding officer, beloved by his men for his attention to detail that extended to their care as well as to training and planning for operations. There is lovely detail that enlivens the formal inspection, the Hessian scrim-screens in the background making it difficult for German observers to see movement on the poplar-edged road. A black-clad local priest stands behind the inspecting party watching the march-past, his bicycle propped against the tree. There are scenes of the inspection of a guard of honour from the NZ Pioneer Battalion, half Maori, half former Otago Mounted Rifles, with Major Peter Buck (Te Rangi Hiroa) as the guard commander.

It all becomes a bit of a jumble after this, a cross section of infantry weapons are fired, including a Lewis gun and rifle grenades. We then see a rare view of no-man's land as the camera pans across the flat low-lying landscape finishing on a dugout entrance built into the tangled brick of a ruined building, while a sentry stands by a knife-rest against a background of a tattered sandbag trench wall. A nonchalant group of smoking, unarmed soldiers wade through a water-filled shell-hole for camera, the one smoking the pipe is Malcolm Ross, the official New Zealand war correspondent. It switches to the bivouac area in Ploegsteert Wood with a fatigue party coming out of the line on a cold, snowy morning. They perk up when they see the camera, the more discerning race round and join the line again so that the folks can get a good look at them when the film is screened in New Zealand.

No. 15 Battery, New Zealand Field Artillery (NZFA), are then shown firing its 18-pounder field guns from concealed

Sir Thomas Mackenzie, High Commissioner for New Zealand in London chats with the New Zealand official war correspondent Hon. Captain Malcolm Ross, an old friend. H-Series, H260, 1/4-009496-G, ATL, Wellington.

positions in the front rooms of brick-fronted houses in a village street. This is matched by the explosion of shells along the German front line, as the camera lens evocatively peers over the top of the sandbag parapet through the barbed wire entanglements into no-man's land. Death delivered to ensure good cinema, and it is. This brief scene is the unique New Zealand front trench scene filmed on the Western Front.

The film would not be of the New Zealand Division without rugby and we see half-time and the final half of the New Zealand trench 'All Blacks', formed from the best pre-war players in the division, taking on the 38th (Welsh) Division, proudly representing a still unbeaten Welsh nation. The 'away' match was played on 15 March 1917 and Russell sits alongside his fellow divisional commander, flanked by officers of the Welsh Division. Russell is the only one who seems to be enjoying the game. With his team winning 10–3 his bonhomie is understandable. The film finishes on this note.

This was the only film specifically taken by British official cameramen of the New Zealand Division. The WOCC found that the demand for filming British divisions and their activities was beyond the resources of the few cameramen available. C.E.W. Bean, the official Australian correspondent, with the support of the Australian Government was setting up an Australian War Records Section and got General Haig's approval for a British photographer, Herbert Baldwin, to become Australia's first official war photographer with his "own developer, his own car [and] his own developing room".[32] The committee had to tell Mackenzie that it could not honour the commitment made and so Mackenzie negotiated with the War Office to appoint an official New Zealand cameraman.[33]

THE FORGOTTEN FRONT: SINAI AND PALESTINE

The New Zealand Mounted Rifles Brigade that served in Sinai and Palestine as part of the ANZAC Mounted Division served on the forgotten front in film terms. There was no official war correspondent with the New Zealanders and there was no New Zealand cinematographer. The British official cinematographer Harold Jeapes filmed the campaign. He was joined by Australian Frank Hurley in December 1917. In June 1918 Hurley was replaced by J.R. Campbell.[34]

Jeapes provides glimpses of the work of the New Zealand Mounted Rifles in a number of films. The film *El Mejdel, Jaffa and West Country Troops* shows the capture of Jaffa by the Wellington Mounted Rifles of the New Zealand Mounted Rifles Brigade on 16 November 1917. It opens with the intertitle 'Jaffa town hall and clock-tower within half an hour of its capture'. We see a patrol of four New Zealand Mounted Rifles enter the square and ride towards camera. The four men represent a section in a mounted rifle troop. In the event of combat, one man would act as horse-holder and take care of all four horses while the other would fight on foot. All four are fully laden with bedrolls strapped in front of the saddles, greatcoats strapped

A heavily laden section of the Wellington Mounted Rifles ride through the town square of Jaffa soon after its capture on 16 November 1917. Still from the British official cameraman Harold Jeapes' *El Mejdel, Jaffa and West Country Troops.* NTSV F246416.

El Mejdel, Jaffa and West Country Troops. NTSV F246416.

behind, and rifles at the trail. We can see that they have been in the saddle for some time. It shows the reality of the horseman's role in this campaign: the man and his horse being an inseparable team. Mateship and teamwork were essential to both survival and success and this scene captures the essence of this relationship.

Individual New Zealanders can be seen in the square, but the camera focuses on a group of officers standing by their horses outside the town hall, which was formerly the Turkish military headquarters. Identified by their service dress jackets and Sam Browne belts, they stand in front of a large group of dismounted riflemen, most probably members of the Wellington Mounted Rifles regimental headquarters.

The scene shifts to a group of New Zealand troopers relaxing on the outskirts of the town, with their horses tethered behind them. Men are cleaning up, smoking and enjoying a drink in the shade. Taking Jaffa was the climax to a week of hard riding and heavy fighting and it shows.[35]

The next detailed look at New Zealanders on film is in the town of Jericho.[36] It opens with a portrait shot of Captain Frank Hurley, attached as official cameraman to the ANZAC Corps formations; Hurley is wearing the slouched hat with the distinctive emu feathers of the Light Horse.

A guard of the Auckland Mounted Rifles Regiment of the New Zealand Mounted Rifles are seen mounting guard outside the headquarters and saluting as a senior officer, possibly Major-General E.C.W. Chaytor, the New Zealand commander of the ANZAC Mounted Division, as he strides past.

A squadron of New Zealand Mounteds is seen galloping through the town. There are detailed close-ups of patrols moving out on horseback. This is followed by a group of New Zealand Army Service Corps soldiers joking for the camera outside of a stores house. It is the daily hustle and bustle of a mounted formation on operations and one sees the casual professionalism of horsemen who know their business and who do not need to act up for the camera.

New Zealanders are also in the newsreel item showing the entry of General Allenby into Jerusalem on 11 December 1917.[37]

The honour guard at the Jaffa Gate is composed of English, Welsh, Scottish, Indian, Australian and New Zealand troops, with 20 soldiers each from Italy and France continuing the line inside the gate. There is a glimpse of the New Zealand troop commander, Second Lieutenant C.J. Harris of the Canterbury Mounted Rifles. His troop of 33 mounted riflemen was made up of a sergeant and ten men from the Auckland Mounted Rifles, nine men from the Canterbury Mounted Rifles, nine men from the Wellington Mounted Rifles, three men from the NZ Machine Gun Squadron and one from the Signal Troop.[38]

This is all there is, but even so they are important reminders on film of perhaps the finest military body that New Zealand has ever raised.[39]

FILMS FOR THE 'DIGGERS'

Film shows were an integral part of the New Zealand Division from the local Egyptian-run cinema at Zeitoun Camp in Egypt in 1914–15 to the YMCA-sponsored screen showings three nights weekly in the large concert hall in the École Professionnelle in Armentières. Film screenings were also on the programme of the New Zealand Divisional Entertainers, known as the 'Kiwis', which was formed in late 1916 at the direction of divisional commander Major-General Sir Andrew Russell.[40]

Going to the 'flicks' for some light relief was very much part of a soldier's life. The rebuilding of the battered and depleted New Zealand Division after the Somme saw Russell turn his

Topical Budget — Jericho. NTSV F246426.

General Allenby's Entry into Jerusalem. NTSV F246417.

attention to the care and welfare of the men. The division returned to the Armentières sector as part of II ANZAC. Impressed by the performances of the 56th Divisional ('Tommy') Concert Party, Russell determined that his New Zealanders would also have their entertainers and form them into a concert party "to be detached from their units and kept out of all 'stunts' in future, as, he said, they were more value to the N.Z.E.F. elsewhere than in the line."[41]

Lieutenant Dave Kenny, a well-known entertainer and pianist from Wellington and now a machine gun officer, was told to form a concert party using the 3rd Field Ambulance Orchestra as a foundation on which to build. With the support of Lieutenant-Colonel J. Hardie Neil this group of medics and, when called on, musicians, singers and comedians, entertained New Zealand units on an ad hoc basis since their arrival in Egypt in early 1916. Kenny sorted out likely members of reputed talent within the division and enlisted them into the party. Most were pleased to join. Sapper George Clyne Lyttleton, formerly a customs officer in Auckland, with a reputation for being an instrumentalist and a comedian, found himself posted to divisional headquarters. "At the least it was a congenial job lasting through most of the winter months and at best it might last the war out."[42] It did and his unpublished record 'Pierrots in Picardy: A Khaki Chronicle by "One of Them"' is an invaluable record of the doings of the New Zealand 'Kiwis'.

A theatre was built by the New Zealand Pioneer Battalion at the corner of the Sailly road at Bac St-Maur, a small village southwest of Armentières. Before it was finished the shows started. Attached to the group was Sergeant Alex Tozer who was in charge of the cinema fit-out. As

The New Zealand Divisional Concert Party known as the 'Kiwis', led by Lieutenant Dave Kenny, sitting centre, second row. Film was an integral part of the Kiwis' performance. H-Series H222,1/2-012914-G, ATL, Wellington.

Lyttleton remembers Tozer "was a Tommy in the N.Z. Engineers (sounds like the beginning of a song) and we had a row the first time we met".[43] Prone to bursts of temper, Tozer was regarded as a shellshock case and everyone in the outfit soon realised it was best not to pick a quarrel with him.

The theatre was put up in a rush and its walls were "a kind of papery scrim covered with tar. This kept the light in, which was important, but it failed to keep out the cold", which was of great importance to the members of the orchestra. "The string players wore mittens at times, the wood wind could hardly blow for shivering and on one or two occasions the brass actually had their valves frozen and couldn't play till they had thawed them out."[44]

The formal opening of the 'Kiwis' was on Christmas Day 1916 with an afternoon show for the children of the district. "There was an immense crowd of them and on the stage an enormous Christmas Tree heavy with gifts … Alec Tozer had rigged up the Cinema temporarily and put on a few films before the show proper. Most of us were back stage helping when the first film began and we were startled by the scream of delighted laughter that arose. We rushed to the front wings to see what this comic could be that was causing such yells of merriment and found it was a street scene from a Pathe Gazette."[45]

The soldiers of the division were a more demanding audience and initially the Kiwis' show was a mixed bag. "Some items went well, others were not so hot." It was Lyttleton's first experience of a New Zealand 'Digger' audience. "I can't say I found them easy. One had a feeling they were thinking: 'Come on now. You claim to be entertainers; entertain us'. With a civilian audience one can always depend on a certain amount of 'polite applause' if nothing else. Not so with the Diggers. Anyone who gets applause from them earns them."[46]

Films formed half the show, with the concert party performing for an hour with a half-hour's worth of films before and after. It was still hard work for the orchestra as they had to play for the films and then get dressed for the show. "This meant getting down in time to make up before the first lot of pictures, playing in the well in khaki, changing into Pierrot costume during the interval, doing the stage show, changing back into khaki — and getting your make-up off if you were lucky — during the second interval and finally playing for the second lot of pictures."[47]

The pictures changed twice a week on Wednesdays and Saturdays and the players would stay on after the show and watch the new films. George Lyttleton records:

> This was great fun; we had the theatre to ourselves and could vent our feelings — real or assumed — in such remarks as seemed good to us.
>
> In those days "Serials" were very popular and part of our programme consisted of a marvellous penny dreadful entitled "The Exploits of Elaine," featuring Pearl White. Pearl was some lil' actress and the trouble that girl got into you wouldn't believe. Of course we were all her champions and tendered sympathy or bellowed advice ("Look behind you, Pearl!" "Don't you believe him, Pearl, he's a dirty dog!") as the occasion demanded. At times she really seemed to act on our warnings and then we cheered like one man. Thinking back, I realise that this was our one hour of relaxation; the show was over and done with, work was ten or twelve hours away — no wonder we enjoyed it.[48]

The Digger audience reacted the same way. Films had been their escape in New Zealand and now in France they were "like a crowd of boys letting themselves go at a cowboy picture" in small town New Zealand.[49]

The New Zealand unofficial cartoonist, Lieutenant G. Pat Hanna, captions his cartoon "Hindenbeggar" drawn on the wall of the officers' club. Hanna would do his lightning sketches with the 'Kiwis' concert party. After the war he formed the 'Diggers', which toured New Zealand and Australia for many years. Photograph taken 1 July 1917 by Henry Armytage Sanders. H-Series 94, 1/2-012805-G, ATL, Wellington.

The Kiwis moved north with the division in its preparation for the 1917 Messines offensive. "What with scenery, music, props, costumes and cinema outfit, it already needed at least two big outfits to shift us" and like all good soldiers the trappings of home were added to the load with members of the cast acquiring camp beds from London, all sensibly overlooked by Dave Kenny, the man in charge.[50]

Individuals who would later involve themselves in film performed with the Kiwis. George Patrick 'Pat' Hanna was a signwriter by trade and he also worked as a cartoonist for the *New Zealand Free Lance*. He was New Zealand diving champion and captain of the national water-polo team in 1912–13. He enlisted with the Samoa Expeditionary Force and served in France with the 1st Otagos. He was commissioned in December 1916 and was appointed bombing officer, as grenades were his speciality. He was known as an entertainer for his monologues and lightning sketches. "While we were at Nieppe, Pat Hanna appeared with us several times … he confined himself to lightning sketches — and very clever they were. Unfortunately, for one show, where some Brass Hats were to be present, he lost confidence a bit and prepared his sheets by putting the lines in <u>very lightly</u> before he went on. Even so the audience could see them and the turn went flat. Pat never appeared again with us. Such a pity, the turn was good and he didn't need the lines, just an attack of nerves made him fear he might get muddled."[51] After the Armistice in 1918, Hanna was appointed recreational and entertainments officer with the New Zealand Division and formed a concert party who would become famous as the 'Diggers' that appeared in concert and film in the 1920s and 1930s.[52]

Sapper Eric Millar reflected the soldier audience's response:

August 24 [1917]. Immediately after tea, Kaye and I took a walk to the Divisional Theatre at Nieppe, where there was a very fine programme, first pictures and then the 'Kiwis', the New Zealand Pierrots. Being wingless birds they cannot escape any half-bricks or other confetti which may come their way. Their stunt was a lot better than I expected; in fact this troupe is reckoned to be one of the cleverest on the whole front. There was a gay pantomime in which the jovial and rotund Dave Kenny of Wellington appeared as a rather matronly Fairy Queen, dressed in white, with a garland of flowers on her perspiring brow.[53]

Kenny did not see out the war, dying from acute appendicitis in the United Kingdom in April 1918. By 1918 the Kiwis were but one of a number concert parties entertaining New Zealanders in France. Musician Tano Fama, from Wanganui, who served as a medic and stretcher bearer in the New Zealand Medical Corps, formed the 'New Zealand Pierrots' at the New Zealand Infantry and Reserve Base Depot at Étaples, which was also home to the 'Te Koas'. Both were sponsored by the YMCA. Groups were formed among the various brigades in the division; one was the 'Tuis' originally with 4th Brigade but transferred to 2nd Brigade when 4th Brigade was disbanded. Also the 'Guns' or 'Gunners' in the artillery, the 'Eyes Front' of the Entrenching Group and the 'Dinks' of 3rd Brigade.[54]

YMCA CINEMAS

The YMCA opened halls and cinemas for troops in the rear areas, including those of the New Zealand Division.

> In S----- [Sailly] we have opened a cinema theatre. Think of it, moving pictures within range of the guns. We have bought an outfit, Pathe's latest 1916 model for £300 and installed it. It has a fine engine, which not only produces power for the operating machine, but also provides electric light for the building. The barn is attached to some stables, but has been gaily decorated with flags, has seating accommodation to hold four to five hundred men and is made as bright as circumstances will permit. If only the roof didn't let in so much water and the cracks in the wall the wind. But the soldiers don't mind; they just put up their collars and laugh to their hearts' content at *Charlie Chaplin's Night Out* and other pictures guaranteed to cheer. There are two changes of programme weekly. These are quite up to the best New Zealand standard, and the pictures are projected quite as clearly as in the Empress or in the King's in Wellington. General Russell has loaned us a cinematograph operator for the work.[55]

The YMCA was appreciated by the soldiers and this message was passed back to New Zealand in the fundraising Red Triangle Days. "We have a free picture show here run by the Y.M.C.A. The money to run it is supplied by the people of New Zealand, so if you have anything to spare for the War Funds give all you can to the Y.M.C.A. It is the best institution over here for looking after the boys. When we are in the trenches they have free tea and biscuits for us and when we come out it is the same, so they are doing good work and deserve all the help they can get."[56]

Entertainment took second place during the major battles and the Kiwis had to find their way to Étaples during the German 'Big Push' in March 1918.

In July 1918 there was the last period of rest and training before what became the final offensive. Film and concerts were held most evenings. The official historian of the New Zealand Rifle Brigade says it best. "In many respects the New Zealanders deserved their reputation for silence; but as far as music was concerned, excepting always the absence of singing on the march, they surely made no little noise in the world. The Artillery, the Entrenching Group [formed from the disbanded 4th Brigade], and each of the twelve infantry battalions in France had its brass band; two of the latter rejoiced in the possession of pipe bands in addition; and there were, of course, the bands of the Base in France and of the Depots in England."[57]

17

"Who is Sanders?"

Sanders is not known in this office, and enquiries at the New Zealand Picture Supplies were resultless, no one of the name being known to the picture business?[1]

PATHÉ TO THE RESCUE

Thomas Mackenzie, the New Zealand high commissioner to the United Kingdom, was a driving force behind the Department of Tourist and Health Resorts' use of films; it was he who ensured that James McDonald was active as a government film-maker. He then took it on himself to see that the New Zealand Division had a cameraman at the front, and approached Pathé Frères' office in London for the use of one of their cameramen. This link to Pathé Frères was well established, going back to 1912 when Mackenzie became high commissioner. His agent in all of this was, of course, trade commissioner T.E. Donne. Between them they ensured a constant stream of film of New Zealanders in the United Kingdom throughout 1915–16. Arranging a cameraman to go to the front was the logical next step. The strength of those links was reflected in the choice and seniority of cameraman that Pathé provided.

The first intimation that the New Zealand Government had that it now employed an official photographer on the Western Front was a cable from Mackenzie on 23 March 1917 stating that "with the approval of the War Office Henry Armytage Sanders has been appointed official photographer to New Zealand Expeditionary Force (NZEF) with rank of Lieutenant."[2] This puzzled the minister of defence, James Allen, and his staff in New Zealand, who assumed that Sanders was a New Zealander, but after making enquiries found that no one in the New Zealand cinema business had heard of him.[3]

On 2 April 1917 Allen, then acting prime minister, asked Mackenzie, "who is Sanders? Has he been appointed, if so on what terms?" Mackenzie replied that Sanders was a photographic and cinematographic expert with seven years' experience with Pathé Frères. He had been given the rank and pay of a lieutenant in the NZEF, with "all photographic materials to be supplied by New Zealand Government who will have sole rights to all photographs".

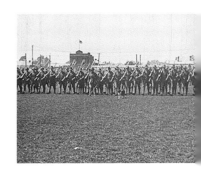

Thirty years old and married with three children, Henry 'Harry' Sanders was a veteran in the news film business. A Londoner, it seems he started as a projectionist and his contemporaries remembered him projecting films for the Boer War correspondent Frederick Villiers. In 1908, at the age of 21, he was working for the Williamson Kinematograph Company, employed in the darkrooms, projection studios and becoming familiar "in all branches of the business".[4] His work with Williamson climaxed with a trip to Iceland filming scenic and travel films, but shortly after this Williamson reduced its film work to concentrate on the manufacture of cameras and printers. In February 1910 Harry Sanders joined Pathé as its first British cameraman, filming British scenes and then sending them to Paris to be incorporated in the *Pathé-Journal*, three copies of which were then posted back to London for local distribution. In June 1910 Pathé expanded its business by launching a British newsreel called *Pathé's Animated Gazette*. This was the first British newsreel and Sanders became chief cameraman under the editorship of Val Steer.[5]

HARRY SANDERS GOES TO WAR

At the outbreak of war in 1914 Sanders was one of the many Pathé cameramen despatched to France and Belgium to film the conflict. The military authorities on the continent were grappling with mobilising their forces to meet the speed of the German advance. Censorship restrictions denying cameramen access to the front had yet to be put into effect, so everything depended on the cameramen's initiative. Every newsreel firm wanted film of the fighting, and in those crazy hectic days of October 1914 Sanders found himself in the path of the German advance through Belgium. The *Bioscope* published Sanders' account of those hours:

Close-up of Lieutenant H.A. Sanders, the New Zealand official cameraman, with his driver/assistant and heavily laden jigger with the cameras and gear. Detail, H-Series H81,1/2-012791-G, ATL.

"The Germans are in the Hôtel de Ville!" Such were the words that greeted me on entering the dining room of my hotel in Ghent. The whole place was in confusion indescribable, and for one who, like myself, was carrying a cinematograph camera and British papers, the position was not enviable. It was imperative that I should decide upon some line of action, and that quick. For up to the present the attitude the Germans would take up with regard to Press and cinematographers, unaccredited to the staff and without authority from the official quarters of any of the Allies to take pictures, has not yet been discovered. And to put it frankly, I was not going to be the first one to find out what that attitude might be![6]

Together with R.A. Coulson, a reporter from the *Daily Sketch*, Sanders hurriedly left Ghent by car, heading for Ostend, along with two Belgian soldiers who refused to get off "either for love, money or threats". They ran into German cycle patrols that they passed at speed in some panic, "with the total disregard for brakes, ditches, or humanity that only fear can engender". The fear was made worse by the fact that the car was flying a miniature Union Jack, which they promptly removed, along with a German rifle previously acquired as a souvenir. "When the Belgians … saw these trophies they thought we were the real thing and implored us not to shoot." The car joined the trail of refugees heading for the coast alongside the soldiers of retreating Allied armies. At Ostend there was a "mad struggle through the waiting crowd, a jump from the quay onto the paddle-boxes, and I felt with relief the deck of the homeward steamer under my feet".[7]

This is the sole account we have in Sanders' own words — it would be marvellous to have a similar account of his time with the New Zealanders, but there are no known diaries and only one or two letters of official correspondence that exist.

The freedom of cameramen to travel to the sounds of the guns and seek pictures vanished once the front stabilised and a blanket embargo forced them back to England. Sanders continued to work as Pathé's chief cameraman and it seems he was acting editor for a time. His occupation, and being a married man with three children, delayed his call-up once Britain introduced conscription. Sanders had no ties with New Zealand when he accepted the job of 'official kinematographer' for the New Zealand Division, nor I suspect any inclination to join the New Zealanders other than that Pathé, the firm he worked for, saw it as an opportunity to get films from the front that were presently denied them.

It was a commercial arrangement between the New Zealand Government and Pathé Frères. Pathé hoped for access to films from the front, New Zealand wanted publicity for its war effort, and the agent to achieve this was Harry Sanders, secure in the knowledge that when the job was done and the war finished, a position would be waiting for him back at the firm. In one sense both would be disappointed because the restrictions imposed by the War Office Cinema Committee (WOCC) governed what Sanders could do and what happened to his pictures, and the inevitable delays this caused limited Pathé's use of his film.

ENLISTING IN THE NZEF

Sanders was interviewed and assessed as suitable by the General Officer Commanding New Zealand Expeditionary Force (GOC NZEF) UK, Brigadier-General G.S. Richardson and T.E. Donne; both making positive recommendations to the high commissioner. This was confirmed in a letter on 23 March 1917 but by then Sanders had already been contacted by the military secretary's branch confirming that he would be enlisted as an 'Honorary Lieutenant' in the NZEF "with pay and field allowance according to Military Scale". The New Zealand High Commission would provide all the photographic material and, being a careful government department, it reminded him that: "On the termination of your appointment you are required to return to the High Commissioner all cameras, lenses, and other materials, including unused plates."[8]

Sanders enlisted in March and joined the New Zealand Division on 8 April 1917, remaining with it until January 1919, finally being discharged from the NZEF on 8 March 1919. Before leaving for France to join the New Zealand Division, Sanders was briefed on the procedure "imposed by the War Office" for developing photographs and film:

1. The plates or films will be sent by the Official Photographer to General Headquarters ('I') for development. The Photographer will not be permitted to develop his own plates or films nor to superintend their development.
2. The photographs will be censored at General Headquarters, France, and forwarded to the War Office (M.I.7.a.) who will despatch them direct to the High Commissioner. The photographs will be the absolute property of the New Zealand Government on condition that any profits derived from their sale will be devoted to such war charities as the New Zealand Government may select.

3. The photographs when published will be shown as 'Official Photographs' and the name of the Official Photographer will not appear.

4. The Photographer must be a commissioned officer and unconnected with the Press.[9]

MALCOLM ROSS ON THE WESTERN FRONT

Mackenzie advised Captain Malcolm Ross, the official war correspondent, of Sanders' appointment, "as he will, no doubt, be able to help him in his work for the Dominion."[10] There is no doubt that both Ross and Sanders collaborated with each other. Ross now had permission to cable important news back to New Zealand in addition to sending detailed articles by mail. There had been a steady dispatch of material since his arrival in France in 1916, its limitations were those largely imposed by British military censorship.

Malcolm Ross provided a flow of articles on the doings of the division for the duration of the war. The pro-Liberal publications that supported Sir Joseph Ward continued to deride Ross's despatches and questioned the value for money that the country received from having an official war correspondent.[11]

The problem that Ross faced was the inevitable delay in the publication of his articles other than the brief cable summaries. This was compounded by the stock phrases demanded by British military censorship such as: "splendid effort", "with dash and great gallantry" and "which the infantry had captured so brilliantly".[12] Ross could provide details of the actions and make general attributions, such as 'a Canterbury Battalion', but was forbidden to identify individuals, which would have brought the reports to life. This has coloured the views of New Zealand historians: only Ron Palenski, in his master's dissertation on Malcom Ross, displays the professional balance of one who has been a journalist, editor of a major daily and historian.[13] Ross's articles gave a detailed account of the New Zealand Division's actions that wasn't available from any other source at the time. He described events so that readers knew which units were involved and could identify where loved ones fought. Forbidden to use names, Ross indicated who he was talking about by identifying where they were from, therefore a New Zealand audience would immediately recognise and understand who he was referring to. Ross's articles in the press — also reprinted in the *Chronicles of the N.Z.E.F.* — provided an important and detailed chronology.[14]

SANDERS AT THE FRONT

Sanders arrived at the New Zealand Division's headquarters at Westhof Farm during preparations for the Messines offensive. Captain G. Cory Wright, the intelligence officer, wrote of his arrival at the division and the impression that he made on at least one of Major-General Sir Andrew Russell's headquarters' staff.

> We have now a divisional photographer appointed to us. He is a regular cockney 'tout', not even a New Zealander and never been to New Zealand; and here he is appointed to the softest job in the whole division, given a commission in my regiment the N.Z.E. (honorary) if you please, given a motor car and driver all to himself, and what is worse for me put into my mess and I have to sit next to him at every meal! I often think there must be men in our division in the ranks who could ably fill that job without giving the pick of all soft jobs to an outsider like that.[15]

Cory Wright resented an outsider being given a 'soft job', and also doubted whether a Cockney 'tout' should be commissioned into the New Zealand Engineers. In a sense it is the inevitable suspicion of the newcomer by the veteran, and particularly of one such as a newsreel cameraman who, with his honorary rank, was neither fish nor fowl. We do not know how well Harry Sanders integrated into the life of the division. What we do know is that he was well catered for with a van and driver provided to allow him freedom of movement. This was essential if he was to get round the division and move his equipment. The little van played a ubiquitous part in many of the films that Sanders would take over the next two years. His team grew to accommodate a stills cameraman, as each event was often photographed and filmed simultaneously. One of the early photos that we have shows Sanders standing by the van while the dogcart is loaded with the camera, boxes of film and photo plates by the driver and general handyman, but someone else is taking the photograph, so — right from the start — Sanders had an assistant. A study of the films and photographs shows him to be a non-commissioned officer (NCO), who, like Sanders, acted both as cameraman and stills photographer. We see Sanders the new boy in this photo, he is not wearing his gas mask satchel on his chest and no doubt someone would soon remind him that this was obligatory in the front line area. He is also wearing a mix of clothing, with his officer's cane tucked into the dogcart. In the film industry Sanders was remembered as "a soft mannered man who always wore white socks and his trousers half-mast".[16] Now he had to learn the rules of surviving on the Western Front.

The photo shows the practical difficulties facing a stills photographer/film cameraman on the Western Front. In terms of filming, Sanders' camera seems to have been a standard upright with an external film magazine on top. The film used was 35 mm orthochromatic film, which is sensitive to the blue and green areas of the spectrum. It was less effective in the red area. "Particularly noticeable is the lack of detail in the sky: clouds did not photograph well. The contrast between light and dark areas of the image tend to be stark and there is little gradation of tone in shadows."[17]

The cameraman also faced the difficulty of the empty battlefield — no man's land was just that, a desolate expanse with only the tangle of barbed wire and, perhaps, ruined buildings to provide a context. It was very difficult to capture shell bursts or the movement of men pepper-potting forward, running from shell hole to shell hole with a camera that had to be exposed above the sandbag parapet. The restricted space and amount of kit needed made it difficult to film in the trenches. Most cameras had no viewfinder and keeping the subject in shot depended on experience and skill.

For photographs Sanders generally used a glass-plate camera using 4½ x 6½ inch (114 x 165 mm) half-plate. He can be identified in this role during the visit of Massey and Ward to France in July 1918 where he is clearly visible in his officer's uniform as he walks towards the film camera holding his camera and thinking about whether or not he got the photograph of Massey that he wanted.[18] These cameras were much more portable than the full-plate cameras but were far more fragile and heavier than the film-loaded cameras.[19] However, getting images for the historic record and for distribution to the newspapers demanded photos of the best quality.

The glass plate was a "piece of clear glass coated with a silver nitrate emulsion". These were tightly wrapped in opaque paper and shipped in boxes. "Before a photographer could expose a photograph, he needed to unwrap an exposed plate and load it into a wooden 'plate carrier', which looked like a small picture frame. This had to be done in total darkness. Once in the carrier, an opaque 'slide' was inserted in front of the plate, ensuring that no light could reach it. Black felt at the edge of the plate carrier also minimised the chances of light entering. Twin slide carriers that held a glass plate on either side was common. When setting off for the day, a photographer had to take enough loaded carriers for the photographs he expected to take."[20]

Tripods were mandatory, but if necessary could be dispensed with when using the lighter half-plate cameras. Nevertheless, Sanders' team had to carry the film camera, loaded film boxes, tripod or tripods, half-plate camera, carrier boxes for the half-plates, all loaded with both film in the film boxes and glass plates in the carrier boxes in quantity sufficient for the day's work. Each activity was a two-person job or perhaps in this case, a team of three with the driver co-opted as the workhorse. Getting all this forward into the trenches was a major undertaking.

Today Sanders' name is attributed to the official photographs, but the reality is that it was very much a team effort. It is also evident that both Sanders and his deputy had dual roles: both took photos and both were skilled cameramen. The frustration is that while we know Sanders had his team, we do not know the names of those who worked for him in 1917–18. They remain anonymous. However, the photos and film provide an invaluable record of the New Zealand Division on the Western Front. Even when it proved impossible to film, we have the photographs of the daily life of the division and its involvement in the major battles.

The photographic field notes have not survived, but they were used to caption and date the H-Series when it was mounted in master albums in 1918–19. These master albums provide captions, dates and locations for each photograph. In most cases the names of VIPs and senior officers are provided, but sadly this was not done for the rank and file, so most New Zealand soldiers who appear in the photographs are unknown. However, the fact that the stills and moving cameraman worked as a team recording the same event means that it is usually possible to date and identify the locations of Sanders' surviving film.

THE H-SERIES PHOTOGRAPHS

The NZEF official photographs taken by Sanders' team are known as the H-Series, each being identified by the letter 'H' as a prefix to a number that for the most part ran in a chronological sequence up to H1325. Today it numbers 1260 negatives, some of which are copy negatives of prints made when the glass-plate negative was broken or lost.[21]

The series is the only comprehensive visual record of life in the New Zealand Division on the Western Front. The prohibition on private photography, observed in the breach on Gallipoli and in Sinai-Palestine, was strictly enforced within the British Expeditionary Force (BEF) in France and Belgium, and so we have comparatively few private photo collections of New Zealanders at the front.

The H-Series passed into the Alexander Turnbull Library Collection via the Returned Services Association (RSA) and today is known as the RSA Collection. Each photo is dated and located and provides a chronological working record of Sanders' efforts during his time as official photographer. It is an invaluable photographic record of the division and also serves as the visual diary of Sanders' camera crew.

The final 200 or so images are not in order and some relate back to Messines in 1917. This is because Sanders was not able to develop his own photographs. This was done at General Headquarters (GHQ) BEF, "and those passed by the Censor are released through the War Office to the High Commissioner for New Zealand. Those not released by the Censor are retained at G.H.Q."[22] The censors would not develop photographs of individuals and graves; these and images held back for security reasons were released at the end of the war and were numbered accordingly.

After passing the military censor the first of his photos arrived in London in late May 1917, and were sent on to New Zealand where they were published in the weekly illustrated papers on 23 August 1917.[23] Thirteenth of May 1917 appears to be his first day photographing the division. It was the day of the Divisional Horse Show held near divisional headquarters at

"New Zealand soldiers interested in the official photographer's cine camera which illustrates their daily life for the people at home." The unknown cameraman is Harry Sanders' other half of the camera team with motion picture camera at the New Zealand Reserve and Infantry Base Depot at Etaples, 15 January 1918. H-Series, H415, 1/2-013042-G, ATL, Wellington.

Westhof Farm and visited by Commander-in-Chief General Sir Douglas Haig and Godley, corps commander II ANZAC, with Russell the divisional commander in attendance.[24] It was a day for fun and sports with a 'tote' set up for betting. Sander's photographs showing both the men and the generals looking relaxed and smiling.

This was the start of a regular supply of H-Series images appearing in the illustrated papers. The first of these showed scenes of New Zealand soldiers rehearsing the attack on Messines.. The images of the New Zealanders advancing by platoons in file as they practise the movement forward by night are iconic in that they show Russell's attention to detail in getting things right during his division's preparations for this attack. Sanders' images of the New Zealand Brigade's tactical formations show how much British tactics had developed since the disastrous attacks by the British Army on the Somme on 1 July 1916.

The 'lemon squeezer' is everywhere evident and for the first time from the front the New Zealand public gained a sense of the size and professionalism of their New Zealand Division in France. One of the photos in *The Weekly News* shows the commander, 3rd Rifle Brigade, Brigadier-General 'Harry' Fulton viewing Messines before the attack from Hill 63, which provided the best observation over the approaches that his riflemen would take to the battered village on the ridge.[25] Perhaps the secrecy surrounding these preparations limited the taking of film. We may never know, all we know is that when the battle for Messines began, Sanders went forward determined to film the action. Cory Wright gives grudging acknowledgement to this in his letter.

The pictures will of course be appreciated in N.Z. and you will probably see many more now of our own troops than formerly in the papers. Pictures and photos are very nice when you have no

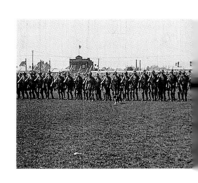

The ruins of Messines under German artillery fire on 8 June 1917, the day after the attack. Sanders went forward intending to film and, as his photos show, was up on the ridge but no film survives. H-Series, H65, 1/2-012776-G, ATL, Wellington.

more serious work on hand but I have had no time to show him round. I sent my batman with him one day. He has a cinema apparatus too and poor old 'Movie' as we call him was up close to the line soon after our last big fight to take photographs and got caught in a shelled area or in a barrage. He had his wits nearly scared away and instead of taking pictures he sat in a shell hole all day. I am inclined to laugh; but it is no joke for the fellow at the time! The point is he should not be there at all just for the pictures![26]

The reality of course was that it was for those very combat 'pictures' that 'Movie' Sanders was there. As he found out, combat was the most difficult aspect of warfare to capture, particularly with the cumbersome equipment of the time. His photographs of Messines show how far forward he got with striking images of the tracks up onto the hill, the wrecked German trenches and bunkers of the front line, and the ruins of the town itself. We have his photographs of the town under German artillery bombardment, but no surviving moving picture film.

The film *The Capture of Messines* was released as a two-reel account of the British victory by the War Office Cinema Committee through Jury's Topical Film Company. It was filmed by the British official cameraman, H.C. Raymond, and tantalisingly shows scenes from Monash's 3rd Australian Division on the New Zealand right, and from the 25th British Division on the New Zealand left flank, and ruins of Messines itself, but no distinctly New Zealand images. Sanders' film of the battle, had it survived, would surely have been included, but it appears not.[27]

No comprehensive list is known of the films that Sanders completed with the New Zealanders in France. We have lists of films that were sent out to New Zealand but all of these films have perished. Twelve almost complete films survive because the negatives of the New Zealand official films were retained by the WOCC and later passed to the Imperial War

Capture of Messines.
IWM Film, IWM 197.

Museum. What survives lack intertitles and when copied on to safety film were doubled up so that we often have two separate films on the one reel. Others may have perished, we simply do not know. One assumes there should be much more for almost two years of filming, but unlike the Australian official cameramen, Hubert Wilkins, and for a brief time Frank Hurley, there are no vivid diary entries nor do we have a series of written accounts similar to his first experience of war recounted for us in the *Bioscope*.[28]

The dates on the H-Series photographs in the master albums provide a diary for Sanders and his team. The photos H15–H52 cover the build-up to the Messines offensive during the period of tactical training in the Lumbres training area and the preparations for battle. The battle itself is recorded in the photographs numbered H53–H67 and H799–H823. These show the heavy artillery firing on Messines before the attack and then scenes from the day after attack itself giving evidence that Sanders was up on the ridge immediately after the position was consolidated. Wounded Germans and New Zealanders are shown making their way down from Messines Ridge. We see the advanced dressing station on the ridge, Messines under German artillery fire and the damaged buildings and concrete bunkers of the German front lines. These have become iconic images in illustrating New Zealand's role in the battle. This pattern was repeated by Sanders for each of the major battles of 1917–18. In each case there is no known film but the photographs provide graphic evidence that Sanders' team moved forward taking pictures in the hours following each attack.

WORK OF THE NEW ZEALAND MEDICAL CORPS

The first of his films were received and passed by the New Zealand censor on 7 November 1917. The titles are not known as they are simply listed as "Government official war films (7000)". Much of Sanders' best filming was not seen by New Zealand audiences until after the war. This is perhaps because although innocuous by today's standards, it was judged too detailed and revealing by military censors. This is the case with the *Work of the New Zealand Medical Corps (NZMC),* which Sanders started to film in late June 1917 immediately after Messines and is the earliest known of his films to have survived.[29]

In many ways it is one of Sanders' best films and has a naturalness lacking in some of the others, where the soldiers ham it up for the camera. Here the fact that badly wounded men have to be attended to limits any sense of artifice. It is a comprehensive look at the casualty evacuation system used in the New Zealand Division at the time of the Messines offensive in June 1917. After the capture of Messines, the New Zealanders were in the line occupying Ploegsteert Wood or 'Plugstreet' as it was known. It was a period of heavy shelling resulting in a steady flow of New Zealand casualties. In the last fortnight of June alone "our casualties were reported to be: 106 killed; 801 wounded. There was an increasing casualty list due to gas poisoning and there were clear signs of nervous exhaustion in many of the sick."[30]

The surviving film lacks intertitles, but Sanders has marked out on the negatives the sequence of scenes to be shown in the cinema. Wounded men were evacuated from the front line by stretcher bearers who carried them along the trench tramways that ran through Ploegsteert Wood and on to the Regimental Aid Post. We see an injured soldier with head wounds carried in at the heavily sandbagged Regimental Aid Post. He is seen by the regimental medical officer who checks his dressings while one of the medics gives him a cigarette. The casualty was then evacuated as quickly as possible, by wheeled stretcher, or 'jigger' as the New Zealanders called them, or by stretcher party or trench tramway, to the Advanced Dressing Station (ADS) at the brewery. At the ADS the wounded were checked and dressed. Serious cases were stabilised before being quickly evacuated by motor ambulance to the Main Dressing

Work of the New Zealand Medical Corps.
NTSV F4310.

Patients moving into the dining hall at No. 3 Field Ambulance at Pont-D'Achelles. A soldier carries his mate who cannot walk because of trench foot. Still from Lt H.A. Sanders' *Work of the New Zealand Medical Corps*. NTSV F4310.

'Diggers' of the New Zealand Division pass their clothes into the steam-cleaner on their way to the bath house. This routine would happen every 8–12 days. Still from Lt H.A. Sanders' *Work of the New Zealand Medical Corps*. NTSV F4310.

Station (MDS), in this case No. 3 Field Ambulance at Pont-D'Achelles. At the MDS casualties were given anti-tetanus shots then examined by surgeons. Serious cases were immediately operated on. The wounded were then evacuated to hospitals in rear.

At the MDS walking wounded continue to arrive while the ambulances bring in stretcher cases. Lightly wounded and sick who will soon recover are held here and the queue for the patients' dining room shows the file of sick and wounded, including one with blackened rotting trench feet being piggy-backed by a mate.

The work of the sanitary section is also shown. Blanket-wrapped men cheerfully hand in their dirty clothes to be steamed in the lorry-mounted Foden thresh chamber as they saunter past the camera into the divisional bathhouse. The machine is a Foden lorry disinfector with two thresh chambers that could each deal with 30 blankets an hour (20 minutes in heating, 20 minutes in steaming and 20 minutes in drying). The process was designed to kill the lice that infected most front-line soldiers and which were responsible for much of the disease and scabies found in the trenches. This was filmed in early September 1917, August being an exceptionally wet month with heavy rains, cold winds and thunderstorms, which swamped Haig's offensive in the Third Battle of Ypres.

It was a miserable wretched month for the New Zealand Division in the Ploegsteert sector with constantly wet trenches that saw an increase in trench feet and sickness. There were also heavy casualties from German shelling. In the first 14 days of August the division suffered 211 killed, 941 wounded and ten missing. On top of this, sickness claimed 1130 casualties. This totalled 2292 soldiers lost to the division, a casualty rate of 20% a month, or about double that recorded for the New Zealanders' first year in France.[31] All of this is captured in crisp detail in Sanders' filming. The filmed images are mirrored in the H-Series photographs covering the period when the New Zealanders were involved in heavy fighting for the villages on the River Lys including the attacks on La Basseville.[32]

What stays in the mind is the scene of off-duty medical staff sitting outside the marquee tents on a summer's day. Their fellow medics are on duty dealing with the wounded and it emphasises that war is a 24-hour business that does not pause. John Singer Sergeant's epic painting *Gassed* in the Imperial War Museum shows the lines of men blinded by mustard gas, sitting waiting in the open air to be treated with bandages over their eyes, while orderlies guide in the next batch of blinded men. In the distance and behind the blinded soldiers in the foreground, one sees men playing soccer. These are off-duty medics enjoying the moment in the sun, knowing that soon enough they will be on duty again. It is that detail, which most people viewing the picture miss or puzzle over, that shows that the painter recognised what Sanders also captured in this film — war never stops and normality, a pause for a smoke or to kick a ball, keeps one sane midst the insanity in a war that in 1917 must have seemed like it would go on forever.

Although no captions survive, we can see the skill with which Sanders shot and edited the film. The film was re-edited by Sanders in 1919 after he returned to Pathé Frères but that version, which came to New Zealand, has been lost. It is a labour of love and Sanders' clever touches are everywhere evident. In later years his peers in the industry regarded Sanders as "undoubtedly the best silent-newsreel editor the profession had known".[33] This is typified by the final and closing scene of motor ambulances arriving with the next batch of New Zealand wounded, while a small party of 'repaired' soldiers, accompanied by the ubiquitous French terrier, march in the opposite direction towards the front line.

It is difficult to understand why the film was not shown, but there is no record of it in the New Zealand Censor records. Nevertheless, the photographs of this period showing scenes at No. 3 Field Ambulance appeared in the illustrated papers in early November 1917.[34]

New Zealand Troops on the March, Inspection by Sir Thomas Mackenzie. NTSV F1070.

VIP VISITS AND PARADES

The first of Sanders' films to be seen in New Zealand are the two he took in September 1917, both of which were 'safe' subjects: the visit of Sir Thomas Mackenzie, the New Zealand high commissioner to London, and the divisional parade for Commander-in-Chief Field Marshal Sir Douglas Haig.

The first of these is of a visit by Sir Thomas Mackenzie to the New Zealand Division on 9–10 September in 1917 while it was in training for the Passchendaele offensive.[35]

The film *New Zealand Troops on the March, Inspection by Sir Thomas Mackenzie* starts with images of a battalion "marching easy". We then see the high commissioner attend the 2nd Otago Battalion church parade together with the divisional commander, Major-General Sir Andrew Russell, and Lieutenant-General Sir Alexander Godley, commanding II ANZAC. There are scenes of the visit to No. 2 Field Ambulance, an inspection of the New Zealand Engineers and an address to 3rd Otago Battalion. Sir 'Tam' "told us truthfully amongst other things, how glad he was that his duties as High Commissioner prevented him from fighting at the front with us".[36] The film also shows Russell inspecting and then addressing the 3rd Auckland Battalion. One can see his meticulous attention to detail. He has the platoon commander accompany him as he inspects each platoon and he would quiz the young officer to ensure that he could give the personal details of each of his men. Malcolm Ross, the official war correspondent, is also present. The final scene shows the VIPs depart with Russell escorting Mackenzie to the leading staff car while his staff run to take their seats. Mr C.J. Wray, Mackenzie's private secretary, is in the rear seat of the second car with Malcolm Ross alongside him. Ross lifts Wray's hat in humorous salute as the car moves off. Sanders' official photographer's van follows on and one can see the silver fern painted below the small side window nearest the camera. This was the identification sign for the New Zealand Division.

It is a cleverly compiled film and captures Mackenzie's keen appreciation of the power of moving pictures. In one of the scenes where he is being introduced to two soldiers of the 2nd Otago, Sir 'Tam' quickly repositions the soldiers so that they do not block the camera's view of his own profile. The divisional commander noted in his diary that: "The whole visit has been successful, fine weather — just enough speechifying but not too much."[37]

Later in the same week on 14 September 1917, Sanders filmed Haig's inspection of the New Zealand Division. Sapper Eric Miller wrote in his diary of the careful preparations the day before, then the early morning start and at:

> 10 a.m., Sir Douglas Haig, accompanied by Winston Churchill, who was attired in civilian riding kit, various aides-de-camp, and a bodyguard of lancers, rode along in front of the battalions, having a few words with each major and colonel. After this there was a grand march past in company column. When passing the saluting base, all eyes seemed fixed, not on the Commander-in-Chief, but on a French staff officer, rigged out in all the colours of the rainbow, and wearing a monocle. D'Artagnan at a fête was dull compared with this bird of paradise. Immediately after the last official photograph had been taken, we set off for home. Our O.C., having had speech with the great General, was exceedingly pleased, and granted us the rest of the afternoon off.[38]

The natural groans from most soldiers at the thought of a parade were dampened by the experience. Private N.M. Ingram wrote in his diary:

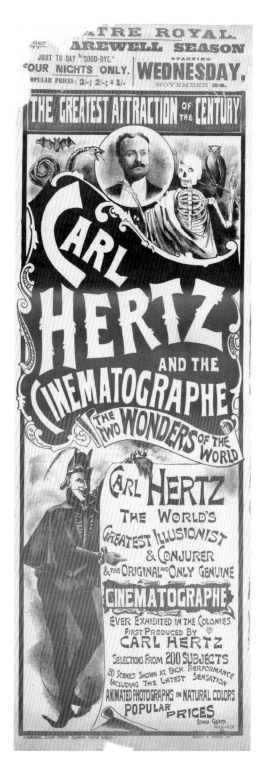

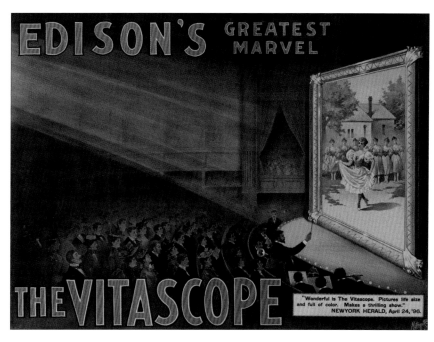

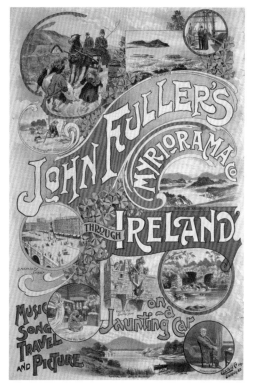

Advertisment for Thomas Alva Edison's Vitascope. Metropolitan Print Company/Library of Congress, Washington, D.C. (LC-DIG-ppsmca-05943).

Poster advertising Carl Hertz and the cinematographe — the two wonders of the world at the Theatre Royal, Hobart, Tasmania, in November 1897. A similar programme was performed in New Zealand. Tasmanian Archive and Heritage Office.

Poster from John Fuller's Myriorama Co., which toured New Zealand in the 1890s and early 20th century with a programme of music, song and entertainment illustrated by magic lantern slides. In this example the theme is 'Through Ireland on a Jaunting Car'. Toitu Otago Settlers Museum, Dunedin.

Still from Edwin S. Porter's
The Great Train Robbery.
Part of a Salvation Army
programme, the film is
a morality tale of good
triumphing over evil.
Library of Congress.

Glass plate lantern slide.
Soldiers of the Cross
was specially scripted by
Herbert Booth with musical
arrangements for choir and
orchestra. Illustrated with film
and lantern slides, it caused
a sensation when narrated by
Booth on his Commandant's
tour to New Zealand in May
and June 1901. The Salvation
Army New Zealand, Fiji & Tonga
Heritage Centre & Archives.

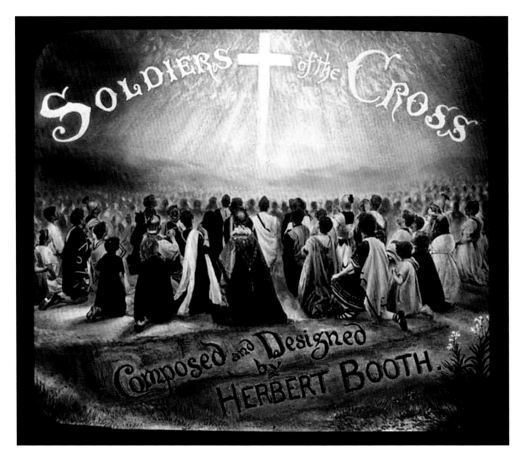

One-armed Boer War veteran
at the medal presentation in
the Octagon, Dunedin on
26 June 1901. Still from Joseph
Perry's *Royal Visit of the Duke
and Duchess of Cornwall
and York to New Zealand*.
NTSV F2468.

Fijians prepare the bed of
hot stones for the firewalkers.
Still from John Henry Brown's
Fiji and the South Seas.
NTSV F7430.

Still showing intertitle
from James McDonald's
*Departure of the British
Antarctic Expedition from
Lyttelton, N.Z., 1st Jan 1908.*
NTSV F8202.

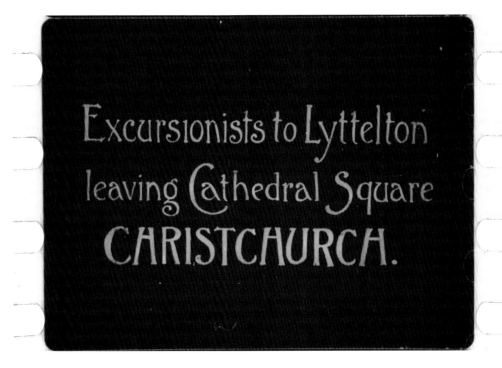

Hand-coloured still of
Charles Newham's *Main
Trunk Express Smash.*
NTSV F4917.

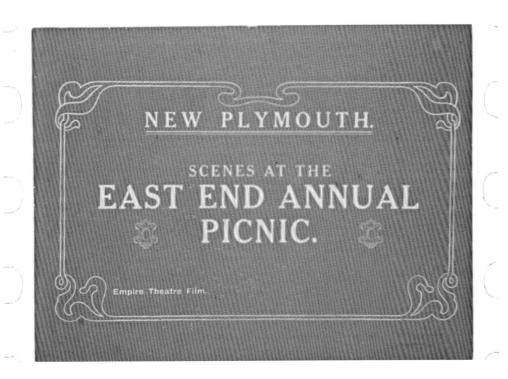

Title still from *Scenes at the East End Annual Picnic*, filmed by Brandon Haughton for the Empire Theatre. NTSV F2655.

Chewing gum race. Still from Brandon Haughton's *Scenes at the East End Annual Picnic*, 1912. NTSV F2655.

A still of the title sequence of W. Franklyn Barrett's *Coasts of New Zealand*. NTSV F41776.

George Tarr's *Hinemoa*, a multi-reel film that opened at the Lyric Theatre, Auckland, on Monday 17 August 1914 in the second week of the war. NTSV.

Tourists in Milford Sound with Mitre Peak in the background. Still from W. Franklyn Barrett's *Coasts of New Zealand*. NTSV F41776.

Still of 'Pelorus Jack' leading the steamer SS *Pateena* through the waters of French Pass. *Coasts of New Zealand*. NTSV F41776.

The Newman's stage coach passes through the gold-mining settlement of Lyell on the Buller River. Still from W. Franklyn Barrett's *Across the Mountain Passes of New Zealand*. NTSV F10078.

Barrie Marschel's 15-minute film *The Kid from Timaru*. Marschel acted as raconteur and recited his story in verse at each performance. Eph-A-CINEMA-1918-01, ATL, Wellington.

Killing the whale. Still from Sydney Taylor's *New Zealand Whale Hunting with Motor Launches in Cook Strait*. NTSV F880.

The review is over! Now that it is a thing of the past I think everyone is glad that they participated in it. It was a grand, brilliant and inspiring sight and will live long in my memory. Never have I seen so many men mustered on parade together at one time. It was a heavy day for us and the march to the parade ground was a long one, by the time we had arrived back to our billets we had been on our feet for 12 hours … It was a brilliant sunny day and when the order 'Present Arms' was given it was a wonderful sight to see the thousands of bayonets flash brilliantly in the rays of the sun … No one likes the parade ground stuff and the sooner it is over the better we are pleased, but to see the whole of the Division on parade at one time and place was well worth the bother."[39]

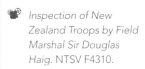

Inspection of New Zealand Troops by Field Marshal Sir Douglas Haig. NTSV F4310.

The *Inspection of New Zealand Troops by Field Marshal Sir Douglas Haig* is not one of Sanders' better films. Yet it captures the size of the division as it marches past Haig on horseback with Minister of Munitions Winston Churchill dressed in tweeds, slumped in the saddle, looking a little like a sack of potatoes, riding alongside him.[40] Haig was pleased with what he saw and wrote in his diary, "The 1st, 2nd and 4th Brigades were on parade. The men were well turned out and handled their arms smartly. They are a study, thick set type of man. After my inspection, the troops marched past by platoons. A very fine show in fine style. Mr Winston Churchill accompanied me and seemed much impressed."[41]

The film arrived in New Zealand in April 1918 and was released for public distribution along with *New Zealand Battalion on the March.*

NEW ZEALAND BATTALION ON THE MARCH

This short film *New Zealand Battalion on the March* survives in an amalgamation of scenes mixed in with another film. It shows scenes of soldiers of the 3rd Brigade on the march. We see a battalion marching through a village, it attracts the interest of the villagers, one or two women come to the doors and look out and the children are attracted to the camera. The soldiers themselves have come out of the trenches and are marching to a rest area. They are tired and it shows. They march in full kit and steel helmets and some respond to the presence of the camera. It is an unvarnished look at a battalion after a hard stint in the trenches. It is interspersed with scenes of another battalion marching along a country road. The band leads the way and it is evident that they have been marching for some time, the officers lead their horses on foot and we can see how much road a battalion takes up with its four infantry companies, each some 220-strong. The distance that a battalion should take up in road space had been carefully calculated. An infantry battalion marching in column of fours as we see here should take up 780 yards (713 metres), an infantry brigade of four battalions 3295 yards (3013 metres), and an infantry division on the march 15½ miles or some 25 kilometres.[42]

The New Zealand Division was organised into three brigades, each of four battalions, and at the time this film was taken in 1917 a fourth brigade had been raised, making the division potentially the strongest in the British Army. One of the four brigades was always detached on other duties, such as cable-laying or trench digging. Russell strongly disliked having this fourth brigade as it made his division the odd one out and he believed the detached brigade suffered by being used on tasks that interfered with its training and preparation for battle.

We have no film of the October 1917 battles but we know Sanders and his team of cameramen were forward: the H-Series photographs are evidence of that. There are images from the New Zealand attack on 4 October 1917 in the Battle of Broodseinde, which is the first time that both Birdwood's I ANZAC and Godley's II ANZAC attacked side by side. It was an outstanding success with the New Zealanders securing the Heights of Abraham on the eastern

side of Gravenstafel Ridge. There are photographs of the division moving into the line, of the German bunkers and of the first German prisoners coming in. We see the New Zealanders move forward into the line for the renewed attack on 11 October and the aftermath of the failed attack in the first battle for Passchendaele on 12 October 1917 — New Zealand's 'Blackest Day' of battle.

Eight hundred and forty two New Zealanders are officially counted as having died on 12 October 1917 with another 2000 wounded or taken prisoner. The October battles cost the division 6000 casualties, including at least 1900 dead.[43] The photographs show the reality that we do not have on film.[44] This and the conditions faced by the shattered New Zealand Division when it wintered in the desolation of the Ypres Salient came close to breaking the spirit of the New Zealanders.

In December 1917 Sanders and his team were detached to the New Zealand Tunnelling Company stationed in Arras. There are photographs showing the tunnellers underground. However, their underground city under Arras that was prepared for the April 1917 offensive had been closed down after the battle and stripped of much of its timber and fittings. There are one or two images but little else to give an effective impression of this work. A film was taken of the destruction of salvaged ammunition to represent a mine explosion, but this has not survived.[45]

THE NEW ZEALAND FIELD ARTILLERY IN FRANCE

Sanders returned to the New Zealand Division on 30 December 1917 and immediately began filming the New Zealand Field Artillery in action in the Salient. There are two existing films of the New Zealand Field Artillery in this period, both survive as an amalgamation of negatives with other films.[46] However, Sanders planned it as a single film of *The New Zealand Field Artillery in France* similar to his film of the New Zealand Medical Corps. He marked the sequence of shots on the negatives and so it is possible to see his intention to provide a comprehensive look at all aspects of the work of the guns: from the horse lines to the guns in action on the gun-line responding to directions telephoned by the gunnery observation officer forward in the front line.

The horses of a New Zealand artillery battery are seen watering at a river. They are magnificent animals in prime condition and their riders lead them back through the muddy fields to the battery horse lines. In this sequence the horses are the stars. Each field artillery battery had 122 horses. A New Zealand Field Artillery Brigade with its mix of three 18-pounder batteries and one 4.5-inch howitzer battery had 198 riding horses, 548 draught horses and two heavy draught horses. The Divisional Ammunition Column to support the field artillery brigades had 56 riding horses, 625 draught horses and 28 heavy draught horses. Despite increased mechanisation, this was a horse-drawn army, and we get a glimpse of this here.[47]

A bugler prepares to blow the lunch time call, but his horse will not wait for the camera and butts him in his keenness to be fed. Once the feed bags are attached the horses attack them with gusto. The gunners depart for lunch and Sanders' final shot in this sequence is that of the bugle hanging from the tethering line alongside the bugler's horse. It is clever cinema.

This is followed by a gunner officer emerging from a sandbagged command post and directing fire using a megaphone. An 18-pounder gun team goes into action, loads and opens fire. There is a close-up of the No. 1 of the gun team adjusting the sights as the gun fires. A forward observation officer directs fire from behind a battered bunker to his signaller using a field telephone. A soldier emerges from a pillbox near the front line and fires a rifle grenade attached to the end of his rifle. The recoil knocks his shrapnel helmet off, and he looks stupidly

The New Zealand Field Artillery in France; New Zealand Rifle Brigade on the March. NTSV F4340.

Watering the horses for an artillery battery. The horses are the stars of this film and as the scene with the bugler in the film indicates, they were well aware of their worth. Still from *New Zealand Field Artillery in France, New Zealand Rifle Brigade on the March*. NTSV F4340.

A New Zealand Field Artillery battery of 18-pounder field guns firing at intense rate at Birr Crossroads alongside the Menin Road in the Ypres Salient over Christmas 1917. Still from *New Zealand Field Artillery in France, New Zealand Rifle Brigade on the March*. NTSV 4340.

at the camera as he realises that he almost killed himself, and then, leaving his rifle outside, sheepishly goes inside.

A scene of gunners being issued Christmas parcels by the YMCA devolves into farce as the men try and extract the Christmas pudding from its tin, all done in frenetic haste for the camera. The film ends with an extended sequence of two of the battery's 18-pounder guns firing at an intense rate — that is flat out. It is at Birr Crossroads, alongside the Menin Road leading from Ypres towards Hooge Crater, which is the New Zealand front line. Infantry pass by in the background, oblivious of the guns firing. One feels the cold as the steady barrage continues. The gun teams are really working hard and it gives a very good impression of the work involved. One can imagine the gunners doing this for hours on end, firing hundreds of rounds, as was the case in the fire plan for each major attack.

There are similar scenes on a second film that are now interspersed with a film of the New Zealand and Reserve Base Depot at Étaples. A 4.5-inch howitzer of a forward New Zealand battery on the Menin Road near Westhoek in the Ypres Salient is shown to cease firing, then the gun crew covers it with white camouflage tarpaulin and a scrim net. The gunners open tinned Christmas cakes and puddings and pass around cigarettes. Once again one is conscious of the bleak openness of the landscape carpeted in snow.

VISIT TO THE NEW ZEALAND INFANTRY BASE DEPOT AT ÉTAPLES

In late January 1918 Sanders visited the New Zealand Infantry and Reserve Base Depot at Étaples and filmed the camp. It was initially issued under the title *Visit to the Infantry Base Depot at Étaples 1918.* Each British Corps and Dominion force had a reinforcement depot at Étaples where they received reinforcements sent over from the training camps in the United Kingdom. The men were given a brief update on current methods being used on the Western Front while holding them until they were called forward to their divisions. The base also housed 16 large British and Dominion hospitals and convalescent camps covering hundreds of acres. Training was conducted on the coastal flats and sand dunes by subject in rotation in what became known as the 'Bull Ring' system. Instruction was carried out by NCO instructors identified by yellow arm bands and who were known as 'Canaries'. Both the 'Bull Ring' and the 'Canaries' were universally hated.[48]

The first scene is double-exposed and shows cookhouse fatigues and a squad of soldiers marching at the New Zealand Depot at Étaples. The New Zealand commandant, Lieutenant-Colonel G. 'Hoppy' Mitchell, escorting the British Base commandant inspects a reinforcement draft in full kit. 'Hoppy' Mitchell, who got his nickname from his Gallipoli wound, invariably in addressing the troops would "explain[ed] that there were six reasons why he was not anxious to take a trip up the line himself, namely, a wife and five children".[49]

Boots are inspected and a soldier with a hole in his hob-nailed 'Bill Massey' boots is sent off to have them repaired or replaced. The camp with its tents and training shelters can be seen in the background. Many of the tents are camouflaged as German aircraft conducted regular night bombing raids. On the end wall of the nearest training shelter can be seen a set of soldier's webbing and equipment laid out as an example of how it was to be put together and worn.

The men shoulder arms and march off to entrain for the front. A bugler sounds a bugle call with the New Zealand Depot accommodation tents and cookhouse as background, and a flag is raised, the film cutting off halfway through the ceremony. The final scene is of soldiers practising Swedish drill. On film the base comes across as a cold soulless place, with snow on the ground. The 'Bull Ring' at Étaples was the final stage in a New Zealand soldier's journey before he joined the division. While overwhelming for the new arrival, it was endured by the returning convalescent who had done it all before. Private Linus Ryan, NZMC, formerly a railway cadet in Christchurch, was shipped to France on 20 June 1917. He recorded:

Next day was a Field Day and a mighty tiring one to wit. We paraded at 7.30 a.m. in Battle Order and our rations for the day were doled out to us. We each carried our small piece of bread and cheese and a tin of bully beef was apportioned to each four men … We passed by many of the so-called "Bull Rings" where troops of various kinds were busily training. A Bull Ring be it known, is the name given by soldiers to an area set aside for training, where conditions approximate as near as possible to the real thing, trenches, listening posts, barbed wire entanglements and so on. Here was given the final polish up to all the training that had gone on before. And so strenuous was the training that night after night the Infantry returned to camp absolutely exhausted.[50]

The sequence of films continues, looking at each aspect of the New Zealand Division in France. It would be interesting to know the schedule for this because the speed of events of 1918 saw no filming by Sanders at the front, other than the visit of the prime minister and Sir Joseph Ward in the rest period in July 1918.

THE SIAMESE TWINS AT THE FRONT

On 30 January 1918 a film of Prime Minister William Massey and his deputy Sir Joseph Ward visiting the New Zealanders at the front was passed by the New Zealand censor. This was a film of the visit to France in November 1916 where they visited the Somme battlefield. They then spent some time with the New Zealand Division that had now returned to the Armentières sector in northern France, speaking to many units and individuals. They met with Commander-in-Chief General Sir Douglas Haig who expressed his satisfaction at the New Zealand Division's performance on the Somme. The visit featured in the New Zealand press with detailed reports of the trip and photographs in the illustrated papers.[51] It was considered important enough for Malcolm Ross to be allowed to cable the daily details to New Zealand and follow it up with a more detailed account by mail.[52]

It was during the trip that "Mr Massey at his own request, made a flight in an aeroplane with an army pilot, an experience which Sir Joseph Ward enjoyed on his previous visit to England some years ago."[53] All of this featured on film, but the reception by New Zealand audiences was not quite what the politicians imagined. The *New Zealand Times* reported:

> MINISTERS in "MOVIES" A picture showing the visit made by Mr. Massey and Sir Joseph Ward to the Western front was screened at a local picture show on Saturday and roused as much laughter as would a Keystone comedy. This seems strange, but anyone gifted with a sense of humour who sees the picture must help to swell the volume of laughter that accompanies its showing. The two leaders are seen arriving by motor car; it is pouring rain, and in his hurry to don his overcoat Mr. Massey has his hat knocked off. Naturally this sets the audience laughing from the start. Then there are various undignified stumblings in the mud of the trenches, the spectacle of the Prime Minister emerging hatless and dishevelled from a dug-out, and through it all the party hurries on as though pursued. Mr Massey is seen donning the overalls preparatory to going aloft in an aeroplane. The spectacle of Mr. Massey in this exceedingly ill-fitted garb arouses shrieks of laughter. Then when the aeroplane returns Mr. Massey becomes entangled in the wirework of the machine, but not a whit disturbed he is seen running along to Sir Joseph to tell him "how he felt." Then, finally, for the edification of the camera man, Sir Joseph Ward assumes the airman's helmet, and cuts such a ludicrous figure that the shout of laughter which follows would do credit to a Charlie Chaplin picture.[54]

The staff of the *NZ Truth* followed up on the story only to find that its distributor, New Zealand Picture Supplies, had withdrawn the film from exhibition. No copy survives, what we have is Massey and Ward's arrival in France in a French newsreel and photos in the New Zealand illustrated weeklies, none of which convey the sense of enjoyment that the audience gained from the screening.[55]

Both politicians were constantly appearing on screen. In January 1918 the New Zealand censors' records show them featuring in this film, plus that of the king inspecting New Zealand troops on Salisbury Plain and Sir Joseph Ward inspecting a parade of the Boy's Brigade in Glasgow.[56]

MASSEY AND WARD VISIT THE FRONT IN 1918

In 1918 there were criticisms, both in the division and at home, concerning the pair making yet another visit to the Western Front. It was a five-day gruelling schedule from 30 June–4 July 1918, which shows as both men are seen to visibly wilt at the pace being set. Malcolm Ross reported that they had:

> an extraordinarily busy time while with the New Zealand Forces. From morning till night their little fleet of cars carried them over country roads, and unit after unit was inspected and addressed. The great desire of Mr Massey and Sir Joseph Ward seemed to be to see as many men as possible, and by the close of the tour they will have seen almost all the New Zealanders. In addition to seeing infantry, artillery, and other units on parade in considerable masses, they went out of their way to visit smaller units and even permitted many personal interviews, renewing acquaintanceships and listening to individual requests.[57]

This is the last surviving film taken by Sanders and his team of the New Zealand Division before the Armistice in 1918.[58] Massey and Ward are seen with the acting divisional commander, Brigadier-General F.N. Johnston (Major-General Russell was on sick leave in England), and accompanied by Brigadier-General G.S. Richardson, General Officer Commanding NZEF UK.[59]

The surviving film is notable for its length as well as showing a number of memorable moments. There is a marvellous scene of Sir Joseph Ward smoking a cigar with the Maori soldier Hemi. Viewers see the earnestness of the personal interviews with both VIPs and the contrasting approaches taken by Massey and Ward. The detailed visit to all of the units effectively illustrates the size of the New Zealand Division, the faces of its men and its obvious professionalism. The film also captures the healthy cynicism of the New Zealand 'Diggers' to the politicians, illustrated

The New Zealand prime minister harangues the troops from the back of a wagon while Captain Harry Sanders (standing on left with camera) acts as stills photographer. Still from *Visit of the Hon. W.H. Massey and Sir J. Ward to the Western Front 30 June–4 July 1918.* NTSV F1068.

Visit of the Hon. W.H. Massey and Sir J. Ward to Western Front 30 June–4 July 1918. NTSV F1068.

by their lukewarm response to calls for three cheers. Notice also the number who smoke, and the number of times the stills cameraman, in this case Captain Harry Sanders looking exceptionally neat in his service dress and lemon squeezer, is caught by the cinema camera.

This was the New Zealand Division after it had held the line on the Somme in March–April 1918 and during its final spell of reorganisation and training before its outstanding performance in the advance of August to November 1918. These are scenes showing what was the strongest and perhaps one of the most professional divisions in the British armies on the Western Front. The only time New Zealanders at home would see this achievement would be on film in the picture palaces.

There are many soldier impressions of the visit; Douglas Knight wrote to his mother:

Massey talks to the New Zealand Tunnelling Company while Harry Sanders takes the photograph that captures his motion picture cameraman in the frame. H-Series H753, 1/2-013355-G, ATL, Wellington.

We, our Brigade, had Church service this morning & it was very poor as far as our singing went … Band played awfully slow too to make matters worse. We were all formed up & Bill & Joe came along in their "civies" & personally I admired old Bill's walk & carriage. Just like a soldier striding forward to meet a great ordeal in a way. Head up & shoulders squared & be 60 odd. Truly he had an ordeal for no one raised so much as a cheer or a smile & as many had skitingly declared they would shoot him & all the rest. Of course all talk but showing the popularity that he & Joe enjoy. Well after the service concluded with the National Anthem, the first part of which Bill kept his hat on, much to our amusement. I expect he got the tip from Joe. He spoke a few words wishing us all the luck etc. & a safe and speedy return after defeating the Hun by giving them a good drubbing & cited as a further incentive the fact of the mine fields off the coast & that two fine boats had already been lost. We smiled for to us to know two fine boats were lost was nothing. We are used to hearing of the loss of twenty two & more sometimes. He was very sorry & touched that we should find cause for merriment in the sad loss for not only did none of the ships sink in 15 min but twenty six valuable lives were lost. We were sorry to have caused him to think us heartless but as you will recognise, what do even twenty six less worry us when thousands die every day all around us & are almost forgotten next day. You see we hold & count life cheap here. We must do or we could not "carry on".[60]

There was a great deal of bitterness among the veterans in the ranks at the abandonment of a furlough scheme for long-serving soldiers to return to New Zealand. This had been cancelled at the request of British authorities in late 1917 and both Massey and Ward bore the backlash in their less than warm reception on this visit.

Sir Joseph Ward offers one of his cigars to Hemi, a soldier in the New Zealand (Maori) Pioneer Battalion. Still from *Visit of the Hon. W.H. Massey and Sir J. Ward to the Western Front 30 June–4 July 1918*. NTSV F1068.

COLONIAL PRESSMEN

There was a visit by five members of the New Zealand Newspapers Proprietors Association to the Western Front in September 1918. This was coordinated by the Ministry of Information, but the visit to the New Zealand Division on 4 September was coordinated by Captain Malcolm Ross, the official war correspondent, with a photographer present. George Fenwick of the *Otago Daily Times* led the delegation and published a detailed account of the visit. They had been welcomed and briefed by Russell, the divisional commander, and had moved forward of the village of Bertincourt, which had been taken by the New Zealanders that morning. "We took our positions beside of a small group of our men in an observation post … Well within the war zone — indeed, close to the actual firing line — it seemed an extraordinary thing that our party of civilians should have the good fortune to arrive there at a junction of affairs which enabled them to stand on ground that had been left by the opposing forces only a few hours previously."[61] There is a sequence of photographs in the H-Series, and the visit was filmed by a British official cameraman. The Australian official correspondent, Captain C.E.W. Bean, is prominent in his slouch hat, but there are no scenes of the visit to the New Zealand Division.[62]

RUGBY IN FRANCE

Rugby was an integral part of a New Zealand soldier's life, both in training in New Zealand and also in Egypt before Gallipoli. This continued in France with impromptu games within units or inter-company competitions. Training weeks were invariably programmed with tactical training in the morning and sports in the afternoons. After the New Zealand Division returned to the Armentières sector in October 1916, Russell placed great emphasis on sport and fitness in a general programme to improve the morale of the division after its Somme experience. This was part of a wide-ranging programme that included improvements to catering standards, accommodation, provision of entertainment and cinema shows, with leave entitlements increased to the United Kingdom, but also provision for three days in Paris.[63] Plugge, removed from command of 1 Auckland Battalion, was promoted acting colonel and appointed as divisional sports coordinator. It was a job at which he excelled. A divisional rugby team was formed. Players were selected from throughout the division and were grouped at the divisional training school. "Representatives will live at the School, and, in addition to being trained as a football team, will receive instruction in Bayonet Fighting, Physical Drill and Bombing. They will be returned to their units at the end of the football season, qualified instructors in these subjects."[64] The New Zealand Divisional All Blacks embarked on a series of games with neighbouring divisions. They played nine games, scoring 372 points to nine against. Their closest encounter was the hard-fought game against the 38th (Welsh Division), which they won 3–0. It was the second time they had met and beaten the Welsh.

It was the first of these games that was filmed in March 1917 by a British official cameraman during the visit to the division of Sir Walter Long, the secretary of state for colonial affairs, detailed in the previous chapter. It was planned that the team would visit the United Kingdom for a fortnight and play four games. This included the unbeaten British Army Service Corps (ASC) team who had defeated all-comers including the New Zealand sides drawn from the training and convalescent camps. It would play the New Zealand Command Team (Sling Camp) drawn from the best New Zealand players in the United Kingdom, a public schools services team and it was also hoped that they would play a Welsh national side. Victory would avenge the defeat of Dave Gallaher's 'Originals' at Cardiff Arms Park in 1905. However, the war intervened and instead they went to Paris to play against a French military selection.

MATCH DE RUGBY: FRANCE — NOUVELLE ZÉLANDE, 1917

The game was played at Vincennes on 8 April 1917 in front of an estimated crowd of 75,000. The New Zealand team arrived a couple of days earlier and spent their time sightseeing and visiting the ground. The French team was assembled straight from the trenches. Their captain was French aviator Maurice Jean-Paul Boyau who would become one of the leading French aces of the First World War with 21 barrage balloons and 14 aircraft to his credit. Before the war he had captained France against Ireland. He was reported missing on 16 September 1918. The game was filmed by a French cameraman and a copy survives in the French Military Archives.[65]

This is the first of three films that survive showing the New Zealand trench 'All Blacks' playing French selections in the First World War. It opens with views of both teams, the French very smart in the kepi headdress while the New Zealanders seem a little more relaxed smiling and throwing the ball around. Colonel Plugge is seen alongside sapper George Murray, the team captain.

There are marvellous scenes of the packed stadium and the arrival of the VIP guests including the Duke of Connaught along with French ministers. The New Zealand flag is raised in the stadium before an expectant crowd. Captain Roger Dansey of the Pioneer Battalion, in service dress and Sam Browne belt, faces the stadium and leads the team in the haka, "Ka mate Ka mate". The French team formally march on, salute the VIPs and the game begins. The New Zealanders won 40–0.

The French team captain and aviator Maurice Jean-Paul Boyau with the ball, about to be tackled by Reg Taylor, a 1913 All Black. Both would be killed in the war, Boyau in September 1918 and Taylor at Messines in June 1917. Bibliothèque nationale de France, Agence Rol 49130.

The *New Zealand Free Lance* published a series of photographs and a letter from one of the players.

> The game need not be described, although it was not the easy run-over the score denotes, as at the end of the first spell the score was only 11–0. The French team had not played together once and were straight from the line whereas our people had played quite a lot. The star on our side was George Murray, who played a most open and brilliant game, and was the hero of the day … Our tries were scored by Murray (3), and about every back scored one. Ryan did some excellent kicking and played a good game. "Ranji," [Wilson] of course and [Tom] French played well among the forwards.[66]

There was great celebration that night. "The French people gave us a ripping time and we all thought that the war was over, as it was never spoken about — perhaps on account of our very small knowledge of French, but we all managed to get through it by our various actions (which was a considerable lifting of the right elbow)."[67] The French presented the New Zealand captain George Murray with a piece depicting a French soldier in the act of throwing a grenade by the noted sculptor, Georges Chauvel. It was titled *Le Lanceur de Granades* but was immediately dubbed the 'coupe de la Somme' and the Somme Cup it became.[68]

The team played one more game before returning to war. It was the last game for some; Reg Taylor, the 1913 All Black, would be killed in action after Messines and Tom French would be badly wounded in the October 1917 battles before Passchendaele.

Although long retired from playing it was on 4 October 1917 at the Battle of Broodseinde that Sergeant Dave Gallaher, former captain of the 1905–06 'Originals', was mortally wounded. He was evacuated from the battlefield to the 3rd Australian casualty clearing station at Poperinge and died there. He is buried at Nine Elms British Cemetery.

 *Match de Rugby: France — Nouvelle Zélande.* NTSV F253654.

Captain Roger Dansey of the New Zealand Pioneer Battalion leads the Divisional All Blacks in the "danse des néo-zélandais". The game, against a French military selection, was played at Vincennes on 8 April 1917 with New Zealand winning 40–0. The trophy awarded by the French became the 'Somme Cup'. Still from *Match de Rugby: France — Nouvelle Zélande*. Bibliothèque nationale de France, Agence Rol 49123.

THE NEW ZEALAND DIVISIONAL RUGBY TEAM, 1918

In February 1918 the Divisional All Blacks were reformed. They played the 38th (Welsh) Division team on 12 February, winning 14–3, in preparation for a game against a French Army team in Paris, at Parc de Princes, on 17 February 1918. This film shows snippets of the match as well as the team sightseeing in Paris as they toured points of interest by charabanc leading up to the game, including the Bois de Boulogne, Arc de Triomphe and Les Invalides on 16 February and the Palace of Versailles on 18 February. It was Sanders' first of two films in 1918 of the trench 'All Blacks'.[69]

An American army officer chosen for his neutrality, Lieutenant A.S. Muhr, refereed the match but forgot how long the game should go for: 30 minutes was played in the first half, 45 for the second. The match was won by New Zealand 5–3 and "[i]t was a case of a magnificent team of athletes [France] playing a half-trained team of footballers [New Zealand]... It was a lucky New Zealand win."[70]

The film opens with a Paris street scene showing the New Zealand team getting into a horsed charabanc outside the Hôtel de Paris for a tour of the sights of the city. After driving through the Bois de Boulogne the team inspect captured war trophies at Les Invalides in a scene where cameraman Harry Sanders has obviously thought out his angles. It cuts to the visit to the Palace of Versailles where everyone in the team puffs away on cigarettes or pipes as they tour the sights.

The film footage of the match at Parc de Princes shows the difficulties of filming a rugby match with a single camera from the sidelines, but the shots of the crowd and of the two teams taking the field capture much of the atmosphere of the occasion as well as the spirit of the two teams. Compare the dour look of the New Zealanders with the French, who walk on brimming with Gallic insouciance, coats still worn or draped over their shoulders. A drunken New Zealand soldier and his Australian counterpart attempt to weave out behind the New Zealand

New Zealand Divisional Rugby Team. NTSV F4332.

team. Sapper George Murray and vice-captain N.A. 'Ranji' Wilson lead the team on to the field; the young woman kicking off is Violet Russell, daughter of Major-General Sir Andrew Russell while 'Ranji' Wilson looks on in bemusement. One senses from the action that this is a tight, hard-fought game. After a scoreless first half, the French scored and took the lead until the last minute of the game when gunner Norman Carnegie scored and was converted, allowing the New Zealanders to squeak home. The film closes with the charabanc driving past the Arc de Triomphe.

The result was widely reported in newspapers who were full of praise for the French performance. The *Evening Standard* wrote:

> No football match played in Paris created greater interest than that between soldiers of New Zealand and French Armies. New Zealand was represented by a team considered by all equal to any Colonial pre-war team, although less trained; but the French fifteen, which included nine aviators, three tank officers, and two second-lieutenants escaped from Germany recently, played better and faster than any pre-war national team. Play was even in the first half, and in the second France kept the direction of the game until the last five minutes.[71]

The New Zealand Division had wintered in Ypres Salient over Christmas 1917 and by March 1918, after a period in reserve, Russell's New Zealanders were at full strength and trained in open warfare tactics. On 23 March the division was rushed forward to fill a dangerous gap on the line of the River Ancre between the British IV and V Corps. The ad hoc New Zealand formations held the German attacks on their front in the critical days of late March and early April 1918. Then, as part of the British IV Corps, Russell's division held the line from April to August 1918, rotating his battalions out of the line for training in mobile warfare. This was supported by artillery batteries who practised leap-frogging forward to maintain fire support as the infantry practised the advance and attack. All this in preparation for the 'counter-offensive' that Russell was sure would come.[72] The H-Series photographs capture all aspects of life and fighting in 1918, but once again we have no film of the division in action over this period.[72]

SEEING THE SIGHTS OF PARIS BEFORE FOOTBALL MATCH, 1918

The successful advance by the British Armies from August 1918 saw rugby again feature on the calendar. *Seeing the Sights of Paris before Football Match* shows scenes from the last tour of France during the First World War by the NZ Divisional All Blacks team before it left for England where it played the NZEF UK All Blacks. The best of both teams were then combined in a NZEF team, which toured the United Kingdom and competed and won the King's Cup at Twickenham in 1919.[74]

The party of 20 members left New Zealand divisional headquarters at Beauvois on 23 October 1918 and arrived in Paris two days later. In Paris the party toured the sights of the city. The match itself was played on 27 October at Parc de Princes "which had been elaborately laid out, the match being the opening of the Great French War Loan".[75]

The New Zealanders won 14–3, but the *Chronicles of the NZEF* reported that:

> as an exhibition of rugby, nothing can be said in its favour, this being due entirely to the different interpretation placed on the rules of the game, and not to lack of ability of the teams. The game can be correctly described as a succession of scrums and quite seventy percent of them were the result of alleged breaches of the 'knock on' rule by the French referees is certainly remarkable.

Seeing Sights of Paris before Football Match. NTSV F4517.

A young Maori corporal of the New Zealand Maori Pioneer Battalion leads the New Zealand Divisional "All Blacks" in the haka, while his mate holds his 'lemon squeezer'. The game was held against a French Army selection at at Parc de Princes, Paris, on 27 October 1918. The New Zealanders won 14–3. Still from *Seeing the Sights of Paris before Football Match*, NTSV F4517.

Irrespective of whether the ball goes forward, drops on the ground or is knocked back, a scrum is ordered. The advantage rule is never applied and consequently the game suffered from every point of view.[76]

There were presentations to the team after the match.

> In the evening the team were guests of the French Rugby Union at a banquet held at the Café de Weber, the French Government being represented by the Minister of the Interior, M. Cains. The Army and Navy were represented by a General and an Admiral and the Prefect of Police was present. Congratulatory speeches were made by the President of the French Rugby Union and by the Minister of the Interior and by Captain Vidal, the referee ... Each member of the team received a present of a pocket wallet from the Rugby Union; the team receiving a beautiful vase valued at 2000 francs.[77]

The film opens with members of the team posing with a mix of American, French and British soldiers outside Café de Weber in Paris. Team members hold miniature trophies and the team manager, Lieutenant-Colonel George 'Hoppy' Mitchell, who we last met at the New Zealand Infantry and Reserve Base Depot at Étaples, holds the trophy. There are fine close-ups of faces: all talking, smiling and smoking. Three British Tommies look suspiciously at the camera as they pass. An amused French soldier is left standing in the doorway while the ubiquitous terrier sniffs for scraps. The circular wrought-iron stairway, marble-topped tables and cane chairs represents everyone's idealised image of a Parisian restaurant.

Café de Weber, Paris, on the morning after the Divisional All Black game in Paris, 28 October 1918. The New Zealand team hold their trophies with a mix of French and British soldiers and civilians, who became part of the celebrations.
UK Series, UK506, 1/2-014271-G, ATL, Wellington.

We see the team take the field at Parc de Princes, ushered on by a Frenchman wearing a bowler hat. There is an excited crowd in the stands. A young Maori corporal in uniform walks out with the team. The bowler-hatted Frenchman leads out the French Army team who look 'very French'. The corporal leads the team in the haka while his offsider, also in uniform, acts as hat-holder. The game is played with the referee neatly attired in a jacket. There are fascinating crowd shots. A French officer, in his formal blues uniform and sword, steps forward to stop a young child running towards the camera. There is a suitably mysterious lady in black sitting behind the right-hand barrier in the foreground. Women in the crowd wave to the camera as it pans across. It is a gem of a film and Sanders clearly enjoyed himself — or at least it may have been Sanders as a photograph of the team outside Café de Weber in the UK Series of numbered photographs may indicate that Tommy Scales or one of his crew may have come to Paris to film the game.[78]

The trench 'All Blacks' played a further two games in France. On 1 November they defeated Tarbes 10–6 before a crowd of 6000. On 3 November they defeated Bordeaux 34–3. "This proved to be a fast open game and the best game of the tour."[79]

Les Annales de la Guerre. No. 74. NTSV F253670.

FILMING VICTORY IN 1918

The films of VIP visits and rugby are all backdrop to the fighting, but we have glimpses only of New Zealanders on film. On 1 January 1918 Godley's II ANZAC was renamed XXII Corps. This was due to the formation of the Australian Corps, which concentrated all of the five Australian divisions in the one formation. The only exception to this was Godley's XXII Corps Mounted Regiment, which retained two squadrons of the 4th Australian Light Horse and one squadron of the Otago Mounted Rifles. In addition, Godley had under his command the New Zealand Cyclist Battalion. In March 1918 the New Zealand Division was detached to the Somme and became part of the British IV Corps for the rest of the war, but the Otago Mounteds and the Cyclists continued to be part of XXII Corps. In 1918 they were to have an interesting war that saw them effectively operate in the mounted role as reconnaissance troops for the first time on the Western Front. In July 1918 Godley's XXII Corps operated as part of General Henri Berthelot's French 5th Army in a major offensive astride the Ardre River southwest of Rheims. The Otago Mounteds and the New Zealand Cyclist Battalion played an important but largely unknown role working in advance of the attacking British infantry: it was a return to the mobile warfare once imagined in 1914 and now in practice in 1918.[80] Godley is seen on film welcoming General Berthelots and then watching the march-past of the Australian Light Horse and the Otago Mounted Rifles. Later in the film we see a brief glimpse of a New Zealand Otago Mounted trooper smiling to camera beside a captured German 155 mm-howitzer.[81] What is most impressive about the film are the shots the French cinematographer takes of the guns and infantry moving forward through the battered and ruined villages, dust rising on the roads, the sense of organised chaos of an army on the march. These are scenes we do not have in Sanders' filming.

Between 21 August and 6 November 1918 the New Zealand Division was the leading division for 49 of the 56 miles advanced on the IV Corps front. In this time it captured 8756 prisoners, 145 guns, three tanks and 1263 machine guns. In an ongoing series of operations the New Zealanders showed their superior training and tactical skill. Russell pushed his artillery well forward as support to his attacking infantry, instructing his brigades to bypass centres of population. Where possible German resistance were also outflanked or bypassed with firm strictures from Russell to his subordinate commanders to avoid needless casualties at all costs.

In early September 1918 the division had taken Bapaume after heavy fighting and was advancing. The Germans mounted a counterattack on the village of Riencourt southeast of Bapaume in which they used four German-designed tanks. Before this, the Germans had relied on using captured British tanks. Two of these cumbersome machines became ditched and were captured by New Zealanders on 2 September 1918.[82] There is a brief glimpse of New Zealand soldiers inspecting one of the tanks.[83]

This was climaxed with the bypassing and surrender of the fortress town of Le Quesnoy and the division's rapid advance through the Forêt de Mormal on 4 November 1918. This was New Zealand's last offensive and they were withdrawn from the line on 6 November 1918. It marked the end of the fighting on the Western Front for Russell's New Zealanders. Once again Sanders or his team were forward with the leading troops. We know there was a cameraman with the Divisional All Blacks and the photos show that there were photographers forward with the division as it bypassed the town: who was where we do not know.[84] It seems that film was also taken, but this has never surfaced. Looking back to 4 November 1918 when he was a platoon commander in the 1st Rifles facing the walls of Le Quesnoy, 'Curly' Blyth remembered:

New Zealand 'Diggers' inspect the captured German tank *Schnuck*. This was one of two German designed tanks captured by the New Zealand Division on 2 September 1918. New Zealanders inspecting the tanks were also filmed by French official cameramen. H-Series, H1035, NAM.

My company had taken the railway line and I was doing a little reconnaissance. [Blyth found the level-crossing mined and informed Battalion Headquarters.] While I was there I came under a certain amount of fire from the Germans in the town and I got down in a small trench to take cover. In two seconds time I found on my left hand side was a photographer busy turning on the handle taking snaps of the whole proceedings. I remember asking him how come he should be right up in the front line like this, and he said it was part of his job, and he proceeded on his way to keep turning the handle while we both took a certain amount of cover.[85]

Sanders' team has left us an invaluable record of the New Zealand Division at war in the H-Series photographs and in his surviving film. Yet it is interesting to note that Major H. Spencer Westmacott, who commanded the New Zealand War Records Section in 1919 and arranged for its return to New Zealand, stated in his final report: "I regret to state that it does not compare favourably as a collection of battle pictures, with that of the Mother Country and that of the Colonies."[86] This is true also for the surviving film. When one views the film taken in the front line by the Australian, British and French official cinematographers then one must still ask why we do we not have similar front line filmed scenes for the New Zealand Division.[87] Sanders deserves the last word. In his correspondence with Westmacott he wrote:

Sanders' image of the New Zealand Rifle Brigade on the railway line west of Le Quesnoy, which was the start line for the attack on 4 November 1918. Sanders also filmed these scenes but there is no record of the film surviving. Photographer Captain H.A. Sanders, H-Series, H1133, 1/2-013688-G, ATL, Wellington.

Arrival of the French President Raymond Poincaré in Le Quesnoy, France, on 10 November 1918. He was there to formally accept the return of the town to France from its liberators, the New Zealand Division. The event was marked by the presentation of the New Zealand flag. Photographer Captain H.A. Sanders, H-Series, H1311, 1/2-013801-G, ATL, Wellington.

I prefer to say nothing more than that the arrangements under which I worked were a constant source of complaint and advice as to their improvement from me, and it is quite unfair to compare the Canadian War Records and the Australian War Records with ours. Unfortunately, you have no knowledge of the conditions under which I worked, as I am aware that, if you did, my work would have been rather commended than criticized. Reflections on my ability are best answered by stating that I was promoted Captain within six months of my appointment, and despite my letter of resignation dated August 21ˢᵗ 1918, it was found inconvenient to replace me until demobilization. I have no grievance against the N.Z.E.F beyond this, and I am rather surprised at the tone of your conversation.'[88]

Filming 'Blighty'

The Dominion forces of Australia, Canada and New Zealand were a rich source of film subjects for the newsreel companies in England, or 'Blighty' as the soldiers called it during the First World War, particularly as these were able to be filmed without the censorship restrictions placed upon cameramen in the overseas operational areas. In New Zealand's case this flow of film enhanced the few films from the front: Ashmead-Bartlett's *With the Dardanelles Expedition* and in 1916 the occasional newsreel clips of New Zealanders from France.

The strong New Zealand links with the firm of Pathé Frères led to New Zealand borrowing a Pathé cinematographer to become the New Zealand official cameraman with the New Zealand Division in March 1917. This triggered negotiations for a second cinematographer to work for New Zealand in the United Kingdom who was employed the following month. This was followed in September 1917 with the establishment of a New Zealand War Records Section. Pathé Frères gave the New Zealand Government three copies of every film taken by the New Zealand official cameraman in the United Kingdom and these films were sent out to New Zealand.

Repeated screenings and the dangerous fragility of nitrate film meant that almost all of the films that came to New Zealand during the war have been lost. We have lists of what was sent out and the film censor records tell when it arrived but only tantalising glimpses of these films survive. However, the release online of the Pathé, Gaumont and Topical Budget newsreel archives in the United Kingdom and the Gaumont Pathé Archive in France have revealed a rich source of New Zealand-related material, copies of which have been added to the New Zealand Ngā Taonga Sound & Vision collections and complement the New Zealand official film material from the Western Front, copies of which have been repatriated from the Imperial War Museum collection.[1]

NEW ZEALAND SICK AND WOUNDED

In 1915–16 there was a steady flow of newsreel film reaching New Zealand featuring New Zealanders in the United Kingdom. The increasing number of New Zealand wounded arriving from Gallipoli saw the formation of the New Zealand War Contingent Committee under the chairmanship of Lord Plunket to raise funds and assist with the welfare of wounded New Zealand soldiers that were scattered the length and breadth of the country. This culminated

Convalescing New Zealand soldiers in the United Kingdom build up strength to return to the front. Still from *After Being Wounded [Recovering New Zealanders hold Sports Meeting].* NTSV F245633.

with the opening of the New Zealand hospital at Walton-on-Thames on 4 August 1915 at Mount Felix, a large private house overlooking the Thames. The original plan was for a convalescent home but the increasing numbers of New Zealand wounded determined the committee to open a New Zealand hospital.

> The wards have been named after Auckland, Hawkes Bay, Wellington, Taranaki, Nelson, Marlborough, Canterbury, Westland, Southland, Dominion, and Otago. There is also the Hinemoa wing, operating theatre, and quarters for matron, resident medical officer, and staff. From the Wellington Ward a splendid view of the lawns and river is obtained. Accommodation is provided at present for 110 beds and this can be extended to 170 if necessary.[2]

The attendance by Lord Plunket and the High Commissioner Thomas Mackenzie before a large gathering of expatriate New Zealanders attracted both photographers and cameramen. Their work featured in New Zealand illustrated papers and picture theatres six weeks later with the *Topical Budget-209* featuring the "Hon. T. Mackenzie at opening of hospital for New Zealand wounded in London."[3] The *Pathé Gazette* news item shows Lord Plunket and the high commissioner walking with nursing staff through the grounds of the hospital before Mackenzie is seen addressing the gathering.[4]

King George V and Queen Mary visited the hospital in the month it opened and provided newsreel scenes of the king being escorted around the hospital meeting wounded. Sometime later in the war the king again visited Walton-on-Thames and was filmed in two widely distributed Pathé newsreel segments.[5]

By the end of 1915 there were 3000 sick and wounded New Zealanders recovering in the United Kingdom.[6] An early newsreel of wounded New Zealanders in England from Gaumont released on 1 November 1915 show *Wounded New Zealanders Spend their Time Profitably*

 New Hospital for Wounded New Zealanders opened by Lord Plunket and by High Commissioner for New Zealand. NTSV F232651.

in basket-making.[7] These were soldiers classed unfit for further active service and awaiting repatriation to New Zealand. The theme is one of the costs of war and how those now unable to fight must be given gainful employment.

The theme of wounded veterans recovering to full health is the subject of a *Pathé Gazette* clip showing a New Zealand sports day on a winter's day in late 1915 or early 1916. It was most likely filmed at Hornchurch, which at the time served as the main depot camp for New Zealanders in the United Kingdom, however, almost all of its members were recovering wounded. The main training camp later became Sling Camp at Bulford with Hornchurch becoming the convalescent camp with an adjacent New Zealand Convalescent Hospital. The newsreel shows men climbing over a rope obstacle course, which clearly exhausts some of them, blindfolded boxers swinging punches and ends with laughing soldiers sitting on a slippery pole pummelling each other with what appear to be flour-filled pillowcases. It is a fun day and a break from the monotony of training.[8] However, there is a subtle difference to the earlier shots of the basket-weavers for now we see veterans who, having 'done their bit', are being rested and recuperating before returning to the front to fight again. These were important images for a home audience and gave a sense of normalcy and comparative safety with the boys being 'home' in 'Blighty' after the anxiety of waiting for news during the Gallipoli Campaign.

GOING HOME

Most Gallipoli wounded never recovered sufficiently to serve again at the front. There are a number of films showing the Anzac veterans being repatriated back to Australia and New Zealand. *New Zealanders Board Ship to Return Home* shows a disembarked trainload of New Zealanders, some on crutches, waiting dockside alongside the ship that will carry them to New Zealand. Their mood is one of patient expectation as they file up the gangway and wave to the camera from the ship's rails. This Pathé film stock is not dated and simply titled 'Old Negatives', but the New

After Being Wounded.
NTSV F245633.

New Zealanders Board Ship to Return Home.
NTSV F245783.

Invalid New Zealanders unfit for active service after their Gallipoli service, on the wharf in England, ready to return home. Still from *New Zealanders Board Ship to Return Home.* NTSV F245783.

Zealand Expeditionary Force (NZEF) adopted the lemon squeezer hat as its distinctive national headdress in August 1916. This is clearly before that date and may be late 1915 or very early 1916.[9]

The second film, *Australian and New Zealand Soldiers Return Home*, shows close-ups of a group of New Zealanders and Australians gathered on deck, talking, sharing a light for cigarettes, obviously pleased to be sailing. We then see their ship, a single-funnel hospital ship pulling away from the wharf. This is the return voyage to New Zealand of NZ Hospital Ship No. 2 *Marama* that sailed from England on 31 August 1916 with 500 patients: 154 of which were New Zealanders, the rest being Australians plus two South Africans.[10] This film was taken as the *Marama* returned to New Zealand on the completion of her first commission as a hospital ship; she travelled 53,251 miles carrying 12,639 patients and 580 passengers, a total of 13,219. The ship's history noted: "Prior to her final departure from Southampton for New Zealand, Messrs. Pathé Frères, by arrangement with the War Office and the New Zealand Government, cinematographed the *Marama* showing the work of embarkation before the vessel left the docks, and the ship herself as she passed down the harbour, in order that a permanent record might be preserved. This policy is being pursued in connection with other matters of personal interest to New Zealanders in England."[11] This is the only film we have of the New Zealand hospital ships *Maheno* and *Marama* in all of the films taken of their work during the First World War.

THE NEW ZEALAND TUNNELLING COMPANY AT FALMOUTH

On 11 April 1916 the first elements of the newly formed New Zealand Division arrived at Marseilles in France, but they were not the first New Zealanders to arrive in France; in March the New Zealand Tunnelling Company had been sent there. This unit had been specially raised from miners in New Zealand in response to a request from the War Office for specialists needed to combat German mining operations under the trenches on the Western Front. This was the first New Zealand unit committed to operations on the Western Front. The unit served as an independent NZEF unit under British Command principally around Arras for most of the war. They did not serve with the New Zealand Division until the final advance in 1918 where they were involved in bridge building as the mobile operations negated the need for the tunnels and dugouts that had been their speciality.

The miners assembled and did initial training at Avondale in Auckland before sailing and then trained at Falmouth in the United Kingdom. In early March they were inspected and pronounced fit for service. On 6 March 1916 they paraded through the streets of Falmouth preceded by a Fusilier band and were inspected by Sir Thomas Mackenzie. Sir 'Tam' takes the salute as Major John Duigan of the New Zealand Staff Corps leads his miners smartly past the dignitaries gathered at the roadside. Duigan would be awarded the DSO for his command of the Tunnellers in France and rose to the rank of major-general and commanded the New Zealand Defence Force at the outbreak of war in 1939.[12] The farewell parade was captured by a Pathé cameraman. There is a very brief newsreel clip titled *15,000 Miles to Serve — 'Tunnellers' from New Zealand inspected by High Commissioner* showing the inspection and then the march past Sir Thomas, including the parade of horse-drawn GS wagons.[13] There is a second clip showing the inspection and march-past.

Pathè also released a third and much longer clip that showed the company lined up for inspection on the parade ground. Sir Thomas inspects the troops and then the company's motor transport. The film shows the march-past, with Sir 'Tam' talking with a mounted Major Duigan. After the troops have passed there is a drive-past of recently issued motor lorries belonging to the company.[14] This is the first film of any New Zealand military unit in history showing motor vehicles integral to the unit, horses being the mainstay of the transport for the New Zealand Division for all of the war. The following day on 7 March the Tunnellers entrained at Falmouth with the "faithful Fusilier band together with half the female population of the county giving it a touching farewell".[15]

Colonial Troops Reviewed. British Pathé, 1936.33.

Sir Thomas Mackenzie, High Commissioner for New Zealand, at the march-past of the New Zealand Tunnelling Company including their motor vehicles before deploying to France. This is the first film of a New Zealand military unit with its motor vehicles. Falmouth, 6 March 1916. Still from *Colonial Troops Reviewed.* NTSV F1936.33.

REORGANISATION OF THE MEDICAL AND TRAINING ESTABLISHMENTS OF NZEF UK

In 1916 the New Zealand administrative structure in the United Kingdom was reorganised to cater for the New Zealand Division's move to France. The key figure in this is Brigadier-General George Spafford Richardson who oversaw the organisation as the officer in charge of administration of the NZEF in the United Kingdom.

Richardson came to New Zealand as a master gunner of warrant officer-rank in 1891 and forged an outstanding military career built on talent and hard work. Born on 14 November 1868 in Ashton, England, of a farming background, he enlisted in the Royal Regiment of Artillery in 1886. Within five years he rose to the rank of staff sergeant instructor in gunnery. Richardson was seconded to New Zealand as an instructor in gunnery and master gunner in 1891 and proved himself invaluable. His engagement continued to be extended and he married a New Zealander. He was commissioned as a captain in the New Zealand Militia in 1907 and in 1909 it was reported that "he was the hardest worked officer in the service". Promoted to major in the New Zealand Staff Corps in 1912, he attended the British Army Staff College at Camberley in the same year. In 1913 he was posted as New Zealand's representative on the Imperial General Staff.

On the outbreak of war, Richardson assisted in the raising of the Royal Naval Division, one of Winston Churchill's schemes. He became the principal administration officer for the division and confirmed his reputation as a superb administrator. He went to Antwerp with the division and then to Gallipoli. By the end of the campaign he was the Deputy Assistant Quartermaster General (DAQMG), the principal administrative officer of the British XII Corps in Salonika in the rank of brigadier-general and awarded a CMG for his Gallipoli service.

In February 1916 he became New Zealand's military representative in London and placed in charge of the administration of the NZEF in the United Kingdom and commanding all New Zealand soldiers in the country. He forged an effective administration that Godley considered "in every way excellent".[16] He is the ubiquitous presence in many of the films taken in the United Kingdom and France as he accompanied VIP parties to the various New Zealand establishments and units.

In 1916 the New Zealand Medical Services transferred its resources from Egypt to the United Kingdom under Director of Medical Services Colonel W.H. Parkes.

No. 1 New Zealand General Hospital was established at Brockenhurst in the New Forest. This was a complex of three separate hospital sites totalling 1100 beds: the Lady Harding's hutted hospital at Brockenhurst in what had been an Indian Army hospital set up for the Indian Corps on its arrival on the Western Front, the 200-bed Balmer Lawn Hospital and the 200-bed Forest Park Hospital, both of these being converted hotels.

The New Zealand War Contingent Association agreed that their hospital at Walton-on-Thames be transferred to the NZEF, becoming No. 2. New Zealand General Hospital. No. 3 General Hospital was established at Codford Camp with 300 beds, this also included the New Zealand Venereal Disease Hospital as a separate annex.

A New Zealand Convalescent Hospital was established at Hornchurch, which until now had been the principal training camp. From 1916 a New Zealand soldier wounded in France would be sent to Brockenhurst if he arrived through the port of Southampton or to Walton-on-Thames if transferred through the port of Dover. Once discharged from hospital the patient was sent to the Convalescent Camp at Hornchurch before being transferred to Codford Camp for a process of fitness and skills training. Once fully fit he would then be sent to the New Zealand

Reserve Group Depot at Sling Camp near Bulford where he joined up with reinforcements from New Zealand.[17]

During the New Zealand Division's involvement in the Somme battles, 300 New Zealand wounded a week arrived in England so that by December 1916 there were 1764 New Zealand patients in the New Zealand hospitals, 1473 in the Convalescent Camp at Hornchurch and 3449 in the Codford Camp. By 1918 there were 6495 NZEF hospital beds in the United Kingdom, each of the general hospitals had over 1500 beds with 1000 at the Convalescent Camp at Hornchurch. In March 1918 there were 1084 New Zealanders in British hospitals throughout Britain and 4646 in New Zealand hospitals: a total of 5730. To cater for those permanently unfit for war service until they could be evacuated back to New Zealand, a New Zealand Discharge Depot was opened at Torquay in May 1917 that took over a number of large homes and hotels. It also became a centre for agricultural activity where men were rehabilitated with farming experience on leased land. This also provided fresh food for the New Zealand camps.

The film "Strawberry Fete" was taken by a local cinematographer in Torquay showing the festivities on Alexandra Day, Wednesday 27 June 1917, for a fundraising fete day "promoted by the Four Allied Trades: Dairymen, Fruiterers, Grocers and Bakers". It was a day of fun, novelty races and afternoon teas with wounded soldiers and nursing staff prominent in the crowd, many of whom are New Zealanders. Maori soldiers of the New Zealand Pioneer Battalion are particularly evident and the film ends with "the evening performance of Maori Nature Dances" as the Pioneers perform a haka for the crowd. It is very evident that Torquay had taken to their hearts in a very short time these convalescing soldiers, waiting return to New Zealand.[18] It showed how effectively New Zealanders mixed in with the local communities around the camps and hospitals where they were based.

MAORI FUNERAL

In September–October 1916 New Zealand households relived the anxiety during the August offensive of the previous year with casualty lists from the Somme battles filling every paper. In early January 1917 the funeral of a New Zealand soldier at Walton-on-Thames was the subject of a *Pathé Gazette* newsreel. It was released under the title *Maori Funeral*. It shows the gun-carriage cortege, led by a New Zealand military band, proceeding from the hospital with those inmates who can march following on in threes, along with nurses and medical staff, with wheelchair and basketchair cases following behind. A party of Maori or Rarotongan soldiers carry the flag-draped coffin to the graveside and at the graveside itself the firing party fires three volleys over the grave while the band plays.[19]

Despite the title it is a military funeral serviced largely by Pakeha, or European New Zealanders, who comprise the firing party and the band members. They were no doubt dispatched from Codford or Hornchurch to carry out the military honours at the funeral. It makes this an interesting film, the word 'Maori' in the title indicated to the world that these were New Zealanders, and to those viewing the film, the nature of the funeral itself showed that in death there was no distinction: here was a New Zealand soldier being buried by his mainly Pakeha comrades. It suggests that for the soldiers abroad Te Rangi Hiroa's assessment of what it meant to be a New Zealand Force was coming true: "No division can truly be called a New Zealand Division unless it numbers Maoris amongst its ranks."[20]

Three Maori members of the Pioneer Battalion are among the 19 New Zealanders buried in the church grounds at Walton-on-Thames, two of these, privates Kingi K. Hamana and Raniera R. Wairua, died in October 1916. The third, Private Terekia Taura from Atiu on Rarotonga in

"Strawberry Fete".
NTSV F110329.

Maori Funeral.
NTSV F48685.

The funeral of Private Terekia Taura from Atiu in the Cook Islands, who died of tuberculosis on 8 January 1917 at No. 2 New Zealand General Hospital and is buried in the church yard at Walton-on-Thames. Still from *Maori Funeral*. NTSV F48685.

the Cook Islands, died on 7 January 1917 and was buried in Walton-on-Thames cemetery the following day.[21] The cold frosty day and the single uniformed Polynesian figure among the immediate close mourners that we see on film suggest that it is a Polynesian who is the subject of the military funeral; had it been a Maori soldier it is likely that there would have been greater numbers walking with the immediate close mourners.

The film images provide an interesting contrast to the photograph of the burial of a Maori soldier at Hornchurch where the catafalque and firing parties are all Maori. Some 2227 Maori served in the New Zealand Pioneer Battalion as well as 458 Pacific Islanders from Rarotonga and Niue, 336 members of the battalion died on active service and 734 were wounded. The *Maori Funeral* film made audiences aware of the particular nature of New Zealand's contribution, and was different enough to attract the newsreel editor's eye.[22]

No one, including politicians, was spared the impact of this war. James Allen, minister of defence, lost his son at Gallipoli. Clutha Mackenzie, son of the high commissioner, was blinded in the battle for Chunuk Bair and evacuated to England in 1915. His father took up a cottage adjacent to the New Zealand hospital at Walton-on-Thames where he could be near to his son and was reported to be "cheering up the [wounded] New Zealanders".[23]

A Pathé newsreel from early 1916 shows the high commissioner with a visiting group of New Zealand parliamentarians being shown round Stonehenge with Brigadier-General George Spafford Richardson, CMG, recently appointed as officer in charge of NZEF Administration in the United Kingdom.

The blind Clutha Mackenzie is one of the party and is led by his father to one of the fallen monoliths, where it is described to him, while the smiling young man taps out its dimensions with his cane. It is this moment on film that no doubt impacted on New Zealand audiences, identifying the Mackenzie family's sacrifice along with their own.[24]

Maori Funeral.
NTSV F48685.

Stonehenge Visited by New Zealand Delegates; After Gallipoli: The Famous Maori Contingent.
NTSV F48689.

RUGBY

Included with the Pathé item on the visit to Stonehenge is the clip titled *After Gallipoli* with the caption: "The famous Maori contingent, now recuperating in England, at a football match." It pans across the faces of four Maori Contingent soldiers, plainly convalescents, before a shot of a Maori rugby team on a misty English morning. The Maori Contingent provided a rich vein of film material. This charity football match at Boscombe, near the New Zealand Engineer Training Depot where Maori Contingent members were trained, provided three separate items for the *Pathé Gazette*, two showing the haka and all emphasising that these were veterans who had fought at Gallipoli.[25]

It was rugby that was the magnet attracting newsreels to New Zealanders in the United Kingdom. Memories of the 1905–06 All Blacks' tour drew the newsreel companies to the New Zealand games. In season, New Zealand teams featuring on film throughout the country every other week, with championship-deciding games being filmed and distributed by all three major newsreel-makers, Pathé, Gaumont and Topical Budget. The earliest surviving of these rugby films is a New Zealand team identified as both 'Blacks' and 'Anzacs' in the papers, drawn from Hornchurch Camp where they had been organised by Major T.H. Dawson, the camp commandant, and Captain Price, the camp adjutant. The team was drawn from the best players available and were listed in *The Sporting Life* report of the game. The Blacks (Anzacs) were: Private Saunders (Auckland) back, Corporal Hesketh (Wellington), Lance-Corporal Griffiths (Wellington), Sapper Burns (Auckland), three-quarters backs. Sergeant Hulton and Lance-Corporal Jeffs (Dunedin), five-eighths; Lance-Corporal Badderley (Wellington), half-back; Sergeant Muir (Auckland), wing-forward; Trooper Ovens (Otago), Sergeant Sheridan (Blenheim), Lance-Corporal Harding (Blenheim), Corporal Hall (Buller), Private Fraser (Otago), Trooper Park (Dunedin) and Corporal Fricker (Auckland), forwards. We see the Blacks file onto the field and scenes from the game.[26] The reports in the British press were reprinted in New Zealand.

> The win was highly creditable, because the Artist's Rifles have not previously been beaten this season, and the critics agree that with practice the New Zealanders would prove doughty opponents to any club team in England. There have been few rugby games of any importance in London this season, consequently this fixture brought together a big crowd, over 3000 persons attending.[27]

This was followed by a Topical Budget film taken on a foggy Saturday on 1 April 1916. Titled *An Anzac Win*, it shows the New Zealand Codford Camp team defeating the United Hospitals team by four tries to nil; "This being their tenth victory out of eleven matches."[28] The newsreels emphasised that these were charity matches played by "New Zealanders who fought in Gallipoli".[29]

The 1915–16 championship decider was played between the New Zealanders and a South African team drawn from recuperating members of the South African Brigade from France that had been the only team to inflict a defeat on the New Zealanders in the season. This was played at Richmond on 8 April 1916 and together with the hundreds of New Zealanders was attended by both Topical Budget and Pathé film crews. "The New Zealanders have their revenge by defeating the South Africans at Richmond by five points to three."[30] Both films show the two teams before the start and scenes of the game itself. In the Pathé newsreel we see Sir Thomas Mackenzie, as always in his tweed suit, smiling and chatting with New Zealanders while cheerfully smoking a cigarette on a cold London day.[31]

Topical Budget No: 233-1, Anzacs Beat Artists. NTSV F246508.

The large numbers of New Zealanders both training and convalescing in the United Kingdom saw a more organised approach to the 1916–17 rugby season.

A meeting of football delegates from the various units was held in Sling Camp on September 21st 1916, when it was resolved to form a New Zealand Reserve Group Football Team, such team to be known as the New Zealand Reserve Group "All Blacks".[32]

In every camp New Zealand teams were active in local competitions, but the Reserve Group 'All Blacks' were selected from the best provincial and former international players available to play in the premiere competition and against selected sides. On Boxing Day 1916 the team played Wales in a charity match drawing 6-all in a game watched by thousands in a packed ground. The film of this game may be the one that survives in the Ngā Taonga Sound & Vision archive that dates from 1916 and gives glimpses of what seems to be periods of play where the Welsh side dominates, and so every New Zealander's dream of beating Wales and revenging the try that all believed Dean to have scored but not awarded, had yet to be fulfilled.[33]

The dominant side this season was not the 'All Blacks' but the Army Service Corps (ASC) Grove Park side, a British Army team which, like the New Zealanders, carefully assembled a team of fine players, including a number of professionals from the Northern Division League, now known as Rugby League. These players, who were normally banned from playing the amateur game, had dispensation while serving in the armed forces. On 13 January 1917 the 'All Blacks' team ran the unbeaten ASC Grove Park team close in losing by one point. The game was watched by a crowd of some 3000 at the Old Deer Park grounds at Richmond. The spectators included Prime Minister Hon. W.F. Massey, High Commissioner Sir Thomas Mackenzie, Brigadier-General G.S. Richardson, Commander NZEF (UK), and Sir Joseph and Lady Ward; Massey's presence being a focus for the cameramen.[34] The New Zealanders included one of

The 1915–16 season deciding match between the New Zealand UK-based 'All Blacks' and the 'Springboks', who had been the only team to defeat the New Zealanders during the season. The game was played at Richmond on 8 April 1916. The New Zealanders won 5–3. Still from *Pathé Gazette: Fighting Men at Play: 'All Blacks' Beat 'Springboks' in Hotly Contested Rugby Match at Richmond.* NTSV F48684.

Sir Thomas Mackenzie discusses the game over a cigarette. Still from *Pathé Gazette: Fighting Men at Play: 'All Blacks' Beat 'Springboks' in Hotly Contested Rugby Match at Richmond.* NTSV F48684.

the famous All Blacks of the 1905 tour, C. 'Bronco' Seeling, who played for Wigan (Northern Union) before enlisting in the NZEF.[35]

In early 1917 it was planned that the unbeaten 'All Blacks' trench team from the New Zealand Division in France would tour England in February and would play the as yet unbeaten ASC Grove Park team and also play Wales in Cardiff. The tour was cancelled at the last minute and so, having advertised the game, the New Zealand Reserve Group team stepped in to see if this time they could upset the champions.

All three newsreel companies covered the game played at Richmond on 17 February 1917. Topical Budget released two clips from the match, the first shows Massey walking along the front of the stands to the cheers of the New Zealanders, most in their hospital 'blues' uniform; deliberately distinctive in that it limited their entry into public houses, but guaranteed a great deal of positive attention from the general public. This extended shot of the New Zealanders is perhaps one of the classic film shots of New Zealand soldier faces of the First World War.[36] In the second clip we see the two teams come on to the field. Given the closeness of the first game between these sides, every New Zealander present hoped for another close game with New Zealand ascendant. The caption spells out the reality: "The all conquering Army Service Corps team defeat the New Zealand team by 21 points to 3, in the rugby match at Richmond".[37]

It was a measure of the strength of the ASC side playing against a New Zealand team featuring a selection of the best of the immediate pre-war players. Former 'All Blacks' included John O'Brien at fullback who was regarded as "a master of positional play to the point of wizardry"; George Loveridge at wing three-quarter; R.W. Roberts at centre three-quarter who captained the New Zealand team in the 1914 tour of Australia; E. Ned Hughes, who played for New Zealand in 1907–08 before turning professional and playing league. Another league player was Charlie 'Bronco' Seeling, one of the 1905 'Originals' with a legendary reputation, "a better forward than Seeling does not exist". There was also the 31-year-old George Sellars at hooker, as

🐾 *Topical Budget No. 287-1, Premier Watches Rugby Match.* NTSV F97873.

"hard as nails", who represented New Zealand, and was a member of the pre-war North Island and NZ Maori sides. Sellars was killed at Messines on 7 June 1917, 11 weeks after this game, while carrying a wounded comrade.[38] Sellars was one of 11 former 'All Blacks' killed in this war, and these newsreels are perhaps the only images we have of him on film.[39]

The *Gaumont Graphic* newsreel focused on the presence of Massey and Ward watching the game, as did the *Pathé Gazette*, making picture-goers in both the United Kingdom and New Zealand aware of the New Zealand political leaders' presence in Britain and giving a sense of New Zealand's contribution to the war effort.[40]

The ASC Grove Park team was dispersed and lost its ascendency in the 1917–18 season. The battle was now between New Zealand and South Africa, all of which claimed newsreel attention.[41] The start of the rugby season in October 1918 coincided with the news that Germany had asked for an armistice, but nothing distracted the New Zealand camps from their usual round of games. The New Zealand Convalescent Camp defeated a New Zealand Headquarters team at Hornchurch by two tries to one (6–3); the game being refereed by Lieutenant E.E. 'General' Booth, an 'Original' All Black from 1905.[42] The Hornchurch team was then defeated by the New Zealand Machine Gunners 6–3.[43]

November 1918 saw the collapse of the Alliance powers and the onset of Spanish Influenza yet New Zealand teams remained prominent in the press and newsreels. *The Sporting Life* reported the defeat of Australia by New Zealand in a charity international match at Herne Hill in a "good hard game in which neither side asked nor conferred favours". The game was filmed by Gaumont.[44]

ANZAC DAY 1916

The newsreel sequence of New Zealanders featuring in the 1915–16 rugby season was immediately followed by the first commemoration of Anzac Day on 25 April 1916, which also featured on film. At home in New Zealand the response was a mix of local spontaneity and government direction. In the United Kingdom there was formal recognition of Australia and New Zealand's achievement with a parade through London, followed by a formal service of remembrance at Westminster Abbey attended by the king and queen. Sir Thomas Mackenzie represented New Zealand and W.M. 'Billy' Hughes represented Australia. Field Marshal the Earl Kitchener, secretary of state for war, Lieutenant-General Sir William Birdwood commanding I ANZAC, Lieutenant-General Sir John Maxwell, General Sir William Robertson, CIGS, and the former commander Mediterranean Expeditionary Force, General Sir Ian Hamilton, with Lord Plunket, the former governor, were among the many dignitaries in attendance.

A Topical Budget newsreel shows the New Zealanders in their smasher hats, with some lemon squeezers sprinkled among them, marching down the Strand through packed inquisitive crowds held back by mounted policemen.[45] Henry Skinner of the Otago Battalion who was to receive a Distinguished Conduct Medal (DCM) for his bravery on Chunuk Bair was among the marchers:

> We detrained at the Temple and fell in, in the street parallel with the Embankment … The order of march was: Mounted Officers, Unmounted Officers, V.C.s and D.C.M.s, … then various companies of infantry, etc. I was on the right flank of the second four of medal men …. We marched along Cheapside into Trafalgar Square, down Whitehall, and round into the square between the House of Lords and the Abbey. The sun was strong, the streets packed with cheering people, and every window crowded with men and women waving and throwing flowers.[46]

Skinner was lucky enough to get a seat in the abbey and the service brought back memories of his Gallipoli experience.

> The pealing notes of the great organ sounded the Dead March and I thought of Tothill, Spottswood [sic], Bob Oliver, Peter Biggar, Ernie Jones, Marshall, David Millar [sic], small of frame but strong in courage, young Anderson, Smith with his talk of about his old mother who was living only to see him back, Archie Veitch, Ernie Davis, Roland Ward, Robbie — crowding out the Abbey and the living crowd about me.[47] On the slopes above the pebbled beach the battered oak scrub will be in leaf and the rhododendrons will be in bloom, and underneath the Spring flowers will be out …. The notes of the Recessional died away and the bugles sang the 'Last Post'. We filed out into the sun and marched to St James Station. Women were kissing everyone, and there were showers of primroses everywhere.[48]

That afternoon Birdwood, accompanied by Sir Thomas Mackenzie and Brigadier-General Richardson, reviewed the New Zealand Command Depot at Hornchurch. This too was filmed and was distributed through the Pathé newsreels in two parts. In the first part we see Birdwood inspecting the ranks, clearly enjoying talking to the men who respond in turn. This is followed by an impressive march-past with line after line of New Zealanders passing in review. Henry Skinner was in the ranks. "The Review was held in a green field beside the camp. The march past seemed to me to be excellently done, though perhaps the cinematograph will say differently, you will see! I was in the rear rank of the first detachment, on the right."[49]

In the second part Birdwood presents medals to the Gallipoli veterans. Skinner was at pains in his letter to tell his family where he was standing in the medal ceremony so that they could see him on film. "I was left-hand man of the rear rank, or right hand of the front when we were turned about. The General asked me where I won the medal. I said 'On Chunuk Bair, sir.' 'That was a hot corner, wasn't it?' 'Yes it was.' 'Are you going back to the Front?' 'I don't know, sir,' 'I hope so, well good luck, and he shook hands."

All of the veterans are keen to see themselves on film. On 28 April Skinner wrote home that "I have just been told that I am the principal figure in one of the films of the Review." In early May he saw the film. "I went to see the Anzac Day pictures at Romford. In the march past in London I just came in to the pictures on the right of the second four of infantry, waving my hand to someone in the crowd. You cannot recognise me. In the cheering one I am on the right of the near group with my face very wrinkled. I am asking Pathé for a photo …"[50]

Considering that each one is a Gallipoli casualty, the scale of the cost of that campaign to New Zealand becomes evident in two newsreels released at the time. Even if the current identification of one of them by Pathé as *Inspection of Australian Troops* so titled no doubt on the researcher's assumption that as Birdwood commanded the Australian Imperial Force (AIF) during the First World War then these must be Australians, it cannot disguise the contemporary publicity that New Zealanders received through the newsreels.[51]

There is a brief scene in *General Birdwood presents Medals* where he talks to some well-dressed ladies, one of whom is the high commissioner's daughter, Helen Mackenzie, who assisted her now blind brother Clutha Mackenzie to produce the *Chronicles of the N.Z.E.F.*, a fortnightly magazine published by the New Zealand War Contingent Association in London as "a paper to gather and dispense all interesting information concerning New Zealand soldiers in Europe, and a gazette of New Zealand patriotic efforts in this country".[52] Helen accompanied her father to many of his engagements and stands out among the faces in the crowd of

General Birdwood presents Medals. NTSV F245688.

Inspection of Australian [New Zealand] Troops [by General Birdwood]. British Pathé 1936.12.

immediate civilian VIPs and can be identified in many of the surviving films. One of these is the presentation of the aircraft *Nottingham* to New Zealand by the city of Nottingham in October 1917. In the Topical Budget news clip we see the vivacious Duchess of Portland breaking with a mallet a bottle of champagne attached to the aircraft's propeller, and there is a brief glimpse of Helen Mackenzie, in the dark hat with the white band in the official party.[53] These scenes are repeated in a Pathé newsreel.[54] Another Pathé newsreel shows Helen Mackenzie attaching a bronze emblem of a kiwi to the aircraft's fuselage while Major Alfred De Bathe Brandon, Royal Flying Corps, DSO MC, looks on.[55] Brandon was one of New Zealand's heroes for his exploits in attacking Zeppelins in their night raids on Britain in 1916.[56]

The Anzac Day parade became an annual event in Britain during the war with the Lord Mayor's Parade usually including the parade of Australian and New Zealand soldiers through London featuring on film each year. In 1918 General Sir William Robertson inspected New Zealand and Australian officer cadets under training at Cambridge University at the Anzac Day memorial service and parade. The university halls of residence were used to accommodate the officer training courses for the British Army. Filmed by Topical Budget and titled *Honours for Anzacs at Cambridge*, the film shows VIPs and cadets filing out from the King's College Chapel after a special service conducted by Australian and New Zealand military chaplains. Robertson takes the salute at the march-past of the cadets with their distinctive white pugarees on their hats that identify them as officer cadets, and he then presents medals.[57]

A longer version of the same parade was released in the French military newsreels *Annales de la Guerre*. This runs for 4 minutes 28 seconds and shows the march-past and the presentation of medals, where one of the New Zealanders waiting to be awarded his medal winks at the camera, followed by scenes of the afternoon sports watched by friends and convalescent soldiers on a lovely spring day and on one where New Zealand beat Australia in the tug-of-war.[58]

The Anzac Day parades featured column after column of Australian soldiers, effectively illustrating the scale of Australia's contribution to the war effort.[59] In 1919 the parade was taken by the Prince of Wales. The film ends with the soldier crowd, including New Zealanders, mobbing the prince with three cheers, while a tweed-coated Sir Thomas Mackenzie can be identified among the VIPs.

FILMING THE VCS

Among the wounded and convalescing New Zealanders in Britain was Sergeant Cyril Bassett who became New Zealand's first Victoria Cross winner in the NZEF during the First World War. This was for his exploits during the 1915 August offensive on Gallipoli when, while a corporal, with a team of signallers, he worked between the New Zealand line on Chunuk Bair and the New Zealand Infantry Brigade Headquarters on Rhododendron Ridge. This was to keep the field telephone line open in the face of what should have been certain death from Turkish snipers. In January 1916 his award of the VC was announced while Bassett was convalescing in the United Kingdom. We see him being congratulated by his barrack mates at Hornchurch and then hoisted on their shoulders. We then see him outside the New Zealand High Commission in the Strand, again being congratulated, along with his friend Sergeant Robert Tilsey of the Auckland Battalion who was awarded the DCM for his bravery on Gallipoli. Tilsey's son remembers his grandmother telling him that she went every day to the local theatre in New Zealand to see her boy on film in the week that the newsreel featured.[60]

The VC winners were obvious subjects for the newsreels. Film and photographs of King George V awarding the VC to Sergeant Sam Frickleton on 18 September 1917 in front of a

Corporal Cyril Bassett, VC, and Sergeant Robert Tilsey (on right) on the steps of the New Zealand High Commission in London after the announcement of his being awarded the VC. Tisley was awarded the DCM. Still from *For Bravery at Gallipoli — VC for Corporal Bassett.* NTSV F245688.

packed stadium at Ibrox Park in Glasgow, where Frickleton was convalescing, featured in the illustrated papers and on the newsreels.[61] This was the first public investiture by a reigning monarch in Scotland since the Union of the Crowns in 1603.[62]

Scottish-born Samuel Frickleton was one of 11 children of a coal-mining family. By 1911 seven of the boys including Sam were working in the mines alongside their father. After the death of their father, four of the boys with their mother migrated to New Zealand where an elder brother was working in the Blackball mine on the West Coast. The five brothers were remembered in Blackball as the 'fighting Frickletons'. All five Frickletons volunteered to serve with the NZEF in the First World War. Sam initially joined the Canterbury Battalion in 1915 but was returned from Egypt with tuberculosis. He was discharged but recovered and enlisted again in April 1916 and served in France as a rifleman with 3rd Rifles. Lance Corporal Frickleton took part in the attack on Messines on 7 June 1917. He knocked out two German machine guns, killing their crews. He was wounded in the hip and was later gassed in this attack. For these acts of gallantry he was awarded the VC. Frickleton was later commissioned but was medically downgraded and returned to New Zealand to a hero's welcome in June 1918. His brother William served in Gallipoli and in France, where he was wounded and died in 1916. All four surviving brothers were wounded and returned to New Zealand medically unfit for further service.[63]

There is also the film of Frickleton, now a sergeant, congratulating Sergeant L.W. Andrew after his receiving the VC from the king at Buckingham Palace, which gave the newsreels two for the price of one. It is the day of Andrew's investiture and both are filmed outside Buckingham Palace. Frickleton congratulates Andrew and they are then surrounded by friends who shake their hands before carrying them both shoulder high. Frickleton can be identified because he is wearing the VC ribbon on his chest, while Andrew has both the ribbon and medal pinned on his chest. The soldier standing beside Frickleton, wearing the badge of the NZ Machine Gun Corps, appears to be one of his brothers.[64]

For Bravery at Gallipoli — VC for Corporal Bassett. NTSV F245688.

HM The King on the Clyde. NTSV F246448.

VC for Anzac Heroes of the Ridge. Sergeants Frickleton and Andrew Being Congratulated by Comrades. NTSV F245768.

Two of the five New Zealanders caught up in the 1916 Easter Rising in Dublin. Sergeant Nevin and Private Waring and the Australian, Private McHugh, rifles under their arms, walking from Trinity College after the rebels surrendered. Still from *Easter Rising Dublin*, 1916. NTSV F246452.

THE EASTER RISING 1916

In 1915–16 the United Kingdom was the haunt of convalescing New Zealand soldiers on leave, visiting relatives and seeing the sights. A group of New Zealanders were in Dublin at the time of the Easter Rising that started on 24 April 1916 and became involved in the defence of Trinity College. The five New Zealanders were Sergeant Frederick Nevin from Christchurch, Corporal Alexander Don from Dunedin, Lance Corporal Finlay McLeod from Wellington, and Corporal John Garland and Private Edward Waring from Auckland. A number of letters were published in the New Zealand press detailing their experiences. Garland's letter summarised the fighting:

> We reported there at 3 pm. There were only about thirty of us and we filled sandbags from 5 pm
> until 9 pm. By that time our strength had grown to nearly sixty including five New Zealanders,
> one Australian, five from South Africa and two Canadians. At 11 pm they woke us up and took
> the colonials whom they called Anzacs (although there were really only six Anzacs) up to the roof
> where we were to snipe. We remained on that roof from midnight Easter Monday till midnight
> on Thursday without a wink of sleep — exactly 72 hours. From the roof we could command a
> view of the main streets — Sackville, Grafton and Dame. Four of us were on the front parapet
> commanding Dame Street, also part of Grafton Street.[65]

The aftermath of the fighting was captured in the film *Easter Rising, Dublin, 1916*. We see two New Zealanders, Sergeant Nevin and Private Waring and the Australian, Private McHugh, rifles under their arms, walking from Trinity College after the rebels surrendered.[66] Waring would serve on the Western Front and was invalided back to New Zealand where he died from Spanish Influenza in November 1918. Nevin, a medical sergeant, returned to New Zealand on HMNZHT *Marama* on which he was serving. [67]

Easter Rising, Dublin 1916. NTSV F246452.

TOMMY SCALES FILMS 'BLIGHTY'

Both Massey and Ward wanted greater publicity in the United Kingdom as to New Zealand's war effort. The appointment of Sanders as cinematographer to the New Zealand Division in France was engineered by Mackenzie, but it seems that he and Pathé took the discussion further, because a month after Sanders was enlisted another Pathé cameraman, Thomas Frederick Scales, was enlisted on special terms to do a similar job for New Zealand in the United Kingdom. Although Scales was signed on in April 1917, this was not discussed with the New Zealand Government until November 1917 when the first batch of films taken by Scales were dispatched to New Zealand.

Mackenzie once again worked through Donne in approaching Pathé Frères "with regard to the taking of Cinematograph Films in this Country that may be of interest to New Zealand".[68] As with Sanders, Pathé offered the use of one of their best cameramen.

> Messrs Pathé Frères are to provide for the use of Sergeant T. Scales, an expert Cinematograph Operator in the New Zealand Expeditionary Force, a camera and all the necessary film stock that may be required from time to time for the taking of film of the New Zealand Depots in this country and any functions of interest to New Zealand that may take place. Also to supply to the New Zealand Government three free copies of whatever film is taken, the exclusive right for showing same to be vested in the New Zealand Government. In return for their doing the above Messrs. Pathé Frères are to hold the negative film and to show same wherever they may desire throughout the World with the exception of New Zealand.[69]

It was the retention by Pathé Frères of the negative film to show in their newsreels worldwide "wherever they may desire" that ensured that we have some record of Scales' work, as very little survived of the many films sent to New Zealand at the time.

What is interesting about this letter is that Mackenzie did not inform his government that Scales had been enlisted until 1 November 1917. However, as Scales' personal file records he was enlisted on 26 April 1917 and immediately put to work. He was appointed as "Cinema Expert for NZ Units in England with rank of T/Sgt while so employed". Special arrangements were made about Scales' pay with the New Zealand authorities agreeing to making up the difference between the pay for his rank of sergeant and what he earned at Pathé. "As he would only accept service on the understanding that he receive a remuneration at the rate of £5 per week, the difference between the pay and allowances of his rank at Expeditionary Force rates and £5 per week was paid to him from the various Depot Regimental Funds."[70]

Scales' terms of reference involved:

1. Arranging and supervising the installation of cinematographs at Camps and Hospitals for the entertainment of troops and patients and for education purposes.
2. Selecting and arranging programmes and their circulation.
3. Taking pictures of life in the camps and any special events of interest to New Zealand.[71]

He was initially attached to the Reserve Group at Sling Camp and operated from here until 28 April 1918 when he was posted to Headquarters NZEF UK working under the direction of Captain R.F. Gambrill. A barrister and solicitor from Gisborne and a pre-war territorial officer, Gambrill served on Gallipoli with the Wellington Infantry Battalion, but was classified administrative duties only after the campaign. He served the remainder of the

war in administrative and instructional posts and was appointed officer in charge of the New Zealand War Records Section on 20 December 1917.[72]

Initially Scales was tasked by the New Zealand High Commission but with the formation of the New Zealand War Records Section, this became his home. Scales was very much on loan from Pathé who provided his camera and film. After he returned to Pathé at the beginning of February 1919, the arrangement continued and the firm would loan a cinematographer and camera to film requested events. Sometimes this was Scales and sometimes it was simply whoever was available.

UK-SERIES PHOTOGRAPHS

Scales also worked with a team as we see the filming of the king's visit involved both a still photographer and Scales as the cinematographer. The photographs identified by the initial 'UK' are in chronological order and are known as the UK-Series. It seems that many of the glass-plate negatives did not survive as the War Records Section documentation mentions having in excess of some 900 images. The existing series has just over 500 glass-plate negatives. It also lacks the detailed captions, locations and dates, which exists for the H-Series. There are captions, but there are gaps and it does not seem that master albums were assembled for the UK-Series as was the case with the H-Series. However, unlike Sanders' team on the Western Front, we know some of the photographers who worked with Scales and who were listed as members of the War Records Section. It seems one of his photographers from 1 May 1918 was Lance Corporal John Gilmour Irwin of 2nd Canterbury, a photoengraver with the *Canterbury Times*, who was wounded on 3 December 1917. He was posted as a lance corporal to the NZ War Records Section in London and would reach the rank of warrant officer.[73]

HIS MAJESTY KING GEORGE V REVIEWING NEW ZEALAND TROOPS ON SALISBURY PLAIN

Within days of being enlisted, Scales filmed *His Majesty King George V Reviewing New Zealand Troops on Salisbury Plain* on 1 May 1917. Some 7000 New Zealanders were on parade, 4000 came from 4th Brigade, a new formation being raised in England from reinforcements in early 1917 under the command of Brigadier-General Herbert Hart, the first New Zealand territorial officer to be promoted overseas in wartime to the rank of brigadier-general and to the command of a New Zealand infantry brigade. It was the New Zealand event in the United Kingdom in 1917 and this film gave it the coverage that the New Zealand prime minister craved. Massey, Ward and Mackenzie were present with their families, together with prominent New Zealand expatriates, their families and New Zealand soldiers' friends and relatives who could make the journey to Bulford Field for the occasion. Hart's diary records:

His Majesty King George V Reviewing New Zealand Troops on Salisbury Plain. NTSV F5540.

> 1st May. Beautiful day. The troops commenced moving out of Sling Camp at 9 o'clock to the review ground at Bulford Field. 7000 New Zealanders were present, 4th [NZ] Brigade 4000. From Sling 1500, Codford Command 1000. Engineers, ASC, Cadets and a few mounted. At 11.30 the King arrived accompanied by Generals Godley, Sclater ... Richardson, & Ian Hamilton also Massey, Sir Joseph Ward, & the High Commissioner. The King inspected the assembled troops then took the march past. Then he presented some medals, the senior officers & ladies present were presented to him & he left by a special train at one o'clock. The politicians then addressed the troops briefly and then returned to Sling Camp.[74]

King George V presents medals to New Zealand soldiers at Bulford Field on 1 May 1917. He is filmed by Sergeant Thomas F. Scales performing his first filming in uniform as the official cameraman, NZEF UK. NAM, author's collection.

King George V presents a decoration to a New Zealand officer cadet. In the background from left to right: Lieutenant-General Sir Alexander Godley, general officer commanding II ANZAC and the NZEF; Brigadier-General Herbert Hart, commanding the newly raised 4th New Zealand Brigade; Sir Thomas Mackenzie, New Zealand high commissioner and William Massey, New Zealand prime minister. Still from Sergeant Thomas F. Scales' *His Majesty King George V Reviewing New Zealand Troops on Salisbury Plain*. NTSV F5540.

All this is evident in the film. It begins with the parade of New Zealand officer cadets with their distinctive white pugarees on their lemon squeezers and canes, being inspected, presumably before the main parade, by Colonel V.S. Smyth, NZSC, commanding the New Zealand Reserve Group at Sling Camp. The filming shifts to Bulford Field and we see the king on horseback with

Brigadier-General Francis Earl Johnston, who commands the parade, being the senior New Zealand officer among those commanding the various New Zealand camps around Salisbury Plain. Lieutenant-General Godley, general officer commanding NZEF and II ANZAC has come over from France for the occasion, with him is General Sir Ian Hamilton and the always smiling Brigadier-General G.S. Richardson, officer-in-charge administration NZEF UK. The king inspects the ranks of New Zealanders and then reviews the march-past.

After this the King is introduced to Massey, Sir Joseph Ward, Mackenzie and their families before presenting medals to New Zealand soldiers on parade. The high commissioner's daughter, the vivacious Helen Mackenzie, stands out as the women are presented, and can be seen again with her father at the lunch following the parade. It is a friendly yet formal gathering that concludes with shots of Mackenzie addressing the troops from the back of a wagon, and there is a glimpse of the dignitaries and families lunching in the officers' mess at Sling Camp.

A New Zealand soldier photographer is very evident on film and one of his photographs shows that the cinematographer is in uniform. This is Scales in action and he already has a photographer as part of his team. The entire film was sent to New Zealand but three separate segments were included in the *Pathé Gazette*.[75] The three segments total no more than one minute and 40 seconds of film but picture-goers around the world saw King George V greeting New Zealand's political leaders and inspecting New Zealand troops — political mana for both Massey and Ward. The complete film itself was passed by censor in New Zealand on 30 January 1918, by which time New Zealand picture-goers would have already seen glimpses of the parade on newsreel.[76]

This newsreel attention was also appreciated by those being filmed. Sergeant George Knight was in the NZEF Officer Training Corps, in training for a commission in the NZEF and was involved in the events of Tuesday 1 May 1917.

In the morning we were all issued with white puggarees & they looked well. We all got sticks & gloves & the mob looked fine. We had ourselves moving pictured as we went on parade. So you must see if you can pick me. I could imagine you all sitting in the Palace & suddenly a shout "There's our George"!!??!! The march past went off well & we all had a good screw at the King. He looks very old and grey. We had addresses by Gen. Richardson, Sir Ian Hamilton, Bill, Joe & Tom McK. I don't dare think how Alex [Lt-Gen. Sir Alexander Godley] would have got on if he had tried I think he would have been hooted. He is very unpopular & Lady G even more so. He was followed by cries of "Make them do it again Alex; I like to see them run."[77]

TOMMY SCALES

The new cinema expert of the NZEF UK, Tommy Scales, was an interesting character. Film was his life or in his own words, "My life of reel thrills". In a later article Scales recounted:

Picture to yourselves Hendon flying around in 1910. Aeronautics was in its infancy then. Crack-ups were frequent. Good pictures were plentiful! Aeroplanes were "meat" to the cine-camera men of those early days. Then came my great chance — the offer of a flip in a Farnham biplane camera and all! Here was a scoop! Rushing precariously through the air, with the camera balanced upon my knee without a tripod. What a thrill! ... I have filmed every Derby since 1906. I have filmed most of the Grand Nationals. I filmed King Edward VII's funeral, King George's coronation, the Prince of Wales' investiture. I have climbed ship's riggings for unique angles, high buildings for elevated shots, narrow scaffoldings — hundreds of feet above the ground — for ship's launchings.[78]

Scales is believed to have been born in 1887 and first worked in film when he joined the Warwick Trading Company in 1905 and worked in the darkroom. He quickly graduated to camera work and in 1906 filmed the Derby. In May 1910 Scales filmed the funeral of Edward VII, and was possibly on the original staff of the Warwick Bioscope Chronicle when it was launched in July 1910. He later reminisced on having taken aerial shots at Hendon in this year, "with the camera balanced upon my knee". From his description it sounds as if he was using an Aeroscope camera. However, soon after this Scales left and joined Barker Motion Photography, which Will Barker had founded after leaving Warwick. He was employed as a cameraman and darkroom technician. It was perhaps for Barker that Scales filmed the coronation of George V in June 1911 and the following month he filmed the investiture of the Prince of Wales. From there he seems to have moved to Gaumont, perhaps to work on the *Gaumont Graphic*, but in 1912 he transferred to Pathé as one of the cameraman on the *Pathé Animated Gazette*.

TOMMY SCALES GOES TO WAR

On the outbreak of war in August 1914 Scales was instructed by Mayell, the editor of the *Pathé Animated Gazette*., "to go to Ostend, Belgium, to get what you can out of the war". He worked with the Belgian Army and in October 1914 the *Kinematograph Weekly* reported that Scales had filmed the British Naval Brigade defending Antwerp, and also worked near Ghent where he "had to carry his life in his hands, to say nothing of a very heavy tripod and camera. On several occasions he had no sooner put up his apparatus and begun to turn on an exciting subject, when the whiz of the enemies [sic] bullets and the bursting of a shell quite close to his camera made him aware of the fact that the kinematograph machine was taken by the enemy for a Belgian quick-firer [cannon]."[79]

Like all good cameramen Scales was prepared to take a chance and on one occasion he took up a position so close to the Belgian guns during a big battle on the Scheldt "that a Belgian officer thought it necessary to warn him of his great peril. As the officer approached him, Mr Scales, with the coolness that is the first quality of a good operator, continued turning despite the warning, and it took all the persuasive eloquence of this gentleman, which would have been wasted had it not been supported by an immediate order to depart under penalty of the film being confiscated."[80]

Scales was almost caught up with the German advance when his driver failed to reach an agreed rendezvous, and it was only the services of two Belgian soldiers, one of whom carried his tripod, that made it possible for him to get away. Like Sanders he ended up in a mad dash by car to Ostend avoiding German mounted patrols en route before escaping to England on one of the last fishing boats to leave the port.[81]

After the crackdown on newsreel cameramen at the front, Pathé arranged for Scales to work with the Belgian Red Cross, taking his camera "as personal baggage". Attempts to film the front line led to Scales being apprehended by a French patrol and arrested as a spy, where he was held for 48 hours before release.[82]

Scales was working for Pathé in England for the *Pathé Animated Gazette*, which came out as a bi-weekly issue. On his enlistment form he states that he was working as a cinematographer for the Whitehead Aircraft Company. It is likely that Pathé were aware that they were likely to lose him to being conscripted into the British Army, when, like a gift from the gods, the New Zealand Government came looking for another cameraman to film New Zealand-related material in Britain.

During his time as official cameraman and 'Cinema Expert' Scales shot thousands of feet of film on New Zealand-related topics. The list of films is long and impressive, covering all

aspects of the NZEF. The list of films, compiled by the New Zealand War Records Section, is long and impressive. Titles include: *NZ Boys arriving at Liverpool and entering Training Camp* (1500'); *NZ Boys at Sling Camp* (1200'); *Anzac Day 1918, Sports in Sling Camp*; *HM King George reviews NZ Troops Salisbury* (800'); *New Zealanders in England*; *No. 1 NZ General Hospital Brockenhurst, Sports, etc*; *NZ Command Depot, Codford*; *NZ Convalescent Hospital, Hornchurch*; *NZ General Hospital, Walton (Part 1)*; *NZ General Hospital, Walton (Part 2)*; *NZ Reinforcements arriving at Liverpool*; *QNZEF, YMCA, Educational Scheme, Classes at Hornchurch*; *NZ YMCA in and around Boscombe*; *NZ YMCA in and around Brockenhurst*; *NZ YMCA in and around Codford*; *NZ YMCA with the Dinkums at Brocton*; *NZ YMCA at Walton* (600'); *NZ YMCA Walton and trip on the river* (600'); *Nott's Battleplane Gift to New Zealand*; *Sir J.G. Ward inspects Boys Lads Brigade Glasgow* (400'); *Sports at Walton on Thames*; and *Thames from Walton to Richmond*.

The list is not complete but it gives some idea of the quantity of film that Scales was releasing through Pathé on New Zealand topics, which were also being sent out to New Zealand. In 1918 the fruits of Scales' first year as a cinematographer was compiled into a major film for public release.

WITH THE NEW ZEALAND EXPEDITIONARY FORCE IN THE UNITED KINGDOM (9000 FEET)

All that survives of *With the New Zealand Expeditionary Force in the United Kingdom* is part of the first reel of a nine-reel film, a mere 531 feet (161.8 metres) of the original 9000-foot (2743-metre) film, each reel of film equating to approximately 1000 feet (305 metres).[83] It opens with the intertitle: "This film has been specially taken to show the arrival, training, Hospital treatment and recreation of our Troops." We meet New Zealand Reinforcement troopship SS *Athenic* of the White Star Line at Liverpool on 16 September 1917 carrying 832 officers and men of the 27th Reinforcements.[84]

What we see in this surviving fragment is a section compiled from of one of Scales' films, *NZ Boys Arriving at Liverpool and Entering Training Camp*, which was originally 1500 feet (457.2 metres) in length. There are close-ups of soldiers waving and poking faces at the camera. Stores and officers' luggage are unloaded with a young Maori soldier, obviously an officer's batman, bringing down luggage, while smartly dressed British draft conducting officers (DCO), identified by armbands, look on. Soldiers in lemon squeezers assemble on the wharf and march off with kitbags to entrain for Sling Camp.

The next intertitle introduces us to Sling Camp, in this case a series of bell tents on the rolling downs. The reinforcements, led by their officers, march across open fields and form up under their officers before being marched away to a meal.

The first inspection of the new arrivals is held by an impassive Brigadier-General Harry Fulton, accompanied by a stern-faced Major Percy W. Skelley, a regular officer of the New Zealand Staff Corps who is the principal administration officer, a medical officer and camp staff, while the camp band plays in the background. Paybooks, which contain the administrative life of every soldier, are checked then it's haircuts and the 'Bill Massey' hobnail boots. Reinforcement officers are inspected by Fulton with Skelley grimly looking on. It was said that, "Second-Lieutenants were Fulton's pet aversions, and they dreaded him."[85]

Harry Fulton, born in India, was the son of a British general, but was a New Zealander by upbringing, raised and schooled in Dunedin where he served as an officer in the Dunedin City Guards. He joined the British Army in 1892 and later transferred to the Indian Army where he saw active service on the frontier. He served as a captain with the 4th New Zealand Contingent in the Boer War, was severely wounded, and was awarded the DSO.

The 832 officers and men of the 27th Reinforcements parade on the wharf before marching to the train. This scene also appears in *With the New Zealand Expeditionary Force in the United Kingdom, Part I*. NTSV F1001. NAM, author's collection.

Chance saw him again in New Zealand on the outbreak of war in 1914. He served with the Samoan Advance Party and then was appointed to raise the Trentham Regiment, which became the New Zealand Rifle Brigade. He took the brigade to France in 1916 and after the battle of Messines was rested with a tour as commander of the 5th Reserve Brigade in Sling Camp until November 1917 when he returned to command the Rifle Brigade. He was mortally wounded at Colincamps on 28 March 1918 when his brigade headquarters was hit by artillery fire. He died the next day. Fulton was the third New Zealand brigadier-general to be killed on the Western Front. One senses from the film that he was a no-nonsense disciplinarian, however, while not loved, he, like Russell, the divisional commander, was highly respected both as a tactician and a commander.[86]

The fragment closes with a group filming of camp staff with the brigadier-general in the centre and Major Skelley who is seen to smile! He too would die, on 9 June 1918 from wounds received in May while serving as brigade major of the 3rd Rifle Brigade.[87]

With the New Zealand Expeditionary Force in the UK, Part I, had its premiere screening at a War Film Exhibition in London from 28–30 January 1918 that was held in conjunction with the Imperial War Museum Exhibition at Burlington House. Incidental music for the film was played by Corporal Daniel Mason and seven others from the band of the New Zealand Command Depot at Codford. Mason would also feature on film as he was the outstanding New Zealand middle distance runner, one of a select group of New Zealand athletes who dominated track meetings in the United Kingdom in 1918. Mason would win gold in the 800 metres at the Inter-Allied Games in 1919.

Richardson sought Internal Affairs' finance for the cost of accommodation and meals for his musicians. It was a hard battle to have the sum of £6 and 14/- paid for as a charge to the Department of Internal Affairs instead of it being taken out of regimental funds; being three days of breakfast @ 1/3, dinner @ 1/9, tea @ 1/3 and supper @ 4d for eight men, plus beds for eight men for three nights @ 1/- in the Salvation Army Hostel on Southampton Row, London.[88] Richardson's argument being, "As the film depicted the life of a New Zealand soldier in England

With the New Zealand Expeditionary Force in the United Kingdom, Part I. NTSV F1001.

from the time of his disembarkation here until re-embarkation for New Zealand, showing the various stages for training for service overseas and of his treatment in Hospital Convalescent Camp, it was a very good piece of propaganda."[89] This administrative wrangle allows us to see the employment of the Codford Camp orchestra and imagine our eight New Zealand soldiers enjoying playing the incidental music to a major New Zealand film in a large London theatre. The film itself was a major achievement and was proof of the range of work that Scales achieved in his first eight months.

NEW ZEALAND BOYS AT SLING CAMP: NEW ZEALANDERS IN ENGLAND

We can judge what was also likely to have been part of this major film by surviving sections of the other Scales films. The *New Zealand Boys at Sling Camp: New Zealanders in England* was shot by Scales in 1917.[90] It exists as fragments only, interspersed with scenes from training in New Zealand. Spliced into the film is an improvised bridge crossing exercise by the New Zealand engineers in training, on the Tauherenikau River in the Wairarapa, most likely filmed by L.W. Mence, the freelance camp photographer at Featherston. Less than one quarter of the Sling Camp scenes survive of the original 1200-foot (366-metre) film. It shows New Zealand recruits training at Sling Camp, the main New Zealand training camp. It features a grenade practice, Lewis gun drill, trench fighting drill and the final inspection and departure of reinforcements for France.

What stands out is the intensity of the training. We see the morning 'Piccadilly' or march-past of platoons where the commandant takes the salute and the non-commissioned officers are spaced on either side of the road, barking out corrections on dress and drill as each platoon marches past. The finale is the final parade and checking of kit before entraining for France. They are much smarter than the reinforcements we saw disembarking from the troopship at Liverpool. The reinforcement draft in full kit marches to Bulford Station and file by file get into the carriages, with the stationmaster keen to get in shot, supervising the loading. The Sling Camp band plays and the soldiers wave to camera as the train pulls out and they head off to the war. Viewing the men on screen it is easy to see faces that may be relatives who served in the NZEF, but because we do not know which draft it is and when it left Codford, it is impossible to know for certain — as much as we want them to be ours.[91]

A New Zealander of the 27th Reinforcements on the SS *Athenic* as it arrives at Liverpool on 16 September 1917. Still from Sergeant Tommy Scales' *With the New Zealand Expeditionary Force in the United Kingdom Part I*. NTSV F1001.

New Zealand Boys at Sling Camp: New Zealanders in England. NTSV F17937.

NEW ZEALAND HOSPITAL WALTON-ON-THAMES AND OATLAND'S PARK. NEW ZEALAND HOSPITAL BROCKENHURST

As with the training there are two brief fragments of the many medically related films taken of New Zealanders in England by Scales. The surviving film shows an ambulance being unloaded while a one-legged soldier on crutches in hospital 'blues' looks on.[92]

The care of sick and wounded New Zealand soldiers was of intense interest to the public back home. 'Our Wounded Heroes' was a popular theme and Scales made films of all of the hospitals and convalescent facilities. In addition, a large number of films were made showing the work in assisting soldiers of the YMCA at the various hospitals and camps. These films were distributed by NZ Picture Supplies and they were shown at very successful YMCA Red Triangle fundraising days, raising thousands of pounds for amenities for soldiers overseas. We have one brief film showing the work of the New Zealand Dental Corps, similar films such as

that showing the work of Mr McKay on constructing and fitting artificial limbs have vanished.[93] The NZEF was the first in the British armies to attach dentists to the units and field ambulances. It was the first to send a dental detachment to Gallipoli. On the transfer of the New Zealand Division to the Western Front, dental clinics were set up in each unit and in all the medical units. The same applied to the camps in the United Kingdom.[94]

There was no requirement to submit copies of films complete in the United Kingdom to the War Office Cinema Committee (WOCC) and so what survives is that material used by Pathé in its *Gazette*. The remains of what came out to New Zealand are fragments only that have survived by chance and good fortune.

FILMING THE SIAMESE TWINS

In 1915–16 Mackenzie as the senior New Zealand Government representative was the ubiquitous presence in almost every film that involved visits or inspections. It was only the arrival of the 'Siamese twins', Prime Minister William Massey and Minister of Finance Sir Joseph Ward, his partner in the wartime National Government who accompanied him on each overseas trip to Britain, that pushed Mackenzie back from the limelight; though inevitably he is seen with them on most occasions.

In late 1916 Massey and Ward arrived on an extended visit to the United Kingdom that included a tour to the Western Front where they visited the New Zealand Division after its efforts on the Somme. It was a busy period and in November 1916 Massey was granted the Freedom of the City of London. Topical Budget filmed him inspecting a New Zealand guard of honour before the ceremony.[95]

In February 1917 Massey featured speaking on behalf of the War Loan to a crowd outside Mansion House with the lord mayor in attendance.[96] The New Zealand politicians featured in many of the films of rugby matches and they remained in the spotlight throughout the war.

MASSEY AND WARD ATTEND IMPERIAL CONFERENCE, JUNE 1918

On 15 June 1918 Massey and Ward arrived at Euston Station, after crossing the Atlantic in an American troopship, to attend the Imperial War Council and Conference. *The New Zealander* reported: "On arrival at Euston … the Ministers were received by a considerable gathering of New Zealanders and a guard of honour of NZ troops, while the NZ Band from Hornchurch played outside the station. There was also an escort of NZMR to the Savoy Hotel where the Ministers are staying."[97]

It is likely that Scales filmed the arrival and a segment survives on a Pathé newsreel. A photographer from Scales' team was also present. There are gloomy shots inside the station in which Massey and Ward can just be distinguished. But all is brightness and light when the band in their lemon squeezers march out the gates at Euston Station followed by the Otago Mounted Rifles and then the Rolls-Royce carrying the prime minister's party, with cheerful Londoners crowding in.[98]

Their arrival at No. 10 Downing Street for the Imperial Conference was also filmed by Topical Budget. We see the various premiers and ministers arrive by vehicle, impassively ignoring the camera and going directly inside, that is until Massey and Ward arrive. Both, on seeing the camera, smile broadly and advance towards it, determined to show the New Zealand public that they are on the job.[99]

Massey and Ward visited all of the New Zealand camps and hospitals during their time in the United Kingdom. There is a film of Massey presenting medals to wounded soldiers in their Hospital Blues uniforms at No. 2 New Zealand General Hospital at Walton-on-Thames.[100]

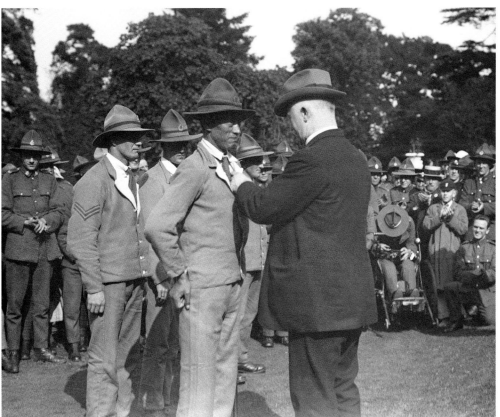

HALCYON DAYS 1918 — NEW ZEALAND TRIUMPHANT

The final year of the war were brilliant days for the sportsmen of the NZEF who were
convalescing, training or attached as instructional staff in the many camps in the United
Kingdom. New Zealanders excelled in a wide range of sports that thrust them into prominence
in the cinemas and in the press. Scales and his photographers were actively filming in all these
areas, providing news for *Pathé Gazette*.

A view of the Thames River from the headquarters of the London Rowing Club in Putney, England. Possibly during the NZEF regatta in 1918. View looks over the wooden landing. Cameraman Thomas F. Scales is carrying a camera on a tripod near the edge of the landing. Civilian and New Zealand military spectators look on. Photograph taken c.1918 by one of Scales' photographers. UK-Series UK3, 1/2-013809-G, ATL, Wellington.

🎞 *Opening of the HQ NZ Rowing Club*, British Pathé: ID 1896.21

🎞 *New Zealand Rowing Team*, NTSV F245781

OPENING REGATTA — NEW ZEALAND HEADQUARTERS ROWING CLUB

On Saturday 29 June 1918 Mr Massey and Sir Joseph Ward, with Sir Thomas Mackenzie, went to the Putney Rowing Club for the opening of the NZ Headquarters Rowing Club.[101]

This was the opening of the season and Massey, Ward and Colonel the Hon. R. Heaton Rhodes watched the races. The official photographer was present and snapped the winners of the departmental fours that was won by the Motor Traction Staff Team from Oatlands Park by a length-and-a-half over the Pay Office, who were three-quarters of a length ahead of the Post Office. The winning crew were Artificer Marshall, Artificer Anderson, Driver Lomas and Artificer Kendrick.[102] The event appeared in the *Pathé Gazette*. We see the Motor Traction Staff Team board their four, and the crossing of the finish line, followed by the winning team posing with a smiling Massey in Panama hat.[103]

It was a golden period for New Zealand rowing in the United Kingdom. In August 1918 at the Services Regatta at Putney, Darcy Hadfield won the senior single sculls and the NZ Command Depot won the senior eights. The crew were C.J. Walsh (bow), P. Monaghetti, T.J. Wright, F.S. Bush, W. Keenan, W. Coombes, C.R. Moore, C. Healey (stroke) and G.H. Wilson (cox). The Senior Fours were crewed by D.C. Hadfield (bow), W. Coombes, C.R. Moore and C. Healey (stroke).[104] At the RAF Regatta in September 1918 at Caversham, Hadfield won the single sculls and New Zealand won the international eights.[105] There is film of the eights in training at Putney. This was the basis of the team that would go on to win the Inter-Allied competition on the Seine in Paris in 1919.[106]

The NZEF Rowing Club held a series of regattas on the Thames at Putney under the auspices of the Putney Rowing Club. On Saturday 28 September 1918 at the NZEF Rowing Club Regatta held at Putney, Private D.C. Hadfield defeated W.D. Kinnear of the RAF and 1912 Olympic Champion. "From the start the Colonial, who has been exceptionally successful at all the leading regattas held on the Thames this season, made the pace, and always had the race in hand, ultimately winning by two and three-quarter lengths."[107] Apart from the handicap sculls all the other events were won by New Zealand crews, "the fine eights not being extended in the senior event, where they met the Sons of the Thames. In the junior eights for which there were seven entries, two New Zealand crews were left to fight out the final."[108]

ATHLETICS

New Zealanders also excelled on the track in the summer of 1918. "Two members of the NZEF, J. Lindsay and Corporal Dan Mason, distinguished themselves at the sports at Villa Park, Birmingham. From the scratch mark Lindsay won his heats in the 100 yards in fine style. In the

300 Yards it was equally easy for him but on account of foot trouble he slowed near the tape and came second. *The Sporting Chronicle* says: 'He is the best class sprinter of recent years. He simply danced his first heat. Enough was seen of him to justify the statement that he is of the very best class, both in speed and in style.'[109] Mason won the 1000 yards steeplechase from scratch and very much impressed the critics as a hurdler.

At Bournemouth in August 1918 the New Zealand athletes won all of the opens, the New Zealand Command Depot won the relay and the Maori Pioneer Team the tug-of-war. Lindsay came second in the 100 yards, Mason winning the 440 and the 880.[110] At the Service Meeting arranged under the auspices of the Amateur Athletics Association (AAA) at Stamford Bridge, Mason won the mile "simply strolling home in the straight". Lindsay came fifth in the final of the 100 yards, Mason second in the 440, but won the 880 yards.[111]

In September Mason won the mile in the first Cinema Gymkhana held at Stamford Bridge raising money for the king's fund for disabled officers and men of the navy, army and air forces. It was a small but select group of runners. "Two hundred yards from home, the dark-skinned New Zealander dashed to the front, and in a hundred yards had his man beat. Up the Straight Mason merely doddled, and yet won in 4 min. 20 1/5 sec. He is the best miler we have seen for many a day."[112]

At the Army Athletic Meeting at Stamford Bridge on Saturday 7 September 1918 Mason was again picked out. "The New Zealander, Cpl Mason, is the great man for middle-distance racing. He is programmed for the quarter-mile, half-mile and mile, and the half-mile in the relay. Obviously he cannot win everything; if he cuts the quarter-mile out, he may do better time in the mile and half-mile than has been seen here for years."[113] Mason did not disappoint, "he had an easy journey in the mile, simply strolling home in the straight". He narrowly lost the 440 yards and won the half-mile to go with his victory in the mile in what *The Sporting Life* described as a "wonderful show".[114]

The film *British Empire and American Services Sports — Stamford Bridge September 7th 1918* gives us a glimpse of Mason and the other New Zealand athletes. Its focus is on the Royal Air Force

British Empire and American Service Sports — Stamford Bridge September 7th 1918. NTSV F246479.

(RAF), but we see a black singlet-clad runner in the 100-yard heats, and an acknowledgement in the intertitle that "One Mile Race won by Cpl J. Mason, New Zealand", and we see him in the pack as they pass the grandstand. But for the bulk of the film it is very much the RAF's day.[115]

With Mason as a member the NZEF team consisting of Sergeant Lindsay, Corporal Stone and Corporal Brian, the New Zealanders finished the season winning the mile relay at the Life Guards' Sports in Hyde Park on Thursday 10 October 1918.[116]

NEW ZEALAND WAR RECORDS SECTION

The New Zealand War Records Section initially functioned within the AIF War Records Section in copying and distributing NZEF war diaries. A shift of location saw the section set up as an independent unit. It eventually became responsible for the collation of war diaries, the collection of war trophies, publicity, work of the Battles Committee for NZEF Battle Honours and work associated with War Memorials, as well as the Photographic and Cinema Section.[117]

Control of the work of Scales and his team passed from the High Commission to the War Records Section, headed by Captain R.F. Gambrill, on 9 September 1917. A publicity branch was established as part of the War Record headed by Lieutenant H.T.B. Drew. Drew would later edit *The War Effort of New Zealand*, one of the series of popular government histories of the war published in 1923.[118]

As Gambrill noted in his report, the glass-plate negatives for the H-Series for the Western Front, received from the War Office and UK-Series negatives, "were neither indexed nor in any order, and in addition a large number had never been dealt with" were put in order. On receipt of negatives from the War Office four prints were sent to New Zealand, two to the High Commission, one to the Ministry of Information, one to the official photographer and one on file. The negatives were then sent to the press for two weeks and resulted in photographs being published in 45 different papers throughout the United Kingdom.

Gambrill also had his staff produce albums of all the official photographs and "is proceeding as fast as the accumulation of back work permits, and the staff are working on Sundays to hasten the completion. It is intended to have a travelling album for the Division as well as a Stationary one at the Divisional Canteens, and one with the Official Photographer. Prints are for sale to the troops at 6d per half plate print and 9d per whole plate."[119] Gambrill was succeeded by Major H. Spencer Westmacott in late 1918.

Film was a different matter. The distribution of Scales' films in the United Kingdom were already part of the Pathé distribution system. This gave New Zealand constant and valued publicity throughout the world. Two copies of these films were sent to New Zealand where they were distributed by New Zealand Picture Supplies in an arrangement with the New Zealand Government. The arrangements for Sanders' films were not so clear. In his May 1918 report, Gambrill wrote: "The official photographer has, I understand, taken some films of our troops in France. I have no record of these here, though doubtless he has a record of them." As far as Gambrill knew, they were "not available for issue to the Dominions concerned until (as at present) the end of the war".[120] As we have seen, this was not the case with films relating to VIP visits and inspections where the WOCC facilitated their release.

In the United Kingdom the official photographer's team was in constant demand. During September 1918 "visits have been made to Brocton, Torquay, Sling, Boscombe, Walton and Hornchurch. Approximately 900 prints have been made from photographs taken and a valuable record of these camps has been obtained." It was the same for film and "under the arrangement

with Pathé Frères Ltd., a film depicting the activities of the N.Z.E.F. in England towards food production is being prepared. Some 2400 feet of film have already been obtained at a cost of operator's time only.
An educational film is also being prepared on similar lines."[121]

CAMP CINEMAS

Picture shows were run in all of the New Zealand camps and hospitals. The greatest problem faced was in finding a supply of films for the cinemas. Various options were tried and in September 1918 arrangements were made with the "Community Motion Pictures Bureau — a branch of the United States Y.M.C.A. — whereby excellent films of good quality are regularly obtained at a cost of £1 per night ... The cinema expert attached to this Section has rendered assistance to all our cinema operators and attends to despatch and care of programmes."[122]

New Zealand convalescent soldiers and 'Limbies' (those with artificial limbs) raising poultry as part of their rehabilitation. These scenes were also filmed in Sergeant Tommy Scales' *Hospital Farmyard*. NTSV F245798, UK-Series, UK140, 1/2-013931-G, ATL, Wellington.

Gambrill also attempted to source films from New Zealand. "The demand for cinema films of New Zealand scenes and life is insistent, and cannot be met here with the few films in possession of the High Commissioner ... The value of these films in keeping our men's minds upon their own country is great, both morally and materially, and the medium of the motion picture is one which reaches all our troops."[123]

FOOD PRODUCTION AND REHABILITATION

The victorious advance from August 1918 saw New Zealanders' doings in France feature in the press. They also featured on film in the United Kingdom where convalescent soldiers at Torquay, Hornchurch and other camps were busily producing food. At Torquay there was almost 500 acres under cultivation producing 2000 tons of potatoes and oats alone, providing both Torquay and Codford Camp with vegetables at the rate of 10 to 20 tons a week.[124] All this work featured in the *Pathé Gazette*. There is a brief clip of New Zealanders in their hospital 'blues' feeding hens.[125] There is also a newsreel titled *New Zealanders Produce their own Food*, showing ploughing by both tractor and horse, and finishing with a group of smiling 'Diggers' who have obviously been working, with their officers, who have not, but who are equally keen to be on camera.[126]

With victory on the horizon, Scales was under pressure to return to Pathé. This was finally approved from 31 January 1919. The letter of approval signed on behalf of Brigadier-General Richardson stated: "I wish to state that your work while in charge of the Photographic and Cinema Branch of the New Zealand War Records Section was performed most efficiently and gave entire satisfaction."[127] In his two years as cinematographer in the United Kingdom, he and his team had produced thousands of metres of film that Pathé gladly used in their newsreels. These and the photographs kept New Zealand in the public eye.

Hospital Farmyard. NTSV F245798.

19

Laughing with Charlie Chaplin

Take the little girl and go to a picture show and see Charlie Chaplin again,
that will make you laugh.[1]

This extract of a letter from a New Zealand soldier at the front to his wife and child in New
Zealand, quoted in Parliament, reflected the role of the pictures in wartime; a brief chance to
escape the worries of the world and the constant gnawing anxiety about loved ones overseas.
By 1915 there were 165 theatres in the country and attendance had become for thousands of
New Zealanders "as much a habit as wearing a hat or drinking tea."[2] In 1916 the *Evening Post*
estimated that 320,000 New Zealanders went to the pictures every week, with the observation
that this was a "very much bigger attendance than those who went to the churches."[3] By August
1917 it was reported during a debate in Parliament that "no less than 550,000 people go to
picture entertainments every week."[4] Going to the pictures was New Zealand's national pastime.

Multi-reel feature or star films were now common with the 1915 Chaplin film from
Keystone, *Tillie's Punctured Romance,* breaking new ground as before this no one could conceive
of a 5700-foot long multi-reel comedy (six reels and approximately 95 minutes in length). The
female stars, Marie Dressler, the highest paid vaudeville comedienne at the time, and Mabel
Norman, to whom Chaplin had previously played a supporting role, were now supplanted by
this funny chap in baggy pants. New Zealand shared the world's delight in his antics, which
mystified some commentators. A Dutch reporter contrasted cinema in Britain to Germany,
noting that film-going in Germany was to see films about the war and the war effort but on
going to a London cinema, all the audience wanted was Chaplin.

> The only sign of war was that some of your generals were thrown on the screen, but they
> received relatively small applause. An English friend of mine explained that the English are not
> enthusiastic in the matter of hand-clapping, but I pointed out that Charlie Chaplin received a
> positive ovation![5]

The Chaplin name in a film's advertising was guaranteed to draw the crowds and it was
now common for the actors' names to be advertised with most feature films. A typical film

Opposite page: This image
reflects the reaction of New
Zealanders to the steady stream
of casualties at the Western
Front that was reported in the
newspapers. This became a
flood in September when the
New Zealand Division was
committed to the Somme.
Auckland Weekly News,
27 July 1916.

The Grand Picture Palace in Dunedin opened on 17 February 1915 as part of the picture theatre building boom. Guy Morris Photo, *Otago Witness*, 31 March 1915, p. 46, Hocken Collections, University of Otago. ID14418.

programme consisted of a multi-reel feature supported by one or two single reel comedies, one or two scenic films, a news-event or a newsreel as standard fare. It was becoming less usual for a short such as a news-event film to get feature billing in the press advertising, but when it did, it was invariably because of its local interest.

New picture theatres continued to spring up in the main centres. In Wellington, the Crown Theatre in Molesworth Street in April 1916, the Queen's Theatre in Cuba Street in December 1916 and the Paramount in Courtney Place in August 1917. In Auckland, Everybody's opened in Queen Street and was one of seven Queen Street picture theatres and Hayward's built the Strand in Queen Street that opened in December 1916.[6]

In Dunedin the King Edward Theatre opened in South Dunedin on 7 December 1914, the Grand opened on 17 February 1915, Everybody's opened on 11 November 1914, the Empire, with a capacity for 1000 patrons, opened on 6 March 1916.[7] In Christchurch Everybody's opened in Cathedral Square on 1 February 1915, the Starland Theatre opened in Colombo Street on 29 May 1916, the Strand opened in Cathedral Square on 5 April 1917, followed by the Liberty on 8 September 1917, and then the Crystal Palace on 6 April 1918.[8]

The scale of theatre construction aroused the ire of Leonard M. Isitt, the member for Christchurch North who questioned the government's priorities and particularly its claim that:

> we could not proceed with certain works because of a shortage of labour, in Christchurch we
> have had three or four valuable blocks of buildings pulled down — in one case a nearly new
> building — in order to put up more picture theatres. At the present time, in Gloucester Street,
> there is a great vacant space where we are to have another picture show erected — a place where
> valuable buildings in good order have been destroyed; and here in Wellington, we have heard
> it declared that, with all the picture-shows you have in this city, there is a movement on foot to

Cadzow's Pictures, People's Picture Palace, Lyndhurst Street, Westport, opposite the public library, later renamed Theatre Royal when purchased by Miss and Mr Morgan and used for silent pictures, grand balls, dances, boxing, wrestling, concerts, indoor basketball and finally as an agricultural warehouse. Kete West Coast: Brian Ryan Collection.

PEOPLE'S PICTURE PALACE, WESTPORT.

CADZOW'S PICTURES

The World's Best Pictures for Westportians, The World's Best People.

Maoriland Worker, 14 February 1917, p. 7.

erect another one at the cost of pulling down good buildings." Isitt, no fan of pictures or picture theatres, asserted that "if the National Government had been alive to its duty, it would have absolutely forbidden the erection of another picture-show or place of amusement or racing stand until the war is over.[9]

Isitt was a flag bearer for the 'Wowsers' as they were called, that puritanical element that saw the need for thrift, temperance and sobriety to match the efforts and suffering being made at the front. For someone like Isitt, picture theatres represented an insidious lure that would weaken society: "young men and women are found in them — night after night, and night after night, sometimes for four and five nights a week … [and] evenings that should be devoted to some self-improvement are absolutely wasted, and the whole atmosphere of a life of that kind is certainly detrimental to such development as will make a man or woman a good and worthy citizen of the country".[10] However, the more general feeling was that the pictures offered a valuable escape from the strains and stress of war, and local businessmen looked at the crowds flocking to the pictures and saw it as a cash business worth investing in.

The Foresters' and Oddfellows' halls that had been venues in the suburbs gave way to specially designed theatres. In Auckland the Broadway opened in Newmarket in 1915, the Parnell Picture Palace in 1916 and the Crystal Palace in Mt Eden in the same year; the Alexandra in Greenlane in 1917 and again, in the same year, the Paragon in Papakura.[11]

It was happening throughout New Zealand. In Lyttelton, Pathé films had screened twice-weekly in the Oddfellows' Hall but a local businessman and also deputy mayor, Mr J.T. Norton, saw a business opportunity and hired prominent Christchurch architects J.S. and M.J. Guthrie to design a picture house for Lyttelton Pictures Ltd.[12] The Harbour Light Cinema, with its two

prominent and distinctive towers, was a brick building with a stucco facade in the Californian style with art nouveau features and seating for 550 patrons in the circle and stalls. It opened on 20 March 1917 with the screening of *The Deep Purple* (five-reel, 1915) starring Clara Kimball Young, followed by Charlie Chaplin; a guaranteed house filler. The local press described it as "the most up to date in the dominion" and at that moment it was, with its Nicholas Power Company projector and Mr Bert Hoyle, "a dapper man, always in grey suit, white shirt and black bow tie who was never seen out without his bowler hat" playing piano in the pit (and who also played the organ at Lyttelton's Holy Trinity Church). Going to the Saturday pictures at the Harbour Light became a highlight in many a family's week with "reserved seats that they always sat in and at half time the cinema-goers would dash across the road to the Kreamy Milk Bar for ices and refreshments. It was the social centre of the port in its picture house years."[13]

The war saw the supply of European films dwindle to a trickle and American output dominate the New Zealand film market. By 1917 film importation and distribution within New Zealand was in the hands of six firms, four of which were based in Wellington and two in Auckland. The Wellington-based firms were New Zealand Picture Supplies Ltd, The Cooperative Film Exchange, Paramount Film Service (New Zealand) Ltd and Fox Film Service (New Zealand) Ltd. The Auckland-based firms were Fraser Films (New Zealand) Ltd and Amalgamated Film.[14] New Zealand Picture Supplies was the largest firm, directly controlling 21 theatres and supplying film to 129 theatres.[15] The Cooperative Film Exchange supplied 56 theatres, Fraser Films supplied 47 theatres, Fox Film Service supplied 15 theatres and the figures for the remaining two were not listed, but likely to be small in number.[16]

In June 1917 Henry Hayward leased Nelson's Empire Theatre by New Zealand Picture Supplies, which would operate as Hayward's Pictures. In an interview with *The Colonist* he said "his company, which represents a capital of over £400,000, has over fifty picture theatres in New

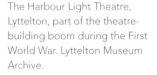

The Harbour Light Theatre, Lyttelton, part of the theatre-building boom during the First World War. Lyttelton Museum Archive.

Zealand, and employs more than 500 people, the last two or three years having shown a remarkable development in its successful operations". Hayward spoke of the future where gramophone sound would be synchronised with the pictures on screen. He believed that the popularity of the pictures was due to the "cheapness of the entertainment", and because "the silent drama enables each person in the theatre to put his or her own interpretation on what appears on the screen". He concluded by saying that: "At least 50 per cent of the population attend the picture theatre, and cinematography consequently has a tremendous influence in the moulding of public opinion."[17]

The lack of film from Europe was partly compensated for by a flow of feature films from Australia full of Anzac achievement and topical dramas based on the war. One of the first of these but without an overtly Australian theme was *It's a Long, Long Way to Tipperary*, a three-reel film by the Higgins brothers in Australia, distributed by Fraser Film Company. Based on the popular song it drew the crowds. At its opening in Auckland at MacMahon's Princess and Queen's theatres in January 1915 the management advertised that the well-known baritone Mr F.G. Bourke would sing the song at the evening sessions and that the "audience is cordially invited to assist its success by singing the refrain".[18]

In June 1915 the Australian war drama *Will They Never Come?* drew Governor Lord Liverpool, Prime Minister William Massey and Minister of Defence James Allen to the opening night at Everybody's Picture Palace in Wellington.[19] In July 1915 Everybody's announced the screening of its successor, *A Hero of the Dardanelles*.

> A Picture of the patriotic hour. A subject that will thrill you and make you feel proud you were born UNDER THE SOUTHERN CROSS. Depicting the gallant story of OUR LADS AT GALLIPOLI. Glorious interpretation of ASHMEAD-BARTLETT's famous despatches. Sequel to the record-breaking inspiring patriotic drama WILL THEY NEVER COME? You may now see the don't care lad of "Will they never come?" realising his responsibilities and gallantly assisting in the LANDING AT GALLIPOLI where he becomes A HERO OF THE DARDANELLES.[20]

This was followed by a stream of similar films: *How We Beat the Emden, Boys of the Dardanelles, Deeds that Won Gallipoli* and in response to the public outcry at her execution by German authorities in Belgium, the *Martyrdom of Nurse Cavell*.[21] At its opening at the King's Theatre in

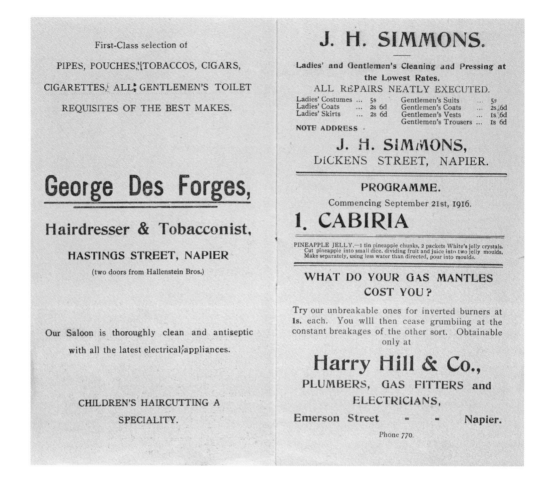

Wellington on 28 February 1916, an invitation to a private screening on the film of 'England's Joan of Arc' was extended to "all Ministers of Religion, Members of Parliament, Nurses, press and Leaders of Patriotic and Red Cross Societies".[22]

July 1915 saw the return of the first of the Gallipoli wounded aboard the *Willochra* with its cargo of 273 wounded and sick. It docked at Glasgow Wharf in Wellington on Thursday 15 July to packed crowds of relatives and next-of-kin who broke through the barriers and swamped the gangway exit. Those fit enough were then taken by motor-car parade through the city streets to the Town Hall. The wounded and their relatives entered the hall to sustained cheering and the peal of the organ while the crowd once again broke through the barriers and rushed the returned men. This enthusiasm was mirrored in every town as men went by special Red Cross train to Auckland and all stations on the way. Over the next days picture theatres screened the film *Our Wounded Heroes Return*, showing the *Willochra* coming up the stream, the disembarkation, some of the wounded and the crowd breaking the barriers at the Town Hall.[23] Welcoming the wounded home became a civic duty. The Wellington welcome for the *Willochra* became the pattern for the remainder of the war, each arrival also featuring on screen in news-events films throughout New Zealand.

LONGFORD AND LYELL FILM IN NEW ZEALAND

One Australian producer/director also looked to New Zealand as a setting for his films. In August 1915 Raymond Longford, working with the love of his life and muse, the actress and — although not credited — assistant director, Lottie Lyell, filmed *A Maori Maid's Love* in Rotorua and returned the following year to film *Mutiny on the Bounty*. They had toured New Zealand together with the Edwin Geach theatre company in 1909 and now the Longford/Lyell partnership followed in Gaston Meliès' footsteps in using New Zealand settings, one for a film with an interracial New Zealand theme, the second using the Maori backdrop to represent the Polynesians of the south sea islands.

Originally titled *The Surveyor's Daughter*, *A Maori Maid's Love* was filmed in Rotorua in 1915 with Lyell playing the heroine's part as the daughter of a Maori woman who has a married white lover.[24] It opened in Sydney in January 1916 to mixed reviews. The Sydney *Sun* reported that: "The scenery, for which New Zealand is justly famous, provides a background for the action of the play … The quaint dignity of the Maoris, their curious and in many cases beautiful tribal customs and habits are utilised in a most artistic way, possibly one of the finest effects being the reproduction of the 'poi' dance. Miss Lottie Lyall makes a fascinating 'Maori Maid', and her two foster-sisters (two genuine, pretty Maori girls) assist her capitally."[25]

Longford both produced and directed the film. He had fallen out with Australasian Films, or 'Combine' as it was known; the all-powerful film distribution agency in Australia, having unsuccessfully sued them over the distribution of his previous film *The Silence of Dean Maitland*.[26] It was their refusal to hire him studio facilities at the former Cosens Spencer facility at Rushcutter's Bay that decided him to film in New Zealand. On completion of *A Maori Maid's Love* he could not get a New Zealand distributor "owing to the opposition of the Hayward–Fuller organisation … whose interests were allied to those of the combine" and so, apart from a private screening, the film was never seen in New Zealand.[27] Despite this and although limited to showings in independent theatres willing to risk the Combine's anger, the film did good business throughout Australia. Mr W.R. Blow, the New Zealand government agent in Sydney wrote that "we have received good advertising from a moving picture entitled 'A Maori Maid's Love'. This picture has been screened all over Australia since December last."[28]

Having made money with *A Maori Maid's Love* Longford's Australian backers, Crick and Jones, financed *The Mutiny on the Bounty*, which was shot on location in Sydney, Norfolk Island and New Zealand. The Australian cast arrived in New Zealand in April 1916 with Mokoia Island and Whakarewarewa Pa at Rotorua becoming the setting for Pitcairn Island and a Tahitian village with locals being enlisted as extras and, in two cases in featured roles, Meta Taupopoki in the role of Otoo, the Tahitian chief, with Mere Amohau as Fletcher Christian's Tahitian lover. Charles Newham and A.O. Segerberg are credited as the cameramen.[29]

Longford and Lyell co-directed filming. In addition to the Maori they also sought extras from convalescing soldiers at King George V Hospital in Rotorua. One of these was Jack Moller, formerly of the Wellington Infantry Battalion, recovering from being shot in the leg on Gallipoli. "A crowd of about 40 of us took part. It was tremendous fun and the film company paid us five shillings a day."[30] Moller enlarged on his role as an extra.

Cartoonist Sir David Alexander Cecil Low, "The Business of Punching Cows". "Well now, Mrs 'Iggins my 'usband may be a bit 'andy callin' me 'cow' when 'e' is drunk, but fancy the lives them fellers wives must lead wif punchin' an' shootin' an' all." *The Bulletin*, Sydney, 4 October 1917, p. 22.

The government's response to the anniversary of "Anzac Day", the Gallipoli landings on 25 April 1916.

Some days we acted as sailors and others as soldiers of those days. We had to have our fair complexions done up with pink grease paint as our features required it, with the Maoris brown features showing up well without it … I can recall a landing we made on Mokoia Island, two of us rowed the boat, and my job was to step ashore and help Lieut Christian who was sitting in the bow ashore. Miss Lottie Lyal [sic] the leading lady was not pleased with our first effort so we had to go out and try again. The second time we struck a tall rock with a tree on top, and my mate got out and pulled the boat around, and we rowed in, in line with the camera and landed. I stepped ashore gave Lieut Christian my hand and helped him land. Miss Lyal [sic] said splendid this time. I thought we had made a mess of it bumping that rock.[31]

Moller later saw the film in his home town of Hawera and thought it "very good".[32] A young Rudall Hayward was also very impressed. "I can remember quite vividly the scenes which showed the lifeboat becalmed at night on the sea and the members of the starving and thirsty crew looking into the distance and seeing a vision which was shown by double exposure into the sail of the boat … [of] their memories of their families in England."[33]

The Mutiny on the Bounty was released as a five-reel (5000 feet) film in New Zealand in October 1916 in the same month that saw the release of D.W. Griffith's *The Birth of a Nation* and the British Government's epic official documentary *The Battle of the Somme*.[34] *The Birth of a Nation* would set new standards for feature film-making, while the multi-reel *The Battle of the Somme* (5000 feet) visually brought home the realities of war to the New Zealand public.

RAWDON BLANDFORD'S *THE TEST*

The Mutiny on the Bounty became just another film that did good business in a month when Griffith's masterpiece and *The Battle of the Somme* claimed all of the attention. It was Longford and Lyell's last film-making foray to New Zealand but Charles Newham was involved in another New Zealand-based fictional melodrama in 1916 as he was cameraman for the filming of *The Test*. This was produced and directed and starred New Zealand stage actor and singer Rawdon Blandford, who toured the New Zealand theatre circuit with J.C. Williamson, and who also had a role in *A Maori Maid's Love*.[35] Rudall Hayward remembered it being "based on a popular sort of poem that used to be recited in those days and it concerned a party of people who went into the bush … and they got lost". The likely hero proved to have feet of clay "and showed his cowardice and unimposing characters came forward and became the leaders of the party".[36] Indeed it is a campfire tale based on William Satchell's poem *The Ballad of Stuttering Jim*, of the death of two lovers from starvation while the third in the triangle hoards and secretly eats the food that would have saved them, and then has to live with the knowledge of what he has done.

The first New Zealand wounded return from Gallipoli via Egypt on the SS *Willochra* in July 1915. *The Press* Collection, 8355-1/1, ATL, Wellington.

Like *Hinemoa* before it, the four-reel film must have been done on a miniscule budget with Rawdon Blandford as producer and Nada Conrade as "principal girl".[37] It screened at the Tivoli Theatre in Auckland in 1916 and does not seem to have been released in Australia.[38] It may have been a film effort that Blandford preferred to forget. In 1933 Blandford, now described as a British film director visiting Australia, was quoted in the press adversely commenting on Australian films. When challenged to name the films he directed, Blandford instead named his Australian film appearances in Franklyn Barrett's *The Breaking of the Drought* (1920), F. Stuart Whyte's *Painted Daughters* (1925) and Raymond Longford's *Peter Vernon's Silence* (1926), but made no mention of directing *The Test*, but there again he may have decided its New Zealand setting would count against it.[39]

THE KID FROM TIMARU

It was not until December 1917 when another New Zealand fictional film was screened to New Zealand audiences. Playwright Barrie Marschel resurrected a verse play he first used on stage during the Boer War in his 15-minute film *The Kid from Timaru*. It was filmed around Timaru and Marschel took it on tour narrating the story, "told as the film unfolds by the man who wrote it".[40] Marschel used soldiers in training for some of his scenes and the advertising gave attention to the fact that it was "Pictured by Permission of Sir James Allen, Minister of Defence, and with the assistance of the Military Authorities of New Zealand." It was the verse epic in film of a "sunny-faced youngster from Timaru" who left his "scrumptious" girl with "Irish eyes" and went to war to fight the Turk for king and country and Timaru. At 900 feet (274 metres) in length it was a fictional short, a throwback to the standard one-reel of four or five years previously, but that did not dampen its reception.[41] It opened to full and enthusiastic houses at Fuller's Pictures at the Theatre Royal in Timaru on Monday 31 December 1917 with Marschel, "an old and firm favourite with Timaruvians, reciting the lines in inimitable style and with telling effect".[42] It then successfully toured New Zealand.[43]

THE WOWSERS AND CENSORSHIP

Prosperity at home sat uncomfortably alongside the sacrifice New Zealanders were making overseas. The country's economic good fortune created a public guilt complex where people felt they should be doing more

Barrie Marschel's 15-minute film *The Kid from Timaru*. Marschel acted as raconteur and recited his story in verse at each performance. Eph-A-CINEMA-1918-01, ATL, Wellington. (see colour section).

for the war effort and in particular should be sharing some of the pain. "We had a meatless day once a week, more for the look of the thing than because of any acute shortage. It was really not hardship as we quite enjoyed the change of food, and thinking out new vegetarian dishes was most interesting. There was no rationing, and we had as many clothes, and as much butter and sugar as we wanted … Middle aged and strong minded ladies employed their spare time in presenting white feathers to undeserving men, many of whom had already been to the war, and had returned permanently disabled."[44] Film played a part in shaping the public mood. "We heard terrible tales of the cruelty and barbarity of the Germans, and of their wanton destruction of everything in their path. We saw moving pictures of the actual fighting on the battlefields and then we saw movies of the results of the use by the enemy of dum-dum and soft nose bullets."[45]

Spy mania swept the country and suspicious lights and behaviour was reported. Those with German backgrounds bore the brunt of public mistrust. Anti-German hysteria was fuelled by the reports of German atrocities in Belgium, the execution of Nurse Edith Cavell and the sinking of the *Lusitania*. We wanted to believe it was true. Aliens of military age were interned on Motuihe Island in the Hauraki Gulf and on Somes Island in Wellington Harbour.

To have a German-sounding name was enough, even if the family had been in New Zealand for many years. There were outbreaks of violence. A butcher's shop in Gisborne belonging to Frederick Wohnsieder was ransacked on New Year's Eve 1914, and further incidents were reported in Wanganui and New Plymouth in 1915 when Hallensteins, the long-established men's outfitters, was attacked. In 1916 Lady Stout and Madame Ida Boeufre founded the Women's Anti-German League; its aim being "to root out the Hun Hog".[46] The League protested "against the employment of Germans, sons of Germans, and naturalised Germans in our army or in any position of trust where they can obtain information detrimental to our country's interest."[47] Supported by the *New Zealand Times* and John Payne, MP for Grey Lynn, the League conducted a campaign to get a New Zealander, Lieutenant E.H. Grierson, dismissed from the forces on the grounds that he was a spy as he had worked for the German Consul in Wellington.[48] A Royal Commission cleared Grierson, but the campaign of hate continued. Recruiting lists were scrutinised for German-sounding names, and suspects were subjected to a barrage of hate mail in letters to the editor of the local papers and though the post.

AMUSEMENTS

THE EMPRESS.
THE EMPRESS.
Last Day of
THE RUSE!   THE RUSE!
A Drama that compels.
A Big and Varied Bill as well.

THE GIANT LAUGHTER FILM
THE GIANT LAUGHTER FILM
THE GIANT LAUGHTER FILM
Starts on Monday at
THE EMPRESS.
THE EMPRESS.
ARE YOU COMING TO SEE?

CHARLIE CHAPLIN
In the biggest piece of Funmaking he has ever done. THINK! A six-reel Keystone, containing the full strength of the biggest mirth-making organisation in the Universe.
6000 feet.   100 Funsters.
"TILLIE'S PUNCTURED ROMANCE."
"TILLIE'S PUNCTURED ROMANCE."
"TILLIE'S PUNCTURED ROMANCE."
"TILLIE'S PUNCTURED ROMANCE."
"TILLIE'S PUNCTURED ROMANCE."
"TILLIE'S PUNCTURED ROMANCE."
"TILLIE'S PUNCTURED ROMANCE."
"TILLIE'S PUNCTURED ROMANCE."
"TILLIE'S PUNCTURED ROMANCE."
"TILLIE'S PUNCTURED ROMANCE."
"TILLIE'S PUNCTURED ROMANCE."
"TILLIE'S PUNCTURED ROMANCE."
A perfectly wonderful record of an excruciatingly farcical romance, presented in a cleverer and more original manner than any other comedy ever filmed.
Starring the Great
MARIE DRESSLER The highest
MARIE DRESSLER salaried
MARIE DRESSLER comedienne
MARIE DRESSLER in the
MARIE DRESSLER whole
MARIE DRESSLER WORLD.
And her marvellous work in this master laughter-piece shows you why. This
GREATEST OF ALL FUN FILMS,
Is in three Episodes. "The Elopement," "The Marriage," "The Bust Up." The whole story will be screened at every session throughout the day and night in 1½ hours.
REMEMBER!
MONDAY MORNING AT 10.
THE CRUSH COMMENCES.
DAY PRICES: 3d, 6d. Res. Section 1s.
AT NIGHT, 6d all over. Res., 1s.

Charlie Chaplin's name was enough to fill a theatre. *New Zealand Times*, 25 September 1915, p. 3.

Convalescing soldiers from King George V Hospital in Rotorua acting as extras in *Mutiny on the Bounty*. One of these was Jack Moller. "A crowd of about 40 of us took part. It was tremendous fun and the film company paid us five shillings a day." *Mutiny of the Bounty*, S1909, no. 12. 647362, NFSA, Sydney Australia.

Soldiers, such as George Bollinger, regimental sergeant-major of the Wellington Infantry Battalion who had fought with distinction for New Zealand on Gallipoli, were not immune, and were accused of enlisting so as to shoot good New Zealanders in the back. This intensified in 1916 when Private William Nimot, the New Zealand-born son of a naturalised German family from Carterton serving with the New Zealand Division in France, deserted to the Germans. It was the only case of desertion to the enemy to occur in the New Zealand forces in the First World War. In France anyone with a German-sounding name was removed from the division and sent back to England. In Carterton the Nimot family was ostracised. It was a stigma that the other sons and daughters had to bear for the rest of the war and after. A debate also began in parliament over the role of foreign teachers of enemy alien background having an undue influence over children. Professor von Zedlitz of the University of New Zealand in Wellington came in for particular attention. This led to a teaching ban on aliens; many of those barred from teaching were later conscripted for service, so they were able to fight for but not teach in their country of adoption.[49]

There was also agitation for the formal introduction of a system of government censorship of films.[50] Censorship had been debated since film was first introduced but nothing had formally been put in place; it being left to theatre owners and film distributors to decide what the public could see.[51] Rudall Hayward recalled his aunts acting in that role for Hayward Pictures "and if they didn't like the moral tone of the film, cuts were made immediately". With marvellous parallels to the compilation of the priest-censored kisses in *Cinema Paradiso*, he also noted that the projectionists would save the cuts and assemble them together always under the generic title *The Earthquake* and show it at "beer parties held by the projectionists."[52]

Tom Pollard, running his picture theatres in Greymouth and Hokitika, was equally particular about the films he screened. At the Opera House in Greymouth he once came on stage and apologised after the screening of a film "which had slipped through without his personal preview. He claimed he would never allow a woman or girl to see a picture he would not like his wife or daughter to view."[53] In the face of growing calls for censorship the picture theatre distributors and managers petitioned the government to retain the status quo. John Fuller junior of Fuller and Sons acted as spokesman. "In Wellington alone there are over 40,000 picturegoers, and these people have a sense of decency, and would soon cry out or stay away if any picture proprietor over-stepped the bounds."[54]

Picture theatre managers wanted it both ways. In 1915 Everybody's Picture Palace in Wellington did great business with *Neptune's Daughter*, featuring the Australian swimming star Annette Kellerman. The advertising for the Saturday matinee emphasised the mermaid story. "'Neptune's Daughter' is a great play for children for the story is such that only good and noble thoughts can be aroused."[55] However, it was not the mermaid story that attracted the adult audience, with the same paper's entertainment reporter delicately making it clear why one should see the film. "Miss Kellerman is admittedly in the forefront as one of the world's greatest swimmers, divers, and natatorial experts, besides being credited with possessing the most truly classical figure known to the modern world — a figure surpassing the lovely lines of the ancient Greek goddesses. In 'Neptune's Daughter', Miss Kellerman, as the daughter of the old sea-god, is said to display to advantage the lavish gifts Nature has showered upon her."[56]

Billposters also came in for criticism. In Auckland, Harold Josey, chairman of the Parnell School Committee protested about:

> the most suggestive posters that are displayed within sight of the Parnell Public School, at the foot of Alpha Road. I am well aware that little children do not see the evil in a picture that an adult would see, but boys and girls in the fifth and sixth standards most certainly do. There were two posters recently placarded up to which others besides myself had strong exception. The first was a picture of two men fighting in a bedroom in the presence of a very scantily-attired female. The second was a man holding a woman in an extremely suggestive attitude and kissing her.[57]

John Fuller wrote of 500,000 New Zealanders acting as self-censors, but for the many that his letters addressed this was not a time or a place for a laissez-faire approach on questions of public morality. After a series of well-reported public conferences and meetings led by the Catholic Federation the government gave way and introduced the Cinematograph-film Censorship Act, 1916. William Jolliffe was appointed film censor with a duty to refuse approval "in the case of any film which, in the opinion of the censor, depicts any matter that is against public order and decency, or the exhibition of which for any other reason is, in the opinion of the censor, undesirable in the public interest."[58] The film censor's position was not an easy one. Many small picture theatres producing local films did not believe that censorship applied to them for something that was filmed today and shown tomorrow and Jolliffe was too busy to follow-up films that had been shown without clearance.

In August 1915 James McDonald, using his experience as former government kinematographer, made suggestions on the procedures that may be best followed in censoring films.

The Australian professional swimmer, Annette Kellerman, pioneered the one-piece female swimsuit to the outrage of many. Her films also excited concern. "In 'Neptune's Daughter', Miss Kellerman, as the daughter of the old sea-god, is said to display to advantage the lavish gifts Nature has showered upon her." George Grantham Bain Collection, Library of Congress.

There are only three concerns importing and distributing films in New Zealand, the chief of which has its headquarters in Wellington. An examination of the films here by a responsible government officer prior to their distribution might effectively stop the exhibition of immoral and vulgar picture, and do away with the necessity of Government Inspectors throughout the country. To each film passed there might be added a few feet, just sufficient to satisfy the public mind, bearing the words passed by the New Zealand Government Inspector (or Censor.)[59]

His recommendations were not forgotten. In August 1918, after Jolliffe, citing workload, submitted his resignation, he was persuaded to remain on the understanding that an assistant censor would be appointed. McDonald was appointed assistant censor.[60] This was a part-time position for two days of the week for which he received £75 per annum.[61] It was an appointment he later came to detest. The increasing length of films added to his workload, and McDonald realised once again that he was seen as the perfect second-in-command, always able to stand-in but never likely to be appointed to the censor's position as in the same way, despite working as acting director; he was never going to be appointed director of the Dominion Museum.[62]

The government responded to each problem as it arose with regulation. War regulations on finance, patriotic societies, six o'clock closing of public houses, censorship, national efficiency and conscription involved government to an unprecedented degree in the lives of its citizens. It set and increased income tax, regulated trade and expanded the bureaucracy of government. In 1917 an amusement tax was introduced that added to the prices of theatre tickets. It reflected the National Government's ongoing search for income to offset the cost of the war. In the same year a "penal tax was imposed on those who had not contributed to the war loan in proportion to their incomes" and a beer tax dependent on alcoholic content was introduced. The graduated income tax first introduced in 1914 increased by 33⅓% and

Greymouth and Hokitika picture theatre manager Tom Pollard, c.1907.
PA1-q-237-237 ATL, Wellington.

William Joliffe, New Zealand's first film censor. James McDonald would
become his deputy in 1917. 1-2-098682-F.W. Joliffe, ATL, Wellington.

applied to incomes from lands and mortgages in order to tax the increased profits from the
sale of wool, meat and dairy produce. It was one way that New Zealanders at home could
share in the burden of war. The contribution of income tax to government tax revenue rose
from 9.2% to 40.4% in the period 1914–15 to 1916–17.[63]

In one sense the amusement tax on entertainment was a safe target but all the same
Minister of Finance Sir Joseph Ward, did not want to adversely affect the film industry. He
made sure that the tax had minimum impact on the cheapest seats, with no tax on admissions
up to and including 6d, and a 1d tax on admissions up to the value of 2/6d and so on up the
scale of admission prices. Ward's avoidance of tax on the cheapest seats reflected the general
feeling that "The sixpenny picture show had been an enormous boon and blessing to a large
number of people, and in war-time it had kept them from fretting."[64]

20

Filming 'God's Own Country'

On Saturday I had my first experience in whaling and it was great the other two boats got there first but waited for our boat to arrive with the camera there were 2 big humpbacks surrounded by hundreds of porpoises … I got some great film.[1]

During the war, local scenic, news-events and industrial films continued to be popular and featured in cinema advertising. These included films of the Auckland Cup at Ellerslie and the Wellington Cup Day at Trentham, the Waitemata Regatta with 'Beautiful Yachting Scenes, Auckland', and scenic films of New Zealand.

SELLING NEW ZEALAND TO THE WORLD

In October 1916 the Lyric Theatre, Auckland, invited patrons to be all seated for Rotorua with the train leaving the Lyric Station at 8 p.m. in *A "Picture" Trip to Rotorua*.

> The Wonderland of New Zealand has, strange to say, been visited by comparatively few residents of the Dominion. The guides of Rotorua inform the visitor that for every New Zealander who goes through to view the thermal marvels of his country, there are three Americans and two Australians.[2]

Now New Zealanders could see all that Rotorua had to offer in this 2000-foot film. "The pictures which were taken by a local cinematograph photographer, Mr Newham, are beautifully clear, and it is to be hoped that the success of the present series will encourage the exhibition of more local pictures of the same class."[3] Newham's film featured in theatres throughout New Zealand. It followed his earlier scenic film *God's Own Country* that also featured scenes of Rotorua but included "views of a trip on the Porokino [Pourakino] River, Southland — the upper reaches of the river, mutton birds and sea scape studies on the West Coast showing Blowhole Bay and The Lion Rock."[4] It appears Newham concentrated on filming Rotorua-related material and produced *A "Picture" Trip to Rotorua*. New Zealand fictional films may have been rare events but travelogues and scenic films drew large local

Opposite page: Medieval pageant in 1914 with knights and their maidens on display at Newtown Park. A motion picture cameraman is in the foreground. *Christchurch Press* Collection, G17718-1/1, ATL, Welllington.

```
WEDNESDAY        POLLARD'S PICTURES        WEDNESDAY
    THE  TRIANGLE  PLAY THAT  SET NEW YORK  TALKING
    THE SWEETEST BROADWAY FOLLIES STAR EVER KNOWN
In the——Spiciest—  Raciest—   and Sweetest Drama Ever Written—

    OLIVE THOMAS      In ——       "BROADWAY ARIZONA."
    OLIVE THOMAS      In ——       "BROADWAY ARIZONA."

A PLAY CROWDED WITH THE SPARKLE & GAIETY OF THE GAYES
From Broadway, —Land of Lights— to  the  Black  Wastes  of  Arizona

"THE TRAGIC MOSQUE"—13th Episode of the "SECRET KINGDOM.
NO 3 AND FINAL SCENES OF NEW  ZEALAND  ALPINE  REGIONS

ELECTION  RETURNS——All returns screened as they arrive
```

Grey River Argus, 29 May 1918, p. 1.

audiences as well as finding a market in Australia and the United States.

A number of these were the work of Syd Taylor, the official cinematographer working for the Department of Agriculture. "Most of my work was movie pictures of N.Z. Industries and Farming and showing pictures in different places in the country districts."[5] In this he mirrored the experience of McDonald before him, but the war saw the government photographer once again at the centre of New Zealand film-making similar to McDonald's halcyon period from 1908–10. In Wellington, Shortt's Theatre was the regular outlet for Taylor's government films: *Grass Seeding in New Zealand, Coal Mining in New Zealand, New Zealand's Thermal Regions* with scenic films of Rotorua, the Buller Gorge and Huka Falls following one another throughout 1915. In addition to Taylor showing films in country halls at the behest of local MPs, his films were distributed through New Zealand by New Zealand Picture Supplies. In 1916 *The New Zealand Fruit Industry*, "kindly loaned by the Agriculture Department" featured in the advertising at Everybody's Theatre in Hastings and it may have been coincidental that the main billing was *The Fruits of Desire.*[6]

THE WONDERLAND OF NEW ZEALAND

The Department of Tourist and Health Resorts saw its European market for New Zealand-bound tourists dry up and throughout the war concentrated its overseas attention on Australia and America, as well as convincing New Zealanders to visit the beauty spots of their own country. This kept Taylor busy and during the summer season he was engaged in filming and editing a constant stream of scenics and industrials. One of the major productions of this period was *The Wonderland of New Zealand*. This was not filmed by Taylor, but was the work of two Kinemacolor cameramen sent to New Zealand by the Natural Color Kinematograph Company of England. Although 7000 feet in length, this needs to be qualified since Kinemacolor films necessarily ran at twice the speed of ordinary black and white films. The film was the equivalent of 3500 feet, giving a running time of approximately 58 minutes.[7] It toured with special projectors and operators as a form of "roadshow" or "special" presentation. It was distributed through New Zealand Government agents to film distributors in Australia and the United States.[8] A great success, it was shown at the San Francisco Exhibition in 1915 and then distributed throughout the United States.

The film also toured Victoria, South Australia and New South Wales. "The kinemacolor pictures were shown in Sydney for three weeks on end at one of the leading picture theatres and it was estimated that they were seen by about twenty-five thousand people."[9]

It also toured New Zealand for three months to good houses. "It reveals the beauties of New Zealand scenery in natural colours, dealing particularly with Mt Cook and the Cold Lakes of the south. The film which is controlled by William J. Shephard who will be remembered for his 'Fighting Forces of Europe' is presented by arrangement with the New Zealand Government."[10]

Shephard aimed for similar success with *The Wonderland of New Zealand*, opening it in Wellington on 9 June 1917 at the Town Hall with the governor, the Earl of Liverpool, and Lady Liverpool in the audience.[11] It screened at the Theatre Royal in Christchurch from 10–15 September, and from the programme detail we see that the Kinemacolor film encompassed all aspects of New Zealand's scenic attractions, covering:

The Home of the Maoris — Rotorua — Whakarewarewa — Maori Types — Washing, Bathing, and cooking in Hot Springs — Ceremonies and Native Scenes

Grain Growing — Stock Raising — Shipping Oysters, Cheese and Hemp

Milford Sound Fiords — Glaciers —Wanganui River — Christchurch and the Avon …

Glimpses of the Great Motor Tour — Queenstown (Lake Wakatipu) — To Mount Cook and the Hermitage.

Sports in New Zealand — Horse Racing — Trotting — Surf Bathing — Trout Fishing.

Rotorua — Government Buildings — Bath House and Gardens — Hot Lakes and Steaming Cliffs.[12]

During 1915 and early 1916 Taylor filmed in the Southern Alps and the Annual Report for 1915–16 reported that a "complete set of films of the alpine region has been secured by the photographer of the Department of Agriculture, and it is intended to have these extensively displayed in Australia as well as in New Zealand through the medium of picture companies".[13] This was released as *The Southern Alps of New Zealand* and successfully toured throughout New Zealand and Australia. In March 1917 Mr Wilson, the general manager, reported that the film was still touring Australia "and I have direct evidence from correspondence received that they have already been the means of inducing Australians to visit New Zealand and personally see this wonderful display of nature's grandeur".[14] He also noted the intention to "take cinematograph-films of the fiordland regions, but unforeseen happenings have caused this project to stand over for another season".[15] *The Southern Alps of New Zealand* remained popular and the New Zealand Government agent in Sydney reported that for 1917, this and the film *Scenes in New Zealand* "have frequently been loaned to various picture proprietors for exhibition in Sydney and the suburbs".[16]

Even disasters had their silver lining. The Waimangu Geyser eruption on 1 April 1917 destroyed the accommodation and killed the wife and child of the caretaker. The tragedy had the effect of drawing sightseers and the general manager reported that "the 'round trip' has, however, again been established, and the traffic shows no sign of falling off. It will be necessary to erect another dwelling for the guide and it is intended to preserve the ruins of the old building as an attraction to visitors, as was done in the case of the remains of the old houses at Wairoa destroyed by the eruption of 1886."[17] This featured in the cinemas and there is a surviving clip from a *Pathé Gazette* titled *Great Volcanic Eruption at Rotorua* showing clouds of white steam rising from the ash-covered site; a mantelpiece standing among the remains of the accommodation house while a sole figure walks among the ruins.[18]

America's entry into the war in 1917 impacted on the number of tourists to New Zealand. Australia was now the main source of visitors with a large number coming "for sight-seeing and health purposes". America's ongoing potential as a source of tourists was still recognised and all of Taylor's scenic films were sent to America "and are being shown in many theatres by the leading firm of Burton Holmes and Co., and several requests for further copies and more varied films have been received".[19] Elias Burton Holmes was a professional lecturer whose illustrated travel lectures made him a household name in America. His travelogue films, such as those provided to him by New Zealand, were released through Paramount to the moving picture

Dominion, 5 June 1917, p. 7.

 *Pathé Gazette: Great Volcanic Eruption at Rotorua.* NTSV F31423.

theatre chains throughout the United States.[20] Holmes' own cameraman also visited and filmed in New Zealand.[21] This was excellent publicity for New Zealand and more than repaid the cost to government of their official photographer — T.E. Donne's dream again being fulfilled.

In terms of revenue, 1916 and 1917 were record years for the Tourist Department with the influx of many Australian tourists. Wilson recognised that "the kinemacolor display of New Zealand scenery … and the exhibition of the scenic films of the Southern Alps were potent factors" in this success. Taylor was tasked accordingly. Wilson wrote: "During the coming season I propose getting the Government photographer to do a considerable amount of travelling and to further develop this method of advertising."[22]

From December 1917 Taylor's film *Alpine Regions of New Zealand* toured New Zealand.[23] It was released in three parts and while generally commented on as "excellent entertainment", came in for occasional critical comment. "'Alpine Regions of New Zealand' (Part No. 1) unfolded a view of an outward bound train from Timaru and scenes on the way to the Hermitage at Mount Cook. Glimpses were also given of the snow-bound heights and glaciers 7000 ft. above sea-level. As appears to be the case in the majority of the films taken in New Zealand, the photography in parts, due to faulty toning, was not a complete success."[24]

Taylor's filming was far from occasional and episodic but kept him fully employed during these years as he met the directions of the general manager for the Department of Tourist and Health Resorts as well as doing an ongoing series of industrial topics on New Zealand's agricultural industries for the Department of Agriculture. His output was impressive both in quantity and in quality, to which his surviving film of whaling in the Cook Strait bears testimony.

WHALE HUNTING IN COOK STRAIT

In early 1918 Taylor was filming in the South Island fjords. He followed this work by filming life at the shore whaling station at Te Awaiti in Cook Strait. Taylor was a keen sailor, having his engineer's ticket for all types of powered boats except steam and a master's ticket for inland waters and extended limits around the coast. His love of the sea is captured in this film. The complete *New Zealand Whale Hunting with Motor Launches in Cook Strait* survives together with 56 minutes of off-cuts, which gives us a glimpse of how he shot and edited his films.[25] Taylor gave a private screening on 7 November 1918 and it was passed by the censor on 10 December.[26] Taken during September's southeasterly gales in Cook Strait, it records the work of the three Picton-built motor launches, the largest being the *Cachelot*, that set out from the whaling station when the lookout on Lookout Point above the Tory Channel reports a whale in sight.

> No sooner is the whale seen than the three launches [leave] … carrying each two men — harpooner and coxswain. It is the former's business to hurl the spring-barbed shaft, the latter's to drive home the bomb lance. The harpooning is not so much as to kill as to secure the cetacean. The bomb does the killing. This bomb is a hollow tube of iron into which fine sticks of gelignite with a detonator behind them are inserted. There is a barbed head to the bomb. At the other end a wooden shaft is screwed in. The charge thus kept in place is fired by the detonator which is ignited by electric spark from a battery to which insulated wires are attached. There may be a pay out of 20 fathoms of this firing wire. The whale having received its mortal wound — and misses and losses are exceedingly rare — is towed back to Te Awaite as fast as possible and there cut up.[27]

New Zealand Whale Hunting with Motor Launches in Cook Strait. NTSV F880.

Whaling in the Tory Channel.
Two whale chasers following
a submerged whale.
Photographer: S.C. Smith,
1/2-046855-G, ATL, Wellington.

Killing the whale. Still from
Sydney Taylor's *New Zealand
Whale Hunting with Motor
Launches in Cook Strait*.
NTSV F880. (See colour section.)

All this is shown dramatically on film, the history of the station and its position in the Sounds, the preparation of the harpoon, the lookout, seeing the 'spout', the race to the boats and the chase as the launches put to sea in speeds of up to 29 knots. Whales are harpooned from the

Cutting up the whale. Still from *New Zealand Whale Hunting with Motor Launches in Cook Strait*. NTSV S4277, No. 1.

chasers in stormy seas, killed with bomb lance to the elation of the crews, and towed back, with an escort of gulls overhead and dolphins or pilot whales alongside, to be cut up and flensed at the trying station on the opposite side of the sound to Te Awaiti. "Blubber is stripped off in great slabs with a short butcher's knife, such as would be used in killing sheep. From the intestines fat is also taken up to two tons in some cases. The bones and the fat-stripped carcase is towed to sea and allowed to sink." At the time of Taylor's filming 40 whales had been taken during the season, with a large whale yielding up to ten tons of whale oil.

Taylor interweaves several strands into his documentary narrative: dramatic in its high speed chases and whaling scenes, scenic in the drama of a wild coast and strait, and educational in his detail of the life of the whale. Nothing escapes his camera from the balletic movements of the harpoon gunner as his feet constantly move to retain his balance in rough seas to the thrashing tail of a giant humpback in its death throes. He himself had a "very lively time of it". The whale chaser he was on was flicked by a humpback in rough seas, and he was lucky it was no more than a tap, "making a rent of five feet, but not so bad as to prevent the launch from reaching home where she sank."[28] He was enjoying himself and this is evident in his letters to 'Em', his wife.

> On Sunday we went after another two [whales] we got away before the other boats and got an iron [harpoon] into one of them before the others came up and what a time we had[.] before we started one whaler said to me that if I see flukes and tails flying round me [']keep turning['] [the camera] and when anything happened they would all yell [']keep turning['] well one got underneath us nearly got us over[.] one end of his tail nearly swept my camera off the deck and I kept turning[,] I think it must have been from fright[.] just after that I got a great piece of film, it will make your hair stand on end, a whale spouted and the small launch charged it at full speed from the opposite direction[.] the gunner made a lovely flying shot[,] got his harpoon home[,] the engineer could not pull up in time so he drove it right over the back of the whale in a smouther [sic] of foam[.] it was great and I have got 1200 ft of film of whales in every position.[29]

Looking back on his life, Taylor set greater store on his work after 1925 as a photographer with the *Otago Daily Times*. His photographs would win a gold and silver medal at the Panama World Exposition, but in his scenes of the shore whaling industry, we see his skill as cameraman, storyteller and editor, telling a story, both terrible and majestic, that holds the audience for its three reels. It was "a bigger job than I thought and it is going to be my masterpiece."[30] In terms of New Zealand documentary narrative, it is, and one must agree with what Elsdon Best wrote in the *Evening Post* at the time. "The pictures are beautiful, clear, well-chosen, and valuable as recording a New Zealand industry which may be truly described as heroic."[31]

LOCAL EVENTS FOR LOCAL THEATRES

The pattern of local films in local theatres continued as before the war with local cameramen busy meeting local interest in each centre. In Christchurch the Grand Theatre provided a cameraman to the Colosseum Skating Rink for the filming of its two day skating carnival in August 1917.

> A MOVING PICTURE will be taken of the Whole Carnival from start to finish. We want you to be in this. The Management have spared no expense in lighting and decorating to perfect this elaborate and costly film, which has never been attempted before in any skating rink in the Australasian Colonies.[32]

It was to be screened first at the Grand Theatre and then to tour "throughout New Zealand at an early date".[33] The Grand made it its business to film and screen local events. Earlier in the same month it advertised the *Grand National Steeplechase* with "Views of the Crowd. Come and See if the Camera caught you".[34] In late 1917 the Grand Theatre's cameraman responded to the request of Mr T.E. Taylor, the leading merchant at Akaroa, who financed the £40–50 needed to make *Picturesque Akaroa and the Bays* showing the "motor drive to Akaroa and all the beauty spots" to advertise the town and the harbour to New Zealand. It had its first screening in January 1918 at Hayward's Weekly Pictures in the Oddfellows' Hall, Akaroa, managed by the same T.E. Taylor who financed it.[35] It fit comfortably into the pattern of the many similar films intent on broadcasting the beauty of their town and district to the rest of New Zealand and possibly the world.

Comparatively few films taken in New Zealand during the war years have survived. One is of the manufacture of Highlander Milk taken by Newham's Dominion (NZ) Film Company showing in detail the process of its production at W.T. Murray & Co. factory at Underwood near Invercargill.[36] Newham gave the intertitles a distinctive tartan pattern as he shot all aspects of the production. The film toured throughout New Zealand with the feature *Big Gun Manufacture* that showed the manufacture of heavy naval guns in the United States.

Murray, the manufacturer of Highlander Milk, made effective use of the screenings, which they no doubt commissioned Newham to film, as it toured New Zealand from November 1915 to June 1916. Commonly screened under the title *Highlander Milk Manufacture*, the *Evening Star* in Dunedin advertised its screening at the New Queen's Theatre. "MAKING HIGHLANDER MILK: A NEW ZEALAND INDUSTRY. A Film, itself of New Zealand manufacture, of interest to all patriotic supporters of Local Industry … During the time the Picture is being shown here, the Proprietors of HIGHLANDER MILK will post, free of charge, a Copy of their HIGHLANDER COOKERY BOOK to anyone sending in the annexed coupon".[37] It is ironic that faults with the soldering process in sealing the cans saw Murray go into

Canning Highlander Milk.
Still from Charles Newham's
Highlander Milk Manufacture.
NTSV F4996.

Highlander Milk advertisement. *Weekly Press,*
Christmas number, 1917, PUBL-0104-1917-12-01 ATL.

liquidation while this film was on the circuit and the manufacture of Highlander Milk ceased until the factory was taken over by the New Zealand Milk Products Company.[38]

Newham also filmed the production of Glaxo dried milk powder at Joseph Nathan's newly built factory at Matangi near Hamilton.[39] The surviving sequence shows scenes of the Glaxo factory in production at Matangi, which opened in late 1919. It was described in the *Auckland Star*:

> Dealing first with the industrial phases of the picture, one of the most interesting was that devoted to the new branch of the dairy industry, under which is to be classified the production of Glaxo or dried milk. The film shows views of Messrs Joseph Nathan and Company's up-to-date and extensive works at Matangi, with adjuncts in the shape of comfortable cottages for the workmen. The bringing in of the milk in its ordinary fluid form by the suppliers was first shown. The process of transforming the milk into its dried state was then exhibited. The Glaxo being seen rolled out of a large machine in thin sheets. The sifting process and the packing of the product in tins (also manufactured there), and the final view of the well appointed engine room and the modern plant, completed the interesting visit to these works.[40]

This was part of the film, *The Land We Live In* that was produced by Messrs Siegel and Wilson, the principals of the New Zealand Educational Film Company that toured the film throughout New Zealand. The film was aimed at both the educational market and the general public. Two years had been spent filming the scenic attractions and the major industries of New Zealand. It was then screened throughout the country in 1919–20 with provision for schools to see the

*Highlander Milk
Manufacture.*
NTSV F4996.

Weighing Glaxo dried milk powder at Joseph Nathan's newly built factory at Matangi near Hamilton. Still from Charles Newham's *The Land We Live In*. NTSV F11142.

afternoon matinee sessions. It had the backing of the Tourist Department and it was intended to "show the film in various parts of the world".[41]

It opened at the Britannia Theatre in Wellington to a special screening for Minister of Education the Honorable Mr J.A. Hanan, senior members of the Education Department and other dignitaries including the mayor of Wellington, Mr J.P. Luke. "All of those present yesterday were unanimous in their high praise of the production. 'It is the best picture I ever saw', said the Mayor."[42]

These and the Brandon Haughton film of *The Production of the Taranaki Herald and Budget* filmed in 1912 are rare surviving examples of New Zealand industrial films of the period.[43]

They were popular films, of great local interest, showing New Zealand manufacturing ingenuity to New Zealanders.[44] Highlander Milk is still produced today, with its distinctive label showing a pipe major of what is believed to be a Southland highland pipe band, but no longer in Underwood; having being long absorbed into Nestlé. Glaxo is now part of one of the largest pharmaceutical companies in the world, and only the empty disused factories at Bunnythorpe and Matangi gives some clue as to its beginnings in New Zealand.

CZAR OF NEW PLYMOUTH

Empire Theatre owner Garnet Saunders faced competition from the People's Picture Palace, which opened in New Plymouth in 1916. Competition merely whetted his appetite; audiences were flocking to the pictures and he was determined to cash in. In addition to the Empire Theatre, he purchased New Plymouth's Theatre Royal, where he originally started screening films, and also began the construction of a new cinema, Everybody's Theatre. He was also contracted to build theatres in Waitara, Inglewood and Stratford; Taranaki, under Saunders, being very much part of the cinema-building boom.

However, there were troubles for Saunders in 1915. A popular film in New Zealand that year was *Armies of Europe at War* which was double-billed with *N.Z. Troopship to the Dardanelles*.

The Land We Live In. NTSV F11142.

1500 School Children at New Plymouth. NTSV F7411.

In New Plymouth the company touring the film negotiated with Saunders for the hire of the Theatre Royal and then complained in a letter to the editor of the *Taranaki Herald* that Saunders had refused to let out the theatre "unless paid an outrageous sum of money". Enraged at suggestions that he had tried to keep the public from seeing the film, Garnet sued Henry Weston, owner of the *Taranaki Herald*, for £1000 for libel. At the hearing in 1916 Garnet was labelled "the Czar of theatres in New Plymouth" and lost the case, being ordered to pay costs.[45] Worse was to follow. On 23 July 1916 the Theatre Royal and the business block of buildings in which it stood were destroyed by a fire that started in the theatre. Undeterred, Garnet built Everybody's Theatre, which opened on 15 December 1916. The local press called it the best theatre in New Zealand with the best orchestra (Garnet, no doubt, finding time for the occasional turn in the pit with his cornet), and "Patrons went away from Everybody's feeling that New Plymouth had a theatre that was the acme of perfection."[46]

In 1917 Garnet Saunders produced *1500 School Children at New Plymouth,* with Brandon Haughton again the most likely candidate behind the camera, taken for the Empire Theatre in New Plymouth. Its shots of the teachers and children at the Central, Fitzroy and West End schools in New Plymouth with the school assemblies, including careful close-ups and carefully worded intertitles such as 'Some good samples of Taranaki's coming manhood' that would make a viewing parent justly proud, would ensure that all the children and their parents would troop to the theatre to see their sons and daughters on film. It followed the themes of Saunders' earlier films and was no doubt repeated many times over in the years to come.[47]

PATRIOTIC INTENT

The *Mardi Gras Festival Napier New Zealand 1915* showing the decorated floats passing through the crowds lining Hastings Street is typical of the many patriotic pageants and parade films taken at the time, and here the annual Mardi Gras festival also becomes a celebration for New

The title still of Harry Thompson's *Mardi Gras Festival Napier New Zealand 1915.* NTSV F5065.

Creamoata on the float and Kaiapoi [Woollen Mills] on the building, feature in the New Zealand of 1915. Still of Harry Thompson's *Mardi Gras Festival Napier New Zealand 1915*. NTSV F5065.

Zealand wartime endeavour with floats celebrating the British Empire and her Allies leading the procession; a Japanese flag is prominent on a small highly decorated motor car, with another horse-drawn float showing the work of the Red Cross. The cameraman is thought to be Harry Thompson of Thompson–Payne Pictures, who was the secretary of the Mardi Gras Committee. The film screened at the King's Theatre, Hastings, on 16 January1916.[48] It is a local film taken to draw local audiences that, by the wording of its title, then found a wider audience.[49]

The film of the 1916 spring annual Daffodil Parade along Queen Street in Nelson also survives, and while the focus is on the gaily decorated motor car floats smothered in flowers, and of the young children dressed as daffodils, bees, fairies, pixies and elves, the influence of the war is everywhere evident. Staff sergeants in uniform marshal the parade, uniformed school cadets are part of the procession, streets are lined with territorial soldiers, and at the conclusion of the Bishop of Nelson's welcome to spring, the commanding officer of the XIII Nelson Infantry Regiment is presented with what seems to be a bunch of daffodils.[50]

There is a film of the presentation and dedication of the Auckland Hospital's first motor ambulance with speeches by dignitaries in front of staff and public on the hospital steps followed by a parade of Red Cross volunteers in the Domain reviewed by the governor.[51]

Similar films were taken of the Queen Carnival competitions run throughout New Zealand by the New Zealand Patriotic Society to raise funds for wounded soldiers, widows and orphans. In Wellington, prominent publicity was given in the press to the willingness of the picture theatres to lend a hand. Writing on behalf of the Wellington Picture Theatres, the chairman, Mr E.J. Righton, said that the proprietors would "take kinematograph pictures of the Carnival 'Queen' and screen them" in the main Wellington theatres including the Empress, Shortt's Britannia, People's Picture Palace, the New Theatre, Everybody's, the King's and the Star Theatre in Newtown. Ballot boxes would be placed in theatre vestibules and voting tickets could be purchased from the theatre ticket booths. In addition, the proceeds of 6000 tickets worth £150 would be donated.[52]

The Dedication Ceremony of the First Ambulance at the Auckland Hospital. NTSV F8174.

In the procession to Newtown Park the picture theatres presented a float representing:

> the setting of an outdoor drama, such as was produced in the early days of film-making … A kinematograph operator will be seen energetically turning the handle of his machine while the 'Blood and Gore Company' stage a moving-picture drama, entitled 'The Scolloped Heart, or the Maiden's Curse'. People will be able to see how snow effects were obtained, how dense volumes of smoke in the picture were produced by simply passing smoke in front of the camera lens, and how 'stodgies' were used for 'marvellous fire effects'. The Story of 'The Scolloped Heart' is a powerful one. It will show how the heroine's child is murdered, not less than three times, and how the faithful Indian rescues the hero on numerous occasions."

The cast was made up of picture theatre staff and included impersonations of the movie stars of the day, Charlie Chaplin, Mabel Normand, 'Fatty' Forde Sterling, Keystone police "and many other well-known picture artists".[53]

At Newtown Park,

> [a] squad of picture-house employees under the direction of Mr John Fuller, will parade with a moving-picture camera and take 'movies' of all and sundry who contribute to the funds. Tickets will be sold at sixpence each, which will permit the buyers to be included in the groups of people kinematographed, and not only would the pictures be screened locally, but they will be exhibited in other parts of the world, where relations and friends will be able to recognise people living in this outlying portion of the British Empire.[54]

The Wellington theatres were true to their word and films of the procession of the great patriotic carnival were screened in the following weeks. The King's Theatre screened film taken by 'Vanie' Vinsen and his team. "The processions on Thursday and Saturday and the great crowds at the Park are very clearly depicted. Among the many novelties shown is a special athletic display by the Metropolitan Fire Brigade." The various queen candidates also appeared. "The majority of them, though new to the animated camera, have depicted themselves very naturally and gracefully, and screen really well."[55]

Anzac Day commemorations on 25 April 1916 grew out of a shared political and public response to the Gallipoli losses and the ongoing awareness of the many thousands of New Zealanders serving overseas. This reflected New Zealand-wide services in every town and district while at the same time Ashmead-Bartlett was lecturing in the main centres and his film *With the Dardanelles Expedition* was showing in local theatres.

GERMANS SABOTAGE MCDONALD'S MASTERTON FILMING?

As we have seen, Sydney Taylor, the government official photographer, was kept particularly busy filming throughout New Zealand and during his absence from Wellington in March 1916 his predecessor, James McDonald, was directed to film the patriotic carnival at Masterton. Nothing went according to plan. McDonald borrowed a camera, which he carefully overhauled and cleaned, exposing several feet of film as a test before leaving for Masterton by train. "Everything seemed to be in perfect working order, and at Masterton everything was favourable to getting a good picture. I had, however, run about 40 ft of film on the procession as it passed along Queen Street, when the perforations in the film gave way, and the film itself buckled round the sprockets." By the time he had cleared this, the procession had passed. McDonald

Film and photographs advertised New Zealand as a tourist destination for Australians and Americans throughout the war. This is Hatrick's Houseboat on the Whanganui River. The vessel was an 18-cabin floating hotel, with electric lights and flushing toilets. Photographer: William Williams, ¼-055110-G, ATL, Wellington.

consulted with the organisers and it was agreed he would film the procession moving round the park. "Scarcely had I started, when the perforation gave way, and the film jammed again. The procession was stopped, and halted until I got the film adjusted and started again, when the same thing happened. The procession was again halted until I could get the film clear. Scarcely had I started when the film jammed again."[56] Filming was abandoned; McDonald used a local photographer's darkroom to check his camera and film and went to film the sports events, only for it to jam again. Rather than test the patience of the performers who had been willing to stop and start on the cameraman's direction in the hope of appearing on film, McDonald called it a day and returned by train to Wellington.

It is a marvellous tale of the travails of a cinematographer and of the public response to the chance to see them on film — something that Masterton missed out on with this occasion. McDonald pursued the matter of the defective film with the New Zealand manager of Kodak Ltd and it was decided that the fault lay in the United States, where "probably some of the factory hands of German descent or pro German sympathy have deliberately tampered with it … This seems a feasible explanation of the defective manufacture which, of course, is liable to occur in a country so permeated with enemy sympathisers."[57] Today it seems difficult to believe that Masterton's wish to show their patriotism to the rest of New Zealand and perhaps the world was thwarted by cunning sabotage, but it made sense to McDonald and it gives us a glimpse of the climate of the times.

Playing sports and going to the races were subjects of intense debate during the war but, although affected, many sports including horseracing continued. Surviving film of sports in New Zealand are rare. There is the Newham film with its distinctive Maori meeting house titling of the rugby league game between Newton and Ponsonby, the previous year's champions, played before a packed crowd in the Auckland Domain in July 1918. It follows the Newham formula in setting the scene with each team coming on to the field, some fast action in a close game that Newton won 11–10 and then a deliberately lengthy pan of the crowd with the faces very evident, before ending with a shot of his Dominion Film Company logo.[58]

Rugby League Football Newton v Ponsonby Auckland Domain. NTSV F14796.

WAR WEARINESS

The impact of the casualty lists from the Somme in 1916 and from Messines and the battles before Passchendaele in 1917 saw the exhaustion of the numbers of single men and the call-up for compulsory service of married men of the 2nd Division. There was growing questioning by the public and in Parliament over how much New Zealand could contribute and whether or not that point had been reached. The war that was to be over by Christmas 1914 seemed as if it would never end. The reports of victories on Gallipoli and in France and Belgium began to ring hollow as list after list of casualties were published. Small town and district New Zealand went to war, and each telegram announcing a death spread ripples throughout every community. No one was untouched, and despite the crowds gathering on each anniversary of the war and vowing to fight until Germany's total surrender, there was growing war weariness. By late 1917 there was a "growing feeling in New Zealand that the willing horse is being worked to death."[59]

The entry of the United States into the war on 21 April 1917 led to a debate in Parliament that our nation's efforts should shift to food production and that there should be no additional increase in our commitment of the New Zealand forces at the front, other than maintaining what we had there already. New Zealand had led the way with our introduction of conscription. Canada had followed belatedly, but the Australian public had refused in two referenda to bring in conscription. An Empire's cause now seemed to be less important than the long-term impact of our casualties on New Zealand. As it turned out James Allen, minister of defence, showed his skill in providing support to Britain while managing to limit the response to the requests for additional manpower, outside of the essential maintenance of numbers to the New Zealand Division in France and the New Zealand Mounted Rifle Brigade in Sinai and Palestine. At a time of costly excess in casualties, Allen demonstrated New Zealand's willingness to serve in the Empire's cause while at the same time protecting New Zealand's interests in a way that avoided the fractures that struck Australia and Canada. This evidence of national self-interest in our political dealings with Britain in 1917–18 was matched by a growing sense of national identity: perhaps more among the soldiers than the public at home.

These concerns were reflected in the 1918 New Year's Day messages by both Prime Minister Massey and Sir Joseph Ward, his deputy in the National Government. Massey spoke of the "blood of Greater Britain" having been

> poured out like water, but the end is not yet fulfilled and more severe tests may be necessary … We know perfectly well that within our imperial gates we have a proportion of pacifists and anti-militarists, and others whose national sympathies are doubtful, some of them dangerous, some of them harmless, but all of them people who in a time like this are a hindrance rather than of any service. Such people have to be taken care of, and if necessary dealt with by a strong hand, while an overwhelming majority of loyalists join the march to victory and permanent peace.[60]

Ward, too, emphasised that New Zealand had more to do and that the real price had been paid by those who had lost loved ones. "Apart from this sad side we have little to remind us here of the war. We go on our way in comparative security and peace."[61] The war was a constant, but even that was toned down on account of growing war weariness. A Mr Gerald Anderson toured New Zealand giving an illustrated magic lantern lecture on 'New Zealanders at War (on Seven Fronts)' with one of the promotional quotes from the Otago leg of the tour stating "A good story delicately handled; nothing morbid or harrowing."[62]

THE YMCA AND RED TRIANGLE DAY

Attention was given to raising funds for the YMCA and its work in the camps and at the front.
The Red Triangle Day appeal of 15 March 1918 committed itself to raise £100,000 for the
welfare of New Zealand soldiers. Film and the picture theatres featured prominently in the
fundraising campaign, including pictures of New Zealanders in training in England and on
operations in France. Towns and districts competed against each other to raise funds and films
of the events provided ample proof of effort.

In Wellington a Monster Aquatic Gala and Sports Day was held at Island Bay beach on the
Saturday with races, tug-of-wars, gymnastic and diving displays. Families were reminded that
"A Shilling ticket entitles you to Return Tram Ride, Courtney Place — Island Bay, Afternoon Tea
on Beach and this Huge Programme" with the exhortation that "Every shilling goes to provide
comfort for the Boys at the front."[63] The Paramount Picture Theatre cameraman took pictures
of the crowd for screening the following week. Over 10,600 people came by tram and enjoyed
themselves despite a cold southerly wind. "The dressing sheds were aflame with bunting, the new
diving pier was also gay with flags, and even the fleeting of fishing vessels moored in the lee of
the island sported the enlivening red, white and green of beloved Italia."[64] In Petone there was a
citizen's parade and a Grand Picture Benefit at Grand Theatre, with half the proceeds being given
to the appeal.[65] New Zealand-wide a total of £110,927 was raised.[66]

None of these films have survived but we do have the film of the Surprise Packet Day,
which was screened at the Queen's Theatre in Cuba Street, Wellington, on 16 October 1917.
A contemporary report described the film as "Commercial travellers and others selling tickets
and distributing the prizes."[67] As Clive Sowry notes in his research, the "'Surprise Packet'

*The Surprise Packet
Day in Wellington.*
NTSV F7107.

scheme was an initiative of Wellington Commercial Travellers. (In recent years similar fund-raising schemes have been known as 'Mystery Envelope' appeals.) The idea was to raise funds for the British Red Cross and to aid blind soldiers and sailors who had suffered in the service of King and Country. The wide range of prizes donated by business houses included such desirable items as a Singer sewing machine and a return saloon passage to Lyttelton, as well as thousands of free admission tickets to picture theatres."[68]

The crowd is made up mainly of married couples, there are some soldiers in the crowd but not many, and the film captures the buoyant mood of the people as they line up to buy tickets, file into the building and emerge carrying all manner of household goods, parcels, books, and in one case a child's cane cot, which severely taxes the couple concerned as we see them standing and mopping their brows. Every scene is a marvellous mix of ages, race and occupation, a microcosm of Wellington society. There are seamen, working men in leather caps and jackets, all smoking furiously, married couples with children, against a backdrop of horse and carts with the occasional motor car and many bicyclists. Middle-aged women with children look curiously towards the camera and a young lad approaches laughing, in contrast to the black mourning band on his sleeve. It was most likely filmed by Sydney Taylor, the government cameraman. Over 60,000 surprise packets were sold, raising £3000 in one day. Late donations of goods were sold by auction, raising for the charity.

The year of 1917 had started with victory at Messines and descended into the gloom and casualty lists of the Passchendaele offensive. There was talk of a compromised peace, against a backdrop of industrial unrest and concern about New Zealand's ability to continue its supply of manpower to the front. The year 1918 began equally grimly with news of the German March Offensive on the Western Front and the call-up of married men of the 2nd Division, and ongoing concerns about the rising cost of living.

Going to the movies allowed an escape from this, if only for an hour or so. Continuous picture shows were packed and there were ongoing complaints about over-crowding, the potential dangers in the event of fire from people standing in the aisles, and the smell of packed humanity in some of the smaller theatres.

Theatre nicknames gave easy clues as to how audiences regarded them. The Globe in Christchurch was known as the 'Rat Hole of Calcutta' and the Queen's Theatre in Dunedin was known as the 'bughouse' from the day it opened in 1912. Indeed, many centres had their 'bughouses' and their 'fleapits'.[69] Adverse comments on theatre cleanliness saw strenuous press advertising to counter this. In March 1916 the People's Picture Palace in Wellington advertised in the *Evening Post*. "SPECIAL ANNOUNCEMENT: The PPP is fumigated weekly under the supervision of COUNCIL INSPECTORS and is several times daily sprayed with Special Disinfectant recommended by the council."[70] Similar pronouncements were made by other theatres. "Shortt's Theatre is washed out with disinfectant every week and thoroughly fumigated every day NO MICROBES HERE!"[71]

Evening Post, 20 March 1916, p. 2.

SHORTT'S THEATRE.

TO-NIGHT!   TO-NIGHT!

Another Record Programme.
Two Star Attractions:
Big U Three-Reel "Feature,"

"EXAMPLE."
"EXAMPLE."
"EXAMPLE."
"EXAMPLE."

A drama full of sensational incidents.
Three-Reel Essanay Comedy,

"FIFTY!"   "FIFTY!"
"FIFTY!"   "FIFTY!"
"FIFTY!"   "FIFTY!"
"FIFTY!"   "FIFTY!"

One long scream of laughter,

"FIFTY!"   "FIFTY!"

A man boasts to his club mates that he is master in his own house.
How he changes his ideas is shown in

"FIFTY!"   "FIFTY!"

Ladies, you must see this comedy—it's a scream.

SPECIAL NOTE.—Shortt's Theatre is washed out with disinfectant every week, and thoroughly fumigated every day.

NO MICROBES HERE!

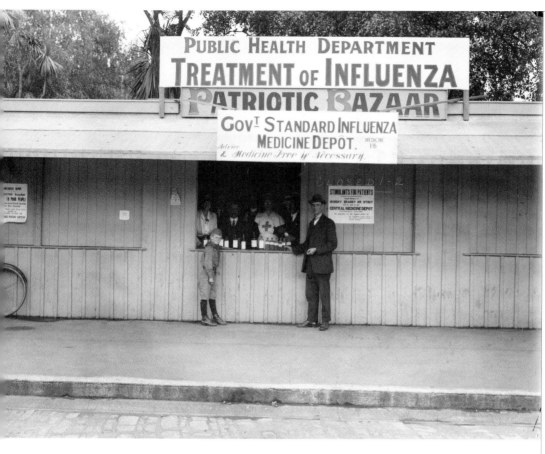

An influenza medicine depot in Christchurch for "poor" people. Taken by an unknown photographer, 4 December 1918. 1/1-008542-G, ATL, Wellington.

Weekly Pictures

ODDFELLOWS' HALL.

—

TO-NIGHT

NOVEMBER 12, 1918.

—

As instructions have been received from the Government to close all Theatres for seven days owing to the influenza epidemic, the Pictures will not be shown To-night.

—

These films are subject to alteration without further notice.

ADMISSION:
Body of Hall 1/1   Children 6d.
Gallery 1/7   Children 10d.

Akaroa Mail and Banks Peninsula Advertiser, 12 November 1918.

PICTURES WILL NOT BE SHOWN TONIGHT

Nothing prepared the public or the theatres for the influenza epidemic of 1918, which arrived with the news of peace. New Zealand celebrated and filmed the Armistice twice, first believing it was signed 24 hours ahead of the reality and then more cautiously rejoicing on 11 November 1918. The Censor's Records lists the film *Peace — Unofficial Celebrations* on 9 November, followed by *Armistice — Official Celebrations* on 17 December 1918 and *Armistice*, a 3500 foot compilation on 17 January 1919.[72] A day of celebrations was followed by word of the rapid spread of the deadly epidemic. Laura Hardy, a housewife of Onehunga, told of "funerals … passing our house continually all day. Coffins were turned out by the hundred and were just made of rough boards … To this sad and sorrowing community came the news of the armistice. There were few families which felt like rejoicing."[73] On 12 November 1918 Hayward's Weekly Pictures at the Oddfellows' Hall in Akaroa posted a notice in the *Akaroa Mail* that "As instructions have been received from the Government to close all theatres for seven days owing to the influenza epidemic, the Pictures will not be shown To-night."[74] It would be a bitter month before pictures were again shown at theatres in New Zealand. The influenza epidemic was war's terrible epilogue for a sorrowing nation. A total of 8573 New Zealanders died; this included 2160 Maori out of an estimated Maori population of 51,000. It was a grim coda to four years of war.

21

Peace, sport and Cologne

News came thro last night that armistice had been signed, and hostilities ceased at 11 a.m. Thank God![1]

In November 1918 Harry Sanders was exhausted and suffering from piles. There was pressure on him to return to Pathé and he was trialling a replacement, but found that he was unsuitable and that the films taken at this time were unusable. However, New Zealand divisional commander Major-General Sir Andrew Russell was keen to give the potential replacement, Bombadier Hilsdon, another chance and so Sanders persevered. We have no film of the events surrounding New Zealand's last battles but we have priceless photos. We know from Lieutenant Laurie Blyth's account that Sanders was filming at Le Quesnoy, but these tantalising descriptions of the cinematographer in action are not matched by surviving film.

The New Zealanders fought their last battle in France from 4–6 November 1918 when they bypassed and then captured the frontier fortress town of Le Quesnoy, fortified by Vauban in the 17th century and now the site of the climax of New Zealand's war on the Western Front. It had been a year of bloody fighting for the 18,000-strong New Zealand Division. It had a critical role in holding the German attack on Amiens in March and had been at the forefront of the advance of General Byng's 3rd Army since the attack on 21 August 1918. Since then the division had led for 79 of the 90 kilometres advanced, inflicting thousands of German casualties in dead and wounded, capturing 8756 prisoners, 145 guns, three tanks and 1263 machine guns.

The cumulative cost of this for the division since its arrival in France in April–May 1916 was 12,483 dead and 35,419 wounded; 47,902 out of the total of 59,483 casualties suffered by New Zealand in the First World War.[2] By November 1918 it was a war-weary division, which embodied the national army of an equally war-weary Dominion. New Zealand in four years mobilised 124,211 volunteers and conscripts from an eligible male population of some 243,376 drawn from a population of 1,158,436 (based on 1914 estimates); 100,444 sailed overseas suffering 18,166 deaths and 41,317 wounded. The nation furthest removed from the centre of the fighting sent to war 9% of its total population. This was 40% of its eligible male population, suffering casualties amounting to 25% of its eligible male population. Six out of every ten

Opposite page: Three 'Diggers' looking across the Rhine to the old city of Cologne with the twin spire of the cathedral and the Hohenzollern Bridge in the foreground. H-Series, H1280, 1/1-002098-G, ATL, Wellington.

who sailed overseas became a battle casualty, thousands more were debilitated by sickness and disease. For many of the New Zealanders who were in France at the Armistice on 11 November 1918, soldiering in war was the only occupation they knew.

Like everyone else, the New Zealanders were stunned by the rapid end to a campaign that was anticipated to go on into 1919. There was a universal feeling of thankfulness for having survived and a great longing to see home.

THE OCCUPATION OF THE RHINE

On 15 November 1918 the New Zealand Division was informed that it would be part of the British Occupation force on the Rhine. Under the Armistice arrangements Germany in the west was to cede Alsace-Lorraine to France and withdraw its armies from all invaded territories behind a line to the east of a designated neutral zone on the right bank of the Rhine, with the Allied powers occupying the left bank and of three bridgeheads at Mainz, Coblenz and Cologne.[3] After intense negotiations with the French who were set on setting up an independent French-orientated Rhineland, it was determined that British forces would occupy the Cologne bridgehead.[4] General Sir Hubert Plumer's 2nd Army was tasked to occupy the bridgehead. Its initial garrison numbered some 275,000 personnel including Australians, Canadians and New Zealanders.[5]

Lieutenant-General Sir Alexander Godley, commanding both the New Zealand Expeditionary Force (NZEF) and XXII Corps that was one of the corps occupying the left bank of the Rhine. He had with him New Zealand and Australian units that had remained with him from their time as II ANZAC and, as he wrote to Allen, the New Zealand minister of defence, "I take with me the Otago Mounted Rifles and the New Zealand Cyclist Battalion and the New Zealand Tunnelling Company."[6]

As it turned out, the New Zealand Tunnelling Company never got to the Rhine, being fully employed on bridge-building in northern France. The New Zealand Division was transferred from IV Corps to Lieutenant-General Sir Charles Fergusson's II Corps. It seems that it was deliberate policy to post a representative cross-section of the Dominion forces as part of the Rhine garrison, as the initial garrison included the Canadian Corps of two divisions, the New Zealand Division as part of II Corps, and briefly during the initial occupation the 13th Australian Light Horse Regiment with Godley's XXII Corps.[7] Both the Canadians and Australians were withdrawn by the end of December, while the New Zealanders trekked in on foot, horse and wagon across Belgium and into Germany with the first elements arriving in Cologne on 22 December 1918.[8]

It was the threat of Bolshevism as much as any fear of a return to war that concerned the Allies. The German garrison in Cologne had mutinied in November. There was a power vacuum in the city and there were great concerns that the Workers and Soviet councils would establish control. Godley wrote to Allen:

> I think we may safely count the war as over now, though there is always a possibility that we may, as an Army of Occupation, have to put down Bolshevism in Germany, but one must hope that a people as educated and as solid as they hitherto have been will not run riot like Russia.[9]

On 3 December the New Zealand infantry brigades began their march to the border and then entrained for Cologne, which was completed on 22 December, while the artillery trekked with horses, gun limbers and wagons to Cologne: crossing the Hohenzollern Bridge to Deutz on the eastern bank of the Rhine on Boxing Day 1918.

The New Zealand Division march across the Hohenzollern Bridge to occupy a zone on the east bank of the Rhine. Still from Captain Harry Sanders' last film with the NZEF, *Arrival of New Zealand Troops at Cologne*. NTSV F4555.

The march through Belgium was a victor's parade with flags and fete meeting the New Zealanders at every town. They also were regaled with stories of German atrocities and met the first of the returning New Zealand prisoners of war, many of whom spoke bitterly of their treatment at German hands. How this would be translated when they marched into Germany was unknown, but the diaries give some indication of the mood of the men. Private N.M. "Monty" Ingram wrote:

> 22nd December 1918. Here we are at long last! We have reached our destination — the end of our long march, — the goal of our endeavour for the past four years, — Germany. The Hun, at last, has foreign troops in occupation of his Fatherland. I hope it hurts his pride.[10]

ARRIVAL OF NEW ZEALAND TROOPS AT COLOGNE, 1918

The division crossed the Belgian frontier into Germany at Herbesthal/Eupen and the infantry and artillery brigades reached Cologne on Boxing Day, 26 December 1918, after a 23-day trek. Captain Harry Sanders was on hand to film the infantry marching over the bridge and the arrival of the artillery columns.[11] *The Chronicles of the NZEF* reported:

> By eleven o'clock we had reached the outskirts of Cologne and entered it through the beautiful suburbs of Lindenthal, passing along many of the main thoroughfares crowded with civilians. All were fashionably dressed, and showed few signs of the hardships of which we had heard. On past the Opernhaus we marched, along the spacious Hohenzollern Ring, the central railway station, passed beneath the glorious cathedral, then across the Rhine by the Hohenzollern Bridge. It is a massive structure of stone, iron girders and spans carrying railway, tramway, wheeled and foot traffic. As the column left the bridge and entered the eastern suburbs of Cologne, the official photographer of the Division took a cinematograph film of the batteries.

New Zealand soldier tourists in France, some of them in their 'hospital blue' uniform, standing on a theatre balcony. The New Zealand cameraman, most likely C.D. Barton, stands below them with his motion picture camera. UK Series, UK486, 1/2-014252-G, ATL, Wellington.

A more interesting spot could not have been chosen, for it has as a background the towers of the Hohenzollern Bridge and the double steeples of the Cathedral.[12]

The surviving film is complete but lacks intertitles. It begins with the Diggers in column of fours crossing through one of the frontier towns. The men are laden with full packs, webbing and rifles, while the officers, leading their horses, march with them. The men are in good humour and wave and point at the camera. It then shifts to the Hohenzollern Bridge as the division makes its way across. An infantry battalion led by its band leads the column. Children walk alongside and stare curiously at the camera. The sheer scale of the New Zealand Division is shown with scene after scene of infantry, transport wagons and artillery filmed with the spires of Cologne Cathedral in the background. The monotony of the endless passage of men, horses and wagons is broken by the occasional tram. The horses pulling the wagons look as bored as the cameraman must himself have felt, but then that is broken with a shot of a horse-drawn field-cooker, steaming away at the end of a column, ready to give a hot brew to the troops at the next halt.

Sanders breaks the pattern by switching scenes to the outside of a German restaurant at Ehrenfeld that has been commandeered as the New Zealand Divisional YMCA with its sign prominently displayed on the window. It is what the YMCA and the soldiers themselves term a 'buckshee stunt': free cakes and a hot drink, something that had been part and parcel of soldier life in Egypt and in France and Belgium. The Diggers file past collecting bread, cakes, coffee and cocoa. They carry their mugs and mess tins full of hot drink and have their cakes or bread placed in their upturned hats. One of the soldiers spits his crust of bread out of his mouth before collecting his cake. The film then returns to the endless crossing of the Rhine.

What Sanders did not film was the reaction of the New Zealand Diggers as they crossed over the Rhine. Lieutenant 'Curly' Blyth was with the 3rd Brigade. "When we marched over the Rhine across the Hohenzollern Bridge it was pretty cold and although we set out in a beautiful fine day. We got halfway across the bridge when we halted. I was part of the combined 1st and 2nd Battalion of the Rifle Brigade, it was part of the cutting down process, amalgamating both battalions. Halfway across we stopped and the ranks of riflemen turned outwards to the edge of the bridge and we relieved ourselves of an ambition which had taken us halfway round the world [and pissed in the Rhine]."[13]

The final scenes in the film are the arrival of trains carrying wagons, equipment and soldiers in the Cologne marshalling yards. Trains are shunted past crowds of waiting New Zealanders who smoke, brew-up, smile and joke at the camera. A soldier with bagpipes jumps down, marches alongside the train playing, before getting on board again. It is the arrival of an army that knows that it has won and all this is proof that the war is over.

Private Ingram was one of the infantry marching through the town from the train station. Bert Stokes in the New Zealand Field Artillery thought that the "German people looked a very dejected lot, poorly dressed, and the little children did not seem to have enough clothes on to protect them from the biting cold wind". As Stokes noted, if the adults ignored the occupiers, the children did not. "We soon found we were the main attraction for the German children who had a hunch that our rations were fairly liberal and were constantly on the outskirts of the barracks begging for food. They were not disappointed as we could not resist the pleading of the youngsters."[14]

This is Sanders' last surviving film with the New Zealanders. Pathé Frères had asked for his release and he requested that he be demobilised but agreed for him to stay on until a suitable replacement was available. In December 1918 the recently arrived gunner C.D. "Charlie" Barton, who the New Zealand military authorities noted "is reputed to be a professional photographer and cinematographer", was sent to France "to assist Capt. Sanders with the ultimate view of replacing him … He should proceed direct to the Division and take cinema camera and films with him."[15]

Barton crossed to France on 14 December 1918 and took over from Sanders on 5 January 1919 when Sanders was admitted to hospital. Barton was promoted to the rank of temporary sergeant as official photographer NZEF.

On 15 January 1919 Sanders was transferred to No. 3 General Hospital, Wandsworth, in London and wrote to Brigadier-General Richardson. "I have brought some films of the entry into Germany (taken under very adverse conditions) with me as I was taken sick and had no means of sending. I can handle this film & get good publicity through Messrs Pathé if the War Office system of handling film has terminated. Could I be advised as to this please?"

"I should further be very grateful if my demobilisation could be expedited so that I could be released after convalescence."[16] Richardson passed this on to Major Spencer Westmacott who had succeeded Gambrill as head of the War Records Section in London. Westmacott replied to Sanders: "As regards the film brought over by you the old arrangements with the War Office are still in force and we are not free to deal with the film as we please."[17]

It was the beginning of a testy relationship between Sanders and Westmacott. Westmacott was conscious of the rapid demobilisation of the NZEF and was keen to have the photographs and films taken during the war edited and catalogued and returned to New Zealand, and pestered Sanders to have this done.

Arrival of New Zealand Troops at Cologne. NTSV F4555.

THE NEW ZEALANDERS IN COLOGNE

The area under control of the New Zealand Division was divisional headquarters at Leverkusen based on the large Bayer chemical works, 1st Brigade Group at Leichlingen, 2nd Brigade Group at Mulheim and 3rd Brigade Group at Mielenforst, with the New Zealand Divisional Artillery at Deutz.[18] The standard of accommodation was superior to anything that the New Zealanders had ever experienced. The artillery found themselves housed in 'first class' army barracks in the suburb of Deutz with "ample room to park our guns and vehicles and the horses were stabled in

what was a ground floor gymnasium with a concrete floor. So for the first time in many a long day our horses were under cover."[19]

The occupying force wanted it to be 'business as usual' within the zones under their control. "The general policy of the Allied Armies is that the life of the civilian population shall so far as possible continue uninterrupted and with the minimum of interference. All civilian institutions will continue to perform their functions under the supervision of and subject to the control of military authorities."[20]

However, Ingram noted that the "Germans seem to bear very little malice towards the British, but appear to hate the French intensely".[21] Bert Stokes had similar experiences:

> Many times we found ourselves sitting at tables with Germans, male and female, who in someway or other we managed to converse with. We usually found the Germans had a better understanding of English than we had of German. I remember on one occasion we sat at a table with a few Germans who had been in the army and had deserted in the last days of the war when there were uprisings in the city and also in the army. During our conversation we found that two of them had been at Passchendaele and we recalled events in that muddy and bloody battle. It all seemed very strange that here we were enemies for four years now discussing quite amicably those past days.[22]

 *Pathé Gazette, No. 556.
The Irony of Fate —
New Zealanders felling
German timber, used
as barricades against
Germans themselves.*
British Pathé 1906.44.

Russell knew the temper of his men, ensured that they were comfortably housed and fed and then insisted that they be kept up to the mark. On 27 December 1918 Lieutenant-General Jacobs, corps commander, II Corps, "came down to tell me of the misconduct of sundry

Three boys with hoops study the cameraman while New Zealand soldiers guard captured German vehicles. Still from *New Zealanders at Auckland* [Cologne]. British Pathé 1854.15.

NZers in Cologne — Inevitable — I hope we shall be able to stop it".[23] Russell spent Saturday afternoon, 28 December, walking the streets of Cologne "to see how our men were saluting".[24]

The discipline of the division was good, but Russell was conscious that his men were under the spotlight of British regulars who were now reverting back to peacetime standards in their expectation of drill, dress and discipline. There was only one serious incident when a soldier in the NZ Machine Gun Battalion attempted to hold up and rob a car and he was killed by a German policeman in the getaway. Another soldier was shot and killed by some German civilians; the principal culprit escaped, but four accomplices were each awarded two years' imprisonment.[25] The New Zealanders in Cologne were determined to see not just the cathedral but other sights, "including some of the areas not actually banned, but nevertheless worth seeing at their busiest time during the early evening. We had seen 'Red lights' in Boulogne and Étaples, but this far exceeded anything we had previously witnessed."[26]

WHATSOEVER A MAN SOWETH

The venereal disease rate in the NZEF was of ongoing concern and in 1917 the New Zealand authorities had adopted a strict but realistic policy. Soldiers going on leave were issued with quantities of prophylactics according to the number of days on leave. This was based on the kit designed by Ettie Rout who was the trailblazer in advocating sex education and the use of prophylactics for soldiers.[27] Those who refused on moral grounds signed the leave book accordingly, and if they succumbed and did not report to the early treatment centre or Lavage Hut within four hours of being with a woman were subject to military discipline if they became infected, but anyone else who followed the rules and still caught something was treated as a normal patient.[28]

New Zealanders at Auckland [Cologne]. British Pathé 1854.15.

The greatest problem facing New Zealanders in 1918 was a shortage in the supply of prophylactics; there was also serious concern about the quality of production. A senior medical officer in Sling Camp reported: "On examining the recent batch of 'French Letters' I found them to be of a most inferior quality as to be a direct danger to the men making use of them."[29]

There were many initiatives, not all of which were publicised in New Zealand. There was tacit support to the work of Ettie Rout and her advice and guidance on what brothels soldiers should use when on leave in Paris. It led to a particular initiative by Brigadier-General Richardson that saw New Zealand jointly produce one of the first films warning of the dangers of venereal disease. On 19 October 1918 Richardson informed the headquarters of the New Zealand Military Forces in Wellington of one of his initiatives. "In order to reduce V.D. in the N.Z.E.F I agreed with the Canadian authorities to co-operate with them in the production of a Cinema Film on the subject. This film has now been completed and will be shown in all our camps. Our share of the cost is £44 and £85 for a separate film for our own use, which amount is small in comparison to its educational value, which I trust will be the means of saving New Zealand many thousands of pounds."[30] The five-reel film concerned the misadventures of a young Canadian soldier in London, who ends up seeing in graphic detail the damage done by sexually transmitted diseases, and the impact of hereditary syphilis on children.[31] The fact that the film featured Canadian soldiers has led to New Zealand's role in this initiative being overlooked.[32]

In January 1919 the film was discussed with Allen who "is of the opinion that the film should be forwarded to New Zealand where it could be used to good effect in our Territorial Camps and elsewhere".[33] The film was purchased by the New Zealand YMCA and shown throughout the country to segregated audiences. On 30 October 1919 the *Evening Post* reported: "Tonight the great V.D. film 'Whatsoever A Man Soweth' will be shown in the Y.M.C.A. to members only."[34] It was advertised in the 'Amusements' column the same day.[35]

CHARLIE BARTON FILMS IN GERMANY AND FRANCE

Sergeant Barton remained in Germany filming and photographing the occupation. However, the rapid demobilisation of the New Zealanders had already started in December with the return of married men, with drafts of 1000 men at a time. Barton filmed the New Zealand *Reception Camp-Spladen-Germany,* and the New Zealand Divisional *Rifle Meeting Bruch — Germany* which are listed as films that were returned to New Zealand but have not survived.

In March 1919 Barton was tasked to take photos of the YMCA's work at New Zealand demobilisation camps in France and Belgium. He was actively employed as a photographer/ cinematographer throughout 1919, but perhaps the only surviving film we have of his work is that of the parade of colonial forces through London, which has clearly been taken from a New Zealand perspective and is listed as one of the films taken for Pathé.[36] He may also have filmed the films of the leave parties touring Paris that show a group of smartly dressed British, Australian and New Zealand soldiers escorted by a party of women wearing what seem to be Red Cross insignia on their cloaks and hats, being shown the sights in a British military motor transport.[37] He also filmed and took photos during his return voyage to New Zealand in late 1919. Back in New Zealand he used to advantage the cachet of 'Official Photographer' and this featured in the credits on his films in the 1920s.

We know two of the photographers attached to the New Zealand War Records Section working with Barton. Private Herbert Huxley Green was a professional photographer working for the *Lyttelton Times*. He marched into camp on 5 January 1917 and served in France with 1 Canterbury Battalion. Green was posted to the New Zealand War Records Section with the rank of corporal on 24 January 1919, was promoted sergeant in August 1919 and worked as an NZEF photographer in England and France throughout 1919, before returning to New Zealand on the SS *Ruahine* on 27 December 1919.[38] Private Lawrence Galatius Hahn was a professional photographer for Steffano Webb in Christchurch. He arrived in England on 30 October 1918 and was posted to Ewshot as a gunner in the New Zealand Field Artillery. He was posted to the New Zealand War Records photographic section on 30 November 1918. Hahn was promoted corporal on 2 December 1918 and then made sergeant on 1 January 1919. A meteoric advance in rank, no doubt made necessary to give him access and credibility on the jobs to which he was sent. He too returned to New Zealand at the end of 1919.[39] The many photographs from 1919 in the UK-Series were taken by these men.[40] On their return to New Zealand they continued to work together and formed the photographic firm of Green & Hahn in Christchurch in the 1920s.[41]

TOMMY SCALES FILMS COLOGNE

Barton was joined in Cologne by Tommy Scales from Pathé Frères, who until 31 January 1919 had been the New Zealand official cameramen in the United Kingdom. In early 1919 Pathé sent Scales, now a civilian, over to film life in the occupation forces. "After the War, news-reel reporting took me to Cologne to make pictures of the Allied re-occupation. From there I motored right through to Ostend, obtaining as many shots as possible. What strange emotions gripped me as I stood on the battlefields of the Somme, Messines and Ypres so soon after the fighting. It was like treading sacred ground."[42]

Naturally enough Scales based himself with the New Zealand Division who, despite him now being a civilian, treated him as one of their own. Barton as official photographer was allocated a Ford car, and Scales was provided with an open Sunbeam tourer, the property of the War Department, for his return trip through Belgium and France. He was to hand the car in at Calais.[43] Barton worked independently from Scales filming the various camps and YMCA establishments.

HAVRINCOURT BRIDGE, COLOGNE AND THE LAST TRAIN HOME

There exists a remarkable series of films on life in the Cologne bridgehead in which New Zealanders feature. The films are titled either *New Zealanders in Cologne* or *Allied Occupation of the Rhineland* and while there is a similar British occupation force's theme to each of the films, there are also strong New Zealand elements. Each provides a montage of shots that often reappear in each film.

The first of the films and perhaps the most important relates almost entirely to New Zealand, apart from one iconic scene featuring a British soldier on sentry duty as Scales films a panorama of the Rhine bridges with the spires of Cologne Cathedral in the background. As with all of the films, it is something of a potpourri, opening with a panning shot of the temporary bridge built over the Canal du Nord at Havrincourt by the New Zealand Tunnelling Company. This brief pan is the only known film of the bridge, which was reputed to be the longest single-span bridge erected in military history to that time. It was certainly the longest bridge of its type erected on the Western Front. The finished bridge was 55 metres in length and was made from two experimental steel span Hopkins bridges that were designed to carry 35-ton tanks over a gap of 36.5 metres. Before this only two Hopkins bridges had been erected under operational conditions to the designed length and one of these had failed. General Little, chief engineer of

the 3rd Army, assessed that the New Zealanders could do the job, even though the company had not been trained in bridge-building. They did not disappoint and indeed under Captain John Holmes achieved a feat that, in the words of the Tunnelling Company history, "verged on the impossible".[44] The New Zealanders joined two bridge sets together and erected the bridge in 104 hours. No reconnaissance was initially possible because it was still in the front line and remained within range of German artillery. In the film one can see the hessian camouflage nets erected between the steel supports to disguise the bridge outline from long range artillery fire. It was the Tunnelling Company's outstanding achievement as bridge builders, but was only one of the many challenging bridge-building tasks undertaken by them in the last months of 1918.[45]

Scales, travelling with a carload of New Zealanders, visited principal New Zealand battle sites on his way back to England and each film contains some of these scenes. The film shows the Cite Bonjean Cemetery at Armentières and then Hyde Park Corner at Ploegsteert Wood showing the entrance to the catacombs built by the Australian Tunnelling Company, which housed 1200 New Zealanders in the lead-up to the attack on Messines on 7 June 1917.[46]

We see the New Zealand Divisional Headquarters at Leverkusen in the snow with two captured German artillery pieces. Scales' camera focuses on the sign that says they were captured at Le Quesnoy and a New Zealander holds up the New Zealand flag so viewers can see that it flies in Germany. The film then shifts to the port of Zeebrugge, scene of the raid by the Royal Navy on 23 April 1918. This was an attempt to block the mouth of the port to prevent its use by German submarines. It was only partially successful, with heavy casualties to the crews of the blockships, but was trumpeted as a British victory in the press. We see the coastal defences on the harbour mole with a greatcoated New Zealander in a lemon squeezer also in the scene.

New Zealanders are shown marching over the Hohenzollern Bridge in Cologne, first infantry and then one of the New Zealand bands leading a mass of New Zealanders with friends, including a number of females. It seems this is the farewell march before entraining to return to England. Scales films the last New Zealand troop train to leave Cologne Station and we see the Diggers waving from the covered wagons and British officers running alongside shaking hands with friends as they leave Cologne on the first stage of the journey back to New Zealand.

The train journey to Rouen took 50–60 hours, which was an improvement on the first trains that took four to five days. The division placed a travelling kitchen and four stoves on each train as well as providing extra straw for bedding. One truck on each train was placed at the disposal of the New Zealand YMCA and was used as a canteen and buffet en route. The YMCA also provided cigarettes and refreshments for the soldiers at the station as their entrained. Indeed, the unsung heroes of New Zealand's demobilisation were the staff of the YMCA. The final demobilisation report concluded: "They have worked hard and have maintained their high reputation right up to the finish."[47]

Appropriately enough the last scene in the film shows companies of New Zealanders halting and entering a New Zealand YMCA in Germany. There is a sign saying 'Victoria Hall — Entertainment Nightly'. Inside, two soldiers distribute a broadsheet as the men queue for coffee and cakes.[48]

The second film opens with a pan across the desolation of the Ypres Salient. It seems to be a shot taken from the area of Hooge Crater, which was a New Zealand brigade headquarters area in the winter of 1917–18, looking back down the Menin Road towards the city.[49] The film reverts to Cologne and we see fully laden British troops march across the Hohenzollern Bridge with the repeat of the city skyline panorama with the sentry in the foreground. There follows repeated scenes of a German airfield with various aircraft in a large hangar. A large two-engine German bomber biplane is flown by someone who appears to be a French pilot, surrounded

by soldiers and civilians of various nationalities. Interspersed with this are scenes that show the mole at Zeebrugge and the sunken Royal Navy blockships; a view of the ruins of Cloth Hall at Ypres with New Zealanders from Scales' touring party in the foreground and a view of the Cite Bonjean Cemetery at Armentières, which pans to a cloth factory that was used as billets by New Zealanders in 1916 and which still stands today. There are 452 New Zealanders buried in the cemetery and the New Zealand Memorial to the Missing lists 47 New Zealanders who have no known graves. It speaks of the cost of the New Zealand Division's introduction to the Western Front in 1916.[50] We then see New Zealanders, in braces and lemon squeezers, felling trees in Germany. This tree-felling sequence was also released as a Pathé newsreel.[51] The film ends with Cologne street scenes with a New Zealand sentry in the foreground.

 New Zealanders in Cologne 1. NTSV F245808.

NEW ZEALANDERS ON GUARD

The third film is principally of a horse racing meeting held by the British Army of the Rhine. Scales films it in all its detail. Some New Zealanders are evident among the crowd.[52] All this is interspersed with scenes of New Zealand soldiers on leave in Cologne, playing rugby and a New Zealand guard mounting sentries in a formal ceremony to guard wagons and artillery limbers, which have been concentrated on the parade ground at Mülheim as the division demobilises. A similar sequence showing New Zealanders guarding captured German motor vehicles was released as a Pathé newsreel.[53] The rugby sequence, which is a game between a New Zealand team and a British Army team, was the subject of a separate newsreel and among the largely British Army crowd with some New Zealanders in their lemon squeezers, we see the distinctive figure of General Sir Hubert Plumer, commanding the British Army of the Rhine.[54]

 New Zealanders in Cologne 2. NTSV F245809.

Walls of Le Quesnoy showing impact of New Zealand artillery fire. The walls were filmed by Tommy Scales on his return from Cologne in 1919. H-Series, H1244, Photographer: Captain H.A. Sanders, 1/2-013791-G, ATL, Wellington.

A GLIMPSE OF LE QUESNOY

The fourth of Scales' Cologne films shows the work of the Royal Navy motor gunboat flotilla patrolling the Rhine. It also includes further shots of the New Zealanders felling trees, guard mounting and scenes from the visits to Ypres and the battlefield in the Salient. The most important sequence shows the walls of Le Quesnoy in the snow, with Scales' touring party walking towards the Valenciennes Gateway into the town. This is the only film that exists of Le Quesnoy shortly after it featured in New Zealand's last battle on the Western Front.[55] There are two further films on the Occupation of the Rhineland that repeat or continue the above themes.[56] Altogether Scales' films amount to some 40 minutes of filming, providing tantalising glimpse of the New Zealand battlefields, not all of which can be identified with certainty, but remain the only views we have on film of the bridge at Havrincourt and the walls of Le Quesnoy.

THE DEMOBILISATION OF THE NEW ZEALAND DIVISION

Equally importantly Scales captures images that show how the vast and complex structure that was the New Zealand Division was telescoped down to nothing in less than three months. At the same time the division had to dispose of its animals, many of whom originally came from New Zealand. A Remount Depot was established and animals were classified into three categories: for retention in the British Army, for sale in the United Kingdom and for sale in Belgium; 3676 were despatched to the United Kingdom for sale and retention, plus 292 evacuated sick, 354 were sold locally to the abbatoir at a price of £22/10/0 including hides. Five horses were returned home to New Zealand.

Motor vehicles were returned, all harnesses, saddlery and equipment was checked and handed in, as were guns, howitzers, limbers and wagons and veterinary and medical supplies.

The double Hopkins-pattern girder bridge erected by the New Zealand Tunnelling Company over the Canal du Nord near Havrincourt. It was longest single-span temporary bridge erected by the British Army on the Western Front. This was filmed by Tommy Scales on his return from Cologne in 1919. Photographer: Captain H.A. Sanders, H-Series, H 1265, 1/2-013797-G, ATL, Wellington.

Sports equipment was sold and the New Zealand Division's printing press, that no one was willing to buy, was donated to the proposed New Zealand War Museum, and the divisional canteens closed. All bands and entertainment troops were demobilised as complete units and their equipment was presented to the YMCA for use on the transports home.[57]

Leaving Cologne was the first step home and despite dock strikes and a shortage of shipping, most were home by mid-1919, far sooner than had been originally anticipated. The New Zealand experience in Germany was a pause on the route home; it did not feature large in the wider New Zealand consciousness at the time, the influenza epidemic being of more concern. For the New Zealanders who experienced Cologne, it made them aware that the 'dastardly Hun' was human too, and if there had been hatred and loathing during the war, this seeped away in the three months garrisoning the Rhine. The Diggers grew to appreciate a beautiful city and despite the restrictions were given a taste of a culture and society very different from New Zealand. For many it was an introduction to a love of classical music and opera that would last a lifetime. Its memory has gone. It did not impact on our literature and that we were there at all is found now in the last pages of a few published war diaries and in the remarkable images of the Pathé newsreel collection and the H-Series photographs. Yet the experience of meeting and talking with the enemy perhaps made it a saner war for some to look back on — who knows? Let us give General Godley the last word in his letter to Allen, New Zealand minister of defence.

> A train full of demobilised New Zealanders passed through here yesterday on its way to the Base from Cologne, and the officer in command told one of my staff who went down to meet it (I was not back from Paris) that when they left Cologne the platform was a seething mass of weeping German maidens.[58]

New Zealanders at Auckland [*It is Mülheim*]. British Pathé 1854.15.

Allied Occupation of Rhineland — [*New Zealanders in Cologne*]. NTSV F245807.

GLORIOUS DAYS OF SPORTING ACHIEVEMENT

These were glorious days of sporting achievement for New Zealand. In rowing New Zealand teams dominated the season with Darcy Hadfield beating all comers in the single sculls and the New Zealand eight beating the more fancied United States team at the international meeting in Paris. A small group of New Zealand runners also dominated the athletics meetings in England with Corporal Daniel Mason unbeatable over the middle distances. Both Mason and Hadfield would break the American dominance at the Inter-Allied Games held in Paris at the Pershing Stadium in April 1919. Sergeant Loveday showed his skills by winning the King's Medal at Bisley. On the rugby field the New Zealand Divisional 'All Blacks' won the King's Cup at Twickenham. This was awarded by King George V before the All Blacks met and defeated a French selection at Twickenham. All this served as a backdrop to the return home of over 50,000 New Zealanders in 1919.

ROWING

In rowing Darcy Hadfield was again the centre of attention. On Monday 7 April 1919 *The Sporting Life* reported large crowds lining the riverbank at Putney and Hammersmith to watch Hadfield train alongside Ernest Barry, the world's sculling champion.

> Hadfield, who is serving in the postal branch of the New Zealand Expeditionary Force in London, has won the New Zealand amateur championships on three occasions. He is a much younger man than Barry, who is at least a dozen years older. In addition, Hadfield has had a thorough preparation during the past twelve months, taking part in most of the regattas of last season as a member of the New Zealand four and eight which practically carried all before them. He also took part in a few sculling races. His best performance was at the New Zealand Expeditionary Force's Regatta held at Putney in September last, where he met and beat W.D. Kinnear, the Olympic champion of 1912, in the final over a mile course.[59]

Hadfield was one of the New Zealand eight selected to compete in the Inter-Allied eights race on the Seine on 27 April and at Henley on 4 July 1919. The eight consisted of: G.H. Wilson

New Zealand eight that would compete in Paris and at Henley on Thames at Putney. This was filmed and titled. *New Zealand Rowing Team.* NTSV F245781. This photograph was taken at the same time. UK-Series, UK185, 1/2-013974-G, ATL, Welllington.

New Zealand Eight wins gold in Inter-Allied Regatta on the Seine, Paris, April 1919. Photographer H.H. Green/ L.G. Hahn, UK-Series UK524, 1/2-014310-G. ATL, Wellington.

(bow), A. White, Lieutenant C.L. Lester, W.G. Coombes, W.J. Patterson, S.B.R. Rutledge, D.C. Hadfield, C.A. Healey (stroke) and A.H. Trussell (cox). "There was a large gathering at the Thames RC to witness the first spin, those present including: Brig-Gen C.W. Melvill, Maj. Cameron (Chairman NZ Sports Control Board), Maj. Hardie, Maj. Cave and Mr C.J. Wray (president of the NZAR Assn)."[60] This was filmed by Pathé. We see the eight crew selected to row at Paris and at Henley in their black singlets with the silver fern. They then carry their shell out to the water and row upriver on a misty Thames day.[61]

At the end of April 1919 there was an Inter-Allied Regatta on the Seine at Paris. The international regatta, which the French were pleased to call 'Henley in Paris', was rowed off on the Seine in something approaching typhoon conditions. The wind and rain did not prevent a large crowd gathering along the riverbanks, from Pont de la Concorde to Jena Bridge, the official course. Six eights had entered for the race, representing France, Alsace-Lorraine, Portugal, New Zealand, Newfoundland and the United States: the last-named starting hot favourites. The race was rowed off in three heats, during which Portugal and Alsace-Lorraine were eliminated. *The Sporting Life* reported:

> The final resulted in a Titanic struggle between New Zealand and America for first place. Close
> pressed up to within a few yards of the post, the All Blacks put a superhuman effort into their
> stroke, and thus managed to get home winners by four yards, with France third, and Newfoundland
> in the rear. The winning crew was composed of Hadfield, Healy, Rutledge, Paterson, Coombes,
> Lester, White, and Wilson, all of whom rowed with excellent judgement, and a sure oar. As cox,
> Russel steered an exceedingly even course, and deserves well of his co-victors.'[62]

This was filmed by Barton, but has not survived, however the race is captured in the UK-Series photographs most likely taken by Corporal Green. This was the New Zealand eights' finest moment.

In the build up to the Royal Henley Peace Regatta, a series of Victory regattas were held. The first at Marlow on Saturday 21 June 1919 saw Hadfield win the senior sculls by two lengths over Major P. Withington, from the United States, and the NZEF eight win the Allied Forces eight from the Australian Imperial Force eight by half a length.[63] Hadfield won again at Walton on 28 June 1919 with the NZ Motor Traction Club coming second to Marlow in the junior clinker fours.

New Zealand champion single sculler Darcy Hadfield at the quayside during the Royal Henley Peace Regatta, England. Photographer: H.H. Green/L.G. Hahn, UK-Series, UK548, 1/2-014324-G. ATL, Wellington.

The Royal Henley Peace Regatta was held in the first week of July 1919 at Henley, arranged and conducted by the Henley Regatta Committee. It included eights, open to any crew of amateur oarsmen of any branch of the service that fought in any country for the Allied cause during the war. For this the King gave a cup: 54 eights entered. Australia defeated Oxford in the final (the NZEF eight losing to Cambridge in the heats). The Kingswood Sculls went to Hadfield, "a beautiful sculler", who in the final easily scored over Lieutenant T.M. Nussey (Army of the Rhine).[64] "The Englishman sculled pluckily but Hadfield was always too good for him and won easily."[65] The Australian eight beat Oxford University Service Crew to win the King's Cup.

ATHLETICS

At the YMCA Sports in May 1919 the New Zealand relay team set a world record for the mile relay. *The Sporting Life* reported:

> Pride of place can be given to the international mile relay in which America and Australia were non-starters. It was a wonderfully close thing between the New Zealanders and England, the former just getting home by a yard in 3 min 30 3/5 sec. The time beats the record of 3 min 31 3/5 sec set up by such men as Mann, Applegarth, D'Arcy and Nicol in July 1914, so some appreciation can be made of the running of both teams. Canada was beaten off 100 yards, but on the times returned their performance was no mean one. The struggle between Hill and Mason in the half-mile was thrilling, and it was when the latter made his burst from the inside position, shutting Hill in and throwing him out of his stride that the latter lost the few yards that would have made all the difference. Lindsay, who ran the last furlong for the New Zealanders, is a flier, and seems to shine in relays.[66]

The New Zealanders won easily again at Woking on 9 June, the NZEF team being, D. Mason, J.R. Wilton, H.E. Wilson and J. Lindsay. "Wilson of the New Zealanders also won the open sprint

New Zealand athletes at a Services Competition in the United Kingdom in 1919. The black-singlet athletes include Gerald Keddell (possibly third from left), Daniel Mason (7th from left) next to Brigadier-General Melvill and Harry Wilson, John Lindsay, James Wilton and then Sergeant E.J. Benjamin, the team coach (in white singlet). Photographer: H.H. Green/L.G. Hahn. Green & Hahn Album, Te Papa.

and hurdles, the latter in a very fast time, which is, however, accounted for by their being only eight flights of low hurdles. Lindsay, another member of the N.Z team, won the scratch 100 yards, in which H.M. Abrahams and F.J. Zoeillin had a splendid race for second place".[67]

INTER-ALLIED GAMES

All of this served as a build-up to the Inter-Allied Games, the first major sporting fixture post-war. This was conceived, organised and dominated by the American forces in Europe. It was suggested by Elward S. Brown, the YMCA official working as director of athletics for the American Expeditionary Forces in France. It was to be a military Olympics for the victors and occupy the "great numbers of troops during the somewhat restless period waiting their return home". With the agreement of the French Government Brown arranged competitive events in 24 sports involving 1500 athletes from 18 countries. In the spring of 1919 a stadium was constructed to hold 25,000 on the outskirts of Paris and was named in honour of the commander-in-chief of the American Expeditionary Force, General John J. Pershing. For two weeks, from 22 June to 6 July 1919, more than 500,000 watched the Americans dominate the athletic events.[68] Pershing proudly wrote to the secretary of war that: "In number of participants and quality of entry, these games probably surpassed any of the past Olympic contests."[69] Teams ranged from the 300-strong United States team to sizeable teams from France, Australia and Canada to the sole Guatemalan participant, with New Zealand entering five athletes in the track events and an eight, a four and a single sculler in the rowing.

The small team of New Zealanders challenged American dominance in the track and field events at the games. It consisted of sergeants Gerald Keddell, John Lindsay, Daniel Mason, Harry Wilson and James Wilton: all of who were given acting rank of sergeant for the competition. In true New Zealand fashion everything was done on the smell of an oily rag. The YMCA reported:

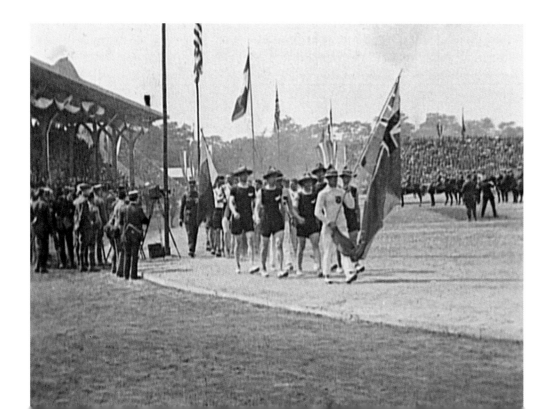

Athletes from Various Allied Countries March at the Opening of the Inter-Allied Games in Paris France. NTSV F232855.

"Recognising the praiseworthy manner in which the NZEF has kept the NZ flag flying in all sports, the NZ YMCA has provided uniform outfits for the All Blacks and for the rowing and running teams. But for this the athletes would have had to wear khaki under conditions which would have militated against their success."[70]

Charlie Barton filmed the New Zealand participation in the games. He filmed the opening ceremony and in the commemorative publication there is a photo of the stadium showing a New Zealand cinematographer wearing a lemon squeezer as a New Zealander, presumably Mason, waits to receive his medal. We know this film was returned to New Zealand but it has not survived. However, we have two American films, each of which includes the parade of athletes on the opening day and shows one of the smallest teams in the competition, which brought glory to New Zealand. Five athletes in black wearing the silver fern, with their trainer, Sergeant Benjamin carrying the New Zealand flag.[71]

James Wilton wrote of the opening. "The parade today was wonderful; the stadium, which holds 25,000 people, was full to overflowing, thousands being turned away. Considering the few that represented New Zealand we were given an excellent reception."[72]

The 100 and 200 metres were won by Lieutenant Charles Paddock, announcing his athletic brilliance to the world, but while another American Edward Teschner came second in both events, John Lindsay won bronze in the 200 metres. The American Earl Eby won gold in the 400 metres with James Wilton, several times New Zealand pre-war quarter-mile champion, winning bronze. Harry Wilson won bronze in the 110-metre hurdles coming third to the Americans, Robert Simpson, holder of the world's 120-yard hurdles record, and Fred Kelly, the 1912 Olympic champion. Fourth in the final was Gerald Keddell, of Southland, the New Zealand record holder, who revolutionised hurdling style in the southern hemisphere. He was the first to demonstrate the straight-leg method, and was 35 years of age when he competed in Paris.[73]

Dan Mason was not placed in the final of the 1500 metres, but won gold for New Zealand in the 800 metres.[74] The Paris edition of the *Chicago Tribune* wrote: "Mason, New Zealand, defeated Earl Eby, U.S. national 600 yard champion, in the 800 metre event for the sensation of the day

The five-man New Zealand athletic contingent at the Inter-Allied Games opening ceremony with the coach, Sergeant E.J. Benjamin, carrying the New Zealand flag, Pershing Stadium. Still from *Athletes from Various Allied Countries March at the Opening of the Inter-Allied Games in Paris France. NTSV F232855.*

and for the greatest surprise of the meet for the Yankee supporters … During the 800-metre final Eby began his final sprint from sixth place. When he cut loose he passed all but the splendid runner from New Zealand. Mason made a splendid spurt to beat the American by a yard."[75]

Comparatively unknown as an athlete before the war, Mason was convalescing at Codford from sinusitis where it was found that he was a skilled violinist and was posted to lead the Codford Camp Orchestra. He was persuaded to run at some local events. He confined his attention at first to the sprints, later competing in the 880 yards and the mile, over which distances he proved himself a remarkable runner. He won innumerable events in various parts of Britain, defeating all the leading performers of the day. It was as a half-miler that Mason made his greatest name, and there seems to be little question that in 1919 he was a world-beater.[76]

Mason's finish in the 800 metres is captured in the official United States film of the games titled *Inter-Allied Games Pershing Stadium*.[77] The film concentrates on the opening and the arrival of the dignitaries with General Pershing, accompanying President Poincaré of France, prominent in all of the opening scenes. New Zealand features in the parade of athletes that highlights once again the small size of the New Zealand team, particularly when compared to Australia and Canada.

The New Zealander's victory is announced by intertitle: "The 800 meters run, won by Mason of New Zealand, with Eby and Spink, both Americans, second and third". We see Mason as he crosses the finish line. The first filmed moment of a New Zealander winning an international athletic race in history — it is a brilliant piece of filming for its time and it is remarkable that the United States' official film includes this New Zealand victory.

First in the 800 metres, New Zealander Dan Mason, with runner-up American Earl Eby, Inter-Allied Games, Pershing Stadium, 4 July 1919. Agence Rol.

Incredibly, New Zealand was third in the overall rankings in the track and field with six points, behind the United States with 92 points, France with 12 in second, and following New Zealand, Australia with five points from two silvers in the 4 x 400 relay and the medley relay, and one bronze in the 4 x 200 metres relay.[78]

Mason and the Frenchman, Jean Vermeulen, who won the modified marathon and the 10,000 metres cross country, were the only individual sportsmen to break the American stranglehold in the running.[79] In 1934 Mason's trainer, formerly Sergeant E.J. Benjamin wrote to the New Zealand Base Records seeking photos of:

[the] New Zealand Army Athletics Team collectively and singly at the Games at the Pershing Stadium in Paris 1919. … I was one of the trainers and Dan Mason was our crack distance runner of the Army. Through the courtesy of the American Army Signalling Corps we have several fine photos, but unfortunately we have not been able to obtain a photo of the Grand Parade of Athletes on the opening day showing the New Zealand Section. We know that the New Zealand Army Officials had a moving picture photographer there and he took untold photos of us, but we were not fortunate enough to see any of them. We are both prepared to pay the necessary expenses to obtain any photos that we are featuring in, so trusting that you might be able to help us obtain some of these valuable mementos of our careers I have written these few lines.

Inter-Allied Games Pershing Stadium. http://www. buyoutfootage.com/.

It was referred to the director of the Dominion Museum and we do not know the outcome.[80]

New Zealand soldier in uniform and lemon squeezer hat, possibly Sergeant Daniel Mason, awaits the presentation ceremony at Pershing Stadium during the Inter-Allied Games. The New Zealand official cameraman, Sergeant Charlie Barton, stands to the left of the flagpole waiting for events to start. SC74654, College Park, USNA.

The New Zealand rowing team also did exceptionally well at the games. The *New Zealand Herald* reported: "New Zealand was the only country to qualify for the final in all events. Hadfield won the international single sculls beating the representatives of Italy, Portugal, America, Belgium, England and Australia. New Zealand crews third in the eights and third in the fours."[81] This was achieved by a team of 11 that included the coxes, all made up to sergeants for the games, except for Lieutenant G.L. Lester. The other members of the rowing team were: W.G. Coombes, G.L. Croll, D.C. Hadfield, G.A. Healey, F.V. Horne, W. Patterson, H.B. Prideaux, A.T. White and G.H. Wilson.[82]

General Petain, the French hero of Verdun, presented gold watches to the outstanding athletes of the games and singled out both Mason and Hadfield for this honour.

RUGBY AND THE KING'S CUP

Success also continued in rugby. Immediately after the Armistice the sporting pages asked if "a series of matches could be arranged between representative sides on international lines … There are numerous high-class players from New Zealand, Australia, and South Africa at present in the country, and now that hostilities have ceased the number of these will be increased. Splendid fifteens could be got together to represent the countries named, while there would be no difficulty raising a British side worthy of being pitted against the best of these."[83] The same article spoke of Lieutenant Ernest Booth, "one of David Gallaher's doughty 'All Blacks'", as already arranging a series of games in South Wales for New Zealand and Australian sides.[84] A match was arranged against a Welsh side to be played in Swansea on Boxing Day with money going to the Prisoner of

War Fund. A strong New Zealand team was beaten 3–0 by Wales in front of a capacity crowd of 20,000 whose enthusiasm saw them constantly encroaching on to the playing field.[85]

An ongoing undercurrent was the position of the Northern Unionists (rugby league) whose members had played alongside amateurs in the same sides during the war, and this had been a feature of the champion ASC side that had dominated the 1916–17 season. Peace saw a return to the status quo and the decision by the Rugby Union Committee that "Northern Union players may still be included in teams with Rugby Unionists in purely Service football — that is, the war-time arrangement may be continued — but that when the Northern Unionists leave the Service they shall no longer be permitted to participate in amateur football."[86]

On 13 January 1919 a committee meeting of the British Army Rugby Union, which had been in abeyance since the outbreak of war, was called to consider a series of games between representative Dominion teams with an invitation to France to send over a team to compete against the winner of the competition. "The opinion of the meeting was unanimous in recommending that in future the Army should always be represented by the best team selected from all ranks and that no Army Cup should be given for any match limited to officers."[87]

New Zealand fielded a series of teams in matches all over the country. The one most eagerly anticipated was that between the New Zealand trench 'All Blacks' and the UK: "The Old Deer Park at Richmond presented an animated scene on Saturday [18 January 1918], the occasion being the meeting of the famous New Zealand Trench Fifteen and their compatriots who have been stationed in the Motherland. Probably the attendance exceeded six thousand, including seemingly the whole of military Maoriland."[88]

It was a dour struggle between two evenly matched sides. "Passing bouts were almost as rare as snakes in Ireland — the tackling was too thorough for this kind of thing — and points were not to be obtained for the mere asking. There was, however, no end of good honest forward work, in which both sets shone, while behind the scrums Capper, Owles, Stohr, Ford and Ryan on the one side, and O'Brien, Storey, Henry, and Juno on the other, particularly distinguished themselves."[89] The trench team won 5–3. A Pathé newsreel survives. Titled *Rugby "Test" Match. [New Zealand Trench Team beat the Home Team by 5 points to 3]*. We see a series of scrums, then shots of the two teams, before a pan of the crowded sideline with lemon squeezers everywhere evident.[90]

The NZEF Board of Control for the All Blacks decided to keep two first-class teams in action in the build-up to the league matches in March and April for the King's Cup when a combined team would be fielded. A series of matches were arranged with various counties and service selections. A *Pathé Gazette* newsreel survives of the New Zealand 'All Blacks' playing Leicester at Welland Road on 11 January 1919, the game being originally scheduled for the previous week but postponed due to snow. It opens with 'Ranji' Wilson leading the trench 'All Blacks' on to the field followed by the Leicester Tigers. The film shows the New Zealanders dominant in a game they won 19–0.[91] This is the sole surviving film of the many taken of the New Zealand games leading up to the King's Cup competition.

On 5 February 1919 the New Zealand Maori Pioneer Battalion XV played their first of a series of games in England defeating the RN Depot 6–3.[92] On Saturday 15 February 1919 they were beaten 6–3 by Llanelly before a crowd of 10,000. "The Maoris team which last week beat Swansea and appeared at Llanelly on Saturday reminds one forcibly of the combination of 1888 as far as dexterity and skill are concerned. They are really a clever fifteen, and play well into each other's hands behind the pack. In weight they averaged considerably over a stone heavier than Llanelly, but like the New Zealanders three weeks ago, they had to bow to Llanelly's plucky little team."[93]

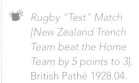

Rugby "Test" Match [New Zealand Trench Team beat the Home Team by 5 points to 3]. British Pathé 1928.04.

Victorious "All Blacks" Beat Mother Country after "ding dong" Match By 6 Points to Three. British Pathé 1906.43.

THE KING'S CUP

The Imperial Services Rugby Tournament involved teams from the Mother Country, Royal Air Force (RAF), New Zealand, Australia and Canada taking part in a round-robin competition to determine the winning team. New Zealand defeated the RAF 22–3 at Swansea on 1 March 1919. *The Sporting Life* reported: "The New Zealanders are a fine side, though the score magnifies their superiority."[94] The New Zealanders then defeated Canada at Portsmouth before a crowd of 3000 on Saturday 8 March 1919.

On Saturday 29 March the New Zealanders defeated South Africa at Twickenham 14–5. The *Daily Telegraph* reported. "It was Rugby with blood and iron in it. I have witnessed no game since the war in which fitter, better-conditioned, more determined men have taken part."[95] *The Times* reported: "NZ has one of the finest sides ever seen in this country, physically perhaps the finest. O'Brien is a classic player."[96]

At Edinburgh on 5 April 1919 New Zealand beat the Mother Country, 6–3. "New Zealand won the great match at Inverleith on Saturday in the Empire Rugby League, and unless the unexpected happens they will become the holders of the King's Cup. The Mother Country was unlucky to lose by a try, but to say this does not detract from the merits of the New Zealand performance … In the first there was no gainsaying the superiority of the 'All Blacks', and they might easily have led by a larger margin at the interval than they did. On the cross-over, however, the boot was on the other foot, and the home players infused as much dash into their play that the Colonials were hard put to it to avoid defeat."[97]

This hard fought game is the sole surviving film of all of the New Zealand games in this competition, although every game was filmed by the newsreel companies. The Pathé newsreel shows the 'All Blacks' assembled for a team photo before the game and we see the movement that leads to the try and then the successful conversion that gives New Zealand the win. The film finishes with shots of a boisterous crowd enjoying the game.[98]

At Bradford on 12 April in a game that was postponed from 22 March because of snow on the ground, Australia defeated New Zealand 6–5.

Australia sprang a big surprise on New Zealand by winning their match in the Inter-Service Rugby Tournament at Bradford last night by two tries (6 points) to one converted try (5 points). This is the first defeat New Zealand have sustained in the tournament. They had only to beat Australia to make themselves winners of the King's Trophy, and the effect of their downfall yesterday is to give the Mother Country an unexpected opportunity to draw level with them. If the Mother Country beat South Africa in next Saturday's match at Twickenham there will be a tie for first place … Yesterday's game at Bradford attracted five thousand spectators. Australia gained a great initial advantage by playing with a powerful wind behind them, New Zealand also facing the setting sun. That the best team won however, there could be no question. The New Zealanders were out-generalled: they could not get the ball in the scrummages, and in loose forward play there was only one team in it.[99]

It set up a final at Twickenham with New Zealand and the Mother Country tied on points after the Mother Country's victory over South Africa. It was played at Twickenham on Wednesday 16 April 1919. The game attracted some 30,000 spectators including Prince Albert and Prince Henry with New Zealand Prime

Official programme: Mother Country versus New Zealand. Te Ara – Encyclopedia of New Zealand.

Army Rugby Union

Mother Country

VERSUS

New Zealand

AT

Inverleith, Edinburgh

On Saturday, 5th April 1919

KICK-OFF AT 3.30 P.M.

Official Programme

PRICE ONE PENNY

Sergeant Major James Ryan, captain of the NZEF All Blacks, receives the King's Cup from His Majesty George V at Twickenham on 19 April 1919 before the start of the New Zealand versus France match. A civilian film cameraman records it for history. The match was also filmed by Sergeant Charlie Barton, NZEF official cameraman. Photographer: H.H. Green/L.G. Hahn, UK-Series, UK414, 1/2-014210-G, ATL, Wellington.

Minister W.F. Massey, Sir Joseph Ward and General Officer Commanding New Zealand Forces Brigadier-General C.W. Melvill. At half-time Prince Albert was introduced to the members of both teams.

"Those who expected a brilliant spectacular display would be disappointed. What they did see was a dour, determined struggle between two sides with but a single thought — the winning of the championship, and incidentally the trophy …" The Mother Country fought hard, "but there was practically none of the passing bouts which had caused such trouble to previous opponents". The black-garbed men saw to that. As a matter of fact, no latitude was allowed on either side. New Zealand 9–Mother Country 3. Despite the promise to pick the best players from all ranks, the British Army side, except for one warrant officer, was a team of officers, with selection based on pre-war performance, which, as it proved, was too long ago. "While admitting that it requires no depth of intellect to criticise after the race is run, one is, nevertheless, inclined to the opinion that the Home Army fifteen might have been somewhat more representative …"[100] The winning New Zealand team was: J. O'Brien, P. Storey, J. Stohr, J. Ford, J. Ryan (captain), W. Fea, C. Brown, M. Cain, E. Hasell, J. Moffatt, J. Kissick, A. Wilson, E. Belliss, A. West and A. Singe.

New Zealand, as winners of the tournament, met France at Twickenham in front of 20,000 spectators including King George V, the Prince of Wales, and his brothers, Field Marshal Sir Douglas Haig, senior army commanders and a host of VIPs. The King presented the King's Cup to the New Zealand captain, Sergeant-Major James Ryan, before the start of the game and was introduced to the two teams. The New Zealanders did not look like losing in what was an enjoyable match, which they won 20–3.[101] This was filmed by Charlie Barton and photographed by Herbert Green. In the photo of King George V presenting the King's Cup to Ryan, we see a newsreel cameraman catching the moment.

Some of the New Zealanders in the crowd at Twickenham on 19 April 1919 for the New Zealand versus France match. Photographer: H.H. Green/L.G. Hahn, UK-Series, UK425, 1/2-014216-G, ATL, Wellington.

The New Zealanders also met Wales at Swansea on Easter Monday 21 April 1919, winning by 6 points to 3, thus avenging the defeat of the 'All Blacks' at Cardiff in 1906.[102]

The New Zealand team continued to tour Great Britain, defeating Coventry 47–0 on Wednesday 23 April 1919 with a strong side. In early May they returned to France to play France at Colombes winning 18–10 before a large crowd including the Australian and New Zealand prime ministers, W.A. Hughes and W.F. Massey.[103] They played 40 games, winning 35, drawing three and losing two.[104] This was followed by the 'Empire Champions' going on a tour to South Africa before returning to New Zealand.

It was capped by Lance Corporal L.G.V. Loveday, MM, an orchestra member of the New Zealand Kiwis, winning the King's Prize at Bisley. His was an interesting military career. A farmer from Ohura and a crack shot, Loveday had spent the war as a musketry instructor in New Zealand and in England. Posted to France in September 1918 he reverted to the rank of private at his own request and joined the 2nd Wellingtons. In the advance through the forest of Mormal on 4 November 1918, Loveday acted as forward scout for his battalion. Colonel H. Stewart's book based on official records states: "Loveday passing through a clearing came on 7 of the enemy. He shot 3 and took the remainder, including 2 officers, prisoners."[105] He was awarded the Military Medal. Promoted lance corporal, Loveday was posted to the Divisional Entertainers in late November 1918. He was promoted to temporary sergeant on becoming a member of the New Zealand Shooting Team for Bisley and reverted to the rank of lance corporal after winning the King's Prize.[106] Loveday would be filmed as one of Hawera's returning heroes in 1919.[107]

New Zealand NZEF 'All Blacks' defeat Wales, 6–3, at Cardiff on 23 April 1919. Photographer: H.H. Green/L.G. Hahn, UK Series, UK427, 1/2-014238-G, ATL, Wellington.

It is unlikely that there has ever been such a sustained period of New Zealand sporting achievement across such a wide spectrum of disciplines in international competition. All of these events were filmed but few films survive. These rare films, photographs and accounts in the press remind us of this now-forgotten excellence.

SAYING GOODBYE

On 3 May 1919 there was an investiture of honours and awards by His Majesty King George V and the march-past of the Dominion troops through London. This was filmed by Charlie Barton and from the prominence given to the New Zealanders, it seems that it may be his film that is one of two that survives in the Pathé vaults. The King invests a cross section of servicemen and nurses, including a very smartly dressed New Zealand officer in service dress and Sam Browne belt. The scene shifts to the royal dais outside Buckingham Palace and the King and members of the royal family. In front of the dais stands Field-Marshal Sir Douglas Haig and his generals, plus Winston Churchill, secretary of state for war. The New Zealanders march past led by their band, and then the Australians. The final scene shows the end of the parade and it is evident that the cameraman is surrounded by New Zealand soldiers who greet their fellows as they march towards them.[108]

The sheer scale of the number of soldiers involved is better appreciated in the Pathé film *Empire Pageant*, which shows the march past the royal dais, but it is the view of the massed columns of men and horse-drawn artillery along the Strand that gives a perspective of the size of the parade.[109]

The members of the New Zealand Division returned to the New Zealand camps in England for demobilisation and despite the inevitable frustrations, 58,832 men were returned to New Zealand. At Christmas 1919 there were only 792 still overseas.[110] The closing of each camp and hospital was

New Zealanders march past the royal dais, London. The parade was also filmed by Sergeant Charlie Barton, official cameraman NZEF. Photographer: H.H. Green/L.G. Hahn, Green & Hahn Album, Te Papa.

Investiture by HM The King at Buckingham Palace, and March of Overseas Troops Through London.
3 May 1919;
NTSV F17841.

marked by commemoration services involving the local community that had developed strong ties with the New Zealanders.

Filming the farewells inevitably featured. After Scales' return to Pathé requests were made to him for filming New Zealand-related events. These were completed by Scales or if he was unavailable by another Pathé cameraman. One of these replaced Scales for the closing ceremonies at Brockenhurst. "Will you please arrange for a cinema operator to be at No. 1 NZ General Hospital, Brockenhurst, on Wednesday, March 5th, to take cinema films of the hospital evacuation from the hospital."[111] The resulting three-minute film survives in the British Pathé archives. The title encapsulates the filming. *Brockenhurst and Lymington — A Token of Appreciation — New Zealanders present flags prior to their departure for home.*[112]

The principal matron, accompanied by Lieutenant-Colonel F.E. Fenwick, commanding No. 1 New Zealand General Hospital Brockenhurst, presents a flag to Brockenhurst Church. Still from *Brockenhurst and Lymington — A Token of Appreciation* (*New Zealanders present flags prior to their departure for home*).
NTSV F245797.

Brockenhurst and Lymington — A Token of Appreciation.
NTSV F245797.

New Zealand Digger at Torquay
feeding his baby for camera as
he and his wife await departure
for home. Still from *Torquay —
Good-Bye "Digger"*.
British Pathé 200.16.

It opens with Lieutenant-Colonel Percival Fenwick, Commanding Officer No. 1
New Zealand General Hospital, Brockenhurst, and his principal matron who is presenting
a New Zealand flag to the mayor of Lymington outside of the town hall in front of a large
crowd made up of hospital staff and the general public. We then see similar scenes at the
church at Brockenhurst where New Zealanders who died in hospital are buried in the church
grounds. Fenwick and a member of the nursing staff present a New Zealand flag into the
safekeeping of the church. The final scenes show Fenwick and his staff walking among the
graves of the New Zealanders buried in the churchyard as the camera pans across the graves
and the church.

The film *Liverpool — Good-Bye to "Blighty" New Zealand Soldiers leave England with their
wives*, shows a passenger ship lined with New Zealand soldiers and their wives while wharfside a handful of family members and lemon squeezer-hatted soldiers wave goodbye.[113]

However, the New Zealand Discharge Depot located in a number of large houses in
Torquay and the surrounding villages, was among the last to close. *Torquay — Goodbye
"Digger" — Mayor bids farewell to last batch of married NZ soldiers who are returning with
their wives and sometimes ... a little "Digger"*, also speaks for itself.[114]

The film shows the departure of 22 officers and 328 other ranks, together with some 60
wives and their children, following a march through the town to a cheering crowd. They
assemble on the wharf and are taken by tender to the SS *Ruahine*, that, because of its size,
was anchored out in the bay. We see the married soldiers holding, and in some cases bottle-
feeding, their children, while their smiling wives and family members look on. It was one of
three sailings from Torquay in November 1919.[115]

🎞 *Liverpool — Good-Bye
to "Blighty"*.
NTSV F245796.

🎞 *Torquay — Good-Bye
"Digger"*, British Pathé
200.16.

22

Filming the Prince of Wales

New Zealand seems to be a Dominion of photographers.[1]

RETURNING HOME

Troopships brought the boys home in 1919 and into 1920. There were 63 arrivals in New Zealand as part of the demobilisation sailings, the bulk from the United Kingdom, four from Suez and one from Samoa. The largest number on one ship came on the SS *Waimana* that sailed as His Majesty's New Zealand Transport No. 257 from the United Kingdom on 10 May 1919 with a complement of 1674 returning soldiers. The SS *Ionic* (HMNZT No. 309) was the last to sail for New Zealand on 31 March 1920 with 24 returning servicemen. There were a total of 43,572 servicemen and nurses not counting wives.[2]

The Maori Pioneer Battalion was the only one to return as a complete unit, the rest returning by draft depending on years of service overseas and marital status. The film of the battalion's arrival in Auckland is also the only one to survive of all the films taken of the soldiers arriving home.

The intertitle of the *Australasian Gazette* announces the "Welcome Home to the Maori Pioneer Battalion from the front". We see smiling soldiers of the Maori Pioneer Battalion on HMNZT No. 228 SS *Westmoreland* on the morning of Sunday 6 April 1919, jam-packed along the ship's rail as they prepare to disembark.[3] The voyage from Liverpool had taken 36 days and the ship's arrival, with its 1033 personnel, was met by three bands and an official reception party while all the ships in the harbour sounded their sirens and a salute rang out from the guns of the saluting battery at Devonport.

The tribes assembled from all over New Zealand in the Auckland Domain to meet their returning warriors. Thousands more spectators gathered in welcome. The *Auckland Weekly News* reported:

> The native welcome to the Maori Battalion at the Domain on Sunday was a most spectacular and interesting ceremony, being carried out in time-honoured manner, with all tradition fully maintained. It was the greatest Maori ceremony of its kind held since the royal visit to Rotorua in 1901. Representatives from every tribe in New Zealand were waiting there to greet

Opposite page: Auckland, 24 April 1920. HRH Prince Edward (left rear) is driven up Queen Street with Admiral Halsey (right) after inspecting the guard of honour. Four motion picture cameras can be identified around his car. Cameraman present included Frank Stewart, Charlie Barton and Henry Gore while Sydney Taylor had filmed the approach of HMS *Renown* into the Waitemata Harbour from the air. Photographer unknown, PA Coll-9055, ATL, Wellington.

 Australasian Gazette 451 [Excerpt], Maori Contingent Home. NTSV F29570.

Members of the New Zealand Maori Pioneer Battalion with their kitbags crowd the rail of the SS *Westmoreland* on its docking in Auckland as they wait to disembark, 6 April 1919. Still from *Australasian Gazette 451: Maori Contingent Home*. NTSV F29570.

The tribes welcome their returning warriors in the Auckland Domain, 6 April 1919. Still from *Australasian Gazette 451: Maori Contingent Home*. NTSV F29570.

the returning braves. Grouped in picturesque native fashion were the welcoming parties of Arawa and Matatua tribes, the Ngapuhi, Maniapoto, Waikato, and Ngatiwhatua, with chiefs and chieftainesses of high rank at their head.[4]

Mita Taupopoki in his distinctive headdress can be identified among the elders. Minister of Defence Sir James Allen took the salute in the presence of the Hon. Maui Pomare and Sir James Carroll. It was a day of welcome, speeches, dances, feasting and sorrow for those who did not return. Though not recorded on film, it was the reception to the tangi that reflected the gulf between New Zealanders at home, compared to the comradeship forged by fire within the New Zealand Division.

> "GOD'S OWN COUNTRY"   ON THE SCREEN
>
> **Two Nights Only**   **friday and Saturday**
>
> **HIS MAJESTY'S**   THE INDEPENDENT PICTURE HOUSE.
>
> NEW ZEALAND FILMS.   NEW ZEALAND SUBJECTS.
>
> **THE MAORI INFERNO**
>
> A Magnificent Series of 70 Views of Rotorua. Why waste money on the trip when you can see this magnificent picture? Geysers in full swing—Boiling Mud-pools—Buried Maori Villages—A Scenic Trip through the Wonderland.
>
> **GISBORNE HUI AROHA.**
>
> Come and See Yourself 'in this Picture.. Views of the Great Gathering on the Show Grounds, Poi Dances, Hakas, and Tangis, Street Scenes in Gisborne, a trip up the Waimata.
> Dress Circle 1s, Stalls 6d.   Book Early at Muir's.
> N.B.—These Films are to leave for England next month.

> The chief ceremony of the afternoon was a tangi for the departed. The soldiers from each tribe sat in the midst of an enclosure in the camp adjoining the sports ground and around them were gathered the sorrowing ones. With low wailing and chants of sorrow, led by their chiefs, the mourners grieved for those who would never return. It was a scene of real pathos and emotion, the significance of which seemed to be lost to the crowds of white people who pressed in upon the mourners, seeming to regard it as a scene of entertainment instead of one of solemnity and grief.[5]

Poverty Bay Herald, 28 August 1919, p. 7.

The film of the welcome of the Maori Pioneers appeared in Auckland cinemas. On 22 April 1919 the *New Zealand Herald* advertised *The Arrival of the Maori Troops* at His Majesty's Theatre. It also featured as a newsreel item in the *Australasian Gazette,* which was not released in New Zealand.

GISBORNE HUI AROHA

The returning Maori soldiers dispersed to their home districts to be welcomed on local marae. A major welcome or 'Hui Aroha' was organised in Gisborne. Tuesday 8 April 1919 was declared a public holiday. The pioneers arrived in Gisborne by Union Steamship Company SS *Mapourika* accompanied by Sir James Allen, Sir James Carroll and Major Peacock and Captain Main and staff from Narrow Neck Camp who had conducted the training of the original two Maori contingents and their reinforcements in New Zealand. This was followed by a parade through Gisborne and a civic reception with a powhiri and tangi at the Gisborne Showgrounds. Sir James Allen presented the French Croix de Guerre to Private Toi Karini of Tolaga Bay who initially worked with the New Zealand Tunnelling Company in the tunnels and quarries under Arras in December 1916. He was severely wounded while the battalion was attached to the French 1st Army in July 1917.[6] A local entrepreneur arranged for the ceremonies to be filmed. It was screened at His Majesty's Theatre in Gisborne for two nights on 29–30 August 1919. The advertising enticed the public: "Come and see yourself in this picture. Views of the Great Gathering on the Show Grounds, Poi Dances, Hakas and Tangis, Street Scenes in Gisborne, a trip up the Waimata".[7] Only a few faded and barely discernible photographed images from the film survive in the Ngā Taonga Sound & Vision archives.

James McDonald from the Dominion Museum, Elsdon Best, the museum's ethnologist, and the Alexander Turnbull Librarian, Johannes Anderson, also went to Gisborne. The trio were less

The dining hall at the Gisborne Showgrounds, Hui Aroha, 8-9 April 1919. Photographer: James McDonald, MA 1000324, Te Papa Tongarewa, Wellington, New Zealand.

interested in the homecoming activities than the opportunities to record Maori elders engaged in songs, games and activities that might otherwise be lost with the death of that generation; photographs, phonographs and films of "various old Native games" were taken.[8] McDonald filmed and photographed the activities and it is from these images that we can get a sense of the scale of the ceremonies. His film was for the historical record and not for public release. In the 1980s, McDonald's films were restored, titled and assembled for viewing.[9]

MAIN BODY TROOPS ARRIVE AT WELLINGTON

The wharfside welcome given to the Maori Pioneers was the pattern for each arriving troopship. On Saturday 15 March 1919 HMNZT No. 221 SS *Hororata* berthed at Wellington carrying 1505 "Four-Chevron Men", being those who enlisted in 1914–15. Each had one red and three blue stripes on their right sleeve, the red indicating an 1914 enlistment and the blue stripe each subsequent year of overseas service.[10] The group received a rapturous reception in Wellington, which was repeated as the draft dispersed to each of the main centres. In Wellington bands played and schoolgirl choirs sang and waved flags on the harbour ferry that circled the ship as it came into dock.

> As the first line [from the ship] thumped on to the wharf the Patriotic Band and 350 voices from the Civil Service Ladies' Choir placed in the balcony of the shed that traversed the berth where the *Hororata* was to lie, struck up "When Johnny Comes Marching Home," and from that out the berthing of the liner was given a musical dressing. The Choir sang "Three Cheers for the Red, White and Blue", "The Soldiers of the King", "The girl I Left Behind Me", "Pack Up Your Troubles", and "I'll Be Waiting". There could be no question that the boys on the transport were charmed and delighted with the novel reception accorded them. Their looks told the story. Whilst the singing was delighting the ears of the home-comers, eager eyes in the wharf were seeking out their loved ones among the lads in khaki who were packed in lines along the vessel's decks. Every porthole framed a face, every ledge formed a seat for a soldier, and they all had eyes for someone ashore as did those on the wharf for those afloat. The greetings were very affecting

in places. There were tears in plenty among the waiting women, but the most touching spectacle was the sight of two little children welcoming their father (a four-chevron man). Such scenes are too sacred to be described, but what an argument they are against war![11]

HAWERA'S HEROES

The *Hororata* arrival scenes were filmed and screened throughout New Zealand.[12] Each community welcomed its returning soldiers. Only a single film of the many local welcomes survives. Hawera feted one of its sons, Lieutenant John Gilroy Grant, VC, on his arrival by train on 29 October 1919. He was joined in the ceremonies by two other local heroes, Lieutenant Harry Laurent, VC, and Sergeant Leslie Loveday, MM, who won the King's Prize for shooting at Bisley in 1919. The film shows Grant being greeted by the mayor, a procession through the town in the fire brigade engine with Grant, a member of the brigade, sitting alongside Laurent, with the firemen proudly in their places, splendid in uniform and helmets. A tree is planted and we see both VC winners with their families.[13] The film of the ceremonies was taken "under the direction of Mr A.M. Conroy [Proprietor of the Opera House] who has given the film to the Borough as a historic record".[14]

HMS *NEW ZEALAND*

The men were not the only veterans to return to New Zealand. HMS *New Zealand* arrived as part of a world tour carrying Admiral Lord Jellicoe, who succeeded Liverpool as governor general of New Zealand the following year. Jellicoe was tasked with inspecting the naval forces of the Empire. The battlecruiser, its crew and the admiral were feted in every port. A veteran of every major engagement in the North Sea the battlecruiser featured in many newsreels. This trip simply added to the number, with films of its departure from Portsmouth and its arrival in New Zealand screening in picture theatres.[15]

HIS EXCELLENCY'S VISIT TO THE COOK ISLANDS AND SAMOA

On 29 May 1919 Sydney Taylor accompanied Lord Liverpool's party to Rarotonga and Samoa on the governor general's farewell tour of the islands on the SS *Tutanekai*. We have Taylor's letters to his 'dear Em', which describe his visit. They give a rare glimpse of a New Zealand cameraman's view of the proceedings, and we can see the result of his efforts in the fragments of film that survive.[16] During the stay in Rarotonga, one evening he and the crew were drawn ashore by the sound of drumming.

> [we] came to a great crowd surrounding half a dozen boys giving some drums <u>hell</u> when we came to compare the size of the boys with the sound they produced, well they were some kids. First one little chap would rattle up his clapper then the one with the big drum would get into his stride, then they would go hell-for-leather, by jove [sic] it was great music, and what perfect

Sidebar

WELLINGTON CITY COUNCIL.

VISIT OF ADMIRAL LORD JELLICOE.

H.M.S. NEW ZEALAND.

The Official Programme will include the following:—

As soon as possible after arrival in Port, a CIVIC RECEPTION will be tendered to the Admiral in the Town Hall.

The City Council will also entertain the Admiral and Staff at luncheon.

A Citizens' Ball (in the Town Hall) will be tendered to the Admiral and Officers on the 25th instant.

The men of H.M.S. New Zealand will be entertained in the Town Hall at luncheon on two days (one half of the full complement on each day).

The Town Hall will be open to the men each day during the ship's stay in port (except on the 26th instant, the date of the Ball) as a Club Room, where games, music, dances, and light refreshments may be indulged in.

Outdoor Sports for the men have also been arranged.

The Council's Observation Cars will be available to convey a number of the men each morning in and around the city.

The Navy League is co-operating with the Citizens in the Entertainments.

Citizens and Shipping Authorities are invited to display as much bunting as possible during the visit, and to give the Admiral, his officers, and men, a hearty welcome to this Port and City.

18th August, 1919.   JOHN P. LUKE, Mayor.

Evening Post, 19 August 1919, p. 7.

 Pathé Gazette: (Excerpt) Jellicoe Departs on HMS New Zealand. British Pathé: 2352.21.

time they kept, then I went to one native and asked him what the great idea was? He looked quite surprised and said why Pakeha te pictures tonight. Having nothing better to do we went in. The place was filled with natives, while waiting for the pictures to start they started to sing, it was lovely to listen to, I was sorry when the pictures started. The Rarotongans are looked on as having the best voices and the prettiest songs in the South Pacific. The Films shown had Joliff's [sic] signature on them and the titles were of course in English, so they have a native translator, he reads out all the titles and the ways they laugh we began to think he was a great humorist [sic] and was giving them his own version of it, while changing spools he would play the accordion, altogether it was a great show and we were very pleased we went.[17]

Taylor found himself in his element.

The people round here are calling me the uncrowned King of Rarotonga the natives think I am the big chief with my camera ... Monday. Well old dear have just returned from the official welcome, then we went to Queen Makea's palace where we had dinner[.] it was a great turnout, when the Governor arrived he had to walk between two rows of warriors after the welcome by the leading chief they presented presents of maps and bed spreads to the distinguished visitors, then they started to dance, which they kept up while we were having dinner, while the dancers rested a native brass band played, they kept it going for three hours. Some of the dances were lovely. They were of the old traditional type, such as attacking an island, capturing a man that ran away with another's wife etc.

After finishing at Makea's Palace we went up to Karika's Palace, the opposition Queen, there we had another dinner, more presentations, but no dancing. At this place I was highly honoured, after his X and Dr Pomare had received their mats, my name was called & I received one the same as theirs. Old Captain Post of this ship was standing behind, was heard to remark, (Well I'm

The welcome to Governor General Lord Liverpool. Still from S.B. Taylor's *His Excellency's Visit to the Cook Islands and Samoa*, 1919. NTSV F6552.

Returned veterans from the Rarotongan Contingent among the crowds, but ignored by the governor general. Still from S.B. Taylor's *His Excellency's Visit to the Cook Islands and Samoa*, 1919. NTSV F6552.

Buggered). He did not seem to think the photographer was anybody but the natives did & they ought to know.

Wednesday night. Have just returned from shore yesterday we went to a big affair and had a very good time, got some good pictures and a few strings of beads, the dancing was much better than the day before ...

This morning we went to Arorangi Palace and had a great turn out, it was the best show of all, the costumes were perfect. I had only five plates & two hundred feet of film, I did not intend to take any film today but when the chiefs heard of it, three of them visited me last night, and said the other tribes would have the laugh on them if there was no moving pictures taken at their place, so went round with one length of film. What I got was good but there was not enough of it, after I finished it, I went round the show & cranked the handle with no film, but everybody was happy ...

By this letter dear you will see that I have been enjoying myself, but I think it would have been much nicer whaling.[18]

There was no official reception by the governor general for the returned soldiers of the Rarotongan Contingent. They had seen the world, given good service, been paid at New Zealand rates serving as New Zealand soldiers. They came home wealthy men by island standards, but now found themselves subject to a cartel of European and foreign traders who controlled the prices paid for local produce and also the prices of products sold in their stores. On demobilisation, each returning veteran received a five guinea mufti-voucher with which to outfit himself in a civilian suit. This would not have been an issue had they been given out in New Zealand but the clothing was not available in the Cook Islands. Some of the traders demanded that the entire balance be spent in their store and refused to refund any unused balance. Soldiers took umbrage and a riot ensued, with traders' stores being looted. A number of soldiers were court-martialled. In response, Liverpool made no formal contact with the

His Excellency's Visit to the Cook Islands and Samoa. NTSV F6552.

Scenes from the Dunedin Peace Day parade, Saturday 19 July 1919. Still from Henry Gore's *Peace Day Procession*. NTSV F3799.

returned soldiers, but as Taylor's film shows, uniformed men in lemon squeezers are present in the crowds.[19]

PEACE DAY PROCESSION, DUNEDIN

The Treaty of Versailles formally ending the Great War was signed on 28 June 1919, almost eight months after the Armistice on 11 November 1918 brought fighting to a close in France and Belgium. Peace celebrations were held in New Zealand in every district and town. Most followed the programme recommended by the government, with three days of celebration from Saturday 19 July to Monday 21 July comprising a Soldiers' Day, a day of thanksgiving and a children's day.[20]

The festivities were embraced by the local population. In Dunedin the *Otago Witness* claimed that: "[h]igh carnival reigned in the streets of Dunedin on Saturday afternoon. A magnificent procession, replete with gorgeous pageantry, tableaux of significant symbolism, handsomely decorated vehicles, a multitude of beautiful displays, and much of the pomp and circumstance of war provided a strikingly spectacular sight and one that has probably never before been equalled in this city, much less excelled."[21]

The *Otago Daily Times* reported:

Peace Day Procession. NTSV F3799.

[i]n the morning the various church services were well attended, the mass service at the Oval at midday was listened to by a large number, and at 2 o'clock the people were streaming into the city by thousands, to line the streets and take up points of vantage to witness the procession … [which] was a magnificent success. It took nearly three-quarters of an hour to pass a given point, and allowing that it had several delays on the route, it can be calculated from this time

that it must have been about two miles in length. The procession ended the day's programme, but in the evening there was another great concourse of people in the streets. The myriads of coloured electric bulbs hung in the main thoroughfares and on the adjacent buildings provided a blaze of light. The illuminations, in fact, are quite a feature of the efforts of the Peace Celebrations Committee.[22]

All this was captured on film by Henry Gore.[23] His *Peace Day Procession* is the only film we have of the three days of celebrations conducted throughout the country. It includes scenes from the afternoon procession and morning memorial service that were held and also shows some of the many illuminations that decorated buildings in the city. It screened as a "Special Local Picture" at the Plaza Theatre in Dunedin from 29 August to 3 September 1919.[24]

FILMING THE PRINCE OF WALES

One significant event marking recognition of New Zealand's role in the Great War came with the visit of Prince Edward, the Prince of Wales, in 1920. The visit was anticipated. George V had told the prime ministers at the Imperial War Conference in 1917 and again in 1918 that his eldest son and heir to the throne would visit the Dominions "when peace comes".[25] The Prince of Wales visited Canada in 1919 in a gruelling itinerary. His visit to New Zealand and then Australia was confirmed by the secretary of state for the colonies in a cable to Governor General Lord Liverpool on 3 January 1920. It was a significant gesture that mirrored the 1901 tour to

Prince's Tour Of New Zealand. NTSV F4097.

The Prince of Wales, escorted by the Hon. Maui Pomare, is greeted at the Rotorua Railway Station before the welcome by the tribes at the Rotorua Racecourse. Note the motion picture camera to the right of frame. Still from Henry Gore's *The Prince of Wales in Maoriland*. NTSV F4095.

A cameraman can be seen to the left of the flagstaff at the presentation of medals to returned servicemen by the Prince of Wales, Hagley Park, Christchurch, Thursday 13 May 1920. *Christchurch Press* Collection, G8475 1/1, ATL, Wellington.

New Zealand of the future King George V, when he acknowledged New Zealand's role in the war in South Africa against the Boers.

The New Zealand leg of the tour proposed a full itinerary by train and vehicle, covering both islands with stops at almost every sizeable town along the way. H. Hector Bolitho's *With the Prince in New Zealand* paints the prince in heroic colours. "We had known the Prince of Wales through the medium of motion pictures and the illustrated journals … We were not disappointed for it was no delicate orchid of an artificial culture that we greeted. It was a sun-browned Prince, not spoiled by the unending tribute of his nation's millions, physically strong and handsome and evidencing the splendid manhood that characterised his service during the war."[26] The crowds that flocked to each appearance and stood at every railway station as he passed viewed him in this light. He was a prince for the motion picture age.

Sydney Taylor, in his role as government cinematograph officer, coordinated the filming of the Prince of Wales' visit. He and his assistant accompanied the prince's party on the royal train. He worked with Frank Stewart and his assistant, Cyril Morton, who were working for New Zealand Picture Supplies,

The reception for the Prince of Wales at Newtown Park, Wellington, 6 May 1920. One motion picture camera is at the flagstaff and the second is partly obscured by the two men on the right. PAColl–9054, ATL, Wellington.

representing the film companies of New Zealand. There was also a cameraman and an assistant from the Advance New Zealand Film Company, which was employed by the New Zealand Returned Soldiers Association, and in addition there was C.D. Barton of the Carlton Hotel, Wellington, and the former official cameraman of the New Zealand Expeditionary Force (NZEF). Taylor's instructions left no doubt that he was the man in charge, stating "The Stationary Picture Photographers have been advised that the condition attached to the granting of facilities to them is that they shall not at any time at any of the functions come within range of the Cinema Film Operators. They have further been advised that in the event of a dispute arising as to a position your decision is to be accepted as final. The Cinema Film Operators are being advised similarly."[27]

A cameraman ensures he has the best spot as the Prince of Wales is cheered from all sides in Nelson, Monday 10 May 1920. Photographer unknown, C19340, ATL, Wellington.

Taylor, Stewart and Barton worked together to ensure that all aspects of the tour were covered. On the arrival of the battlecruiser HMS *Renown* in Auckland, Taylor was aloft, filming the approach of the warship into the Waitemata Harbour.[28]

According to Frank Stewart, he and Charlie Barton were some of the 14 motion picture operators at the Auckland reception. Four can be seen in the photo at the beginning of this chapter. The numbers decreased as the prince travelled south: there were six at Rotorua. This presence was not always appreciated. Cyril Morton remembered "when we were shooting a reception in a big marquee an aide-de-camp came from the dais to stop us because people could scarcely hear the Prince above the noise of the camera. Our films were silent, but our cameras were not."[29] Five films are listed in the Film Censor's records: 26 April 1920, *Prince's Arrival at Auckland*, (400'); 27 April, *Prince's Visit to Auckland*, (250'); 3 May, *Rotorua Welcomes Our Prince*, (800'); 8 June; *Prince of Wales Football Match*, (450'); and on 15 July 1920 the combined efforts of Taylor, Stewart and Barton with, *Prince's Tour of New Zealand*, (4000').[30] There were many other films taken by cameramen for immediate screening in the local picture theatres that were not seen by the film censor.

The photographs tell the story and it is hard not to find a motion picture camera in the crowd in every main centre gathering on the month-long tour. The group was in Auckland for Anzac Day, Pukekohe, Hamilton and Rotorua, there was a rail strike and then they were back to Auckland. The the tour went to Taumarunui, New Plymouth, Stratford, Hawera, Patea, Wanganui, Marton, Feilding, Palmerston North, Napier. Hastings, Waipawa, Waipukurau, Dannevirke, Woodville, Masterton, Carterton, Featherston, Cross Creek and Wellington. Then south to Picton on the HMS *Renown*, then by road to Havelock, Nelson, Glenhope, Murchison, Reefton, Westport, Hokitika and Greymouth. Train through Jackson to Otira, Christchurch for three days, then Ashburton, Temuka, Timaru, Waitaki, Oamaru, Dunedin, Milton, Balclutha and Invercargill.

There is a rich surviving film record of the tour, both in New Zealand and in the British film archives. Taylor, Stewart and Barton's *Prince's Tour of New Zealand* survives.[31] An eight-minute section of Henry Gore's *The Prince of Wales in Maoriland* shows the Auckland and Rotorua reception.[32] There is a film of the Rotorua welcome that may be *Rotorua Welcomes Our Prince*.[33] There is also a Pathé newsreel, *Prince in New Zealand: Wellington's Wonderful Welcome*, which despite its title shows scenes from Wellington, Rotorua and Auckland. There are New Zealand scenes in the 'official' British film, *50,000 Miles with the Princes of Wales*, filmed by Captain William Barker, the noted film producer, who came out of retirement to cover the tour.[34]

The camera in the crowd (bottom right) at the reception to the Prince of Wales at the Rotorua Racecourse, 29 April 1920. Photographer unknown, C19141, ATL, Wellington.

MCDONALD FILMS AT ROTORUA

James McDonald also filmed during the prince's tour. Although assistant-director, his duties at the museum were marked with acrimony and frustration as it became obvious to him that he would never receive the recognition he considered his due. It was against this background that McDonald and his colleagues at the Dominion Museum undertook a series of ethnological expeditions, the films and photographs of which have become the foundation of McDonald's reputation. In 1920 they went to Rotorua to attend the welcome of the Prince of Wales; once again they ignored the welcome ceremonies involving the prince and concentrated on the welcome by the Arawa tribe to the tribes arriving at the Rotorua Racecourse, and the traditional skills and arts of the Maori.[35]

> The ancient Maori method of making fire by friction was demonstrated by Ranguia, one of the younger men of the [Tuhoe] party, and a complete cinematograph record of his remarkably smart performance was secured. A number of new string games were recorded and photographed. In addition to the work done at the reception camp visits were made to Whakarewarewa and Ohinemutu, where photographs were taken of Maori carving. Of special interest are those of the lizard, probably one of the oldest world-wide symbols to be found in the decorative art of pre-historic peoples … The mural decorations of the new Maori church at Ohinimutu, in which all of the old tukutuku or laced patterns known to the Arawa people have been wrought in patterns of Harapaki work, were also photographed'.[36]

SCREENING THE WAR FILMS

One of McDonald's responsibilites at the Dominion Museum was the cataloguing and storage of the war film collection, the last of which arrived in New Zealand in zinc-lined boxes in late 1919. It was an impressive collection, numbering over a 120 different titles, many of which had duplicate copies. It covered much of the production of the War Office Cinema Committee taken during the war. It also included the Pathé material taken by Sanders on the Western Front, and by Tommy Scales in the United Kingdom. There was also a great deal of additional material taken by Scales in Cologne and by Barton in France and the United Kingdom in 1919.[37] Much of the film taken by Barton in 1919 had not been titled. It is clear that McDonald, with his myriad responsibilities, had little time to deal with it.

The acting chief clerk to the under secretary at the time said, "Mr McDonald informed me that he has about 30,000 ft. of positive film and about 10,000 feet of negative film which he received from the Defence Department. It deals largely with sports gatherings, industries at War Hospitals and Soldiers in training. The great majority of the matter is of passing interest only and Mr. McDonald does not consider any of it worth duplicating."[38]

The government had an exclusive distribution agreement with New Zealand Picture Supplies over the screening of the NZEF films in theatres, but by 1920 this film was being returned to the museum.[39] In addition, both the YMCA and Returned Soldiers' organisations were keen to show the films to remind the public of what their men had experienced overseas and the work done by agencies such as the YMCA. In June 1919, on the anniversary of Founder's Day, the YMCA under James Hay, who had been the YMCA commissioner with the New Zealand Division in France, showed a number of New Zealand official war films taken by Sanders and Scales in the Wellington Town Hall under the title *Our Boys in Blighty*.[40] Similar screenings were conducted in following years but the organisers found that it was difficult to get suitable venues outside of the established picture theatres, who were already committed to their regular programmes.

In 1920 a Mr Naughton arranged the loan of a compilation film that he titled *The Diggers Day at Work and Play*.[41] This was New Zealand official film taken on the Western Front and in the United Kingdom, and included the Inter-Allied Sports and various rugby, rowing and sports meets in 1919. McDonald doubted the programme's viability. "Judging by the difficulty experienced by the YMCA in making satisfactory arrangements to show the Government War Films in public halls throughout the Dominion, Mr Naughton is up against a stiff proposition."[42] The film screened in the Wellington Town Hall from 28–31 December 1920.[43] The film was in constant demand and loaned out to Returned Soldiers' Association meetings and anniversaries. Viewing copies of the war film collection were also sent to Samoa at the request of Brigadier-General G.S. Richardson on his appointment as administrator in 1923, to provide entertainment for him and his staff.[44]

In 1924 the exhibition copies of the war films were transferred to the publicity office for care and storage, but remained the responsibility of the Dominion Museum. In 1931 the director reported that the films were stored in the Public Works Department shed in Sydney Street, Wellington. Where duplicates existed, one copy was kept as a master and not used. "They are consequently all in good order though possibly the film may have deteriorated during the last ten years, as so far as I am aware, they have not been treated in any way. They

Y.M.C.A. FOUNDER'S DAY.
————
TOWN ———— HALL.
————
THURSDAY, 5th JUNE,
At 7.30 p.m.
————
MOVING PICTURE DISPLAY,
"OUR BOYS IN BLIGHTY."
————
Addresses by
SIR JAMES ALLEN,
GENERAL RICHARDSON.
————
WELCOME TO MR. J. L. HAY
(Newly-appointed General Secretary).
Soloist: Miss Eileen Driscoll, Wellington's
Leading Mezzo-Soprano.
Mr. George Holloway, Accompanist.
His Worship the Mayor in the Chair.
————
ADMISSION FREE.
S. G. CRESSWELL,
Acting-General Secretary.

Evening Post, 4 June 1919, p. 2.

Otago Daily Times, 28 April 1921, p. 1.

are stored in close-fitting tin boxes."[45] The viewing copies had been loaned many times and it was increasingly obvious that many were in "such poor conditions from continual use that they were not suitable for the purpose of showing in connection with other films through our main theatres".[46] It was decided that all the film be transferred to the control of the publicity department, and it is here that the trail ends. Today only fragments remain and the existing collection of New Zealand-related films of the First World War in Ngā Taonga Sound & Vision archive has been largely drawn from overseas collections.

ANZAC DAY AND THE WAR MEMORIALS

There are few films of the Anzac Day services in New Zealand from this period. One of the first is a film taken in Dunedin in 1921. Titled *Anzac Day at Dunedin*, it was screened at O'Brien's Empire Theatre on 28 April 1921.[47] A gloomy wet day does not discourage large crowds from gathering. The horse-drawn gun carriage, clad with bouquets of flowers, and accompanying escort is part of the so-called "Boxer Service" — the RSA Dominion president Dr Ernest Boxer's promotion of a uniform nationwide observance based on a symbolic re-enactment of a military burial. The film captures the columns of men in civilian hats marching in the rain. Later that same day another familiar post-war ritual is filmed: the official unveiling of the North East Valley War Memorial.[48] This too is rare film of a war memorial unveiling in New Zealand. It is not the case for New Zealand memorials on the Western Front.

Harry Sanders and Tommy Scales clearly treasured their wartime links with New Zealand. The evidence for this is in the Pathé archives. There is a remarkable collection of films of the

Unveiling of the North East Valley War Memorial, Dunedin, 25 April 1921. Still from *Anzac Day at Dunedin*. NTSV F10327.

 *Anzac Day at Dunedin.* NTSV F10327.

Harry Sanders' editorial influence is evident in this item title. Still from *Memorial to 7,000 'Diggers'*. British Pathé 286.01.

General Godley (left) listens as Sir James Allen addresses the crowd at the unveiling of the New Zealand Battlefield Memorial at Longueval on the Somme, 8 October 1922. Still from *Memorial to 7,000 'Diggers'*. British Pathé 286.01.

opening of the New Zealand Battlefield memorials in Belgium and France for the Somme, Messines and Gravenstafel. There is also the newsreel of the 1924–25 All Blacks visiting Dave Gallaher's grave at Nine Elms Cemetery, Poperinge. The wording of the titles shows that the newsreel editor was well-versed in the New Zealand story and it seems exceptional that the opening of the New Zealand memorials in particular were filmed in such detail. The answer is the fact that Harry Sanders was then senior editor of the *Pathé Gazette* and Tommy Scales was an editor and still active behind the camera.

New Zealand is unique among the Dominions after the war in establishing national battlefield memorials on all of the principal battlefields where it was engaged. Canada and Australia established one national memorial covering the Western Front — the Canadian Memorial at Vimy and the Australian Memorial at Villers-Bretonneux. New Zealand also broke ranks on the question of memorials to the missing and decided against being included on the Imperial monuments at Thiepval on the Somme and the Menin Gate at Ypres, but insisted on memorials sited in the area where New Zealanders fought in the particular battle. These are located at Armentières, Messines, Tyne Cot (within the larger Memorial Wall but in a separate New Zealand alcove), Polygon Wood, Caterpillar Valley Cemetery, Grévillers and Marfaux south of Reims.[49]

On Gallipoli New Zealand is the only country other than Turkey to have its own battlefield monument on Chunuk Bair. It has no names on the British Imperial monument at Cape Helles but has its own national monuments to the missing at Twelve Tree Copse, Lone Pine (which it shares with Australia), Hill 60 and Chunuk Bair.

The New Zealand Battlefield Memorial on the Somme was unveiled on 8 October 1922 and the title of the newsreel indicates Harry Sanders' intimate knowledge of the New Zealand Division: *To the memory of 7,000 'DIGGERS' — NZ Division Memorial unveiled on the site of Switch Trench — scene of continuous fighting for 23 days in Somme Battle*.[50] Sir Francis Dillon Bell, Sir James Allen and General Sir Alexander Godley addressed a small crowd on a blustery October

Memorial to 7,000 'Diggers'. British Pathé 286.01.

King Albert of Belgium
addresses the crowd at the
unveiling of the New Zealand
Battlefield Memorial, Messines,
1 August 1924. Still from
*New Zealand Memorial Long
Version.* NTSV F245642.

day at Longueval, while children from the village placed flowers around the memorial — a scene repeated in 2004 at the ceremony for the return of the Unknown Warrior.[51]

There are two newsreel items in the British Pathé collection of the unveiling of the New Zealand memorials in Belgium on 1–2 August 1924. Both show the unveiling of the New Zealand Memorial at Messines by King Albert of Belgium escorted by New Zealand High Commissioner to London Sir James Allen, on the morning of 1 August 1924. The group includes Sir Thomas Mackenzie, Major-General Sir Edward Chaytor and Brigadier-General W.G. Braithwaite, who commanded the 2nd New Zealand Infantry Brigade in the October battles in 1917. In the long version we see the official New Zealand party visit Tyne Cot Cemetery, near Passchendaele, which was under construction with temporary headstones still evident.

Lieutenant-Colonel the Reverend Frank Dunnage conducts the dedication. The women with the official party include Mrs Fulton, widow of Brigadier-General H. Fulton who commanded the 3rd Rifle Brigade at Messines and who was killed on the Somme in 1918.

It then shows the unveiling of the New Zealand Memorial at the Gravenstafel crossroad on 2 August 1924. There is a small crowd gathered at the New Zealand flag-draped memorial on a wet blustery day with harvested stooks in the fields beyond. This was the first objective for the New Zealand Division's successful attack on 4 October 1917. To the east it overlooks the disastrous 12 October battlefield. We see the official party in front of the memorial, with Reverend Dunnage reading the dedication. Sir James Allen stands bare-headed in the rain with Sir Thomas Mackenzie, the burgomaster (mayor) of the district, General Godley and Major-General Sir Edward Chaytor.[52] The *New Zealand Memorial Short Version* is an abbreviated version that does not include the Gravenstafel ceremony.[53]

 *New Zealand Memorial
Long Version.*
NTSV F245642.

The final newsreel item is appropriately titled *For Remembrance*. It shows the 1924–25 All Blacks — the 'Invincibles', who won all 38 matches in Australia, New Zealand, Great Britain France and Canada — laying wreaths at Dave Gallaher's grave at Nine Elms Cemetery, Poperinge, and then visiting the New Zealand Memorial at Messines in Belgium on a cold January day.[54]

The wealth of New Zealand-related material from the First World War and its aftermath survives in the vaults of the overseas archives. Much of this has been repatriated and can be viewed through Ngā Taonga Sound & Vision archives, but many important films remain yet to be returned to New Zealand. We are fortunate that so many of these that are in overseas collections can be seen online.[55]

New Zealand has a rich history of filming and picture-going in the 1920s, the last decade of the silent era. Many of the cameramen who were the pioneers of filming in New Zealand and who have featured in this story continued to be very active, but this story ends here with a final coda.

On 17 April 1929 an obituary appeared in the *Northern Advocate*, announcing the death on 7 April of Alfred Henry Whitehouse, aged 73 years, at the Knox Home in Auckland. He had been an inmate of the home for 10 years.[56]

> Mr Whitehouse was very fond of travelling and went round the world three times, when transport conditions were very much different from what they are today. He invariably brought home some new invention. He was the first to introduce moving pictures to New Zealand, after paying a personal visit to Mr Edison. Later he brought out an improved phonograph.[57]

For Remembrance. British Pathé 368.22.

Whitehouse was never a cameraman with 'his hand on the crank' as Clive Sowry reminded me. However his initiative began a tale that continues to this day. In remembering this cobbler turned film entrepreneur we also recall the faces behind the cameras: W.H. Bartlett, Joseph Perry, T. J. West, Edwin Hardy, John Henry Brown and his brother W. Franklyn Barrett, Brandon Haughton, Henry Gore, Frank Stewart, Charles Newham, Charles Barton, Joseph 'Vanie' Vinsen, Henry Sanders, Thomas Scales, James McDonald and Sydney Taylor. They live on in the film that survives and the stories it tells of a very different New Zealand, a long time ago.

Endnotes

AJHR   *Appendices to the Journals of the House of Representatives*
NZPD   *New Zealand Parliamentary Debates*

1. 'A Marvellous Counterfeit'

1. P.A. Harrison, 'The Motion Picture Industry in New Zealand 1896–1930', unpublished MA Thesis, University of Auckland, April 1974, p. 1.

2. Oral History, Memoirs of H.J.L. Corrick, Audio 0318, NTSV.

3. This is brilliantly explored and illustrated in Brian Coe, *The History of Movie Photography*, Eastview Editions, Westfield, NJ, 1981. David Robinson, 'Magic lantern shows,' in Richard Abel (ed.), *Encyclopedia of Early Cinema*, London and NY, 2005, pp. 404–408.

4. Rebecca Solnit, *River of Shadows: Eadweard Muybridge and the Technological Wild West*, Viking, NY, 2003, pp. 179–203

5. Coe, op. cit., pp. 38–53. Pierre Marchand, translated Claire Llewellyn, *One Hundred Years of Cinema*, Kingfisher Kaleidoscopes, London, 1995, pp. 2-4, 46-47. Lighting, 'Inventing Entertainment: The Motion Picture and Sound Recordings of the Edison Companies', The Library of Congress, http://rs6.loc.gov/ammem/edhtml/edhome.html. Accessed 15 April 2011.

6. Charles Musser, *The Emergence of Cinema: The American Screen to 1907*, History of the American Cinema Series, Charles Scribner's Sons, New York, 1990, p. 55.

7. Coe, op. cit., pp. 60–67. 'The Motion Picture and Sound Recordings of the Edison Companies,' op. cit.

8. 'Dickson, William Kennedy Laurie,' in Abel, (ed.), *Encyclopedia of Early Cinema*, p. 186.

9. David Robinson, *From Peep Show to Palace: The Birth of American Film*. Columbia University Press, New York, 1996. p. 34.

10. 'The World's Columbian Exposition', http://en.wikipedia.org/wiki/World_Columbian_Exposition.

11. Musser, *The Emergence of Cinema, Vol. 1*, pp. 72–75.

12. Clive Sowry, 'Whitehouse, Alfred Henry 1856–1929,' in Claudia Orange (ed.), *The Dictionary of New Zealand Biography: Vol. Two: 1870–1900*, Bridget Williams Books and Department of Internal Affairs, Wellington,1993, pp. 574–75. Clive Sowry, 'Film Pioneers of New Zealand: Edison's Kinetoscope,' *The Big Picture*, Issue 8, Autumn 1996, pp. 11–12.

13. *Waikato Times*, 16 April 1878, p. 2.

14. Ibid, 25 January 1890, p. 3.

15. *NZ Observer and Free Lance*, 21 December 1895, p. 9.

16. Musser, *The Emergence of Cinema, Vol. 1*, pp. 56–62.

17. *NZ Observer and Free Lance*, 21 December 1895, p. 9. See also Sowry, 'Whitehouse', in Orange (ed.), op. cit., pp. 574–75.

18. Bartlett, William Henry, (1870–1943), born Auckland, opened Auckland Studio in 1894 taking over a business that had been in existence since 1860s, successful photographer whose work appeared in the *Auckland Weekly News*. At times had branches in New Plymouth, Whangarei and Wellington, Photographer's Directory, Auckland Public Library. http://canterburyphotography.blogspot.co.nz/2013/07/bartlett-william-henry.html. Accessed 1 August 2017.

19. Sowry, 'Whitehouse', in Orange (ed.), op. cit., pp. 574–75.

20. 'Dickson, William Kennedy Laurie,' Abel, (ed.) *Encyclopedia of Early Cinema*, p. 186.

21. *Serpentine Dance* [Annabelle Moore nee Whitford, dancer], 1895, Cameramen: W.K.L. Dickson, William Heise, Production Co.: Edison Manufacturing Co., Duration: 0:00:54, NTSV F2909.

22. Most of these films can be viewed by accessing 'Inventing Entertainment: The Motion Picture and Sound Recordings of the Edison Companies', The Library of Congress, http://rs6.loc.gov/ammem/edhtml/edhome.html. The sequence of the 'Annabelle Serpentine Dance' is illustrated in Musser, *The Emergence of Cinema, Vol. 1*, pp. 79.

23. *NZ Observer and Free Lance*, 14 December 1895, p. 9.

24. Ibid, 21 December 1895, p. 9.

25. *Hastings Standard*, 15 July 1896, quoted in Harrison, 'The Motion Picture Industry in New Zealand 1896–1930, op. cit., p. 5.

26. *Hawkes Bay Herald*, 8 July 1896.

27. *Wanganui Chronicle*, 28 May 1896. See 'Princess Ali', Thomas A. Edison Inc., William Heise producer, filmed Black Maria, 9 May 1895, 'Inventing Entertainment: The Motion Picture and Sound Recordings of the Edison Companies', op. cit.

28. *Wanganui Chronicle*, 4 June 1896.

29. *Hawkes Bay Herald*, 8 July 1896.

30. *Hastings Standard*, 21 July 1896, quoted in Harrison, 'The Motion Picture Industry in New Zealand 1896–1930, op. cit., p. 6.

31. Jacques Rittaud-Hutinet with Yvelise Dentzer, *Letters: Auguste and Louis Lumière*: Faber and Faber, London and NY, 1995, fn. p. 22.

32. Charles Musser, 'Edison Manufacturing,' in Richard Abel, (ed.), *Encyclopedia of Early Cinema*, pp. 200–203.

33. Coe, op. cit., pp. 66–75.

34. 'People We Meet. No. VIII — Professor G.P. Hausmann, Conjurer and Illusionist,' *Otago Witness*, 7 July 1898, p. 39. Clive Sowry, 'The Kinematograph Arrives in New Zealand, in *The Big Picture*: Issue 9, Winter 1996, pp. 22–23.

35. Terry Ramsaye, *A Million and One Nights: A History of the Motion Picture*: Simon and Schuster, NY, 1926, p. 278.

36. P. Rompter, 'Wellington Wing Whispers dated 8 October 1896,' *Otago Witness*, 15 October 1896, p. 39.

37. *Auckland Star*, 14 October 1896, quoted in Dave McWilliams, 'Auckland Film History — No. 1', *Auckland Star*, 26 July 1941.

38. 'MacMahon, James, (1858?–1915)', 'MacMahon, Charles (1861?–1917)', *Australian Dictionary of Biography — Online edition*, accessed 1 August 2008: http://www.adb.online.

anu.edu.au/biogs. The MacMahon Brothers introduced the kinetoscope to Sydney audiences on 30 November 1894 and then toured them successfully throughout Australia. Chris Long, 'Silent film, to 1914,' in Brian McFarlane, Geoff Mayer and Ina Bertrand (eds), *The Oxford Companion to Australian Film*: OUP, Melbourne, 1999, pp. 452–55.

39. Rompter, "Wellington Wing Whispers', *Otago Witness,* p. 39. Clive Sowry, 'Film Pioneers of New Zealand — Macmahon's [sic] Cinematographe,' *The Big Picture*: Issue: 10, Spring 1996, pp. 22–23.

40. *Evening Post*, Wellington, 29 October 1896, quoted in Clive Sowry, 'Eighty Years of Film Exhibition in Wellington', *Sequence: Journal of the Wellington Film Society*, October 1976, p. 21.

41. Rompter, 'Wellington Wing Whispers,' *Otago Witness*, p. 39. Appropriately enough Newhaven's victories at the VRC Derby at Flemington, Melbourne on 31 October 1896 and in the Melbourne Cup on 3 November 1896 featured in some of the earliest film shot in Australia by Maurice Sestier, the Lumière representative and cameraman in Australia, directed by the Sydney society photographer H. Walter Barnett. Chris Long, 'Australia's First Films: Facts and Fables: Part Three: Local Production Begins,' *Cinema Papers*: 93, pp. 34–41, 60–61.

42. Rompter, 'Wellington Wing Whispers,' *Otago Witness*, p. 39.

43. 'People We Meet. No. VIII — Professor G.P. Hausmann, Conjurer and Illusionist,' op. cit., p. 39. Clive Sowry, 'The Kinematograph Arrives in New Zealand, *The Big Picture*, pp. 22–23.

44. Graham Shirley and Brian Adams, *Australian Cinema: The First Eighty Years*, Angus & Robertson and Currency Press, Sydney, 1983, p. 5.

45. Ina Bertrand (ed.), *Cinema in Australia: A Documentary History*, New South Wales University Press, Kensington, NSW, 1989, pp. 16–17. 'Hertz, Carl (1859–1924)', Stephen Herbert and Luke McKernan, *Who's Who in Victorian Cinema*: BFI Publishing, London, pp. 65–66. Clive Sowry, 'Film Pioneers of New Zealand: The Illusionist and the Cinematographe,' *The Big Picture*: Issue 11, Summer 1997, pp. 20–21.

46. *Otago Witness*, Thursday, 22 April 1897, p. 39. To see how this was reported in the trade press, see John Barnes, *The Beginnings of the Cinema in England 1894–1901, Vol. 2, 1897*, University of Exeter Press, 1996, pp. 161–62.

47. Sowry, 'Film Pioneers: The Illusionist and the Cinematographe,' *The Big Picture*, pp. 20–21.

48. *North Otago Times*, 29 April 1897, p. 3.

49. *Otago Witness*, 21 April 1898, p. 39.,

50. 'The Kinetoscope,' *Evening Post*, 12 December 1896.

51. *Evening Post*, 18 November 1896, p. 4; and 11 December 1896.

52. Musser, *The Emergence of Cinema, Vol. 1*, pp. 81–89. Chris Long, 'Australia's First Films Fact and Fable: Part One: The Kinetoscope in Australia', *Cinema Papers*, 91, pp. 36–43.

53. Sowry, 'Film Pioneers: Edison's Kinetoscope,' *The Big Picture*, pp. 11–12.

54. *Evening Post*, 9 September 1897, p. 4.

2. Whitehouse films New Zealand

1. David Low, *Low's Autobiography*, Michael Joseph, London, 1956, p. 18.

2. Erik Olssen and Marcia Stenson, *A Century of Change: New Zealand 1800–1900*, Longman Paul, Auckland, 1989, p. 400. Matthew Wright, *Illustrated History of New Zealand*; David Bateman, Auckland, 2013, chapters 6 and 7. Bronwyn Dalley & Gavin McLean, *Frontier of Dreams: The Story of New Zealand*, Hodder Moa, Auckland, 2005, chapters 7 and 8.

3. See, Tom Brooking, *Richard Seddon: King of God's Own: The Life and Times of New Zealand's Longest Serving Prime Minister*, Penguin, Auckland, 2014.

4. See chapters 13 and 15, Olssen and Stenson, *A Century of Change*, op. cit. Discussion with Professor Tom Brooking, Department of History, University of Otago, 2007. See also, Tom Brooking, *Richard Seddon*, op. cit.

5. Angela Ballara. 'Tunuiarangi, Hoani Paraone', from the *Dictionary of New Zealand Biography, Te Ara — the Encyclopedia of New Zealand,* updated 30 October 2012. URL: http://www. TeAra.govt.nz/en/biographies/3t44/tunuiarangi–hoani– paraone, accessed 30 November 2016.

6. For Lieutenant-Colonel A. Pitt's biography, see Peter Cooke and John Crawford, *The Territorials: The History of the Territorial and Volunteer Forces of New Zealand*, Random House, Auckland, 2011, p. 100.

7. Garry James Clayton, *Defence Not Defiance: The Shaping of New Zealand's Volunteer Force*, D. Phil Thesis, University of Waikato, 1992, p. 401.

8. Colonel Peter Walton, *A Celebration of Empire: A Centenary Souvenir of the Diamond Jubilee of Queen Victoria 1837–1897*, Spellmount Publishers in association with the Victorian Military Society, Staplehurst, 1997, p. 47. This distinguished the New Zealand Contingent from all other colonial contingents

who generally wore their slouch hats with their brims turned up to the left, with the exception of the Victoria Mounted Rifles. Their hats were broader than the New Zealanders' and were distinctive with a curious thick pagri, almost in the form of a plaited rope, around the rim of the hat.

9. For detail on the selection and raising of the Jubilee Contingent see Clayton, *Defence Not Defiance*, op. cit., pp. 401–407.

10. *Christchurch Press*, 20 August 1897, p. 5. Clive Sowry, 'Film Pioneers of New Zealand: Exhibiting Films in Jubilee Year,' *The Big Picture*, Issue 12, Autumn 1997, pp. 20–21.

11. *New Zealand Times*, 14 September 1897, quoted in Clive Sowry, 'Eighty Years of Film Exhibition in Wellington, Part Two; 1897–1900, *Sequence*, July 1977, pp. 18–19.

12. *Auckland Star*, 12 October 1897, p. 5.

13. *Otago Witness*, 2 September 1897, p. 39. The Dunedin performance mentions 23 scenes of the Diamond Jubilee Procession and it is interesting to speculate who filmed them as R.W. Paul advertised 12 scenes, each of 40 feet; Lumière advertised eight that could be linked to make a 'continuous exhibition of over six minutes duration.' W. Watson & Son advertised 1000 feet of film in 75 foot lengths making 13 scenes, and J. Wrench & Son issued the procession in seven films, each 75 feet and one of 100 feet. John Barnes, *The Beginnings of the Cinema in England 1894–1901, Vol. 2, 1897*, University of Exeter Press, Exeter, 1996, pp. 223–37.

14. *Auckland Star*, 2 December 1897, quoted in P.A. Harrison, 'The Motion Picture Industry in New Zealand 1896–1930', unpublished MA Thesis, University of Auckland, April 1974, p. 22.

15. Barnes, *The Beginnings of the Cinema in England , Vol. 2*, op. cit., pp. 178–199.

16. *Queen Victoria's Diamond Jubilee Procession, 22 June 1897*, Camera: R.W. Paul and others, Production Co.: R.W. Paul, Duration: 0:01.02, NTSV F11225. See R.W. Paul, *The Collected Films 1895–1908*, DVD with booklet, BFI, www.bfi.org.uk.

17. A copy of the letter is attached with Whitehouse to Colonial Secretary, IA1 1899/2243, ANZ. See also *New Zealand Herald*, 1 November 1897, p. 5.

18. *Auckland Star*, 28 November 1897, quoted in Harrison, thesis, op. cit., p. 19.

19. Ibid, 15 May 1897, Supplement p. 2, quoted in Harrison, thesis, op. cit., p. 22.

20. Ibid, 23 February 1897, p. 2.

21. Ibid.

22. A.H. Whitehouse Programme included in Harrison, 'The Motion Picture Industry in New Zealand 1896–1930', op. cit. p. 20.

23. Clive Sowry, 'Film Pioneers of New Zealand – Macmahon's [sic] Cinematographe,' *The Big Picture*: Issue 10, Spring 1996, pp. 22–23.

24. Harrison, thesis, op. cit., p. 13.

25. Charles Musser, *The Emergence of Cinema, Vol. 1*: pp. 82–84. *Wanganui Herald*, 7 June 1897, p. 2.

26. Barnes, *The Beginnings of the Cinema in England, Vol. 2*, pp. 150–152. *Wanganui Herald*, 19 March 1897, p. 2.

27. N.A.C. McMillan, 'Fitzsimmons, Robert 1863–1917,' *Dictionary of New Zealand Biography, Te Ara — the Encyclopedia of New Zealand*. http://www.dnzb.govt.nz, accessed 10 July 2006.

28. Rector had planned to film Fitzsimmons' heavyweight fight against Peter Maher on 21 February 1896 but was frustrated by dark skies and rain. Luke McKernan, 'Fitzsimmons, Robert (1862–1917),' Stephen Herbert & Luke McKernan (eds), *Who's Who of Victorian Cinema*, BFI Publishing, London, p. 50. Terry Ramsaye, *A Million and One Nights*, op. cit., pp. 284–89.

29. *Evening Post*, 27 October 1897, p. 2.

30. Ibid.

31. *Fitzsimmons vs Corbett World Heavyweight Title Fight 17th March 1897*, 1897, Cameraman: Unknown, Production Co.: Veriscope, USA, Duration: 0:12.45, NTSV F26977.

32. *Tuakepa Times*, 11 December 1897, p. 2 and 11 December 1898, p. 3. *Wanganui Herald*, 19 November 1898, p. 5 and 22 November 1898, p. 3.

33. *Grey River Argus*, 25 July 1899, p. 4. *Taranaki Herald*, 7 July 1899, p. 1.

34. Musser, *The Emergence of Cinema, Vol. 1*, pp. 202–203.

35. *West Coast Times*, 7 May 1902, p. 3. *Grey River Argus*, 16 May 1902, p. 4. Clive Sowry, 'Eighty Years of Film Exhibition in Wellington, Part Four: 1902–1903,' *Sequence*, May 1978, pp. 20–21.

36. Pasquin, 'Theatrical and Musical Notes', *Otago Witness*, 22 January 1902, p. 60.

37. Ibid.

38. McMillan, 'Fitzsimmons, Robert,' op. cit., accessed 10 July 2006.

39. Gordon Ingham, 'Everyone's Gone to the Movies. The Sixty Cinemas of Auckland — And Some Others', n.d, MS, NTSV, p. 5.

40. Wellington newspaper advertisement quoted in Clive Sowry, 'Eighty Years Ago —New Zealand's First Films', *Sequence*, November 1978, p.18.

41. *Auckland Star*, 24 December 1898, p. 4.

42. Ibid, 30 December 1898, p. 8.

43. Ibid, 10 January 1899, p. 4.

44. Ibid, 14 February 1899, p. 4.

45. Sowry, 'New Zealand's First Films,' *Sequence*, November 1978, op. cit., p. 18.

46. *Bay of Plenty Times*, 9 December 1898, quoted in Rorke, 'A.H. Whitehouse', op. cit., pp. 17–23.

47. Clive Sowry note to author.

48. *Bay of Plenty Times*, 27 October 1899, p. 2.

49. 'An Evening with Edison,' *Evening Post*, 11 November 1899, p. 5. See also Clive Sowry, 'Eighty Years of Film Exhibition in Wellington, Part Two: 1897–1900', *Sequence*: July 1977, pp. 18–19.

50. 'Cromwell,' *Otago Witness*, 28 August 1901, p. 31.

51. The films appear in the Warwick Trading Catalogue as number 5518 *Departure of the New Zealand Mounted Rifles from the Docks* (24 November); 'These troopers are seen leading their horses and walking from the Docks to the Railway Station, where men, horses and kits are entrained for the front', and number 5519 *New Zealand Mounted Rifles Leading their Charges after Disembarking* (24 November), 100 feet, 'A continuation of the preceding picture which is of increased interest on account of the splendid portraits of these Australians, who have already rendered such valuable services in the field of battle.' John

51. Barnes, *The Beginnings of the Cinema in England 1894–1901, Vol. 4, 1899*, University of Exeter Press, Exeter, 1996, pp. 164, 292.

52. Lieutenant-Colonel A. Pitt, 'Report of the Visit to England of the New Zealand Diamond Jubilee Contingent', *AJHR*, A–J 1897, Vol. III, H14, Archives New Zealand.

53. *Evening Post*, 15 February 1900, p. 6.

54. Ibid, 25 January 1900, p. 6.

55. Corporal F. Twisleton, *With the New Zealanders at the Front: A Story of Twelve Months Campaigning in South Africa*, Whitcombe & Tombs, Christchurch, Wellington and Dunedin, 1903, p. 7.

56. *The Departure of the Second Contingent for the Boer War*, 1900, Producer: A.H. Whitehouse, Cameraman: W.H. Bartlett, Production Co.: A.H. Whitehouse, Duration 0:00:45, NTSV F22555. See accompanying notes. Discussions with Clive Sowry, 1994.

57. Stephen Herbert and Luke McKernan (eds), *Who's Who of Victorian Cinema*, op. cit., p. 5.

58. Twisleton, *With the New Zealanders at the Front*, op. cit., p. 8.

59. *Taranaki Herald*, 2 August 1901, p. 2.

60. Ibid, 1 July 1901, p. 3.

61. Pasquin, 'Theatrical and Musical Notes,' *Otago Witness*, 11 January 1900, p. 50. Clive Sowry, 'Film Pioneers of New Zealand: Northcote's Kinematograph on tour. Letters from an early film exhibitor,' *The Big Picture*, Issue 13, Spring/Summer 1997, pp. 24–25.

62. 'Around the World', from *Otago Witness Specials, Otago Witness*, 21 June 1900, p. 51.

63. Whitehouse requested permission to show his films in Paris under New Zealand Government authority and also sought assistance to film a 'Maori War Dance'. A.H. Whitehouse, Northcote, Auckland to J. Carroll, Colonial Secretary, IA 1899/2243 dated 29 June 1899, ANZ, in Judith Shanahan, 'Early Cinema in New Zealand,' National Film Library dated 11 September 1961, Film History, NTSV.

64. Footlight, 'Dramatic and Musical,' *The Free Lance*, 15 December 1900, p. 12.

65. Dave McWilliams, 'Motion Picture History in Auckland 1896–1941: Written in four parts and published in *The Auckland Star*,' Reference 791.43, M17, Auckland Public Library.

66. Another son, Mr Clifton Manfield Whitehouse, also worked with his father. He wrote about his father in 'A Pioneer of Circuit Exhibition: The trials and problems of the early days,' *N.Z. Motion Picture Exhibitors' Bulletin*, 22 September 1956, pp. 5–6. See also the mention of A.H. Whitehouse being accompanied by a Mr Whitehouse on his first visit to Tauranga in November 1897, together with his second wife Ada, who he married the previous year. He was accompanied by Mr Whitehouse again in October 1898, but this time his wife stayed at home having recently given birth to a child; Jinty Rorke, 'A.H. Whitehouse – An Early Film Pioneer,' *Historical Review: Bay of Plenty Journal of History*, 32–1, May 1984, pp. 17–23.

67. *Hawera and Normanby Star*, 27 December 1902, p. 2.

68. Ibid, 12 November 1904, p. 2 and 24 January 1907, p. 7.

69. Merrilyn George, *Ohakune: Opening to a New World*, Kapai Enterprises, Ohakune, 1990, p. 372.

70. Ibid, pp. 192, 372.

71. Ibid.

72. George Cain, *Packsaddle to Rolls Royce*, Foveaux Publishing, Auckland, 1976, pp. 49–50. Part of this is quoted in Nerida Elliot, 'ANZAC, Hollywood, and Home: Cinema and Film Going in Auckland 1909 to 1939,' a thesis presented in partial fulfilment of the requirements for the degree of Master of Arts , University of Auckland, 1989, p. 18, quoted in John Stuart Reynolds, 'Going Far? John Reid's *Runaway* in the context of his attempt to establish a feature film industry in New Zealand,' a thesis submitted in fulfilment of the requirements for a PhD degree in Film, Television, and Media Studies, University of Auckland, 2002, p. 32.

73. Whitehouse, 'A Pioneer of Circuit Exhibition' op. cit., pp. 5–6. C.C. Whitehouse was Clarence Craddock Whitehouse (1879–1921); C.M. Whitehouse was Clifton Manfield Whitehouse (1898–1980), note from Clive Sowry.

74. Flyer, A.H. Whitehouse material, NTSV.

75. Clive Sowry, 'A Very Special Collection', *Archifacts*, No. 16, December 1980, pp. 378–86.

76. *New Zealand Footballers: The All Blacks Arrival & Reception at Auckland,* 1906, Cameraman: Brandon Haughton, Production Co.: Chubb's Biograph Company, J. & N. Tait *Living London* tour, Duration: 0:03.28; NTSV F4361.

77. *The Theatre*, Sydney, 1 May 1906, pp. 21–22. Clive Sowry film notes to author.

78. *Auckland Weekly News*, 8 March 1906.

79. *Evening Post*, Wellington, 26 and 27 1906, p. 2. For details on the Tait brothers see 'Tait, Charles (1868–1933), *Australian Dictionary of Biography — Online edition*, http://www.adb. online.anu.edu.au/biogs. Accessed 20 April 2009. Charles Urban's multi–reel *Living London* film produced by his Urbanora Company in 1904 did great business throughout the world. Sections of the film were identified in the Australian National Film Archive. 'London Loves,' London Film Festival, published 22-10-2008, http://www.londonfilmfestivals.com/news.

80. *Auckland Weekly News*, 8 March 1906.

81. Ibid.

82. *Entry of Scots Guards into Bloemfontein,* 1900, Cameraman: Walter Beevor; Production: R.W. Paul Animatograph Works, UK, Duration: 0:01.26, NTSV F8627. *Farrier Shoeing Horses in Camp/A Camp Smithy*, 1899, Cameraman: Unknown, Production: R.W. Paul, UK, Duration: 0:00.48, NTSV F7369.

83. *Entry of Scots Guards into Bloemfontein,* 1900, BFI screenonline. http://www.screenonline.org.uk/film/id/1229666/index.html; accessed 10 June 2017.

84. *Mr Edison at work in his Chemical Laboratory,* 1897, Cameraman: James H. White; Production Co.: Edison Manufacturing Company, USA; Duration: 0:00.28; NTSV F5271. *Railway Track viewed from a Train,* Cameraman: Unknown, Production Co.: Warwick Trading Company, UK, Duration: 0:00.44, 1898, NTSV F2143. *Windsor from a Moving Train,* 1900; Cameraman: Williamson?, Production Co: Warwick Trading Company?, Duration: 0:00.50, NTSV F972. *Street Scene — Decoration of London Streets for Edward VII* Coronation, 1902, Cameraman: Unknown, Production: R.W. Paul?, UK, Duration: 0:00.47, NTSV F3372.

85. *Hanging out the Clothes,* 1897, Cameraman: Unknown, Production: G.A. Smith, Duration: 0:00.42, NTSV F6415.

86. Clive Sowry gives a fascinating account of the detective work involved in identifying this collection in his article 'A Very Special Collection', *Archifacts,* op. cit.

87. Rudall Hayward interview with Walter Harris, NTSV.

88. Dave McWilliams, 'Auckland Film History – No. 4', *The Auckland Star,* Saturday, 16 August 1941,

89. *Auckland Star,* 23 December 1899, p. 8. 'The management have secured the outfit of A.H. Whitehouse,' *Taranaki Herald,* 1 September 1900, p. 3.

90. *Auckland Star,* 6 July 1900, p. 8.

91. Zealandia Living Pictures,' *Auckland Star,* 5 July 1900, p. 3.

92. *Auckland Star,* 6 July 1900, p. 8.

93. 'Zealandia Living Pictures,' op. cit.

94. *The World's First Lady Mayor,* 1900, Camera: Enos Sylvanus Pegler, Production Co: Zealandia Living Picture Company, Duration: 00:01:10, NTSV F90103. See accompanying notes.

95. *Manawatu Times,* 6 July 1901, p. 3

96. 'Obituary,' *Auckland Star,* 21 October 1938, p. 3.

3. Joseph Perry and the Limelight Brigade

1. 'Kai Pai,' New Zealand *War Cry,* March 1905. A collection of cuttings from New Zealand *War Cry,* Original in Salvation Army Archive, Bourke Street, Melbourne, Australia.

2. William D. Routt, 'Story of the Kelly Gang, The', in McFarlane, Mayer and Bertrand, *The Oxford Companion to Australian Film;* pp. 473–74.

3. *The Great Train Robbery,* 1903, Director: Edwin S. Porter, Production Co.: Thomas A. Edison, Duration: 0:12:09; Library of Congress.

4. Prior to 1905, there are instances of films taken in New Zealand being screened before the end of the tour, having been sent back to Melbourne for developing and printing and then returned to the travelling company. Clive Sowry note to author.

5. William Booth resigned from the ministry of the Methodist New Connection Church in 1861 and established the East London Revival Society, which after several changes of name became known in 1878 as the Salvation Army. Renate Howe, 'Booth, Herbert Henry (1862–1926)', *Australian Dictionary of Biography,*

Vol. 7, 1891–1939, A–Ch, Bede Nairn and Geoffrey Serle (eds), Melbourne University Press, Melbourne, 1979, pp. 344–45.

6. Chris Long, 'Australia's First Films, Facts and Fable: Part Seven: Screening the Salvation Army', *Cinema Papers 97/98,* pp. 34–41, 64–66.

7. *Otago Daily Times,* 6 January 1883, quoted in Cyril R. Bradwell, *Fight the Good Fight: The Story of the Salvation Army in New Zealand 1883–1983,* A.H. & A.W. Reed, Wellington, 1982, p. 7.

8. This summary is drawn from Bradwell, *Fight The Good Fight,* pp. 14–28.

9. 'Limelight: The Biographies, Joseph Perry', http://www.abc.net. au/limelight/docs/guide. This is no longer accessible.

10. Ibid.

11. Ina Bertrand, 'Perry, Joseph Henry (1863–1943)', *Australian Dictionary of Biography, Vol. 11, 1891–1939, Nes–Smi,* Geoffrey Serle (ed.), Melbourne University Press, Melbourne, pp. 204–206.

12. 'Limelight: The Biographies, Frank Barritt', http://www.abc. net.au/limelight/docs/guide. This is no longer accessible. P.T. Barnum (1810–1891) was a successful American showman and entrepreneur, who founded the circus he billed as 'The Greatest Show on Earth' in 1871. http://www.biography.com/people/pt-barnum-9199751, accessed 16 May 2016.

13. 'Limelight: Picture Show Tours', http://www.abc.net.au/ limelight/docs/tours. This is no longer accessible.

14. 'Introduction' Salvation Army Heritage Centre, 69 Bourke Street, Melbourne', quoting from Barbara Bolton, *Booth's Drum,* Hodder & Stoughton, Australia, 1980.

15. 'Orizaba George Perry (1888–1950)', 'Reginald Harry Perry (1890–1981)' and 'Stanley Wesley Perry (1893–1975)'. After leaving the Salvation Army, Orrie and Reg became cameraman and assistant for Johnson and Gibson, starting with the 1910 remake of *The Story of the Kelly Gang.* After one film for the Tait Brothers, the two firms combined into Amalgamated Films, and the brothers shot six more narrative feature films for the new company in 1911, and a further two in 1912. This ended the Perry family involvement with film production. The sons all entered cinema management, starting at the Melbourne Majestic, which was opened by Amalgamated Pictures in 1912 with Orrie as manager, and Reg and Stan as operators. In 1915 Orrie moved to Sydney where he managed major theatres such as the Capitol and State, before entering radio production. Reg stayed in Melbourne, acting as Entertainments Officer for the Armed Forces during World War I and then managing several suburban theatres before moving to South Australia as State Manager for Universal Pictures. Stan rose through the ranks of Hoyts Theatres Ltd to become resident manager for Western Australia. Bertrand, 'Perry, Joseph Henry', *Australian Dictionary of Biography, Vol. 11,* pp. 204–206.

16. This is drawn from the meticulous detail in Long, 'Screening the Salvation Army', *Cinema Papers 97/98,* op. cit., pp. 34–41, 64–66.

17. Quoted in 'Introduction' in Bolton, *Booth's Drum,* op. cit.

18. 'The Limelight Crusade', *War Cry,* 11 January 1896.

19. 'Destruction of Limelight Apparatus', *War Cry,* 9 May 1896.

20. 'The Lorgnette', *NZ Observer and Free Lance*, 17 October 1896, p. 15.
21. 'The Triple Alliance: The Graphophone, Cinematographe and Limelight on Salvation Service', *The Victory*, August, 1898, pp. 300–304.
22. The Watson 'Motorgraph' was the first film projector advertised for sale ex–stock from an Australian supplier. See Long, 'Screening the Salvation Army', *Cinema Papers 97/98*, op. cit., pp. 34–41, 64–66. John Barnes, *The Beginnings of the Cinema in England, Vol. 1*, p. 164–65.
23. Long, 'Screening the Salvation Army', *Cinema Papers 97/98*, op. cit., pp. 34–41, 64–66. Graham Shirley and Brian Adams, *Australian Cinema: The First Eighty Years*, Angus & Robertson and Currency Press, Sydney, 1983, p. 10.
24. 'Limelight: The Salvation Army, Publications, 'Full Salvation/ The Victory', http://www.abc.net.au/limelight/docs/ lime/2_1_5_2.htm. This is no longer accessible. See also Bradwell, *Fight the Good Fight*, op. cit., p. 72.
25. 'The Triple Alliance: The Graphophone, Cinematographe and Limelight on Salvation Service', *The Victory*, August, 1898, pp. 300–304.
26. 'Limelight, The Lumiere Cinematographe', http://www.abc.net. au/limelight/docs/capture. This site is no longer accessible.
27. 'The Triple Alliance', *The Victory*, op. cit., pp. 300–304.
28. Shirley and Adams, *Australian Cinema*, op. cit., p. 11.
29. *War Cry*, 13 July 1901, p. 4.
30. Ibid, 3 December 1898, p. 4
31. Ibid, 10 December 1898, p. 9. Chris Long letter to NZFA dated 2 September 1991. Long, 'Screening the Salvation Army', *Cinema Papers 97/98*, op. cit., pp. 34–41, 64–66, which refers to the earliest known reference of these Maori films being in the *Australian Photographic Review*, 21 January 1899, p. 2.
32. *War Cry*, 15 June 1901.
33. Bradwell, *Fight the Good Fight*, p. 72.
34. Chris Long, Australia's First Films Milestone and Myths: Part Eight: 'Soldiers of the Cross', *Cinema Papers*, 99, pp. 60–67, 82–83.
35. Ibid.
36. 'Limelight, Picture Show Tours,' http://www.abc.net.au/ limelight/docs/tours. This site is no longer accessible.
37. 'Sidney Cook', see also 'Cook's Pictures', Australian Variety Theatre Archive, https://ozvta.com/entrepreneurs–a–f/, accessed 30 November 2016. Eric Reade, *The Australian Screen: A Pictorial History of Australian Film Making*, Lansdowne Press, Melbourne, 1975, pp. 27, 31, 33.

4. Joe Perry films the duke

1. William Peart, Chief Secretary Salvation Army, Australasia, to Premier of New Zealand dated 5 March 1901, Royal Visit, 1901/953, in IA 1 1908/864, ANZ.
2. 'Limelight: 'Films of the time', http://www.abc.net.au/ limelight/docs/films, accessed 28 September 2008. This is no longer accessible.
3. 'Limelight, Warwick Bioscope', http://www.abc.net.au/ limelight/docs/capture. This is no longer accessible. John

Barnes, *The Beginnings of Cinema in England, 1894–1901: Vol. 4, 1899*, University of Exeter Press, Exeter, 1996, p. 173. Barnes, *The Beginnings of Cinema in England, Vol. 5, 1900*, University of Exeter Press, Exeter, 1997, pp. 88, 92–94. The cameras were the product of the London-based Warwick Trading Company under its American-born managing director, Charles Urban. The Warwick Trading Company began life as an agent of an American company but developed into one of the commercial powerhouses of the British film industry at the beginning of the twentieth century. It was both one of the leading film makers, specialising in topical and news films, and equipment suppliers. Barnes, *The Beginnings of Cinema in England, Vol. 4*, op. cit., pp. 159–85.
4. Peart to Premier of New Zealand, 5 March 1901, op. cit. ANZ.
5. Sir Donald Mackenzie Wallace, *The Web of Empire: A Diary of the Imperial Tour of their Royal Highnesses the Duke and Duchess of Cornwall and York in 1901*, Macmillan, London, 1902, p. 3. Harold Nicolson, *King George the Fifth: His Life and Reign*, Constable, London, 1952, pp. 66–68. Chris Long and Clive Sowry, 'Australia's First Films: the Royal Visit Films of 1901,' *Cinema Papers*, March 1995, pp. 40–43, 56–57.
6. Michael Bassett, *Sir Joseph Ward — A Political Biography*, Auckland University Press, 1995, pp. 120–21.
7. *War Cry*, 10 December 1898, p. 10.
8. Bassett, op. cit., p. 110.
9. Ibid, p. 111.
10. Ibid.
11. Ibid, pp. 117–18.
12. Ibid, p. 118.
13. Ibid, p. 118.
14. Margaret McClure, *The Wonder Country: Making New Zealand Tourism*, Auckland University Press, Auckland, 2004, p. 26.
15. McClure, *The Wonder Country*, op. cit., pp. 26–27.
16. E.S. Dollimore, 'Thomas Edward Donne (1859–1945) A Biographical Essay,' ABKB 7709 W5035 1j 33, pp. 1–25, ANZ.
17. Pollen, Under-Secretary, Colonial Secretary's Office to Peart dated 30 March 1901, 1901 Royal Visit, IA 1 1908/864, ANZ.
18. Perry to Colonial Secretary's Office dated 22 May 1901, 1901 Royal Visit, IA 1908/864, ANZ.
19. *War Cry*, 13 July 1901, p. 4; 'New Zealand's Share in the Royal Visit,' *Evening Post*, 24 May 1901, p. 5.

20. 'New Zealand's Share in the Royal Visit,' *Evening Post*, 28 May 1901, p. 5.

21. Perry to Pollen, Colonial Secretary dated 22 May 1901, 1901/953 in IA 1 1908/864; Perry to Pollen dated 1901/953 in IA 1 1908/864, ANZ.

22. Perry to Seddon dated 17 July 1901, 1901/2779a, in IA 1, 1908/864, ANZ.

23. *Royal Visit of the Duke and Duchess of Cornwall and York to New Zealand*, 1901, Cameramen: Joseph Perry and others, Production Co: Limelight Department, Salvation Army, Duration: 0:08:10, NTSV F2468.

24. 'The Duke in Geyserland,' *Evening Post*, 15 June 1901, p. 5.

25. Chris Long and Clive Sowry, 'Australia's First Films: Foreign Producers in Australia, 1901,' *Cinema Papers*, June 1995, pp. 40–43, 55.

26. *Otago Witness*, 3 July 1901, p. 28.

27. Minute from Hugh Pollen to J. Mackay, Government Printer, 1901/3728 dated 27 March 1902 with annotated reply. IA 1 1901/3728, ANZ.

28. Ibid.

29. It was not the only time that Maggie Papakura would meet the royal couple. She attended their coronation in 1911 when they were crowned King George V and Queen Mary, and met Captain Staples-Brown again (whom she met at Whakawerawera in 1907) and married him. She was presented to the royal couple at least on two further occasions. June Northcroft-Grant, 'Papakura, Makereti'. First published in *The Dictionary of New Zealand Biography, Te Ara — the Encyclopedia of New Zealand, Vol. 3*, 1996. https://teara.govt.nz/en/biographies/3p5/papakura-makereti (accessed 8 August 2017).

30. R.A. Loughnan, *Royalty in New Zealand: The Visit of their Royal Highnesses The Duke and Duchess of Cornwall and York to New Zealand, 10th to 27th June 1901. A Descriptive Narrative*, Government Printer, Wellington, 1902.

31. Loughnan, *Royalty in New Zealand*, op. cit., p. 93.

32. Ibid, p. 98.

33. 'Maoriland — Ancient and Modern,' As Seen by the Royal Visitors,' *Evening Post*, 27 July 1901, p. 11.

34. Perry to Seddon dated 17 July 1901, 1901/2779a, in IA 1, 1908/864, ANZ.

35. Loughnan, *Royalty in New Zealand*, op. cit., p. 98.

36. Ibid, p. 186.

37. E.F. Knight, *With the Royal Tour: A Narrative of the Recent Tour of the Duke and Duchess of Cornwall and York through Greater Britain, including His Royal Highness's Speech delivered at the Guildhall, on December 5, 1901*, Longmans, Green and Co, London, 1902, p. 223.

38. Chris Long and Clive Sowry, 'Australia's First Films: Our First Producers Abroad,' *Cinema Papers*, August 1995, pp. 36–39, 57–58. 'The Royal Visit,' *Hawera and Normanby Star*, 28 June 1901, p. 3.

39. 'The Embarkation Scene at Lyttelton,' *Evening Post*, 28 June 1901, p. 5.

40. Long and Sowry, 'Our First Producers Abroad,' *Cinema Papers*, op. cit., pp. 36–39, 57–58.

41. Martha Rutledge, 'Barrett, Walter Franklyn (1873–1964)', *Australian Dictionary of Biography, Vol. 7, 1891–1939, A-Ch*, Bede Nairn and Geoffrey Serle, (eds). Melbourne University Press, p. 190.

42. Rutledge, 'Barrett, Walter Franklyn (1873–1964)', *Australian Dictionary of Biography, Vol. 7, ibid*. Graham Shirley and Brian Adams, *Australian Cinema, The First Eighty Years*, Angus & Robertson and Currency Press, Sydney, 1983, p. 5, also discussions on Franklyn Barrett with Clive Sowry.

43. 'The Royal Bioscope,' *Wanganui Herald*, 25 July 1901, p. 3. Long and Sowry, 'Foreign Producers in Australia, 1901', op. cit., pp. 40–43, 55.

44. 'The Bioscope Company,' *Evening Post*, 29 July 1901, p. 5. Clive Sowry, 'Eighty Years of Film Exhibition in Wellington, Part Three: 1901', *Sequence*, October 1977, pp. 18–19.

45. *Evening Post*, 30 July 1901, p. 5.

46. Long and Sowry, 'Our First Producers Abroad,' *Cinema Papers*, op. cit., pp. 36–39, 57–58.

47. Clive Sowry, 'Eighty Years of Film Exhibition in Wellington, Part Four: 1902–1903', *Sequence*, May 1978, pp. 20–21. *Evening Post*, 10 April 1902.

48. *Evening Post*, 26 October 1901, p. 5.

49. Ibid, 2 November 1901, p. 6. Macdonald had the rare distinction of rising from the ranks to knighthood and Major-General. He was in New Zealand and fêted throughout the country while en route to Ceylon where rumours of his alleged homosexuality led to his suicide in a Paris hotel on 25 March 1903. 'Sir Hector Macdonald', *Encyclopædia Britannica Online*, <http://www.britannica.com/EBchecked/topic/1359877/Sir-Hector-Macdonald. Accessed 21 October 2008.

50. P. Rompter, 'Wellington Wing Whispers,' *Otago Witness*, op. cit., p. 57; 'The Manawatu Show,' *Evening Post*, 15 November 1901, p. 2.

51. *Evening Post*, 20 November 1901, p. 6.

52. See 'A view of Palmerston North Station, North Island, New Zealand about 1900.' Photo taken by A.B. Harris, published in *The New Zealand Railways Magazine*, Vol. 11, Issue 4, 1 July 1936, p. 46. New Zealand Electronic Text Centre. This would be when it was the junction point for New Zealand Rail and the privately owned Wellington and Manawatu Railway Company. For a view of the distinctive American-style clerestory roof cars of the Wellington and Manawatu Railway Company, see 'Engine 11 of the Wellington Manawatu Railway Co. pulling a train out of Thorndon, Wellington, 1892, Ref: ½-018847-F; Alexander Turnbull Library. The verandah design, the position of the clocks and a sense of the track layout can be gauged from the images in J.D. Mahoney, *Down at the Station: A Study of the New Zealand Railway Station*, Dunmore Press, Palmerston North, 1987, pp. 124–29.

53. *Biograph Pictures of the Palmerston Show: Departure of the Wellington Train From Palmerston North Station after the Show*, 1901, Cameraman: J.H. Brown, Production Co.: Empire Specialty Company, Duration: 0:01:35, NTSV F2142.

54. Sowry, 'Eighty Years of Film Exhibition in Wellington, 1902–1903', *Sequence*, op. cit., pp. 20–21.

55. Sowry, 'Eighty Years of Film Exhibition in Wellington, 1901', *Sequence*, op. cit., pp. 18–19. *Evening Post*, 11 and 12 December 1901, p. 6.

56. Rompter, 'Wellington Wing Whispers,' *Otago Witness*, op. cit., p. 57.

57. *Fiji and the South Seas,* 1902–1907, Cameramen: J.H. Brown and W. Franklyn Brown [Barrett], Production Co.: Charles Urban Trading Company, UK, Eclipse, France, Duration: 0:04:18, NTSV F7430.

58. *Wanganui Herald*, 10 July 1903, p. 5.

59. Ibid, 13 July 1903, p. 5.

60. Ibid, 14 July 1903, p. 7.

61. Ibid, 11 July 1903, p. 4, 13 July 1903, p. 5.

62. Ibid, 13 July 1903, p. 5.

63. Footlight, 'Dramatic and Musical,' *New Zealand Free Lance*, 1 June 1901, p. 7.

64. *Wanganui Herald*, 31 July 1901, p. 3.

65. Ibid, 22 July 1901, p. 2.

66. *Taranaki Herald*, 6 May 1901, p. 2.

67. This increased to £745.12.03 with the addition of three additional Rotorua scenes. Salvation Army to New Zealand Government, 1902/883, ANZ.

68. Perry to Seddon dated 22 November 1901, 1901 Royal Tour, IA1908/864, ANZ.

69. *Evening Post*, 3 April 1902.

70. J. Mackay to Pollen dated 8 May 1902, 1902/883, in IA 1 1908/864, ANZ.

71. *Evening Post*, 3 April 1902. As it turned out, while the film was shown throughout New Zealand a number of times, the projectors were overlooked and remained in storage. One was finally passed on for the use of the Department of Tourist and Health Resorts in 1907 and the second was sold for £40 to John Fuller and Sons on 13 April 1908. Donne to Hugh Pollen, Under-Secretary, Colonial Secretary's Department dated 23 March 1907, IA 1 1902/883 and Minute by Hugh Pollen dated 13 April 1908, IA 1 1908/864, ANZ.

72. There is no record of the Perrys' film being shown in the United Kingdom. Alfred West's *Scenes from the Royal Tour* taken by the 'King's Kinematographist' was shown to the royal family at Sandringham and featured in his programme, so the New Zealand scenes were seen by British audiences.

5. Limelight and salvation

1. *The Modern Bioscope Operator*, Ganes Limited, London, 1911, p. 5.

2. *Biorama Ramblings: Being an account of the travels of the Territorial Biorama Company during a tour of four months duration through the Colony of New Zealand. The Author being one known as the Rambler, August to November 1902 & 1905.* A collection of cuttings from the New Zealand *War Cry*. Original in Salvation Army Archive, Bourke Street, Melbourne, with annotations by Chris Long. 'Wellington's Celebrations,' *Evening Post*, August 9, 1902, p. 5.

3. Clive Sowry, 'Eighty Years of Film Exhibition in Wellington, Part Four, 1902–1903, *Sequence*, May 1978, pp. 20–21.

4. E.S. Dollimore, 'Thomas Edward Donne (1859–1945) A Biographical Essay,' p. 13, ABKB 7709 W5035 1j 33, ANZ.

5. Ibid.

6. T.E. Donne, General Manager to Engineer in Charge, Rotorua 08/153 dated 11 February 1909, TO 1 1911/486, ANZ.

7. Tom Brooking, *Richard Seddon: King of God's Own: The Life and Times of New Zealand's Longest Serving Prime Minister*, Penguin, Auckland, 2014, p. 347.

8. Christopher Tobin, *The Original All Blacks: 1905–1906*, Hodder, Moa, Beckett, Auckland, 2005, pp. 53–54.

9. Ibid, p. 53.

10. *Evening Post*, 17 January 1906, p. 8. *Otago Witness*, 7 February 1906, p. 59; 4 April 1906, p. 60.

11. The Stonham–Morrison Co., His Majesty's Theatre, Dunedin advertised 'N.Z. Footballers in the match against Wales,' starting September 17, 1906, Theatre Brochure, Peter Harcourt Early Film and Theatre Programme Collection, 0443, NTSV.

12. *New Zealand vs England 1905*, Cameraman: Unknown, Production Co.: Unknown, United Kingdom, Duration: 0:03:41, NTSV F27366. There is another surviving film from the tour of the 'Originals'. It shows the All Blacks vs Glamorgan match in December 1905, and runs for about three and a half minutes. It is incorporated into the 1925 film *The Invincible All Blacks Record Tour 1924–5*, 1924, Cameraman: Unknown, Production Co.: Unknown, Duration: 0:36:01 (it follows the intertitle "A Peep into the Past", which starts at 0:15:49), NTSV F7026. Clive Sowry film notes to author.

13. *New Zealand Footballers: The All Blacks Arrival & Reception at Auckland, 1906*, Cameraman: Brandon Haughton, Production Co.: Chubb's Biograph Company, J. & N. Tait's *Living London* tour, Duration: 0:03.28, NTSV F4361.

14. *Funeral Procession of Premier R.J. Seddon*, 28 June 1906, Cameraman: W.F. Barrett, Production Co.: Globe Syndicate Pictures, Duration: 0:03.07, NTSV F31276. The cameraman was originally identified as Leonard Corrick, but the Corrick family were touring South Australia at this time having finished a season in Adelaide before moving on to Broken Hill. See 'The Ghost Walk', *Otago Witness*, 27 June 1906, p. 68. Descendants of Corrick Family (interviewed by Jane Paul, Film Researcher, NTSV, stated that W. Franklyn Barrett filmed the funeral. Appears as W.F. Barrett in film advertisement for above, *Evening Post*, 17 July 1906, p. 6. Barrett showed the film at His Majesty's

Theatre, Wellington for Globe Syndicate Pictures in July 1906. Versions of the film were also being shown throughout New Zealand in the same month. See *Grey River Argus*, 6 July 1906, p. 2. E S Dollimore, 'Thomas Edward Donne (1859–1945) A Biographical Essay,' p.13, ABKB 7709 W5035 1j 33, ANZ.

15. Clive Sowry film notes to author.
16. *War Cry*, 9 March 1907, p. 6.
17. Ibid.
18. *West Coast Times*, 2 November 1906, p. 4
19. Eric Reade, *The Australian Screen*, op. cit., p. 26.
20. *Sights and Scenes at the New Zealand Exhibition*, 1906, Cameraman: E.J. Hardy and others, Production Co.: West's Pictures — T.J. West, Duration: 0:07.54, NTSV F2656.
21. *Otago Daily Times*, 7 February 1907, p. 1; *Timaru Herald*, 14 March 1907, p. 1.
22. J. Cowan, *Official Record of the New Zealand International Exhibition of Arts and Industries, held at Christchurch, 1906–7*: Government Printer, Wellington, 1910, pp. 80–113.
23. Cowan, *Exhibition of Arts and Industries, 1906–07*, op. cit., p. 93.
24. Perry to Seddon dated 12 March 1902, IA 1908/864, ANZ.
25. Dean Rapp, 'The British Salvation Army, The Early Film Industry and Urban Working–Class Adolescents, 1897–1918,' *Twentieth Century British History*: Vol. 7, No. 2, 1996, pp. 157–188. See extracts from the Salvation Army publications on the effectiveness of moving picture exhibitions from *The Field Officer* and *The Officer* in Colin Harding and Simon Popple, *In the Kingdom of the Shadows: A Companion to Early Cinema*: Cygnus Arts, London, 1996, pp. 80–84.
26. *Evening Post*, 24 April 1907, p. 2, 'Perry's Biorama', Princess Theatre, commencing Wednesday 3 July 1907, Dunedin, theatre brochure, Peter Harcourt Early Film and Theatre Programme Collection, 0443, NTSV.
27. 'Perry's Electric Biorama, A Record House, A Brilliant Entertainment, A Festive Treat.' *Grey River Argus*, 2 January 1909, p. 3.
28. Clive Sowry, 'Eighty Years of Film Exhibition in Wellington, Part Eight: 1907,' *Sequence*, February 1980, pp. 4–5.
29. *War Cry*, 9 March 1907, p. 6.
30. *Evening Post*, 14 September 1905.
31. *War Cry*, 9 March 91907, p. 6.
32. Ibid.
33. Ibid.
34. *Coasts of New Zealand*, 1910, Cameraman: W. Franklyn Barrett, Production Co.: Pathé Frères, Duration: 0:04.51, NTSV F9043. *Coasts of New Zealand [Pelorus Jack Excerpt]*, Duration: 0:00.45, NTSV F3812.
35. *War Cry*, 9 March 1907, p. 6.
36. Ibid.
37. *Biorama Ramblings*, op. cit.
38. *Biorama Ramblings* with annotations by Chris Long, op. cit., this is the only known mention of the hand-tinting of Salvation Army film.
39. *Across the Mountain Passes of New Zealand, 1910*, Cameraman: W. Franklyn Barrett, Production Co.: Pathé Frères, Duration: 0:04:01, NTSV F10078.

40. *Biorama Ramblings* with annotations by Chris Long, op. cit., March 1905.
41. Ibid.
42. Ibid, 15 April 1905.
43. Ibid, 22 April 1905.
44. Ibid.
45. Ibid.
46. Clive Sowry film notes to author.
47. Ibid, 2 September 1905.
48. Ibid.
49. *Biorama Ramblings*, annotations by Chris Long, op. cit., 2 September 1905.
50. Clive Sowry film notes to author.
51. The first recorded story film is believed to be that shot by W.F. Brown alias W. Franklyn Barrett, who filmed an 800 foot adaption of the play 'A Message from Mars' in Wellington in 1902–03. However we also know that the Brown brothers shot 'Ally Sloper at Day's Bay' also known 'Ally Sloper's Half-Holiday' in the same period. Neither of these have survived. Graham Shirley and Brian Adams, *Australian Cinema: The First Eighty Years*, Angus & Robertson and Currency Press, Sydney, 1983, pp. 38–39.
52. *Biorama Ramblings*, annotations by Chris Long, op. cit., 2 September 1905.
53. Ibid, 7 October 1905.
54. Ibid, 14 October 1905.
55. Ibid.
56. Ibid, 1902. The 'tank' referred to is that holding the oxygen under pressure that was mixed with hydrogen and played on the limestone block to illuminate the projector.
57. Ibid, 2 September 1905.
58. *War Cry*, 1 May 1909.
59. *Evening Post*, 6 and 8 November 1909, pp. 6 and 2. Sowry, 'Eighty Years of Film Exhibition in Wellington, Part Ten: The Lasting Picture Show', *Sequence*, September 1980, pp. 20–21.
60. 'The Biograph Supply Department', *War Cry*, May 8, 1909, p. 17.
61. Ibid.
62. Cyril R. Bradwell, *Fight the Good Fight*, op. cit., p. 73. Rapp, 'The British Salvation Army', op. cit., pp. 157–88.
63. 'Perry's Pictures,' *Hawera and Normanby Star*, 21 June 1910.

6. The government appoints a kinematographist

1. T.E. Donne, 'The New Zealand Government Department of Tourist and Health Resorts,' TO 1, 1908/495, ANZ.
2. *American Fleet at Auckland*, 1908, Cameraman: James McDonald, Production Co.: Department of Tourist and Health Resorts, Duration: 0:03:16, NTSV F10262.
3. See: *Te Hui Aroha Ki Turanga : Gisborne Hui Aroha*, 1919, Cameraman: James McDonald, Production Co.: Dominion Museum, Duration: 0:10.41, NTSV F7882; *He Pito Whakaatu i te Hui i Rotorua: Scenes at the Rotorua Hui*, 1920, Cameraman: James McDonald, Production Co.: Dominion Museum, Duration: 0:26.40, NTSV F2808; *Welcome at the Rotorua Race Course to the Tribes arriving for the Visit by the Prince of*

Wales, 1920, Cameraman: James McDonald, Production Co.: Dominion Museum, Duration: 0:04.41, NTSV F847; *He Pito Whakaatu i te Noho a te Māori i te Awa ō Whanganui: Scenes Of Maori Life On The Whanganui River,* 1921, Cameraman: James McDonald, Production Co; Dominion Museum, Duration: 0:54.19, NTSV F2816; *Scenes of Maori Life on the East Coast,* 1923, Cameraman: James McDonald, Production Co.: Dominion Museum, Duration: 0:24.56, NTSV F2815. McDonald took these films as an ethnological record for the Dominion Museum Collection and it was only in the 1980s that the surviving films were structured and titled. Jonathan Dennis and Sharon Dell, *James McDonald Kai-Whakaahua: Photographs of the Tangata Whenua*, National Library Gallery, December 1989–20 January 1990. National Library of New Zealand, Wellington, 1989.

4. David Thomas, 'McCubbin, Frederick (1885–1917)', Margaret Rose, 'Richardson, Charles Douglas (1853–1932), *Australian Dictionary of Biography — Online edition*, http://www.adb.online.anu.edu.au/biogs. Accessed 12 June 2008.

5. Nominal Roll of Persons Employed in Each Department (other than Postal and Railways) giving length of service as on 31st March 1907 and salaries for financial year 1907–1908 chargeable on the Consolidated Fund, *AJHR*, 1907, Wellington, H-5, p. 6.

6. David Colquhuon, 'Cowan, James, 1870–1943', *The Dictionary of New Zealand Biography, Vol. Three, 1901–1920*, Auckland University Press and Department of Internal Affairs, Auckland, 1996, pp. 119–21.

7. *New Zealand Mail,* 7 March 1906.

8. Tangiwai [James Cowan], 'Pictures of New Zealand Life'. *The New Zealand Railways Magazine*, 1 July 1935, p. 51. 'Overland from Westland,' *Otago Witness*, 21 March 1906, p. 33.

9. Tangiwai, 'Pictures of New Zealand Life,' ibid.

10. H. Wise and Co., New Zealand Index, *Otago Daily Times* and *Otago Witness*, Dunedin, 1917, p. 354.

11. James Cowan, *The New Zealand Wars: A History of the Maori Campaigns, and the Pioneering Period: Vol. 1: 1845–64, Vol. II: The Hauhau Wars, 1864–72*, Government Printer, Wellington, 1983.

12. James Cowan, *Official Record of the New Zealand International Exhibition of Arts and Industries, held at Christchurch, 1906–7.*

13. *New Zealand Mail,* 7 March 1906.

14. Cowan, *Exhibition of Arts and Industries, 1906–7*, op. cit.

15. Ibid, p. 107.

16. It seems that the Colony of Queensland can claim that first when Frederick Charles Wills (1870–1955) was appointed as official artist and photographer on 13 March 1897. In 1898 the Queensland government agreed to Wills taking motion pictures 'on the Lumière Cinematographe principle', which they financed for 12 months, to show at the Greater Britain Exhibition in London in 1899. With Henry William Mobsby as his assistant, Wills produced some 30 one-minute films of topical events and agricultural processes around Queensland, which included Queensland troops embarking for the Boer War. The only showing of these films was a private one in the Department of Agriculture boardroom on 17 November 1899. Although dispatched to Britain they were never publically displayed. Pat Laughren, 'Mobsby, Henry William (1860–1933)', *Australian Dictionary of Biography — Online edition*, http://www.adb.online.anu.edu.au/biogs. Accessed 12 June 2008.

17. Local and General', *The Dominion*, 21 December 1907, p. 4.

18. Ibid.

19. Appendix 1, Annual Report of General Manager of Tourist and Health Resorts, 1909, H-2, *AJHR*.

20. Ibid.

21. *New Zealand's Thermal Wonderland,* 1907–1910, Cameraman: James McDonald, Production Co.: Department of Tourist and Health Resorts, Duration: 0:02:25, NTSV F31561.

22. *Maori Women Performing Action Song at Pohutu Geyser,* 1907–1908. Cameraman: James Donald, Production Co.: Department of Tourist and Health Resorts, Duration: 0:00:51, NTSV F30560.

23. *Poi Dances at Whakarewarewa.* 1910, Cameraman: Unknown; Production Co.: Unknown, Duration: 0:02.15, NTSV F3990.

24. *Maori War Canoe Race,* 1912. Cameraman: Unknown, Production Co.: Unknown, Duration: 0:02:39, NTSV F5035.

25. Donne to Shackleton dated 28 December 1907, TO 1, 1907/320, ANZ.

26. District Agent, Christchurch to Donne dated 2 January 1908, TO 1, 1907/320, ANZ.

27. *Departure of the British Antarctic Expedition from Lyttelton, N.Z.,* 1 January 1908, Cameraman: James McDonald, Production Co.: Department of Tourist and Health Resorts, Duration: 0:05:20, NTSV F8202.

28. Stanley Newman, (ed.), *Shackleton's Lieutenant: The Nimrod Diary of A.L.A. Mackintosh, British Antarctic Expedition, 1907–1909*, Polar Publications, Christchurch, 1990, pp. 22–25.

29. Newman (ed.), *Shackleton's Lieutenant*, op. cit., pp. 22–25

30. P.L. Brocklehurst diary entry quoted in Beau Riffenburgh, *Nimrod: Ernest Shackleton and the Extraordinary Story of the 1907–1909 British Antarctic Expedition*, Bloomsbury, London, 2004, p. 280.

31. *The Sketch* article quoted in Riffenburgh, *Nimrod,* p. 281.

32. *The Terra Nova,* 1913, Cameraman: Unknown, Production Co.: Unknown, Duration: 0:01:24, NTSV F1547.

33. Shackleton to Donne, British Antarctic Expedition 1907, Christchurch dated 1 April 1909. TO 1, 1907/320, ANZ.

34. Donne to Ward, dated 2 April 1909, TO1, 1907/320, ANZ.

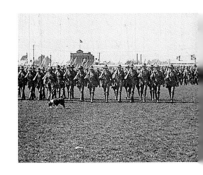

35. Donne to Shackleton, dated 15 April 1909. TO 1, 1907/320, ANZ.

36. 'Foreign News,' *The Bioscope*, 16 December 1909, p. 23.

37. G.P. Taylor, 'New Zealand, the Anglo–Japanese Alliance, and the 1908 Visit of the American Fleet.' Unpublished manuscript, University of Waikato, Robin Kay Papers, W5596/1, AAAA 21464, ANZ.

38. *American Fleet at Auckland*, 1908, op. cit., NTSV F10262.

39. Seddon believed it would detract from the Maori welcome at Rotorua, *Evening Post*, 24 May 1901, p. 2. 'King Dick sits on King Mahutu,' *New Zealand Free Lance*, 1 June 1901, p. 8.

40. *Otago Witness*, 12 August 1908.

41. Department of Tourist and Health Resorts to F.S. Mathews, Permanent Secretary to the Minister of Finance, dated 13 June 1914, AD 12/238, ANZ.

42. T.E. Donne, 'The New Zealand Government Department of Tourist and Health Resorts,' TO 1, 1908/495, ANZ.

43. Ibid.

44. *American Officers' Visit to Rotorua*, 1908, Cameraman: James McDonald, Production Co.: Department of Tourist and Health Resorts, Duration: 0:01:10, NTSV F3033.

45. *Auckland Weekly News*, 20 August 1908.

46. *Evening Post*, 14 August 1908.

47. Clive Sowry, 'Eighty Years of Film Exhibiton in Wellington, Part Nine, 1908', *Sequence*, March 1980, pp. 4–5.

48. *Evening Post*, 28 September 1908.

49. *Dominion Day Celebrations (Wellington): Children's Demonstration, [Basin Reserve Wellington], Living New Zealand Series, 26 September 1908*, Cameraman: James McDonald, Production Co.: Department of Tourist and Health Resorts, Duration: 0:02:51, NTSV F8276.

50. *Dominion Day Celebrations (Wellington) [March of Volunteers Past Government Buildings, Lambton Quay, Wellington], Living New Zealand Series, 26 September 1908*, 1908, Cameraman: James McDonald, Production Co: Department of Tourist and Health Resorts, Duration: 0:03:26, NTSV F5064.

51. *Evening Post*, 28 September 1908.

52. *New Zealand Free Lance*, 3 October 1908.

53. *Dominion Day Celebrations: [Newtown Park, Wellington], 26 September 1908*, 1908, Cameraman: James McDonald, Production Co.: Department of Tourist and Health Resorts, Duration: 0:03:00, NTSV F8277.

54. *Proclamation of King George V, Wellington*, 1910, Cameraman: James McDonald; Production Co.: Department of Tourist and Health Resorts; Duration: 0:00.40 sec, NTSV F4102. The confirmation of McDonald as cameraman is from Clive Sowry's research. Clive Sowry notes to author.

55. Donne, 'The New Zealand Government Department of Tourist and Health Resorts,' TO 1, 1908/495, ANZ.

56. *Sir Joseph and Lady Ward*, 1909? Cameraman: James McDonald, Production Co.: Department of Tourist and Health Resorts; Duration: 0:00:46, NTSV F3032.

57. B.W. Hempseed, *Richard Arnst: The Single Sculls World Champion from New Zealand*, Acorn Press, Christchurch, 'Richard Arnst' (1883–1953), New Zealand Sports Hall of Fame, http://www.nzhalloffame.co.nz. Accessed 8 August 2017.

58. Arthur P. Bates & Phil Thomsen (eds), *Whanganui River memories: being a selection of true stories from the Whanganui River area from the archives of The Friends of the Whanganui River*, Heritage Press, Palmerston North, 1999.

59. *Wanganui Herald*, 21 June 1909.

60. *World's Sculling Championship Wanganui River*, 1909, Cameraman: James McDonald, Production Co.: Department of Tourist and Health Resorts, Duration: 0:02:26, NTSV F41774: 'World Sculling Championship,' *Wanganui Herald*, 22 June 1909, pp. 4–5.

61. *Wanganui Herald*, 22 June 1909.

62. *New Zealand Times*, quoted in Sowry, *Eighty Years of Film Exhibition in Wellington*, 'The Lasting Picture Show', op. cit.

63. *Wanganui Herald*, 18 August 1909.

64. 'Thompson Payne Pictures', Gaiety Theatre advertisement, *Hawkes Bay Herald*, 4 October 1909.

65. *Wanganui Herald*, 24 August 1909.

66. 'The Great Sculling Match,' *The Bioscope*, 15 September 1910, pp. 7, 10.

67. *World Sculling Championship, 11 June 1921*, Cameraman: S.B. Taylor, Production Co.: New Zealand Department of Agriculture, Duration: 0:04.18, NTSV F1156.

68. Hempseed, *Richard Arnst*, op. cit.

69. R.J. Polaschek, *Government Administration in New Zealand*, NZIPA, Oxford University Press, London, 1958, p. 37.

70. Margaret McClure, *The Wonder Country: Making New Zealand Tourism*, Auckland University Press, Auckland, 2004, p. 63.

71. 'Our Tourist Traffic,' *New Zealand Free Lance*, 1 May 1909, p. 6.

72. 'Foreign News,' *The Bioscope*, 13 January 1910, p. 29.

73. Michael Bassett, *Sir Joseph Ward*, op. cit., p. 180.

74. *A Day with the Boy Scouts: Kitchener Inspecting Boy Scouts in Dunedin: Living New Zealand Series, 20 February 1910*, 1910, Cameraman: James McDonald, Production Co.: Department of Tourist and Health Resorts, Duration: 0:01.54, NTSV F6078. *Otago Witness*, 23 February 1910.

75. *A Day with the Boy Scouts: Inspection by Lord Kitchener [Hagley Park, Christchurch, 22 February 1910], Living New Zealand Series, 22 February 1910*, Cameraman: James McDonald, Production Co.: Department of Tourist and Health Resorts, Duration: 002.05, NTSV F6076. Both F6076 and F6078 may have been screened as a single film under the above title.

76. Christchurch *Press*, 23 February 1910; *Otago Witness*, 2 March 1910.

77. 'New Year Honours,' *Evening Post*, 3 January 1916, p. 2.

78. *Pathé Gazette, c.1912, Men of the Times. Hon. T. Mackenzie, A Minister of Many Portfolios, Wellington, N.Z.*, NSFA No. 74137, Australia, c.1912. The same Archive title number (74137), includes a similar item, most probably taken around the same time, titled *Maori Legislators. Mr A.T. Ngata, Mr C.R. Parata, Sir J. Carroll, and Dr. T.E. Rangihiroa: Wellington. N.Z.*, where only Ngata and Carroll are seen on the surviving film. The remaining items cover boy scouts, rifle shooting and rowing events in Australia. See, http://colsearch.nfsa.afc.gov.au.

79. *A Reunion of New Zealand's Pioneer Miners*, 1912. Cameraman: James McDonald; Production Co.: Department of Tourist and Health Resorts; Duration: 0:02:58; NTSV F202128. The film of the Dunstan miners' celebration at Clyde in November 1912 has been identified and retitled *Dunstand Miners Jubilee Celebrations* [formerly *Highland Sports*], November 1912. Cameraman: James McDonald, Production Co.: Department of Tourist and Health Resors on behalf of Department of Mines, Duration: 0:02:31, NTSV F6536. Another surviving McDonald film from this year is *Floral and Garden Fete at Oamaru, NZ, 1912*, Cameraman: James McDonald, Production Co.: Department of Tourist and Health Resorts, Duration: 0:05:36, NTSV F7548.

80. *The Evening Star*, 6 June 1912, p. 6.

81. Memo J. Hislop, Under-Secretary, Department of Internal Affairs to Mr Hamilton, dated 14 November 1912, IA 1912/3582, ANZ. 'Jubilee Celebrations', *Otago Daily Times*, 19 November 1912, p. 6.

82. Tom Brooking, 'Thomas Noble Mackenzie, 1853–1930', Claudia Orange (ed.), *The Dictionary of New Zealand Biography, Vol. Three, 1901–1920*, Auckland University Press, Department of Internal Affairs, Auckland and Wellington, 1996, pp. 303–304.

83. Dave McWilliams, 'Motion Picture History in Auckland, 1896–1941', *The Auckland Star*, 26 July, 2, 9 and 16 August 1941. Auckland Public Library, 791.43 M17.

84. *Hawera and Normanby Star*, 19 October 1910, p. 1; *Grey River Argus*, 1 September 1910, p. 5.

85. *Hawera and Normanby Star*, 13 December 1910, p. 5.

86. Sidney [sic] B. Taylor transcript of brief handwritten memoir notes. Sydney Benjamin Taylor (1887–1973), 'Photographs, Letters and Memorabilia of A Professional Photographer', ANZC 380, Christchurch Central Library. Also obituary, *Otago Daily Times*, 29 November 1973, which has his place of birth as Mosgiel in contradiction to his application to leave New Zealand under War Regulations of 29 May 1919, where Taylor states his place of birth as Port Chalmers. S.B. Taylor Notes, NTSV.

87. S.B. Taylor is listed as 'Photographer' with the Department of Agriculture, Industries and Commerce, dating from 24 June 1912 at a salary of £210. A Mr C. Perry is listed as 'Despatcher' on a salary of £160 in the Provisional Classification of the Public Service published as a Supplement to the *New Zealand Gazette*, No. 63, dated 20 August 1913, p. 2567. By 1916 Taylor's salary had risen to £220, and Perry was now classified as Assistant Photographer on a salary of £175. 'List of Persons Employed in the Public Service on the 31st Day of March 1916, Supplement to the *New Zealand Gazette*, No. 50, 28 April 1916.

88. Memo for the Ministry of Internal Affairs dated 9 October 1912. Kinematograph Films, etc, Dominion Museum, Te Papa.

89. Memo from J. Hislop, Under-Secretary, Department of Internal Affairs to Director, Dominion Museum date 2 November 1912, IA 1912/2559, 'Kinematograph films, etc, Dominion Museum, Te Papa.

90. Director Dominion Museum to Under-Secretary Department of Internal Affairs dated 9 November 1912, Dominion Museum File, "Kinematograph films etc.', Te Papa.

91. 'All Sorts of People', *New Zealand Free Lance*, 20 July 1913, p. 4.

92. Clive Sowry film notes to author.

93. *1863–1913 Otago Boys' High School Jubilee Celebrations at Dunedin August 1st to 5th 1913*, 1913, Cameraman: James McDonald, Production Co.: Department of Agriculture, Duration: 0:07.09, NTSV F28248. This was screened at Fuller's Kings Theatre, Dunedin on 7 August 1914. *Otago Daily Times*, 7 August 1914, p. 1.

94. Cowan, *The New Zealand Wars, The Hauhau Wars, 1864–72*, op. cit., pp. 209, 293.

95. *Tutange of Patea, 1912*, Cameraman: James McDonald, Production Co.: Dominion Museum, Duration: 0:00:38, NTSV F1862.

7. T.J. West conquers Australasia

1. Footlight, 'Dramatic and Musical,' *New Zealand Free Lance*, 2 December 1905, p. 14.

2. *Biorama Ramblings: Being an account of the travels of the Territorial Biorama Company during a tour of four months duration through the Colony of New Zealand. The Author being one known as the Rambler, August to November 1902 & 1905*. A collection of cuttings from the New Zealand *War Cry*. Original in Salvation Army Archive, Bourke Street, Melbourne, with annotations by Chris Long, 7 October 1905.

3. Geoffrey B. Churchman, *Celluloid Dreams: A Century of Film in New Zealand*, IPL Books, Wellington, 1997, p. 18–19.

4. Henry J. Hayward, *Here's to Life! The Impressions, Confessions and Garnered Thoughts of a Free–Minded Showman*: Oswald & Sealy, Auckland, 1944, p. 47.

5. John Barnes, *The Beginnings of the Cinema in England. Vol. 4, 1899*, University of Exeter Press, Exeter, 1996, p. 103. Some authorities say West was born in Scotland as he has been pictured wearing a kilt and did the Christmas season in Edinburgh each year. However, West talks about his schoolboy days in Bedford in his reminiscences, T.J. West, 'Pictorial Reminiscences extending over 40 years —1873–1913,' *Kinematograph Year Book, Film Diary and Directory*, The Kinematograph & Lantern Weekly Ltd, London, 1914, pp. 101–103.

6. Ibid.

7. Advertisement at Opera House Wellington, 6 July 1905, illustrating Clive Sowry, 'Eighty Years of Film Exhibition

in Wellington, Part Six: West's Pictures and the Brescians', *Sequence*, March 1979, pp. 20–21.

8. Hayward, *Here's to Life!* op. cit., pp. 81–82.

9. Ibid.

10. Alex Rankin, 'Stock Actualities, Lectures and Extended Film Runs (1902–1909)' from his 'The History of Cinema Exhibition in Exeter 1895–1918', Dissertation, University of Exeter, 2001, Bill Douglas Centre, Teaching and Learning Articles, http://www.ex.ac.uk/bdc/teaching_article_02_chapterthree. Accessed 4 June 2008.

11. 'West's Pictures,' *The Bioscope*, 10 December 1908, p. 4.

12. This was epitomised by the Spithead reviews by the reigning sovereign of Britain's naval might, the most impressive of which had been on the 26 June 1897 when Queen Victoria reviewed the assembled ships of the Royal Navy off Spithead for her Diamond Jubilee celebrations from the Royal Yacht *Campania*. This vast armada of 165 ships flying the White Ensign was filmed and the images released around the world. Three different films of the Review are listed in John Barnes, *The Beginnings of the Cinema in England 1894–1901, Vol. 2, 1897*, University of Exeter Press, 1996, p. 266.

13. *Evening Post*, 3 October 1903, p. 6.

14. Barnes, *The Beginnings of the Cinema in England,* Vol. 4, op. cit. See note to 'West, Alfred John (1857–1937), in Stephen Herbert and Luke McKernan (eds), *Who's Who of Victorian Cinema*, op. cit., pp. 149–50. It is clear from the following report in 1910 that this never stopped. 'The star pictures will depict "Life in the British Navy" which is over 3000 ft in length. The pictures show British warships of today, bluejackets training and life in the fighting-top of a battleship. These pictures were specially taken to the order of Mr T.J.West, and have proved a trump card in all the principal cities of the world where they have been presented under Mr West's management.' *Wanganui Chronicle*, 21 December 1910, p. 8.

15. 'Theatrical and Musical Notes,' *Otago Witness*, 11 January 1905, p. 60.

16. Passenger list of the RMS *Corinthic*, London to New Zealand in February 1905, Iddenden Family website, Kiwi Konnections, http://freepages.genealogy.rootsweb.com/~patricia/corinthi.htm. Accessed 5 June 2008. It seems from this that Mr A.N. Miller was West's second cameraman and later became a regional manager.

17. P. A. Harrison, 'The Motion Picture Industry in New Zealand 1896–1930', unpublished MA Thesis, University of Auckland, April 1974, p. 33.

18. Sowry, 'Eighty Years of Film Exhibition in Wellington, West's Pictures and the Brescians', op. cit. *Otago Witness*, 12 April 1905, p. 61; 19 April 1905, p. 65.

19. *Otago Witness*, 5 April 1905, p. 60.

20. *Otago Witness* 12 April 1905, p. 61.

21. *Otago Daily Times*, 14 April 1905, p. 6.

22. Jonathan Dennis, 'Aotearoa New Zealand in the Silent Period,' *Aotearoa and the Sentimental Strine*, op. cit., p. 7.

23. Luke McKernan (ed.), *A Yank in Britain: The Lost Memoirs of Charles Urban, Film Pioneer*, Projection Box, Hastings, 1999, pp. 75–80

24. Rudall Hayward interview with Walter Harris, NTSV.

25. Ibid.

26. *Evening Post*, 7 July 1905, p. 5.

27. Hayward, *Here's to Life!*, op. cit., pp. 84–85.

28. 'The Exhibition,' *Bush Advocate*, 15 February 1907, p. 5.

29. 'Sideshows and Attractions,' *Evening Post*, 1 November 1906, p. 7. *Sights and Scenes at the New Zealand Exhibition*, Cameraman: E.J. Hardy and others, Production Co.: T.J. West, Duration: 0:07.54, NTSV F2656. 'The Exhibition,' *Evening Post*, 28 January 1907, p. 3. The *Exhibition* film was also incorporated into the touring show, 'West Pictures and the Brescians,' *Otago Witness*, 6 February 1907, p. 61.

30. *Hawera and Normanby Star*, 1 December 1906, p. 1. *Evening Post*, 24 December 1906, p. 2. His Majesty's Theatre, Dunedin, 'West's Pictures and Brescians, Host of Star Pictures Including 'Sights and Scenes At the NZ International Exhibition,' 12 February 1907, Theatre Brochure, Peter Harcourt Early Film and Theatre Programme Collection, 0443, NTSV.

31. 'West's Pictures,' *Hawera and Normanby Star*, Hawera, 19 October 1908. Research notes by Betty Arnold, NTSV.

32. Rudall Hayward interview, op. cit. with Walter Harris, NTSV.

33. Ibid. West followed the same pattern in Australia. On his first visit with the Brescians to Sydney and then to Melbourne he incorporated locally made films into the programme. These included *The Audience Leaving the Theatre Royal* and *Fire in Clarence Street*. He is believed to have shot the first film of a football match in Melbourne. Graham Shirley and Brian Adams, *Australian Cinema: The First Eighty Years*, op. cit., p. 22.

34. *02976, Sights in New Zealand* (525'), 20 January 1906, (E), Urban, Ph. T.J. West, Maori dances, hot springs, etc. (16 scenes), Dennis Giford, *The British Film Catalogue, Non–Fiction Films Vol. 2*, BFI Publishing, London, 1999. Mr Jones' feat was repeated for Perry's Biorama on 25 August 1906 and shown in Nelson to 'storms of applause' on 27 August 1906. Clive Sowry, 'Nelson's first Movie,' *Nelson Evening Mail*, 30 April 1994, p. 11; clipping, NTSV.

35. *Otago Witness*, 4 October 1905, p. 41.

36. *Sights in New Zealand,* 1905–1906, Principal Cameraman: E.J. Hardy and others, Production Co.: West's Pictures, Duration: 0:04:08, NTSV F3005.

37. Luke McKernan, 'Urban, Charles', pp. 650–651 and Laurent Mannoni, 'Eclipse,' p. 199, in Abel (ed.), *Encyclopedia of Early Cinema*, op. cit. 'Urban, Charles', Herbert and McKernan, *Who's Who of Victorian Cinema*, op. cit., pp. 144–45. 'Charles Urban, Motion Picture Pioneer,' http://www.charlesurban.com. Accessed 30 January 2009.

38. It may also have been influenced by the prominence given to film in the Maskelyne and Devant's Mysteries tour that Hayward toured throughout New Zealand. See Barnes, *The Beginnings of the Cinema, Vol. 2*, op. cit., pp. 161–62.

39. Hayward, *Here's to Life!*, op. cit., pp. 86–87.

40. Diane Collins, 'Shopfronts and picture showmen: film exhibition to the 1920s' in James Sabine (ed.), *A Century of Australian Cinema*, Australian Film Institute, William Heinemann, Port Melbourne, 1995. Collins talks of West

owning a string of cinemas in Britain before moving to Australia in 1904. This is not correct but it may have been part of T.J. West's 'gift of the gab', pp. 33–34.

41. Ketupa.net media profile. Pathé, Gaumont, Seydoux,' http://www.ketupa.net/pathe.htm. Accessed 30 January 2009.

42. Richard Abel, *The Ciné Goes to Town: French Cinema 1894–1914*, University of California Press, Berkeley, 1994, pp. 30–31.

43. 'Foreign News,' *The Bioscope*, 12 August 1909, p. 41

44. Ibid, 21 October 1909, p. 45.

45. Shirley & Adams, *Australian Cinema*, op. cit., p. 22. Advertisement for West's Pictures listed 10 picture theatres in Australia, plus two open air theatres, one being constructed in Paddington, Sydney, and six touring circuits, together with three theatres in New Zealand: Albert Hall, Auckland; King's Theatre, Wellington; King's Theatre, Christchurch and a theatre being constructed in Dunedin. *The Bioscope*, 27 October 1910, p. 92.

46. 'Foreign News,' *The Bioscope*, 26 August 1909, p. 31. Ina Bertrand (ed.), *Cinema in Australia*, op. cit., pp. 55, 73.

47. Collins, 'Shopfront and picture showmen' in Sabine, *A Century of Australian Cinema*, op. cit., pp. 33–36. See also Eric Reade, *History and Heartburn: The Saga of Australian Film 1896–1978*, Associated Universities Presses, East Brunswick, NJ, 1981, pp. 9–10. Diane Collins, 'Spencer, Cosens (1874–1930)', *Australian Dictionary of Biography*, National Centre of Biography, Australian National University, http://adb.anu.edu.au/biography/spencer–cosens–8604/text15027, accessed 11 December 2015. This article was first published in hardcopy in *Australian Dictionary of Biography*, Vol. 12, Melbourne University Press, 1990.

48. Diane Collins, *Hollywood Down Under: Australians at the Movies: 1896 to the Present Day:* Angus & Robertson, North Ryde, 1987, pp. 7–8.

49. 'The Bioscope in Australia,' *The Bioscope*, 9 September 1909, p. 19

50. 'Foreign News,' *The Bioscope*, 23 September 1909, p. 45. Jean–Jacques Meusy, 'Film d'Art,' Abel (ed.) *Encyclopedia of Early Cinema*, op. cit., pp. 237–38.

51. 'Foreign News,' *The Bioscope*, 25 August 1910, p. 49.

52. Eric Reade, *The Australian Screen: A Pictorial History of Australian Film Making*, Lansdowne Press, Melbourne, 1975, pp. 28, 31, 33– 34, 36

53. Ibid, 1975, pp. 42, 47, 54. *Beauty by Biograph* entries, 1922–1923, Film Censor's Register, Archives New Zealand.

54. Hayward, *Here's To Life!*, op. cit., 1944, p. 88.

55. Clive Sowry film notes to author.

56. 'Foreign News,' *The Bioscope*, 8 July 1909, p. 223.

57. This competition between rival companies was waged as fiercely in the correspondence columns of the press. See John Fuller Jnr's 'Letter to the Editor', *Evening Post*, 2 August 1909 and Linley and Donovan's reply in 'Letters to the Editor,' *Evening Post*, 4 August 1909.

58. *Auckland Star*, 7 November 1911, p. 7

59. Ibid, p. 12.

60. Margaret Williams, 'MacMahon, Charles (1861?–1917)' and 'MacMahon, James (1858?–1915)', *Australian Dictionary of Biography — Online edition*, http://www.adb.online.anu.edu.au/biogs. Accessed 20 February 2009.

61. Geoffrey B. Churchman, *Celluloid Dreams: A Century of Film in New Zealand*, IPL Books, Wellington, 1997, p. 16.

62. For J.D. Williams see Jill Julius Matthews, 'Modern nomads and national film history: the multi-continental career of J.D. Williams,' *Connected Worlds: History in Transnational Perspective*, ANU–E Press, http://epress.anu.edu.au. Collins, 'Shopfronts and picture showmen: film exhibition to the 1920s', *A Century of Australian Cinema*, op. cit., pp. 34–36, 39. 'where everybody goes' featured on front of J.D. Williams theatres. See also Shirley & Adams, *Australian Cinema*, op. cit., p. 23. Reade, *The Australian Screen*, op. cit., pp. 41, 47–48, 51–58, 60–61, 75–76, 89. Collins, *Hollywood Down Under*, op. cit., pp. . 9–10. J.D. Williams later became a significant figure in the American movie industry as one of the principals of Associated First National Pictures Incorporated, *Silent Era*, accessed 23 October 2008, http://www.silentera.com/PSFL/companies/A/associatedFirstNational.html. See also Terry Ramsaye, *A Million and One Nights, op. cit.*, pp. 679–80, 789–90, 793, 826.

63. Gordon Ingham, 'Everyone's Gone to the Movies: The Sixty Cinemas of Auckland — And Some Others', n.d., MS, NTSV, p. 9.

64. Ibid.

65. 'Moving Pictures Come to Auckland,' MS 1469 Auckland War Memorial Museum Library.

66. Charles Musser, *The Emergence of Cinema*, op. cit., pp. 429–31. Lauren Rabinovitz, 'Hale's Tours' in Abel, *Encyclopedia of Early Cinema*, op. cit., pp. 293–94.

67. Rudall Hayward interview with Walter Harris, NTSV.

68. Clive Sowry. 'Hayward, Henry John', first published in *The Dictionary of New Zealand Biography, Te Ara — the Encyclopedia of New Zealand, Vol. 3*, 1996. https://teara.govt.nz/en/biographies/3h11/hayward-henry-john, accessed 10 August 2017.

69. Peter Downes, 'Fuller, John 1850–1923,' in Claudia Orange (ed.), *Dictionary of New Zealand Biography, Vol. Two, 1870-1900*, Bridget William Books/Department of Internal Affairs, Wellington, 1993, pp. 161–62. John Fuller (1879–1959), *Australian Dictionary of Biography*, http://www.adb.online.anu.edu.au/biogs/. Accessed 8 February 2009.

70. B.J. Foster, 'Sir Benjamin John Fuller, (1875–1952)', A.H. McLintock, *An Encyclopaedia of New Zealand*, Vol. 1, Government Printer, Wellington, 1966, pp. 763–64.

71. Clive Sowry, 'Eighty Years of Film Exhibition in Wellington, Part Nine, 1908,' *Sequence*, March 1980, pp. 4–5.

72. Luke McKernan, 'Urban, Charles,' and Paolo Cherchi Usai, 'Color,' in Abel (ed.), *Encyclopedia of Early Cinema*, op. cit., pp. 138–41, 650–51.

73. 'Kinemacolour: An Innovation,' *Evening Post*, 5 December 1911, p. 2.

74. Rudall Hayward interview with Walter Harris, NTSV.

75. Downes, Peter, 'Pollard, Tom 1857–1922,' *Dictionary of New Zealand Biography, Vol. Two, 1870–1900*, Bridget William Books and Department of Internal Affairs, op. cit., p. 392. See Peter Downes, *The Pollards: A Family and its Child and Adult Opera Companies in New Zealand and Australia, 1880–1910,* Steele Roberts, Wellington, 2002, and Peter Downes, *Shadows on the Stage: Theatre in New Zealand, The First Seventy Years,* John McIndoe, Dunedin, 1975.

76. Maurice Hurst, *Music and the Stage in New Zealand: The Record of a Century of Entertainment, 1840–1943*, Beggs, Auckland, 1944, pp. 37, 39. Peter Harcourt, *A Dramatic Appearance: New Zealand Theatre 1920–1970*, Methuen, Wellington, 1978, p. 19.

77. *Evening Post*, 7 November 1913, p. 3.

78. See advertisement detail. 'His Majesty's Theatre,' *Evening Post*, 9 December 1910, p. 8. Ivo Blom, 'Ambrosio,' in Abel, (ed), *Encyclopedia of Early Cinema*, op. cit., pp. 18–19.

79. Ivo Blom, 'All the Same or Strategies of Difference. Early Italian Comedy in International Perspective,' in Anna Antonini (ed.), *Il Film e i suoi multipli/Film and its Multiples*, Forum, University of Udine, 2003, pp. 465–480. See 'Entertainments,' *Evening Post*, 24 January 1911, p. 2.

80. 'Jean (III),' Filmography, IMDb, http://www.imbd.com. Accessed 14 February 2009.

81. 'Florence Turner,' Biography, IMDb, http://www.imdb.com. Larry Trimble would become Turner's exclusive director and both Jean and Turner would feature in the Trimble directed *Auld Lang Syne* in November 1911 which was Vitagraph's first two–reel film. Ben Brewster, 'Vitagraph Company of America,' in Abel (ed.), *Encyclopedia of Early Cinema*, op. cit., pp. 679–81.

82. Brewster, 'Vitagraph Company of America,' in Abel (ed.), *Encyclopedia of Early Cinema*, op. cit., pp. 679–681. The first motion picture star is a subject of ongoing debate. See Jane Gaines, 'Star System,' ibid, pp. 608–610.

83. Reade, *The Australian Screen*, op. cit., pp. 40–41.

84. Advertisement, *Evening Post*, 12 December 1910, p. 8, column 4.

85. *Sydney Street Siege aka aka Sidney Street Siege*, 1911, Cameraman: Unknown, Production Co.: Pathé Gazette, Duration: 0:01:32, British Pathé 2961.31.

8. The permanent picture show

1. F.H. Richardson, 'Lessons for Operators: Chapter IX — The Picture', *The Moving Picture World*, 9 May 1908, pp. 412–13.

2. P. A. Harrison, 'The Motion Picture Industry in New Zealand 1896–1930', unpublished MA Thesis, University of Auckland, April 1974, p. 57.

3. 'Flickering dreams — Garnet Saunders and the New Plymouth theatre industry', Puke Ariki — Taranaki Stories, http://www.pukeariki.com/en/stories/entertainmentAndLeisure/g.saunders.htm. Brian Scanlan, 'Saunders' timing perfect,' *Taranaki Herald*, 9 July 1983. Jonathan Dennis, 'Aotearoa New Zealand in the Silent Period,' *Aotearoa and the Sentimental Strine*, op. cit., p. 7.

4. Caleb Wyatt, Scrapbook of New Plymouth film clippings, NTSV.

5. *Taranaki Herald*, 15 June 1910.

6. 'Flickering dreams', Puke Ariki — Taranaki Stories, op. cit.

7. Richard Abel, *The Ciné Goes to Town*, op. cit., pp. 41, 51.

8. Caleb Wyatt, 'Garnet Saunders, cinema pioneer', *The Weekender*, New Plymouth, 19 April 1992, p. 17.

9. Caleb Wyatt interview with Sarah Davey, NTSV, all details of Garnet Saunders are from Sarah Davey research notes deposited with NTSV.

10. 'An Interesting Venture,' *Poverty Bay Herald*, 5 October 1910, p. 5.

11. *Waikato Times*, 3 January 1906, p. 3.

12. 'Perry's Biorama', Princess Theatre, commencing 3 July 1907, Dunedin, Theatre brochure, Peter Harcourt Early Film and Theatre Programme Collection, 0443, Ngā Taonga Sound & Vision archive. See 'Perry's Electric Biorama,' *Grey River Argus*, 2 January 1909, p. 3.

13. 'Personal Items,' *New Zealand Herald*, 6 July 1908, p. 6.

14. 'An Interesting Venture,' *Poverty Bay Herald*, 5 October 1910, p. 5. Haughton's film, *Labor Day in Gisborne*, although badly decomposed, survives in Ngā Taonga Sound & Vision Archive. It was first screened at Pathé Pictures, Gisborne on 18 October 1910. *Poverty Bay Herald*, 18 October 1910, p. 2. *Labor Day in Gisborne*, 1910, Cameraman: Brandon Haughton, Production Co.: Pathe Pictures; Duration: 0:03:49, NTSV F5636.

15. 'Local and General,' *Taranaki Daily News*, 11 January 1912, p. 4.

16. *Scenes at the East End Annual Picnic, New Plymouth*, 1912, Cameraman: Brandon Haughton, Production Co.: Garnet Saunders: Empire Theatre Film Co., Duration: 0:04:15, NTSV F2655.

17. *Taranaki Herald*, 1 February 1912.

18. *The Production of the Taranaki Herald and Budget*, 1912, Cameraman: Brandon Haughton, Production Co.: Garnet Saunders, Empire Theatre Film Co., Duration: 0:02:06, NTSV F4106.

19. *Taranaki Daily News*, 31 January 1912, p. 1.

20. Ibid, p. 4.

21. *Taranaki Jockey Club's Annual Meeting*, 1912, Cameraman: Brandon Haughton, Production Co.: Garnet Saunders: Empire Theatre Co., Duration: 0:02:10, NTSV F1465.

22. H. Wise and Co., *The New Zealand Index, Otago Daily Times and Otago Witness*, Dunedin, 1917, pp. 290–292.

23. *Taranaki Herald*, 15 February 1912.

24. *Evening Post*, 18 August 1911, p. 11.

25. 'Circular Road Race,' *Taranaki Daily News*, 6 September 1912, p. 5.

26. *Taranaki Circular Road Race,* 1912, Cameraman: Brandon Haughton, Production Co.: Egmont Film Company — Garnet Saunders, Duration: 0:02:11, NTSV F9312.

27. *Taranaki Daily News*, 28 November 1912, p. 1; 30 November 1912, p. 4.

28. *Grand School Carnival*, 1912, Cameraman: Brandon Haughton, Production Co.: Egmont Film Company — Garnet Saunders, Duration: 0:03:43, NTSV F4154.

29. *Taranaki Daily News*, 22 November 1912, p. 4.

30. *Scenes In Taranaki New Zealand,* 1912, Cameraman: Charles Newham?, Production Co.: Dominion Film (NZ)?, Duration: 0:05:00, NTSV F55926.

31. This was released by Heron Films in the UK on 20 March 1913 and is probably Newham footage as other New Zealand titles released by Heron correspond to what Newham was filming. Clive Sowry film notes to author.

32. *Taranaki Daily News*, 1 November 1919, p. 4.

33. *Hawera & Normanby Star*, 23 March 1922, p. 8.

34. *Evening Post*, 7 May 1928, p. 2.

35. 'The King's Theatre,' *Dominion*, 15 March, p. 6.

36. *New Zealand Times*, 15 March 1910, quoted in Clive Sowry, 'The King's Theatre — Eighty Years Ago', *Sequence*, April 1980, pp. 4–5.

37. Reported in the *Hawera & Normanby Star*, 6 October 1910, p. 4.

38. Simon Price, *New Zealand's First Talkies: Early film-making in Otago and Southland, 1896–1939*, Otago Heritage Books, Dunedin North, 1996, pp. 89–90.

39. 'Entertainments,' *Evening Post*, 17 March 1910, p. 2.

40. Diane Collins, *Hollywood Down Under*, op. cit., pp. 80–82.

41. 'Fitting the Music to the Picture,' *The Bioscope*, 3 June 1909, p. 23

42. 'Cinema', A.H. McLintock (ed.), *An Encyclopaedia of New Zealand*, originally published in 1966; *Te Ara — The Encyclopaedia of New Zealand*, updated 18 September 2007, http://www.TeAra.govt.nz/1966/C/Cinema/en. Accessed 20 March 2009.

43. To put music in silent films in context and the question of how silent, silent films may have been, see the brilliant study by Rick Altman, *Silent Film Sound*, Columbia University Press, NY, 2004.

44. Louis Daly Austin (1877–1967), '80 Years of music and the theatre,' Papers MS-Group-0984, ATL, Wellington.

45. Thompson, John Mansfield, 'Austin, Louis Daly Irving 1877–1967', *Dictionary of New Zealand Biography*, *Te Ara — the Encyclopedia of New Zealand*, updated 22 June 2007, http://www.dnzb.govt.nz. Accessed 20 March 2009.

46. The King's Theatre, 154–156 Gloucester Street was the first purpose-built cinema in Christchurch. It opened on 24 March 1910 under West's Pictures. It became Hayward-West's Pictures on 12 November 1910. The cinema was closed the following week as it failed to attract the crowds. It was leased by Radium Picture Propriety but this too was unsuccessful and Hayward-West reopened it (as they owned the building) for Saturday matinees and as a back-up when their main theatres, His Majesty's and the Opera House, were required for live shows. It had eight days use in 1916. It was demolished in 1918. 'History of Cinemas: King's Cinema, Christchurch, New Zealand Cinemas'. http://www.geocities.com/hd7393/nzcinframeset.htm. See Also Louis Daly Austin, Part Two of 80 Years of music and the theatre, Ref. MS-Papers-7069-2, ATL, Wellington, pp. 15–18.

47. Louis Daly Austin, 'Part Two of 80 Years of music and the theatre', op. cit., pp. 23–24, 28; Thompson, 'Austin, Louis Daly Irving', op. cit. If Austin's tales of the mirrors at the skating rink seems far-fetched, at the opening of Fuller's management of His Majesty's Theatre in Wellington on 16 March 1910 the press reported that the crowd was so large that 200–300 people sat on the stage behind the screen with a reverse view of the films. 'Entertainments,' *Evening Post*, 17 March 1910, p. 2.

48. Louis Daly Austin, 'Part Two of 80 Years of music and the theatre', op. cit., pp. 35–40.

49. *Evening Post*, 2 October 1915, p. 11.

50. *Free Lance*, 25 November 1911, p. 7. quoted in Judith Shanahan, 'Early Cinema in New Zealand,' National Film Library dated 11 September 1961, Film History, NTSV.

51. 'W.B.H.' [Walter Harris], 'Cinema,' *An Encyclopaedia of New Zealand*, Vol. 1, op. cit.' pp. 349–51.

52. E. Trevor Hill, '"The Movie Monger": A volume of plaudits deserved and otherwise by a praise agent bent on capturing the nimble shilling & life long patrons,' Unpublished ms. D0783, NTSV.

53. Ina Bertrand, 'David and Goliath: the Grand Theatre Company and the National Exhibition Chains,' in T. O'Regan & B. Shoesmith (eds), *History on/and/in Film*. Perth: History & Film Association of Australia, 1987. pp. 106–109.

54. Graham Shirley and Brian Adams, *Australian Cinema*, op. cit., p. 36.

55. Ina Bertrand and William D. Routt, *The Story of the Kelly Gang: 'The Picture That Will Live Forever,'* The Moving Image, No. 8, Australian Teachers of Media, St Kilda, Victoria, 2007. *The Story of the Kelly Gang*, National Film and Sound Archives, Madman Films, 2007.

56. Chris Long, 'Documentary and non–fiction, silent', and 'Silent Film to 1914,' Brian McFarlane, Geoff Mayer and Ina Bertrand (eds) *The Oxford Companion to Australian Film*, op. cit., pp. 109–15, 452–55. Eric Reade, *History and Heartburn*, op. cit., pp. 8–13.

57. Obituary, *The Kinematograph Year Book 1917*, p. 82; Obituary, *The Kinematograph Year Book 1918*, p. 113. In 1917 *The Kinematograph Year Book* listed West's Ltd with its head

office, 337 Pitt Street, Sydney, NSW, with its London office c/– T.J West, 58 Dean Street, Shaftesbury Avenue, London. The following cinemas were listed in Australasia: Princess, Glaciarium and Olympia in Sydney; Olympia and Princess in Brisbane; Palace in Melbourne; Melrose and Subiaco in Perth; Princess in Fremantle; Olympia and Pavilion in Adelaide; Albert Hall in Auckland and the King's Theatre in Wellington.

58. 'Obituary', *Auckland Star*, 2 December 1916, p. 6.

59. Patrick McInroy, 'The American Melies,' *Sight and Sound*: Autumn, 1979, pp. 250–54.

60. Jonathan Dennis, 'Aotearoa New Zealand in the Silent Period,' op. cit., pp. 7–8.

61. 'Personal Matters,' *Evening Post*, 13 September 1912, p. 7.

62. Ibid, 17 September 1912, p. 7.

63. Ibid.

64. For a detailed assessment of Méliès' work in New Zealand, see Babington, *A History of The New Zealand Fiction Feature Film*, op. cit., pp. 33–36.

65. Correspondence of Gaston and Hortense Méliès to Paul Méliès dated 2 October 1912, Rotorua, New Zealand, NTSV. See also Dennis, 'Aotearoa New Zealand in the Silent Period', op. cit., pp. 7–8.

66. Doré Hoffman, 'Melies in New Zealand,' *Moving Picture World*, 8 February 1913, pp. 553–54.

67. Méliès' correspondence mentions that the two-reel *A Tale of Old Tahiti*, the one–reel *A Woman's Mission* and the one-reel *Ballad of the South Seas*. All had scenes retaken or finished in New Zealand. Films de Fiction Realises en Oceanie et en Asie de Juillet 1912 a Mai 1913 par Gaston Méliès, Méliès material, NTSV.

68. Letter 12 October 1912, Méliès material, NTSV, quoted in Babington, *A History of The New Zealand Fiction Feature Film*, op. cit., p. 35.

69. Dennis, 'Aotearoa New Zealand in the Silent Period, op. cit., p. 8.

70. W. Stephen Bush, 'Loved by a Maori Chieftess,' *Moving Picture World*, 8 March 1913, p. 1001.

71. *Moving Picture World*, 1913, p. 595.

72. Ibid, 12 April 1913, p. 231.

73. Ibid, 1913, p. 655.

74. Correspondence of Gaston and Hortense Méliès to Paul Méliès dated 2 October 1912, Rotorua, and 2 November 1912, Brisbane, New Zealand, NTSV.

75. Frank Thompson, *Texas' First Picture Show: The Star Film Ranch*, Republic of Texas Press, Plano, 1996, p. 67.

76. Ibid, p. 70.

77. This film was released in the United Kingdom in three parts: *A Trip through New Zealand*, 453 feet, *An Ostrich Farm in New Zealand*, 245 feet, and *A Present Day Maori Village*, 321 feet. Clive Sowry 'The "Lost" Méliès New Zealand Films,' NTSV. See individual films, Progressive Silent Film List, Silent Era, http://www.silentera.com. See also the list of films in Thompson, *Texas' First Picture Show*, op. cit., p. 233.

78. Clive Sowry, 'The "Lost" Méliès New Zealand Films', NTSV.

79. Thompson, *Texas' First Picture Show*, op. cit., p. 70.

80. Bruce Babington, *A History of the New Zealand Fiction Feature Film*, op. cit., p. 32.

81. Frank Thompson, *Texas' First Picture Show*, op. cit., p. 70.

82. *Scenes in Samarang* and *An Ostrich Farm in New Zealand* were shown to New Zealand audiences, but there is no evidence of his New Zealand sourced fictional material being screened in New Zealand. *Evening Post,* 16 April 1914, p. 2.

9. Charlie Newham films Wanganui

1. Bernard E. Jones, *The Cinematograph Book: A Complete Practical Guide to the Taking and Projecting of Cinematograph Pictures*, Cassell and Co., London, Revised edition, 1920, p. 33.

2. 'Advertising New Zealand,' *New Zealand Herald*, 18 January 1909, p. 6.

3. Chris Long, 'Silent Film to 1914', in McFarlane, Mayer and Bertrand (eds), *The Oxford Companion to Australian Film*, op. cit., pp. 452–55. T.J. West does not merit an entry in this volume.

4. Henry J. Hayward, *Here's To Life!* op. cit., p. 87.

5. Long, 'Silent Film to 1914', op. cit., pp. 452–55.

6. Ibid, pp. 452–55.

7. *New Zealand Herald*, 3 June 1911, p. 8, in Judith Shanahan, 'Early Cinema in New Zealand,' National Film Library dated 11 September 1961, Film History, NTSV.

8. Walter Frank Brown, musician, 180 Willis Street, which he shared with John Henry Brown, photographer; *Stones Wellington, Hawke's Bay and Taranaki Directory*, Dunedin, 1905, p. 115.

9. In 1902–1903 he and his brother produced a series of short comedies based on the adventures of a comic strip hero 'Ally Sloper'. Shirley and Adams, *Australian Cinema*, op. cit., p. 20

10. *Hawera & Normanby Star*, 4 July 1906, p. 1. The Unique Pantoscope Company under Franklyn Barrett's direction did a run at the Criterion Theatre in Sydney in September 1906. Eric Reade, *The Australian Screen*, op. cit., p. 27.

11. *Funeral Procession of the Late Rt. Hon. R.J. Seddon 21 June 1906*, 1906, Cameraman: W. Franklyn Barrett, Production Co.: Wide-world Pantoscope Company/Globe Syndicate Pictures, Duration: 0:0:3.07, NTSV F31276. Title as advertised, *Wanganui Herald*, 27 June 1906, p. 1.

12. *Manawatu Standard*, 22 June 1906, p. 5.

13. *Feilding Star*, 21 June 1906, p. 2.

14. *Evening Post*, 10 July 1906, p. 5.

15. *Taranaki Herald*, 21 December 1909, p. 2.

16. 'A Film Artist's Tour in New Zealand,' *Evening Post*, 17 December 1909, p. 3. See also 'Foreign News,' *The Bioscope*, 10 February 1910, p. 31.

17. Inter-title wording in *Coasts of New Zealand*, 1910, Cameraman: W. Franklyn Barratt, Production Co.: Pathé Frères, Duration: 0:04:51, NTSV F41776.

18. 'A Film Artist's Tour in New Zealand', op. cit., p. 3.

19. 'Kinematography,' *The Dominion*, 8 February 1910, p. 7.

20. *Across the Mountain Passes of New Zealand*, 1910, Cameraman: W. Franklyn, Production Co.: Pathé Frères, Duration: 0:04:01,

NTSV F10078. What seems to be a third film, *Among the Gorges of New Zealand*, is simply a renamed 16 mm version of *Across the Mountain Passes of New Zealand*.

21. *Coasts of New Zealand* was advertised as *On New Zealand's Coasts* and emphasising 'Pelorus Jack', featured at Fuller's Pictures, His Majesty's Theatre, Wellington, *Evening Post*, 31 August 1911, p. 8. *Across the Mountain Passes of New Zealand* featured at West's Pictures, Royal Albert Hall, Auckland in late March 1911. *Auckland Star*, 27 March 1911, p. 7.

22. Eric Reade, *History and Heartburn: The Saga of Australian Film 1896–1978*, Associated Universities Presses, East Brunswick, NJ, 1981, pp. 10–11.

23. *Auckland Star*, 3 September 1910, p. 12.

24. Vaughan Yarwood, 'Smokestacks and paddle-wheels', *New Zealand Geographic*, Issue 048, Oct–Dec 2000, https://www.nzgeo.com/stories/smokestacks–and–paddle–wheels/, accessed 9 December 2016.

25. *Wanganui Chronicle*, 29 August 1910, C.F. Newham, Photographers' Index, Wanganui Regional Museum.

26. Ibid, 10 September 1910.

27. Ibid, 9, 10, 12 September 1910, 14 October 1910.

28. Clive Sowry, 'Newham, Charles Frederick 1880–1960', *Dictionary of New Zealand Biography, Te Ara — the Encyclopedia of New Zealand*. www.dnzb.govt.nz, accessed 20 September 2002.

29. 'Local and General,' *Wanganui Chronicle*, 14 October 1910, p. 4.

30. *Opening of the Wanganui Rowing Season, Wanganui River, October 15, 1910*, 1910, Cameraman: Charles Newham, Production Co.: Hayward's Pictures, Duration: 0:01.06, NTSV F38482.

31. *Wanganui Chronicle*, 15, 17–18, 20–21 February, 8 April 1911.

32. Ibid, 'Local and General', 19 April 1911, p. 4.

33. Ibid, 20 April 1911, pp. 7–8.

34. *Fashions in Melbourne: Harem Skirts at Georges, c1911*, Cameraman: Pathé ; Production Co.: Pathé, 0:00.44, NFSA 74917. Harem skirts appear to have been a fad of the time. Charles Urban Trading Company lists the film *Julie Trys a Harem Skirt* in 1911 and it may have been this or a similar film that prompted the display. Charles Urban Trading Company, filmography, Screenonline, screenonline.org.uk. Accessed 14 June 2009.

35. 'Local and General, *Wanganui Chronicle*, 16 March 1911, p. 4. For Pathe's Wellington office, see Clive Sowry, 'Film Identification by Examination of Physical Characteristics,' *Archifacts: Bulletin of the Archives and Records Association of New Zealand*, 1988/2, June 1988, pp. 1–12.

36. *Fielding Races*, 1911, Cameraman: Charles Newham, Production Co.: Dominion (NZ) Film; Duration: 0:05:30, NTSV F38481.

37. *Pathé Gazette: Fielding Races*, 1911, Cameraman: M. Dahmen, Production Co.: Pathé Frères for Hayward's Pictures, Duration: 0:03:34, NTSV F7384.

38. *Fielding Star*, 1 December 1911, p. 3.

39. Ibid, 6 December 1911, p. 4.

40. Bruce Ralston, 'Wilkinson, Charles Anderson 1868–1956,' *Dictionary of New Zealand Biography, Te Ara — the Encyclopedia of New Zealand*. www.dnzb.govt.nz, accessed 20 September 2002.

41. *World Championship Axemen's Carnival, Taumata park, Eltham New Zealand*, 1911, Cameraman: Charles Newham, Production Co.: Dominion (NZ) Film; Duration: 0:10:40; NTSV F1152. It is listed as filmed in 1910 but Bob Anderson's research into the McCauley family history states that it was won in 1911. Bob Anderson, 'History of the McCauley Family, accessed 21 June 2008, http://www.bobanderson.co.uk/familyhistory/mccauleys.php. This is confirmed by results 'Eltham Axemen's Carnival,' *Grey River Argus*, 30 December 1911, p. 7.

42. 'The World's Chopping Championship,' *Hawera & Normanby Star*, 18 December 1908, p. 5.

43. Ralston, 'Wilkinson, Charles Anderson', op. cit.

44. Interview with George Tarr, 'Film Making in New Zealand', T259, Radio Sound Archives, Copy NTSV.

45. 'George Herrman Tarr (1882–1968)', New Zealand Biographies, Vol. 7, 1968, p. 97, ATL, Wellington.

46. Interview with George Tarr, 'Film Making in New Zealand', op. cit.

47. *Hawkes Bay Herald*, 4 October 1911.

48. *Fishing Industry in New Zealand, 1916*, Cameraman: Charles Newham, Production Co.: New Agency Film Co. Ltd, Duration: 0: 05:50; NTSV F97914. The New Agency Film Co.'s *Fishing Industry of New Zealand* was a 1916 reissue of the Heron film of 1912 *Trawling in Napier, New Zealand*, which in turn was derived from Newham's 1911 film *Napier Day by Day*. Clive Sowry film notes to author.

49. *The Wreck of the* Star of Canada, 1912, Cameraman: Charles Newham, Production Co.: Dominion (NZ) Film Co.; Duration: 0:06:53; NTSV F38455. A local engineer successfully dismantled the ship's two-storeyed wheelhouse and captain's cabin and sold it to Mr William Good, a local jeweller, who erected on an empty section next to his home. This was added to in 1927 and filmed in 1928. *"Star of Canada" House*, 1928, Cameraman: Unknown, Production Co.: Unknown, Duration: 0:01:05; NTSV F9892. For details of the grounding see 'Steamer Ashore,' *Evening Post*, 24 June 1912, p. 7; Gavin McLean, *New Zealand Tragedies, Shipwrecks and Maritime Disasters*, Grantham House, 1991, pp. 147–48.

50. *Wanganui Chronicle*, 17 May 1913, p. 4.

51. Ibid, 'Personal,' 30 May 1913, p. 4.

52. Rudall Hayward interview with Ray Hayes. NTSV.

53. Rudall Hayward interview with Walter Harris. NTSV.

54. *Main Trunk Express Smash*, 1914, Cameraman: Charles Newham, Production Co.: Dominion (NZ) Film, Duration: 0:03:00, NTSV F4917.

55. *Trawling in the Hauraki Gulf*, 1912, Cameraman: Charles Newham?, Production Co.: Dominion (NZ) Film?, Duration: 0:01:08; NTSV F1776.

56. *Auckland Cup*, 1912, Cameramen: Unknown, Production Co.: Unknown, Duration: 0;05:06, NTSV F10454.

57. 'Donaldson, John (Jack), (1886–1933),' 'Postle, Arthur Benjamin, (1881–1965),' *Australian Dictionary of Biography*, http://www.adb.online.anu.edu.au/biogs. Accessed 23 January 2009.

58. *A 75-yard Dash between Donaldson and Postle*, 1912, Cameraman: Unknown, Production Co.: John Fuller & Sons, Duration: 0:00:54, NTSV F31417. *Donaldson, the Champion Runner of the World*, 1911, Cameraman: Unknown, Production Co.: Unknown, Duration: ?; NTSV F8283.

59. *Plunket Shield Cricket Match Auckland v Canterbury/Domain Fete Christchurch*, 1912, Cameraman: Unknown, Production Co.: Unknown, Duration: 0:04:49; NTSV F3985.

60. *Football: England v Auckland July 25, 1914*, 1914, Cameraman: Unknown, Production Co.: Unknown, Duration: 0:03:47; NTSV F27357. See John Coffey and Bernie Wood, *The Kiwis: 100 Years of International Rugby League*, Hodder Moa, 2007, pp. 51–55.

61. Chris Pugsley, 'HMS *New Zealand*: Gift to the Empire', *New Zealand Defence Quarterly*, No. 7, Summer 1994, pp. 20–26.

62. Bassett, *Sir Joseph Ward*, op. cit., pp. 179–80.

63. Pugsley, 'HMS *New Zealand*', op. cit., pp. 20–26.

64. *The Launch of the HMS* New Zealand, Hayward's Pictures, Empire Theatre, Napier, *Hawkes Bay Herald*, 6 August 1911. 'Fuller's Theatre Royal, Wellington', *Evening Post*, 15 September 1911.

65. *New Zealand Leads the Way/Scenes on Board HMS* New Zealand/*Britannia Rules the Waves*, 1913–1916, Cameramen: Unknown, Production: Jury's Imperial Pictures, 0:03.08, NTSV F4387.

66. *HM the King Inspects "The New Zealand" at Portsmouth Photographed Exclusively by the Topical Film Co. by His Majesty's Permission, 5 February 1913*, 1913, Cameraman: Unknown, Production Co.: Topical Film Co., Duration: 0:03:35; NTSV F29375. This, apart from the additional scenes, is identical to *King George V Inspects HMS New Zealand, 5 February 1913*, 1913, Cameramen: Unknown, Production Co.: Jury's Imperial Pictures, Duration: 0:02.33, NTSV F5539.

67. *Evening Post*, 7 February 1913, p. 7.

68. 'Resentment in Australia,' *Evening Post*, 7 February 1913, p. 7.

69. Geoffrey W. Rice, *Heaton Rhodes of Otahuna: the illustrated biography*; Canterbury University Press, 2008, pp. 168–69.

70. Unknown, *Onward: HMS New Zealand*, Swiss & Co, Naval Printers, Fore Street, Devonport, pp. 3–4.

71. *Evening Post*, 12 April 1913, p. 6.

72. Ibid, 14 April 1913.

73. *Nelson Evening Mail*, 1 May 1913.

74. Ibid, 23 May 1913.

75. *Auckland's Reception to the Battleship HMS* New Zealand, 1913; Cameraman: Charles Newham; Production Co.: Dominion (NZ) Film; Duration: 0:01:34; NTSV F10484. *New Zealand Herald*, 1 May 1913, p. 5.

76. *New Zealand Herald*, 30 April 1913, p. 9.

77. A copy of James McDonald's official film HMS *New Zealand* was presented to the ship's captain, His Highness Prince George of Battenberg, as a gift to the officers and men of HMS *New Zealand* to be shown at film evenings on board ship. The film was produced in two parts (Part I 1850 feet, Part II 450 feet, totalling 2,400 feet including a concluding congratulatory message from Prime Minister William Massey. The copy including the addition of the message cost £44.13.6d and the correspondence reported that 'It is being shown to the ship's company who greatly appreciate it.' AD12/172 HMS *New Zealand*, ANZ.

78. 'Local and General, *Dominion*, 22 July 1913, p. 4.

79. Ibid.

80. *HMS New Zealand, June 1913*, 1913, Cameraman: H.C. Gore, Production Co.: Plaza Picture Theatre?, Duration: 0:01:02, NTSV F38483. There is also a brief but fuzzy scene on *Personal Record. Gore, H.C. Assorted Scenes*, Cameraman: H.C. Gore, Production Co.: various, Duration: 0:02:22, NTSV F24833.

10. Local, topical and professional

1. 'Amusements', *Evening Star*, 15 October 1910, p. 5; Simon Price, *New Zealand's First Talkies: Early film-making in Otago and Southland, 1896–1939*, Otago Heritage Books, Dunedin North, 1996, pp. 21–26.

2. Price, *New Zealand's First Talkies*, op. cit., pp. 21–26.

3. Ibid. Discrepancies in dates have been reconciled with the Dunedin cinema histories in B.T. Knewstubb, *Cinema: Dunedin and Districts 1897–1974*, Dunedin, 1974.

4. 'Private Company', *Otago Daily Times*, 4 August 1913, p. 4.

5. 'The Queen's Theatre, *Dominion*, 2 December 1916, p. 9.

6. *Otago Daily Times*, 28 October 1912, p. 6.

7. *Dunedin Brass Band Contest, Quickstep*, 1912, Cameraman: H.C. Gore, Production Co.: New Queen's Theatre, Dunedin, Duration: 0:03:28, NTSV F9933. *Otago Daily Times*, 28 October 1912, p. 1.

8. *Wreck of the SS* Tyrone, 1913, Cameraman: H.C. Gore, Production Co.: New Queen's Theatre, Dunedin, Duration: 0:02:55, NTSV F1208.

9. *Otago Daily Times*, 1 October 1913.

10. *Dominion*, 22 July 1913.

11. *The Fisher Monoplane, 1913*, Cameraman: C.D. Barton; Production Co.: C.D. Barton; Duration: 0:03:24, NTSV F7306.

12. 'The Fisher Monoplane: Cinematograph Pictures,' *New Zealand Times*, 22 July 1913, p. 11.

13. *Evening Post*, 19 February 1914, p. 2.

14. *Public Reception and Welcome Home to Sir Walter Buchanan at Carterton, July 10 1913*, 1913, Cameraman: C.D. Barton, Production Co.: C.D. Barton; Duration: 0:04:09, NTSV F14622.

15. Alan Williams, 'The Unions,' Bryce Fraser (ed.), *The New Zealand Book of Events*, Reed Methuen, Auckland, 1986, pp. 230–35. See Melanie Nolan (ed.), *Revolution: The 1913 Great Strike in New Zealand*, Canterbury University Press, Christchurch, 2005; and Erik Olssen, *The Red Feds; Revolutionary Unionism and the New Zealand Federation of Labour, 1908–1914*, Auckland, 1988.

16. Rudall Hayward interview with Walter Harris. NTSV.

17. Ibid.

18. Ibid.

19. H. Roth, *Trade Unions in New Zealand*, A.H. & A.W. Reed, Wellington, 1973, p. 35.

20. *Federation of Labour (formerly Unity Congress)*, 1913, Cameraman: C.D. Barton; Production Co.: C.D. Barton; Duration: 0:02:36, NTSV F1956.

21. *Auckland Star*, 28 August 1913, p. 12.

22. Roth, *Trade Unions*, op. cit., p. 22.

23. *Wellington. 'The Elections'. A Dash Of Politics At Lunch*, 1911, Cameraman: Unknown, Production Co.: Pathé's Animated Gazette (Australasian Edition), Duration: 0:00:54, NTSV F862. See *Evening Post*, 6 December 1911.

24. Barry Gustafson. 'Massey, William Ferguson', first published in the *Dictionary of New Zealand Biography, Te Ara — the Encyclopedia of New Zealand, Vol. 2*, 1993, and updated online in November, 2013. https://teara.govt.nz/en/biographies/2m39/massey-william-ferguson, accessed 11 August 2017.

25. *Auckland Bakers' Strike: Procession of Chinese Bakers In New Zealand, 1912*, Cameraman: unknown, Production Co.: Pathé Freres, Duration: 0:00:54; NTSV F46203. There is one film at the same period showing a Labor Day procession similar in style to the above, this is *Labor Day in Gisborne, 12 October 1910*, Cameraman: Brandon Haughton, Production Co.: Pathé Pictures Gisborne, Duration: 0:02:31, NTSV F5636.

26. M.K. Organ, 'Strike 1912: Looking for Australia's Earliest Worker's Film', *Illawarra Unity — Journal of the Illawarra Branch of the Australian Society for the Study of Labour History*, Vol. 5 Issue 1, 2005, Article 4.

27. *Nelson Evening Mail*, 13 and 15 May 1911.

28. Thompson of Thompson-Payne Picture Company to Godley, 13 January 1914, AD1 12/45, ANZ.

29. Major-General A.J. Godley to Colonel Hon J. Allen, Minister of Defence, dated 6 June 1914, AD1 12/238, ANZ.

30. General Manager, Department of Tourist and Health Resorts to Permanent Secretary, Minister of Finance, 6 June 1914, AD1 12/238, ANZ.

31. Memo Under-Secretary, Department of Internal Affairs to Commandant New Zealand Military Forces, 11 September 1914, AD1 12/238, ANZ.

32. 'Easter Encampments,' *The Press*, March 27, 1913, p. 10.

33. *The Press*, 31 March 1913, p. 1.

34. *2500 Territorials March into Christchurch, 1913*, Cameraman: Unknown, Production Co.: West-Hayward's Pictures, Duration: 0:01:30, NTSV F56660. There are also fragments from a Henry Gore film advertised as *Dunedin Territorial Parade* (or *The Defenders of New Zealand*). It was screened at the New Queen's Theatre, Dunedin, on 8 May 1913 (see *Otago Daily Times*, 8 May 1913, p. 1; *Evening Star*, 8 May 1913, p. 5). It was filmed on 8 February 1913. There is a brief glimpse of mounted riflemen on horseback, seen turning from Stuart Street into Cumberland Street, Dunedin, followed by infantry marching. These scenes are also in the NTSV film No. F984, which shows the titles from "Winifred of Wanganui" and a "troop parade". *Dunedin Territorial Parade* (or *Defenders of New Zealand* — formerly *Otago Expeditionary Force Section 2*) 1913, Cameraman: H.C. Gore, Production Co.: New Queen's Theatre, Dunedin, Duration: 0:00:07, NTSV F1821.

35. 'Report by the Inspector General of Overseas Forces on the Military Forces of New Zealand', by General Sir Ian Hamilton, *The Times Documentary History of the War, Vol. X, Overseas, Part 2, The Times*, London, 1919, p. 487.

11. New Zealand goes to war

1. Cecil Malthus, *Anzac: A Retrospect*, Reed Books, Auckland, 2002, p. 17.

2. *Evening Post*, 6 August 1914.

3. *Taranaki Herald*, 7 October 1912, p. 7.

4. 'Of particular interest was a film depicting the unveiling of the Captain Cook Memorial at Ship's Cove. This picture was taken by Mr V. Vinsen, The King's Theatre expert.' *Evening Post*, 18 February 1913, p. 2.

5. R. Palamountain's letter on Joseph Sylvanus (Vanie) Vinsen, NTSV.

6. *Evening Post*, 6 August 1914.

7. Rudall Hayward interview with Walter Harris. NTSV.

8. *Evening Post*, 6 August 1914, p. 4.

9. 'Local and General,' ibid, p. 6.

10. *Auckland Star*, 15 August 1914.

11. Programme, 'The Maori,' Rotorua Maori Mission Choir and Entertainers, Town Hall, Wellington, 26 July 1910, Photo image: 71610-ac-1-1, ATL, Wellington.

12. Interview with George Tarr, 'Film Making in New Zealand', T259, Radio Sound Archives, Copy NTSV.

13. Interview with Sarah Rogers (Hera Tawhai), 'Film Making in New Zealand', T259, Radio Sound Archives, Copy NTSV.

14. Interview with George Tarr, op. cit.

15. This was the Italian two–reel film *Marcantonio E Cleopatra* made by Cines in 1913 and released in the US by George Kleine as *Antony and Cleopatra*, it ran for about 63 minutes. David Robinson, *From Peepshow to Palace: The Birth of American Film*, Columbia University Press, NY, 1996, pp. 136, 173.

16. Interview with George Tarr, op. cit.

17. *Auckland Star*, 18 August 1914.

18. Interview with George Tarr, op. cit.

19. *Evening Post*, 25 August 1914, p. 3

20. Rudall Hayward interview with Ray Hayes, NTSV.

21. *Evening Post*, 6 May 1915, p. 2.

22. 'Her Brother's Redemption', Film Brochure, NTSV. *Mataura Ensign*, 23 July 1915, p. 4.

23. *Evening Post*, 6 May 1915, p. 3.

24. 'Tarr, George Herman, 1882–1968', 1968, *New Zealand Biographies*, Vol. 7, p. 97, ATL, Wellington.

25. 'Amusements,' *Auckland Star*, 5 and 11 August 1914.

26. N. Annabell, *Official History of the New Zealand Engineers during the Great War 1914–1919*, Evans, Cobb & Sharpe, Wanganui, 1927, p. 1.

27. Lieutenant-Colonel A.D. Carbery, *The Medical Services in the Great War 1914–1918*, Whitcombe & Tombs, Wellington, 1924, p. 14.

28. *Manawatu Times*, 29 August 1914, p. 8.

29. *Off to the Front* [formerly *Loading Troopship on Wellington Waterfront*] 1914, Cameraman: Unknown, Production Co.: Hayward's Pictures, Duration: 0:01:24, NTSV F38442.

30. *Evening Post*, 11 August 1914, p. 2.

31. 'In New Zealand. Expeditionary Force,' *Ashburton Guardian*, 14 August 1914, p. 5.

32. 'New Zealand's military role in Samoa,' Ian McGibbon (ed.), *The Oxford Companion to New Zealand Military History*, OUP, Auckland, 2000, pp. 475–77.

33. *Auckland Star*, 11 August 1914.

34. 'Pages for Women', *Auckland Weekly News*, 24 September 1914, p. 65.

35. *Auckland's Expeditionary Force: The Minister for Defence Reviews the Troops*, [formerly *Territorials New Zealand Brigade*] *19 September 1914*, Cameraman: Unknown, Production Co.: Dominion Picture Theatres Co. Ltd., Duration: 0:02:29, NTSV F38469. Illustrations in *Auckland Weekly News*, 24 September 1914, p. 42, *Evening Post*, 19 September 1914, p. 8.

36. Clive Sowry suggests Frank Stewart as the more likely candidate for cameraman, as he is known to have been filming for the Queens Theatre some months earlier. Clive Sowry's film notes to author.

37. 'Ready for the Front,' *Auckland Weekly News*, 24 September 1914, p. 17.

38. Tony Fagan interview, 'Gallipoli: The New Zealand Story', documentary material, TVNZ Collection, Kippenberger Archives, NAM.

39. 13/254, 2 Lt Henry Frederick, Earnest, Mackesy, AMR, born Kansas, 1882, KIA 7 August 1915, Gallipoli, Personal File, ANZ; 13/634, Major Frank Chapman, AMR, KIA 8 August 1915, Gallipoli, Personal File, ANZ.

40. 3/306 Colonel Charles Mackie Begg, CB, CMG, died of disease, UK, 2 February 1919, Personal File, ANZ.

41. 'Pages for Women,' *Auckland Weekly News*, 24 September 1914, p. 65.

42. 'Amusements,' *Auckland Star*, 21 September 1914, p. 10.

43. *The Exploits of the* Emden, *1928*, Director: Ken G Hall, Production Co.: First National Pictures, (Australia). A montage of documentary footage and recreation based on a German film *Unsere* Emden (1926). NFSA 6979. See 1914 footage: Sight and Sounds of the First World War, anzacsightsound.org, http://anzacsightsound.org/videos/exploits–emden accessed 20 December 2016. See also *The Exploits of the Emden*, 1928, Australian Screen, http://aso.gov.au/titles/features/the–exploits–of–the–emden/. Accessed 20 December 2016.

44. 'From Queen Street to the Front', anzacsightsound.org, Sights and Sounds of World War 1.

45. 'Amusements,' *Auckland Star*, 24 September 1914, p. 10.

46. *Auckland Star*, 17 August 1914.

47. *Auckland Star*, 1 October 1914.

48. *Auckland Star*, 14 October 1914.

49. 'Stage Jottings', *Auckland Star*, 17 May 1930, p. 2.

50. 'Just as the Sun Went Down,' words and music. An earlier version was also recorded by 71st Regt (US) Band for Edison in 1896, so it is obviously a song and a theme that had been around for a long time, possibly since the American Civil War. http://www.archive.org/details/DudleyMacdonough.

51. 'Moving Pictures Come to Auckland,' MS 1469 Auckland War Memorial Museum Library.

52. *Auckland Star*, 14 October 1914.

53. *Manawatu Times*, 4 May 1910, p. 1.

54. *Auckland Star*, 24 June 1911, p. 12

55. *Auckland Star*, 28 August 1911, p. 7.

56. *New Zealand Herald*, 2 September 1913, p. 5.

57. *Auckland Star*, 10 September 1913, p. 5.

58. *Auckland Weekly News*, 1 October 1914.

59. *Evening Post*, 24 September 1914.

60. Ibid.

61. *New Zealanders for the Front: Official Farewell*, 1914, Cameraman: James McDonald, Production Co.: Department of Agriculture, Duration: 0:02:00, NTSV F1820.

62. Christopher Pugsley, *The Anzac Experience: New Zealand, Australia and Empire in the First World War*, Oratia Books, Auckland, 2016, pp. 235–42.

63. Colonel Robin, QMG memo to Minister of Defence 22 August 1914, quoted in Christopher Pugsley, *Gallipoli: The New Zealand Story*, Oratia Books, Auckland, 2016, p. 53.

64. *Evening Post*, 25 September 1914.

65. *Otago Daily Times*, 4 September 1914, p. 1.

66. *Civic Farewell at Tahuna Park, Section 1* [formerly *Otago Expeditionary Force, Section 1*], *September 1914*, Cameraman: H.C. Gore, Production Co.: Plaza Pictures, Duration: 0:03:55, NTSV F1147.

67. *Otago Witness*, 23 September 1914, p. 27, Supplement, p. 41.

68. *Civic Farewell at Tahuna Park, Section 2 [Otago Expeditionary Force, Section 3], 21 September 1914*, Cameraman: H.C. Gore Production Co.: Plaza Pictures, Duration: 0:00:07, NTSV F54107. This is an extract from film, *Personal Record Gore, H.C. [Assorted Scenes]*, 1914, Cameraman: H.C. Gore; Production Co.: Various, Duration: 0:02:20, NTSV F24833.

69. Clutha Mackenzie, *Tales of a Trooper*, John Lane, London, 1921, p. 20, quoted in Pugsley, *Gallipoli*, op. cit., p. 66.

70. Shots of the New Zealand Contingent appear in *London Scottish Cadets: Troops at Lord Mayor's Show, 12 November 1914*, 1914, Cameraman: Unknown, Production Co.: *Gaumont Graphic*, BGT407040506, Gaumont-Graphic Newsreel, Reuters-ITN.

71. *Gaumont Graphic 380: New Zealand Infantry*, 1914, Cameraman: Unknown, Production Co.: Gaumont, Duration: 00 00.12, NTSV F194541.

72. Advertisement, 'Gaumont War Graphic: Types of Britain's Defenders at the Lord Mayor's Show, including New Zealand Infantry,' Everybody's Theatre, Wellington, *Evening Post*, 12 January 1915, p. 2.

73. 2nd Lt C.W. Saunders, DCM, NZE, Diary, quoted in Pugsley, *Gallipoli*, op. cit., p. 65.

74. *Lord Mayor's Show*, 1916?, Cameraman: Unknown, Production Co.: Pathé Gazette, Duration: 02.53, 1936.11, British Pathé.

75. *New Zealand Reinforcements Leaving, 13 February 1915*, 1915, Cameraman: Unknown, Production Co.: Pathé Gazette, Duration: 0:01.10, British Pathé 1860.48, NTSV F245692.

76. 'A Description concerning the Maori Contingent of Aotearoa and Te Waipounamu who took part in the Great War Collated by the Committee of the Maori Members of Parliament,' in Christopher Pugsley, *Te Hokowhitu A Tu: The Maori Pioneer Battalion in the First World War*, Libro, Auckland, 2015, p. 30.

77. Ibid.

78. George Knight to 'My Dear Home', on board *Aparima* 17 February 1915, Nancy Croad (ed.), *My Dear Home: The Letters of the three Knight brothers who gave their lives during WW1*, Croad, Auckland, 1995, p. 32.

79. *New Zealand Reinforcements Leaving, 13 February 1915*, op. cit.

80. *Evening Post*, 18 February 1915, pp. 2–3; 29–31 March 1915, p. 2.

81. *Evening Post*, 24 May 1915, p. 3.

82. Florence Ripley Mastin, 'At the Movies,' Catherine Reilly, *Scars upon my Heart: Women's poetry and verse of the First World War*, Virago Press, London, 1981, p. 70.

12. Sailing off to see the world

1. 'The Grey Fleet,' *Dominion*, 29 August 1914, p. 8.

2. Lt Colvin S. Algie, Auckland Battalion, entry 25 October 1914, Diary, 23 September 1914–7 August 1915, MS Papers 1374, ATL, Wellington.

3. Major Fred Waite, *The New Zealanders at Gallipoli*, Whitcombe & Tombs, Wellington, 1919, p. 17.

4. *Life on New Zealand Troopships [Daily Routine and Life of our Troops En Route To Egypt, Departure of the New Zealand and Australian Troopships King George's Sound, Western Australia]*, 1915, Cameraman: Captain Holmes, Ship's Master, SS *Waimana*:

Production Co.: Unknown, Duration: 0:11:10, NTSV F8201. The *Waimana* can be identified by the presence of the Auckland Battalion on the wharf. It is also the last of the New Zealand ships in the left file and this is confirmed on the film as the cameraman on the bridge shows the departure of the other ships of the New Zealand convoy forming file after the Australian ships have sailed. See Map 1. C.E.W. Bean, *The Story of ANZAC*, Vol. 1; (5th edition), Angus & Robertson, Sydney, p. 104.

5. See 'Joining the Flotilla', http://anzacsightsound.org/videos/the–first–troopships–depart. *WWI Troops Embarkation and Charity Bazaars, Sydney c.1915, 1914*, Cameraman: Bert Ive and others; Production Co.: Unknown; Duration: 0:07:41; NFSA 45988. *Departure of 37 Transports from Albany, 1 November 1914*, Cameraman: Unknown, Duration: 012.47, F00161 AWM; *Life on Board the "A3" Orvieto*, 1914, Cameraman: Unknown, Duration: 005.51, F00160, AWM. Accessed 4 March 2017.

6. *Evening Post*, 20 January 1915, p. 3.

7. *Evening Post*, 9 March 1915, p. 2.

8. 'NZ Troopship to the Dardanelles,' *Evening Post*, 30 September 1915, p. 2.

9. Major Fred Waite, *The New Zealanders at Gallipoli*, op. cit., p. 38

10. Ibid, p. 31.

11. *Evening Post*, 28 April 1915, p. 2.

12. *Our Boys in Egypt, A.H. Noad Film: Gallipoli*, 1914?–1927? Cameramen: Various, Production Co.: Arthur Tinsdale, Embassy Pictures; Duration: 1:03:23, AWM F00176. The New Zealand Field Artillery sequence is at F00176: TCR01:18:11:09–TCR01:18:22:13.

13. Christopher Pugsley, *Gallipoli: The New Zealand Story*, op. cit., pp. 85, 360.

14. *Inspection of the New Zealand and Australian Division, March 1915*, 1915, Cameraman: Unknown, Production Co.: Pathé?, Duration: 0:07:40, NTSV F6824.

15. Major H. Hart Diary, WIB, 28 March 1915, QEII/AT.

16. Ibid. See also John Crawford (ed.), *The Devil's Own War: The First World War Diary of Brigadier-General Herbert Hart*, Exisle, Auckland, 2008, p. 49.

17. 3 April 1915, NZ Defence Forces, *NZEF War Diary 1914*, Government Printer, Wellington, 1915.

18. J.B. Condliffe, *Te Rangi Hiroa: The Life of Sir Peter Buck*, Whitcombe & Tombs, 1926, p. 27, quoted in Christopher Pugsley, *Te Hokowhitu A Tu: The Maori Pioneer Battalion in the First World War*, Libro International, Auckland, 2015, p. 34.

19. Pugsley, *Te Hokowhitu A Tu*, op. cit., p. 35.
20. Viola Shafik, 'Egypt and other Arab countries,' Richard Abel (ed.), *Encyclopedia of Early Cinema*, Routledge, London, 2005, pp. 215–16.
21. Godley to Allen dated 10 April 1915, Semi-official Papers, Hon. Sir James Allen, 1912–1919, 16145. See also Correspondence between General Sir Alexander Godley [Commander New Zealand Expeditionary Force] and Colonel Hon. Sir James Allen, Minister of Defence, 2 April–18 December 1915, R24048325, ANZ.
22. Advertisement, 'NZ Troopship to the Dardanelles,' *Evening Post*, 30 September 1915, p. 2. See also advertisement, Shortt's Theatre, 'The Heroes of the Dardanelles,' and The Empress Theatre, 'Trentham to Mena's Great Camp,' *Evening Post*, 12 July 1915, p. 2, as characteristic of the same recycled film.
23. *Evening Post*, 30 September 1915, p. 2.
24. *Evening Post*, 4 October 1915, p. 8.

13. The French film the Dardenelles

1. Michael Paris, 'Film/Cinema (France),' *1914–1918 Online — International Encyclopedia of the First World* War; http://encyclopedia.1914–1918, online.net/article/filmcinema_france, accessed 10 March 2017. Pierre Sorlin, 'French Newsreels of the First World War,' *Historical Journal of Film, Radio and Television*, 24:4, 2004, pp. 507–15. Laurent Véray 'Cinema,' in Jay Winter (ed.) *The Cambridge History of the First World War, Vol. III, Civil Society*, CUP, Cambridge, 2014, pp. 475–503.
2. Steve Russell, 'Seeking the Lost: Early NZ–related film material in French audio–visual archives'. Report to the New Zealand-France Friendship Fund, Steve Russell, Mediaplex Manager, Ngā Taonga Sound & Vision archive; NTSV.
3. *With the Allied Fleets in The Dardanelles*, 1915, Cameraman: Unknown, Production Co.: Gaumont, Duration: 0:03:24, NTSV F29386.
4. *With the Allied Fleets in The Dardanelles*, 1915, Cameraman: unknown, Production: Gaumont, UK, Cameraman: Unknown, Duration: ?, BFI 603107.
5. Christopher M. Bell, *Churchill and Sea Power*, Oxford University Press, Oxford, 2013, pp. 59–71.
6. Paul G. Halpern, *The Naval War in the Mediterranean 1914–1918*, Naval Institute Press, Annapolis, 1987, pp. 55–59.
7. 'Amusements,' *Star*, (Christchurch), 17 August 1915, p. 8.
8. *Dominion*, 24 August 1915, pp. 7–8.
9. *Wanganui Chronicle*, 24 September 1915, p. 6.
10. Brigadier-General C.F. Aspinall-Oglander, *Military Operations Gallipoli: Vol. I, Inception of the Campaign to May 1915*; William Heinemann Ltd, London, 1929, pp. 96–98.
11. Halpern, *The Naval War in the Mediterranean*, op. cit., p. 76.
12. Elizabeth Greenhalgh, Th*e French Army and the First World War*, Cambridge University Press, Cambridge, 2014, pp. 101–104.
13. Ibid, pp. 101–104.
14. Ibid, p. 105.
15. *Les Curaissés "Le Gaulois" et "Le Bouvet" qui ont pris part au bombardment des Dardanelles*, 1915, Cameraman: Unknown, Production Co.: Gaumont Journal Actualité, Duration: 0:00:43, Gaumont Pathé Archives 1509GJ00010.
16. R.D. Layman, *Naval Aviation in the First World War: Its Impact and Influence*; Caxton Publishing, London, 1996, pp. 138–149.
17. David Méchin, 'Escadrille MF 98T – F398, Escadrille 524', http://albindenis.free.fr/Site_escadrille/escadrille524.htm, accessed 26 January 2017.
18. André Jouineau, *Officers and Soldiers of the French Army during the Great War, Vol. II. 1915–1918*; Histoire & Collections, Paris, 2009, pp. 45–46.
19. *A Marseille, Des Aviateurs embarquent a bord du parquebot "Britannia" pour les Dardanelles*, 1915, Cameraman: Unknown, Production Co.: Gaumont Journal Actualité, Duration: 0:00:38, Gaumont Pathé Archives 1526GJ00002.
20. *The Dardanelles*, 1915, Cameraman: Unknown, Production Co.: Pathé Journale Actualité, Duration: 0:00:29, Gaumont Pathé Archives No. 1915 22.
21. *The Allies in the East [Other Segments]*, 1916, Cameraman: Unknown; Production Co.: Spencers Australia, Duration: 0:14:21, NFSA 323. *The Allies in the East*, 1916, Cameraman: Unknown, Production Co.: Gaumont, Duration: 0:08:21, NFSA 309. *The Allies in the East*, 1916, Cameraman: Unknown, Production Co., Gaumont UK, Duration: 0:04:48, BFI 19359.
22. *Southland Times*, 7 April 1916, p. 3.
23. Pugsley, *Gallipoli*, op. cit., p. 364.
24. *Gaumont Actualities No.5022, 1920*, filmed 1915–16, Cameraman: Unknown; Production Co.: Gaumont Journal Actualité , France, Duration: 0:10:23:10; Gaumont Pathé Archives No. 2000GS05022.
25. Brigadier- General C.F. Aspinall-Oglander, *Military Operations Gallipoli: Vol. II, May 1915 to the Evacuation*; William Heinemann Ltd, London, 1932, pp. 461–62.
26. Jouineau, *Officers and Soldiers of the French Army during the Great War*, op. cit., pp. 52–63; Aspinall-Oglander, *Military Operations Gallipoli: Vol. II*, op. cit., pp. 494–95.
27. *Southland Times*, 21 August 1915, p. 5.
28. Alan Gray, 'One of the French Foreign Legion's Finest — A Kiwi,' enclosed in Anna Leask, 'Gallipoli 100: Our forgotten 'French' hero,' nzherald.co.nz, 14 April 2015, http://www.nzherald.co.nz/nz/news/article.cfm?c_id=1&objectid=11432103, accessed 20 January 2017.
29. Ibid.
30. Aspinall–Oglander, *Military Operations Gallipoli: Vol. II*, op. cit., pp. 33–34.
31. Commandant (Lieutenant-Colonel) James Waddell, personal file, Service historique de la Défense, Château de Vincennes (SHD), copy in author's collection.
32. Aspinall-Oglander, *Military Operations Gallipoli: Vol. II*, op. cit., pp. 101–104.
33. 9/229, Tpr Waddell, David Barnett, OMR, Personal File 9/229–Army, ANZ.
34. *Fielding Star*, 22 March 1917, p. 2.

35. The *Médaillé Extraordinaire* exhibition examining the achievements of Lieutenant-Colonel James Waddell and his service in the French Army opened in Belloy-en-Santerre, Picardy, on 4 July 2016. It ran until August 2016 and then was toured through the Santerre Region. It was curated by Jasmine Millet. *Médaillé Extraordinaire* is one of only two New Zealand-led projects given the official seal of France's Mission du centenaire de la Première Guerre mondiale. Story Shop, '*Médaillé Extraordinaire* exhibition opens in France,' 29 June 2016, http://storyshop. co.nz/new–blog/2016/6/28/mdaill–extraordinaire–exhibition–opens–in–france, accessed 26 January 2017.

14. Ashmead–Bartlett films Gallipoli

1. 15/93A, Private Russell John James Weir, NZ & A Divisional Headquarters quoted in Christopher Pugsley and Charles Ferrall, *Remembering Gallipoli: Interviews with New Zealand Gallipoli Veterans*; Victoria University Press, Wellington, 2015, p. 73.

2. Christopher Pugsley, *On the Fringe of Hell: New Zealanders and Military Discipline in the First World War*, Hodder & Stoughton, Auckland, 1991, p. 73.

3. Ellis Ashmead-Bartlett, *Ashmead-Bartlett's Despatches from the Dardanelles*, George Newnes, London, 1915.

4. Ron Palenski, 'War Stories: Malcolm Ross — how New Zealand got it wrong and Australia got it right,' Unpublished MA Dissertation, Department of History, University of Otago, pp. 4–10.

5. 'Conditions of Employment of Official War Correspondent.' Government Printer, Wellington, 1915. Malcolm Ross Correspondence, Folio 8, Sir James Allen Papers, 4/74, ANZ. 'War Letters — The New Zealand Correspondent — Questions in Parliament,' *Evening Post*, 15 September 1915.

6. Ibid.

7. Janet McCallum, 'Ross, Forrestina Elizabeth and Ross, Malcolm', from the *Dictionary of New Zealand Biography, Te Ara — the Encyclopedia of New Zealand*, http://www.TeAra.govt.nz/en/biographies/2r28/ross–forrestina–elizabeth, accessed 30 May 2017.

8. 'The Wounded,' *Evening Post*, 7 July 1915, p. 11.

9. 'What is Wanted,' *Evening Post*, 28 August 1915.

10. Ibid.

11. Geoffrey W. Rice, *Heaton Rhodes of Otahuna: the illustrated biography*, Canterbury University Press, 2008, pp. 176–78.

12. 'The Wounded. What is being Done,' *Evening Post*, 7 July 1915, p. 11; Rice, *Heaton Rhodes of Otahuna*, op. cit., pp. 201–207.

13. Malcolm Ross, 'At Gallipoli,' *Evening Post*, 5 July 1915, p. 3.

14. Malcolm Ross, 'With the Troops … A Daring New Zealander,' *Evening Post*, 21 July 1915, p. 7.

15. His first despatch 'In Action … "The White Ghurkar," in four columns appeared in the *Evening Post*, 3 July 1915, p. 18. His second letter dated 20 May, with the editor acknowledging that the landing detail was abridged, appeared in *Evening Post*, 5 July 1915, p. 3. 'With the Forces … The Hospital in Egypt,' dated 24 May appeared *Evening Post*, 16 July 1915, p. 10.

16. 'On Gallipoli,' *Evening Post*, 14 August 1915.

17. Malcolm Ross, 'With the Troops,' *Evening Post*, 13 October 1915.

18. Ross to Allen dated 25 September 1915, Malcolm Ross Correspondence, Folder 8, Allen Papers 4/74, 16145, ANZ.

19. Ibid.

20. Ibid.

21. Ashmead-Bartlett, Ellis (1881–1931), AIM25, Institute of Commonwealth Studies, http://www.aim25.ac.uk, accessed 8 April 2008.

22. Fred and Elizabeth Brenchley, *Mythmaker: Ellis Ashmead–Bartlett: The Englishman Who Sparked Australia's Gallipoli Legend*; John Wiley & Sons, Milton, Queensland, 2005. Philip Dutton, 'More vivid than the written word': Ellis Ashmead-Bartlett's film *With the Dardanelles Expedition 1915; Historical Journal of Film, Radio and Television*, 24:2, 2004. Kevin Fewster, 'Ellis Ashmead–Bartlett and the making of the Anzac legend; *Journal of Australian Studies*; 6:10, 1982, pp. 17–30.

23. Ashmead-Bartlett's agent secured a contract from Alfred Butt, the theatre impresario.

24. Ashmead-Bartlett, *The Uncensored Dardanelles*, Hutchinson & Co., London, 1928, p. 121.

25. Ibid.

26. *With the Dardanelles Expedition/Heroes of Gallipoli*, 1915, Cameramen: Ellis Ashmead-Bartlett, Ernest Brooks, Production Co.: Alfred Butt, retitled and captioned by C.E.W. Bean for Australian War Memorial in the 1920s, Duration: 020.02, F00069, Australian War Memorial. A digital restoration of this film was carried out by Weta Workshops in New Zealand and can be found at F10581 AWM. Further scenes from *With the Dardanelles Expedition* have been identified in the AWM Film Collection. A.H. Noad film (A.C. Tinsdale's *Gallipoli 1928*); Cameramen: various, Director: Arthur Charles Tinsdale; Production Co.: Embassy Films, Duration: 1:01:53, AWM F00176. *A Study into Ellis Ashmead-Bartlett's Gallipoli Footage and its Various Versions and Interpretations; 2013*, AWM PAFU 0696; compiled by Michael Kosmider and Esa Makela to accompany Michael Kosmider, *Archival Films of Gallipoli*, Michael Kosmider, July 2014, with supporting documents and DVD.

27. Ashmead-Bartlett, *The Uncensored Dardanelles*, op. cit., pp. 136, 139.

28. Ibid, pp. 155–56.

29. Ibid, pp. 160–61.

30. John Crawford with Peter Cooke, *No Better Death: The Great War Diaries and Letters of William G. Malone*, Reed, Auckland, 2005, p. 239. No date is given for the visit, and at this time Malone was not keeping a daily entry.

31. Field-Marshal Lord Birdwood, *Khaki and Gown: An Autobiography*, Ward Lock & Co., London, 1941, p. 297.

32. Ashmead–Bartlett, *The Uncensored Dardanelles*, op. cit., p. 161.

33. Ibid, p. 162.

34. Ibid, pp. 168, 172–73.

35. Ibid, p. 176.

36. Ibid, pp. 177–78.

37. Ibid, p. 186.

38. Ibid, pp. 212–13.

39. Ibid, pp. 235–36.

40. Stephen Badsey, *The British Army in Battle and Its Image 1914–1918*, Birmingham War Series, Continuum, London, 2009, pp. 126–27.

41. Ashmead–Bartlett, *The Uncensored Dardanelles*, op. cit., p. 244.

42. Ibid, p. 244.

43. ICS 84 A/12/3, Ellis Ashmead-Bartlett Diary of 1916, Australia, New Zealand, America, pp. 18–19.

44. ICS 84 A/12/3, Ellis Ashmead-Bartlett Diary of 1916, Australia, New Zealand, America, p. 28.

45. 'Observor [sic] of the War: Mr Ashmead-Bartlett,' *Grey River Argus*, 14 February 1916, p. 3.

46. 'A Glorious Effort and a Splendid Failure,' *Grey River Argus*, 22 April 1916, p. 3.

47. Ellis Ashmead-Bartlett Diary of 1916, op. cit., pp. 72–73.

48. Ibid, p. 74e.

49. Ibid, pp. 65–66.

50. Fraser Film advertisement, *Sun*, Sydney, 12 March 1916, reproduced in Ina Bertrand (ed.), *Cinema in Australia: A Documentary History*, op. cit., p. 87.

51. Reade, *The Australian Screen*, op. cit., p. 75.

52. *Evening Post*, 10 April 1916, p. 3.

53. Fraser Film advertisement, *Sun*, Sydney, 12 March 1916, op. cit.

54. 'The Picture Houses,' *Poverty Bay Herald*, 27 June 1916, p. 5.

55. Ibid.

56. Advertisement, *Poverty Bay Herald*, 24 June 1916, p. 1. In the advertisement on 27 June it was advertised as *Ashmead Bartlett's Dardanelles Expedition*.

57. This paragraph is drawn from George Imashev and his research published as 'Gallipoli: The film "With the Dardanelles Expedition: heroes of Gallipoli"', The Joint Imperial War Museum/Australian War Memorial Battlefield Study Tour to Gallipoli, September 2000, George Imashev, 2001, pp. 1–3. Kosmider, *Archival Films of Gallipoli*, op. cit.

58. C.E.W. Bean Diary, January 1918, entry 1 January 1918, AWM 38, Official History, 1914–1918 War: Records of C.E.W. Bean, Official Historian, 3DRL606/96/1. See also Jeff Maynard, *The Unseen Anzac*, Scribe, Brunswick, Victoria, 2015, p. 109.

59. C.E.W. Bean Diary, January 1918, entry 1 January 1918, op. cit.

60. Maynard, *The Unseen Anzac*, op. cit. pp. xiv–xv, 168–69.

61. C.E.W. Bean, *Gallipoli Mission*: Australian War Memorial, Canberra, 1948.

62. *With the Dardanelles Expedition: Heroes of Gallipoli*, digital restoration by Weta Digital, 2005, Duration: 0:18:00; AWM F10581.

63. Imashev, 'Gallipoli: The film *With the Dardanelles Expedition: Heroes of Gallipoli*', op. cit., pp. 1–3. 'The Picture Houses,' *Poverty Bay Herald*, 27 June 1916, p. 5.

64. *With the Dardanelles Expedition: Heroes of Gallipoli* timings are based on the time code readings taken from the digitally restored version, AWM F10581.

65. AWM F10581: TCR01:17:29:00–TCR01:17:51:08.

66. 5th Royal Irish Fusiliers Sequence: AWM F10581: TCR01:18:00:21–TCR01:18:23:06 and Hill 112: AWM F10581: TCR01:18:32:22–TCR01:19:08:18.

67. Bean seems to have missed the presence of slouch-hatted Australian soldiers evident in the background in the evacuation of the wounded sequence at Suvla. AWM F10581: TCR01:14:39:06–TCR01:14:52:12.

68. Imashev, 'Gallipoli: The film *With the Dardanelles Expedition: heroes of Gallipoli*'. Email correspondence to author from Stephanie Boyle, Acting Senior Curator, Film and Sound, AWM, 13 March 2009.

69. Kosmider, *Archival Films of Gallipoli*, op. cit., p. 32–33.

70. *A.H. Noad Film, 1915–1928,* Cameramen: Various, Producer: A.C. Tinsdale, Embassy Films, Duration: 1:01:53, AWM F00176.

71. *Comparison of Ellis Ashmead Bartlett's Gallipoli Footage in AWM Films F00069 with The Dardanelles Expedition: Heroes of Gallipoli And F00176 A.H. Noad Film*; Duration: 0:08:11, AWM F08484.

72. Paul Byrnes, 'The hunt for a lost Anzac film,' *Sydney Morning Herald*, 19 April 2015. http://www.smh.com.au/entertainment/movies/the–hunt–for–a–lost–anzac–film–20150416–1mk1dm.html, accessed 26 December 2016. Paul Byrnes, 'Gallipoli on Film,' *Australian Screen Online*, http://aso.gov.au/titles/collections/gallipoli–on–film/Australian Screen, accessed 13 February 2017.

73. 'Gallipoli Film,' *Press*, 30 December 1927, p. 7. 'Anzac Crusaders,' *Press*, 21 January 1928, p. 11. *Auckland Star*, 11 February 1928, p. 5.

74. Kosmider, *Archival Films of Gallipoli*, op. cit. Byrnes, 'The hunt for a lost Anzac film, op. cit.

75. 'Home Front. Turkey in the First World War. Birth of Turkish Cinema', http://www.turkeyswar.com/homefront/cinema.html. Accessed 29 August 2017.

76. Author correspondence with William Sellars. AWM 30 prisoner of war statements Item number, B1.11, page 3, AWM.

77. *Pathé Journal Actualité: Guillaume Ii En Turquie, 1917,* German intertitles, Duration: 00:03:32, Gaumont Pathé 191529.

15. Filming the camps

1. 'The Old Nineteens', *The Camp Courier (Circulating in Trentham, Featherston and Papawai Camps, and Posted to All Parts of the British Empire)*, Trentham New Zealand, 9 December 1916, p. 2.

2. Chief of General Staff, New Zealand Military Forces, *War, 1914–1918. New Zealand Expeditionary Force. Its Provision and Maintenance.* Government Printer, Wellington, 1919.

3. Letter dated 20 December 1914, Croad, *My Dear Home*, op. cit., p. 5.

4. Herbert, along with his brother George, sailed with the Third Reinforcements as a member of the Otago Infantry Battalion and would die in the fruitless New Zealand Infantry Brigade attack on Krithia at Gallipoli on 8 May 1915. Letter dated 1 January 1915, Croad, *My Dear Home*, op. cit., p. 7.

5. Secretary of Agriculture, Industries and Commerce to Commandant NZ Defence Forces dated 7 January 1915, AD1 12/238, ANZ.

6. Ibid.

7. *Vast Training Camp aka Aerial Camp View*, 1915, Cameraman: Sydney Benjamin Taylor, Production Co.: Pathé Gazette from film provided by Department of Agriculture, Duration: 0:00.50, (British Pathé 1862:12 — released January 1917), NTSV F245690. *New Zealand Recruits*, 1915, Cameraman: Sydney Benjamin Taylor, Production Co.: Pathé Gazette from film provided by Department of Agriculture, Duration: 0:00.57, (British Pathé 1862:31 — released January 1917), NTSV F245691.

8. Lieutenant-Colonel A.D. Carbery, *The Medical Services in the Great War 1914–1918*, Whitcombe & Tombs, Wellington, 1924, pp. 67–71.

9. Lieutenant-Colonel J.L. Sleeman, 'The Supply of Reinforcements during the War,' in H.T.B. Drew, *The War Effort of New Zealand: A Popular History of (a) Minor Campaigns in which New Zealanders took part; (b) Services not fully dealt with in the Campaign Volumes; (c) The Work at the Bases*, Whitcombe & Tombs Ltd, Wellington, 1923, pp. 1–21. Will Lawson, *Historic Trentham 1914–1917*, Wellington Publishing Co, Wellington, 1917. Neil Frances, *Safe Haven: The Untold Story of New Zealand's Largest Ever Military Camp: Featherston*; Fraser Books, 2012.

10. *Looking North Up Molesworth Street*, 1917–18, Cameraman: Unknown, Production Co.: Unknown, Duration: 0:00:24, NTSV F38467.

11. *Evening Post*, 20 December 1916, p. 3.

12. Pugsley, *Te Hokowhitu A Tu*, op. cit., p. 44. P.S. O'Connor, 'The Recruitment of Maori Soldiers 1914–1918,' *Political Science*, XIX, 2, 1967, pp. 48–83.

13. *Gaumont Graphic 485, New Zealand: Major General Henderson Inspects Maori Troops*, 1915, Cameraman: Unknown, Production Co.: (Gaumont Graphic, Ref. No.: 1549GJ00005), Duration: 0:00.47, NTSV F48604.

14. *Gaumont Graphic 495, New Zealand: Parade by Second Maori Contingent*, 1916, Cameraman: Unknown, Production Co.: Gaumont Graphic, Duration: 0:00:46, Gaumont Pathé 1606GJ00003. Clive Sowry film notes to author.

15. *Major General Henderson Inspects Maori Troops*, 1915, op. cit. See BGT407040844 0 *Maori Troops In New Zealand: Major General Henderson Inspects the Second Contingent of Maori Troops before they Leave New Zealand for the Front, 15 November 1915*, 1915, 1549GJ 00005. *Nouvelle Zelande: Le Major General Henderson Passe En Revue Un Contingent Maori Avant Son Depart Pour Le Front*, Journal Gaumont, France; BGT407040891 495.1. *New Zealander's Response: The 2nd Maori Contingent on Parade*, 1916, 1606GJ 00003. *Nouvelle Zelande: Parade par pe Deuxieme Contingent de Soldats Maori*, 1916; Reuters-ITN Archives. These films have now been transferred to http://reuters.screenocean. com. However, the identification numbers may not match.

16. David Mulgan, *The Kiwi's First Wings: The Story of the Walsh Brothers and the New Zealand Flying School 1910–1924*, Wingfield Press, Wellington, 1960, p. 21. Peter Aimer. 'Aviation', *Te Ara – the Encyclopedia of New Zealand*, updated 21– Sep–2007 URL: http://www.TeAra.govt.nz/EarthSeaAndSky/ SeaAndAirTransport/Aviation/en. Accessed 12 October 2016.

17. Mulgan, *The Kiwi's First Wings*, op. cit., pp. 28–32.

18. E.F. Harvie, *George Bolt: Pioneer Aviator: Foundations of a Future*, A.H. & A. W. Reed, Wellington, 1974, p. 61

19. Mulgan, *The Kiwi's First Wings*, op. cit., pp. 44–49.

20. 'Snap Shots of Napier including — Boxing Day doings, The Flights, Capturing Whales, Marine Parade, etc,' Everybody's Napier, *Hawke's Bay Herald*, 12 January 1918.

21. Mulgan, *The Kiwi's First Wings*, op. cit., pp. 73–76.

22. Hugh Blackwell Diary, 15–17 February 1917, provided by Errol Martyn. *Auckland from the Skies* (former NZFA title: *Flying School at Kohimarama*, also advertised as *Auckland from Aloft*), 1918, Cameraman: C.F. Newham, Production Co.: Dominion (NZ) Film; Duration: 0:35:58, NTSV F7556. There are two versions of this film; (a) the ex–print version with intertitles, copied in the 1960s; and (b) the original negatives (without intertitles), which were held by White's Aviation, passed on to MoTaT and later to the National Film Unit when Conon Fraser was making the *Off the Ground* series in about 1979. The negatives were not in the same order as the film-as-released. Clive Sowry film notes to author. It appears in the NZ Film Censor's records under the title, *Aviators in Training*, 3 April 1918, Register of Films Viewed by the Film Censor's Office IA 60 6/2.

23. Harvie, *George Bolt*, op. cit., p. 47.

24. Ibid.

25. *Auckland from Aloft*, Everybody's Theatre, *Evening Post*, 29 April 1918, p. 2.

26. Charles Wheeler to J. Allen, Minister of Defence, dated 20 January 1917, AD 12/238, ANZ.

27. Director Dominion Museum to Col. Gibbon, Department of Defence dated 6 December 1917, AD 12/238 ANZ.

28. J. Allen Thompson to Col. Gibbon dated 17 February 1918, AD 12/238, ANZ.

29. Clive Sowry film notes to author. Register of Films Viewed by the Film Censor's Office IA 60 6/3. *Snow Man's Land*, 300 feet, 16 August 1918, ANZ.

30. L.W. Mence to Sir James Allen dated 31 January 1919, AD 12/238, ANZ.

31. Hislop, Under-Secretary, Department of Internal Affairs to GOC NZ Military Forces dated 23 August 1919, AD 12/238, ANZ

32. *Snow Man's Land (Expeditionary Force Training, Featherston Camp)*, 1917–1918, Cameraman: L.W. Mence, Production Co.: L.W. Mence, Duration: 0:04:58, NTSV F1475.

33. *Fell Engine On The Rimutaka Incline*, 1918, Cameraman: L.W. Mence, Production Co.: L.W. Mence?, Duration: 0:02.46, NTSV F7389.

34. *New Zealand Boys at Sling Camp: New Zealanders in England, 1917*, Cameraman: T.F. Scales, New Zealand scenes, L.W. Mence, Production Co.: NZ Official/ Pathé Gazette, Duration: 0:03.2, NTSV F17937. This film was a compilation of scenes copied from films (probably negatives that were subsequently destroyed) held by the Dominion Museum. The copying was done about or prior to 1959 during the production of *Pictorial Parade No. 96 The New Army*, although no scenes from it were used in the *Parade*. The film was held by the National Film Unit as library material under the title *Trenches, River Crossing, Parade, Railway* until transferred to the Ngā Taonga Sound & Vision archive in 1983. It is important to distinguish this film as a roll of library material rather than as a film that was released in its present form. Clive Sowry film notes to author.

35. *Evening Post*, 24 September 1915.

36. *Evening Post*, 6 November 1916, p. 7. *Ballot at the Government Statistician's Office*, 1916, Cameraman: Sydney Benjamin Taylor; Production Co.: Department of Agriculture, Duration: 0: 04.00, NTSV F9351. *Photo Session Following Ballot at the Government Statistician's Office*, 1916, Cameraman: Sydney Benjamin Taylor; Production Co.: Department of Agriculture; Duration: 0:04.10, NTSV F3484.

37. *Truth*, 18 November 1916.

38. *Auckland Weekly News*, 23 November 1916, *Canterbury Times*, 22 November 1916.

39. *The First Ballot, 24 September 1940*, Released: 11 October 1940; Cameraman: Unknown; Production Co.: New Zealand Government Film Studios: Duration: 0:01.59; NTSV F7472. 'Semple, Hon. Robert', from *An Encyclopaedia of New Zealand*, edited by A.H. McLintock, originally published in 1966. *Te Ara — The Encyclopedia of New Zealand*, updated 18–Sep–2007, URL: http://www.TeAra.govt.nz/1966/S/SempleHonRobert/en. Accessed 12 October 2016.

40. *Evening Post*, 23 September 1915, p. 2.

41. Sergeant J.W. Wilder, entry 27 August 1915, Diary 3 April–27 August 1917, Kippenberger Archive, NAM. Quoted in Pugsley, *Gallipoli*, op. cit., p. 326.

16. Filming Diggers on the Western Front

1. Florence Ripley Mastin, 'At the Movies,' in Catherine Reilly, *Scars upon my Heart*, op. cit., p. 70.

2. Chief of General Staff, New Zealand Military Forces, *War, 1914–1918. New Zealand Expeditionary Force. Its Provision and Maintenance*. Government Printer, Wellington, 1919, Table III, p. 14.

3. Christopher Pugsley, *On the Fringe of Hell: New Zealanders and Military Discipline in the First World War*; Hodder & Stoughton, Auckland, 1991, pp. 57–76.

4. Stephen Badsey, 'Introduction,' in Roger Smither (ed.), *Imperial War Museum Film Catalogue, Vol. I, The First World War Archive*; Greenwood Press, Westport, Connecticut, 1994, pp. vii–xi.

5. Draft, 'Fred and Ita': including the letters and diary of Fred Cody, edited by his daughter, Patricia Fry, p. 35.

6. *Ruines — Arras, Bailleul, Nieppe, Ypres, Albert, Béthune, Armentiéres*, 1916, Cameraman: French Official, Production Co.: France, Duration: 0:22:42, NTSV F253663.

7. Colonel H. Stewart, *The New Zealand Division, 1916–1919*; Whitcombe & Tombs, Wellington, 1921, p. 58.

8. George Edmund Butler, *A roadside cemetery near Neuve Eglise*, April 1917. Ref: AAAC 898 NCWA 471; George Edmund Butler, *The church, Neuve Eglise*, c.1918. Ref: AAAC 898 NCWA 450, ANZ.

9. *With the Australian Forces in France [Parts 1 And 2]*, 1916, Cameraman, British Official, Production Co.: Jury's Imperial Pictures for British Topical Committee for War Films; Duration: 0:40:00, NTSV F246429. (Part I has not been accessioned.)

10. James Cowan, *The Maoris in the Great War: A History of The New Zealand Native Contingent and Pioneer Battalion: Gallipoli, 1915, France and Flanders, 1916–18*, Whitcombe & Tombs, Wellington, 1926, pp. 78–79; Colonel H. Stewart, *The New Zealand Division, 1916–1919*, Whitcombe & Tombs, Wellington, 1921, p. 24.

11. *Sons of Our Empire, Episode 5*, 1917, Cameraman: Geoffrey H. Malins, Production Co.: War Office Cinematographic Committee (WOCC) by Topical Film Company; Duration: 0:32:00; (IWM 130-10), NTSV F246428.

12. *Sons of Our Empire, Episode 3*, 1917, Cameraman: G.H. Malins, Production Co.: WOCC by Topical Film Company, Duration: 0:42:00, (IWM 130-6); NTSV F246427.

13. Lieutenant-Colonel W.S. Austin, *The Official History of the New Zealand Rifle Brigade*, L.T. Watkins Ltd, Wellington, 1924, p. 67fn.

14. *The King Visits His Armies in the Great Advance*, 1916, Cameraman: G.H. Malins, Production Co.: WOCC by Topical Film Company; Duration: 0:40:00; (IWM 192-01); NTSV F246451.

15. *New Zealand Herald*, 21 December 1916, p. 5.

16. *Sons of Our Empire, Episode 5*, NTSV F246428.

17. Major General L.M. Inglis Papers, 'The Year of the Somme', pp. 63–64, AT Ms papers 421.

18. This numbers some 38 photos including the visit of the New Zealand Prime Minister W. Massey and Sir Joseph Ward to the battlefield. IWM Collections, Search, 'New Zealanders, Somme, 1916', http://www.iwm.org.uk/collections/search?query=New+Zealanders%2C+Somme&=Search, accessed 6 March 2017.

19. Godley to Allen, letter dated 15 October 1916, Godley Papers, WA1 252/3, ANZ. See also Allen Papers, R22319699, ANZ.

20. O.E. Burton, *The Silent Division: New Zealanders at the Front 1914–1919*, Angus & Robertson, Sydney, 1935; reprinted O.E. Burton, *The Silent Division: New Zealanders at the Front 1914–1919 & Concerning One Man's War*, (John H. Gray, ed.), John Douglas Publishing, Christchurch, 2014.

21. C.E.W. Bean, *The Australian Imperial Force in France 1917*, 9th edition, Angus & Robertson, Sydney, 1939, pp. 732–33.

22. *The Battle of the Somme, 1916*, b/w, five reels, 4694'. Cameramen: Geoffrey H. Malins and J.B. McDowell; Production Co.: British Topical Committee for War Films, Jury Imperial Pictures; Duration: 1:19:00; (IWM 191); NTSV F231397. Roger Smither (ed.), *Imperial War Museum Film Catalogue, Vol. 1, The First World War Archive*, Greenwood Press, Westport, Connecticut, 1994, pp. 67–68. Stephen Badsey, *The British Army in Battle and its Image 1914–1918*, Birmingham War Studies Series, Continuum, London, 2009, pp. 107–136.

23. Andrew Macdonald, *On My Way to the Somme: New Zealanders and the Bloody Offensive of 1916*; HarperCollins, Auckland, 2005, p. 269.

24. *Auckland Star*, 21 October 1916. See also *Nelson Evening Mail*, 22 December 1916.

25. 'Entertainments. Hayward's Pictures, "The Battle of the Somme"'. *Ashburton Guardian*, 30 October 1916, p. 3.

26. *Grey River Argus*, 30 November 1916, p. 3.

27. Badsey, Introduction,' in Smither, *Imperial War Museum Film Catalogue, Vol. 1*, op. cit., pp. vii–xi.

28. High Commissioner to Minister of Defence dated 6 January 1917, D12/113, ANZ.

29. Circular Memorandum, H.G. Reid, AA & QMG, HQ NZ Division dated 6 March 1917, WA1 22/6/14, ANZ.

30. Ibid.

31. *Review of New Zealand Troops by Sir Walter Long*, 1917, Cameraman: Unknown, Production Co.: WOCC, Topical Film Company, Duration: 0:16:00, (IWM 196), NTSV F4330. See also Smither, *Imperial War Museum Film Catalogue, Vol. 1*, op. cit., p. 70.

32. Jeff Maynard, *The Unseen Anzac*; Scribe, Brunswick, Victoria, 2015, p. 57.

33. High Commissioner to Minister of Defence dated 6 January 1917; Allen to G.W. Russell dated 8 January 1917, and Minister of Defence to High Commissioner dated 11 January 1917; D12/113, ANZ.

34. Smither, *Imperial War Museum Film Catalogue, Vol. 1*, op. cit., pp. ix–x.

35. *El Mejdel, Jaffa And West Country Troops*, 1917, Cameraman: Harold Jeapes; Production Co.: WOCC, Topical Film Company; Duration: 0:15:53; (IWM 12). NTSV F246416.

36. *Topical Budget — Jericho*, 1917, Cameraman: Harold Jeapes; Production Co.: WOCC, Topical Film Company, Duration: 0:14:57, (IWM 22), NTSV F246426.

37. *General Allenby's Entry into Jerusalem*, 1917, Cameraman: Harold Jeapes, Production Co.: WOCC, Topical Film Company, Duration: 0:13:47, (IWM 13), NTSV F246417.

38. Lieutenant-Colonel C. Guy Powles, *The New Zealanders in Sinai and Palestine*, Whitcombe & Tombs Ltd, Auckland, 1922, p. 170.

39. Terry Kinlock, *Echoes of Gallipoli: in the words of New Zealand's Mounted Riflemen*; Exisle, Auckland, 2005. Terry Kinlock, *Devils on Horses: in the words of the Anzacs in the Middle East 1916-1919*; Exisle, Auckland, 2007.

40. Ernest McKinlay, *Ways and By-Ways of a Singing Kiwi with the N.Z. Divisional Entertainers in France*, privately printed, Dunedin, 1939, p. 33.

41. Ibid, p. 48.

42. Sapper G.C. Lyttleton, 'Pierrots in Picardy: A Khaki Chronicle by "One of Them,"' unpublished manuscript, RV 5344, NAM, p. 40.

43. Ibid, p. 41.

44. Ibid, p. 42.

45. Ibid, pp. 42–43.

46. Ibid, p. 43.

47. Ibid, p. 48.

48. Ibid, p. 51.

49. McKinlay, *Ways and By-Ways of a Singing Kiwi*, op. cit., p. 59

50. Lyttleton, 'Pierrots in Picardy', op. cit., p. 53.

51. Ibid, p. 58.

52. Peter Downes. 'Hanna, George Patrick', from *The Dictionary of New Zealand Biography, Te Ara — the Encyclopedia of New Zealand*, http://www.TeAra.govt.nz/en/biographies/4h14/hanna–george–patrick, accessed 8 March 2017. Lieutenant Colonel J. Studholme, *New Zealand Expeditionary Force, Record of Personal Services during the War of Officers, Nurses and First-Class Warrant Officers, and other facts relating to the NZEF*, Government Printer, Wellington, 1928, p. 141.

53. Eric Miller, *Camps, Tramps and Trenches: The Diary of a New Zealand Sapper, 1917*, A.H. & A.W. Reed, Dunedin, 1939. pp. 123–24.

54. McKinlay, *Ways and By-Ways of a Singing Kiwi*, op. cit., p. 92. W.S. Austin, *The Official History of the New Zealand Rifle Brigade*; op. cit., pp. 323–24.

55. *Red Triangle Day Magazine*, YMCA, 15 March 1918, p .4.

56. Private Relph quoted in YMCA *Red Triangle Day* advertisement, YMCA Clippings, author's collection.

57. Austin, *The Official History of the NZ Rifle Brigade*, op. cit., p. 322.

17. "Who is Sanders?"

1. Memo GOC NZ Military Forces for Ministry of Defence dated 30 March 1917, D12/113, ANZ.

2. High Commissioner to Minister of Defence dated 23 March 1917, D12/113, ANZ.

3. Memo GOC NZ Military Forces, 30 March 1917, op. cit.

4. 'Henry Armytage Sanders', (sometimes Armitage), *Who's Who of British Newsreels*, British Universities Newsreel Database, British University Film and Video Council, newsreel@bufvc.ac.uk; http://joseph.bufvc.ac.uk/BUND/staff/detail.php?id=33185, accessed 29 August 2008. Frank Gray, 'James Williamson,' Richard Abel (ed.), *Encyclopedia of Early Film*, Routledge, London and New York, 2005, p. 695.

5. 'Henry Armytage Sanders', *Who's Who of British Newsreels*, op. cit.

6. 'In Search of "Copy", The Adventures of H.A. Sanders of the "Pathé Gazette.", *The Bioscope*, 22 October 1914, p. 299. See also Kevin Brownlow, *The War The West and the Wilderness*, Secker and Warburg, London, 1978, p. 12.

7. 'In Search of "Copy", *The Bioscope*, op. cit., p. 299.

8. T.E. Donne to H.A. Sanders dated 23 March 1917, IA ZWR 12/113, ANZ. See also Official Films, 10/1/4/90, ZWR, 4/90, Box 10/1/2, R24428246, ANZ.

9. Ibid.

10. Ibid.

11. 'The Dominion's War Correspondent,' *Auckland Star*, 30 June 1916, p. 2.

12. See for example, 'Malcolm Ross Message,' *Hawera & Normanby Star*, 7 July 1916, p. 5. Allison Oosterman, 'From Picardy to Picton,' in Nathalie Philippe et al (eds), *The Great Adventure Ends: New Zealand and France on the Western Front;* John Douglas, Christchurch, 2013, pp. 230–31.

13. Allison Oosterman, 'From Picardy to Picton', The Great Adventure Ends, op. cit., pp. 223–40; Andrew Macdonald, *On My Way to the Somme*; HarperCollins, Auckland, 2006, p. 201. Palenski, R., *Malcolm Ross: a forgotten casualty of the Great War*, 2007, Thesis, Master of Arts, University of Otago. Retrieved from http://hdl.handle.net/10523/338 https.

14. See for example, 'Battle of Messines' and 'New Zealanders at Messines,' *Timaru Herald*, 3 August 1917, pp. 3, 5.

15. Captain S. Cory-Wright to his father, France, dated 14 July 1917, RV 6294, NAM.

16. 'Henry Armytage Sanders', *Who's Who of British Newsreels*, op. cit.

17. Alistair H. Fraser, Andrew Robertshaw and Steve Roberts, *Ghosts on the Somme: Filming the Battle June–July 1916*; Pen & Sword Military, Barnsley, 2009, p. 11.

18. *Visit of the Hon. W.F. Massey and Sir J. Ward to the Western Front 30 June–2 July 1918;* 1918, Cameraman: Hon. Lt. H.A. Sanders,

Production Co.: NZ Official, negative deposited with WOCC, Duration: 0:21:43, (IWM 269) NTSV F1068. Sequence from 0:15:16 to 0:15:27.

19. There are also about 35 quarter-plate negatives in the H-Series and these seem to be in the early part of the sequence scattered across May to November 1917, the earliest being image H13: https://natlib.govt.nz/records/23243397. Natalie Marshall, Curator, Photogaphs, ATL, Wellington, to author, 6 June 2017. A very comprehensive sampling of the H-Series images and the private collections from the Western Fron are in Glyn Harper, *Images of War: New Zealand and the First World War in Photographs*, HarperCollins, Auckland, 2nd edition, 2013. However, the images came from the National Army Museum collections in the Kippenberger Archive and the captions were not cross-referenced to the Master Albums in the Alexander Turnbull Library, resulting in a number of omissions and anomalies. See also Sandy Callister, *The Face of War: New Zealand's Great War Photography*, Auckland University Press, Auckland, 2008, pp. 49–65.

20. Jeff Maynard, *The Unseen Anzac*, Scribe, Brunswick, Victoria, 2015, p. 72.

21. Natalie Marshall, Curator, Photographs, ATL, Wellington, to author, 6 June 2017.

22. 'War Records Section,' Attached to Report No. 26 of GOC NZEF UK dated 8 May 1918, WA1 10/7, ZMR 1/1/32, (R24428496), ANZ.

23. 'New Zealanders in France,' *Weekly News*, 23 August 1917.

24. H-Series Photo Album, Vol. 7, No. 2, ATL, Wellington. 'This Album contains prints of the New Zealand Official Photographs and is the property of the New Zealand War Records Section, 29 Bloomsbury Square, London. Copies of any of the prints herein may be obtained on application to the New Zealand War Records Section, post free, on the following terms:– Size ½ plate 6d per print, whole plate 9d per print, 12x10 1/9d, 15x12 3/–'. The Album shows images H1–H14 of the Divisional Horse Show and though these are not dated, the horseshow took place on 13 May 1917 at Westhof Farm. The Lumbres training photos run from H15–H35, H-Series, ATL, Wellington. See also Lieutenant J.R. Byrne, *New Zealand Artillery in the Field 1914–1918*, Whitcombe & Tombs, Wellington, 1922, p. 164.

25. H41, 1/4-009463-G, ATL, Wellington.

26. Cory-Wright to his father, op. cit.

27. *Capture of Messines*, 1917, Cameraman: H.C. Raymond, Production Co.: Topical Film Company, William F. Jury, producer for WOCC ; Duration: 0:29:00; (1766'); (IWM 197); Smither, *Imperial War Museum Film Catalogue, Vol. 1*, op. cit., pp. 70–71.

28. Maynard, *The Unseen Anzac*, op. cit. David P. Miller, *From Snowdrift to Shellfire: Capt. James Francis (Frank) Hurley 1885–1962*, David Ell Press, Sydney, 1984.

29. *Work of the New Zealand Medical Corps*, 1917, Cameraman: Lt H.A. Sanders, NZ Official, negative deposited with WOCC, Duration: 0:14:26, NTSV F4310.

30. Lieutenant-Colonel A.D. Carbery, *The Medical Services in the Great War 1914–1918*, Whitcombe & Tombs, Wellington, 1924, p. 318.

31. Carbery, *The New Zealand Medical Services in the Great War*, op. cit., p. 327.

32. See H162–H164, H182, H205–H207, H233, and H248, H-Series, ATL, Wellington.

33. 'Sanders, Henry Armytage', *Who's Who of British Newsreels*, op. cit.

34. *Otago Witness*, 7 November 1917, p. 34 (supplement). H98–H222 covers the period June–July 1917 encompassing all the detail of a busy time in the trenches and life behind the lines. Selections appeared in the illustrated press in New Zealand about six to eight weeks later.

35. *NZ Troops on the March, Inspection by Sir Thomas Mackenzie*, 1917, Cameraman: Lt H.A. Sanders, Production Co.: NZ Official, negative deposited with WOCC; Duration: 0:06:18; NTSV F1070. The H-Series photos relating to this visit are H259–H278, ATL, Wellington.

36. Eric Miller, *Camps, Tramps and Trenches: The Diary of a New Zealand Sapper, 1917*, A.H. & A.W. Reed, Dunedin, 1939. pp. 134–35.

37. 'The Russell Saga,' Vol. III, Diaries and Notes of Major-General Sir Andrew Hamilton Russell, KCB, KCMG, ADC, (d)9, (F), Extracted and compiled by R.F. Gambrill, Russell Family, Diary entry 10 September 1917.

38. Miller, *Camps, Tramps and Trenches*, 13–14 September, op. cit., p. 136.

39. N.M. Ingram, *ANZAC Diary: A Nonentity in Khaki*, The Book Printer, Maryborough, Victoria, no date, pp. 42–43.

40. *Inspection of New Zealand Troops by Field Marshal Sir Douglas Haig*, 1917, Cameraman: Lt H.A. Sanders; Production Co.: NZ Official, negative deposited with WOCC; Duration: 0:05:45, NTSV F4094. The H-Series photographs relating to this film are H224–H235 ATL, Wellington.

41. Haig Diaries, Vol. XX, September 17, entry Friday 14 September 1917, National Library of Scotland.

42. General Staff, War Office, *Field Service Pocket Book, 1914*, reprinted with amendments 1916, HMSO, London, 1917, p. 42A.

43. Ian McGibbon, *New Zealand's Western Front Campaign*; Bateman, 2016, p. 142.

44. H279–H307, ATL, Wellington.

45. H351–H355, ATL, Wellington.

46. *The New Zealand Field Artillery in France; New Zealand Rifle Brigade on the March*, 1917–18, Cameraman: Captain H.A. Sanders; Production Co.: New Zealand Official, negative deposited with WOCC; Duration: 0:09:43, NTSV F4340. The H-Series Photographs for this film are H393–H403, ATL, Wellington. *New Zealand Field Artillery in Action, New Year's Day 1918; Visit To New Zealand Infantry Base Depot Etaples;* 1918, Cameraman: Captain H.A. Sanders; Production Co.: New Zealand Official, negative deposited with WOCC; Duration: 0:06:30; NTSV F4339. The H-Series Photos for this film are H424–H428 ATL, Wellington.

47. General Staff, *Field Service Pocket Book, 1914*, op. cit., pp. 8–9.

48. McGibbon, *NZ's Western Front Campaign*, op. cit., pp. 36–37; Christopher Pugsley, *On the Fringe of Hell: New Zealanders and Military Discipline in the First World War*; Hodder & Stoughton, Auckland, p. 221.

49. Miller, *Camps, Tramps and Trenches*, op. cit., p. 91.

50. Quoted in Pugsley, *On the Fringe of Hell*, op. cit., p. 221.

51. *The Canterbury Times*, 17 January 1917.

52. 'Mr Massey and Sir Joseph Ward in France,' *Ashburton Guardian*, 6 November 1916, p. 5.

53. 'Visit to the Front,' *Poverty Bay Herald*, 20 December 1916, p. 4.

54. 'A "Movie" Mystery,' *NZ Truth*, 13 April 1918, p. 5.

55. See images, *Auckland Weekly News*, 5 April 1917.

56. Films Examined — Register of Films Viewed by the Film Censor's Office, IA60, 6/1–6/4. Entry 30 January 1918, ANZ.

57. Malcom Ross, *Chronicles of the NZEF*, Vol. IV, No. 48, 19 July 1918.

58. *Visit of the Hon. W.H. Massey and Sir J. Ward To Western Front 30 June–4 July 1918*, Cameraman: Captain H.A. Sanders, op. cit. NTSV F1068.

59. Imperial War Museum Catalogue (IWM 269) — notes provided by Christopher Pugsley; www.iwm.org.uk; accessed 30/01/2013.

60. Douglas Knight to Dear Mother, Somewhere in France, 28 June 1918, Croad, *My Dear Home*, op. cit., p. 180.

61. Sir George Fenwick, *American Notes 1924 and France and Belgium in War Time; Otago Daily Times and Witness* newspapers, Dunedin, 1927, pp. 90–93.

62. *Colonial Pressmen*, 1918, Cameraman: British Official; Production Co.: WOCC Ministry of Information; Duration: 0:17:21; (IWM 314); NTSV F246464. The H-Series photos of the visit are H995–H1008. H1006 shows the group at Haplincourt with German soldier's corpse nearby which is mentioned in Fenwick's diary; Fenwick, *American Notes*, op. cit., pp. 90–93.

63. Pugsley, *On the Fringe of Hell*, op. cit., pp. 173–77.

64. Ibid, p. 177.

65. *Match de Rugby. France — Novelle Zélande, Entrainement Sportif de Chasseurs Alpine; 1917*, Cameraman: Unknown, Production Co.: French Official, Duration: 0:04:46 (Film length – 0:09:22), NTSV F253654.

66. *The Free Lance*, 29 June 1917, pp. 16–17.

67. Ibid.

68. Ron Palenski, *Rugby: A New Zealand History*, Auckland University Press, Auckland, 2015, pp. 168–71.

69. *New Zealand Divisional Rugby Team, 1918*, Cameraman: Captain H.A. Sanders; Production Co.: New Zealand Official, negative deposited with WOCC; Duration: 0:09:32; (IWM 172); NTSV F4332.

70. 'Football: The Divisional Team,' *Chronicles of the NZEF*, Vol. IV, no. 39, 13 March 1918, pp. 56–57.

71. 'Football,' extracts *Sporting Life* and *Evening Standard*, quoted in *Chronicles of the NZEF*, Vol. IV, no. 38, 27 February 1918, p. 34.

72. Russell Diary 1 June 1918, "The Russell Saga", Vol. III, compiled by R.F. Gambrill, The Russell Family.

73. H-Series; Life in the Ypres Salient, H427–H433, H546, H567, Training and commitment to the Somme March–July 1918, H 448–H615, ATL, Wellington.

74. *Seeing The Sights of Paris before Football Match, 1918*; Cameraman: Captain H.A. Sanders; Production Co.: New Zealand Official, negative deposited with WOCC; Duration: 0:03:34; NTSV F4517.

75. 'Sport,' *Chronicles of the NZEF*, Vol. V, no. 58, 6 December 1918, p. 230.

76. Ibid.

77. Ibid.

78. See UK Series, UK506, 1/2-014271-G, ATL, Wellington.

79. 'Sport,' *Chronicles of the NZEF*, op. cit., 6 December 1918, p.230.

80. Christopher Pugsley, "'The Infantry said we were mad and by Jove we were!": With the Otago Mounted Rifles on the Western Front.' Don Mackay (ed.), *The Trooper's Tale: The History of the Otago Mounted Rifles*; Turnbull Ross Publishing, Dunedin, 2012, pp. 210–47.

81. *Les Annales de la guerre. No. 74;* 1918; Cameraman: French Official, Production Co.: French Official, Duration: 0:07:20, NTSV F253670.

82. Colonel H. Stewart, *The New Zealand Division, 1916–1919*, Whitcombe & Tombs, Wellington, 1921, pp. 454–55.

83. *Soldats Britanniques et Néo–Zélandais Lors de la Deuxiéme Batille de la Scarpe Septembre 1918*; Cameraman: French Official, Production Co.: French Official, Duration: 0:08:27, NTSV F253578. See IWM 508–74, Roger Smither (ed.), *Imperial War Museum Film Catalogue, Vol. 1, The First World War Archive*, Greenwood Press, Westport, Connecticut, 1994, pp. 233–34.

84. H-Series Photos covering July to November 1918, H777–H1159, ATL, Wellington.

85. Interview with author, Lieutenant-Colonel L.M. "Curly" Blyth, 5 June 1992.

86. 'Report on the Work of the New Zealand War Records Section,' 16 September 1919, War Museum Minutes, IA 29/119, see WA 10/3/ZWR 7/1, R24428310, ANZ.

87. Paul Byrnes, 'AWM Western Front,' Australian Screen Online, http://aso.gov.au/titles/collections/awm–western–front/, accessed 24 March 2017.

88. Sanders to Westmacott dated 6 August 1919, 'Proposal to purchase Official Cinema Films taken in France of New Zealand Troops.' New Zealand War Records Section, WA1, Box 10/1/2, ZWR 4/90, R24428246, ANZ.

18. Filming 'Blighty'

1. A difficulty is identifying and dating the material. The Gaumont Graphic and Topical Budget material also includes the date it was released, but this is not the case for much of the wartime Pathé material, which has to be dated from other sources. Gaumont Graphic newsreel may be accessed on http://www. reuters.screenocean.com; British Pathé may be accessed on http://www. britishPathé.com/. Gaumont Pathé Archives, France, may be accessed on http://www.gaumontpathearchives.com/.

2. *Evening Post*, 28 September 1915, p. 4.

3. The Empress Theatre, Wellington, advertised 'Topical Budget No. 209, War Facts of the Moment and Hon. T. Mackenzie at opening of hospital for New Zealand wounded in London.' *Evening Post*, 19 October 1915, p. 2.

4. *Pathé Gazette: New Hospital for Wounded New Zealanders Opened by Lord Plunket and by High Commissioner for New Zealand*, 1915; Cameraman, Pathé Gazette; Production Co: Pathé Gazette; Duration: 0:00:46, NTSV F232651.

5. *King and Queen Visit Hospital, NZ Hospital — Walton-on-Thames, Surrey*, 1917? Cameraman: T.F. Scales, Production Co.: Pathé Gazette, Duration: 0:00:29, Pathé Gazette 1886.47. *King and Queen Visit Anzac Hospital — Walton-on-Thames Surrey*, 1917?, Cameraman: T.F. Scales?, Duration: 0:00:29, Production Co.: Pathé Gazette, (Pathé Gazette, 1894.05), NTSV F245767.

6. Lieutenant-Colonel A.D. Carbery, *The New Zealand Medical Services in the Great War 1914–1918*, Whitcombe & Tombs, Christchurch, 1924, pp. 264–65.

7. *Gaumont Graphic 481(1), Wounded New Zealanders Spend Their Time Profitably, 1 November 1915*, 1915, Cameraman: Unknown, Production Co.: Gaumont Graphic, Duration: (59 feet), Gaumont Graphic BGT407040825, http://www. reuters.screenocean.com.

8. *After being Wounded* [*Recovering New Zealanders hold Sports Meeting*], 1916, Cameraman: Unknown, Production Co.: Pathé Gazette, Duration: 0:01:55, (British Pathé 1868.07), NTSV F245633. There is also a very brief clip of a New Zealand swimming sports meeting at one of the convalescent camps. *New Zealand Sports*, 1917?, Cameraman: Pathé Gazette, Production Co: Pathé Gazette; Duration: 00:33; British Pathé 1872.19.

9. *New Zealanders Board Ship to Return Home*, 1915–1916, Cameraman: Unknown, Production Co.: Pathé Gazette, Duration: 0:00:54, (British Pathé 2336.03) NTSV F245783.

10. *Australian and New Zealand Soldiers Return Home, HMNZHT No. 2 'Marama' With 500 Patients, 31 August 1916*, 1916, Cameraman: Unknown, Production Co.: Pathé Gazette, Duration: 0:00:32, (British Pathé 1926.14), NTSV F245636.

11. Earl of Liverpool, *The Voyages of His Majesty's Hospital Ships "Marama" and "Maheno" (2nd Vol.)*; Whitcombe & Tombs, Wellington, 1917, p. 71.

12. Ian McGibbon. 'Duigan, John Evelyn', from the *Dictionary of New Zealand Biography, Te Ara — the Encyclopedia of New Zealand*, http://www.TeAra.govt.nz/en/biographies/4d24/ duigan-john-evelyn, accessed 6 June 2017.

13. *15,000 Miles to Serve* — 'Tunnellers From New Zealand Inspected By High Commissioner, 6 March 1916*, 1916, Cameraman: Unknown, Production Co.: Pathé Gazette, Duration: 0:00:17, British Pathé, 1856.27.

14. *Colonial Troops Reviewed, 6 March 1916*, 1916, Cameraman: Unknown, Production Co.: Pathé Gazette, Duration: 0:02:01, British Pathé, 1936.33.

15. J.C. Neill, *The New Zealand Tunnelling Company 1915–1919*, Whitcombe & Tombs, Christchurch, 1922, p. 20.

16. This is based on Ian McGibbon, 'Richardson, George Spafford', from the *Dictionary of New Zealand Biography, Te Ara — the Encyclopedia of New Zealand*, http://www.TeAra.govt.nz/en/biographies/3r16/richardson-george-spafford, accessed 21 March 2017.

17. Lieutenant-Colonel Myers, 'New Zealand Hospitals in the United Kingdom,' Lieutenant H.T.B. Drew (ed.), *The War Effort of New Zealand: A Popular History of (a) Minor Campaigns in which New Zealanders took part; (b) Services not fully dealt with in the Campaign Volumes (c) The Work at the Bases;* Whitcombe & Tombs, Wellington, 1923, pp. 115–26; Lieutenant-Colonel A.D. Carbery, *The New Zealand Medical Services in the Great War 1914–1918*, Whitcombe & Tombs, Wellington, 1924, pp. 274–76. John R. Pike, 'The New Zealand Discharge Depot in Torquay, 1917–1919', *The Volunteers: The Journal of the New Zealand Military Historical Society;* 42:3 March 2017, pp. 8–20.

18. *"Strawberry Fete". Promoted by the Four Allied Trades: Dairymen, Fruiterers, Grocers and Bakers, held at Torquay on Alexandra Day, 27 June 1917*, 1917. Cameraman: Unknown, Production Co.: Unknown, Duration: 0:13:22, NTSV F110329.

19. *Maori Funeral*, 1916–1917, Cameraman: Unknown, Production Co.: Pathé Gazette, Duration: 0:02:05, (British Pathé 2346.10), NTSV F48685.

20. J.B. Condliffe, *Te Rangi Hiroa: The Life of Sir Peter Buck*, Whitcombe & Tombs, 1926, p. 27, quoted in Christopher Pugsley, *Te Hokowhitu A Tu*, op. cit., p. 34.

21. Biographical details in Howard Weddell, *Soldiers from the Pacific: The Story of the Pacific Island Soldiers in the New Zealand Expeditionary Force in World War One*; Defence of New Zealand Study Group, 2nd edition, 2016, p. 211. See also Deborah Ancell, 'Son of Cook Islands: Private Terekia Taura's WW1 Story,' in *Remembering: The New Zealanders at Walton-on-Thames*, New Zealand Women's Association, pp. 10–11.

22. Pugsley, *Te Hokowhitu A Tu*, op. cit., p. 81.

23. *Evening Post*, 21 September 1915, p. 8.

24. *Stonehenge Visited by New Zealand Delegates, and after Gallipoli: The Famous Maori Contingent*, 1916, Cameraman: Unknown, Production Co.: Pathé Gazette, Duration: 0:02:07, (British Pathé 1848.27), NTSV F48689.

25. *Maori Soldier R&R aka Maori Contingent Resting, New Zealand Maori Soldiers who took part with the ANZAC Forces in the Gallipoli Campaign are Resting for a while in England*, 1916, Cameraman: Unknown, Production Co.: Pathé Gazette, Duration: 0:00:18, British Pathé 1850.05; and *Maori 'Haka' War Cry*, 1916, Cameraman: Unknown, Production Co.: Pathé Gazette, Duration: 0:00:35, (British Pathé 2346.12), NTSV F48689; *Boscombe — New Zealand Maori 'Haka' for Deserving Charity — Pathé Gazette* , 1916, Cameraman: Unknown, Production Co.: Pathé Gazette, Duration: British Pathé 1902.42.

26. *Topical Budget No: 233-1, Anzacs Beat Artists, 9 February 1916*, 1916, Cameraman: Unknown, Production Co.: Topical Film Co., Duration: 0:03:55, NTSV F246508. See Luke McKernan, 'Topical Budget (1911–1931), BFI screenonline, http://www.screenonline.org.uk/film/id/583128/. Accessed 20 August 2017.

27. *New Zealand Herald*, 29 March 1916, p. 12.

28. *Topical Budget 241-1 An Anzac Win, 5 April 1916*, 1916, Cameraman: Unknown, Production Co.: Topical Film Co., Duration: 0:01:35, NTSV F97870.

29. *Topical Budget No: 233-1, Anzacs Beat Artists, 9 February 1916*, op. cit.

30. *Topical Budget 242-1 New Zealanders Win at Rugby, 12 April 1916*, 1916, Cameraman: Unknown, Production Co.: Topical Film Co., Duration: 0:01:06, NTSV F97871.

31. *Fighting Men at Play: "All Blacks" Beat "Springboks" in hotly contested Rugby Match at Richmond, 8 April 1916*, 1916, Cameraman: Unknown, Production Co.: Pathé Gazette, Duration: 001:25, (British Pathé 1860.43), NTSV F48684.

32. 'Football,' *Chronicles of the NZEF*, 29 September 1916, p. 62.

33. *New Zealand v Wales at Pontypridd*, 1916, Cameraman: Unknown, Production Co.: Gaumont Graphic; Duration: 0:01:17: NTSV F48603.

34. *Gaumont Graphic 604 (1) Rugby Football — Asc (Grove Park) v New Zealand, 4 January 1917*, 1917, Cameraman: Unknown, Production Co.: Gaumont Graphic, Duration: ?, BGT407050745, Reuters–ITN. This has now been transferred to http://reuters.screenocean.com and may have been renumbered.

35. 'All Blacks' Fine Fight,' *Chronicles of the NZEF*, 17 January 1917, p. 230.

36. *Topical Budget 287-1 Premier Watches Rugby Match*, 1917, Cameraman: Unknown, Production Co.: Topical Film Co., Duration: 0:00:41, NTSV F97873.

37. *Topical Budget 287-1 All Blacks v ASC*, 1917, Cameraman: Unknown, Production Co.: Topical Film Co., Duration: 0:01:14, NTSV F97890.

38. Individuals' details taken from R.H. Chester, N.A.C. McMillan and R.A. Palenski, *The Encyclopedia of New Zealand Rugby*, Moa Publications, Auckland, 1987.

39. A.C. Swan, *History of New Zealand Rugby Football, Vol. 1 1870–1945*, Moa Publications, Auckland, facsimile of 1948 edition, 1992, p. 727.

40. *Gaumont Graphic 627 (8) — Hon. W.F. Massey and Sir Joseph Ward (New Zealand)*, 1917, Cameraman: Unknown, Production Co.: Gaumont Graphic, BGT407051154, Reuters–ITN. This has now been transferred to http://reuters.screenocean.com and may have been renumbered.

41. *Gaumont Graphic 702 — South Africans v New Zealanders, 8 December 1917*, Cameraman: Unknown, Production Co.: Gaumont Graphic, BGT 407052001, Reuters–ITN. This has now been transferred to http://reuters.screenocean.com and may have been renumbered.

42. 'New Zealand Rugby Sides at Hornchurch', *The Sporting Life*, London, 7 October 1918.

43. 'First Rugby Defeat for NZ Hornchurch', *The Sporting Life*, London, 22 October 1918.

44. 'Rugby Football at Herne Hill', *The Sporting Life*, London, 11 November 1918. *Gaumont Graphic 799(2) — Rugby International NZ (6) v Aust (0) at Herne Hill in aid of 'Daily Express' Cheery Fund, 9 November 1918*, 1918, Cameraman: Unknown, Production Co.: Gaumont Graphic, Duration: ? BGT 407052623, Reuters–ITN. This has now been transferred to http://reuters.screenocean.com and may have been renumbered.

45. *Topical Budget 244-1 Anzac Day, 25 April 1916*, 1916, Cameraman: Unknown, Production Co.: Topical Film Co., Duration: 0:01:03, NTSV F97877. 'The Service at the Abbey.' *Grey River Argus*, 28 April 1916, p. 3.

46. 8/1837 Lance-Corporal Henry Devenish Skinner, DCM, Otago Battalion, letter diary beginning 27 April 1916. Copy in author's collection. See also Papers of Henry Devenish Skinner (1886-1978), Hocken Collection, University of Otago, Dunedin.

47. 8/2320 Pte Compton Tothill, OIR, KIA 6/8/1915; 8/2318 Pte James Gilchrist Spotswood, OIR, KIA 7/8/1915; 8/1816 Pte Robert Oliver, OIR, KIA 7/8/1915; 8/1889 Pte Peter Biggar, OIR, KIA 7/8/1915; 8/1760 Pte Alfred Ernest Jones, OIR, KIA 1/7/1915; 8/1796 Pte Edward Daniel Marshall, OIR, DOW at sea ex–Gallipoli 12/7/1915; 8/1803 Pte David Pryde Miller, OIR, KIA 27/9/1915; 8/1159 Pte Archibald Veitch, OIR, KIA 6/8/1915; 8/1725 Pte Ernest Davis, OIR, KIA 9/8/1915; 8/2325 Pte Roland Leslie Ward, OIR, KIA 16/8/1915. New Zealand Expeditionary Force, *Roll of Honour*, W.A.G. Skinner, Government Printer, Wellington, 1924.

48. Skinner, letter diary, op. cit.

49. Ibid.

50. Ibid.

51. *Inspection of Australian [New Zealand] Troops [By General Birdwood]*, *25 April 1916*, 1916, Cameraman: Pathé, Duration: 0:02.08, British Pathé 1936.12; *General Birdwood presents Medals, 25 April 1916*, 1916, Cameraman: Pathé, Duration: 0:01:06, (British Pathé 1662.31), NTSV F245688. Distinguished Conduct Medal (DCM) recipients were: Sergeant–Majors J.F. Hill, L.S. Graham and P.C. Boate; Sergeants A.W. Abbey, P.H.G. Bennett, W.H. Spencer, B.N. Tavender, K.W. Watson and J. Comrie, Corporals G.A. Tempany and H.D. Skinner; Privates A.J. Findlay, T. Stockdill, L. Crawford-Watson and Driver N. Clark.

52. *Reference Guides, Researching New Zealand and World War One (1914–1918)*, Hocken Library, Dunedin, p. 8, http://www.library.otago.ac.nz/pdf/Reference World War I July07.

53. *War Office Official Topical Budget 323-1 — Nottingham's Gift to New Zealand.* [*The Duke of Portland and Lord Desborough were present when the Duchess of Portland christened the aeroplane that the Midland City presented to New Zealand, 30 October 1917*]; 1917, Cameraman: Topical Budget, Production Co.: Topical Budget, Duration: 0:00:52, NTSV F49969.

54. *Pathé Gazette, Aeroplane Christened at Military Rally*, 1917, Cameraman: T.F. Scales?, Production Co.: Pathé Gazette, Duration: 0:01:26,; British Pathé 1886.08. T.F. Scales may be the cameraman as the film is listed in the New Zealand films taken on behalf of the New Zealand High Commission. 'Aeroplane "Nottingham"', *Auckland Star*, 19 December 1917, p. 2.

55. *Pathé Gazette, Nottingham gives Plane to Anzacs [New Zealand]*, 1917, Cameraman: T.F. Scales?, Production Co.: Pathé Gazette, Duration: 0:00:34, British Pathé 1894.27. This is duplicated in *Pathé Gazette, Anzac Battle Plane Gift*, 1917, British Pathé 1886.38.

56. Geoffrey Bentley. 'Brandon, Alfred de Bathe', from *The Dictionary of New Zealand Biography, Te Ara — the Encyclopedia of New Zealand*, http://www.TeAra.govt.nz/en/biographies/3b46/brandon-alfred-de-bathe, accessed 24 April 2017.

57. *War Office Topical Budget 349-1, Honours for Anzacs at Cambridge, 29 April 1918*, 1918, Cameraman: Unknown; Production Co.: Topical Film Co., Duration: 0:04:18; NTSV F246480. 'Anzac Day,' *The New Zealander*, London, No. 38, 10 May 1918.

58. *Annales De La Guerre (Additional Material)*, 1918, Cameraman: T.F. Scales?, Production Co.: Pathé Gazette/ French Official, Duration 0:45:53, Parade Section 0:01:48–0:06:24, (IWM 511), NTSV F246478. 'Anzac Day,' *The New Zealander*, op. cit.

59. *Pathé Gazette No. 559, Anzac Day London 25 April 1919*, 1 May 1919, Cameraman: Unknown, Production Co.: Pathé Gazette, Duration: 0:02:39, (British Pathé 2338.44), NTSV F245629. Clive Sowry film notes to author. Scenes of this film are also included in *Anzac Day — Prince of Wales Takes the Salute*, 1919, Cameraman: Pathé; Production Co.: Pathé Gazette; Duration 0:01:58; British Pathé 1918.10.

60. *For Bravery at Gallipoli — VC for Corporal Bassett*, 1916, Cameraman: Unknown, Production Co.: Pathé Gazette, Duration: 0:01:15, (British Pathé 1662.02), NTSV F245688. Tilsey Family correspondence with author.

61. *HM The King on the Clyde, 17–20 September 1917*, 1918, released 1918, Cameraman: Unknown, Production Co.: Department of Information? GB, Duration: 0:27:00, (IWM140), NTSV F246448. Smither (ed.), *Imperial War Museum Film Catalogue, Vol. 1*, op. cit., pp. 48–49.

62. 'The Glasgow Story, Royal Visit 1917', http://www.theglasgowstory.com/image/?inum=TGSA00591, accessed 20 August 2016.

63. 'Samuel Frickleton', http://www.nzhistory.net.nz/people/samuel–frickleton, Ministry for Culture and Heritage, updated 13 June 2016, accessed 20 August 2016.

64. *VC for ANZAC Heroes of the Ridge. Sergeants Frickleton and Andrew being congratulated by comrades*, 1917, Cameraman:

Unknown, Production Co.: Pathé Gazette, Duration: 0:00:43, (British Pathé 1894.07), NTSV F245768.

65. Hugh Keane, 'New Zealanders in the 1916 Irish Rebellion', http://irishvolunteers.org/new-zealanders-in-the-1916-irish-rebellion-by-hugh-keane/ accessed 7 January 2017.

66. *Easter Rising, Dublin 1916*, 1916, Cameraman: Unknown, Production Co.: UK, Duration: 0:14:03, (IWM 194), NTSV F246452.

67. Keane, New Zealanders in the 1916 Irish Rebellion', op. cit.

68. Mackenzie to Prime Minister and Defence Department, 'Cinematograph Films', dated 1 November 1917, ZWR 9/18, Personal Papers, 32700 Sgt T. F. Scales, ANZ.

69. Ibid.

70. Colonel George T. Hall, AQMG NZEF to HQ NZ Military Forces, Wellington, dated 29 March 1919, T.F. Scales Personal File, ANZ.

71. XFG 4/2255, 29 March 1919, ZWR9/18 NA WA 10/1/4, ANZ.

72. Gambrill, Reginald Frank — WWI 10/2145, WWII 804574 — Army, ANZ.

73. Irwin, John Gilmour — WW1 21842 — Army, personal file, ANZ.

74. 1 May 1917, H. Hart Diary: 20 December 1916–3 October 1917, NZ NAM. See also John Crawford, *The Devil's Own War: The First World War Diary of Brigadier-General Herbert Hart*, Exisle Publishing, Auckland, 2008.

75. *King with the New Zealanders,* 1917, Cameraman: Sergeant T.F. Scales, Production Co.: NZ Official/Pathé, Duration: 0:00:57, British Pathé 1866.37. *King with the New Zealanders*, 1917, Cameraman: Sergeant T.F. Scales, Production Co.: NZEF Official/Pathé, Duration: 0:00:26, British Pathé 1866.20. *King on Horseback*, 1917, Cameraman: Sergeant T.F. Scales, Production Co.: NZEF Official/Pathé, Duration: 0:00:17, British Pathé 2328.07.

76. *His Majesty King George V Reviewing New Zealand Troops on Salisbury Plain, 1 May 1917*, Cameraman: Sergeant T.F. Scales, Production Co.: NZ Official/Pathé Gazette, Duration: 0:07:33, NTSV F5540.

77. George Knight to 'My Dear Home', NZ OTC Sling, 6.4.17, (6.5.17), Croad, *My Dear Home*, op. cit., p. 130.

78. Tommy Scales, 'My Life of Reel Thrills,' *The Sunday Sun*, Newcastle, 20 January 1935, p. 8.

79. 'In The Firing Line', The Kinematograph and Lantern Weekly, 15 October 1914, p. 13.

80. Ibid.

81. Tommy Scales, 'My Life of Reel Thrills,' op. cit.

82. Ibid.

83. *With The New Zealand Expeditionary Force in the United Kingdom, Part I, 1917*, Cameraman: Sergeant T.F. Scales, Production Co.: NZ Official/Pathé Gazette, Duration: 0:07:53, NTSV F1001. This film is copied from the nitrate film (probably subsequently destroyed) and held by the Dominion Museum. The copying was done about or prior to 1959 during the production of *Pictorial Parade No. 96 The New Army*, one scene from it being used in the *Parade*. The film was held by the National Film Unit as library material until transferred to the New Zealand Film Archive in 1983. Clive Sowry film notes to author.

84. Chief of General Staff, New Zealand Military Forces, *New Zealand Expeditionary Force. Its Provision and Maintenance*, Government Printer, Wellington, 1919, Table XXXV, p. 54, and Table XXXVII, p. 57.

85. Major C.B. Brereton, *Tales of Three Campaigns*, Selwyn & Blount, UK, 1926, p. 249.

86. W.S. Austin, *The Official History of the New Zealand Rifle Brigade*, L.T. Watkins Ltd, Wellington, 1924, pp. 490–91; Ian McGibbon, *The Oxford Companion to New Zealand Military History*, op. cit., pp. 188–89.

87. Stewart, *The New Zealand Division*, op. cit., p. 387.

88. War Films Exhibition File, IA 29/119, ANZ.

89. Richardson to HQ NZ Military Forces Wellington, XFQ 4/5279, 9 November 1918, 1A29/119, ANZ.

90. *New Zealand Boys at Sling Camp/New Zealanders in England, 1917*, Cameraman: T.F. Scales, Production Co.: NZ Official/Pathé Gazette,; Duration: 0:04:30, NTSV F17937.

91. Steve Russell, 'Private Arthur Andrew Smith, 14th (Southland) Company, 3rd Battalion Otago Regiment, unpublished MS, Russell Family.

92. *Pathé Gazette No. 463A: New Zealand Hospital Walton-On-Thames and Oatland's Park. New Zealand Hospital Brockenhurst*, 1918, Cameraman: Sergeant T.F. Scales, Production Co.: NZ Official/Pathé Gazette, Duration: 0:00:38, NTSV F4338. This item was issued in the UK during the week of 31 January to 4 February 1918. Clive Sowry film notes to author.

93. *Pathé Gazette No. 463A: Little-Heard-Of-Parade*, 1918, Cameraman: Sergeant T.F. Scales, Production Co.: Pathé Gazette, Duration: 0:00:56, (BritishPathé 1880.16), NTSV F245766. Clive Sowry film notes to author.

94. Lieutenant-Colonel T.A. Hunter, 'New Zealand Dental Corps,' in Drew, *The War Effort of New Zealand*, op. cit., pp. 138–48.

95. *Topical Budget 272-1 City Freedom For Rt Hon. W.F. Massey ("Lord Mayor And Mr Massey Inspect New Zealand Guard of Honour Before Ceremony")*, 8 November 1916, Cameraman: Unknown, Production Co.: Topical Film Co., Duration: 50 ft, NTSV F232644.

96. *Topical Budget 286-2 New Zealand's Message to London*, 17 February 1917, Cameraman: Unknown, Production Co.: Topical Film Co., Duration: 0:00.57, NTSV F97872.

97. 'The Ministers,' *The New Zealander*, London, No. 41, 21 June 1918.

98. *Pathé Gazette No.483B: Hun Colonies [Massey and Ward at Euston Station, 15 JUNE 1918]*, 1918; Cameraman: Sergeant T.F. Scales,

Production Co.: Pathé Gazette, Duration: 0:01:15, (British Pathé 1896.10), NTSV F245775. Clive Sowry film notes to author.

99. *Topical Budget 355-2 — Fate of German Colonies, June 1918,* 1918, Cameraman: Unknown, Production Co.: Topical Budget, Duration: 0:01:10, NTSV F97891.

100. *Walton. The Rt Hon. W.F. Massey — Premier of New Zealand, presents medals to brave Anzacs.* Cameraman: T.F. Scales, Production Co: Pathé Gazette, Duration: 0:00:37, (British Pathé: 1934.05), NTSV F245782.

101. 'The Ministers', *The New Zealander,* London, No. 42, 5 July 1918.

102. 'Soldier Sports', ibid.

103. *Opening of the HQ NZ Rowing Club,* 1918, Cameraman: Sergeant T.F. Scales, Production Co.: Pathé Gazette, Duration: 0:00:52, British Pathé: 1896.21.

104. 'Rowing Regatta', *The New Zealander,* London, No. 45, 16 August 1918.

105. 'Soldier Games', ibid, No. 48, 27 September 1918.

106. *New Zealand Rowing Team,* 1918, Cameraman: Sergeant T.F. Scales, Production Co.: Pathé Gazette, Duration: 0:00:53, (British Pathé 1906.29), NTSV F245781.

107. 'New Zealand Regatta at Putney', *The Sporting Life,* London, 30 September 1918.

108. Ibid.

109. 'Soldier Sports', op. cit.

110. 'Soldier Games', op. cit., No. 46, 30 August 1918.

111. 'Service Athletics', *The New Zealander,* London, No. 47, 13 September 1918.

112. Success of the First Cinema Gymkhana: Fine Running in Mile by Cpl D Mason', *The Sporting Life,* London, 4 September 1918.

113. 'To–Day's Big Army Athletic Meeting', *The Sporting Life,* London, 7 September 1918.

114. 'Services Athletics at Stamford Bridge', *The Sporting Life,* London, 9 September 1918.

115. *British Empire and American Service Sports — Stamford Bridge September 7th 1918,* 1918, Cameraman: Ministry of Information, Production Co.: Ministry of Information, Duration: 0:05:14, NTSV F246479.

116. 'Army Athletics,' *The Sporting Life,* London, 11 October 1918.

117. 'Report on the Work of War Records Section, NZ War Records Section dated 7 October 1918, WA 1/4/31, ANZ.

118. Drew, *The War Effort of New Zealand,* op. cit.

119. 'Report on the Work of War Records Section, NZ War Records Section dated 7 October 1918, WA 1/4/31, ANZ.

120. 'War Records Section,' Attached to Report No.26, GOC NZEF UK dated 7 May 1918, WA1 10/7/ZMR 1/1/32. (R24428496), ANZ.

121. Ibid.

122. 'Report on the Work of War Records Section, NZ War Records Section dated 7 October 1918, WA 1/4/31, R24428157, ANZ.

123. Ibid.

124. 'Our Farms, Helping the Food Supplies, Success in Torquay, New Zealanders in Devon,' New Zealand War Records Section Military Publicity Department, 11 September 1918, 'New Zealand at Home, Big Drafts for France. The Unfit Produce Food,' New Zealand War Records Section Military Publicity

Department,' London 13 September 1918, AD 1, 1092, 39/377, see also 10/2 ZWR 4/13, R24428239, ANZ.

125. [*Hospital Farmyard*], 1918, Cameraman: Sergeant T.F. Scales, Production Co.: Pathé Gazette, Duration: 0:00:47, (British Pathé 2354.38), NTSV F245798.

126. *Pathé Gazette No. 492A. New Zealanders Produce their own Food,* 1918, Cameraman: Sergeant T.F. Scales, Production Co.: Pathé Gazette, Duration: 0:00:40, (British Pathé 1934.07), NTSV F245804. Clive Sowry film notes to author.

127. Lieutenant-Colonel T.G. Hall to T.F. Scales Esquire dated 31 January 1919, T.F. Scales Personal File, ANZ.

19. Laughing with Charlie Chaplin

1. Quoted by John Payne, MP, *NZPD,* 31 August 1917, CLXXIX, p. 842 and quoted in P. A. Harrison, 'The Motion Picture Industry in New Zealand, 1896–1930', unpublished MA Thesis, University of Auckland, April 1974, p. 69. Bruce W. Hayward and Selwyn P. Hayward, *Cinemas of Auckland 1896–1979,* Lodestar Press, Auckland, 1979, p. 10.

2. *Evening Post,* 12 June 1916 quoted in P.A. Harrison, 'The Motion Picture Industry in New Zealand, 1896–1930', op. cit., p. 66.

3. Ibid.

4. *NZPD,* 21 August 1917, CLXXIX, p. 449.

5. 'The Impression of a Neutral,' *Grey River Argus,* 4 November 1915, p. 7.

6. Hayward and Hayward, *Cinemas of Auckland,* op. cit., p. 10. Harrison, 'The Motion Picture Industry in New Zealand, 1896–1930', op. cit., pp. 64–65.

7. B.T. Knewstubb, *Cinemas: Dunedin and Districts 1897–1974,* Dunedin, 1974, Clive Sowry film notes to author.

8. 'Christchurch Cinemas', http://www.canterburyfilmsociety.org.nz/localcinemas/cinemas.html, accessed 13 June 2008.

9. Leonard Issit, 30 August 1917, *NZPD,* CLXXIX, p. 817, quoted in Harrison, 'The Motion Picture Industry in New Zealand 1896–1930', op. cit., pp. 69–70.

10. Ibid.

11. Hayward and Hayward, *Cinemas of Auckland,* op. cit., p. 12.

12. 'Christchurch Cinemas', accessed 13 June 2008, op. cit. The Guthries would design a number of Christchurch picture theatres during these boom years, including the Starland (1916), the Joyland (1916) in New Brighton, the Premiere Picture Palace (1916) in New Brighton, and the Crystal Palace, 'The Theatre Magnificent' (1918), with its distinctive tower and seating for 1088 people in Cathedral Square.

13. 'Historic Lyttelton Buildings, 24 London Street — The Harbour Light Theatre, Christchurch Heritage', http://www.ccc.govt.nz/Christchurch/Heritage/HistoricLytteltonBuildings/24LondonStreet.asp, accessed 9 June 2008.

14. Draft of 'Report of Mr Jolliffe, Censor of Films, Wellington on the Cinematograph industry in New Zealand,' to National Efficiency Board, dated 1917. Memo to and from Mr Jolliffe (Censor of Films) 1917, IA 83, 4/7, ANZ.

15. New Zealand Picture Supplies to W. Jolliffe, Censor of Films, dated 21 March 1917; IA 83, 4/7, ANZ.

16. Tables listed in 'Memo to and from Mr Jolliffe (Censor of Films) 1917, IA 83, 4/7, ANZ. For the quantity of film imported by each firm see Cinematograph Film Censorship Applications for Examination, September 1916–July 1920, IA 83, 28, ANZ.

17. 'Animated Pictures,' *The Colonist*, 22 June 1917, p. 7.

18. 'Amusements,' *Auckland Star*, 11 January 1915.

19. *Evening Post*, 5 June 1915, p. 2.

20. Ibid, 30 July 1915, p. 2.

21. Eric Reade, *The Australian Screen*, op. cit., pp. 65–76, 278–79. Ina Bertrand, 'The ANZAC and the Sentimental Bloke: Australian Culture and Screen Representations of World War One,' in Michael Paris (ed.), *The First World War and Popular Cinema: 1914 to the Present*, Edinburgh University Press, Edinburgh, 1999, pp. 74–93.

22. *Evening Post*, 28 February 1916, p. 2.

23. 'Entertainments,' *Evening Post*, 20 July 1915, p. 3.

24. Helen Martin and Sam Edwards, *New Zealand Film 1912–1996*, Oxford University Press New Zealand, Auckland, 1997, p. 25.

25. 'A Maori Maid's Love,' *The Sun*, 9 January 1916, quoted in Marilyn Dooley, *Photo Play Artiste Miss Lottie Lyall (1890–1925)*, NFSA, p. 26, http://www.nfsa.afc.gov.au/the_collection/collection_spotlights/lottie_lyall.html. Accessed 15 April 2008.

26. This successfully toured New Zealand and was the first film to be screened at the Grand Theatre, Dunedin, on its opening on 17 February 1915, Knewstubb, *Cinemas: Dunedin and Districts*, op. cit., p. 4.

27. John Tulloch, *Legends on the Screen: The Australian Narrative Cinema 1919–1929*, Currency Press, Sydney, 1981, p. 155. Martin and Edwards, *New Zealand Film 1912–1996*, op. cit., p. 25.

28. 'Report of the New Zealand Government Agent, Sydney' in 'Annual Report of the General Manager of Tourist and Health Resorts, 1916', *AJHR*, H-2, p. 6.

29. Dooley, *Photo Play Artiste Miss Lottie Lyall*, op. cit., p. 26. Martin and Edwards, *New Zealand Film 1912–1996*, op. cit., p. 26.

30. Jack Moller interview cutting re *Mutiny on the Bounty*, NTSV.

31. Jack Moller to Mr Don Stafford dated 21 September 1985. Dooley, *Photo Play Artiste Miss Lottie Lyall*, op. cit., p. 26.

32. Moller to Stafford, 1985, op. cit. Dooley, *Photo Play Artiste Miss Lottie Lyall* op. cit., p. 26.

33. Rudall Hayward interview with Walter Harris, NTSV.

34. *The Mutiny on the Bounty* featured at the Queen's Dominion Picture Theatre, Auckland, *Auckland Star*, October 28, 1916. *The Birth of a Nation* featured at J.C. Williamson's His Majesty's Theatre, Auckland, *Auckland Star*, 3 October 1916 and *The Battle of the Somme* opened at the Lyric Theatre and Everybody's Theatre, *Auckland Star*, 21 October 1916.

35. Bruce Babington, *A History of New Zealand Fiction Feature Film*, Manchester University Press, Manchester, 2007, pp. 41–42; Jonathan Dennis, 'Aotearoa New Zealand in the Silent Period', *Aotearoa and the Sentimental Strine*, op. cit., p. 13. Rawdon Blandford toured New Zealand with J.C. Williamson in the musical *The Bluebird* in 1913, *Evening Post*, 19 April

1913, p. 6. He also appeared in Franklyn Barrett's film *The Breaking of the Drought* (1920) after appearing on stage in Sydney in the play of the same name, F. Stuart Whyte's *Painted Daughters*, (1925) and Raymond Longford's *Peter Vernon's Silence*, (1926). IMdb, http://www.imdb.com/name/nm0926669/. Accessed 5 June 2008. Graham Shirley and Brian Adams, *Australian Cinema*, op. cit., pp. 60–66. Reade, *The Australian Screen*, op. cit., pp. 96, 121, 128, 161–62.

36. Rudall Hayward interview with Walter Harris, NTSV.

37. 'New Zealand Films,' *Theatre*, Sydney, 1 May 1916, pp. 42–43.

38. Rudall Hayward interview with Walter Harris, NTSV.

39. Reade, *The Australian Screen*, op. cit., pp. 96, 121, 128, 161–62.

40. See advertisement Everybody's Theatre, *Hawkes Bay Herald Tribune*, 6 March 1918. For the antecedents of *The Kid from Timaru* see Peter Harcourt, 'Theatre,' in Bryce Fraser (ed.) *The New Zealand Book of Events*, Reed Methuen, Auckland, 1986, p. 398.

41. *The Kid from Timaru, 21 December 1917*, Films Examined — Register of Films Viewed by the Film Censor's Office, IA60 6/2, ANZ.

42. *Timaru Herald*, 1 January 1918, pp. 1–2.

43. See advertisement, Everybody's Theatre, *Poverty Bay Herald*, 9 March 1918, p. 4.

44. 'The reminiscences of Laura Mary Hardy as told to her daughter', MS136, Auckland Museum.

45. Ibid.

46. Christopher Pugsley, *On the Fringe of Hell: New Zealanders and Military Discipline in the First World War;* Hodder & Stoughton, Auckland, 1991, p. 78.

47. *Auckland Weekly News*, 21 October 1915. See Pugsley, *On the Fringe of Hell*, op. cit., p. 78.

48. *Grey River Argus*, 17 March 1916, p. 2; 8 May 1916, p. 3;

49. 'Alien Teachers,' *Evening Post*, 8 October 1915, p. 4. See Chapter Five: 'An evident taint of enemy blood,' in Pugsley, *On the Fringe of Hell*, op. cit., pp. 77–90.

50. *Evening Post,* 29 September 1915, p. 4.

51. Harrison, 'The Motion Picture Industry in New Zealand 1896–1930', op. cit., pp. 73–81.

52. Rudall Hayward interview with Walter Harris, NTSV.

53. Maurice Hurst, *Music and the Stage in New Zealand: The Record of a Century of Entertainment*: Charles Begg & Co., Auckland, 1944, pp. 20–25.

54. 'Picture Shows in Wellington,' *The Evening Post*, 6 October 1915.

55. *Evening Post*, 4 October 1915, p. 3

56. *Evening Post*, 23 September 1915, p. 3.

57. 'The Censorship of Films,' *Auckland Star*, 5 October 1916.

58. The 'duty of censors' is prescribed in clause 4 of the Cinematograph-film Censorship Act, 1916. (1916, No. 10.) The quotation is from subclause 3. Clive Sowry film notes to author.

59. J. Allan Thomson, Director Dominion Museum to Minister of Internal Affairs dated 28 August 1915, J. McDonald Personal File, 6/2/1, Te Papa.

60. Correspondence Jolliffe to G.W. Russell, Minister of Internal Affairs, May–August 1918, Jolliffe Papers, General 1916–1925, IA 83 4/9, ANZ.

61. J. Hislop, Under-Secretary Department of Internal Affairs to Director Dominion Museum dated 10 August 1918, J. McDonald Personal File, 6/2/1, Te Papa.

62. See correspondence concerning appointment of Mr W.A. Tanner as Assistant Censor Cinematograph Films, McDonald to Director Dominion Museum dated 5 January 1925 and following folios, J. McDonald Personal File, 6/2/1, ANZ.

63. Len Cook, 'Taxes,' in Bryce Fraser (ed.) *The New Zealand Book of Events*, Reed Methuen, Auckland, 1986, p. 205.

64. See Harrison, 'The Motion Picture Industry in New Zealand 1896–1930', op. cit., pp. 80–84 and following pages.

20. Filming 'God's Own Country'

1. Sydney Taylor to wife, 'Em', Te Awaiti, 1918. 'This is the life', letter no. 2, Sydney Taylor Papers, Canterbury Public Library, Manuscripts 'New Zealand Whale Hunting with Motor Launches in Cook Strait,' S.B. Taylor Papers, ANZC 380, Christchurch Central Library.

2. *Auckland Star*, 2 October 1916. It appeared in Wellington at Fuller's His Majesty's Theatre with *The Battle of the Somme*, *Evening Post*, 16 October 1916.

3. 'Entertainments', *New Zealand Herald*, 3 October 1916, p. 5.

4. *Wanganui Chronicle*, 27 March 1916, p. 6.

5. Sydney Benjamin Taylor, (1887–1973), CPL ZMS 186, ATL, Wellington.

6. *Hawkes Bay Herald*, 14 September 1916.

7. Clive Sowry film notes to author.

8. See advertisement, 'Everybody's Theatre', *Hawkes Bay Herald*, 17 August 1917.

9. 'Annual Report of the General Manager of the Tourist and Health Resorts Department, 1918', *AJHR*, H-2, p. 9.

10. 'Mimes and Movies', *Star*, 11 May 1917, p. 3. See chapter 11.

11. *Dominion*, 8 June 1917, p. 4. See also *Wonderland of New Zealand*, 12 June 1917, 7000 feet, Register of Films viewed by the Film Censor's Office, IA 60 6/1–6/4 ANZ.

12. Theatre Royal, Christchurch, William J. Shephard presents By Special Arrangement with and under the auspices of the New Zealand Government, Kinemacolor (Nature in Nature's Own Colors) "The Wonderland of New Zealand and the World Reviewed', 10–15 September 1917, Theatre Brochure, Peter Harcourt Early Film and Theatre Programme Collection, 0443, NTSV.

13. 'Annual Report of the General Manager of the Tourist and Health Resorts Department, 1916', *AJHR*, H-2, p. 6.

14. 'Annual Report of the General Manager of the Tourist and Health Resorts Department, 1917', *AJHR*, H-2, p. 2.

15. Ibid.

16. Ibid, p. 9.

17. Ibid, p. 2.

18. *Pathé Gazette: Great Volcanic Eruption at Rotorua*, 1917, Cameraman: Unknown, Production Co.: Pathé Gazette, Australia, Duration: 0:01.26, NTSV F31423. *Hawkes Bay Herald*, 9 June 1917 advertised 'The Recent Eruption at Waimangu' at Everybody's Theatre in Hastings for that evening's programme.

19. 'Annual Report of the General Manager of the Tourist and Health Resorts Department, 1918', *AJHR*, H-2, p. 9.

20. Charles Musser, 'Holmes, Elias Burton, in Richard Abel (ed), *Encyclopedia of Early Cinema*, op. cit., pp. 303–304.

21. Clive Sowry film notes to author.

22. 'Annual Report of the General Manager, 1918', op. cit., p. 9.

23. 'Everybody's Napier', *Hawkes Bay Herald*, 23 March 1918.

24. 'Entertainments,' *Ashburton Guardian*, 22 February 1918, p. 3.

25. *New Zealand Whale Hunting With Motor Launches In Cook Strait*, 1918, Cameraman: S.B. Taylor, Production Co.: Dept of Agriculture, New Zealand Government, Duration: 0:34.08, NTSV F880. *New Zealand Whale Hunting with Motor Launches in Cook Strait Offcuts*, 1918, Cameraman: S.B. Taylor, Production Co.: Dept of Agriculture, New Zealand Government, Duration: 0:56:00, NTSV F884.

26. 10 December 1918, 'Whaling in Cook Strait,' 4000 feet, Register of Films Viewed by the Film Censor's Office, 1A 60 6/3, ANZ.

27. 'Whalers,' *Evening Post*, 7 November 1918, included in Elsdon Best Scrapbook, Vol. 6, qms, BES (213), ATL.

28. Ibid.

29. Taylor to wife, 'Em', Te Awaiti, 1918, Taylor Papers, op. cit.

30. Ibid.

31. 'Whalers' in Elsdon Best Scrapbook, op. cit.

32. *Lyttelton Times*, 28 August 1917, p. 1.

33. Ibid.

34. Ibid, 20 August 1917, p. 1. It was screened at Everybody's Theatre, Hastings on 20 October 1917, *Hawkes Bay Herald*, 20 October 1917.

35. *Akaroa Mail*, 22 January 1918.

36. *Highlander Milk Manufacture*, 1915, Cameraman: C.F. Newham, Production Co.: Dominion (NZ) Film Co., Duration: 0:17.00, NTSV F4996.

37. *Evening Star*, 10 December 1915, p. 5.

38. Harry and Andrew Mowbray, 'Matangi Factory, Historic Places Trust Restoration Proposal,' Mowbray Group, 452 Tauwhere Road, Matangi, 2004, p. 4.

39. *The Land We Live in (formerly Wellington and Assorted Scenes)*, 1918–1919, Cameraman: C.F. Newham, Production Co.: NZ Educational Film Co., Duration: 0:21:40, NTSV F11142. Sections of scenic films by other cameraman have been added to the surviving footage. Clive Sowry film notes to author.

40. *Auckland Star*, 9 July 1919, p. 7.

41. *Nelson Evening Mail*, 1 March 1919, p. 5.

42. 'The Land We Live In', *Dominion*, 25 July 1919, p. 9.

43. See chapter eight.

44. In September 1918 the Paramount Theatre, Wellington, advertised 'Splendid Industrial Film "Lilywhite Flour" Every stage of the process of producing the flour that is now a household favourite in N.Z. is depicted in striking effects. See the dainty afternoon tea scene. Film is an all N.Z. production by John Swinson Co. (NZ Films)'. *Evening Post*, 2 September 1918, p. 2.

45. 'Flickering dreams — Garnet Saunders and the New Plymouth theatre industry,' PukeAriki — Taranaki Stories, as at 2 July 2007, http://www.pukeariki.com/en/stories/entertainmentAndLeisure/gsaunders.htm. See 'Libel Action', *Taranaki Daily News*, 5 February 1916, p. 7.

46. 'Flickering dreams', op. cit.

47. *1500 School Children at New Plymouth*, 1917, Cameraman: Brandon Haughton, Production Co.: Garnet Saunders, Empire Theatre Film Co., Duration: 0:02:28; NTSV F7411.

48. *Hastings Standard*, 14 January 1916, p. 1.

49. *Mardi Gras Festival Napier New Zealand*, 1915, Cameraman: Harry Thompson?, Production Co.: Thompson–Payne, Duration: 0:10:42, NTSV F5065.

50. *Nelson Daffodil Parade*, 1916, Cameraman: Unknown, Production Co.: Unknown, Duration: 0:03:37, NTSV F23360.

51. *The Dedication Ceremony of the First Ambulance at the Auckland Hospital*, 1915, Cameraman: Unknown, Production Co.: Auckland Animated Gazette, Duration: 0:01:00, NTSV F8174.

52. 'A Worthy Cause,' *Evening Post*, 11 May 1915, p. 6.

53. 'A Wild West Show — Kinematograph Burlesque,' *Evening Post*, 2 June 1915, p. 10.

54. Ibid.

55. 'Entertainments,' *Evening Post*, 7 June 1915, p. 2.

56. Memo for Under-Secretary, Department of Internal Affairs dated 14 March 1916, 'Kinematograph Film of Patriotic Carnival at Masterton', J. McDonald Personal File, DM 6/1/6, Te Papa.

57. Ibid.

58. *Rugby League Football Newton v Ponsonby Auckland Domain*, July 1918, Cameraman: C. F. Newham, Production Co.: Dominion (NZ) Film Company, Duration: 0:02:17, NTSV F14796.

59. James Allen, Acting Prime Minister and Minister of Defence to Lieutenant General Sir Alexander Godley, Commander NZEF dated October 1917, Allen Papers, Correspodence with General Godley, R22319701, ANZ.

60. 'The Prime Minister, A New Year Exhortation,' *Timaru Herald*, 1 January 1918.

61. 'Sir Joseph Ward, A New Year Message,' *Timaru Herald*, 1 January 1918.

62. *Lyttelton Times*, 16 July 1917, p. 1.

63. *New Zealand Times*, 9 March 1918, YMCA clippings, author's collection.

64. *Dominion*, 11 March 1918, YMCA clippings, author's collection.

65. *Hutt and Petone Chronicle*, 12 March 1918, YMCA clippings, author's collection.

66. *Waimate Advertiser*, 19 March 1918, YMCA clippings, author's collection.

67. *Evening Post*, 16 October 1917, p. 8.

68. *The Surprise Packet Day in Wellington*, 1917, Cameraman: S.B. Taylor, Production Co.: Department of Agriculture, Industries, and Commerce, Duration: 0:02:16, NTSV F7107.

69. 'History of Cinemas — Queens, Dunedin,' New Zealand Cinemas, http://www.geocities.com/hd7393/nzcinframeset.htm. Accessed 14 April 2008.

70. *Evening Post*, 20 March 1916, p. 2.

71. Ibid.

72. 'Films Examined — Register of Films Viewed by The Film Censor's Office', IA60, 6/1–6/4; ANZ.

73. 'The reminiscences of Laura Mary Hardy as told to her daughter,' MS136, Auckland Museum.

74. *Akaroa Mail and Bank's Peninsula Advertiser*, 12 November 1918, p. 3.

21. Peace, sport and Cologne

1. Major-General Sir Andrew Russell Diary, 11 November 1918. The Russell Family Saga, Vol. 3, Russell Family.

2. Lieutenant-Colonel John Studholme, *New Zealand Expeditionary Force, Record of Personal Services during the War of Officers, Nurses and First-Class Warrant Officers, and other facts relating to the NZEF*, Government Printer, Wellington, 1928, p. 18.

3. David G. Williamson, *The British in Germany 1918–1930: The Reluctant Occupiers*, Berg, NY, Oxford, 1991, p. 14.

4. Williamson, *The British in Germany*, op. cit., p. 15.

5. Sir James E. Edmonds, *The Occupation of the Rhineland 1918–1929*, HMSO, London, 1987, p. 63.

6. Godley to Allen, New Zealand Minister of Defence, dated 15 November, 1918, Allen Papers, ANZ.

7. Sketch No. 2, 'Cologne Bridgehead Defences, December 1918', Edmonds, *The Occupation of the Rhineland*, op. cit., p. 60.

8. Godley to Allen, 15 November 1918, op. cit.

9. Ibid.

10. N.M. Ingram, *ANZAC Diary: A Nonentity in Khaki*, The Book Printer, Maryborough, Victoria, no date, p. 149.

11. *Arrival of New Zealand Troops at Cologne*, 1918, Cameraman: Captain H.A. Sanders, Production Co.: NZ Official, Duration: 0:12:01, NTSV F4555.

12. 'With the Artillery to the Rhine', *Chronicles of the NZEF*, Vol. V, no. 612, 25 January 1919, p. 303.

13. Interview with author, Lieutenant-Colonel L.M. 'Curly' Blyth, 5 June 1992.

14. 25038, Bombadier Bert Stokes, NZFA, Letters, Diaries and Memoirs, copies in author's collection, p. 65.

15. I.C. War Records Section to HQ NZEF UK, ZWR 4/5 dated 5 December 1918,' New Zealand War Records Section, WA1, Box 10/1/2, ANZ.

16. Captain H.A. Sanders to Brigadier-General Richardson dated 15 January 1919, New Zealand War Records Section, WA1, Box 10/1/2, ANZ.

17. Major H.S. Westmacott, IC War Records Section to Captain H.A. Sanders dated 18 January 1919, New Zealand War Records Section, WA1, Box 10/1/2, ANZ.

18. New Zealand Division, Report on Operations for November and December 1918, Progress reports of NZEF [New Zealand Expeditionary Force] operations. March 1918–April 1919 (R3885335), ANZ.

19. Stokes, op. cit., p. 65.

20. Edmonds, *The Occupation of the Rhineland*, op. cit., p. 63.

21. Ingram, *ANZAC Diary*, op. cit., pp. 150–51.

22. Stokes, op. cit., p. 66.

23. The Russell Family Saga, op. cit., 27 December 1918.

24. Ibid, 28 December 1918.

25. New Zealand Division, Mulheim to HQ NZEF dated 26 March 1919, NZ Div., Reports on Demobilisation, WA1 22/6/50, ANZ.

26. Stokes, op. cit., p. 68.

27. Jane Tolerton. 'Rout, Ettie Annie', from the *Dictionary of New Zealand Biography, Te Ara — the Encyclopedia of New Zealand*, http://www.TeAra.govt.nz/en/biographies/3r31/rout–ettie–annie, accessed 20 April 2017.

28. Christopher Pugsley, *On the Fringe of Hell*, op. cit., pp. 154–66.

29. Ibid, p. 163.

30. Brigadier-General i/c Administration, NZEF to Headquarters NZ Military Forces, Wellington dated 19 October 1918, AD1 24/46/30, ANZ.

31. Kevin Brownlow, *Behind the Mask of Innocence: Films of Social Conscience in the Silent Era*; University of California Press, Oakland, 1990, pp. 63–65. Rachel Low, *The History of the British Film, 1914–1918*; British Film Institute, London, 1973, p. 149.

32. *Whatsoever A Man Soweth*, 1917–1918, Cameraman: Joseph Best; Production Co.: Joseph Best — sponsored by Canadian Expeditionary Force and New Zealand Expeditionary Force; Duration: 0:37:34; BFI http://www.screenonline.org.uk.

33. Memo to Richardson from Major–General A.W. Robin, GOC NZ Military Forces dated 16 January 1919, AD1 24/46/30, ANZ.

34. *Evening Post*, 30 October 1919, p. 8.

35. Ibid, p. 2.

36. AA & QMG, Headquarters NZ Division to Official Photographer, NZ Reception Camp, Rouen, dated 2 March 1919, NZ War Records Section; Personal Papers of C.D. Barton, NZFA 79006, ZWR 9/83, ANZ.

37. *Paris Leave Club*, 1919, Cameraman: Sergeant C.D. Barton?, Production Co.: NZ Official/Pathé Gazette, Duration: 0:08:17, (British Pathé 1936.01), NTSV F245805. *Anzacs Sight-Seeing In Paris*, 1919, Cameraman: Sergeant C.D. Barton?, Production Co.: NZ Official/Pathé Gazette, Duration: 0:00:47, British Pathé 1890.10.

38. Green, Herbert, Huxley, 1st Cant, WW1 44060 — Army, ANZ.

39. Hahn, Lawrence Galatius, NZFA, WW1 78328 — Army, ANZ.

40. The UK-Series numbered 625 negatives when transferred to the Alexander Turnbull Library. The Library holds 538 negatives. 523 have been described and 521 have been digitised. Natalie Marshall, Curator Photographs, ATL, to author, 8 June 2017.

41. 'Early New Zealand Photographers and their Successors: Green & Hahn'; http://canterburyphotography.blogspot.be/2008/12/green–hahn.html; accessed 15 September 2016.

42. Tommy Scales, 'My Life of Reel Thrills,' *The Sunday Sun*, Newcastle, 20 January 1935, p. 8.

43. New Zealand Division, Mulheim to HQ NZEF dated 26 March 1919, NZ Div., Reports on Demobilisation, WA1 22/6/50, ANZ.

44. J.C. Neill, *The New Zealand Tunnelling Company 1915–1919*; Whitcombe & Tombs, Wellington, 1922, p. 117.

45. Neill, *The New Zealand Tunnelling Company*, op. cit., pp. 110–27.

46. Colonel H. Stewart, *The New Zealand Division*, op. cit., pp. 154–55.

47. NZ Division, Mulheim to HZ NZEF, 26 March 1919, op. cit. ANZ.

48. *New Zealanders in Cologne 1*, 1919; Cameraman: T.F. Scales, Production Co.: Pathé Gazette, Duration: 0:06:28, (British Pathé 2358.07), NTSV F245808.

49. *New Zealanders in Cologne 2*, 1919, Cameraman: T.F. Scales, Production Co.: Pathé Gazette, Duration: 0:07:04, (British Pathé 2344.25), NTSV F245809.

50. Cite Bonjean, Military Cemetery, Armentieres; http://www.cwgc.org/find–a–cemetery/cemetery/27801/, accessed 1 April 1917.

51. *Pathé Gazette No. 556: The Irony of Fate — New Zealanders Felling German Timber, used as Barricades against Germans themselves*, 21 April 1919, Cameraman: T.F. Scales, Production Co.: Pathé Gazette, Duration: 0:00:39, British Pathé 1906.44. Clive Sowry film notes to author.

52. *New Zealanders in Cologne*, 1919, Cameraman: T.F. Scales, Production Co.: Pathé Gazette, Duration: 0:08:22, (British Pathé 2358.13), NTSV F245814.

53. *New Zealanders at Auckland* [Cologne], 1919, Cameraman: T.F. Scales, Production Co.: Pathé Gazette, Duration: 0:00:47, British Pathé 1854.15.

54. *Soldiers Watching (Rugby) Football (Cologne)*, 1919, Cameraman: T.F. Scales, Production Co.: Pathé Gazette, Duration: 0:00:50, British Pathé 1906.28.

55. *Allied Occupation of Rhineland — [New Zealanders in Cologne]*, 1919, Cameraman: T.F. Scales, Production Co.: Pathé Gazette, Duration: 0:08:11,; (British Pathé 2340.26), NTSV F245807.

56. *Occupation of the Rhineland*, 1919–1920, Cameraman: T.F. Scales, Production Co.: Pathé Gazette, Duration: 0:06:22, British Pathé 2456.22. There is also the confusingly titled

New Zealanders in Cologne 2, 1918–1919, 1919, Cameraman: T.F. Scales, Production Co.: Pathé Gazette, Duration: 0:02:38, British Pathé 2456.22. This repeats the New Zealand Hohenzollern Bridge and train departure scenes from *New Zealanders in Cologne 1*, 1919; (British Pathé 2358.07), NTSV F245808, but is marred by a series of vertical lines on the film.

57. NZ Division, Mulheim to HQ NZEF, 26 March 1919, op. cit.

58. Godley to Allen dated 7 February 1919, Godley Papers, ANZ.

59. 'Notable Scullers on the Thames,' *The Sporting Life*, London, 7 April 1919.

60. 'Rowing,' *The New Zealander*, London, No. 62, 11 April 1919.

61. *New Zealand Rowing Team, 1919*, Cameraman: Pathé, Production Co.: Pathé Gazette, Duration: 0:00:53, (British Pathé 1906.29), NTSV F245781.

62. 'French Sport and Sportsmen: Huge Crowd to Witness "Henley in Paris",' *The Sporting Life*, London, 1 May 1919.

63. 'Marlow Regatta,' *The Sporting Life*, London, 23 June 1919.

64. *Whitaker's Almanack*; J. Whitaker & Sons, London, 1920, pp. 757–58.

65. 'Colonial Wins at Henley,' *The Sporting Life*, London, 7 July 1919

66. 'Fine Running at Y.M.C.A. Sports: Remarkable Relay by New Zealanders' *The Sporting Life*, London, 26 May 1919.

67. 'New Zealanders win at Woking,' *The Sporting Life*, London, 10 June 1919.

68. William J. Baker, *Sports in the Western World*, University of Illinois Press, 1988, pp. 209–210.

69. Mark A. Robison, 'Recreation in World War I and the Practice of Play in *One of Ours*,' Steven Trout (ed.), *Cather Studies, Vol. 6: History, Memory and War*, University of Nebraska Press, 2006, p. 166.

70. *The New Zealander*, London, No. 69, 18 July 1919.

71. *Athletes from Various Allied Countries March at the Opening of the Inter-Allied Games in Paris France, 1919*, Camera: Unknown, Production Co.: Unknown, Duration: ?, NTSV F232855.

72. 'Inter-Allied War Games,' *Otago Daily Times*, 8 September 1919, p. 10.

73. 'Dan Mason,' *Evening Post*, 30 November 1935, p. 24.

74. Joseph Mills Hanson, (ed.), *The Inter-Allied Games. Paris 22nd June to 6th July 1919*, The Games Committee, Paris, 1919, p. 490, http://www.archive.org/details/cu31924014114353, accessed 1 April 2017.

75. 'The Final,' *Northern Advocate*, 12 September 1919, p. 3.

76. 'Dan Mason,' *Evening Post*, 30 November 1935, p. 24.

77. *Inter-Allied Games Pershing Stadium*, 1919, Cameraman: Unknown, Production Co.: US Official, Duration: 0:12:04:10, http://www.buyoutfootage.com/pages/titles/pd_na_653.php#. WOJreYVOI2w; accessed 1 April 2017.

78. Hanson, *The Inter–Allied Games*, op. cit.

79. 'Inter-Allied Games', gbrathletics, www.gbrathletics.com. Accessed 1 April 2017.

80. Sergeant E.F. Benjamin and Sergeant D.L. Mason to OC Base Records, undated letter, referred to Dominion Museum 10/10/34. D23/1/5, ANZ.

81. 'Soldier Athletes', *New Zealand Herald*, 4 October 1919, p. 10.

82. Hanson, *The Inter–Allied Games*, op. cit., p. 456.

83. Venater, 'Rugby Reflections' *The Sporting Life*, London, 13 November 1918.

84. Ibid.

85. 'Victory for Wales', *The Sporting Life*, 27 December 1918.

86. 'Rugby Reflections', *The Sporting Life*, 29 January 1919.

87. 'Important Decisions by Army Rugby Union', *The Sporting Life*, 14 January 1919.

88. 'NZ Rugby Rivals at Richmond', *The Sporting Life*, 20 January 1919.

89. Ibid.

90. *Pathé Gazette No. 531: Rugby "Test" Match* [*New Zealand Trench Team Beat Home Team by 5 Points To 3*], January 1919, Cameraman: T.F. Scales, Production Co.: Pathé Gazette, Duration: 0:00:49, British Pathé 1928.04. Clive Sowry film notes to author.

91. *The "All Blacks" Win. (Leicester Beaten by 19 Points To Nil.)*, 1919, Cameraman: T.F. Scales?, Production Co.: Pathé Gazette, Duration: 0:01:12, British Pathé 1902:37. (This is the same film as British Pathé 1928.02.)

92. 'Maoris Fine Rugby Win', *The Sporting Life*, London, 6 February 6, 1919.

93. 'Maoris Beaten', *The Sporting Life*, London, 17 February 1919.

94. 'Empire Rugby at Swansea', *The Sporting Life*, 3 March 1919.

95. 'Service Rugby', *The New Zealander*, No. 62, 11 April 1919.

96. Ibid.

97. 'Empire Rugby League', *The Sporting Life*, 7 April 1919.

98. *Pathé Gazette No. 533, Victorious "All Blacks" Beat Mother Country After "Ding Dong" Match By 6 Points To Three*. 10 January 1919, Cameraman: Pathé, Production Co.: Pathé Gazette, Duration: 0:00:48, British Pathé 1906.43. Clive Sowry film notes to author.

99. 'Big Surprise in Rugby Tournament', *The Sporting Life*, London, 9 April 1919.

100. 'Twickenham Rugby Finale,' *The Sporting Life*, 23 April 1919.

101. 'French Rugby Team Beaten,' *The Sporting Life*, 21 April 1919.

102. *Whitaker's Almanack*, 1920, pp. 754–55.

103. 'French Sport and Sportsmen: New Zealand Win Again at Rugby', *The Sporting Life*, 8 May 1919.

104. Stewart, *The New Zealand Division*, op. cit., p. 614.

105. Ibid, p. 583.

106. Ibid, p. 613. Stewart incorrectly gives his initials as M. Loveday. See Loveday, Leslie George Vivian — WW1 10/3938 — Army, ANZ.

107. *Civic Reception of Lieut. J. Grant VC,* 1919, Cameraman: Unknown, Production Co.: A.M. Conroy, Opera House, Hawera, Duration: 0:05:00; Ref: 500,002, www.audiovisual. archives.govt.nz, ANZ.

108. *Investiture By HM The King At Buckingham Palace, and March of Overseas Troops Through London, May 3rd 1919,* Cameraman: C.D. Barton?, Production Co.: C. & E. Films, Duration: 0:03:12, NTSV F17841.

109. *Empire Pageant,* 1919, Cameraman: Pathé, Production Co.: Pathé Gazette, Duration: 0:03:05, British Pathé 1918.11.

110. W.H. Montgomery, 'Repatriation,' in Drew, *The War Effort of New Zealand,* op. cit., p. 164.

111. Major S. Westmacott, IC NZ War Records Section to Messrs Pathe Freres Ltd, Editorial Branch, 28 February 1919, ZWR 4/13, WA1 10/1/2, ANZ.

112. *Pathé Gazette No. 541, Brockenhurst and Lymington — A Token of Appreciation (New Zealanders present flags prior to their departure for home);* 1919, Cameraman: Pathé, Production Co.: Pathé Gazette, Duration: 0:03:20, British (Pathé 1904.28), NTSV F245797. Clive Sowry film notes to author.

113. *Pathé Gazette No. 535, Liverpool — Good–Bye to "Blighty". (New Zealand Soldiers Leave England with their Wives.);* 6 February 1919, Cameraman: Pathé, Production Co.: Pathé Gazette, Duration: 0:00:23, (British Pathé 1904.09); NTSV F245796.

114. *Pathé Gazette No. 613, Torquay — Good-bye "Digger" — Mayor bids farewell to last Batch of married NZ soldiers who are returning with their wives and sometimes … a little "Digger",* 6 November 1919, Cameraman: Pathé, Production Co.: Pathé Gazette, Duration: 0:01:23, British Pathé 200.16.

115. John R Pike, 'The New Zealand Discharge Depot in Torquay, 1917–1919', *The Volunteers: The Journal of the New Zealand Military Historical Society;* 42:3, March 2017, pp. 8–20.

22. Filming the Prince of Wales

1. H. Hector Bolitho, *With the Prince in New Zealand;* Edwin Sayes, Auckland, 1920, p.15.

2. Barry O'Sullivan, Matthew O'Sullivan, *New Zealand Army: Personal Equipment 1910-1945,* Willson Scott, Christchurch, 2005, pp. 318 20.

3. *Australasian Gazette 451 [Excerpt], Maori Contingent Home,* 1919, Cameraman: Unknown, Production Co.: *Australasian Gazette,* Duration: 0:01:14,NTSV F29570. The *Australasian Gazette 451* was not released in New Zealand. It was not released in Australia until 11 October 1919. Clive Sowry film notes to author.

4. 'The Maori Battalion,' *Auckland Weekly News,* 10 April 1919, p. 17. Illustrations: pp. 31, 34–35, 38–39.

5. Ibid.

6. 'Hui Aroha,' *Poverty Bay Herald,* 9 April 1919, p. 5. The paper misspells his name. It is also misspelt and the Belgian Croix de Guerre is incorrectly listed instead of the French, in Wayne Mc Donald, *Honours and Awards to the New Zealand Expeditionary Force in the Great War 1914-1918,*(revised 2nd edition), Richard Stowers, Hamilton, p. 137. See Karini, Toi — WW1 20680 — Army, ANZ.

7. *Poverty Bay Herald,* 28 August 1919, p. 7.

8. Report of the Director of the Dominion Museum, Annual Report of the Department of Internal Affairs, *AJHR,* 1919, H-22.

9. *Te Hui Aroha ki Turanga (Gisborne Hui Aroha),* 1919, Cameraman: James McDonald, Production Co.: Dominion Museum, Duration: 0:13:03, NTSV F7882.

10. Wayne Stack, *The New Zealand Expeditionary Force in World War 1;* Osprey, Men-at-Arms, Oxford, 2011, p. 39.

11. 'The "Four-Chevron Men"', *Dominion,* 17 March 1919, p. 6.

12. 'Amusements', *Evening Post,* 2 April 1919, p. 5.

13. 'Hawera's VC', *Wanganui Chronicle,* 30 October 1919, p. 2.

14. 'Local and General', *Taranaki Daily News,* 3 November 1919, p.4. *Civic Reception of Lieut. J. Grant VC,* 1919, Cameraman: Unknown, Production Co.: A.M. Conroy, Opera House, Hawera, Duration: 0:05:00, Ref: 500,002, www.audiovisual. archives.govt.nz, ANZ.

15. Two films, each of 500 feet, are listed in the Censors Register (IA 60 6/4, ANZ) on 21 August 1919, *Arrival of HMS New Zealand* and *HMS New Zealand. The Arrival of HMS New Zealand in Wellington* featured in the cinemas throughout New Zealand. See advertisement Crystal Palace Picture Theatre, Christchurch, *Sun,* 30 August 1919, p.1. See also *Pathé Gazette (Excerpt) HMS New Zealand;* 1913? Cameraman: Unknown; Production Co.: Pathé Gazette; Duration: 0:00:46; British Pathé: 1924.06. *Pathé Gazette: (Excerpt) Jellicoe Departs on HMS New Zealand,* 1919; Cameraman: Unknown; Production Co.: Pathé Gazette; Duration: 0:01:20; British Pathé 2352.21. *Pathé Gazette: (Excerpt) Welcome Home! Admiral Jellicoe Returns in HMS New Zealand at Conclusion of his World Tour,* 1920; Cameraman: Unknown; Production Co.: Pathé Gazette; Duration: 0:00:41; British Pathé 204.43.

16. *His Excellency's Visit to the Cook Islands and Samoa,* 1919, Cameraman: S.B. Taylor, Production: Department of Agriculture, Duration: 0:06:33, NTSV F6552.

17. Sydney Taylor to his wife, 'My dear Em', Rarotonga dated 4 June 1919. (Though dated 4 June it becomes a 30-page running diary covering events of the trip.) Sydney B. Taylor, Photographs, Letters and Memorabilia of a Professional Photographer, (1887–1973), ANZC 380, Christchurch City Libraries.

18. Ibid.

19. Weddell, *Soldiers from the Pacific,* op. cit., pp.112–121.

20. 'Peace celebrations in 1919', https://nzhistory.govt.nz/war/1919-peace-celebrations, Ministry for Culture and Heritage, updated 27 August 2014, accessed 19 July 2017.

21. *Otago Witness,* 23 July 1919.

22. *Otago Daily Times,* 21 July 1919, p. 5.

23. *Peace Day Procession,* 1919, Cameraman: Henry H. Gore; Production Co.: Henry C. Gore, Plaza Cinema, Duration: 0:08:18, NTSV F3799.

24. *Otago Daily Times,* 29 August 1919, p.1 and 3 September 1919, p. 1.

25. 'Royal Visits', in An Encyclopaedia of New Zealand, edited by A.H. McLintock, originally published in 1966. *Te Ara — The Encyclopedia of New Zealand,* updated 18-Sep-2007, http://www. TeAra.govt.nz/1966/R/RoyalVisits/en, accessed 23 January 2009.

26. Bolitho, *With the Prince in New Zealand,* op. cit., p.15.

27. Hislop, Under-Secretary, Department of Internal Affairs to Taylor, Government Cinematograph Operator, memo dated 10 April 1920. Sydney B. Taylor, Photographs, Letters and Memorabilia of a Professional Photographer, op. cit.

28. Sydney B. Taylor, ibid.

29. The Prince's Visit', *Evening Post*, 25 November 1920, p. 8. "Origins of New Zealand's National Film Unit" by C.J. Morton (c.1963). Original typescript at Archives New Zealand, Wellington. AAPG 6025/16a, ANZ.

30. Films Examined — Register of Films Viewed by the Film Censor's Officer, IA 60, 6/4, ANZ.

31. *Prince's Tour of New Zealand*, 1920, Cameramen: S.B. Taylor, C.D. Barton, Frank Stewart, Production Co.: NZ Government/ NZ Picture Supplies Ltd, Duration: 0:41:57, NTSV F4097.

32. *The Prince of Wales in Maoriland*, 1920, Cameraman: H.C. Gore, Production Co.: H.C. Gore & Co., Duration: 0:08:47, NTSV F4095.

33. *The Prince of Wales at Rotorua*, 1920, Cameraman: S.B. Taylor, C.D. Barton, Frank Stewart, Production Co.: NZ Government/ NZ Picture Supplies Ltd, Duration: 0:15:00, NTSV F4094.

34. *Prince in New Zealand: Wellington's Wonderful Welcome*, 1920, Cameraman: Unknown, Production Co.: Pathé Gazette, Duration: 0:04:50, NTSV F102444. *50,000 Miles with the Prince of Wales*, 1920, Cameraman: Captain William Barker, Production Co.: Topical Film Company, Duration: 1:43:00, IWM 843. See Smither, *Imperial War Museum Film Catalogue, Volume I*, op cit., p. 343.

35. *He Pito Whakaatu i te Hui i Rotorua: Scenes At The Rotorua Hui*, 1920, Cameraman: James McDonald, Production Co.: Dominion Museum, Duration: 0:26:40, NTSV F2808.

36. Report of the Director of the Dominion Museum, Annual Report of the Department of Internal Affairs, *AJHR*, 1920, H-22, p. 14.

37. Index to Cinematograph Films, IA 29/113, 'Loan of Cinematograph Films' DM 3/4/4, ANZ.

38. Acting Chief Clerk to Under-Secretary, Department of Internal Affairs, memo dated 4 May 1921, IA 29/113, 'Loan of Cinematograph Films', DM3/4/4, ANZ.

39. Correspondence and Telegrams — Memorandum of Agreement by New Zealand Government to lease to New Zealand Picture Supplies Ltd, exclusive right to show in New Zealand films released by the British War Office — 13 February 1918, IA 34/12/16. (R18919876) ANZ.

40. *Evening Post*, 4 June 1919, p. 2.

41. Ibid, 27 December 1920, p. 2.

42. Acting Director, Dominion Museum to Under-Secretary Department of Internal Affairs, Memo dated 2 September 1920, IA 13/11/65 on 'Loan of Cinematograph Films,' DM 3/4/4, Te Papa.

43. *Evening Post*, 27 December 1920, p. 2.

44. Under-Secretary Department of Internal Affairs to Acting Director Dominion Museum, memo dated 11 December 1923, 'Loan of Cinematograph Films', DM, 3/4/4, ANZ.

45. Director Dominion Museum to Under-Secretary, Internal Affairs Department, memo dated 29 September 1931,' Loan of Cinematograph Films', DM 3/4/4, Te Papa.

46. Under-Secretary Department of Internal Affairs to Director Dominion Museum, memo dated 27 July 1927, 'Loan of Cinematograph Films,' DM 3/4/4, Te Papa.

47. *Otago Daily Times*, 28 April 1921, p. 1.

48. *Anzac Day Service*, 1921, Cameraman: Unknown, Production Co.: Unknown, Duration: 0:02:53, NTSV F10327.

49. Ian McGibbon, *New Zealand Battlefields and Memorials of the Western Front*, Oxford University Press, Auckland, 2001.

50. *Memorial to 7,000 'DIGGERS': to the memory of 7000 Diggers — NZ Division Memorial Unveiled on Site of Switch Trench — Scene of Continuous Fighting for 23 Days in Somme Battle, 16 October1922*, 1922, Cameraman: Pathé Gazette, Production Co.: Pathé Gazette, Duration: 0:03:08 British Pathé 286.01.

51. 'New Zealand on Somme', *New Zealand Herald*, 10 October 1922, p. 7.

52. *New Zealand Memorial Long Version, 12 August 1924*, Cameraman: Pathé Gazette, Production Co.: Pathé Gazette, Duration: 0:05:29,; (British Pathé 350.14), NTSV F245642.

53. *New Zealand Memorial Short Version, 12 August 1924*, 1924, Cameraman: Pathé Gazette, Production Co.: Pathé Gazette, Duration: 0:00:47, British Pathé 350.15. There is also a short documentary that surveys the major monuments on the Western Front in 1917 and starts with the New Zealand Battlefield Monument at Messines. *New Zealand Memorial at Messines*, 1927, Cameraman: Unknown, Production Co.: Unknown, Duration: 0:02:53, NTSV F13776.

54. *For Remembrance. Victorious All Blacks make pilgrimage to grave of Dave Gallagher* [sic] — *Captain of the first All Blacks' Team, Poperinghe, Belgium*; 15 January 1925, Cameraman: Pathé Gazette; Production Co.: Pathé Gazette; Duration: 0:01:41; British Pathé 368.22.

55. See Filmography. For filming between the wars, see Diane Pivac, 'The Rise of Fiction between the Wars,' and Clive Sowry, 'Non-Fiction Films: Between the Wars,' in Pivac et. al., *New Zealand Film: An Illustrated History*, op. cit., chapters 2 and 3.

56. Jinty Rorke, 'A.H. Whitehouse — An Early Film Pioneer,' *Historical Review: Bay of Plenty Journal of History*, 32-1, May 1984, pp. 17–23.

57. 'Albertlander Passes: Introducer of Motion Pictures', *Northern Advocate*, 17 April 1929, p. 4.

Bibliography

AJHR   *Appendices to the Journals of the House of Representatives*
ATL   *Alexander Turnbull Library*
AWM   *Australian War Museum*
NFSA   *National Film and Sound Archive, Australia*
NTSV   *Ngā Taonga Sound & Vision — New Zealand Archive of Film, TV & Sound*
NZFA   *New Zealand Film Archive*

Books

Abel, Richard, *The Ciné Goes to Town: French Cinema 1894–1914*, University of California Press, Berkeley, 1994.

Abel, Richard (ed.), *Encyclopedia of Early Cinema*, Routledge, London and New York, 2005.

Altman, Rick, *Silent Film Sound*, Columbia University Press, NY, 2004.

Annabell, N., *Official History of the New Zealand Engineers during the Great War 1914–1919*, Evans, Cobb & Sharpe, Wanganui, 1927.

Antonini, Anna (ed.), *Il Film e i suoi multipli/ Film and its Multiples*, Forum, University of Udine, 2003.

Ashmead-Bartlett, Ellis, *Ashmead-Bartlett's Despatches from the Dardanelles*, George Newnes, London, 1915.

Ashmead-Bartlett, Ellis, *The Uncensored Dardanelles*, Hutchinson & Co., London, 1928.

Aspinall-Oglander, Brigadier-General C.F., *Military Operations Gallipoli: Vol. I, Inception of the Campaign to May 1915*, William Heinemann Ltd, London, 1929.

Aspinall-Oglander, Brigadier-General C.F., *Military Operations Gallipoli: Vol. II, May 1915 to the Evacuation*, William Heinemann Ltd, London, 1932.

Austin, Lieutenant-Colonel W.S., *The Official History of the New Zealand Rifle Brigade*, L.T. Watkins Ltd, Wellington, 1924.

Babington, Bruce, *A History of the New Zealand Fiction Feature Film*, Manchester University Press, Manchester, 2007.

Badsey, Stephen, *The British Army in Battle and Its Image 1914–1918*, Birmingham War Series, Continuum, London, 2009,

Baker, William J., *Sports in the Western World*, University of Illinois Press, 1988.

Barnes, John, *The Beginnings of the Cinema in England. Volume 1, 1894–1896*, University of Exeter Press, Exeter, 1998.

Barnes, John, *The Beginnings of the Cinema in England 1894–1901, Volume 2, 1897*, University of Exeter Press, 1996.

Barnes, John, *The Beginnings of the Cinema in England 1894–1901, Volume 3, 1898*, University of Exeter Press, 1996.

Barnes, John, *The Beginnings of the Cinema in England 1894–1901, Volume 4, 1899*, University of Exeter Press, Exeter, 1996.

Barnes, John, *The Beginnings of Cinema in England, 1900, Volume 5*, University of Exeter Press, Exeter, 1997.

Bassett, Michael, *Sir Joseph Ward — A Political Biography*, Auckland University Press, 1995.

Bean, C.E.W., Diary, January 1918, AWM 38, Official History, 1914–1918 War: Records of C.E.W., Official Historian, 3DRL606/96/1.

Bean, C.E.W., *Gallipoli Mission*, Australian War Memorial, Canberra, 1948.

Bean, C.E.W., *The Australian Imperial Force in France 1917*, 9th edition, Angus & Robertson, Sydney, 1939.

Bean, C.E.W., *The Story of ANZAC*, Vol. 1; (5th edition), Angus & Robertson, Sydney.

Bell, Christopher M., *Churchill and Sea Power*, Oxford University Press, Oxford, 2013.

Bertrand, Ina (ed.), *Cinema in Australia: A Documentary History*, New South Wales University Press, Kensington, NSW, 1989.

Bertrand, Ina and William D. Routt, *The Story of the Kelly Gang: 'The Picture That Will Live Forever,'* The Moving Image, No. 8, Australian Teachers of Media, St Kilda, Victoria, 2007.

Birdwood, Field-Marshal Lord, *Khaki and Gown: An Autobiography*, Ward Lock & Co., London, 1941.

Bolitho, H. Hector, *With the Prince in New Zealand*, Edwin Sayes, Auckland, 1920.

Bolton, Barbara, *Booth's Drum*, Hodder & Stoughton, Australia, 1980.

Bowser, Eileen, *History of the American Cinema. Vol. 2. The Transformation of Cinema 1907–1915*, University of California Press, Berkeley, 1994.

Bradwell, Cyril R., *Fight the Good Fight: The Story of the Salvation Army in New Zealand 1883–1983*, A.H. & A.W. Reed, Wellington, 1982.

Brenchley, Fred and Elizabeth, *Mythmaker: Ellis Ashmead–Bartlett: The Englishman Who Sparked Australia's Gallipoli Legend*, John Wiley & Sons, Milton, Queensland, 2005.

Brereton, Major C.B., *Tales of Three Campaigns*, Selwyn & Blount, UK, 1926.

Brittenden, Wayne, *The Celluloid Circus: The Heyday of the New Zealand Picture Theatre, 1925–1970*, Godwit, Auckland, 2008.

Brooking, Tom, *Richard Seddon: King of God's Own: The Life and Times of New Zealand's Longest Serving Prime Minister*, Penguin, Auckland, 2014.

Brownlow, Kevin, *Behind the Mask of Innocence: Films of Social Conscience in the Silent Era*, University of California Press, Oakland, 1990.

Brownlow, Kevin, *The War The West and the Wilderness*, Secker and Warburg, London, 1978.

Burton, O.E., *The Silent Division: New Zealanders at the Front 1914–1919*, Angus & Robertson, Sydney, 1935; reprinted O.E. Burton, *The Silent Division: New Zealanders at the Front 1914–1919 & Concerning One Man's War*, (John H. Gray, ed.), John Douglas Publishing, Christchurch, 2014.

Byrne, Lieutenant J.R., *New Zealand Artillery in the Field 1914–1918*, Whitcombe & Tombs, Wellington, 1922.

Cain, George, *Packsaddle to Rolls Royce*, Foveaux Publishing, Auckland, 1976.

Callister, Sandy, *The Face of War: New Zealand's Great War Photography*, Auckland University Press, Auckland, 2008.

Carbery, Lt Col. A.D., *The New Zealand Medical Service in the Great War 1914–1918*, Whitcombe & Tombs, Christchurch, 1924.

Chester, R.H., N.A.C. McMillan and R.A. Palenski, *The Encyclopedia of New Zealand Rugby*, Moa Publications, Auckland, 1987.

Chief of General Staff, New Zealand Military Forces, *New Zealand Expeditionary Force. Its Provision and Maintenance*, Government Printer, Wellington, 1919.

Chief of General Staff, New Zealand Military Forces, *War, 1914–1918. New Zealand Expeditionary Force. Its Provision and Maintenance,* Government Printer, Wellington, 1919.

Churchman, Geoffrey B., *Celluloid Dreams: A Century of Film in New Zealand*, IPL Books, Wellington, 1997.

Clayton, Garry James, *Defence Not Defiance: The Shaping of New Zealand's Volunteer Force*, D. Phil Thesis, University of Waikato, 1992.

Coe, Brian, *The History of Movie Photography*, Eastview Editions, Westfield, NJ, 1981.

Coffrey, John and Bernie Wood, *The Kiwis: 100 Years of International Rugby League*, Hodder Moa, 2007.

Collins, Diane, *Hollywood Down Under: Australians at the Movies: 1896 to the Present Day,* Angus & Robertson, North Ryde, 1987.

Condliffe, J.B., *Te Rangi Hiroa: The Life of Sir Peter Buck*, Whitcombe & Tombs, Auckland, 1966.

'Conditions of Employment of Official War Correspondent.' Government Printer, Wellington, 1915.

Cooke, Peter and John Crawford, *The Territorials: The History of the Territorial and Volunteer Forces of New Zealand*, Random House, Auckland, 2011.

Cowan, J., *Official Record of the New Zealand International Exhibition of Arts and Industries, held at Christchurch, 1906–7*, Government Printer, Wellington, 1910.

Cowan, James, *The New Zealand Wars: A History of the Maori Campaigns, and the Pioneering Period: Volume 1: 1845–64, Volume II: The Hauhau Wars, 1864–72*, Government Printer, Wellington, 1983.

Crawford, John (ed.), *The Devil's Own War: The First World War Diary of Brigadier-General Herbert Hart*, Exisle, Auckland, 2008.

Crawford, John with Peter Cooke, *No Better Death: The Great War Diaries and Letters of William G. Malone*, Reed, Auckland, 2005.

Croad, Nancy (ed.), *My Dear Home: The Letters of the three Knight brothers who gave their lives during WW1*, Croad, Auckland, 1995.

Dennis, Jonathan and Clive Sowry, *The Tin Shed: The origins of the National Film Unit*, National Film Unit, New Zealand Film Archives, Wellington, c.1981.

Dennis, Jonathan and Sharon Dell, *James McDonald Kai-Whakaahua: Photographs of the Tangata Whenua*, National Library Gallery, December 1989–20 January 1990. National Library of New Zealand, Wellington, 1989.

Dennis, Jonathan, 'Aotearoa New Zealand in the Silent Period', *Aotearoa and the Sentimental Strine: Making Films in Australia and New Zealand in the Silent Period*, Moa Films, Wellington, 1993.

Downes, Peter, *Shadows on the Stage: Theatre in New Zealand, The First Seventy Years,* John McIndoe, Dunedin, 1975.

Downes, Peter, *The Pollards: A Family and its Child and Adult Opera Companies in New Zealand and Australia, 1880–1910*, Steele Roberts, Wellington, 2002.

Drew, H.T.B., *The War Effort of New Zealand: A Popular History of (a) Minor Campaigns in which New Zealanders took part; (b) Services not fully dealt with in the Campaign Volumes (c) The Work at the Bases*, Whitcombe & Tombs, Wellington, 1923.

Earl of Liverpool, *The Voyages of His Majesty's Hospital Ships "Marama" and "Maheno" (2nd Volume)*, Whitcombe and Tombs, Wellington, 1917.

Edmonds, Sir James E., *The Occupation of the Rhineland 1918–1929*, HMSO, London, 1987.

Fenwick, Sir George, *American Notes 1924 and France and Belgium in War Time*, Otago Daily Times and *Witness* newspapers, Dunedin, 1927.

Fielding, Raymond, *The American Newsreel 1911–1967*, University of Oklahoma Press, Norman, 1972.

Frances, Neil, *Safe Haven: The Untold Story of New Zealand's Largest Ever Military Camp: Featherston*, Fraser Books, 2012.

Fraser, Alistair H., Andrew Robertshaw and Steve Roberts, *Ghosts on the Somme: Filming the Battle June–July 1916*, Pen & Sword Military, Barnsley, 2009.

Fraser, Bryce (ed.), *The New Zealand Book of Events*, Reed Methuen, Auckland, 1986.

General Staff, War Office, *Field Service Pocket Book, 1914*, reprinted with Amendments 1916, HMSO, London, 1917.

George, Merrilyn, *Ohakune: Opening to a New World*, Kapai Enterprises, Ohakune, 1990.

Giford, Dennis, *The British Film Catalogue, Non-Fiction Films Volume 2*, BFI Publishing, London, 1999.

Greenhalgh, Elizabeth, Th*e French Army and the First World War*, Cambridge University Press, Cambridge, 2014.

H. Wise and Co., *New Zealand Index, Otago Daily Times* and *Witness* newspapers, Dunedin, 1917.

Halpern, Paul G., *The Naval War in the Mediterranean 1914–1918*, Naval Institute Press, Annapolis, 1987.

Hampseed, B.W., *Richard Arnst: The Single Sculls World Champion from New Zealand*, Acorn Press, Christchurch.

Hanson, Joseph Mills (ed.), *The Inter-Allied Games. Paris 22nd June to 6th July 1919*, The Games Committee, Paris, 1919, http://www.archive.org/details/cu31924014114353.

Harcourt, Peter, *A Dramatic Appearance: New Zealand Theatre 1920–1970*, Methuen, Wellington, 1978.

Harding, Colin and Simon Popple, *In the Kingdom of the Shadows: A Companion to Early Cinema*, Cygnus Arts, London, 1996.

Harper, Glyn and the National Army Museum, *Images of War: New Zealand and the First World War in Photographs*, HarperCollins, Auckland, Second edition, 2013.

Harvie, E.F., *George Bolt: Pioneer Aviator: Foundations of a Future*, A.H. & A.W. Reed, Wellington, 1974.

Hayward, Bruce W. and Selwyn P. Hayward, *Cinemas of Auckland 1896–1979*, Lodestar Press, Auckland, 1979.

Hayward, Henry J., *Here's to Life! The Impressions, Confessions and Garnered Thoughts of a Free-Minded Showman*, Oswald & Sealy, Auckland, 1944.

Herbert, Stephen and Luke McKernan (eds), *Who's Who of Victorian Cinema*, British Film Insititue Publishing, London, 1996.

Hurst, Maurice, *Music and the Stage in New Zealand: The Record of a Century of Entertainment*, Charles Begg & Co., Auckland, 1944.

Ingram, N.M., *ANZAC Diary: A Nonentity in Khaki*, The Book Printer, Maryborough, Victoria, no date.

Jones, Bernard E., *The Cinematograph Book: A Complete Practical Guide to the Taking and Projecting of Cinematograph Pictures*, Cassell and Co., London, Revised edition, 1920.

Jouineau, André, *Officers and Soldiers of the French Army during the Great War, Vol. II. 1915–1918*, Histoire & Collections, Paris, 2009.

Kinlock, Terry, *Devils on Horses: in the words of the Anzacs in the Middle East 1916-1919*, Exisle, Auckland, 2007.

Kinlock, Terry, *Echoes of Gallipoli: in the words of New Zealand's Mounted Riflemen*, Exisle, Auckland, 2005

Knewstubb, B.T., *Cinema: Dunedin and Districts 1897–1974*, Dunedin, 1974.

Knight, E.F., *With the Royal Tour: A Narrative of the Recent Tour of the Duke and Duchess of Cornwall and York through Greater Britain, including His Royal Highness's Speech delivered at the Guildhall, on December 5, 1901*, Longmans, Green and Co., London, 1902.

Koszarski, Richard, *History of the American Cinema, Volume 3. An Evening's Entertainment: The Age of the Silent Feature Picture 1915–1928*, Charles Scribner's Sons, New York, 1990.

Lawson, Will, *Historic Trentham1914–1917*, Wellington Publishing Co., Wellington, 1917.

Layman, R.D., *Naval Aviation in the First World War: Its Impact and Influence*, Caxton Publishing, London, 1996.

Loughnan, R.A., *Royalty in New Zealand: The Visit of their Royal Highnesses The Duke and Duchess of Cornwall and York to New Zealand, 10th to 27th June 1901. A Descriptive Narrative*, Government Printer, Wellington, 1902.

Low, David, *Low's Autobiography*, Michael Joseph, London, 1956.

Low, Rachel, *The History of the British Film, 1914–1918*, British Film Institute, London, 1973.

Macdonald, Andrew, *On My Way to the Somme: New Zealanders and the Bloody Offensive of 1916*, HarperCollins, Auckland, 2005.

Mackay, Don (ed.), *The Trooper's Tale: The History of the Otago Mounted Rifles*, Turnbull Ross Publishing, Dunedin, 2012.

Mahoney, J.D., *Down at the Station: A Study of the New Zealand Railway Station*, Dunmore Press, Palmerston North, 1987.

Malthus, Cecil, *Anzac: A Retrospect*, Reed, Auckland, 2002.

Marchand, Pierre, translated Claire Llewellyn, *One Hundred Years of Cinema*, Kingfisher Kaleidoscopes, London, 1995.

Martin, Helen and Sam Edwards, *New Zealand Film 1912–1996*, Oxford University Press New Zealand, Auckland, 1997.

Maynard, Jeff, *The Unseen Anzac*, Scribe, Brunswick, Victoria, 2015.

McClure, Margaret, *The Wonder Country: Making New Zealand Tourism*, Auckland University Press, Auckland, 2004.

McDonald, Wayne, *Honours and Awards to the New Zealand Expeditionary Force in the Great War 1914-1918*, (revised 2nd edition), Richard Stowers, Hamilton.

McFarlane, Brian, Geoff Mayer and Ina Bertrand (eds), *The Oxford Companion to Australian Film*, OUP, Melbourne, 1999.

McGibbon, Ian, *New Zealand Battlefields and Memorials of the Western Front*, Oxford University Press, Auckland, 2001.

McGibbon, Ian, *New Zealand's Western Front Campaign*, Bateman, 2016.

McGibbon, Ian, *The Oxford Companion to New Zealand Military History*, OUP, Auckland, 2000.

McKernan, Luke (ed.), *A Yank in Britain: The Lost Memoirs of Charles Urban, Film Pioneer*, Projection Box, Hastings, 1999.

McKernan, Luke, 'Fitzsimmons, Robert (1862–1917),' Stephen Herbert & Luke McKernan (eds), *Who's Who of Victorian Cinema*, BFI, London.

McKinlay, Ernest, *Ways and By-Ways of a Singing Kiwi with the N.Z. Divisional Entertainers in France*, privately printed, Dunedin, 1939.

McLean, Gavin, *New Zealand Tragedies, Shipwrecks and Maritime Disasters*, Grantham House, 1991.

McLintock, A.H., *An Encyclopaedia of New Zealand*, Volume 1, Government Printer, Wellington, 1966.

Miller, David P., *From Snowdrift to Shellfire: Capt. James Francis (Frank) Hurley 1885–1962*, David Ell Press, Sydney, 1984.

Miller, Eric, *Camps, Tramps and Trenches: The Diary of a New Zealand Sapper, 1917*, A.H. & A.W. Reed, Dunedin, 1939.

Mulgan, David, *The Kiwi's First Wings: The Story of the Walsh Brothers and the New Zealand Flying School 1910–1924*, Wingfield Press, Wellington, 1960.

Musser, Charles, *The Emergence of Cinema: Volume 1: The American Screen to 1907*, History of the American Cinema Series, Charles Scribner's Sons, New York, 1990.

Nairn, Bede and Serle, Geoffrey (ed.), *Australian Dictionary of Biography,* Melbourne University Press, Melbourne, 1979.

Neil, J.C., *The New Zealand Tunnelling Company 1915–1919,* Whitcombe & Tombs, Christchurch, 1922.

New Zealand Expeditionary Force, *Roll of Honour,* W.A.G. Skinner, Government Printer, Wellington, 1924.

Newman, Stanley (ed.), *Shackleton's Lieutenant: The Nimrod Diary of A.L.A. Mackintosh, British Antarctic Expedition, 1907–1909,* Polar Publications, Christchurch, 1990.

Nicolson, Harold, *King George the Fifth: His Life and Reign,* Constable, London, 1952.

Nolan, Melanie (ed.), *Revolution: The 1913 Great Strike in New Zealand,* Canterbury University Press, Christchurch, 2005.

Nominal Roll of Persons Employed in Each Department (other than Postal and Railways) giving length of service as on 31st March 1907 and salaries for financial year 1907–8 chargeable on the Consolidated Fund, *AJHR,* 1907, Wellington.

NZEF War Diary 1914, Government Printer, Wellington, 1915.

O'Connor, P.S., 'The Recruitment of Maori Soldiers 1914–1918,' *Political Science,* XIX, 2, 1967.

O'Sullivan, Barry and Matthew O'Sullivan, *New Zealand Army: Personal Equipment 1910-1945,* Willson Scott, Christchurch, 2005.

Olssen, Erik, *The Red Feds; Revolutionary Unionism and the New Zealand Federation of Labour, 1908–1914,* Auckland, 1988.

Olssen, Erik and Marcia Stenson, *A Century of Change: New Zealand 1800–1900,* Longman Paul, Auckland, 1989.

Orange, Claudia (ed.), *Dictionary of New Zealand Biography: Volume Two: 1870–1900,* Bridget Williams Books and Department of Internal Affairs, Wellington, 1993.

Palenski, Ron, *Rugby: A New Zealand History,* Auckland University Press, Auckland, 2015.

Paris, Michael (ed.), *The First World War and Popular Cinema: 1914 to the Present,* Edinburgh University Press, Edinburgh, 1999.

Philippe, Nathalie, Christopher Pugsley, John Crawford and Matthias Strohn (eds), *The Great Adventure Ends: New Zealand and France on the Western Front,* John Douglas, Christchurch, 2013.

Polaschek, R.J., *Government Administration in New Zealand,* NZIPA, OUP, London, 1958.

Powles, Lieutenant Colonel C. Guy, *The New Zealanders in Sinai and Palestine,* Whitcombe & Tombs, Auckland, 1922.

Price, Simon, *New Zealand's First Talkies: Early film-making in Otago and Southland, 1896–1939,* Otago Heritage Books, Dunedin North, 1996.

Pugsley, Christopher and Charles Ferrall, *Remembering Gallipoli: Interviews with New Zealand Gallipoli Veterans,* Victoria University Press, Wellington, 2015.

Pugsley, Christopher, *Gallipoli: The New Zealand Story,* Oratia Books, Auckland, 2016.

Pugsley, Christopher, *On the Fringe of Hell: New Zealanders and Military Discipline in the First World War,* Hodder & Stoughton, Auckland, 1991.

Pugsley, Christopher, *Te Hokowhitu A Tu: The Maori Pioneer Battalion in the First World War,* Libro, Auckland, 2015.

Pugsley, Christopher, *The Anzac Experience: New Zealand, Australia and Empire in the First World War,* Oratia Books, Auckland, 2016.

Ramsaye, Terry, *A Million and One Nights: A History of the Motion Picture through 1925,* Simon & Schuster, NY, 1964 reprint.

Reade, Eric, *History and Heartburn: The Saga of Australian Film 1896–1978,* Associated Universities Presses, East Brunswick, NJ, 1981.

Reade, Eric, *The Australian Screen: A Pictorial History of Australian Film Making,* Lansdowne Press, Melbourne, 1975.

Reilly, Catherine, *Scars upon my Heart: Women's poetry and verse of the First World War,* Virago Press, London, 1981.

Rice, Geoffrey W., *Heaton Rhodes of Otahuna: the illustrated biography,* Canterbury University Press, 2008.

Riffenburgh, Beau, *Nimrod: Ernest Shackleton and the Extraordinary Story of the 1907–1909 British Antarctic Expedition,* Bloomsbury, London, 2004.

Rittaud-Hutinet, Jacques with Yvelise Dentzer, *Letters: Auguste and Louis Lumière,* Faber and Faber, London and NY, 1995.

Robinson, David, *From Peep Show to Palace: The Birth of American Film.* Columbia University Press, New York, 1996.

Roth, H., *Trade Unions in New Zealand,* A.H. & A.W. Reed, Wellington, 1973.

Sabine, James (ed.), *A Century of Australian Cinema,* Australian Film Institute, William Heinemann, Port Melbourne, 1995.

Serle, Geoffrey (ed.), *Australian Dictionary of Biography,* Melbourne University Press, Melbourne, 1988.

Shirley, Graham and Brian Adams, *Australian Cinema: The First Eighty Years,* Angus & Robertson and Currency Press, Sydney, 1983.

Smither, Roger (ed.), *Imperial War Museum Film Catalogue, Volume 1, The First World War Archive,* Greenwood Press, Westport, Connecticut, 1994

Solnit, Rebecca, *River of Shadows: Eadweard Muybridge and the Technological Wild West,* Viking, NY, 2003.

Sowry, Clive, *Filmmaking in New Zealand: A brief historical survey,* New Zealand Film Archive: Friends of the Film Archive (NZ), Wellington, 1984.

Stack, Wayne, *The New Zealand Expeditionary Force in World War 1,* Osprey, Men-at-Arms, Oxford, 2011

Stewart, Colonel H., *The New Zealand Division, 1916–1919,* Whitcombe & Tombs, Wellington, 1921.

Streible, Dan, *Fight Pictures: A History of Boxing and Early Cinema,* University of California Press, Berkeley, 2008.

Studholme, J., *New Zealand Expeditionary Force, Record of Personal Services during the War of Officers, Nurses and*

First-Class Warrant Officers, and other facts relating to the NZEF, 1928.

Swan A.C., *History of New Zealand Rugby Football, Volume 1 1870–1945*, Moa Publications, Auckland, facsimile of 1948 edition, 1992.

The Modern Bioscope Operator, Ganes Limited, London, 1911, p. 5

Thompson, Frank, *Texas' First Picture Show: The Star Film Ranch*, Republic of Texas Press, Plano, 1996.

Tobin, Christopher, *The Original All Blacks: 1905–1906*, Hodder, Moa, Beckett, Auckland, 2005.

Trout, Steven (ed.), *Cather Studies, Volume 6: History, Memory and War*, University of Nebraska Press, 2006.

Tulloch, John, *Legends on the Screen: The Australian Narrative Cinema 1919–1929*, Currency Press, Sydney, 1981.

Twisleton, Corporal F., *With the New Zealanders at the Front: A Story of Twelve Months Campaigning in South Africa*, Whitcombe & Tombs, Christchurch, Wellington and Dunedin, 1903.

Unknown, *Onward: HMS New Zealand*, Swiss & Co., Naval Printers, Fore Street, Devonport.

Waite, Major Fred, *The New Zealanders at Gallipoli*, Whitcombe & Tombs, Wellington, 1919.

Wallace, Sir Donald Mackenzie, *The Web of Empire: A Diary of the Imperial Tour of their Royal Highnesses the Duke and Duchess of Cornwall and York in 1901*, Macmillan, London, 1902.

Stones Wellington, Hawke's Bay and Taranaki Directory, Dunedin, 1905.

Walton, Colonel Peter, *A Celebration of Empire: A Centenary Souvenir of the Diamond Jubilee of Queen Victoria 1837–1897*, Spellmount Publishers in association with the Victorian Military Society, Staplehurst, 1997.

Weddell, Howard, *Soldiers from the Pacific: The Story of Pacific Island Soldiers in the New Zealand Expeditionary Force in World War One*, Defence of New Zealand Study Group, Wellington, 2015.

Whitaker's Almanack, J. Whitaker & Sons, London, 1920.

Williamson, David G., *The British in Germany 1918–1930: The Reluctant Occupiers*, Berg, NY, Oxford, 1991.

Other sources

Aimer, Peter, 'Aviation', *Te Ara — the Encyclopedia of New Zealand*, updated 21–Sep–2007 URL: http://www.TeAra.govt.nz/EarthSeaAndSky/SeaAndAirTransport/Aviation/en.

Anderson, Bob, 'History of the McCauley Family', http://www.bobanderson.co.uk/familyhistory/mccauleys.php, accessed 21 June 2008.

'Arnst, Richard.' (1883–1953), New Zealand Sports Hall of Fame, http://www.nzhalloffame.co.nz.

Ashmead-Bartlett, Ellis, Diary of 1916, Australia, New Zealand, America. ICS 84 A/12/3, School of Commonwealth Studies, Library, University College of London.

Ballara, Angela, 'Tunuiarangi, Hoani Paraone', *Dictionary of New Zealand Biography. Te Ara — the Encyclopedia of New Zealand*, updated 30 October 2012, http://www.TeAra.govt.nz/en/biographies/3t44/tunuiarangi–hoani–paraone, accessed 30 November 2016.

Barrett, Franklyn W, Australasian Cinema, New: 8 November 2012|Now: 18 November 2013|garrygillard [at] gmail.com.

http://australiancinema.info/directors/barrettfranklyn.html, accessed 18 December 2016.

Bentley, Geoffrey, 'Brandon, Alfred de Bathe', *The Dictionary of New Zealand Biography. Te Ara — the Encyclopedia of New Zealand*, http://www.TeAra.govt.nz/en/biographies/3b46/brandon-alfred-de-bathe, accessed 24 April 2017.

BFI, *R W Paul: The Collected Films 1895-1908*, dvd and booklet.

Brooking, Tom, 'Thomas Noble Mackenzie, 1853–1930', Claudia Orange (ed.), *Dictionary of New Zealand Biography, Volume Three, 1901–1920*, Auckland University Press, Department of Internal Affairs, Auckland and Wellington, 1996.

Bush, W. Stephen, 'Loved by a Maori Chieftess,' *Moving Picture World*, 8 March 1913.

Byrnes, Paul, 'AWM Western Front,' Australian Screen Online, http://aso.gov.au/titles/collections/awm–western–front/, accessed 24 March 2017.

Byrnes, Paul, 'Gallipoli on Film,' Australian Screen Online, http://aso.gov.au/titles/collections/gallipoli–on–film/Australian Screen, accessed 13 February 2017.

Cite Bonjean, Military Cemetery, Armentieres; http://www.cwgc.org/find–a–cemetery/cemetery/27801/ accessed 1 April 1917.

Cody, J F, Draft, 'Fred and Ita': including the letters and diary of Fred Cody, edited by his daughter, Patricia Fry. Copy in author's possession.

Collins, Diane, 'Spencer, Cosens (1874–1930)', *Australian Dictionary of Biography*, National Centre of Biography, Australian National University, http://adb.anu.edu.au/biography/spencer–cosens–8604/text15027, published first in hard copy 1990, accessed online 11 December 2015. This article was first published in hard copy in *Australian Dictionary of Biography*, Volume 12, Melbourne University Press, 1990.

Correspondence of Gaston and Hortense Méliès to Paul Méliès dated 2 October 1912, Rotorua, and 2 November 1912, Brisbane, New Zealand, NTSV.

Cory-Wright, Captain S., to his father, France, dated 14 July 1917, RV 6294, NAM.

Dennis, Jonathan, and Clive Sowry, 'Hinemoa,' *Onfilm*, Dec 1983; p.40

Dooley, Marilyn, *Photo Play Artiste Miss Lottie Lyall (1890–1925)*, NFSA, Australia, accessed 15 April 2008, http://www.nfsa.afc.gov.au/the_collection/collection_spotlights/lottie_lyell.html.

Downes, Peter, 'Fuller, John 1850–1923,' *Dictionary of New Zealand Biography*, updated 7 April 2006, http://www.dnzb.govt.nz/.

Downes, Peter. 'Hanna, George Patrick', from *Dictionary of New Zealand Biography. Te Ara — the Encyclopedia of New Zealand*, http://www.TeAra.govt.nz/en/biographies/4h14/hanna–george–patrick, accessed 8 March 2017.

Dutton, Philip, 'More vivid than the written word': Ellis Ashmead-Bartlett's film *With the Dardanelles Expedition 1915; Historical Journal of Film, Radio and Television*, 24:2, 2004

Fagan, Tony, interview, 'Gallipoli: The New Zealand Story', documentary material, TVNZ Archive, National Army Museum, Waiouru.

Fechner, Christian, *Georges Méliès*. dvd and booklet, StudioCanal, 2011.

Fewster, Kevin, 'Ellis Ashmead–Bartlett and the making of the Anzac legend'. *Journal of Australian Studies*, 6:10, 1982.

Frickleton, Samuel, http://www.nzhistory.net.nz/people/samuel–frickleton, Ministry for Culture and Heritage, updated 13 June 2016, accessed 20 August 2016.

Fuller, John, (1879–1959), *Australian Dictionary of Biography*, http://www.adb.online.anu.edu.au/biogs/.

'From Queen Street to the Front', anzacsightsound.org, Sights and Sounds of World War I.

'The Glasgow Story, Royal Visit 1917', http://www.theglasgowstory.com/image/?inum=TGSA00591, accessed 20 August 2016.

Gray, Alan, 'One of the French Foreign Legion's Finest — A Kiwi,' enclosed in Anna Leask, 'Gallipoli 100: Our forgotten 'French' hero,' nzherald.co.nz, 14 April 2015. http://www.nzherald.co.nz/nz/news/article.cfm?c_id=1&objectid=11432103, accessed 20 January 2017.

Green HH and L G Hahn, 'Early New Zealand Photographers and their Successors: Green & Hahn'; http://canterburyphotography.blogspot.be/2008/12/green–hahn.html; accessed 15 September 2016.

Hamilton, General Sir Ian, 'Report by the Inspector General of Overseas Forces on the Military Forces of New Zealand', *The Times Documentary History of the War, Vol. X, Overseas, Part 2*, The Times, London, 1919.

Hardy Laura May, 'The reminiscences of Laura May Hardy as told to her daughter,' MS136, Auckland Institute and Museum Library

Harrison, P.A., 'The Motion Picture Industry in New Zealand 1896–1930', unpublished MA Thesis, University of Auckland, April 1974.

Hill, E. Trevor, '"The Movie Monger": A volume of plaudits deserved and otherwise by a praise agent bent on capturing the nimble shilling & life long patrons,' D0783, NTSV.

'Historic Lyttelton Buildings, 24 London Street — The Harbour Light Theatre, Christchurch Heritage', accessed 9 June 2008, http://www.ccc.govt.nz/Christchurch/Heritage/HistoricLytteltonBuildings/24LondonStreet.asp.

'History of Cinemas — Queens, Dunedin,' New Zealand Cinemas, http://www.geocities.com/hd7393/nzcinframeset.htm.

'History of Cinemas: King's Cinema, Christchurch, New Zealand Cinemas'. http://www.geocities.com/hd7393/nzcinframeset.htm.

Hoffman, Doré, 'Melies in New Zealand,' *Moving Picture World*, 8 February 1913.

Imashev, George, 'Gallipoli: The film *With the Dardanelles Expedition: heroes of Gallipoli*', The Joint Imperial War Museum/Australian War Memorial Battlefield Study Tour to Gallipoli, September 2000, George Imashev, 2001.

Ingham, Gordon, 'Everyone's Gone to the Movies: The Sixty Cinemas of Auckland — And Some Others', no date, MS, NTSV.

'Inventing Entertainment: The Motion Picture and Sound Recordings of the Edison Companies', The Library of Congress, http://rs6.loc.gov/ammem/edhtml/edhome.html.

'Joining the Flotilla', http://anzacsightsound.org/videos/the–first–troopships–depart.

'Just as the Sun Went Down,' words and music, http://www.archive.org/details/DudleyMacdonough.

Keane, Hugh, New Zealanders in the 1916 Irish Rebellion,' http://irishvolunteers.org/new-zealanders-in-the-1916-irish-rebellion-by-hugh-keane/, accessed 7 January 2017.

Kosmider, Michael, 'Archival Films of Gallipoli', Michael Kosmider, July 2014, with supporting documents and DVD. AWM.

Kosmider, Michael, 'Images and Notes: Supplement to the "Archival films of Gallipoli." Michael Kosmider, July, 1914.

Kosmider, Michael, 'A study into Ellis Ashmead-Bartlett's Gallipoli footage and its various versions and interpretations.' PAFU0696, dvd, AWM.

Laughren, Pat, 'Mobsby, Henry William (1860–1933)', *Australian Dictionary of Biography — Online edition*, http://www.adb.online.anu.edu.au/biogs, accessed 12 June 2008.

Lighting, 'Inventing Entertainment: The Motion Picture and Sound Recordings of the Edison Companies', The Library of Congress, http://rs6.loc.gov/ammem/edhtml/edhome.html.

Long, Chris and Clive Sowry, 'Australia's First Films: Foreign Producers in Australia, 1901', *Cinema Papers*, June 1995.

Long, Chris and Clive Sowry, 'Australia's First Films: Our First Producers Abroad', *Cinema Papers*, August 1995.

Long, Chris and Clive Sowry, 'Australia's First Films: the Royal Visit Films of 1901', *Cinema Papers*, March 1995.

Long, Chris, 'Australia's First Films Fact and Fable, Part One: The Kinetoscope in Australia', *Cinema Papers 91*.

Long, Chris, 'Australia's First Films, Facts and Fable, Part Seven: Screening the Salvation Army', *Cinema Papers 97*.

Long, Chris, 'Australia's First Films: Facts and Fable, Part Three: Local Production Begins,' *Cinema Papers 93*.

Long, Chris, 'Australia's First Films Milestone and Myths, Part Eight: Soldiers of the Cross', *Cinema Papers 99*.

'MacMahon, James, (1858?–1915)', 'MacMahon, Charles (1861?–1917), *Australian Dictionary of Biography — Online edition*, accessed 1 August 2008, http://www.adb.online.anu.edu.au/biogs.

'The Maori,' programme, Rotorua Maori Mission Choir and Entertainers, Town Hall, Wellington, 26 July 1910. Photo image: 71610-ac-1-1, ATL.

Matthews, Jill Julius, 'Modern nomads and national film history: the multi-continental career of J.D. Williams', in *Connected Worlds: History in Transnational Perspective*, ANU–E Press, http://epress.anu.edu.au.

McCallum, Janet, 'Ross, Forrestina Elizabeth and Ross, Malcolm', *Dictionary of New Zealand Biography. Te Ara — the*

Encyclopedia of New Zealand, http://www.TeAra.govt.nz/en/biographies/2r28/ross-forrestina-elizabeth, accessed 30 May 2017.

McGibbon, Ian, 'Duigan, John Evelyn', *Dictionary of New Zealand Biography. Te Ara — the Encyclopedia of New Zealand*, http://www.TeAra.govt.nz/en/biographies/4d24/duigan–john–evelyn, accessed 6 June 2017.

McGibbon, Ian, 'Richardson, George Spafford', *Dictionary of New Zealand Biography. Te Ara — the Encyclopedia of New Zealand*, http://www.TeAra.govt.nz/en/biographies/3r16/richardson-george-spafford, accessed 21 March 2017.

McInroy, Patrick, 'The American Melies', *Sight and Sound*, Autumn 1979.

McMillan, N.A.C., 'Fitzsimmons, Robert 1863–1917', *Dictionary of New Zealand Biography*, http://www.dnzb.govt.nz, accessed 10 July 2006.

McWilliams, Dave, 'Motion Picture History in Auckland, 1896–1941', written in four parts and published in *The Auckland Star*, reference 791.43, M17, Auckland Public Library.

Méchin, David, 'Escadrille MF 98T — F398, Escadrille 524', http://albindenis.free.fr/Site_escadrille/escadrille524.htm, accessed 26 January 2017.

Mowbray, Harry and Andrew, Matangi Factory, Historic Places Trust Restoration Proposal, Mowbray Group, 452 Tauwhere Road, Matangi, 2004.

Newham, C.F Photographers' Index, Whanganui Regional Museum.

Organ, M.K., 'Strike 1912: Looking for Australia's Earliest Worker's Film', *Illawarra Unity — Journal of the Illawarra Branch of the Australian Society for the Study of Labour History*, Volume 5, Issue 1, 2005, Article 4.

Ng Taonga Sound & Vision, *For King & Country: New Zealand's First World War on Film*. dvd, 2015.

Palenski, R., *Malcolm Ross: a forgotten casualty of the Great War*. Thesis, Master of Arts, University of Otago, 2007. Retrieved from http://hdl.handle.net/10523/338 https.

'Peace celebrations in 1919', https://nzhistory.govt.nz/war/1919-peace-celebrations, Ministry for Culture and Heritage, updated 27 August 2014, accessed 19 July 2017.

Pike, John R., 'The New Zealand Discharge Depot in Torquay, 1917–1919', *The Volunteers: The Journal of the New Zealand Military Historical Society*, 42:3, March 2017.

Pugsley, Christopher, 'Gallipoli Footprints,' in Charles Ferrall and Harry Ricketts (eds), *How We Remember: New Zealanders and the First World War*, Victoria University Press, Wellington, 2014.

Pugsley, Christopher, 'HMS *New Zealand*: Gift to the Empire', *New Zealand Defence Quarterly*, No. 7, Summer 1994.

Pugsley, Christopher, 'Images of Te Hokowhitu A Tu in the First World War,' in Santanu Das (Ed) Race, *Empire and First World War Writing*, Cambridge University Press, Cambridge, 2011.

Pugsley, Chris, 'The Magic of Moving Pictures: Film Making 1895-1918,' in Diane Pivac, Frank Stark and Lawrence McDonald, (ed) *New Zealand Film: An Illustrated History*, Te Papa Press, Wellington, 2011, pp.29-51.

Pugsley, Christopher, '"Who is Sanders?" New Zealand's Official Cameraman on the Western Front 1917-1919.' *Stout Centre Review*, 5:1, March 1995,

Ralston, Bruce, 'Wilkinson, Charles Anderson 1868–1956', *Dictionary of New Zealand Biography*, www.dnzb.govt.nz, accessed 20 September 2002.

Rankin, Alex, 'Stock Actualities, Lectures and Extended Film Runs (1902–1909)', from his 'The History of Cinema Exhibition in Exeter 1895–1918'. Dissertation, University of Exeter, 2001, Bill Douglas Centre, Teaching and Learning Articles, http://www.ex.ac.uk/bdc/teaching_article_02_chapterthree.

Rapp, Dean, 'The British Salvation Army, The Early Film Industry and Urban Working-Class Adolescents, 1897–1918,' *Twentieth Century British History*, Volume 7, No. 2, 1996.

Richardson, F.H., 'Lessons for Operators: Chapter IX — The Picture', *The Moving Picture World*, 9 May 1908.

Rorke, Jinty, 'A.H. Whitehouse — An Early Film Pioneer,' *Historical Review: Bay of Plenty Journal of History*, 32-1, May 1984.

Rose, Margaret, 'Richardson, Charles Douglas (1853–1932), *Australian Dictionary of Biography — Online Edition*, http://www.adb.online.anu.edu.au/biogs.

'Royal Visits', in *An Encyclopaedia of New Zealand*, edited by A.H. McLintock, originally published in 1966. *Te Ara — The Encyclopedia of New Zealand*, updated 18-Sep-2007, http://www.TeAra.govt.nz/1966/R/RoyalVisits/en, accessed 23 January 2009.

Rutledge, Martha, 'Barrett, Walter Franklyn (1873–1964)', *Australian Dictionary of Biography, Volume 7, 1891–1939, A–Ch*, Bede, Nairn and Geoffrey Serle (eds), Melbourne University Press.

Sanders, Henry Armytage, (sometimes Armitage), *Who's Who of British Newsreels*, British Universities Newsreel Database, British University Film and Video Council, newsreel@bufvc.ac.uk; http://joseph.bufvc.ac.uk/BUND/staff/detail.php?id=33185, accessed 29 August 2008.

Saunders Garnet, 'Flickering dreams — Garnet Saunders and the New Plymouth theatre industry', Puke Ariki — Taranaki Stories, http://www.pukeariki.com/en/stories/entertainmentAndLeisure/g.saunders.htm.

'Semple, Hon. Robert', *An Encyclopaedia of New Zealand*, A.H. McLintock (ed.), originally published in 1966. *Te Ara — The Encyclopedia of New Zealand*, updated 18 September 2007, http://www.TeAra.govt.nz/1966/S/SempleHonRobert/en.

'Sidney Cook', see also 'Cook's Pictures', Australian Variety Theatre Archive, https://ozvta.com/entrepreneurs–a–f/, accessed 30 November 2016.

Sorlin, Pierre, 'French Newsreels of the First World War,' *Historical Journal of Film, Radio and Television*, 24:4, 2004.

Sowry, Clive, 'Eighty Years Ago — New Zealand's First Films', *Sequence: the Journal of the Wellington Film Society*, November 1978.

Sowry, Clive, 'Eighty Years of Film Exhibition in Wellington,' *Sequence: the Journal of the Wellington Film Society*, October 1977.

Sowry, Clive, 'Eighty Years of Film Exhibition in Wellington, Part Two: 1897–1900', *Sequence: the Journal of the Wellington Film Society*, July 1977.

Sowry, Clive, 'Eighty Years of Film Exhibition in Wellington, Part Three: 1901', *Sequence: the Journal of the Wellington Film Society*, October 1977.

Sowry, Clive, 'Eighty Years of Film Exhibition in Wellington, Part Four: 1902–1903', *Sequence: the Journal of the Wellington Film Society*, May 1978.

Sowry, Clive, 'Eighty Years of Film Exhibition in Wellington, Part Six: West's Pictures and the Brescians', *Sequence: the Journal of the Wellington Film Society*, March 1979.

Sowry, Clive, 'Eighty Years of Film Exhibition in Wellington, Part Eight: 1907', *Sequence: the Journal of the Wellington Film Society*, February 1980.

Sowry, Clive, 'Eighty Years of Film Exhibition in Wellington, Part Nine: 1908', *Sequence: the Journal of the Wellington Film Society*, March 1980.

Sowry, Clive, 'Eighty Years of Film Exhibition in Wellington, Part Ten: The Lasting Picture Show', *Sequence: the Journal of the Wellington Film Society*, September 1980.

Sowry, Clive, 'A Very Special Collection', *Archifacts: Bulletin of the Archives and Records Association of New Zealand*, No. 16, December 1980.

Sowry, Clive, 'Film Identification by Examination of Physical Characteristics', *Archifacts: Bulletin of the Archives and Records Association of New Zealand*, 1988/2, June 1988.

Sowry, Clive, 'Film Pioneers of New Zealand — Macmahon's Cinematographe', *The Big Picture*, Issue 10, Spring 1996.

Sowry, Clive, 'Film Pioneers of New Zealand: Edison's Kinetoscope,' in *The Big Picture*, Issue 8, Autumn 1996.

Sowry, Clive, 'Film Pioneers of New Zealand: Northcote's Kinematograph on tour. Letters from an early film exhibitor,' *The Big Picture*, Issue 13, Spring/Summer 1997.

Sowry, Clive, 'Film Pioneers of New Zealand: The Illusionist and the Cinematographe,' *The Big Picture*, Issue 11, Summer 1997.

Sowry, Clive, 'Newham, Charles Frederick 1880–1960', *Dictionary of New Zealand Biography*, www.dnzb.govt.nz, accessed 20/9/2002.

Sowry, Clive, 'The Kinematograph Arrives in New Zealand, *The Big Picture*, Issue 9, Winter 1996.

Sowry, Clive, 'The "Lost" Méliès New Zealand Films,' NTSV.

Sowry, Clive, 'New Zealand's First Films,' *Archifacts: Bulletin of the Archives and Record Association of New Zealand*, No. 2, n.s., June 1977.

Sowry, Clive, 'Non-Fiction Films: Between the Wars,' Diane Pivac, Frank Stark and Lawrence McDonald, (ed), *New Zealand Film: An Illustrated History*, Te Papa Press, Wellington, 2011, pp.79-101.

Sowry, Clive, 'Tarr, George Herrmann', first published in the *Dictionary of New Zealand Biography*, vol. 3, 1996. Te Ara - the Encyclopedia of New Zealand, https://teara.govt.nz/en/biographies/3t6/tarr-george-herrmann (accessed 19 September 2017).

Spr G.C. Lyttleton, 'Pierrots in Picardy: A Khaki Chronicle by "One of Them"', Unpublished ms, RV 5344, NAM.

Story Shop, '*Médaillé Extraordinaire* exhibition opens in France', 29 June 2016, http://storyshop.co.nz/new–blog/2016/6/28/mdaill–extraordinaire–exhibition–opens–in–france.

Theatre Royal, Christchurch, 'William J. Shephard presents By Special Arrangement with and under the auspices of the New Zealand Government, Kinemacolor (Nature in Nature's Own Colors) "The Wonderland of New Zealand and the World Reviewed", 10–15 September 1917'. Theatre brochure, Peter Harcourt Early Film and Theatre Programme Collection, 0443, NZFA.

Thomas, David, 'McCubbin, Frederick (1885–1917)', *Australian Dictionary of Biography — Online Edition*, http://www.adb.online.anu.edu.au/biogs.

Thompson, John Mansfield, 'Austin, Louis Daly Irving 1877–1967,' *Dictionary of New Zealand Biography*, updated 22 June 2007, http://www.dnzb.govt.nz.

Tolerton, Jane, 'Rout, Ettie Annie', *Dictionary of New Zealand Biography, Te Ara — the Encyclopedia of New Zealand*, http://www.TeAra.govt.nz/en/biographies/3r31/rout–ettie–annie, accessed 20 April 2017.

Whitehouse, C.M., 'A Pioneer of Circuit Exhibition: The trials and problems of the early days', *NZ Motion Picture Exhibitors' Bulletin*, 22 September 1956.

Williams, Margaret, 'MacMahon, Charles (1861?–1917)', *Australian Dictionary of Biography — Online Edition*, http://www.adb.online.anu.edu.au/biogs/.

Williams, Margaret, 'MacMahon, James (1858?–1915)', *Australian Dictionary of Biography — Online Edition*, http://www.adb.online.anu.edu.au/biogs/.

'The World's Columbian Exposition', http://en.wikipedia.org/wiki/World_Columbian_Exposition.

Wyatt, Caleb, Scrapbook of New Plymouth film clippings, NZFA, 16 June 1910.

Yarwood, Vaughan, 'Smokestacks and paddle-wheels', *New Zealand Geographic*, Issue 048, Oct.–Dec. 2000, https://www.nzgeo.com/stories/smokestacks–and–paddle–wheels/, accessed 9 December 2016.

Suggested websites

anzacsightsound.org. Sights and Sounds of World War 1: http://anzacsightsound.org/explore/entire-war/all

Archives New Zealand: http://archives.govt.nz/

Auckland War Memorial Museum, Online Cenotaph: http://www.aucklandmuseum.com/war-memorial/online-cenotaph

Australian War Memorial: https://www.awm.gov.au/

BFI (British Film Institute): http://www.bfi.org.uk/

British Pathé: https://www.britishpathe.com/

Collections, National Library and Alexander Turnbull Library: https://natlib.govt.nz/collections

Gaumont Pathé Archives: http://www.gaumontpathearchives.com/

Imperial War Museums, United Kingdom: http://www.iwm.org.uk/

Library of Congress > Films, Videos: https://www.loc.gov/film-and-videos/

Museum of New Zealand, Te Papa Tongarewa: https://www.tepapa.govt.nz/

National Film and Sound Archive of Australia: https://www.nfsa.gov.au/

New Zealand WW100. http://ww100.govt.nz/

Ngā Taonga Sound & Vision: http://www.ngataonga.org.nz/collections/search

NZONSCREEN: https://www.nzonscreen.com/

Reuters — screenocean: http://reuters.screenocean.com/

Te Ara — The Encyclopedia of New Zealand: https://teara.govt.nz/en

Journals, newspapers, magazines and other printed sources

Akaroa Mail and Banks Peninsula Advertiser
Appendices to the Journals of the House of Representatives
Ashburton Guardian
Auckland Animated News
Auckland Star
Auckland Weekly News
Australasian Gazette/Australian Gazette
Bay of Plenty Journal of History
Bush Advocate
Canterbury Times
Christchurch Press
Chronicles of the NZEF
Dominion
Evening Post
Evening Star
Gaumont Graphic
Hastings Standard
Hawera and Normanby Star
Hawkes Bay Herald
Hutt and Petone Chronicle
Illawarra Unity — Journal of the Illawarra Branch of the Australian Society for the Study of Labour History

Limelight
Lyttelton Times
Moving Picture World
Nelson Evening Mail
New Zealand Animated News
New Zealand Free Lance
New Zealand Graphic
New Zealand Herald
New Zealand Times
North Otago Times
Northern Advocate
NZ Observer and Free Lance
Otago Daily Times
Otago Witness
Pathé Gazette
Pathé Animated Gazette
Pathé-Journal
Poverty Bay Herald
Red Triangle Day Magazine
Southland Times
Sydney Morning Herald
Taranaki Daily News
Taranaki Herald
The Bioscope
The Camp Courier
The New Zealander
The Sporting Life
The Sporting Life, London
The Sunday Sun, Newcastle
The Victory
The Wairarapa Age
The Weekender
Theatre
Timaru Herald
Waimate Advertiser
Wanganui Chronicle
Wanganui Herald
War Cry
Weekly Press

Chronological Filmography

This filmography is a snapshot of what New Zealand-related film is known to survive at the date of publication. Ongoing research continues to reveal new material and confirm or question existing identification.

Each entry is in the order of title, year of release (in some cases day and month), cameraman, production company, duration of film, archive source, and film identification number.

1897

Fitzsimmons vs Corbett World Heavyweight Title Fight 17th March 1897, 1897, Cameramen: Unknown, Production Co.: Veriscope, USA, Duration: 0:12.45, NTSV F26977.

Queen Victoria's Diamond Jubilee Procession, 22 June 1897, Cameramen: R.W. Paul and others, Production Co.: R.W. Paul, Duration: 0:01.02 mins, NTSV F11225.

1900

The Departure of the Second Contingent for the Boer War, 1900, Cameraman: W.H. Bartlett, Production Co.: A.H. Whitehouse, Duration 0:00.45, NTSV F22555.

The World's First Lady Mayor, 1900, Camera: Enos Sylvanus Pegler, Production Co.: Zealandia Living Picture Company, Duration, 00:01:10, NTSV, F90103.

1901

Biograph Pictures of the Palmerston Show: Departure of the Wellington Train from Palmerston North Station after the Show, 1901, Cameraman: John Henry Brown, Production Co.: Empire Specialty Company, Duration: 0:01:35, NTSV F2142.

Royal Visit of the Duke and Duchess of Cornwall and York to New Zealand, 1901, Cameramen: Joseph Perry and others, Production Co.: Limelight Department, Salvation Army, Duration: 0:08:10, NTSV F2468.

1902

Fiji and the South Seas, 1902–1907, Cameramen: J.H. Brown and W. Franklyn Brown [Barrett], Production Co.: Charles Urban Trading Company, UK, Eclipse, France, Duration: 0:04:18, NTSV F7430.

1905

All Blacks versus Glamorgan, 1905 (excerpt) see *The Invincible All Blacks Record Tour 1924-5*, 1924, NTSV F7026.

New Zealand vs England, 1905, Cameraman: Unknown, Production Co.: Unknown, United Kingdom, Duration: 0:03:41, NTSV F27366.

Sights in New Zealand, 1905–1906, Principal Cameraman: E.J Hardy and others, Production Co.: West's Pictures, Duration: 0:04:08, NTSV F3005.

[Parade Auckland] 1905, Cameraman: Unknown, Production Co.: Unknown, Duration: 0:00:03, NTSV F20240.

1906

Funeral Procession of the Late Rt. Hon. R. J. Seddon 21 June 1906, 1906, Cameraman: W. Franklyn Barrett, Production Co.: Wide-world Pantoscope Company/Globe Syndicate Pictures, Duration: 0:0:3.07, NTSV F31276.

New Zealand Footballers: The All Blacks Arrival & Reception at Auckland, 1906, Cameraman: Brandon Haughton, Production Co.: Chubb's Biograph Company/ J & N Tait *Living London* Tour, Duration: 0:03.28, NTSV F4361.

Sights and Scenes at the New Zealand Exhibition, 1906, Cameraman: E. J. Hardy and others, Production Co.: West's Pictures — T.J. West, Duration: 0:07.54, NTSV F2656.

1907

Maori Women Performing Action Song at Pohutu Geyser, 1907–1908. Cameraman: James McDonald, Production Co.: Department of Tourist and Health Resorts, Duration: 0:00:51, NTSV F30560.

New Zealand's Thermal Wonderland, 1907–1910, Cameraman: James McDonald, Production Co.: Department of Tourist and Health Resorts, Duration: 0:02:25, NTSV F31561

1908

American Fleet at Auckland, 1908, Cameraman: James McDonald, Production: Department of Tourist and Health Resorts, Duration: 0:03:16, NTSV F10262.

American Officers' Visit to Rotorua, 1908, Cameraman: James McDonald, Production Co.: Department of Tourist and Health Resorts, Duration: 0:01:10, NTSV F3033.

Departure of the British Antarctic Expedition from Lyttelton, N.Z., 1st Jan 1908, 1908, Cameraman: James McDonald, Production Co.: Department of Tourist and Health Resorts, Duration: 0:05:20, NTSV F8202.

Dominion Day Celebrations: [Newtown Park, Wellington, 26 September 1908], 1908, Cameraman: James McDonald, Production Co.: Department of Tourist and Health Resorts, Duration: 0:03:00, NTSV F8277.

Dominion Day Celebrations (Wellington): Children's Demonstration, [Basin Reserve Wellington, 26 September 1908], Living New Zealand Series, 1908, Cameraman: James McDonald, Production Co.: Department of Tourist and Health Resorts, Duration: 0:02:51, NTSV F8276.

Dominion Day Celebrations (Wellington) [March of Volunteers Past Government Buildings, Lambton Quay, Wellington, 26 September 1908], Living New Zealand Series, 1908, Cameraman: James McDonald, Production Co.: Department of Tourist and Health Resorts, Duration: 0:03:26, NTSV F5064.

[*Mt Eden School*] 1908, Cameraman: Unknown, Production Co.: Unknown, Duration: 0:04:15, NTSV F53909.

[*Wanganui River Steamboat Trip*], 1908–1913, Cameraman: Unknown, Production Co.: Unknown, Duration: 0:04:27, NTSV F31567.

Wellington: A Panoramic View of New Zealand's Capital, 1908–1914, Cameraman: Unknown, Production Co.: Unknown, Duration: 0:01:39, NTSV F31566.

1909

Sir Joseph and Lady Ward, 1909, Cameraman: James McDonald, Production Co.: Department of Tourist and Health Resorts, Duration: 0:00:46, NTSV F3032.

World's Sculling Championship Wanganui River, 1909, Cameraman: James McDonald, Production Co.: Department of Tourist and Health Resorts, Duration: 0:02:26, NTSV F41774

1910

Across the Mountain Passes of New Zealand, 1910, Cameraman: W. Franklyn Barrett, Production Co.: Pathé Frères, Duration: 0:04:01, NTSV F10078. [Film also produced as a renamed 16 mm version called *Among the Gorges of New Zealand*.].

A Day with the Boy Scouts: Inspection by Lord Kitchener [Hagley Park, Christchurch, 22 February 1910], Living New Zealand Series, 1910, Cameraman: James McDonald, Department of Tourist and Health Resorts, Duration: 002.05, NTSV F6076.

A Day with the Boy Scouts: Kitchener Inspecting Boy Scouts in Dunedin: Living New Zealand Series, 1910, Cameraman: James McDonald, Production Co.: Department of Tourist and Health Resorts, Duration: 0:01.54, NTSV F6078.

Among the Gorges of New Zealand, 1910, see *Across the Mountain Passes of New Zealand*.

Coasts of New Zealand, 1910, Cameraman: W. Franklyn Barrett, Production Co.: Pathé Frères, Duration: 0:04.51, NTSV F9043.

Labor Day in Gisborne, 1910, Cameraman: Brandon Haughton, Production Co.: Pathe Pictures, Duration: 0:03:49, NTSV F5636.

[*Motor Car Racing*] 191–, Cameraman: Unknown, Production Co.: Unknown, Duration: 0:00:13, NTSV F23401.

Opening of the Wanganui Rowing Season. Wanganui River. Oct. 15th 1910. Newham Series, 1910, Cameraman: Charles F. Newham, Production Co.: Hayward's Pictures, Duration: 0:01.06, NTSV F38482.

[*Personal Record, Hinge Leslie, Hinge Family*], 1910, Cameraman: Unknown, Production Co.: Amateur, Hinge Family, Duration: 0:01:11, NTSV F2473

Poi Dances at Whakarewarewa. 1910, Cameraman: Unknown, Production Co.: Unknown, Duration: 0:02.15, NTSV F3990.

Proclamation of King George V, Wellington, 1910, Cameraman: James McDonald, Production Co.: Department of Tourist and Health Resorts, Duration: 0:00.40 sec, NTSV F4102.

Tid-Bits of Travel, Hunua Falls, 1910, Cameraman: Unknown, Production Co.: Major Wilson Films, Duration: ? NTSV F228360.

1911

Fashions in Melbourne: Harem Skirts at Georges, c1911, Cameraman: Pathé, Production Co.: Pathé, 0:00.44, NFSA F74917.

Feilding Races, 1911, Cameraman: M. Dahmen, Production Co.: Pathé Frères for Hayward's Pictures, Duration: 0:03:34, NTSV F7384.

Fishing Industry in New Zealand, 1911–1916, Cameraman: Charles Newham, Production Co.: New Agency Film Co. Ltd, UK, Duration: 0:05:50, NTSV F97914. The New Agency Film Co.'s *Fishing Industry of New Zealand* was a 1916 reissue of the Heron, UK, film of 1912 *Trawling in Napier, New Zealand*, which in turn was derived from Newham's 1911 film *Napier Day by Day*.

[*Maori Craft Activities*], 191–? Cameraman: Unknown, Production Co.: Unknown, Duration: 0:00:40, NTSV F37776.

[*Maori Women Performing Action Song at Pohutu Geyser*] 191–? Cameraman: Unknown, Production Co.: Unknown, Duration: 0:00:51, NTSV F30560.

[*Picnic and Sports*] 1911, Cameraman: Unknown, Production Co.: Unknown, Duration: 0:01:20, NTSV F3896.

Pictures of Feilding Races, [formerly *Wanganui Spring Hurdles*], 1911, Cameraman: Charles F. Newham, Production Co.: Dominion (NZ) Film, Duration: 0:05:30, NTSV F38481.

[*Replica model armoured sternwheel steamer NZ Wars*] 191– ?, Cameraman: Unknown, Production Co.: Unknown, Duration: 0:01:12, NTSV, F2331.

[*Sand Yacht & Ice Yacht*] 191–?, Cameraman: Unknown, Production Co.: Unknown, Duration: 0:00:26, NTSV F23400.

Sydney Street Siege, 1911, Cameraman: Unknown, Production Co.: Pathé Gazette, Duration: 0:01:32, British Pathé 2961.31.

Wellington. 'The Elections'. A Dash of Politics at Lunch, 1911, Cameraman: unknown, Production Co.: Pathé's Animated Gazette (Australasian Edition), Duration: 0:00:54, NTSV F862.

World's Championship Axemen's Carnival, Taumata Park Eltham New Zealand, 1911, Cameraman: Charles F. Newham, Production Co.: Dominion (NZ) Film, Duration: 0:10:40, NTSV F1152.

1912

A 75-yard Dash between Donaldson and Postle, 1912, Cameraman: Unknown, Production Co.: John Fuller & Sons, Duration: 0:00:54, NTSV F31417.

Auckland Bakers' Strike: Procession of Chinese Bakers in New Zealand, 1912, Cameraman: unknown, Production Co.: Pathé Gazette, Duration: 0:00:54, NTSV F46203.

[Auckland Cup 1912], 1912, Cameramen: Unknown, Production Co.: Unknown, Duration: 0:05:06, NTSV F10454.

Auckland, N.Z. Swimming Races in the Harbour, 1912, Cameraman: Unknown, Production Co.: Pathé, Australia, Duration: 0:00:33, NTSV F31419.

[Christchurch Scenes ca. 1912] 1912, Cameraman: Unknown, Production Co.: Unknown, Duration: 0:00:49, NTSV F8962.

[Dunedin 1912], 1912, Cameraman: Unknown, Production Co.: Unknown, Duration: 0:08:31, NTSV F8350.

Dunedin Brass Band Contest, Quickstep, 1912, Cameraman: Henry C. Gore, Production Co.: New Queen's Theatre, Dunedin, Duration: 0:03:28, NTSV F9933.

Dunstan Miners' Jubilee Celebrations, [formerly *Highland Sports*] November 1912. Cameraman: James McDonald, Production Co.: Department of Tourist and Health Resorts on behalf of Department of Mines, Duration, 0:02:31, NTSV F6536.

Floral and Garden Fete at Oamaru, NZ, 1912, Cameraman: James McDonald, Production Co.: Department of Tourist and Health Resorts, Duration: 0:05:36, NTSV F7548.

The Funeral of the Late Father Venning, 1912, Cameraman: Unknown, Production Co.: Harrington's Ltd, N.Z., Duration: 0:00:39, NTSV F31418.

Grand School Carnival 1912, Cameraman: Brandon Haughton, Production Co.: Garnet Saunders, Egmont Film Company, Duration: 0:03:43, NTSV F4154.

Maori War Canoe Race, 1912. Cameraman: Unknown, Production Co.: Unknown, Duration: 0:02:39, NTSV F5035.

[New Plymouth Harbour — Waves breaking on the coast — formerly *Saunders' Neg.]* 1912, Cameraman: Brandon Haughton, Production Co.: Garnet H. Saunders, Duration: 0:01:00, NTSV F2637.

[Panorama of Auckland] 1912, Cameraman: Unknown, Production Co.: Unknown, Duration: 0:00:19, NTSV F3723.

Pathé Gazette, Maori Legislators. Mr A.T. Ngata, Mr C.R. Parata, Sir J. Carroll and Dr T.E. Rangihiroa: Wellington, N.Z., c1912, Cameraman: Unknown, Production Co.: Pathe Gazetté, Duration: 0:00:41, (NFSA 74137), NTSV F31421.

Pathé Gazette, Wellington. N.Z. Men of the Times. Hon. T. Mackenzie, A Minister of Many Portfolios. c1912? , Cameraman: Unknown, Production Co.: Pathe Gazette, Duration:0:00:22, (NSFA 74138), NTSV F31420.

Personal Record, [*Women in Garden c1912*], 1912, Cameraman: Unknown, Production Co.: Amateur, Duration: 0:00:12, NTSV F1018.

[Picnic by Peregrine to Brown's Island] 1912, Cameraman: Unknown, Production Co.: Unknown, Duration: 0:01:28, NTSV F3897.

Plunket Shield Cricket Match Auckland v Canterbury/Domain Fete Christchurch, 1912, Cameraman: Unknown, Production Co.: Unknown, Duration: 0:04:49, NTSV F3985.

The Production of the Taranaki Herald and Budget, 1912, Cameraman: Brandon Haughton, Production Co.: Garnet Saunders, Empire Theatre Film Co., Duration: 0:02:06, NTSV F4106.

A Reunion of New Zealand's Pioneer Miners, 1912. Cameraman: James McDonald, Production Co.: Department of Tourist and Health Resorts, Duration: 0:02:58, NTSV F202128.

Scenes at the East End Annual Picnic, New Plymouth, 1912, Cameraman: Brandon Haughton, Production Co.: Garnet Saunders, Empire Theatre Film Co., Duration: 0:04:15, NTSV F2655.

Scenes In Taranaki New Zealand, 1912, Cameraman: Charles F. Newham?, Production Co.: Dominion Film (NZ)?, Duration: 0:05:00, NTSV F55926.

[Sculling and Steamer on Lake Wakatipu], 1912–1916, Cameraman: Unknown, Production Co.: Unknown, Duration: 0:02:51, NTSV F57921.

Taranaki Circular Road Race, 1912, Cameraman: Brandon Haughton, Production Co.: Garnet Saunders, Egmont Film Company, Duration: 0:02:11, NTSV F9312.

Taranaki Jockey Club's Annual Meeting, 1912, Cameraman: Brandon Haughton, Production Co.: Garnet Saunders, Empire Theatre Co., Duration: 0:02:10, NTSV F1465.

Trawling in the Hauraki Gulf, 1912, Cameraman: Charles Newham?, Production Co.: Dominion (NZ) Film?, Duration: 0:01:08, NTSV F1776.

Tutange of Patea, 1912, Cameraman: James McDonald, Production Co.: Dominion Museum, Duration: 0:00:38, NTSV F1862.

The Wreck of the Star of Canada, 1912, Cameraman: Charles F. Newham, Production Co.: Dominion (NZ) Film Co., Duration: 0:06:53, NTSV F38455.

1913

1863–1913 Otago Boy's High School Jubilee Celebrations at Dunedin August 1st to 5th 1913, 1913, Cameraman: James McDonald, Production Co.: Department of Agriculture, Duration: 0:07.09, NTSV F28248.

2500 Territorials Marching Home from Camp, 1913, Cameraman: Unknown, Production Co.: West-Hayward's Pictures, Duration: 0:01:30, NTSV F56660.

Auckland's Reception to the Battleship HMS New Zealand, 1913, Cameraman: Charles F. Newham: Production Co.: Dominion (NZ) Film, Duration: 0:01:34, NTSV F10484.

Federation of Labour (formerly *Unity Congress*), 1913, Cameraman: Charles D. Barton, Production Co.: C.D. Barton, Duration: 0:02:36, NTSV F1956.

Dunedin Coursing Club, 4th June 1913, 1913, Cameraman: Unknown, Production Co.: Unknown, Duration: 0:02:45, NTSV F28578.

Dunedin Territorial Parade (or *Defenders of New Zealand* — formerly *Otago Expeditionary Force Section 2*) 1913, Cameraman: Henry C. Gore, Production Co.: New Queen's Theatre, Dunedin, Duration: 0:00:07, NTSV F1821.

The Fisher Monoplane [also known as *Experimental Flights of the Fisher Monoplane*], 1913, Cameraman: Charles D. Barton, Production Co.: C.D. Barton, Duration: 0:03:24, NTSV F7306.

HM the King Inspects "The New Zealand" at Portsmouth. Photographed exclusively by the Topical Film Co. by His Majesty's Permission, 1913, Cameraman: Unknown, Production Co.: Topical Film Co., Duration: 0:03:35, NTSV F29375.

HMS New Zealand, June 1913 [H.C. Gore Extracts], 1913, Cameraman: Henry C. Gore, Production Co.: Plaza Picture Theatre? Duration: 0:01:02, NTSV F38483.

King George V Inspects HMS New Zealand, *5 February 1913*, 1913, Cameramen: Unknown, Production: Jury's Imperial Pictures, Duration: 0:02.33, NTSV F5539.

Kijkjes uit Manawatu, [Scenes in the Manawatu] 1913, Cameraman: unknown, Production Co.: Kalem, Duration: 0:04:00, NTSV, F58412.

Nelson Trotting Club Handicap. Start, Finish & Winner, 1913, Cameraman: Unknown, Production Co.: Permanent Pictures, Theatre Royal, Nelson, Duration 0:00:53, NTSV F2231.

New Zealand Leads the Way/Scenes on Board HMS New Zealand/ Britannia Rules the Waves, 1913, Cameramen: Unknown, Production: Jury's Imperial Pictures, 0:03.08, NTSV F4387.

The Terra Nova, 1913, Cameraman: Unknown, Production Co.: Unknown, Duration: 0:01:24, NTSV F1547.

Pathé Gazette: (Excerpt) HMS New Zealand, 1913? Cameraman: Unknown, Production Co.: Pathé Gazette, Duration: 0:00:46, British Pathé: 1924.06.

Public Reception and Welcome Home to Sir Walter Buchanan at Carterton, July 10 1913, 1913, Cameraman: Charles D. Barton, Production Co.: C.D. Barton, Duration: 0:04:09, NTSV F14622.

Wreck of the SS Tyrone, 1913, Cameraman: Henry C. Gore, Production Co.: New Queen's Theatre, Dunedin, Duration: 0:02:55, NTSV F1208.

1914

A.H. Noad Film: Gallipoli, 1914–1928, Cameramen: Various, Producer: A.C. Tinsdale, Embassy Films, Duration: 1:01:53, AWM F00176.

Auckland's Expeditionary Force: The Minister for Defence Reviews the Troops, [formerly *Territorials New Zealand Brigade*] 1914, Cameraman: Frank Stewart? Production Co.: Dominion Picture Theatres Co. Ltd, Duration: 0:02:29, NTSV F38469.

Civic Farewell at Tahuna Park, Section 1 [formerly Otago Expeditionary Force, Section 1], 1914, Cameraman: Henry C. Gore, Production Co.: Plaza Pictures, Duration: 0:03:55, NTSV F1147.

Civic Farewell at Tahuna Park, Section 2 [formerly Otago Expeditionary Force, Section 3], 1914, Cameraman: Henry C.

Gore Production Co.: Plaza Pictures, Duration: 0:00:07, NTSV F54107.

Departure of 37 Transports from Albany, 1 November 1914, Cameraman: Unknown, Production Co.: Unknown, Duration: 012.47, AWM F00161.

Football: England v Auckland July 25, 1914, 1914, Cameraman: Unknown, Production Co.: Unknown, Duration: 0:03:47, NTSV F27357.

Gaumont Graphic, 380, New Zealand Infantry, 12.11.14, 1914, Cameraman: Unknown, Production Co.: Gaumont, Duration: 00 00.12, NTSV F194541.

Life on Board the "A3" Orvieto, 1914, Cameraman: Unknown, Production Co.: Unknown, Duration: 005.51, AWM F00160.

London Scottish Cadets: Troops at Lord Mayor's Show, 12 November 1914, 1914, Cameraman: Unknown, Production Co.: *Gaumont Graphic*, Reuters-ITN. BGT407040506. This has been transferred to http://www.reuters.screenocean.com and may have been renumbered.

Main Trunk Express Smash, 1914, Cameraman: Charles F. Newham, Production Co.: Dominion (NZ) Film, Duration: 0:03:00, NTSV F4917.

[*Mining and Town Scenes*] 1914, Cameraman: Unknown, Production Co.: Unknown, Duration: 0:01:37, NTSV F29378.

New Zealanders for the Front: Official Farewell, 1914, Cameraman: James McDonald, Production Co.: Department of Agriculture, Duration: 0:02:00, NTSV F1820.

Off to the Front [formerly *Loading Troopship on Wellington Waterfront*] 1914, Cameraman: Unknown, Production Co.: Hayward's Pictures, Duration: 0:01:24, NTSV F38442.

Personal Record Gore, H.C. [Assorted Scenes], 1914, Cameraman: H.C. Gore, Production Co.: Various, Duration: 0:02:20, NTSV F24833.

WWI Troops Embarkation and Charity Bazaars, Sydney c.1915, 1914–1915, Cameraman: Bert Ive and others, Production Co.: Unknown, Duration: 0:07:41, NFSA 45988.

1915

The Dardanelles, 1915, Cameraman: Unknown, Production Co.: Pathé Journale Actualité, Duration: 0:00:29, Gaumont Pathé Archives No. 1915 22.

The Dedication Ceremony of the First Ambulance at the Auckland Hospital, 1915, Cameraman: Unknown, Production Co.: Auckland Animated Gazette, Duration: 0:01:00, NTSV F8174.

Le croiseur anglais combattant : "Le New-Zeland", ayant pris part à la bataille navale de la Mer du Nord, 1915, Cameraman: Unknown, Production Co.: Journal Gaumont, France, Duration: 0:00:30, Gaumont Pathé, 1505GJ 00014.

Gaumont Graphic, 481(1), Wounded New Zealanders Spend Their Time Profitably, 1 November 1915, 1915, Cameraman: Unknown, Production Co.: Gaumont Graphic, Duration: (59 feet), Reuters –ITN, BGT407040825. This has now been transferred to http://reuters.screenocean.com and may have been renumbered.

Highlander Milk Manufacture, 1915, Cameraman: Charles F. Newham, Production Co.: Dominion (NZ) Film Co., Duration: 0:17.00, NTSV F4996.

Inspection of the New Zealand and Australian Division, 1915, Cameraman: Unknown, Production Co.: Pathé? Duration: 0:07:40, NTSV F6824.

Life on New Zealand Troopships [*Our Boys en route to Egypt*], 1915, Cameraman: Captain Holmes, Ship's Master, SS *Waimana*, Production Co.: Unknown, Duration: 0:07:29, NTSV F8201.

A Marseille, des Aviateurs Embarquent a bord du Parquebot "Britannia" pour les Dardanelles, 1915, Cameraman: Unknown, Production Co.: Gaumont Journal Actualité, Duration: 0:00:38, Gaumont Pathé Archives 1526GJ00002.

Mardi Gras Festival Napier New Zealand, 1915, Cameraman: Harry Thompson?, Production Co.: Thompson–Payne, Duration: 0:10:42, NTSV F5065.

New Zealanders Board Ship to Return Home, 1915–1916, Cameraman: Unknown, Production Co.: Pathé Gazette, Duration: 0:00:54, (British Pathé 2336.03) NTSV F245783.

New Zealand Recruits, 1915–1917, Cameraman: Sydney Benjamin Taylor, Production Co.: Pathé Gazette from film provided by Department of Agriculture, NZ, Duration: 0:00.57, (British Pathé 1862:31 — released January 1917), NTSV F245691.

New Zealand Reinforcements Leaving, 1915, Cameraman: Unknown, Production Co.: Pathé Gazette, Duration: 0:01.10, (British Pathé 1860.48), NTSV F245692.

[*Otago Rowing Association Annual Regatta*], 1915, Cameraman: Unknown, Production Co.: Unknown, Duration: 0:03:15, NTSV F3619.

Our Boys in Egypt 1915 [The New Zealand Field Artillery Cairo parade sequence is from time code: 18:11:09 to 18:22:13 a total of 13 seconds], *A.H. Noad Film: Gallipoli,* 1915–1928, Cameramen: Various, Producer: A.C. Tinsdale, Embassy Films, Duration: 1:01:53, AWM F00176

Personal Record, Hopkins, William. [*Circus, Canoe Hurdling, Women's Action Song, Ngaruawahia*] 1915, Cameraman: William Hopkins, Production Co.: Amateur, Duration: 0:04:58, NTSV F51482

Vast Training Camp aka Aerial Camp View, 1915–1917, Cameraman: Sydney B. Taylor, Production Co.: Pathé Gazette from film provided by Department of Agriculture, NZ, Duration: 0:00.50, {British Pathé 1862:12 – released January 1917), NTSV F245690.

With the Allied Fleets in the Dardanelles, 1915, Cameraman: Unknown, Production Co.: Gaumont, UK, Duration: 0:03:24, NTSV F29386.

With the Allied Fleets in the Dardanelles, 1915, Cameraman: Unknown, Production Co.: Gaumont, Duration:? BFI 603107.

1916

15,000 Miles to Serve — '*Tunnellers from New Zealand inspected by High Commissioner, 6 March 1916,* 1916, Cameraman: Unknown, Production Co.: Pathé Gazette, Duration: 0:00:17, British Pathé, 1856.27.

After Being Wounded — [*Recovering New Zealanders hold Sports Meeting*], 1916, Cameraman: Unknown, Production Co.: Pathé Gazette, Duration: 0:01:55, (British Pathé 1868.07), NTSV F245633.

The Allies in the East, [*Other Segments*], 1916, Cameraman: Unknown, Production Co.: Spencers, Australia, Duration: 0:14:21, NFSA 323.

The Allies in the East, 1916, Cameraman: Unknown, Production Co.: Gaumont, Duration: 0:08:21, NFSA 309.

The Allies in the East, 1916, Cameraman: Unknown, Production Co.: Gaumont, UK, Duration: 0:04:48, BFI 19359.

Australian and New Zealand Soldiers Return Home, [*HMNZHT (His Majesty's New Zealand Hospital Transport) No. 2 'Marama' With 500 Patients, 31 August 1916*], 1916, Cameraman: Unknown, Production Co.: Pathé Gazette, Duration: 0:00:32, (British Pathé 1926.14), NTSV F245636.

Australian Gazette-275, Mr E Ashmead Bartlett, who has come to tell us of the Anzac's immortal deeds at Gallipoli, 1916, Cameraman: Unknown, Production Co.: Australian Gazette, Duration: 0:00:28, NFSA 102837.

Ballot at the Government Statistician's Office, 1916, Cameraman: Sydney B. Taylor, Production Co.: Department of Agriculture, Duration: 0:04.00, NTSV F9351.

The Battle of the Somme, 1916, b/w, five reels, 4694'. Cameramen: Geoffrey H. Malins and J.B. McDowell, Production Co.: British Topical Committee for War Films, Jury Imperial Pictures, Duration: 1:19:00, (IWM 191), NTSV F231397.

Colonial Troops Reviewed, 6 March 1916, 1916, Cameraman: Unknown, Production Co.: Pathé Gazette, Duration: 0:02:01, British Pathé, 1936.33.

Easter Rising, Dublin 1916, 1916, Cameraman: Unknown, Production Co.: UK, Duration: 0:14:03, (IWM 194), NTSV F246452.

Fighting Men at Play: "All Blacks" Beat "Springboks" in hotly contested Rugby Match at Richmond, 8 April 1916, 1916, Cameraman: Unknown, Production Co.: Pathé Gazette, Duration: 001:25, (British Pathé 1860.43), NTSV F48684.

For Bravery at Gallipoli — VC for Corporal Bassett, 1916, Cameraman: Unknown, Production Co.: Pathé Gazette, Duration: 0:01:15, (British Pathé 1662.02), NTSV F245688.

Gaumont Graphic, 485, New Zealand: Major General Henderson Inspects Maori Troops, 1916, Cameraman: Unknown, Production Co.: Gaumont Graphic, Duration: 0:00.47 (Gaumont Pathé, 1549GJ00005), NTSV F48604.

Gaumont Graphic, 495(1), New Zealand: Parade by Second Maori Contingent, 1916, Cameraman: Unknown, Production Co.: Gaumont Graphic, Duration: 0:00:46, (Gaumont Pathé 1606GJ00003), NTSV 246326.

Nouvelle Zelande: Le Major General Henderson passe en revue un Contingent Maori avant son Depart pour le Front, 1916,

Cameraman: Unknown, Production Co.: Journal Gaumont, France, Duration: 0:01:04, Gaumont Pathé, 1549GJ 00005.

Nouvelle Zelande: Parade par le Deuxieme Contingent de Soldats Maori, 1916, Cameraman: Unknown, Production Co.: Journal Gaumont, France, Duration: 0:00:46, Gaumont Pathé, 1606GJ 00003.

General Birdwood presents Medals, 25 April 1916, 1916, Cameraman: Pathé, Duration: 0:01:06, (British Pathé 1662.31), NTSV F245688.

Inspection of Australian [New Zealand] Troops [By General Birdwood], 25 April 1916, 1916, Cameraman: Pathé, Duration: 0:02.08, British Pathé 1936.12.

The King Visits His Armies in the Great Advance, 1916, Cameraman: G.H. Malins, Production Co. WOCC by Topical Film Company, Duration: 0:40:00, (IWM 192-01), NTSV F246451.

Lord Mayor's Show, 1916? Cameraman: Unknown, Production Co.: Pathé Gazette, Duration: 02.53, British Pathé 1936.11.

Maori Soldier R&R aka Maori Contingent Resting, New Zealand Maori Soldiers who took part with the ANZAC Forces in the Gallipoli Campaign are Resting for a while in England, 1916, Cameraman: Unknown, Production Co.: Pathé Gazette, Duration:0:00:18, British Pathé 1850.05.

Maori Funeral, 1916–1917, Cameraman: Unknown, Production Co.: Pathé Gazette, Duration: 0:02:05, (British Pathé 2346.10), NTSV F48685.

Nelson Daffodil Parade, 1916, Cameraman: Unknown, Production Co.: Unknown, Duration: 0:03:37, NTSV F23360.

New Zealand v Wales at Pontypridd, 1916, Cameraman: Unknown, Production Co.: Gaumont Graphic, Duration: 0:01:17: NTSV F48603.

Personal Record Hayward, R., Wellington, October 1916, Cameraman: R. Hayward, Production Co.: R. Hayward, Duration: 0:02:00, NTSV F27365.

Photo Session Following Ballot at the Government Statistician's Office, 1916, Cameraman: Sydney B. Taylor, Production Co.: Department of Agriculture, Duration: 0:04.10, NTSV F3484.

Review of New Zealand Troops by Sir Walter Long, 1917, Cameraman: Unknown, Production Co.: WOCC, Topical Film Company, Duration: 0:16:00, (IWM 196), NTSV F4330.

Ruines — Arras, Bailleul, Nieppe, Ypres, Albert, Béthune, Armentiéres, 1916, Cameraman: French Official, Production Co.: France, Duration: 0:22:42, NTSV F253663.

Topical Budget No: 233-1, Anzacs Beat Artists, 9 February 1916, 1916, Cameraman: Unknown, Production Co.: Topical Film Co., Duration: 0:03:55, NTSV F246508.

Topical Budget 241-1 An Anzac Win, 5 April 1916, 1916, Cameraman: Unknown, Production Co.: Topical Film Co., Duration: 0:01:35, NTSV F97870.

Topical Budget 242-1 New Zealanders Win at Rugby, 12 April 1916, 1916, Cameraman: Unknown, Production Co.: Topical Film Co., Duration: 0:01:06, NTSV F97871.

Topical Budget 244-1 Anzac Day, 25 April 1916, 1916, Cameraman: Unknown, Production Co.: Topical Film Co., Duration: 0:01:03, NTSV F97877.

Topical Budget 272-1 City Freedom For Rt Hon. W.F. Massey ("Lord Mayor And Mr Massey Inspect New Zealand Guard of Honour Before Ceremony"), 8 November 1916, Cameraman: Unknown, Production Co.: Topical Film Co., Duration: 50 ft, NTSV F232644.

Stonehenge visited by New Zealand Delegates, After Gallipoli: The Famous Maori Contingent, 1916, Cameraman: Unknown, Production Co.: Pathé Gazette, Duration: 0:02:07, (British Pathé 1848.27), NTSV F48689.

With the Australian Forces in France [Parts 1 And 2], 1916, Cameraman, British Official, Production Co.: Jury's Imperial Pictures for British Topical Committee for War Films, Duration: 0:40:00, NTSV F246429. (Part I has not been accessioned.)

With the Dardanelles Expedition: Heroes of Gallipoli, 1916, Cameramen: Ellis Ashmead-Bartlett, Ernest Brooks, Production Co.: Alfred Butt, retitled and captioned by C.E.W. Bean for Australian War Memorial in the 1920s, Duration: 0:20.02, AWM F00069.

With the Dardanelles Expedition: Heroes of Gallipoli, 1916 [Digital restoration by Weta Digital], Cameramen: Ellis Ashmead-Bartlett, Ernest Brooks, Production Co.: Alfred Butt, retitled and captioned by C.E.W. Bean for Australian War Memorial in the 1920s, Duration: 0:18:00, AWM F10581.

1917

1500 School Children at New Plymouth, 1917, Cameraman: Brandon Haughton, Production Co.: Garnet Saunders, Empire Theatre Film Co., Duration: 0:02:28, NTSV F7411.

Australian Gazette 542, Perilous Voyage, 1917, Cameraman: Unknown, Production Co.: Australian Gazette, Duration: 0:01:18, NTSV F31427.

The Capture of Messines, 1917, Cameraman: H. C. Raymond,, Production Co.: Topical Film Company, William F. Jury, producer for WOCC, Duration: 0:29:00, (1766'), IWM 197.

El Mejdel, Jaffa and West Country Troops, 1917, Cameraman: Harold Jeapes, Production Co.: Topical Film Company for WOCC, Duration, 0:15:53, (IWM 12), NTSV F246416.

Gathering of the Clans — Colonials attend Sunday Service [London] 1917–1918, Cameraman: Unknown, Production Co.: Pathé Gazette, Duration: 0:00:41, British Pathé 1896.12.

Gaumont Graphic 604 (1) Rugby Football — ASC (Grove Park) v New Zealand, 4 January 1917, 1917, Cameraman: Unknown, Production Co.: Gaumont Graphic, Duration:?, Reuters –ITN, BGT407050745. This has now been transferred to http://reuters. screenocean.com and may have been renumbered.

Gaumont Graphic 627 (8), Rugby Football — ASC (Grove Park) v New Zealand, 26 March 1917. Cameraman: Unknown, Production Co.: Gaumont Graphic, Duration: ?, Reuters –ITN, BGT407051154. This has now been transferred to http://reuters. screenocean.com and may have been renumbered.

Gaumont Graphic 627 (8) — Hon. W.F. Massey and Sir Joseph Ward (New Zealand), 1917, Cameraman: Unknown, Production Co.: Gaumont Graphic, Duration ?, Reuters –ITN, BGT407051154. This has now been transferred to http://reuters.screenocean. com and may have been renumbered.

Gaumont Graphic 639 (6), Football – France v New Zealand for Somme Cup, 7 May 1917. Cameraman: Unknown, Production Co.: Gaumont Graphic, Duration ?, Reuters –ITN, BGT407051244. This has now been transferred to http://reuters.screenocean. com and may have been renumbered

Gaumont Graphic 702 — South Africans v New Zealanders, 8 December 1917, Cameraman: Unknown, Production Co.: Gaumont Graphic, Duration: ?, Reuters –ITN, BGT 407052001. This has now been transferred to http://reuters.screenocean. com and may have been renumbered.

General Allenby's Entry into Jerusalem, 1917, Cameraman: Harold Jeapes, Production Co.: WOCC, Topical Film Company, Duration: 0:13:47, (IWM 13), NTSV F246417.

Glasgow Boys Brigade 1917, 1917, Cameraman: Sergeant Thomas F. Scales, Production Co.: NZ Official/ Pathé Gazette, Duration: 0:00:56, British Pathé, 1874.47.

His Majesty King George V Reviewing New Zealand Troops on Salisbury Plain, 1 May 1917, 1917, Cameraman: Sergeant Thomas F. Scales, Production Co.: NZ Official/Pathé Gazette, Duration: 0:07:33, NTSV F5540.

Inspection of New Zealand Troops by Field Marshal Sir Douglas Haig, 1917, Cameraman: Lt Henry A. Sanders, Production Co.: NZ Official, negative deposited with WOCC, Duration: 0:05:45, (IWM 156), NTSV F4094.

King and Queen Visit Anzac Hospital, — Walton-on-Thames Surrey, 1917?, Production Co.: Pathé Gazette, Cameraman: Sergeant Thomas F. Scales, Duration: 0:00:29, (British/Pathé, 1894.05 and 1886.47) NTSV F245767.

King and Queen Visit Hospital, NZ Hospital — Walton-on-Thames, 1917?, Cameraman: Sergeant Thomas F. Scales, Production Co.: Pathé Gazette, Duration: 0:00:29, Pathé Gazette 1886.47. This is the same as Pathé Gazette, 1894.05.

King on Horseback, 1917, Cameraman: Sergeant Thomas F. Scales, Production Co.: NZ Official/Pathé, Duration: 0:00:17, British Pathé 2328.07.

King with the New Zealanders, 1917, Cameraman: Sergeant Thomas F. Scales, Production Co.: NZ Official/Pathé, Duration: 0:00:57, British Pathé 1866.37.

King with the New Zealanders, May 1917, Cameraman: Sergeant Thomas F. Scales, Production Co.: NZEF Official/Pathé, Duration: 0:00:26, British Pathé 1866.20.

Looking North Up Molesworth Street, [Wellington, New Zealand] 1917–1918, Cameraman: Unknown, Production Co.: Unknown, Duration: 0:00:24, NTSV F38467.

Match de Rugby entre la France et Nouvelle Zélande pour la "Coupe de la Somme". Avant le match, danse, 1917, Cameraman: Unknown, Production Co.: Journal Gaumont, France, Duration: 0:01:36, Gaumont Pathé, 1715GJ 00013.

Match de Rugby. France — Nouvelle Zélande, Entrainement Sportif de Chasseurs Alpine, 1917, Cameraman: Unknown, Production Co.: French Official, Duration: 0:04:46 (Film length – 0:09:22), NTSV F253654.

New Zealand Boys at Sling Camp: New Zealanders in England, 1917, Cameraman: Thomas F. Scales, New Zealand scenes, L.W.

Mence, Production Co.: NZ Official/Pathé Gazette, Duration: 0:04:30, NTSV F17937.

The New Zealand Field Artillery in France, New Zealand Rifle Brigade on the March, 1917–1918, Cameraman: Captain Henry A. Sanders, Production Co.: NZ Official, negative deposited with WOCC, Duration: 0:09:43, (IWM 166), NTSV F4340.

New Zealand Sports, 1917? Cameraman: Sergeant Thomas F. Scales, Production Co.: Pathé Gazette, Duration: 00:33, British Pathé 1872.19.

New Zealand Troops: Gen Sir William Birdwood, 2 March 1917, Cameraman: Unknown, Production Co.: Gaumont Graphic, Duration: ?, Reuters –ITN, BGT407051085. This has now been transferred to http://reuters.screenocean.com and may have been renumbered.

New Zealand: The River Avon, 22 January 1917, Cameraman: Unknown, Production Co.: Gaumont Graphic, Duration: ? Reuters –ITN, BGT407050828. This has now been transferred to http://reuters.screenocean.com and may have been renumbered.

Pathé Gazette, Aeroplane Christened at Military Rally, 1917, Cameraman: Sergeant Thomas F. Scales?, Production Co.: Pathé Gazette, Duration: 0:01:26, British Pathé 1886.08.

Pathé Gazette, Anzac Battle Plane Gift, 1917, Cameraman: Sergeant Thomas F. Scales?, Production Co.: Pathé Gazette, Duration: 0:00:34, British Pathé 1886.38. This is identical to British Pathé 1894.27.

Pathé Gazette, Great Volcanic Eruption at Rotorua, 1917, Cameraman: Unknown, Production Co.: Pathé Gazette, Australia, Duration: 0:01.26

Pathé Gazette, Nottingham gives Plane to Anzacs [New Zealand], 1917, Cameraman: Sergeant Thomas F. Scales?, Production Co.: Pathé Gazette, Duration: 0:00:34, British Pathé 1894.27. This is identical to British Pathé 1886.38.

Pathé Journal Actualité: Guillaume Ii En Turquie, 1917, German intertitles, Duration: 00:03:32, Gaumont Pathé 191529.

Returning Home: Wounded Anzacs, with trophies of war, on their way back to New Zealand, 4 January 1917. Cameraman: Unknown, Production Co.: Gaumont Graphic, Duration:0:00:15, Reuters –ITN, BGT407050747. This has now been transferred to http://reuters.screenocean.com, ID. 208555.

Sir J Ward Inspects Glasgow Boys' Brigade, 1917, Cameraman: Sergeant Thomas F. Scales, Production Co.: NZ Official/Pathé

Gazette, Duration: 0:00:56, British Pathé, 1872.11. [This is identical to *Glasgow Boys Brigade 1917*].

Snow Man's Land (Expeditionary Force Training, Featherston Camp) 1917–1918, Cameraman: L.W. Mence, Production Co.: L.W. Mence, Duration: 0:04:58, NTSV F1475.

Sons of Our Empire, Episode 3, 1917, Cameraman: G. H. Malins, Production Co.: WOCC by Topical Film Company, Duration: 0:42:00, (IWM 130-6), NTSV F246427.

Sons of Our Empire, Episode 5, 1917, Cameraman: Geoffrey H. Malins, Production Co.: by Topical Film Company, Duration: 0:32:00, (IWM 130-10), NTSV F246428.

"Strawberry Fete". Promoted by the Four Allied Trades: Dairymen, Fruiterers, Grocers and Bakers, held at Torquay on Alexandra Day, 27 June 1917. 1917, Cameraman: Unknown, Production Co.: Unknown, Duration: 0:13:22, NTSV F110329.

The Surprise Packet Day in Wellington, 1917, Cameraman: Sydney B Taylor, Production Co.: Department of Agriculture, Duration: 0:02:16, NTSV F7107.

Topical Budget 286-2 New Zealand's Message to London, 17 February 1917, Cameraman: Unknown, Production Co.: Topical Film Co., Duration: 0:00.57, NTSV F97872.

Topical Budget 287-1 Premier Watches Rugby Match, 1917, Cameraman: Unknown, Production Co.: Topical Film Co., Duration: 0:00:41, NTSV F97873.

Topical Budget 287-1 All Blacks v ASC, 1917, Cameraman: Unknown, Production Co.: Topical Film Co., Duration: 0:01:14, NTSV F97890.

Topical Budget, Jericho, 1917, Cameraman: Harold Jeapes, Production Co.: WOCC, Topical Film Company, Duration: 0:14:57, (IWM 22), NTSV F246426.

VC for ANZAC Heroes of the Ridge. Sergeants Frickleton and Andrew being congratulated by comrades, 1917, Cameraman: Sergeant Thomas F. Scales, Production Co.: Pathé Gazette, Duration: 0:00:43, (British Pathé 1894.07), NTSV F245768.

New Zealand Troops on the March, Visit of Sir Thomas Mackenzie, KCMG, High Commissioner for New Zealand, to the New Zealand Division, September 9th and 10th 1917, 1917, Cameraman: Captain Henry A Sanders, Production Co.: NZ Official negative deposited with WOCC, Duration: 0:06:18, (IWM 157) NTSV F1070.

War Office Official Topical Budget 323-1 — Nottingham's Gift to New Zealand. [The Duke of Portland and Lord Desborough were present when the Duchess of Portland christened the aeroplane that the Midland City presented to New Zealand, 30 October 1917], 1917, Cameraman: Topical Budget, Production Co.: Topical Budget, Duration: 0:00:52, NTSV F49969.

[Wellington Scenes] 1917, Cameraman: Unknown, Production Co.: Unknown, Duration: 0:17:57, NTSV F 11033.

Whatsoever A Man Soweth, 1917–1918, Cameraman: Joseph Best, Production Co.: Joseph Best — sponsored by Canadian Expeditionary Force and New Zealand Expeditionary Force, Duration: 0:37:34, BFI http://www.screenonline.org.uk.

With The New Zealand Expeditionary Force in the United Kingdom, Part I, 1917, Cameraman: Sergeant Thomas F. Scales,

Production Co.: NZ Official/Pathé Gazette, Duration: 0:07:53, NTSV F1001.

Work of the New Zealand Medical Corps, 1917, Cameraman: Lt Henry A. Sanders, Production Co.: NZ Official, negative deposited with WOCC, Duration: 0:14:26, NTSV F4310.

1918

Annales de la Guerre. No. 74, 1918, Cameraman: French Official, Production Co.: French Official, Duration: 0:07:20, NTSV F253670.

Annales de la Guerre (Additional Material) 1918, Cameraman: Thomas F. Scales?, Production Co.: Pathé Gazette, Duration 0:45:53, Parade Section 0:01:48–0:06:24, (IWM 511), NTSV F246478.

The Aratiatia Rapids of New Zealand, 1918, Cameraman: Unknown, Production Co.: Unknown, Duration: 0:01:18, NTSV F10349.

Auckland from Aloft, 1918, see *Auckland from the Skies.*

Auckland from the Skies (former: *Flying School at Kohimarama,* also advertised as *Auckland from Aloft*) 1918, Cameraman: Charles F. Newham, Production Co.: Dominion (NZ) Film, Duration: 0:35:58, NTSV F7556.

British Empire and American Service Sports — Stamford Bridge September 7th 1918, 1918, Cameraman: Ministry of Information, Production Co.: Ministry of Information, Duration: 0:05:14, NTSV F246479.

[Children's Contest], 1918, Cameraman: Henry C. Gore, Production Co.: Unknown, Duration: 0:00:38, NTSV F9319.

Colonial Pressmen, 1918, Cameraman: British Official, Production Co.: WOCC Ministry of Information, Duration: 0:17:21, (IWM 314), NTSV F246464.

[Crowd in Trafalgar Square Nelson] 1918, Cameraman: Unknown, Production Co.: Unknown, Duration: 0:00:19, NTSV F12175.

England: New Zealand Rugby XV, 21 December 1918. Cameraman: Unknown, Production Co.: Gaumont Graphic, Duration: ? Reuters –ITN, BGT407052677. This has now been transferred to http://reuters.screenocean.com and may have been renumbered.

Fell Engine On The Rimutaka Incline, 1918, Cameraman: L.W. Mence, Production Co.: L.W. Mence?, Duration: 0:02.46, NTSV F7389.

Flying School at Kohimarama, 1918, see *Auckland from the Skies.*

Gaumont Graphic 744(4) Fetes at Bournemouth: New Zealand Engineers hold sports in aid of POW Fund, 19 August 1918, Cameraman: Unknown, Production Co.: Gaumont Graphic, Duration: ? Reuters –ITN BGT407052487. This has now been transferred to http://reuters.screenocean.com and may have been renumbered.

Gaumont Graphic 799(2) — Rugby International NZ (6) v Aust (0) at Herne Hill in aid of 'Daily Express' Cheery Fund, 9 November 1918, 1918, Cameraman: Unknown, Production Co.: Gaumont Graphic, Duration: ? Reuters –ITN, BGT 407052623. This has now been transferred to http://reuters.screenocean.com and may have been renumbered.

HM The King on the Clyde, 17–20 September 1917, 1918, Cameraman: Unknown, Production Co.: Department of Information? GB, Duration, 0:27:00, (IWM140), NTSV F246448.

[Hospital Farmyard], 1918, Cameraman: Sergeant Thomas F. Scales, Production Co.: Pathé Gazette, Duration: 0:00:47, (British Pathé 2354.38), NTSV F245798.

King visits Liverpool and Manchester — New Zealand Troops March Past, 1918, Cameraman: Unknown, Production Co.: Gaumont Graphic, Duration: 0:06:43, NTSV F48602.

The Land We Live in (formerly Wellington and Assorted Scenes), 1918–1919, Cameraman: Charles F. Newham, Production Co.: NZ Educational Film Co., Duration: 0:21:40, NTSV F11142.

New Zealand Divisional Rugby Team, 1918, Cameraman: Captain Henry A. Sanders, Production Co.: NZ Official, negative deposited with WOCC, Duration: 0:09:32, (IWM 172), NTSV F4332.

New Zealand Field Artillery in Action, New Year's Day 1918, Visit To New Zealand Infantry Base Depot Etaples, 1918, Cameraman: Captain H.A. Sanders, Production Co.: New Zealand Official, negative deposited with WOCC, Duration: 0:06:30, (IWM 160), NTSV, F4339.

New Zealand: Regatta at Putney, 28 September 1918. Cameraman: Unknown, Production Co.: Gaumont Graphic, Duration:? Reuters –ITN, BGT407052557. This has now been transferred to http://reuters.screenocean.com and may have been renumbered.

New Zealand Whale Hunting with Motor Launches in Cook Strait, 1918, Cameraman: Sydney B. Taylor, Production Co.: Department of Agriculture, Duration: 0:34.08, NTSV F880.

New Zealand Whale Hunting with Motor Launches in Cook Strait, Offcuts, 1918, Cameraman: Sydney B. Taylor, Production Co.: Department of Agriculture, Duration: 0:56:00, NTSV F884.

Opening of the HQ NZ Rowing Club, 1918, Cameraman: Sergeant Thomas F. Scales, Production Co.: Pathé Gazette, Duration: 0:00:52, British Pathé: 1896.21.

Paris, Au Parc des Princes: Un Grand Match de Football Rugby au Profit de la Maison des Journalistes, 1918, Cameraman: Unknown, Production Co.: Journal Gaumont, France, Duration: 0:00:43, Gaumont Pathé, 1844GJ 00002. This has now been transferred to http://reuters.screenocean.com and may have been renumbered.

Pathé Gazette No. 463A, Little-Heard-Of-Parade, 1918, Cameraman: Sergeant Thomas F. Scales, Production Co.: Pathé Gazette, Duration: 0:00:56, (British Pathé 1880.16), NTSV F245766.

Pathé Gazette No. 463A, New Zealand Hospital Walton-On-Thames and Oatland's Park. New Zealand Hospital Brockenhurst, 1918, Cameraman: Sergeant Thomas F. Scales, Production Co.: NZ Official/Pathé Gazette, Duration: 0:00:38, NTSV F4338.

Pathé Gazette No.483B: Hun Colonies [Massey and Ward at Euston Station, 15 June 1918], 1918, Cameraman: Sergeant Thomas F. Scales, Production Co.: Pathé Gazette, Duration: 0:01:15, (British Pathé 1896.10), NTSV F245775.

Pathé Gazette No. 492A. Somewhere in England. New Zealanders Produce their own Food, 1918, Cameraman: Sergeant Thomas F. Scales, Production Co.: Pathé Gazette, Duration: 0:00:40, (British Pathé 1934.07), NTSV F245804.

Pathé Gazette, Boscombe, New Zealand Maori 'Haka' for Deserving Charity — Pathé Gazette, 1918, Cameraman: Thomas F. Scales?, Production Co.: NZ Official/Pathé Gazette, Duration:0:00:26, British Pathé Collection 1902.42.

[Personal Record: Wellington Rugby, Hawera Storefront and Children] 1918, Cameraman: Unknown, Production Co.: Unknown, Duration: 0:01:38, NTSV F245076.

Rugby: French Army v New Zealand Rugby Army Team, 18 February 1918, Cameraman: Unknown, Production Co.: Gaumont Graphic, Duration: ? Reuters –ITN, BGT407052153. This has now been transferred to http://reuters.screenocean.com and may have been renumbered.

Rugby League Football Newton v Ponsonby Auckland Domain, July 1918, Cameraman: Charles F. Newham, Production Co.: Dominion (NZ) Film Company, Duration: 0:02:17, NTSV F14796.

Seeing the Sights of Paris before Football Match, 1918, Cameraman: Captain Henry A. Sanders, Production Co.: New Zealand Official, negative deposited with WOCC, Duration: 0:03:34, NTSV F4517.

Soldats Britanniques et Néo–Zélandais Lors de la Deuxiéme Batille de la Scarpe Septembre 1918, 1918, Cameraman: French Official, Production Co.: French Official, Duration: 0:08:27, (IWM 508–74), NTSV F253578.

Topical Budget 349-1, Honours for Anzacs at Cambridge, 29 April 1918, 1918, Cameraman: Unknown, Production Co.: Topical Film Co., Duration: 0:04:18, NTSV F246480.

Topical Budget 355-2 — Fate of German Colonies, June 1918, Cameraman: Unknown, Production Co.: Topical Budget, Duration: 0:01:10, NTSV F97891.

[Town Scenes, Auckland] 1918, Cameraman: Unknown, Production Co.: Unknown, Duration: 0:00:30, NTSV F51483.

Visit of the Hon. W.F. Massey and Sir J. Ward to the Western Front 30 June–2 July 1918, 1918, Cameraman: Hon. Lt. Henry A. Sanders, Production Co.: NZ Official, negative deposited with WOCC, Duration: 0:21:43, (IWM 269) NTSV F1068.

Walton. The Rt Hon WF Massey – Premier of New Zealand, presents medals to brave Anzacs. 1918, Cameraman: Sergeant Thomas F. Scales, Production Co.: Pathé Gazette, Duration: 0:00:37, [British Pathé: 1934.05], NTSV F245782.

Wellington and Assorted Scenes, see *The Land We Live In.* 1918–1919, NTSV F11142.

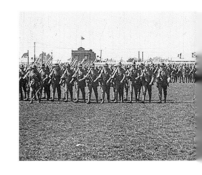

1919

The "All Blacks" Win. (Leicester Beaten by 19 Points To Nil.), 1919, Cameraman: Thomas F. Scales? Production Co.: Pathé Gazette, Duration: 0:01:12, British Pathé 1902:37. (This is the same film as British Pathé 1928.02.)

Allied Occupation of Rhineland — [New Zealanders in Cologne], 1919, Cameraman: Thomas F. Scales, Production Co.: Pathé Gazette, Duration: 0:08:11, (British Pathé 2340.26), NTSV F245807.

Anzac Day — Prince of Wales takes the Salute, 1919, Cameraman: Unknown, Production Co.: Pathé Gazette, Duration: 0:01:58, (British Pathé 1918.10), NTSV F245629.

Anzacs Sight-Seeing in Paris, 1919, Cameraman: Sergeant Charles D. Barton?, Production Co.: NZ Official/Pathé Gazette, Duration: 0:00:47, British Pathé 1890.10.

Arrival of HMS New Zealand, 1919, Cameraman: Unknown, Production Co.: Unknown, Duration: 500 feet, Listed New Zealand Censors Register IA 60 6/4, ANZ, 21 August 1919, no copy known to exist.

Arrival of New Zealand Troops at Cologne, 1919, Cameraman: Captain Henry A. Sanders, Production Co.: NZ Official negative deposited with WOCC, Duration: 0:12:01, (IWM 385), NTSV F4555.

Athletes from Various Allied Countries March at the Opening of the Inter-Allied Games in Paris France, 1919, Cameraman: Unknown, Production Co.: Unknown, Duration: ?, NTSV F232855.

Australasian Gazette 451 [Excerpt], Maori Contingent Home, 1919, Cameraman: Unknown, Production Co.: Australasian Gazette, Duration: 0:01:14, NTSV F29570.

Civic Reception of Lieut. J. Grant VC, 1919, Cameraman: Unknown, Production Co.: A.M. Conroy, Opera House, Hawera, Duration: 0:05:00, Ref: 500,002, www.audiovisual.archives.govt.nz, ANZ.

Empire Pageant, 1919, Cameraman: Pathé, Production Co.: Pathé Gazette, Duration: 0:03:05, British Pathé 1918.11.

The Garden Fete at 'Terangi': Residence of S. Solomon Esq. Cinematographed by H.C. Gore, Dunedin, 1919, Cameraman: Henry C. Gore, Production Co.: H.C. Gore, Duration: 0:03:00, NTSV F7816.

Gaumont Graphic 815(2) Maori War Dance. Maoris from the New Zealand Pioneer Batt give the Haka war dance in Native Costume, 18 Jan 1919. Cameraman: Unknown, Production Co.: Gaumont Graphic, Duration: 0:02:00. Reuters –ITN, BGT407052726. This has now been transferred to http://reuters.screenocean.com. ID, 593676.

Gaumont Graphic 850(4), New Zealanders Farewell Colours at Stafford, 13 May 1919, Cameraman: Unknown, Production Co.: Gaumont Graphic, Duration: ? Reuters –ITN, BGT407053857. This has now been transferred to http://reuters.screenocean.com and may have been renumbered.

His Excellency's Visit to the Cook Islands and Samoa, 1919, Cameraman: Sydney B. Taylor, Production: Department of Agriculture, Duration: 0:06:33, NTSV F6552.

HMS New Zealand, 1919, Cameraman: Unknown, Production Co.: Unknown, Duration: 500 feet, Listed New Zealand Censors Register IA 60 6/4, ANZ, 21 August 1919, no copy known to exist.

Inter-Allied Games Pershing Stadium, 1919, Cameraman: Unknown, Production Co.: US Official, Duration: 0:12:04:10, http://www.buyoutfootage.com/pages/titles/pd_na_653.php#.WOJreYVOI2w.

Investiture by HM The King at Buckingham Palace, and March of Overseas Troops Through London, May 3rd 1919, 1919, Cameraman: Sergeant Charles D. Barton?, Production Co.: C. & E. Films, Duration: 0:03:12, NTSV F17841.

Lord Jellicoe's World Tour, 20 February 1919. Cameraman: Unknown, Production Co.: Gaumont Graphic, Duration: 0:03:14, Reuters –ITN, BGT407052763. This has now been transferred to http://reuters.screenocean.com, ID. 651965.

New Zealand Rowing Team, 1919, Cameraman: Unknown, Production Co.: Pathé Gazette, Duration: 0:00:53, (British Pathé 1906.29), NTSV F245781.

New Zealand: The Land of the Digger, Part 7, 1919, Cameraman: unknown, Production Co.: Unknown, Duration: 0:02:24, NTSV F4386.

New Zealanders at Auckland, 1919, Cameraman: Thomas F. Scales, Production Co.: Pathé Gazette, Duration: 0:00:47, British Pathé 1854.15.

New Zealanders in Cologne, 1919, Cameraman: Thomas F. Scales, Production Co.: Pathé Gazette, Duration: 0:08:22, (British Pathé 2358.13), NTSV F245814.

New Zealanders in Cologne 1, 1919, Cameraman: Thomas F. Scales, Production Co.: Pathé Gazette, Duration: 0:06:28, (British Pathé 2358.07), NTSV F245808.

New Zealanders in Cologne 2, 1919, Cameraman: Thomas F. Scales, Production Co.: Pathé Gazette, Duration: 0:07:04, (British Pathé 2344.25), NTSV F245809.

New Zealanders in Cologne 2, 1918–1919, 1919, Cameraman: Thomas F. Scales, Production Co.: Pathé Gazette, Duration: 0:02:38, British Pathé 2456.22. [Scenes from *New Zealanders in Cologne 1, 1919*, (British Pathé 2358.07), NTSV F245808 but marred by vertical lines].

Occupation of the Rhineland, 1919–1920, Cameraman: Thomas F. Scales, Production Co.: Pathé Gazette, Duration: 0:06:22, British Pathé 2456.22.

Paris Leave Club, 1919, Cameraman: Sergeant Charles D. Barton?, Production Co.: NZ Official/ Pathé Gazette, Duration: 0:08:17, (British Pathé 1936.01), NTSV F245805.

Pathé Gazette No. 531: Rugby "Test" Match [New Zealand Trench Team beat the Home Team by 5 points to 3.] January 1919, Cameraman: Thomas F. Scales, Production Co.: Pathé Gazette, Duration: 0:00:49, British Pathé 1928.04.

Pathé Gazette No. 533, Victorious "All Blacks" Beat Mother Country after "ding dong" Match By 6 Points to Three. 10 January 1919, Cameraman: Pathé, Production Co.: Pathé Gazette, Duration: 0:00:48, British Pathé 1906.43.

Pathé Gazette No. 535: Liverpool — Good–Bye to "Blighty". New Zealand Soldiers leave England with their wives, 6 February 1919, Cameraman: Pathé, Production Co.: Pathé Gazette, Duration: 0:00:23, (British Pathé 1904.09), NTSV F245796.

Pathé Gazette No. 541, Brockenhurst and Lymington — A Token of Appreciation (New Zealanders present flags prior to their departure for home), 1919, Cameraman: Pathé, Production Co.: Pathé Gazette, Duration: 0:03:20, British (Pathé 1904.28), NTSV F245797.

Pathé Gazette No. 556, The Irony of Fate — New Zealanders felling German timber, used as barricades against Germans themselves, 21 April 1919, Cameraman: Thomas F. Scales, Production Co.: Pathé Gazette, Duration: 0:00:39, British Pathé 1906.44.

Pathé Gazette No. 559, Anzac Day London 25 April 1919, 1 May 1919, Cameraman: Unknown, Production Co.: Pathé Gazette, Duration: 0:02:39, (British Pathé 2338.44), NTSV F245629.

Pathé Gazette No. 613, Torquay — Good-bye "Digger" — Mayor bids farewell to last batch of married NZ soldiers who are returning with their wives and sometimes … a little "Digger", 6 November 1919, Cameraman: Pathé, Production Co.: Pathé Gazette, Duration: 0:01:23, British Pathé 200.16.

Pathé Gazette: (Excerpt) Jellicoe Departs on HMS New Zealand, 1919, Cameraman: Unknown, Production Co.: Pathé Gazette, Duration: 0:01:20, British Pathé 2352.21.

Peace Day Procession, 1919, Cameraman: Henry C. Gore, Production Co.: Henry C. Gore, Plaza Cinema, Dunedin, Duration: 0:08:18, NTSV F3799.

Rugby Football, 1919, Cameraman: Thomas F. Scales?, Production Co.: Pathé Gazette, Duration: 0:01:12, British Pathé 1928.02. [This is identical to *The "All Blacks" Win,* British Pathé 1902:37.]

Soldiers watching [Rugby] Football [Cologne], 1919, Cameraman: Thomas F. Scales, Production Co.: Pathé Gazette, Duration: 0:00:50, British Pathé 1906.28.

Te Hui Aroha ki Turanga (Gisborne Hui Aroha), 1919, Cameraman: James McDonald, Production Co.: Dominion Museum, Duration: 0:13:03, NTSV F7882.

1920

50,000 Miles with the Prince of Wales, 1920, Cameraman: Captain William Barker, Production Co.: Topical Film Company, Duration: 1:43:00, IWM 843.

Gaumont Actualities No.5022, 1920, filmed 1915–16, Cameraman: Unknown, Production Co.: Gaumont Journal Actualité, France, Duration: 0:10:23:10, Gaumont Pathé Archives No. 2000GS05022.

He Pito Whakaatu i te Hui i Rotorua: Scenes At The Rotorua Hui, 1920, Cameraman: James McDonald, Production Co.: Dominion Museum, Duration: 0:26:40, NTSV F2808.

Lord Jellicoe and the H.M.S. New Zealand docks in Portsmouth, 3 February 1920, Cameraman: Unknown, Production Co.: Gaumont Graphic, Duration: 0:00:57, http://reuters.screenocean.com, ID. 649817.

Pathé Gazette: (Excerpt) Welcome Home! Admiral Jellicoe returns in HMS New Zealand at conclusion of his World Tour, 1920, Cameraman: Unknown, Production Co.: Pathé Gazette, Duration: 0:00:41, British Pathé 204.43.

The Prince of Wales at Rotorua, 1920, Cameramen: Sydney B. Taylor, Charles D. Barton, Frank Stewart, Production Co.: NZ Government/NZ Picture Supplies Ltd, Duration: 0:15:00, NTSV F4094.

The Prince of Wales in Maoriland, 1920, Cameraman: Henry C. Gore, Production Co.: H.C. Gore & Co., Duration: 0:08:47, NTSV F4095.

Prince in New Zealand: Wellington's Wonderful Welcome, 1920, Cameraman: Unknown, Production Co.: Pathé Gazette, Duration: 0:04:50, NTSV F102444.

Prince's Tour of New Zealand, 1920, Cameramen: Sydney B. Taylor, Charles D. Barton, Frank Stewart, Production Co.: NZ Government / NZ Picture Supplies Ltd, Duration: 0:41:57, NTSV F4097.

Welcome at the Rotorua Race Course to the Tribes arriving for the Visit by the Prince of Wales, 1920, Cameraman: James McDonald, Production Co.: Dominion Museum, Duration: 0:04.41, NTSV F847

1921

Anzac Day at Dunedin [formerly *Anzac Day Service*], 1921, Cameraman: Unknown, Production Co.: O'Brien's Empire Theatre, Dunedin, Duration: 0:02:53, NTSV F10327.

Anzac Day Service, see *Anzac Day at Dunedin,* 1921.

He Pito Whakaatu i te Noho a te Māori i te Awa ō Whanganui: Scenes Of Maori Life On The Whanganui River, 1921, Cameraman: James McDonald, Production Co, Dominion Museum, Duration: 0:54.19, NTSV F2816.

World Sculling Championship, 11 June 1921, Cameraman: Sydney B. Taylor, Production Co.: Department of Agriculture, Duration: 0:04.18, NTSV F1156.

1922

Memorial to 7,000 'DIGGERS': to the memory of 7000 Diggers — NZ Division Memorial Unveiled on site of Switch Trench — scene of continuous fighting for 23 days in Somme Battle, 1922, Cameraman: Pathé Gazette, Production Co.: Pathé Gazette, Duration: 0:03:08, British Pathé 286.01.

1923

Scenes of Maori Life on the East Coast, 1923, Cameraman: James McDonald, Production Co.: Dominion Museum, Duration: 0:24.56, NTSV F2815.

1924

New Zealand Memorial Long Version, 12 August 1924, Cameraman: Pathé Gazette, Production Co.: Pathé Gazette, Duration: 0:05:29, (British Pathé 350.14), NTSV F245642.

New Zealand Memorial Short Version, 12 August 1924, Cameraman: Pathé Gazette, Production Co.: Pathé Gazette, Duration: 0:00:47, British Pathé 350.15.

1925

For Remembrance. Victorious All Blacks make pilgrimage to grave of Dave Gallagher [sic] — *Captain of the first All Blacks' Team, Poperinghe, Belgium,* 15 January 1925, Cameraman: Pathé Gazette, Production Co.: Pathé Gazette, Duration: 0:01:41, British Pathé 368.22.

The Invincible All Blacks Record Tour 1924–5, 1925, Cameraman: Unknown, Production Co.: Unknown, Duration: 0:36:01, (New Zealand All Blacks v Glamorgan match, December 1905 follows the intertitle "A Peep into the Past", which starts at 0:15:49), NTSV F7026.

1927

A.H. Noad Film/Gallipoli: 1914–1928, Cameramen: Various, Production Co.: Arthur Tinsdale, Embassy Pictures, Duration: 1:03:23, AWM F00176.

New Zealand Memorial at Messines, 1927, Cameraman: Unknown, Production Co.: Unknown, Duration: 0:02:53, NTSV F13776.

1928

"Star of Canada" House, 1928, Cameraman: Unknown, Production Co.: Unknown, Duration: 0:01:05, NTSV F9892.

1940

The First Ballot, 24 September 1940, Released: 11 October 1940, Cameraman: Unknown, Production Co.: New Zealand Government Film Studios: Duration: 0:01.59, NTSV F7472.

2013

Comparison of Ellis Ashmead Bartlett's Gallipoli Footage in AWM Films F00069 with The Dardanelles Expedition: Heroes of Gallipoli and F00176 A.H. Noad Film, Duration: 0:08:11, AWM F08484.

A Study into Ellis Ashmead-Bartlett's Gallipoli Footage and its Various Versions and Interpretations, 2013,, compiled by Michael Kosmider and Esa Makela to accompany Michael Kosmider, *Archival films of Gallipoli,* Michael Kosmider, July 2014, AWM, PAFU 0696.

Index of Films

Index